OXFORD JUNIOR ENCYCLOPAEDIA

VOLUME II
NATURAL HISTORY

OXFORD JUNIOR ENCYCLOPAEDIA

GENERAL EDITORS
LAURA E. SALT & GEOFFREY BOUMPHREY
ILLUSTRATIONS EDITOR: HELEN MARY PETTER

VOLUME II
NATURAL HISTORY

OXFORD UNIVERSITY PRESS

Oxford University Press, Ely House, London W. 1

GLASGOW NEW YORK TORONTO MELBOURNE WELLINGTON
CAPE TOWN IBADAN NAIROBI DAR ES SALAAM LUSAKA ADDIS ABABA
DELHI BOMBAY CALCUTTA MADRAS KARACHI LAHORE DACCA
KUALA LUMPUR SINGAPORE HONG KONG TOKYO

First published 1949
Reprinted with corrections 1951, 1955,
1957, 1961,
Revised 1974

Printed in Great Britain
at the University Press, Oxford
by Vivian Ridler
Printer to the University

PREFACE

IN authorizing the preparation of this work the Delegates of the Oxford University Press had foremost in mind the need to provide a basic book of reference for school libraries. In form it was to be a genuine encyclopaedia, in treatment and vocabulary suitable for the young reader. To many children (and indeed to many adults) reading is not a natural activity: they do not turn to books for their own sake. But they can be trained to go to books for information which they want for some particular purpose—and thus, very often, to form a habit which will be of lifelong value. Their capacity to read continuously for any length of time being limited, they can absorb knowledge better if they get it in small quantities: therefore they will often read reference books when they may reject the reading of more extended matter. Again, it is probably true to say of such readers that their approach is from the particular to the general, and from the application to the principle, rather than the reverse, that their main interest is in the modern world around them, and that since they are not very good at conceiving things outside their own experience, their capacity for grasping abstract ideas is limited. On the other hand, once their interest is aroused, they will often pursue a subject to remarkable lengths, so long as its development is logical and the treatment avoids dullness.

But such generalizations can easily be overdone: many children using the books will not be of this type. Moreover, it was evident from the first that a project involving so great an amount of work, however exactly it might meet its principal mark, would be fully justified only if it could be of service to a far wider circle of readers. Even for the age-group first in mind, anything like 'writing down to children' must plainly be taboo—but clear exposition and simple language are no bad qualities in writing for any audience. Here, then, it seemed was the opportunity to provide a work of reference suitable for many readers to whom the large, standard encyclopaedias are too heavy and technical, and the popular alternatives for the most part neither sufficiently complete nor authoritative. The fact that the plan allowed for an exceptionally large proportion of illustrations to text (between one-quarter and one-third of the total space) is an advantage to any reader, since pictures may, in many instances, save whole paragraphs of involved explanation. With these secondary aims well in mind, then, the General

Editors have ventured to hope that the encyclopaedia may find usefulness not only among certain younger children, but also among older students in clubs, libraries, and Young People's Colleges, and even to no small extent among their parents and other adults who may wish for a simple approach to some unfamiliar or forgotten subject.

SCOPE AND EMPHASIS. Within certain limits the OXFORD JUNIOR ENCY-CLOPAEDIA purports to be reasonably comprehensive, though (in common with all general encyclopaedias) not exhaustive. Chief among these limits is that matter already easily available in school text-books is included only so far as its presence is necessary for the proper understanding of the subject under discussion. Thus, although an immense field of history is surveyed, it will be found mainly under headings dealing with its effects, or in the biographies of those who lived to make it. Purely technical or scientific subjects, also, are omitted except when they have some general interest. In natural history and kindred studies the immense variety of forms necessarily led at times either to their treatment by groups or to their omission on purely arbitrary decisions as to which species would, in all probability, never be looked for, or because there was nothing particularly interesting to say of them. In point of general balance the stress is laid rather on the modern world, though due space is given to the factors which have shaped it, no less than to those which are changing it.

ARRANGEMENT. The encyclopaedia is planned to consist of twelve volumes and an index. Each of the twelve main volumes is arranged alphabetically, and each deals with a particular range of related subjects (*see* PLAN OF VOLUMES, p. xii). Within its terms of reference, then, each volume is self-contained, and, owing to the great number of single-line cross-references, can well be used alone. The index covers all entries in the encyclopaedia. This arrangement, which has the incidental advantage of making the encyclopaedia easier to revise, arose mainly from one consideration. If articles were to be kept really short—and, in fact, few approach and almost none exceeds 2,000 words—many subjects could be dealt with comprehensively only by referring the reader to other relevant articles—itself a desirable thing to do. It was clearly preferable for these to be under his hand, rather than be dispersed through any of the twelve volumes at the caprice of the alphabet.

This the present arrangement achieves to a great extent. If it has led to a small amount of overlapping, that again is not without its advantages.

Cross-references, then, play an indispensable part in the make-up of the encyclopaedia. They are of two kinds: references in the text to further articles amplifying the particular point under review, and references at the end of an article to others taking the whole subject farther. Therefore, a reader looking up any wide subject, such as ANATOMY, and following up its cross-references either in the text or at the end of the article, can discover under what main headwords the subject is treated. These, again, will refer him to any subsidiary articles, as also, in many cases, to those of a complementary nature. Thus he may be guided either from the general to the particular or vice versa. It is believed that the titles of the twelve volumes (see p. xii), in conjunction with their sub-titles, will usually lead the reader straight to the volume containing the information he wants. In selecting headwords, the rules generally followed have been to prefer the familiar, or even the colloquial, reserving the technical alternative for a single-line entry, and to group narrow subjects under a headword of wider scope. Thus, for POLLINATION, *see* REPRODUCTION IN PLANTS, section 5; for LEPIDOPTERA, *see* BUTTERFLIES or MOTHS; for DUNLIN, *see* WADING BIRDS; and for GAZELLE, *see* ANTELOPE.

L. E. S., G. M. B.

Oxford

LIST OF CONTRIBUTORS

VOLUME EDITOR

Dr. M. Burton, Deputy Keeper at the British Museum (Natural History).

CONTRIBUTORS

General Biology and Zoology

Dr. M. Burton, British Museum (Natural History).

John Buxton, Fellow of New College, Oxford.

T. J. S. Rowland, M.A.

Mammals

D. Seth-Smith, F.Z.S., M.B.O.U., *Late* Curator of Mammals and Birds, Zoological Society. The 'Zoo Man' of the B.B.C. Children's Hour.

R. W. Hayman, Senior Experimental Officer, Dept. of Zoology, British Museum (Natural History).

Fish

A. Fraser-Brunner, F.Z.S., Associate in the Dept. of Zoology, British Museum (Natural History).

Birds

D. Seth-Smith, F.Z.S., M.B.O.U., *Late* Curator of Mammals and Birds, Zoological Society. The 'Zoo-Man' of the B.B.C. Children's Hour.

John Buxton, Fellow of New College, Oxford.

P. H. Trahair Hartley, M.A., Dept. of Ornithology, Oxford.

Reptiles

Dr. Malcolm Smith.

Crustaceans and Molluscs

F. Martin Duncan, F.Z.S., Gen. Ed. and Librarian of Zoological Society (1919–45).

Insects

A. J. A. Woodcock, M.Sc., F.R.E.S.

G. J. Arrow, F.Z.S., F.R.E.S., Late Deputy Keeper, Dept. of Entomology, British Museum (Natural History).

L. Hugh Newman, F.R.E.S., Author of *Wings in the Sun*; *Butterfly Haunts*, &c.

G. E. J. Nixon, B.A.

B. M. Hobby, D.Phil., Hope Dept. of Entomology, Oxford University Museum.

Prof. G. D. Hale Carpenter, Hope Professor of Zoology (Entomology), Oxford (1933–48).

Spiders

Theodore H. Savory, M.A., F.Z.S., Author of *The Biology of Spiders*; *Arachnida*, &c.

Plants

T. H. Hawkins, M.Sc., M.Ed., F.L.S.

L. J. F. Brimble, B.Sc., F.L.S., Joint Editor of *Nature*.

Assistant Editors—Nora C. Day; Hester Burton.

Assistant Illustrations Editor—Ursula Aylmer.

Valuable help in the early stages of planning this volume and in the selection of authors was given by Brian Vesey-Fitzgerald, F.L.S., F.R.E.S., Editor-in-Chief of *The Field* (1938–46). The work of revising the Volume for the 1955 revision was carried out by Dr. B. M. Hobby, D.Phil., Hope Dept. of Entomology, Oxford University Museum, and Miss S. M. Littleboy, Dept. of Botany, Oxford.

Further revision in 1960 was carried out by Dr. B. M. Hobby and Miss S. M. Littleboy; by Denis F. Owen, Edward Grey Institute of Field Ornithology; and by the following members of the Hope Department—M. F. Claridge, F.R.E.S., Peggy E. Ellis, Ph.D. (Lond.), M. W. R. de V. Graham, D.Phil., A. J. Pontin, D.Phil., G. C. E. Scudder, D.Phil., F.R.E.S.

ACKNOWLEDGEMENTS

THE EDITORS wish to thank all those who have lent photographs, or allowed them to be used at reduced fees for this educational project. They have had particular assistance from Harold Bastin; S. Beaufoy, F.R.P.S.; S. C. Bisserôt, A.R.P.S.; Eric J. Hosking, F.R.P.S.; John Markham, F.R.P.S.; G. K. Yeates, F.R.P.S.; and the Zoological Society of London. They would also like to express their thanks to the Hope Dept. of Entomology, Oxford University Museum, for providing the specimens for the colour plates, opp. pages 64 and 336.

The editors also wish to thank Dr. Marion Nixon; Prof. David Nichols; Mary Gregory, Jodrell Laboratory, Royal Botanic Gardens, Kew; and John Burton, Natural History Unit, B.B.C., Bristol; for help in correcting and updating the 1974 reprint.

COLOUR PLATES

PLAN OF VOLUMES

GENERAL INDEX VOLUME
Covering entries in all 12 volumes

HOW TO USE THIS BOOK

THIS VOLUME is one of twelve, each on a separate subject, the whole set forming what is called an encyclopaedia, or work from which you can find out almost anything you want to know. (The word comes originally from the Greek *enkuklios*, circular or complete, and *paideia*, education.) Each of the twelve volumes is arranged alphabetically within itself, as twelve dictionaries would be.

The difference between a dictionary and an encyclopaedia is that while the first gives you no more than the meanings and derivations of words, the second tells you a very great deal more about their subjects. For instance, from a dictionary you could learn that a SALAMANDER is a lizard-like animal, and little more; but an encyclopaedia will tell you where and how they live, and will give details of interesting species, such as the Giant Salamander of Japan or the Hell-bender of the Mississippi. Then a dictionary contains nearly every word in the language; but an encyclopaedia deals only with words and subjects about which there is something interesting to be said, beyond their bare meanings. So you should not expect to find every word in an encyclopaedia—every subject is there, but not every word.

There are two ways in which you can find a subject in the OXFORD JUNIOR ENCYCLOPAEDIA. The first way is to study the Plan of Volumes on the opposite page, and then to decide in which volume the subject comes. The second way is to make use of the Index. Very often you will be able to tell from the title alone which volume contains the information you need; but if not, the list of sub-headings on the plan opposite will help to direct you. For example, if you want to find out about an animal or plant, you would look it up in Volume II, Natural History; but if you wanted to know how that animal or plant is used in something like farming, fishing, or trapping, you would find it in Volume VI. If your subject were something in nature that does not have life—such as the sun, or a particular country or river, or a kind of stone—you would find it in Volume III, with tides, earthquakes, the weather, and many other things. Matters connected with communication of any kind—of people, or goods, or even of ideas—are in Volume IV. So you would look there for languages, and printing, and broadcasting, as well as for ships, and trains, and roads. But if it is the engineering side of any of these things that interests you, Volume VIII, Engineering, is the place to try.

Business and trade are in Volume VII; and how we are governed and protected by the State, the law, and the armed forces is in Volume X. All kinds of sport and games, as well as acting, dancing, concerts, and musical instruments, are in Volume IX; and Volume XI deals with almost everything connected with our homes, from the building and furnishing of the house to the clothes and health of those who live in it. The titles of Volumes V and XII, Great Lives and The Arts, explain themselves; and a rather fuller account of the volume you are reading now is given on page xv. If you cannot find your subject readily by this means, then you must make use of the Index. An article on page xv of the Index Volume will tell you how to do this.

To find your subject in the volume, think of its ordinary name, and then look it up as though you were using a dictionary—the As on the first page and the Zs (if there are any) on the last. If you cannot find it, try a more general word. For instance, if you want to read about the Bladder-Wrack and cannot find it under its name (as you cannot), try either ALGAE or SEAWEEDS—either of which will lead you to it. If you cannot think of a more general word, you should at once use the Index.

As you read any article, you will probably come across the title of other articles in some way connected with what you are reading. You will know that they are titles of other articles because they will be printed in capital letters. Either they will be followed by (q.v.) in brackets (this is short for the Latin *quod vide*, and means 'which see'), or else they themselves will be in brackets, with the word *see* in front of them. You can look up these other articles at once if you want to know more about the particular point dealt with, or you can save them up until you have finished the article you are reading. At the end of any article you may find the words 'See also', followed by one or more titles in small capital letters. If you look these titles up, they will tell you still more about the subject that interests you. These last 'cross-references' are very useful if you want to look up a particularly wide subject (such as ANATOMY or BIRDS), because they show you at once the titles of all the main articles dealing with it. You can then decide for yourself which to read.

WHAT YOU WILL FIND IN THIS VOLUME

THIS VOLUME IS ABOUT LIVING THINGS, PLANTS AND ANIMALS, WHICH EXIST IN A NATURAL STATE ON THE EARTH.

PLANTS. The thousands of different PLANTS in the world all belong to a number of big groups, such as FLOWERING PLANTS, CONIFERS, FERNS, SEAWEEDS, FUNGI, and BACTERIA. You will find articles on these groups but not on every individual plant. You can read about the various parts of plants, the FLOWERS, SEEDS, FRUIT, LEAVES, STEMS, and ROOTS, which all serve different and essential purposes, and about the GROWTH OF PLANTS, REPRODUCTION IN PLANTS, RESPIRATION IN PLANTS, and other such subjects. You can find out about plants which have special devices for living, by looking up headwords such as CLIMBING PLANTS, PARASITIC PLANTS, and PLANT DEFENCES; and others which prefer a certain type of environment such as DESERT PLANTS, SEASHORE PLANTS, and WATER PLANTS.

ANIMALS. There is a vast range of animal life in the world, from the highly specialized animals which include Man himself, as well as APES, ELEPHANTS, and CATS, to the simple creatures such as SPONGES and CORALS which hardly seem like animals at all, and the microscopic AMOEBA. This book describes the way of life and behaviour of all the better-known species of MAMMALS, BIRDS, FISH, REPTILES, INSECTS, and other animals. It also tells you about the ANATOMY OF ANIMALS, the different methods of GROWTH, REPRODUCTION, and MOVEMENT, and how the parts of the body, such as the BRAIN and the HEART, have developed. Animals respond to their environment through their SENSES, and are protected from their natural enemies by CAMOUFLAGE. Their song and courtship display are part of ANIMAL LANGUAGE, and the instinctive behaviour is directed in the higher animals by a dawning INTELLIGENCE.

The chart on the next page gives a simple picture of how by EVOLUTION plants and animals have developed into their many varied and complex forms; and it gives the general headings under which the plants and animals will be found.

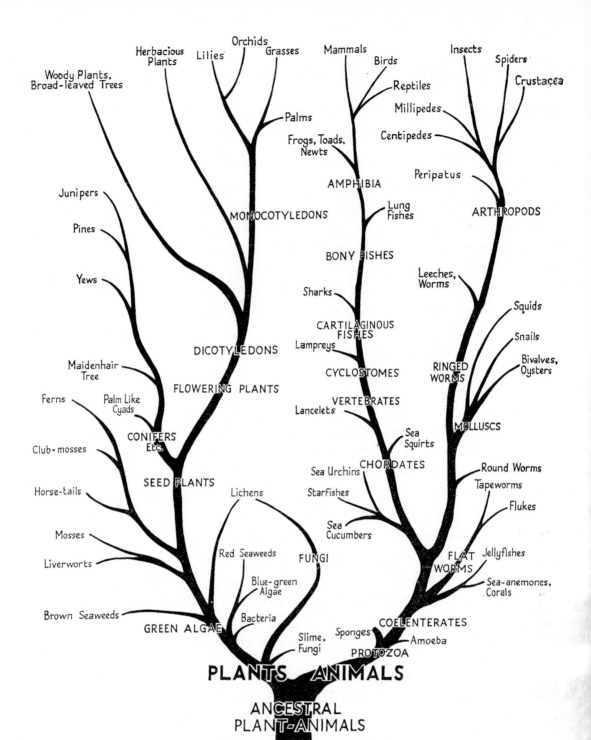

LIVING PLANTS AND ANIMALS

Designed by Dr. B. M. Hobby

This very much simplified evolution chart gives a guide as to what is to be found in this volume. It suggest how plants and animals may have grown up from the beginning. It might be compared with the chart in Vol. III, p. 139.

A

AARD-VARK (Dutch for earth-pig), or Ant-bear. This mammal is the only member of the order of animals called the Tubulidentata; at one time it was included with the ANT-EATERS, SLOTHS, and ARMADILLOS (qq.v.) in the order Edentata. It has no front teeth, and the rest of its teeth are simple and peg-like; but apart from the lack of front teeth, its long snout, and its habit of eating ants and termites, it bears little

AARD-WOLF. This mammal of South and East Africa looks very like a small HYAENA (q.v.). It is about the size of a fox, but stands higher on account of its longer legs. It has a yellowish or reddish-brown, shaggy, woolly coat, marked with about half a dozen vertical stripes on each side of its body. The tail is fairly long and bushy, and on the nape of the neck and along the back there is a distinct mane. The

AARD-VARK

AARD-WOLF

resemblance to these others. It is to be found mainly in open country in Africa, south of the Sahara, and is an animal of very extraordinary, ungraceful appearance. It is large and heavy, about 2 metres long, including the long, thick tail. It has a rounded back, long tubular snout, and ears which are very long and donkey-like, evidently adapted for picking up the slightest sound of approaching danger. In hot districts it is nearly hairless, in cooler districts its skin is covered with coarse, yellowish-brown hair—but this is short and sparse on the back and hardly noticeable at first sight. The Aard-varks dig themselves deep burrows with their powerful claws. They stay hidden in these until after dark, when they come out to attack the nests of termites, picking up the insects with their long, sticky tongues. They are much esteemed as food by the natives, who dig them out of their burrows.

muzzle is more pointed and the ears longer than those of the hyaena.

The exact position of Aard-wolves in the animal world has been rather a puzzle to zoologists. They appear to be related to Hyaenas, but their way of life is very different. Unlike Hyaenas, Aard-wolves have weak jaws, and their teeth show that their diet is very different from that of ordinary flesh-eating mammals. Their main food seems to be termites and other insects, fruit, and grubs. They live in burrows often dug by Aard-varks, several often sharing one hole. Like most burrowing animals, they are timid and cowardly, and make off at a rapid pace when they are driven from their earths. They venture out only at night, and on this account are rarely seen.

ADDER (also known as the VIPER). The old English name of Adder is preferable, since there are many species of VIPER (q.v.) (Viperidae) throughout the world. It is the only poisonous snake found in England, and can easily be distinguished from the GRASS SNAKE or the SMOOTH SNAKE (qq.v.), the other two English kinds. It is a short snake, seldom more than 38 centimetres long; it has a fairly thick body, a short tail, and a head very distinct from the neck. In colour it is brownish or reddish, with a dark zigzag stripe or series of spots down the middle of the back, which vary in distinctness, but are never absent. The belly is either dark greyish with light spots, or almost entirely black. Owing to the many colour variations, the adder has at times been given different names; but there is only one species. The particularly large red ones that are occasionally seen are always females, for the females grow to a larger size than the males.

The adder is widely distributed over most of Europe, and is found all over England and Scotland, usually in pine and heather country. It feeds mainly upon lizards and small mammals, and gives birth to from six to twelve living young at a time. The popular legend that the adder in time of danger will swallow its young, or allow them to crawl down its throat in order to protect them, still needs confirmation: for no one has been able to prove it by finding an adder with the young in its stomach. The bite of the adder can be fatal to human beings, and sheep and dogs not infrequently die from it.

See also SNAKE.

AGAMA. This is a lizard of the family Agamidae, found in the tropical and sub-tropical regions of Africa and Asia. Agamas differ from all other lizards in having their teeth fixed to the parapet of the jaw, and these can be divided roughly into incisors, canines, and molars. Except by their teeth, there is little to distinguish them from the IGUANAS (q.v.). In the breeding season many Agama males are very beautifully coloured. They are found living under all sorts of conditions, in desert country and among rocks, in the forests, and in the open country.

An Indian species, known as the Bloodsucker, is found frequently in gardens on bushes and shrubs. It feeds on insects and grubs, and in spite of its name is harmless. In the breeding season the male becomes bright red in colour— and this may have given rise to its name, for it certainly never sucks blood.

Zoological Society of London
A FRILLED LIZARD

The Frilled Lizard from the north of Australia is one of the largest members of the family (*see* Colour Plate, opp. p. 400). It has an expansion of skin on each side of the neck, which is its frill. This can be erected by means of special bones in the throat, which extend into the skin like the ribs of an umbrella. When the lizard is excited and standing at bay, the frill is spread out, giving it a formidable appearance. Another Australian species, known as the Moloch, was called by the early settlers Spiny Lizard or Thorny Devil. It grows to 20 cm in length, of which the tail forms nearly half. It has a small head, short limbs, and a flattened body, and is covered all over the upper surface with large, horny spines. Though fearsome to look at, it is quite harmless. It moves slowly, catching ants with its sticky tongue and consuming up to 1,000 at a meal.

See also LIZARDS.

AGOUTI. This RODENT (q.v.), about the size of a rabbit, is related to the CAVY (q.v.) and lives in the forests of South America and in the West Indies. It has slender legs, looks rather like a small antelope, and can run very fast. Its colour varies greatly, but is usually olive-brown, with yellow-orange hindquarters. Whenever the animal is alarmed, the brightly coloured patch of hair opens out and becomes very conspicuous. This is regarded by some as a signal, warning other Agoutis of approaching danger, and indicating the direction they should follow—as when rabbits show the white undersides of their tails.

During most of the day Agoutis lie concealed in hollow trees or in burrows in their forest homes, and come out in the early morning or at night to eat leaves, plants, and fallen fruits—at which time they can sometimes be seen in the open. With their sharp incisor teeth they can pierce the shells of the toughest nuts. In cultivated districts they eat sugar-cane and bananas. They are active animals, either trotting or springing along at high speed; they swim well, but cannot dive. For most of the year the two sexes live apart, but at the mating season each male selects a female and follows her with

AGOUTI

squeaks and grunts, staying by her until after the birth of their offspring. She has her young in a lair or in a nest carefully made of leaves, roots, and hair, and she prevents the male from coming near them until some days after their birth.

Agoutis are hunted a great deal for their flesh. They live well in captivity, and have been bred in Zoological Gardens.

ALBATROSS, *see* PETREL.

ALGAE. In structure and organization algae are the simplest of all plants. There are a great many different kinds of algae, ranging in size from the unicellular plant called Protococcus, which forms the green powdery growth seen on tree trunks and damp wood, to the many seaweeds, some of which are very large indeed. Algae do not bear seeds but reproduce themselves by swimming spores and other kinds of small reproductive bodies which grow directly

into new plants (*see* REPRODUCTION OF PLANTS). They are able to make their own food by PHOTOSYNTHESIS (q.v.) because they all contain the green pigment chlorophyll, although the colour may be concealed by other pigments, especially in the red and brown seaweeds.

Protococcus is a good example of one of the simplest living things. On tree trunks it is usually found on the windward and northern sides, where it is protected from direct sunlight and is kept damp by the rain driven against the trunk by the prevailing wind. If the green film is scraped off and examined under a microscope, it will be found to consist of many tiny, round, green cells, each one a plant in which all the functions of life are carried out. Protococcus itself cannot move, but it has many freshwater or sea relatives which can swim rapidly by the beating of delicate whip-like hairs of protoplasm.

Spirogyra is a well-known example of the thread-like forms. It consists of a long string of cells containing one or more spirals coloured green by the presence of chlorophyll. There are many other thread-like forms which contain their green pigment in structures varying in shape from small disks to bands and stars. Most of these algae live in slow-moving freshwater streams or stagnant pools; they float up to the surface in spring and summer, sinking to the bottom again during the winter.

Probably the best-known algae are, however, the seaweeds (*see* SEASHORE PLANTS). These are of three kinds—red, green, and brown. Green seaweeds are found in very shallow water and

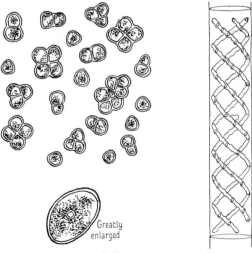

Greatly enlarged

PROTOCOCCUS (*left*), AND SPIROGYRA (*right*)

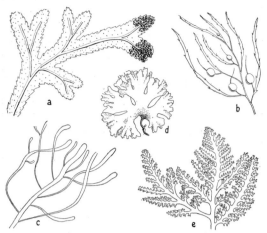

BROWN SEAWEEDS: (*a*) Serrated Wrack (*Fucus serratus*) and (*b*) Sargasso; GREEN SEAWEED: (*c*) *Enteromorpha compressa*; RED SEAWEEDS: (*d*) *Lithophylum versicolor* and (*e*) *Laurencia pinnatifida*

are exposed most of the time to the atmosphere. Brown seaweeds grow abundantly between tide-marks, where they are exposed at low tide. Red seaweeds, which are particularly beautiful, are the least frequently seen, because they occur in deeper water. Some seaweeds are very large, even reaching a length of very nearly half a kilometre—yet their organization is still simple, and they show no division into roots, stems, and leaves. The Sargasso Sea (q.v. Vol. III), in the North Atlantic Ocean, is the centre of a vast eddy in which a particular brown seaweed accumulates. Here, it floats at the surface and used to be a great nuisance to navigation. Sea-weeds were once used as a source of iodine, but to-day are used mainly as manure or for making power alcohol, chiefly in Ireland. In recent years, 'agar', a jelly-like substance used widely in commerce, has been obtained from seaweeds.

ALLIGATOR, *see* CROCODILES.

ALPACA, *see* LLAMA.

ALPINE PLANTS. The 'alpine region' refers to land above the upper limit of coniferous trees —that is, about 1525 metres or more above sea-level—as in the PYRENEES (q.v. Vol. III) and all the lofty mountains of central Europe. In alpine regions, with their high day temperature and dry atmosphere, the plants grow in compact cushions to suit the peculiar conditions under which they live. Because the soil is frozen

in winter, there is little moisture and the plants have to live under their warm covering of snow, in darkness, for a large part of the year. One of the peculiarities of alpine flora is, therefore, their tendency to 'rush into flower' at the earliest possible moment when the snow melts in springtime, their short but brilliant flowering period being usually confined to this time. To carry them over the long period when they are buried under the snow, most of the plants are provided with some form of underground organs in which reserve stocks of food can be stored.

Many alpine flowers are dazzling blues—although not so many as the casual observer is inclined to believe—and these are specially noticeable because of the intense depth of colour and the large number of individual flowers. Among the many strikingly beautiful alpine flowers, the best known are the deep blue Gentians, Anemones, pale violet Soldanellas, Campanulas or Bell-flowers, many kinds of yellow-gold Saxifrages, and, of course, the well-known Edelweiss and the Alpenrose, after which so many Swiss inns are named, and which might be called the national flowers of Switzerland. As well as these there are many other less well-known gems. The weirdly shaped, vivid, rose-coloured Sempervivum is a wonderful example of adaptation to meet the demands of environment. When the soil is quite dry and the sun so hot that all other flowers have flagged, the Sempervivum stands erect and full of living sap. It has a supply of water in its thick rosettes of leaf-heads. These are covered with sticky hairs and hair-threads which form a net, like a cobweb, over the plant to hold in the moisture and counteract the effect of the sun. Lovers of the Alps or Dolomites also know the golden Alpine Poppy, the red cushions of Moss Campion, the unbelievable sky-blue of the rare Fairy Forget-me-not, the rose-red, purple-stamened Dolomites Potentilla, and a whole galaxy of others.

The Edelweiss, about which so much romance has been woven and which is commonly believed to grow only in places which even the most hardy mountaineer can barely reach, is a complete fraud: it is not a rare plant, indeed it is almost common. Every season huge masses of Edelweiss are gathered by the Swiss peasants, or even cultivated in the lowlands of northern Switzerland for sale to the tourist. The Edelweiss may be local in its distribution, but where it does occur it grows freely. The characteristic

British Museum (Nat. Hist.)

Saxifraga signatella (S.E. Tibet)

British Museum (Nat. Hist.)

Meconopsis bella (Himalayas)

Paul Popper

Gentiana acaulis

Paul Popper

Edelweiss

ALPINE PLANTS

whiteness—the word means 'precious white'—is due to a thick covering of long woolly hairs, which are really empty cells. The stem and leaves of the Edelweiss are in fact green, but the greenness is masked by these grey-white hairs. The leaves, like those of many alpine plants, are arranged in a rosette just above the soil. A single stalk springs from the centre of the rosette, bearing what appears to be a solitary flower, but is really a complicated structure consisting of several flower heads, as found in daisies and dandelions. Edelweiss grows in southern Europe, India, and Siberia.

The Alpenroses, of which there are two, the Common and the Hairy, are more common than the Edelweiss. Alpenroses are really small-flowered evergreen Rhododendrons, growing to a height of up to a metre or more. They grow in great abundance on the higher pastures among the alpine thickets, or on the borders of the coniferous forests, especially where these fringe the margins of alpine lakes. The Common Alpenrose is easily recognized, because the undersides of the older leaves have a rusty-brown appearance, due to the presence of numerous scales, which protect the leaf pores or stomata, and so decrease the water-loss caused by TRANSPIRATION (q.v.) during their intense spring-flowering period. The Hairy Alpenrose, more common on limestone soils, is like the Common Alpenrose, except that all the leaves are green beneath and fringed with hairs along their margins.

See also Vol. III: ALPS; CARPATHIANS; PYRENEES.

AMOEBA. This genus of animals belonging to the phylum PROTOZOA (q.v.) is familiar to the general reader because it was long thought that the original animals from which all others descended must have looked rather like an Amoeba. Some flagellata Protozoa, however, show very obvious similarities both to plants and animals, and it is now believed that the common ancestors of both groups must have been one of these.

Four relatively large freshwater species of Amoebae are found in Britain. They are not easy to find as they are usually smaller than a pin's head, only just visible as whitish specks when viewed against a black background. They may be found in the late summer by skimming the surface of the mud at the bottom of well-aerated ponds and slow-moving streams con-

taining decaying leaves. Most of the specimens used in biology classes are cultured in shallow dishes of soft water containing a few boiled wheat grains, which provide nourishment for the minute living things.

Under the microscope a young and active Amoeba is seen as a mass of jelly-like substance known as protoplasm, constantly moving and changing in shape as it pushes out blunt finger-like pseudopodia, first in one direction and then in another. The protoplasm consists of cytoplasm and nucleus. The cytoplasm has a thin, transparent, surface membrane which is in contact with the water of the pond. Within this layer, the cytoplasm contains foodstores in the form of tiny granules whose shapes differ in different species of Amoebae. The nucleus controls the Amoeba's heredity, reproduction, and chemical changes; it rolls about inside the Amoeba, and can be seen after an Amoeba has been killed and stained with a special dye.

An Amoeba has no sense organs, but its whole body is sensitive to light, heat, and poisons, from which it moves away. This sensitiveness, known as irritability, is one of the fundamental properties of living things. An Amoeba feeds by putting out pseudopodia, flowing round its prey, and enclosing it in a spherical space known as a 'vacuole': in this way it devours from fifty to a hundred flagellates a day. Digestive juices pass into the food vacuole and dissolve the prey, which is then absorbed, while the undigested remains are cast out.

Oxygen for respiration enters through the

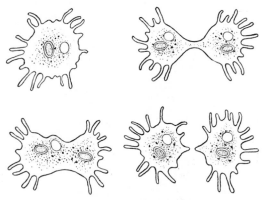

AMOEBA DIVIDING INTO TWO

The microscopic Amoeba multiplies by simply dividing into two. A 'waist' appears, which becomes narrower until it parts in the middle and there are two Amoebae where formerly there was one

hatch into tiny Amoebae. The whole life-cycle takes from 4 to 6 months.

Amoeba is often termed unicellular; but as it corresponds to the whole body of an animal such as a cat, and not with one of its numerous cells, it is far better to regard Amoeba as non-cellular.

See also PROTOZOA.

AMPHIBIA. These are a class of vertebrate animals that live both in the water and on land. They are descended from fishes which lived about 350 million years ago in fresh waters liable to dry up, so that an ability to do without water from time to time was a great advantage in the struggle for existence. The early Amphibia had long bodies and tails and, in place of fins, four limbs each with five digits. They were heavily built and slow and clumsy on the land, though more active in the water. They breathed by means of lungs and had skins resistant to the drying power of the air. Many species, some of them three metres or more in length, were in existence when the great coal-producing forests flourished, and some of them gave rise to the much more efficient REPTILES (q.v.). Most of these early Amphibia were unable to compete successfully with the Reptiles either on the land or in the water, and about 200 million years ago they became extinct. A few forms survived, however, and from these are derived the modern SALAMANDERS and NEWTS (recognized by their tails and usually four limbs, sometimes rather small), the jumping and tail-less FROGS and TOADS (qq.v.), and the limbless Apoda (Caecilians).

Modern Amphibia usually have moist skins through which they breathe. With few exceptions they are restricted to damp environments where, however, they have flourished and have produced numerous species with many interesting adaptations. They feed on insects, snails, worms, and such food, and in turn are eaten by fish, snakes, and birds. They thus form an important link in many food chains. They are mostly small, though the Giant Salamander of the Far East may reach 150 cm and the Giant Frog of West Africa is 30 cm long. They usually lay their eggs in water; for the eggs, having no shell, would dry up on land. Fertilization normally takes place in the water, and the eggs hatch into young, called tadpoles. These, with a few exceptions, live in the water, breathing

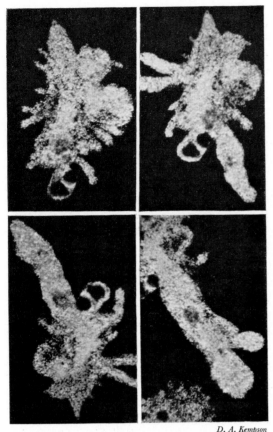

D. A. Kempson

AMOEBA IN MOVEMENT (GREATLY ENLARGED)

An Amoeba is throwing out a pseudopodium, which flows away and gradually increases in size, carrying the rest of the animal with it

Amoeba's surface from solution in the water. Water also enters and is periodically ejected by a 'contractile vacuole', which slowly swells for several minutes until almost as large as the nucleus, and then suddenly bursts. An Amoeba reproduces in two ways, both asexual. In one way the nucleus and cytoplasm split into two, producing two exactly similar daughter Amoebae, which then proceed to feed, grow larger, and to repeat the process. In the other way the nucleus of an ageing Amoeba forms hundreds of spores which are scattered in the water when the parent Amoeba disintegrates. Even though during the summer months the pond may dry up, the Amoeba spores do not die because they have protective coats which prevent loss of water. They are distributed by the wind or on the muddy feet of birds or mammals, and upon finding water eventually

chiefly by means of gills; indeed, some amphibia, such as the Siren and the Mexican Axolotl, never lose their gills. Some species, such as the Black Salamander of Europe, are 'viviparous'— their young develop inside the mother's body. The SURINAM TOAD (q.v.) has the curious habit of carrying the young in pits on its back, and the male Midwife Toad of Europe carries the eggs about wrapped round its legs.

The Apoda or Caecilians are limbless Amphibia which burrow in the ground like earthworms. They live in wet tropical regions of Asia, Africa, and America. Although blind, they have sensitive tentacles which enable them to feel their way about. They have extremely

AN APODAN

The female lays her eggs in an underground chamber and coils herself round them for their protection

short tails, and some species retain small scales, resembling those of their fish ancestors, embedded in the skin. All are moist and slimy. The large yolky eggs are fertilized within the body of the mother. Some species lay their eggs in an underground chamber, and the parents guard them. The tadpoles continue to live underground, not taking to the water until they are almost mature.

ANACONDA, *see* BOA.

ANATOMY is the study of the organs of the body, the word itself meaning 'to cut up'. The reason why this word is used in this connexion is that the organs cannot be studied in detail until they are artificially separated from one another. Selected organs, such as HEART and TEETH (qq.v.) are dealt with elsewhere. Here we are making a comparative study of animals, to show how their anatomy becomes more elaborate as we ascend the evolutionary scale from simple types such as an Amoeba to higher ones such as a rabbit.

An AMOEBA (q.v.) carries out the same fundamental processes as a rabbit. It moves, breathes, feeds, excretes, grows, and reproduces; but all these functions are carried out by a single mass of protoplasm not divided into separate CELLS (q.v.), though some parts, such as the food vacuoles and contractile vacuole, do have special functions. A rabbit's body, on the other hand, has numerous organs, such as lungs, kidneys, and gut, each having separate functions to perform and each being composed of thousands of cells differing in shape, size, and function. This specialization is termed division of labour. Its simple beginnings are shown in the noncellular Amoeba, but with the evolution of multicellular animals limitless new developments became possible.

This evolution can best be understood by comparing it with what has happened in human society. Primitive man, when he lived with his family alone in a cave, had to do everything for himself. He hunted his own food, fetched his own wood for the fire, made his own pots, tools, weapons, clothes, and so on. As the families came together to form communities, it followed that some men were better hunters, while others were better at making pots; and so the work was divided, making a more efficient system.

In a modern society this division of labour has now reached such a degree that men who have specialized in certain trades or professions, and worked at these for many years, find it difficult to work efficiently at anything else. In a precisely similar way, as the multicellular animals have developed, so their cells have become specialized.

We speak of a primitive society and a civilized (or specialized) society, the second growing out of the first as a result of the division of labour, or of specialization. In the same way we speak of primitive or specialized animals: the lower we go in the animal kingdom, the more primitive its members; the higher we go, the more specialized. If we compare the eyes of different animals, we can see the kind of thing that happens with all organs as we pass from the primitive to the specialized. An Amoeba has no eyes, yet it is not insensitive to light, and will move rapidly away if a strong beam of light is allowed to play on it. The response to light is vested in the whole body. Certain other noncellular animals, especially among those known as the Flagellates, are light-loving, and these have a few grains of a dark, usually red, pigment which is sensitive to light. This is not an eye in the sense in which we usually speak, but it is the beginning of an eye—and the group of pigment granules is known as an eye-spot.

Some of the multicellular animals are without eyes or eye-spots, yet still react to light. It is found, for example, that SPONGES (q.v.) grow best in a moderate light (although, being permanently fixed, they cannot alter their position once they have passed the post-larval stage); so, although they have no eyes, they clearly must be responsive to light stimuli throughout the tissues of the body. Other permanently fixed animals are also without eyes; and it soon becomes apparent, as might be expected, that the development of eyes goes hand in hand with locomotion. Moreover, the faster an animal moves—especially where speed of movement is needed for catching prey, as in insects, birds, and mammals—the better will be the eyesight.

The eyes of slow-moving worms are not obvious; but certain cells of the skin contain pigment cells, and these are scattered singly and evenly over the whole body. In other worms these cells are seen to be collected in groups, with slender nerve fibres running from them to the main nerve cord—here is the beginning of a retina. In other cases the pigmented cells are sunk in a pit in the skin—a sort of rounded chamber lined by pigmented cells. At this point we can see that the eyeball is foreshadowed— and, sure enough, other animals related to worms have developed a lens. It is not possible to describe every type of eye, nor to name the animals that possess them. Summarizing, however, we may say that, as we pass from the lowest to the highest animals, we see the eye develop, first as an eye-spot, then as a group of pigmented cells, and then, as the group of cells grows larger to form a retina, a lens is added, an optic

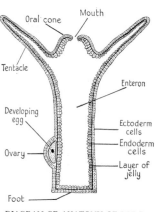

DIAGRAM OF ANATOMY OF HYDRA

nerve, and all the accessories seen in the eye of the highest mammal (*see* SENSES, Section 2).

In the same way we can follow the building up of a digestive system and a BLOOD SYSTEM (q.v.)—the one for taking in food, and the other for passing it round the body. For this purpose we need not go lower in the animal scale than the SEA-ANEMONES or HYDRA (qq.v.). A sea-anemone is nothing more than a cylindrical bag, with an opening or mouth at one end, surrounded by tentacles. The inside of the bag is capacious, and the wall is composed of only two layers of cells, the inner layer being purely digestive, the outer forming the skin. Food taken into this large digestive cavity is absorbed by the cells

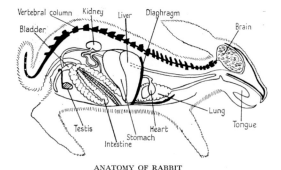

ANATOMY OF RABBIT

of the inner layer, and some is passed on to the cells of the outer layer. The important point is that no cell is so far away from the digestive cells that it cannot absorb food direct from it. The next stage in development after the sea-anemones and their relatives is seen in animals with a narrow tube for the digestion of food, the so-called alimentary tract. These animals have highly developed MUSCLES (q.v.), and grow larger and thicker. This fact alone means that many cells in the body are too far away to have food passed direct to them. Blood-vessels are necessary, therefore, to carry the food round to all parts of the body.

As we go up the scale, and animals develop limbs and become more active, the need for muscles gets greater, the bulk of the body increases in proportion to the space occupied by the alimentary tract, and a more complicated system of blood-vessels becomes necessary. Also, the more active the animal, the more food is needed—and, again, this is an added reason for a more efficient blood system (*see* NUTRITION IN ANIMALS).

With a wider network of blood-vessels comes the greater need for an efficient pump to drive the blood through them. So, in the WORMS (q.v.), the heart is no more than the slightly dilated parts of some of the blood-vessels which, by having more muscular walls than the rest, are able to pulsate and drive the blood along. In the vertebrates, however, a very muscular heart appears, a simple S-shaped tube in fishes, a three-chambered heart in amphibia, and four-chambered in birds and mammals (*see* HEART).

No matter which of the organs we choose, whether the stomach, heart, BRAIN (q.v.), kidneys, or any others, it is possible to show how, as the animal becomes more specialized and complicated, so each organ becomes more elaborate. On the whole, however, there is an orderly pattern along which these specializations proceed, although there are, of course, many exceptions.

Perhaps the chief exceptions in this broad plan concern the NERVOUS SYSTEM, the skeleton, and the organs of RESPIRATION (qq.v.)—that is, gills and lungs. Two points are worth mentioning, however. Firstly, the nervous system of invertebrates is ventral, and the 'brain' is primitive, while that of the vertebrates is dorsal with a more developed brain. Then, the skeleton of invertebrates is usually on the outside of the body. As to the respiratory system, the fact of whether an animal has gills or lungs depends mainly on whether it lives in water or out of it. But again there are exceptions to this, as in the LUNG-FISHES (q.v.) and others.

Briefly, then, the internal organs are, on the whole, built on a regular pattern which becomes more complicated as the animal becomes more specialized. Exceptions do occur, however—one large group, the INSECTS (q.v.), being particularly marked in its departure from the general plan, especially in the breathing and blood-systems. Insects have neither gills nor lungs, but tracheae (although some aquatic larvae have ex-ternal structures which are called gills); and instead of blood-vessels in the form of a system of tubes, they have large blood spaces or sinuses.

See also Vol. XI: ANATOMY (Human).

ANCHOVY, *see* HERRING.

ANGEL-FISH, *see* CICHLIDS.

ANGLER-FISH. In shallow waters round the coasts of Britain and also those of Europe and America is found a curious fish which lies on the bed of the sea and catches smaller fishes by means of a 'rod and line'. Its head is broad and flat, and the wide mouth is armed with long, sharp teeth. Any small animal finding its way between these jaws will be unable to escape, for the teeth can be depressed backwards to form a barrier like a row of fixed bayonets. The 'rod' is the first ray of its first dorsal (back) fin, which is placed rather more forward than usual, near the nose, and is very long, with a tassel of skin at the end. The Angler-fish is so flat that when it lies on the sea-floor it is not easily seen. It also has a CAMOUFLAGE (q.v.) of small flaps of skin that resemble bits of weed. Hidden in this way, it waves its 'bait' to and fro—and when a small fish approaches the tempting morsel, the great jaws close upon it with a snap. It does not rely entirely on its angling, however, but

A. Fraser-Brunner

ANGLER-FISH USING ITS BAIT TO ATTRACT ITS PREY

A. Fraser-Brunner

FEMALE DEEP-SEA ANGLER-FISH CARRYING A LIGHT ON HER NOSE
Firmly attached beneath her are three dwarf males

themselves—though this does sometimes result in their death (*see* DEEP-SEA FISHES).

In some of these oceanic Anglers the male is very small and permanently fixed to the female. It has, in fact, no independent life and cannot even feed for itself, but gets all its nourishment from the blood of the female, which flows into its own blood-vessels. Not all the males are attached in this way—indeed, it is very difficult to understand how this comes about, but it avoids the need to find a mate. It is hard to study creatures living at these great depths, and we have still a lot to learn about them.

sometimes attacks sea-birds from below, dragging them down to the sea-floor. This Angler-fish, 60 to 90 cm long (brought to market under the name Monk), is one of the several kinds of fish sold in shops as 'Rock Salmon'.

The most characteristic feature of the Angler-fish and its relative, the Frog-fish, is the gill-opening without a cover that lies behind the pectoral fins. The paired fins are borne at the end of limb-like structures, which allow the Angler-fish to 'walk' on the sea bottom. They are also used to move sand: the pelvic fins shovel forwards and outwards, while the pectoral ones push the sand away. The fish lies in this hollow, its back almost flush with the surface. Most Frog-fishes inhabit tropical shores. They have smaller lures on the nose and patches of colour which camouflage them as they creep about among the weed. One kind, however, lives in the open sea on the drifting seaweed of the SARGASSO SEA (q.v. Vol. III) and elsewhere.

In the very deep sea, where it is very cold and the light of day does not penetrate, there are many kinds of Angler-fish of various weird shapes, with terrifying faces and even more frightful teeth. They are not flattened and do not lie on the bottom, but swim about in the blackness waving their 'baits', which are often very elaborate, and give off a bright light to attract their prey. Their stomachs are so elastic that they can swallow fishes larger than

ANIMAL DISTRIBUTION. The different species of animals do not occur everywhere throughout the world, but are restricted to particular areas by natural barriers, such as oceans, deserts, and mountains, and within those areas by the nature of the soil or water, the climate (especially rainfall and temperature), the kind of food available, and competition from other species. Some species, the Death's Head Hawk Moth, for example, have a very wide distribution, ranging from Europe to China and Japan, Southern India, Malaya, and North and South Africa, and covering thousands of square kilometres; others have a very limited distribution: for instance, one kind of Leaf-hopper breeds in a single tree on a mountain in Hawaii.

In the latter part of the 19th century it was realized that the land masses of the world could be divided into five regions, within each of which the majority of the land animals were more or less distinct from that of any other region. An English ornithologist, Sclater, named these regions as follows:

1. Holarctic, which may be divided into

    (i) Palaearctic, the northern region of the Old World.
    (ii) Nearctic, the northern region of the New World.

2. Ethiopian, including most of Africa and Arabia.

3. Oriental (or Indian), including those parts of Asia south of the Palaearctic region.

4. Australasian, the continent of Australia, New Zealand, and adjacent islands, including some of the East Indian Islands.

5. Neotropical, the continent and islands of America south of the Tropic of Cancer.

The Oriental and Australasian faunas meet in the East Indian Archipelago, and it is not easy to decide where to draw the line between them. One such division passes between the islands of Bali and Lombok and was named Wallace's Line by T. H. Huxley, after the great naturalist, A. R. Wallace (qq.v. Vol. V). The naturalists Weber and Pelseneer proposed lines farther east, which in some respects are more satisfactory than that suggested by Wallace.

The natural distribution of any one species of animal changes as conditions become more or less favourable for its survival. Occasionally some chance event, such as a great gale, enables a species to pass one of the great barriers that formerly restricted its range and to colonize another zoological region. The African bird, the cattle egret, for example, has recently reached Brazil, probably blown there by a gale, and is now spreading rapidly into Neotropical and Nearctic regions.

This natural distribution of species has also been greatly changed by man, particularly in historical times, when he himself has increased enormously in numbers and has colonized most habitable parts of the globe. Man has always killed animals for food, and for their skins, or for other products, and has decimated certain species, such as bison and whales. More recently, by killing for sport man has reduced, for example, the big game of Africa. Again, man has altered whole environments by felling trees, ploughing the soil, draining marshes, planting crops, and building cities, making vast areas no longer suitable for animals that formerly lived there. In some cases other species with different requirements have moved in to take their place. In this way many species that were formerly widespread and common, for example, the Swallowtail Butterfly and the Passenger Pigeon, have in recent years become local, rare, or extinct; and others, once restricted in distribution, have found new sources of food in agri-cultural crops, and have increased enormously in numbers and range, often becoming widespread Pests (q.v. Vol. VI).

Man has also carried species accidentally to new lands in trade goods, food stores, and on plants, with the result that some species, such as the brown rat and the saw-toothed grain beetle, are now world-wide in distribution, and their original homes difficult or impossible to identify. Man has also deliberately introduced animals and plants from one country to another; for example, he introduced into Australia rabbits from Europe and the prickly pear from the Argentine—introductions which had appalling consequences for the native fauna and flora, which were unable to compete with the newcomers. Sometimes species have been introduced to control other species (see Biological Control, Vol. VI).

Many governments have attempted to preserve species in danger of extinction by laws protecting them. Nature reserves and National Parks (q.v. Vol. IX) are designed to preserve the entire animal and plant communities in selected habitats, such as bogs, sand dunes, and forests.

The distribution of marine (or sea) animals bears some resemblance to that of land animals, but with certain important differences. To understand their distribution, it is necessary to remember that marine animals are divided into three kinds, according to habit. The 'planktonic' animals are those that float on the surface, but drift with the currents, such as jelly-fishes, as well as the teeming microscopic forms. The 'nektonic' animals are those that are free-swimming and capable of propelling themselves against a current. The 'benthic' animals are those which live on the bottom—either fixed, such as sponges and corals, or burrowing, such as worms and some shell-fish, or creeping about the bottom, such as starfish and most molluscs.

The distribution of the Plankton (q.v.) is largely determined by the ocean currents, and that of the nekton is mainly governed by temperature. The distribution of the benthic animals, however, is closely similar to that of land animals. This is a very simplified version of a very complicated subject. To begin with, there is no hard-and-fast line to be drawn between plankton, nekton, and benthos. For example, the larva of a coral is a free-swimming larva and therefore planktonic; but the adult is benthic. The larval fish is planktonic, and the adult nektonic. Moreover, we have outstanding exceptions, such as the large blue whales of the Antarctic. These are powerful swimmers, therefore nektonic; but they feed on krill, a minute shrimp-like animal which drifts in its millions with the currents. Thus the whales follow the krill and their distribution, which is planktonic.

ANIMAL LANGUAGE. Man alone is able to convey precise information to his fellows through speech. But although only he, when hungry, can ask for the particular food he wants, many other animals can show that they are hungry, and to that extent have a language or means of communication. Thus, when hungry, a lamb will bleat, a lion will roar, a dog will fawn upon its master. The difference between human and animal language is, therefore, that whereas an animal can show by voice, gesture, or other sign that it is in a certain emotional or physical state—such as hungry, tired, frightened, playful, and so on—man is able to express such feelings in precise terms, and to indicate not only that he is hungry, but what he wishes to eat, not only that he is afraid, but of what he is afraid.

Apart from speech, however, man still retains certain features of animal language. Laughter, usually considered as peculiarly human, is language of this sort: a Zulu, hearing an Englishman laugh, understands his feeling; though if the Englishman tried to describe why he laughed, the Zulu would probably not understand. So it is with tears, sobs, screams, and other primitive language sounds, as well as gestures and bodily movements: these are universal just because they are primitive, and because they indicate the emotional state of the person who makes them.

It is not only by such simple sounds as most of the mammals produce that animals can show their state of feeling: the song of birds, for example, is far more elaborate and highly developed. It is produced in the lower part of the trachea, in a portion known as the syrinx—a great variety of sounds resulting, continuous chirrups, raucous croaks, sweet and varied musical notes, cries of alarm, and shrieks of rage. True birdsong has two main purposes. Many male birds sing in order to warn off other males of their own kind from intruding into their breeding territory. Many also sing to attract a mate to the territory (*see* ANIMAL TERRITORY). Some birds,

therefore, like the Nightingale, sing only during the breeding season; others, which sing all the year round, are at their best at this period. Song is most used by birds which would otherwise find it difficult to communicate with each other—birds living scattered in the woods, hedges, and fields, and small birds with inconspicuous plumage. Large conspicuous birds or those living in flocks do not usually sing.

Another form of animal language is that known as display. The strutting PEACOCK with his fanned and gorgeous tail, the magnificent BIRD OF PARADISE displaying his plumes in dance, the great crested GREBES shaking their fantastically adorned heads at one another, or the BLACKBIRD (qq.v.) with the feathers of his rump raised up and his tail pressed on the ground—all these are showing their readiness to mate and breed. These displays are confined to this special use just as much as song is confined to its uses, or as other forms of display are employed to frighten off an intruder, to lure away an enemy, or even to submit to a superior. The ROBIN, for instance, will raise up his beak and sway from side to side, waving his red danger signal at a rival; a SNIPE disturbed at her nest will flutter away as if she were injured, with dragging wings, and so lure an inquisitive dog or man far from her eggs; and a JACKDAW will bow his head and expose the pale grey patch on his nape in submission, like a dog with its tail between its legs. Other forms of display are used when birds are looking for a site for their nest, when they are warning their chicks to hide, or inviting them to fly. The cock REDSTART (qq.v.) has a series of displays by which he induces the hen to begin the nest, which she alone builds, in a hole which he alone selects. If one of his displays fails, he will try the others.

Though these displays seem so clearly directed to achieve their end, it must not be supposed that the bird can perceive that end, or that he deliberately tries to bring it about. The displaying bird is doing no more than expressing his own emotional or physiological state. The hen responds because this expression brings something new into her environment, and her response is likewise no more than an expression of her state, though that may have been changed by her perception of the male's display.

The language of birds, because of the complexity of their lives, is more elaborate and more apparently purposeful than the language of other

G. K. Yeates

Male Blackcock displaying its tail feathers on the 'lek', or communal mating ground

Eric Hosking

White Storks performing greeting ceremony

Eric Hosking

Little Terns courtship feeding

COURTSHIP DISPLAY OF BIRDS

groups of animals. Yet it is no more remarkable than the language of many insects. In this, though sound plays some part, as with crickets and grasshoppers, and though some beetles make gestures with their armoured legs, and other insects with their wings or tails, the most elaborate displays are connected with scent and the sense of smell. This sense lies in the antennae, but the scent scales are situated in various parts of the body. In most British butterflies the male's scent scales are on the upper part of the wing. In some species, such as the GRAYLING (q.v.) (whose scent is like the wood of an old cigar-box), the male will stand before the female, waving his wings slowly to direct the scent towards her, and she will touch the scented

Harold Bastin

The Ruff displaying before the Reeve (hen)

patches with her antennae. Many female butterflies and moths have scents which lead the males to them, but these scents are not perceptible by man. The scents of the male, on the other hand, can be detected by man, and it is a surprising fact that most of them are pleasing to us as well as to the female insect.

It is not possible here to do more than suggest something of the immense variety of means by which animals of all classes communicate with one another. But it must be remembered that, since no animal except man has the power to reflect, and therefore the power to foresee, animal language is limited to the expression of an emotional or physiological state. They are not able to form ideas, or to define their needs or desires as we can; but by expressing their own feelings, they affect the consciousness of their companions, mates, offspring, or enemies, and so avoid the chaos which would ensue if they had no language.

See also Colour Plate opposite p. 16.

ANIMAL TERRITORY. Many animals live in flocks, herds, or shoals, while others live a more or less solitary life for most of the year. But whether they live with others of their own kind or not, during the breeding season almost all animals keep their own small family isolated to some extent. This is more obvious in those which have only one mate, such as the fox, but is no less true of deer and seals, which are polygamous.

The segregation of a mated pair, or of a group of animals, is brought about because the male adopts an area which he regards as his own property or territory, and which he will defend against any intruder of his own species. The area defended may be extremely small, or it may cover a wide tract of land; but in either case it will be sufficient to secure freedom for its owner to breed without disturbance, and without the wasteful fighting which animals of all kinds (except man) have learnt to avoid. The supreme climax of life for living creatures, whether plant or animal, is the reproduction of their own kind, and their survival is, obviously, dependent on their success in achieving this. If, as was once supposed, male animals regularly fought for their mates, there would soon be very few males left. Where fighting does take place, it is usually for the sake of a territory, and not for a mate. The habit of holding a territory is clearly related to the supply of food, and is therefore supremely important during the breeding season when the young are arriving—for not only do they require, proportionately to their size, a greater quantity of food, but they are also often unable to move about in search of it. Moreover, although the habit is most marked in birds, in certain mammals, and in such insects as dragonflies, it is obvious that to a lesser degree all species must have developed this habit of spacing themselves out—which is all the habit of holding territory amounts to.

As this behaviour was first noticed in birds, and has been most carefully studied in them, it may be as well to give examples from these. In spring, birds begin to return to the places where they will breed, either from overseas (*see* MIGRATION) or from the flock in which they gathered during the winter. The first to arrive, whether a Swallow or a Cuckoo from Africa, a Chaffinch from the flock in the neighbouring rick-yard, or a Lapwing from a flock in the meadows, will almost always be a male. And, often quite gradually, this male bird will settle down in some place where it is going to breed—at first, perhaps, returning for part of the day to the flock which it has just left, or associating with several other birds with which it arrived from migration. But soon, especially if the weather is fine, it will grow more and more intolerant of the presence of others of its kind. Now, if a Finch or Lapwing had to drive off all the trespassing Finches or Lapwings by fighting, it would soon become exhausted. Also, since the male has arrived first, some means must be found whereby the female, when she arrives, can find a mate. The remarkable songs of male birds meet these difficulties. The bird, once established in its territory, begins to sing, thereby warning other males of its kind not to trespass within hearing, at the same time informing arriving females where a mate of their own kind is to be found. Many birds, when singing, make themselves as conspicuous as possible—by perching on the topmost twig of a tree, like the Thrush, by flying high in the air over the fields, as the Skylark does. The Lapwing, which does not sing, often indulges in some aerobatic display.

Some birds of prey hold a territory covering many hectares of moorland in which all the food for the pair and for their chicks will be found. The Finches and Thrushes of our gardens lay claim, perhaps, to only half a hectare of territory, for these birds have a very varied diet, and they can find all they require in a small area. The Swallows and many sea-birds hold a territory covering only a metre or so about the nest, for these birds range far and wide through the air or over the sea for their food, and all they require is space enough to lay their eggs without disturbance. But the principle is the same in all.

Those birds with no song usually have a very small territory, which they defend by visual means. The Razorbill and Guillemot, for instance, defend their cliff territory by gesture and display; Ducks can see any intruder coming over the open water, and can warn them off by visual means. Also, the pairing of these birds takes place during the winter in the flock, so that there is no question of the male needing to make his presence known to the female.

Mammals achieve the same isolation during breeding by much the same means. They have no song, but the stag roars, and so warns off his rivals, and other mammals, as well as reptiles and fishes, make threatening sounds or gestures which serve the same purpose as the song of birds. Insects, too, often have their own territory, the grasshopper's reeling and the cricket's chirrup serving to warn off rivals and to attract mates.

Normally, territory is defended only against animals of the same species. Thus in the same garden, Blackbird and Thrush, Robin, Dunnock, and Wren, Chaffinch and Greenfinch, Swallow and House Martin, may all have breeding territories overlapping one another, without any rivalry between them. Tits of different species, which all require holes in which to breed, may quarrel over some particular hole or nest-box, and contests of this sort do take place. But for most birds any number of suitable places are available, and if rivals of their own species are kept away, no trouble arises from others.

When the breeding season is over and the young are independent of their parents, territory is held no longer, except by a very few species—of which, in Britain, the ROBIN (q.v.) is the best known. Robins of both sexes hold territory outside the breeding season, and the song of the hen Robin assists in its preservation. (Song is quite exceptional in hen birds of other species.) After the breeding season, a hundred or more seals may be seen basking together on the same rock, huge flocks of Geese and Waders come to our estuaries and feed peacefully side by side, and in the stubbles and rick-yards the little birds that sang so vigorously not long before to segregate themselves from their fellows, now peck about together without concern.

See also ANIMAL LANGUAGE.

ANOA, *see* BUFFALO.

ANT-EATER. This mammal belongs to the order of animals called Edentata (without teeth), which includes also the SLOTHS and ARMADILLOS (qq.v.). Members of this order are to be found only in South or Central America. All Edentata have relatively small brains and are without front teeth, or, like the ant-eater, have no teeth at all.

Ant-eaters live in tropical forests or low, wet lands near rivers. The best-known of them (though none are at all common) is the Great Ant-eater. This is a large animal, standing about 60 cm high and measuring about 180 cm from head to tip of tail. It is a most fantastic-looking creature. It has an extremely long, narrow head; its body is covered with dark grey hair, marked with black bands margined with white; it has an enormous mass of long, stiff hair on its tail, making it appear like a huge brush; its front legs are long and very powerful; and its front feet have curved claws, one of which is much longer than the others.

The Great Ant-eater lives entirely on the ground, and only comes out by night. During the day it curls itself up, covering its body with its great tail, the hairs of which fall down on either side, hiding it very effectively among the

AUSTRALIAN BIRDS IN COURTSHIP DISPLAY

Above: The Satin Bower-bird decorates his 'bower' with shells
Below: The Lyre-bird displays his magnificent tail to the female

THE LESSER ANT-EATER

Booth Steamship Co.

tall grasses where it makes its lair. Its food consists chiefly of termites and ants and their larvae. It rips open their nests with the long curved claw of its front foot; then, when the ants rush out, it licks them up with its immensely long, sticky tongue, which goes in and out of its mouth with lightning speed. Except during the mating season the ant-eaters generally live alone. They are not at all aggressive animals, but, if cornered, they are said to turn and attack fiercely, their method of attack being to catch their enemies in their great muscular arms and crush them by hugging.

Another species, the Lesser Ant-eater (Tamandua), is only about half the size, and has a shorter head, short, bristly hair, and a long, but not hairy, tail. It spends most of its life in trees, and climbs with the use of its prehensile tail as well as its claws. It is rather more common than its larger relation and is sometimes seen abroad during the day. The third species, the Pigmy or Two-toed Ant-eater, is very much smaller, no larger than a rat. It lives only in the hottest forest regions of South and Central America, and because of its size, its nocturnal habits, and the fact that it lives in the trees, it is very rarely seen. It hangs on to the branches of trees with its curved claws and its prehensile tail, and sleeps by day in a hollow tree-trunk.

The Aard-Vark or Ant-bear and the Pangolin (qq.v.) used to be included in the order Edentata, but are now classified differently.

ANTELOPE. 1. Antelopes are among the most graceful animals in the world. They live in various types of country—plains, forests, mountains, and marshes. They are herbivorous—that is, they eat mostly grass and the leaves of trees —ruminating or chewing the cud in the same way as the Deer and Cattle, Sheep, and Goats (qq.v.). Whereas deer shed their antlers annually, the antelope's horns are part of the skull itself and remain throughout its life, as in cattle and sheep. The horns vary a great deal in shape and size: with some species they are curved or twisted in spirals, with others they are quite straight. Those of the handsome African Kudus are sometimes over a metre long, whereas those of the Duikerboks are only from 7 to 10 cm. Antelopes also vary greatly in size, from the Eland, nearly 2 metres high, to the tiny Pigmy Antelopes of Africa, only 30 cm high and little larger than a rabbit. The following are some of the best-known.

2. The Gazelles are a large group of smallish, sandy-coloured antelopes, found in Africa and parts of Asia. One species, called the Gerenuk, has such a long neck that it is often likened to a miniature giraffe. Another species, the Springbok of South Africa, gets its name from its habit of suddenly leaping into the air when it is running. Vast herds of Springboks used to migrate from one district to another, in masses so dense that if they met a flock of sheep, the sheep would be inevitably swept along with them. Now, the Springboks are comparatively rare.

3. The Gnus or Wildebeests are large, ungainly antelopes, with short, broad heads, long, hairy tails and manes, and broad heavy horns, rather like those of a buffalo. Their eyes are small, and their general appearance is uncouth and clumsy. There are few uglier beasts.

Paul Popper

GROUP OF GRANT'S GAZELLES IN KENYA

Large herds used to be seen on the veld in South Africa; but today only a few are kept in game preserves, though large herds are still found in East Africa. The Hartebeests of south, east, and west Africa are also fairly large, over a metre high, with long, narrow faces, and horns curved sharply backwards.

4. The largest antelopes, the Elands, are found only in Africa. They stand nearly 2 metres high, and both sexes have twisted horns from 60 to 90 cm long. They live both in semi-desert and in wooded country. Among the small antelopes are the Steinboks, the Grysboks, and the Klipspringers, which live in the mountains of Africa. The Klipspringer, whose name means 'rock-jumper', is able to bound up the sides of very steep cliffs, and has very small hoofs which enable it to stand safely on narrow ledges. Indeed, the hoofs are so small that the animal can take advantage of a projection of rock no larger than a 20p piece to obtain a foothold in leaping. The Marshbucks, or Situtungas, which also live in Africa, have long, spreading hoofs which enable them to walk on marshy land and on the soft banks of streams and lakes.

Of the Indian antelopes, the largest is the Nilgai, sometimes called the 'Blue Bull', from the colour of the adult males. It stands about 1·5 metres high, has a mane on its neck, and a fringed tail, and is a rather ungainly animal. Only the males have horns—short, curved, and very sharp.

See also CHAMOIS.

ANTLER-MOTH, *see* NIGHT-FLYING MOTHS.

ANTS. These insects belong to one large family, the Formicidae, which together with BEES and WASPS, ICHNEUMON and Braconid Flies, CHALCID FLIES, GALL-WASPS, and SAWFLIES (qq.v.) is included in the order Hymenoptera. They are easily distinguished from other insects by the narrow waist formed by one or two small abdominal segments.

About 8,000 different kinds of ants are known, most of which are found in the tropics. With very few exceptions, they are social insects, living in communities which may contain as few as a dozen individuals or as many as several hundred thousand. The colony is made up of one or more perfect females, usually called 'queens', a large number of imperfect females, called 'workers', and, at the right time of the year, many males. These three different forms

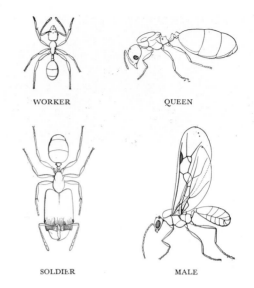

WORKER   QUEEN

SOLDIER   MALE

of ants are known as 'castes'. The worker ant, like the workers of the Hive Bee, the Bumble Bees, and the Social Wasps, does not produce offspring. Many kinds of ants have two forms of the worker caste, simple workers and 'soldiers'. The soldiers have enormous heads, which seem out of all proportion to the size of the rest of the body. Although these curious workers are called soldiers, their role is by no means only to protect the colony. The huge head has made possible the development of powerful muscles. These give great strength to the pair of large mandibles, with which the soldier is able to crush seeds and insects. Only the queens and males have wings, but the queens remove theirs immediately after the marriage flight. The workers and queens of some kinds of ants are armed with a sting, which they use for defence. Many species have no sting, but are able, instead, to squirt formic acid from the tail-end of the body. If one of the nests of the Wood-Ant is disturbed, the acid squirted up by the seething mass of ants may be seen rising as a fine spray.

The queen ant, one of which has been kept alive in captivity for 17 years, lays eggs, which hatch into legless grubs or larvae. These larvae are looked after by the worker ants, who carry them about and place them in whatever parts of the nest seems at the time best for them. The workers are very sensitive to warmth and humidity, both of which are necessary for the growth of the larvae. For warmth they rely very much on the heat brought by the sun's rays—which is why, in warm, damp weather, the ant larvae will be found near the surface of the soil; but in cold or very dry weather, the workers carry the larvae deep down into the ground, where the soil is moist and the temperature higher. The grubs receive either liquid or solid food from the workers. The liquid food is stored by the ants in their crop, and taken back to the nest to be shared out amongst the brood. During feeding, the worker places its mouth against that of the larva, and forces up from its crop a droplet of liquid, which is eagerly swallowed by the grub. The solid food is cut up into small fragments and placed within reach of the grubs.

When the larvae become full grown, they change into pupae. The larvae of some kinds of ants, among which is the Wood Ant, spin a cocoon before pupating. (It is the cocoons of the Wood Ant which are sold for feeding Goldfish, as 'ants' eggs'.) Others make the change without any protection. After a time there emerges from the pupa an adult ant, which may be a queen, a male, or a worker. It is important to notice that each individual ant-larva is not confined during its growth within a cell, like the larvae of the social bees and wasps. The absence of the cell-building habit in ants has certainly been useful to them, because, if for some reason a nesting site becomes unsuitable, many kinds of ants are able to move to a new one, taking with them their eggs, larvae, and pupae.

The marriage flight of ants in Great Britain usually takes place simultaneously over wide areas, embracing several counties, on still, sultry days towards the end of summer. This promotes outbreeding between different colonies. The flights that we are likely to observe will be those of the common Black Garden Ant. The tiny males and huge females leave the nests in enormous numbers, flying into the air in clouds. Pairing takes place in flight, and afterwards the females drift slowly down, with the males still attached to their bodies. Once the female reaches the ground, she quickly throws off the male, removes her wings, and is then ready to set about the business of starting a home.

The methods by which queen ants make their homes are many, and only a few can be mentioned here. The fertilized female or queen may found her colony without any help at all, just as the queen Wasp and the queen Bumble Bee do. Or she may rely on the help of ants from strange colonies, belonging to a different species from herself. Or she may return to the nest from which she first came, which now, having perhaps several queens, may become so populous that a number of smaller colonies are split or budded off from it.

Among the ants which found their colonies without help is the common Black Garden Ant, mentioned earlier. The fertilized queen burrows into the ground, and hollows out for herself a small cell or chamber. She carefully blocks the entrance to this cell, and does not leave it again until she has brought up her first brood of workers. For roughly 9 months she remains a voluntary prisoner, and takes no food at all. How, then, does she feed her small brood of larvae? It must be remembered that when our queen ant set to work to bring up a family, her body was plump and well nourished. Now, by drawing on these fat reserves and on materials formed from the breakdown of her wing muscles, she is able to keep up a constant supply of the saliva on which she feeds her larvae. These larvae produce undersized, but vigorous, ants which soon tunnel to the surface to find food for themselves and their mother.

More exciting and adventurous ways of starting family life are shown by the queens of those species of ants which must have help during this critical period of their lives. The queen of the Slave-maker Ant (*Formica sanguinea*) must seek out a nest of *Formica fusca* and steal some of its pupae. She hides these away in some little cavity in the ground, taking care of them until they become adult ants, capable of bringing up the offspring of their foster-mother. The queens of other species somehow manage to get themselves accepted by the workers of an alien colony as members of the community. Such an ant is *Lasius fuliginosus*, a shiny, jet-black ant which is fairly common in Great Britain, and whose rather slow-moving workers march in long files to and from their nest. The fertilized queen enters the nest of *Lasius umbratus* (a yellow ant which spends most of its life underground), and is treated as a friend by the yellow ants. What happens to their own queen-mother is not quite clear; but after a while, black *fuliginosus* workers appear among the yellow ants. The two species, so sharply contrasted in colour, work peacefully together, until finally the yellow ants die out, and the colony consists only of the black *fuliginosus*.

Ants obtain food in three different ways, almost like the methods used by human beings at different cultural levels. The most primitive are the hunters which catch, kill, and bring back to the nest small animals of many kinds, especially insects. The gleaners return with seeds and fruits, nectar of flowers, and the excretions of aphids and scale insects. The most advanced are the 'agriculturalists' which tend special fungus gardens in underground chambers connected to the open air by ventilating passages. Hunting ants usually have a better developed sting than do gleaners and agriculturalists.

If a plant infested with APHIDS (q.v.) is looked at closely, ants will often be seen crawling about over the dense mass of greenfly, gently tapping them with their antennae and quickly sucking up the sugary droplets ejected from the vent. The Common Yellow Ant, a mound builder of English pastures, lives almost entirely on the secretions of underground aphids which feed on the roots of plants. The ants tend the aphids much as men tend a herd of cattle.

Ant societies seem to be much older than those of wasps and bees, and the various castes have been found preserved as fossils in AMBER (q.v. Vol. III) thought to have been formed 35 million years ago.

See also INSECTS.
See also Vol. VI: INSECT PESTS.

ANTS, HABITS OF. So varied are the habits of ants that no more than a few of them can be discussed here.

In South America some of the most abundant ants are the so-called Umbrella, or Leaf-cutting Ants, known as *Atta*. They are to be seen in great columns, each ant carrying a large piece of leaf over its head. The Attas are expert gardeners, and grow a fungus in large hollows which they dig out in the soil. But a fungus will grow only on dead and decaying organic matter, and so the ants chew up into tiny fragments the pieces of leaf, and with them make a mushroom bed in which the spores of the fungus will germinate. Certain parts of the fungus form the main diet of the ants and their larvae. Now the Attas usually live in dry desert regions, where food in the form of insects is not easy to obtain: by cultivating a fungus and getting their nourishment from it, they are not worried by a shortage of other kinds of food.

In the drier parts of the world, where plant as well as animal life is scarce, other kinds of ants have solved the food problem quite differently from the Attas. In the deserts of North America, for example, live the Harvesting Ants, known as *Pogonomyrmex*. Although they will eat insects whenever they can get them, they normally rely for food on the seeds of various plants, which they gather and store. Even more remarkable are the Honey-pot Ants, likewise inhabitants of desert regions in various parts of the world. These ants set aside some of their sister workers to become living reservoirs of food. They feed them with juices until their abdomens become enormously swollen—so much so, indeed, that in the case of one species living in North America, *Myrmecocystus horti-deorum*, the self-sacrificing workers are unable to move. They hang motionless from the roof of their underground chambers, like so many barrels of wine, waiting to be tapped when other sources of food dry up.

The three kinds of ants that have just been mentioned all nest in the ground. This habit is shared by most species of ants; but there are a great many kinds that make their homes only in trees and shrubs. Perhaps the best known of these is *Oecophylla smaragdina*, an ant to be found in numbers all over the tropics of the Far East. Its nest is just a mass of leaves, drawn together and held fast by means of fine silken threads. Now, no adult ant has spinning glands; but the larvae of *Oecophylla* spin cocoons, and so they are used by the worker ants as living tools for spinning together the leaves out of which the nest is made.

The Doryline or Driver Ants of Africa have strange nomadic habits, and work together in an uncanny way. Except for short periods, when they settle down in one spot, they are ever on the move, marching in long files many thousands strong and sweeping every living thing out of their path. They are meat-eaters, and will devour any animal that, by sheer weight of numbers, they can torment to death. If a human dwelling happens to stand in the path of the moving column, the ants will enter it and quickly rid it of spiders, cockroaches, and beetles. The astonishing fact about these ants is that the workers of which this vast crawling army is composed are entirely blind—and yet they have no difficulty in keeping together, or in uniting their efforts for a particular purpose. They communicate with each other by means of sense

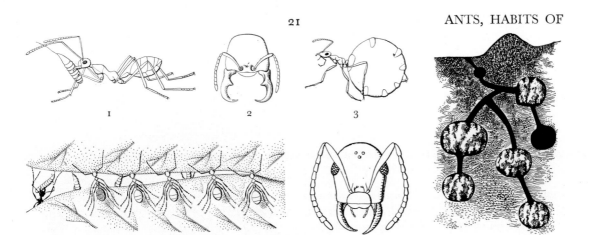

HABITS OF ANTS

1. Worker of Tree Ant, using larva for spinning threads; 2. Head of Driver Ant, showing tong-like mandibles; 3. Worker of Honey-pot Ant, showing swollen abdomen; 4. Workers of Tree Ant using larvae to fasten edges of leaves together; 5. Head of Slave-maker Ant, showing sickle-shaped mandibles; 6. Fungus gardens of Leaf-cutter Ant

organs of which we understand very little at present.

Some ants have acquired the habit of keeping other ants as slaves. Some kinds cannot live at all without their slaves; others need them only when their colonies are small, but can do without them when the colonies become sufficiently populous. Of the latter type is the large handsome *Formica sanguinea*, in appearance very much like the common Wood Ant, but much brighter in colour and more rapid in its movements. It usually lives in dry places, such as the sandy heaths of southern England, and can often be seen on hot sunny days running nimbly over the ground. It often makes its nest in the stump of a pine tree. If we break off a piece of the decayed bark, we may very likely find a great many ants, with their brood, crowded beneath it. They will come out in a flurry of angry excitement, and we shall notice that, in addition to the large numbers of pugnacious red-coloured slave-makers, there are many smaller ants, bronzy black in colour. These are the slaves, and they belong to a species called *Formica fusca*. These timid workers are no worse off in the colony of *Formica sanguinea* than they would be in their own: they tend the brood, forage for food, and altogether take a full share in the running of the community. What is interesting about these slave ants is not that they settle down so peacefully among strangers, but the manner in which they have been brought into the strange colony —the details of the slave-raid itself. Scouts

of the red slave-maker having discovered the whereabouts of a nest of *Formica fusca*, the raid is made on some warm summer's day. The *sanguinea* ants come out of their holes in great numbers and, forming themselves into a rather loose band, make their way towards the nest of the black ant. As soon as they reach it, they rush boldly in, scattering the inhabitants, who begin to flee in confusion. Each *sanguinea* ant seizes a cocoon of the *fusca* and at once makes for home with it. Should a bolder *fusca* worker attempt to prevent a raider from carrying off its booty, a savage bite from the powerful mandibles of the slave-maker quickly puts it out of action. From these stolen cocoons eventually emerge the adult *fusca* workers, who from that time live in complete harmony with their captors.

Another and much more thorough-going slave-maker, *Polyergus rufescens*, is to be found on the continent of Europe, but not in Great Britain. The workers of this species are able neither to dig their nest nor to look after their brood—in fact, they are scarcely able even to feed themselves. They have become parasitic upon the ants they enslave, and cannot live without them. These Amazons of the ant world are blood-red in colour and have long, sickle-shaped mandibles, well fitted to pierce the heads of the ants whose colonies they plunder and pillage. The timid, black *Formica fusca* is again usually the victim. The raids made by *Formica sanguinea* seem clumsy affairs by comparison with the extremely well-organized raids of *Polyergus rufescens*.

Arriving in almost military formation at a nest of the *fusca*, the Amazon ants pour into it, killing or driving out the numerous *fusca* workers, and seizing their cocoons. The late August Forel, a great expert on ants, made a series of observations on a colony of the Amazons, and estimated that the number of slave-makers in it was round about 1,000, and that the number of cocoons of slave-ants taken by them in one season was not far short of 20,000. Of all these stolen cocoons, only a small proportion eventually produce adult ants, the others being either killed by rough handling or consumed as food.

One species of ant, occurring in north Africa, and called *Bothriomyrmex decapitans*, has a particularly interesting method of starting its colony. After her marriage flight, the queen *Bothriomyrmex* wanders about over the ground until she finds a nest of another ant, *Tapinoma nigerrimum*. She is seized at once by the workers of *Tapinoma* and dragged into their nest. They treat her roughly, and unless she can find a means of protecting herself, she is likely to be severely mauled. She therefore mounts on to the back of the much larger *Tapinoma* queen, where for some reason she is safe from further attack. But for the *Tapinoma* queen this unwelcome load means certain death. Slowly and deliberately the *Bothriomyrmex* female begins to saw off with her strong mandibles the head of her rival. By the time this murderous deed is accomplished, she has acquired the nest odour of the *Tapinoma* colony and now moves about among the workers without fear of being molested by them. The workers bring up her brood, and the colony eventually becomes pure *Bothriomyrmex decapitans* —for the *Tapinoma* population, having now no queen of its own, gradually dies out.

APES (Anthropoid). **1.** Under the term 'ape' might be included not only the anthropoid or manlike apes, but also all the MONKEYS (q.v.), which belong to the same order as Man—the Primates. But this article is concerned only with the manlike apes—the Chimpanzee, Gorilla, Orang-utan, and Gibbon. Structurally, these animals are very much like man. They have hands adapted for grasping, though their feet, in contrast to man's, are adapted for grasping as well as for walking—the big toe being opposed to the other toes, as man's thumb is opposed to his fingers. In contrast to monkeys, they have no tails or cheek pouches, and have larger and

Harold Bastin

CHIMPANZEE

more developed brains than any other animal except man—but even then the relative size of the brain is half or less than half that of man. The skulls of the manlike apes are very little different in shape from those of the ape-men, the earliest ancestors of modern man (*see* EVOLUTION OF MAN, Vol. I). The apes have longer arms and shorter legs than man, because they are adapted in varying degrees for life in trees. They produce only one young one at a birth, as do all kinds of monkeys except Marmosets.

2. CHIMPANZEE. Of all the large manlike apes, the Chimpanzee of the tall equatorial forests of west and central Africa comes nearest to man in bodily structure, and has been the longest known to Europeans. A fully grown male is not more than 1·5 metres high, weighs 82 kg, and when standing upright his arms reach only a short distance below the knee. The young animal has a bare face which is nearly white, though it usually darkens and often becomes completely black later on. Chimpanzees keep together in family parties, building a resting platform rather low in the trees. They eat fruit, nuts, and many kinds of green food, and seem continually to shift their haunts in order to find fresh feeding-grounds. Sometimes they visit and pillage deserted native plantations. They utter loud cries, which may be heard resounding through the forest at all hours of the night. Young chimpanzees are affectionate and intelligent, though apt to become rather uncertain in temper as they grow older. They used to be regarded as delicate, and were given hot-house treatment in zoos, which caused them to die very early; but now that they are given normal conditions, they live healthily for many years, and prove to be comparatively hardy.

3. GORILLA. This is the largest of the manlike apes, a full-grown male being nearly 2 metres high and weighing 254 kg. Gorillas live in family parties in the densest parts of the forests of Equatorial Africa, travelling from district to district in search of food, such as wild fruits, the juicy stalks of wild celery, the roots of plants, and leaves. They walk on all-fours, with their hands closed and the knuckles resting on the ground. Until quite recently, this huge ape was regarded as being very savage, and was supposed to live in the trees. This myth has now been completely exploded—gorillas are now known to be rather playful, docile, and peaceful animals, never attacking a man unless they are wounded, or in order to defend their young. Moreover, they do not live in trees—indeed they very rarely climb high up in trees, but spend most of their time on the ground, making beds or nests at the foot of trees or in the shelter of dense growths.

4. ORANG-UTAN. This manlike ape is found only in the swampy forests of Sumatra and Borneo. Its name, a Malayan word, means 'Man of the Woods'. Its brain is more like that of man than any other ape; but otherwise it is less like a human being in structure than are the Gorilla and Chimpanzee, and is far better adapted than they are for a life in trees, its legs being short and weak, but its arms long and very strong. The adult male is nearly 1·5 metres high, weighs about 76 kg, and grows large, fleshy flaps from the side of his face. He has a long, thick, reddish-brown coat—unusual for an animal living in such a hot climate, but it probably serves to protect the ape against the deluges of rain in the wet seasons and also against mosquitoes. The Orang-utan never leaps or jumps, and never seems to be in a hurry: the idea that he will make his way overhead in the forest as fast as a man can run on the ground below is not confirmed by modern observers, who all agree that he is slow and deliberate. He eats various fruits and leaves, gathering them with his long arms as he swings from bough to bough. He collects branches and leaves and builds a large sleeping-platform in the trees.

Orang-utans live well under modern zoo conditions, one having recently lived to be over 30 years old in the London Zoo.

5. GIBBON. These, the smallest of the manlike apes, live in the forests of south-east Asia. The largest is less than a metre high. Their arms are so long that, when standing upright, they can touch the ground with their fingers. They are the only apes which walk normally in an upright position. Sometimes they use their arms when walking; but they can walk perfectly well with their hands clasped behind their necks. Gibbons live in family parties in the trees, rarely coming to the ground. They are extraordinarily agile, and swing from branch to branch and tree to tree without seeming to make any effort. They move so fast that they often succeed in capturing birds flying among the trees. As well as birds, they eat fruit and leaves. Their cries in the morning are loud and almost unearthly. On the whole, tamed Gibbons have an amiable and affectionate nature, though they appear to take a mischievous pleasure, as children sometimes do, in doing what they know is forbidden. Despite the greatest care, they do not live long in captivity in Europe.

See also LEMURS.

APHIS (order Hemiptera). Aphides are usually only about 2–3 mm. in length, but they breed quickly, produce dense infestations, and carry virus diseases from infected to healthy plants, so that in spite of their small size they are some of the worst insect pests. They are usually green, brown, or black and are often known as Plant-Lice, Green-flies (those that attack Roses), Black Dolphin or Black Blight (those that attack Broad Beans). Some, such as the Cabbage Aphis, secrete a white waxy substance which gives them a powdery appearance or completely conceals them, as it does the Woolly Aphis of apple trees. They are soft-bodied and are preyed upon by many insects, such as LADY-BIRDS, LACEWINGS, and HOVER-FLIES (qq.v.) as well as by birds such as FLY-CATCHERS, SPARROWS, and WARBLERS (qq.v.). They thus form an important link in many food-chains.

They are sluggish, slow-moving insects, but some are sufficiently active to escape many of the attacks of other insects or to defend themselves by smearing the heads of their enemies with wax secreted from two tubes which can be seen protruding from the fifth abdominal segment. Others are protected by being so dis-tasteful that a Lady-bird larva vomits if it eats them.

Aphides, like all Bugs (q.v.), have beak-like mouth-parts with which they pierce leaves, stems, buds, fruits, bark, or roots and suck the plant juices through the wounds. This damages the plant and may cause malformations such as galls or curled and twisted leaves. These juices contain far more sugar than the aphides require, and the excess is excreted through the vent as 'honey-dew', sometimes in such vast quantities as to drip from the leaves like rain. This sugary excretion is attractive to many kinds of insects, especially to Ants (q.v.): some species of ants tend and protect groups of aphides much as man does a herd of cows. When the 'honey-dew' accumulates on leaves it blocks the pores, and as it is sticky it picks up dust and also fungus spores which quickly develop.

In the autumn, male and female Aphides are found together on the same tree; and, after pairing, the female lays her eggs in places of safety, such as chinks in the bark. These eggs hatch in the following spring, and the minute Aphides immediately attack the food-plant, puncturing its tissues and sucking its juices. They grow up quickly, and, like all bugs, cast the skin or 'moult' at stages through their growth. When adult, they are all wingless females. These rapidly produce offspring with-out pairing, for as yet there are no males—a kind of Reproduction in Animals (q.v.) called 'parthenogenesis'. These offspring are born alive (viviparously) instead of hatching from eggs. Generation after generation of female Aphides may be produced in this way in rapid succession, and enormous numbers of all sizes gather together on one particular stem or leaf. Overcrowding and lack of food now causes the development of other youngsters, born par-thenogenetically and viviparously, as described above. These grow up into winged females, and fly away to other plants, often in such enormous numbers that they make a dense mass. New colonies are thus founded in fresh situations; and further series of generations follow rapidly until, in late summer, males appear again, and eggs are laid as in the previous year.

Some species of Aphis are found, so far as we know, on only one species of plant. Others, when they fly away, travel to a different species from the one they left, and their descendants find their way back to the original kind of plants. Thus the black Bean Aphis produces on the bean winged females in the summer. These fly to the spindle-tree, where they produce female offspring that are able to lay eggs. These females are joined by males that have also flown there from bean plants; eggs are laid, and the colony of adults dies out. In spring, the eggs on the spindle-tree hatch and, in the new colonies which soon develop, winged females appear and fly to the beans. They reach the bean plants singly, not being at first noticed; but soon the young shoots are covered with masses of black Aphides.

In recent years much research has been de-voted to the flight and dispersal of Aphides, especially of the Bean Aphis. Adult winged females are too soft to fly until a period after the last moult, which varies with the tempera-ture. They never take to the wing at night or at temperatures below 17° C., and usually leave the host plants in two main waves, one in the morning and one in the afternoon. They are carried aloft by ascending currents of air, often reaching heights of 1000 or more metres; but they seldom remain airborne for more than 3 or 4 hours, and sooner or later are caught in descending air currents which bring them down to earth, where they seek suitable host-plants. Nevertheless, prolonged journeys of hundreds of miles over the sea have been recorded. Many species undertake several flights of this kind, but in most the wing muscles soon degenerate and provide nutriment for reproduction. Older females cannot fly.

See also Vol. VI: Aphid Pests

ARCHER-FISH. This is a small fish, rather like the Perch (q.v.), usually 15 to 20 cm long, which inhabits the fresh waters of the East Indian region. It is yellow, with broad black bands or spots, and gets its name from its habit of lying just below the surface of the water be-neath overhanging plants, on which it can watch for insects to settle. When its prey appears, it shoots a jet of water upwards along a groove in the roof of its mouth, knocking the insect into the water, where it is eaten. The fish can aim accurately over a distance of at least 150 cm.

ARMADILLO. This mammal, found mainly in South America, belongs to the same order as the Ant-Eater (q.v.). Armadillos are unique among mammals in possessing a more or less complete shield of bony scales in the skin, which forms an armour over the head, shoulders, back, and even legs and tail. The shield is made up of movable bands of scales, so that the armadillo can move its body freely or roll itself into a ball like a hedgehog. In some species a good deal of hair comes up between the scales—this is particularly true of the Long-haired Armadillo from Chile and Argentina, and of the Hairy Armadillo.

Paul Popper

LITTLE MULE ARMADILLO

There are several kinds of armadillos living in various parts of South and Central America and in the south of North America. They are mostly quite small: the largest, the Giant Armadillo, which inhabits the forests of Surinam and Brazil, is less than a metre from snout to base of tail. Traces, however, have been found of an extinct type reaching some 2 metres in length. Armadillos are inoffensive creatures, living mainly on insects, especially ants. They dig into the ground with their very powerful claws and make burrows for their families. Except in the mating season, they usually live a solitary existence, and prefer flat, open country.

The smallest known species is the Pichiciago (Fairy Armadillo), which is only 12·5 cm long, and has a pink scaled shield over its head and body and white fur underneath. It is to be found, though not at all commonly, in parts of Argentina, where it makes its burrow in the scorching hot sand. It hates both cold and wet.

ASH, *see* WOODLANDS, Section 4; *see also* Vol. VI: TREES, BROADLEAVED.

ASS. The Wild Ass or Donkey belongs to the same family as the HORSE (q.v.). The Abyssinian Wild Ass appears to be the direct ancestor of the domestic DONKEY (q.v. Vol. VI). It was domesticated in very early times by the ancient Egyptians, was brought to England in the 9th or 10th century, and is now used as a beast of burden in many parts of the world. Some of the domestic breeds, such as those produced in Spain, Italy, and the United States, are very fine, and much larger than the wild animal. There are only small numbers of African Wild Donkeys alive today. They are fine, strong, bluish-grey animals, large specimens standing about 12 hands at the withers. They move swiftly and gracefully, and their voice is the well-known bray.

A. Fraser Brunner

ARCHER-FISH CATCHING PREY

The Asiatic Wild Ass, which is generally a sandy-red colour, seems to be more or less untamable. It lives on open plains, often where there is little vegetation, its fleetness and sureness of foot enabling it to outrun most of its enemies. It is a remarkably silent animal, only occasionally uttering a stifled, suppressed bray. The largest species is the Kiang, which lives in Tibet and Mongolia, up to about 5000 metres above sea-level. These are powerfully built animals, standing about 13 hands at the withers. They are never found far away from water, and, unlike the African ass, are strong and fearless swimmers, boldly crossing broad and swift-flowing rivers.

AUKS. 1. The Auk family (Alcidae) also includes the Razorbills, Guillemots, and Puffins. They all live in the cold regions of the northern hemisphere, some species migrating in the winter as far south as the Bay of Biscay or the coasts of Virginia. They all have heavy, compact bodies, and legs placed far back, with webbed feet. They feed on crustacea and small fish, and breed in colonies on rocky coasts, spending much of the rest of the year out at sea. All, except the Black Guillemot, usually lay only one egg. Birds of this family are sometimes mistaken for PENGUINS (q.v.), which, however, are found only in the southern hemisphere.

The largest member of the family, the Great Auk, became extinct in the 19th century, after a relentless persecution for the sake of its feathers (*see* FEATHER HUNTING, Vol. VI). It was about the size of a goose, with such small wings that it could not fly. It was, however, an excellent swimmer and diver, and in winter carried out long migrations that way. The Little Auks, dapper little birds some 20 cm long, fly each year in thousands from the Arctic regions, where they breed, down to the North Sea. Sometimes strong gales at sea force them close in shore, to escape the stormy waves.

2. THE RAZORBILL (or Lesser Auk) is often confused with the Guillemot, which it much resembles in size, build, and habits, and with which it often lives. It differs from the Guillemot in being rather smaller (43 centimetres against 45 cm), in its characteristic thick bill, and in certain of its habits. For instance, it feeds its young with small fish which it carries across the bill, several at a time—while the Guillemot carries one only, held lengthwise. The Razorbills congregate in large numbers at many points on the British coast and adjacent islands, generally preferring rough, stony ground, and sheer cliffs. They pair for life, and generally return to their last year's nesting site. Courtship is carried on by rubbing bills and nibbling at plumage, and the male shares in incubating and feeding the young. When the young Razorbill is about 3 or 4 weeks old, and before it can fly, its parents push it off its nesting ledge into the sea. As its nest may be as high as 150 metres above the sea, this leap is very perilous: its fluttering, weak wings may carry it clear of projecting rocks, but many come to grief.

3. THE GUILLEMOTS arrive in even greater numbers than the Razorbills to their nesting cliffs, crowding together so thickly that there seems to be no possible room for new-comers. But still more come, alighting on the backs of their fellows and waddling over them until they find a cranny into which to squeeze. This crowded community life gives them comparative protection from the attacks of their enemies, chiefly the Herring Gull. The Guillemots are true ocean birds, with legs so well adapted for swimming and diving that the birds are awkward on land and do not stand erect easily. They carry out an entertaining courtship, which involves odd bowing movements. The hen lays an egg (large for the size of the bird) on a bare cliff, with no attempt at a nest. During incubations she often holds the egg on her feet—after the manner of Penguins. The Black Guillemot is a smaller species, about 35 centimetres long, which breeds on the rocky coasts of north Ireland, west Scotland, and the Scottish Isles.

4. THE PUFFIN is still smaller, about 30 cm, and is a strange-looking bird, with its grotesque, gaudy, orange and blue bill. It breeds on most rocky coasts of Britain, especially in the north and west. The Puffin lays her single egg in a burrow in the turf near the cliff top, and the male helps to dig the burrow, as well as to incubate and feed the young. He will fight fiercely for possession of his hole. Like most members of the Auk family, the Puffins are silent birds, but occasionally utter a deep, grumbling note.

AVOCET, *see* WADING BIRDS.

Eric Hosking

GUILLEMOTS ON THE PINNACLES, FARNE ISLANDS

Kittiwakes can be seen on the side of the rocks

Eric Hosking

PUFFINS

B

BABOON. These grotesque MONKEYS (q.v.) with their long, dog-like faces live in Africa and south-west Arabia. They are often very fierce, flying into a great rage if anything excites them. Instead of running away from a human being, as most animals instinctively do, they will turn round and face him with threatening gestures. The male baboons have most formidable tusk-like teeth—a baboon's bite is, in fact, almost as severe as a leopard's. As their arms and legs are about the same length, they feel much more at home on the ground than in trees, and though they can climb trees, most of them prefer homes in rocky places. On fairly flat ground they gallop almost as fast as a horse. They eat practically any food they come across—fruit, leaves, nuts, insects, young birds, and birds' eggs, and they frequently raid cultivated crops. They live in troops, with a powerful male as the leader. The baby baboon is at first carried by its mother, who holds it with one hand clasped to her breast, but later on it rides on her back as the troop moves from one place to another.

The Gelada of Ethiopia is blackish brown and has a short muzzle and a massive mane on its shoulders. The Drill and the Mandrill are also large, powerful baboons, differing from the typical baboons in having very short tails and a greater inclination to resort to trees. They live in West Africa, and spend much of their time on the ground; but they are never far away from the forest trees, in which they sleep and take refuge from danger. The Mandrill is a grotesque-looking animal, having on its face large blue swollen ridges, a bright carmine-red nose, and a yellow beard. The hair on its hind-quarters is very scanty, showing rainbow-coloured skin underneath. The Drill has a shiny black, bare face, bordered with whitish fur.

BACTERIA. These are among the very smallest of all living things, and it is only recently, by using modern apparatus such as the ELECTRON MICROSCOPE (q.v. Vol. VIII), that we have been able to magnify them sufficiently to get some idea of their structure and life-history. Enormous numbers of them exist everywhere—in the air, in the soil, in water, and even in the bodies of living things. Here, some may be harmful in causing BACTERIAL DISEASES (q.v. Vol. XI), but others may be useful and even essential for the help they give in digesting food. Others, again, perform valuable work in breaking down dead tissue (*see* SAPROPHYTES).

Bacteria are probably related to a group of ALGAE (q.v.) called the blue-green algae. Some are ball-shaped, 'cocci'; some are rod-shaped, 'bacilli'; and some are spiral-shaped, 'spirilla'. Some are able to move by means of 'flagella', which are minute hair-like projections from the cell surface. Under unfavourable conditions bacteria reproduce by forming spores which have thick protective walls round them. Under favourable conditions they simply divide into two very rapidly, sometimes once an hour. The record for reproduction is held by a common bacteria called *Bacillus subtilis* which can divide three times in every hour.

See also PARASITIC PLANTS; NITROGEN SUPPLY IN PLANTS; YEASTS; VIRUS.

BADGER. The badger lives in woods and forests in the British Isles, but only in small numbers. It belongs to the order CARNIVORA (q.v.), flesh-eaters. It is a thick-set, bear-like animal nearly a metre long, with thick, coarse,

Neave Parker

A BADGER

greyish fur, and a white face with broad black stripes. It is very keen of scent and hearing, and is an intelligent, courageous, and resourceful animal. Its tough, loose skin enables it to wriggle round when seized and bite its aggressor.

Badgers live in deep burrows, called 'sets', in rocky hills and banks. The set has one or more chambers, with several entrance passages, and many workings on various levels. At the main entrance there is always a huge mound of excavated soil. Badgers are very clean animals: they bury their dung in an earth closet dug far away from the set, and clean their claws, like cats, on a tree before going underground. At nightfall they come out to seek their food and also to play: to see them tumbling and rolling on the ground is a very amusing sight. They eat almost everything—roots, fruit, honey, slugs, snails, wire-worms, any kind of insect, moles, snakes, young birds, and rabbits.

In very cold climates badgers hibernate from November to March; but in England they sleep for short periods only in a deep set, bedded with dry bracken and grass. They block up the entrance to keep themselves warm; but they come out in mild weather, and sometimes even when there is snow on the ground. A regular spring-cleaning takes place about March, when they drag their bedding out into the sun, and make new chambers, lining them with fern and grass in preparation for the breeding season. Their two to four cubs are born in the spring or summer. These are silver-grey, and blind at birth. They do not come out of the set for two months, during which time the mother washes them and looks after them most carefully.

Badgers are to be found in Asia and North America as well as in Europe. They are trapped for their fur, badger-hair being used for shaving-brushes. In Germany the small dachshund is used for driving the animal out of its set. If captured young, badgers are easily tamed and can make very good pets.

The Ratels of India and Africa, sometimes known as the Honey Badgers, belong to the badger family. They generally hunt in pairs, and are very bold for their size, attacking all sorts of animals, including poisonous snakes. They are very fond of honey and take no notice of the attacks of the bees. The Ratel, like the badger, soon becomes tame in captivity. It has the amusing habit of turning complete somersaults as it walks up and down its cage.

BAGWORMS. These caterpillars construct silken bags, strengthened with pieces of stick, leaves, lichen, or other objects, within which they live, and which protect them as they move over their food plants—the lichens on rocks, fences, and tree-trunks, and grasses, flowers, and leaves. The bags sometimes resemble the cases of the CADDIS-FLY (q.v.) (which, however, are found in water). The family of moths to which the Bagworms belong (*Psychidae*) is widespread, but only about 20 small species occur in Britain. The largest, found in Australia, makes bags over 12 cm long. The caterpillar eventually changes to a chrysalis, which has hooks enabling it to move within the bag and enabling the moth to make its escape. The males fly swiftly, chiefly by day, and have dull-coloured and very hairy wings, though some species, owing to imperfect scaling,

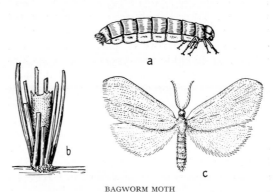

BAGWORM MOTH
(*a*) Typical wingless female; (*b*) Bag (or case);
(*c*) Typical male

have transparent wings. The females, the most degenerate of all moths, are without wings, and sometimes lack even antennae, mouth-parts, and legs. On hatching they remain inside the bag, where they are sought by the males, mate, and lay their numerous eggs. Some species appear to have no males, and the eggs develop without fertilization (*see* REPRODUCTION IN ANIMALS). The young caterpillars are sometimes blown considerable distances by the wind, the long strands of silk which they spin serving as parachutes. By this means the Bagworms colonize new areas, which might otherwise never be reached by an insect with a flightless female. The tiny lichen-feeding bagworms, for instance, to be found on the huge stones of Stonehenge, are 2·5 km away from the nearest tree occupied by these moths.

BAMBOO, *see* Grasses; *see also* Vol. VI: Bamboos.

BARNACLE. This animal is a Crustacean (q.v.), although this is not immediately obvious. It used to be classified as a Mollusc (q.v.), but study of its tiny larvae has shown clearly that it is really related to the crustacea. The Barnacle larva, with its minute triangular body, single central eye, and two pairs of jointed complex antennae, with which it swims freely through the water, is totally unlike its parent. After a while it reaches the second stage of its life-history, when the body and limbs are enclosed in a semi-transparent bivalve shell. Through this shell can be seen a pair of large compound eyes and six pairs of branched swimming feet; while in front, a pair of antennules, each bearing a sucker-like disk, project beyond the valves of the shell. After swimming about for a short period the larva becomes attached to some object, such as a rock or piece of submerged timber. It is held to its support by these sucker-disks, as well as by a cement secreted from glands at the base of the antennules, so that these fasten the front of its head to the support. The bivalve-shell is now cast off, and the beginnings of the shell-valves of the adult appear. The six pairs of swimming legs develop into graceful, feathery limbs, and the compound eyes disappear. The adult barnacle now remains for the rest of its life firmly attached by its head to the base it has selected, dwelling within the safe recesses of its shell and kicking its food into its mouth by means of the feathery legs, which serve as a casting-net for the capture of food.

The Goose or Ship Barnacles pass through a similar life-history, but choose floating timbers

THREE STAGES OF THE BARNACLE

(*a*) 1st larval stage; (*b*) 2nd larval stage; (*c*) Adult Acorn Barnacles on rock

and the bottoms of ships, to which they attach themselves by a long muscular stalk—really the greatly elongated front part of the head. The body is enclosed in an oval shell composed of five separate pieces, hinged together to leave a slit through which the feathery-looking feet can be protruded. The Goose Barnacles gained their popular name from the once-prevalent idea that they finally developed into birds, the Barnacle Geese (q.v.).

BASILISK, *see* Lizards; *see also* Vol. I: Fabulous Creatures.

BAT. This is the only member of the order Chiroptera (hand-winged), and the only mammal which can really fly (*see* Flight). Bats' wings are formed by a delicate membrane which connects up their enormously long fingers, and is carried back to join their hind limbs. On their toes are very sharp claws by which they hang downwards when resting. The hair may be either silky, woolly, or coarse—or, in some species, may be lacking entirely. In all but the Flying Foxes the eyes are small, and the sight is believed to be very poor. The insect-eating bats have been shown to possess the remarkable power of finding their way about

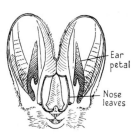

HEAD OF A BAT, SHOWING NOSE LEAVES AND EAR PETALS

(probably used in echo-location)

and of locating their insect food by echo-location. So, even if blindfolded, they can fly at a great speed without colliding with any obstacle (*see* Ultrasonics, Vol. VIII).

Bats frequently live together in large numbers. In the north-temperate zones they hibernate, mostly leaving their summer resorts in the winter, and retreating to caves or other shelters, where they hang upside-down by their feet, their wings often wrapped round their bodies. Their temperature drops to that of their surroundings, and their breathing becomes light and slow (*see* Hibernation). In the summer many bats sleep most of the day and night, only coming out for food in the evening and morning. Others, however, fly throughout the night.

Once a year (about June or July in Britain) one young is born, blind and naked. At its birth

Steven Henty

A FLYING FOX

S. C. Bisserôt

A MOUSE-EARED BAT IN FLIGHT

the mother turns head upwards and drops the young bat into a pouch made by bending her tail forward. Then she lifts it up, cleans it, and places it at one of the two teats on her breast. It clings on with its teeth, and holds on to its mother's fur with its thumbs and hind claws. There it stays for about a fortnight, without hampering her flight. After this time, however, she hangs it up by its feet in some safe place, while she goes away on a flight, replacing it at her breast on her return. Towards autumn the young bat begins to fly.

The order of bats (Chiroptera) is divided into two groups—the insect-eaters and the fruit-eaters: all British bats are insect-eaters, about 16 species having been seen at different times; but only the four described below—Pipistrelle, Long-eared Bats, Noctules, and Horseshoe Bats—are at all common. The first three belong to one family, the Vespertilionidae, called the 'typical' bats, members of which are found all over the world. They can bring their tails forward so as to form a pouch, in which they imprison large insects.

The Pipistrelle, which has a wing-span of about 20 cm, is the most common bat in the British Isles. Large colonies live in church roofs and towers, and in any cranny in houses, trees, and rocks. The Long-eared Bats, which have a wing-span of some 25 centimetres, are also fairly common. Their ears are almost as long as their bodies, and so sensitive that they are kept constantly quivering. In warm weather they sleep

out, hanging from tree-trunks, and on colder days they take shelter in some warm spot. They hibernate, usually alone in hollow trees or in old buildings, from about mid-October to mid-April. They are the lightest sleepers of all British bats, and often come out in the winter, sometimes at mid-day, to drink. Noctules or Great Bats have a wing-span of from 33 to 38 centimetres, and live in many wooded districts of England and Wales. They make short flights, sometimes of less than an hour. On their return they land head upwards, but at once turn upside-down and, hanging by one foot, perform an elaborate toilet. When this is over, they hang upside-down by both feet to rest. Their daily sleep in the summer is much like hibernation: it is very sound, their temperature falls, and their breathing becomes very short.

The Horseshoe Bats are a separate family. They derive their name from a growth of skin in the shape of a horseshoe on the face, which may be connected with the detection of obstacles or insects by echo-location. It has been seen in captivity that they do not put their prey in a tail pouch like the typical bats, but, instead, master large insects by pressing them with their mouths against their wings. Whether they do this in the wild is, however, not known. The females have two 'dummy' nipples on their groins as well as the two breast teats common to all bats. The mothers put the new-born young on to one of these dummies so that when she hangs head down, it is head up. She transfers it to the true teats for feeding only. There are two species, the Greater Horseshoe Bat (wing-span 33 cm), and the Lesser Horseshoe Bat (wing-span 21 cm).

In December 1956 a colony of Mouse-eared Bats was found hibernating in underground quarries on the South Coast of England. These bats are palish brown on the back and have whitish undersides. They have a wing span of at least 38 cm, and fly soon after dusk with heavy flapping of their wings.

The so-called Vampires are small bats living in the forests of South and Central America and the West Indies. The appearance of some species, with their long, leathery ears and nose-leaf (an erect growth of skin on their face), is so hideous and diabolical that it fully accounts for their evil reputation. Some are purely insect-eaters, others live on a mixed diet of fruit and insects, and only one species lives entirely on the blood of other animals. The blood-suckers attack their sleeping victims during the night, make slight incisions in the skin with their very sharp teeth, and then lap their blood. Some of them attack human beings whilst they are asleep.

The other large group of bats, the fruit-eaters, are often called Flying Foxes on account of their fox-like heads. They live in Africa, southern India, and Australasia, and are typi-

GREATER HORSESHOE BAT

S. C. Bisserôt

cally much larger than insect-eating bats, some having a wing-span of a metre. During the day they hang by their toes from the branches of the forest trees, looking, with their wings wrapped round their bodies, rather like clusters of pears. At dusk they begin to move about amongst the branches with raucous squeaks and grunts. Presently, one flies off, to be followed by the whole party, which may number a hundred or more. Like a flock of large crows, they wing their way to some part of the forest where there is ripening fruit. Sometimes they have to travel several miles in their search, and in cultivated districts they cause, of course, immense damage.

The insect-eating bats are believed to be of value in helping to fight malaria by destroying mosquitoes. Sometimes, however, bats tend to be a nuisance because of the swarms of parasites they often carry.

BEAR. 1. Bears are found in most parts of the world, though in many countries they are now scarce and rarely found outside the large game reservations. They live in widely different climatic regions: the huge white Polar Bears live in Arctic regions; the Black and Brown Bears in the temperate zones; while in tropical countries are the oriental Sloth Bears and the Spectacled Bears. Those that live in cold climates hibernate through the winter (*see* HIBERNATION). Bears belong to the Order of CARNIVORA (q.v.), flesh-eaters, but in fact they eat a great variety of food—even the large Brown Bears eat great quantities of fruit and other vegetable food—and spend much of their time tearing to pieces old logs and digging in the ground in order to find grubs, worms, and insects. The female generally has a litter of two or three cubs, which are at first extremely small—Polar Bear cubs are only about 30 cm long.

2. POLAR BEARS. These are among the largest of the bears, often being nearly 3 metres long. They are provided with hair on the soles of their feet, which enables them to secure a good grip on the ice. If they are hungry they can be most formidable foes. In the winter they eat the flesh of seals and walruses, and in coastal districts a large amount of fish; but in the summer they keep to a vegetable diet. In autumn the female Polar Bear, having fed well and laid up a good stock of fat, retires to a cave beneath the snow and gives birth to her cubs in mid-winter. Polar Bears show a strong love for their offspring:

Paul Popper

BLACK BEAR CUBS CLIMBING A PINE-TREE IN SEARCH OF A HONEYCOMB

still lives in many parts of Canada, and in some places in the United States; but it is now protected and may only be hunted at certain times. In some of the National Parks it has become tame enough to take food from visitors. In the Yellowstone Park in the U.S.A. Black Bears sometimes hold up cars to beg for food, and, if not given any, they have been known in their anger to try to tear the car to pieces. They rarely kill wild animals, but often become very destructive to sheep and raid farm-yards. They usually make their winter dens under the upturned roots of a fallen tree or beneath a pile of logs. They scrape together a few bushes or leaves to make a bed, and wait for the first snow-storm to complete the roof and fill in the remaining chinks.

There are Black Bears also in Asia—from Persia, right through the Himalayas, to China; and there is a smaller species in Japan. They live in the mountains or forests, where they climb the trees in search of fruit. In Malaya are found the small Honey Bears or Sun Bears, which have short, sleek, black coats. They, too, are excellent climbers and in their search for honey are very clever at finding bees' nests.

5. TROPICAL BEARS. The Sloth Bear of India and Ceylon is a fairly large, shaggy animal,

when starved and living under the greatest hardships, they have often been seen carefully dividing among their cubs a small amount of food caught after long hours of hunting, keeping only a small piece for themselves.

3. BROWN BEARS. These are found in a few places in western and in most of eastern Europe, and in Asia and North America, their size and the shade of their coats varying according to where they live. In Alaska there are Brown Bears, called Kodiaks, which are sometimes as much as 3 metres long, and weigh over 680 kg— the largest of all the bears. The Grizzly Bear of the Rocky Mountains is another huge animal, immensely strong. Although such enormous creatures, these giant brown bears are timid, inoffensive beasts, unless wounded, cornered, or protecting their young, and they will generally do their best to escape man. The ferocity of the Grizzly has been greatly exaggerated; but once the Grizzly or the Alaskan Bear is aroused and angered he is a dangerous and deadly enemy. A Grizzly was once seen to break the neck of a bull bison with a single blow of its paw.

4. BLACK BEARS. The American Black Bear, a much smaller animal than the Brown Bear,

Mansell Collection

A POLAR BEAR

with a large white **V** mark on its chest. It is particularly fond of Termites (q.v.), and with its large, strong claws it tears the nests to pieces, then, blowing away the dust, it scoops up the insects with its long tongue and protruding lower lip. The young cubs are generally carried on their mother's back when the animals are on the move: it is an amusing sight to watch them dismount at the feeding ground and scramble back to their seats at the first alarm.

The only bear to be found in South America is the Spectacled Bear, which lives in the mountains of Peru and Colombia. It is a small inoffensive black bear, with a white breast and pale-coloured rings round its eyes, which give it a clownish appearance. It lives in remote areas, and avoids man as much as possible. Its food is fruit and other vegetable matter.

BEAVER. This large, stout Rodent (q.v.) lives mainly in the water. He is about 76 cm long—larger than an otter—and has a thick, warm, brown coat, the upper hairs of which form a waterproof covering to his woolly under-coat. It is this under-coat which is used in the Fur Trade (q.v. Vol. VII). The beaver's hind-

Camera Press

BEAVER

feet are webbed for swimming, and his tail, which is wide and flat, acts as a rudder. His front (incisor) teeth are very strong and sharp. There are still many beavers in North America, although they have been severely trapped for their fur (*see* Fur Hunting, Vol. VI). In Europe they are found in Scandinavia, and also on the Rhône and the Elbe, and they were once quite common even in England—many places in England, for example, Beverley and Beaverbourne, derive their name from the beaver.

The beaver shows almost incredible engineering skill and intelligence in constructing dams in the streams and rivers in which he lives. His main purpose in building the dam seems to be to ensure a sufficient depth of water around his house for him to swim in when the surface is frozen over in the winter. The way in which he seems to choose the very best spot for building the dam is almost uncanny.

Beavers obtain material to build their dams and also their houses (called 'lodges') by felling trees with their sharp teeth. If there are no suitable trees near the water, building material is often brought some distance over land. In this case the beavers usually construct canals to float down the material, since their heavy bodies, short legs, and webbed hind feet are not well adapted for carrying loads across country. They strip off the boughs, and cut up these and the trunk itself into convenient lengths. Most of the work is done at night, numbers of the beavers working together. The large logs form the base of the dam and the smaller wood is worked in later with turf and clay to make it watertight.

The beaver 'lodge' is a permanent house, with the entrance beneath the surface of the water, and the beaver lives there both summer and winter. The lodge usually contains two rooms, one used as a living-room, and the other as the pantry, where the beaver stores his winter food supply of twigs and branches. He also sinks food supplies in the water conveniently near the lodge, and in this way he is well provided for in the winter months, when ice and snow make it impossible to travel outside. In the autumn the beavers plaster their houses with mud, which, when frozen in the winter, forms a wind-proof and cold-proof covering, and protects them from their enemies—bears, wolverines, and foxes. At the close of winter or early in spring from three to four young are born in the lodge.

BED-BUG. This Bug (q.v.) belongs to the family called Cimicidae, which includes also parasites of those bats, martins, and swallows which nest in caves. Man probably first became associated with these parasites in prehistoric times, when he also dwelt in caves. The Bed-bug, although it is to be found all over the world, almost certainly evolved in a warmish climate, perhaps in the Middle East.

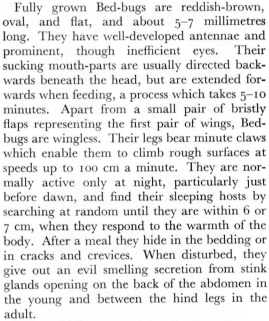

BED-BUG
×3

Unlike Mosquitoes (q.v.), Bed-bugs of both sexes are blood-suckers. Although usually dependent on man, they are also able to live on the blood of hens, mice, and other animals, and may be pests in poultry houses and zoos, as well as in human dwellings.

Fully grown Bed-bugs are reddish-brown, oval, and flat, and about 5–7 millimetres long. They have well-developed antennae and prominent, though inefficient eyes. Their sucking mouth-parts are usually directed backwards beneath the head, but are extended forwards when feeding, a process which takes 5–10 minutes. Apart from a small pair of bristly flaps representing the first pair of wings, Bed-bugs are wingless. Their legs bear minute claws which enable them to climb rough surfaces at speeds up to 100 cm a minute. They are normally active only at night, particularly just before dawn, and find their sleeping hosts by searching at random until they are within 6 or 7 cm, when they respond to the warmth of the body. After a meal they hide in the bedding or in cracks and crevices. When disturbed, they give out an evil smelling secretion from stink glands opening on the back of the abdomen in the young and between the hind legs in the adult.

Their method of reproduction is unlike that of other insects, for when the male and female mate, the sperms are placed in a special cavity on the underside of the female's abdomen, and not in the genetical duct. The sperms then migrate through the body to the oviducts, where they fertilize the eggs. Each female lays about three eggs a day and about 300 in all, the number depending upon the temperature and the amount of blood the bug has sucked. The white, elongated eggs are usually hidden in crevices and stuck down with a quickly-drying cement. Each egg has a little lid which the young nymph pushes back as it emerges about

a week later. The young look very much like their parents, except for their size and pale colour. They take 1 to 6 months to mature, casting their coats five times during this period, and needing at least one blood meal between each moult. Larger nymphs and adults are able to live in moist, cool conditions for a whole year without food, and so remain alive in unoccupied houses for a long time.

See also Vol. XI: Household Pests.

BEECH, *see* Woodlands, Section 3; *see also* Vol. VI: Trees, Broadleaved.

BEE-EATER. This is the name of a large family of smallish birds, the species of which inhabit southern Europe, central Asia, south Africa, Madagascar, and Australia. They have long, curved beaks, long tails, and very brilliant colouring—predominantly blue and green, with black, yellow, and chestnut markings. They live on insects—principally, as their name suggests, on bees, which they catch in the open in full flight. The quick, darting flight of these vivid little birds in pursuit of their prey is an attractive sight. The European Bee-eater, a rather larger species, measuring 25 cm from beak to tail, not only takes its food on the wing, but also visits the bee-hives and captures the bees as they fly in or out. They visit southern Europe regularly in the summer, spending the winter in various

C. K. Yeates

BEE-EATERS

parts of Africa, and breeding in central Asia. In 1955, a few pairs of Bee-eaters bred in Southern England. They have a peculiar cry, a single note repeated continuously. Like most Bee-eaters, they lay their glossy, white eggs at the end of long tunnels which they dig with their beaks, preferably in sandy river banks. These tunnels are generally fouled by the discarded indigestible parts of the bodies of bees and wasps.

The Swallow-tailed Bee-eaters of Africa measure about 21 cm, and the Square-tailed Bee-eaters, species of which are also to be found in India and southern Asia, are all rather smaller. Other species, such as the Bearded Bee-eaters, one of which has magnificent scarlet throat-feathers, inhabit the forests of the East Indies and other countries of southern Asia.

Related to the Bee-eaters are the Motimots of Central and South American forests. These are rather larger birds, some 39 cm, with long beaks and very long tails. They are gaudy creatures, with magnificent green, blue, silver, and purple colouring. In the West Indies is another closely related family, the Todres, little green and red birds, which are now becoming rather scarce, because of the raids made on their burrows by mongooses, who eat their eggs.

BEES. 1. These insects belong to the huge Order Hymenoptera, which also includes WASPS and ANTS (qq.v.). Insects of this order usually have two pairs of transparent wings, the front pair bearing a special fold on the hind margin, and the hind pair bearing a row of small hooks on the leading edge. When the insects are at rest there is no connexion between the two pairs of wings, but when the front wings are drawn over the hind ones, as they are in preparation for flight, the hooks catch in the fold and the wings of each side lock together as one.

Hymenoptera undergo complete METAMOR-PHOSIS (q.v.). This means that during their life-history they pass through four stages—egg, larva or grub, pupa, and adult insect. The females of all, except those of Stingless Bees, are able to sting. The sting is really an egg-laying organ which has changed in function to become a defensive weapon. 'Drones', or male bees, are harmless insects, whose only job is the insemination of the females, who are then able to lay fertilized eggs.

Bees have evolved from wasps which abandoned hunting and changed to a diet of nectar and pollen some 80 million years ago. The subsequent evolution of both bees and flowers has been greatly influenced by their dependence upon one another, for in visiting flowers bees bring about pollination, a necessary process in the development of seeds and fruits. They are thus highly important and beneficial insects to flowering plants—and consequently also to man. Bees are well adapted for their mode of life; for example, the hairs with which they are clothed are branched, and consequently pollen grains firmly adhere to them. Often the hairs are grouped in special regions, for example, on the legs of Lawn Bees or on the underside of the abdomen of Leaf-cutter and Mason Bees. Others, such as Bumble and Honey Bees, have a smooth, slightly hollowed-out surface on the outer side of the hind leg, called a pollen-basket, which is fringed with long hairs, and into which the bee packs the pollen in a solid mass.

As in all INSECTS (q.v.), the mouth parts of bees consist of three pairs of appendages. In bees the outside pair are jaws, not only used for biting but for many other jobs. Within comes a pair of maxillae (or upper jaws) which, together with a labium (or lip) and hairy 'tongue', form a tube or proboscis through which the bees suck nectar. When this is not in use, the maxillae and inner parts separate and fold back beneath the head, where they are held in place by the jaws. In primitive species the 'tongue' is very short; in others it is as long as the body. Flowers with deep nectaries, such as Red Clover, can only be pollinated by long-tongued Bumble-bees.

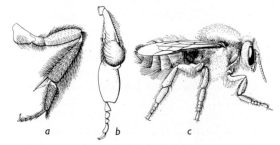

Fig. 1 *a*. HIND LEG OF A SOLITARY BEE, *Panurgus*, SHOWING THE LONG POLLEN-COLLECTING HAIRS

Fig. 1 *b*. HIND LEG OF A HONEY-BEE, SHOWING THE POLLEN BASKET WITH SOLID LUMP OF POLLEN

Fig. 1 *c*. LEAF-CUTTER BEE, SHOWING THE LONG POLLEN-COLLECTING HAIRS ON THE ABDOMEN

The worker Honey Bee sucks up nectar into her crop or honey-stomach, where it undergoes chemical changes. On returning to the hive, she brings it up again and gives it to others who treat it in such a way that much of its water evaporates. It is then deposited as 'green', partially ripened honey in one of the cells. Honey provides the energy necessary for everything that bees do; pollen is the source of protein and is necessary for growing larvae and the well-being of the whole community.

The average flying speed of Honey Bees, carrying a full load of pollen almost equal to their own weight, is about 22·5 km per hour, but they rarely travel more than 3 km in search of food. The celebrated French naturalist, FABRE (q.v. Vol. V), caught, marked, and then released forty Mason Bees 5 km from their nest, and only nine were able to find their way home.

Most kinds of bees are solitary. In these the female makes a cell in a burrow in the ground or in an old log. She provisions each cell with bee bread, a mixture of pollen and honey, and lays an egg upon it. She then closes the cell and flies away paying no further attention to it. Bumble-bees, Honey Bees, and Stingless Bees are social species which give more attention to their offspring. The mother Bumble-bee, for instance, stays with her young throughout their lives, feeding them from day to day while they are still larvae. When they become adult, they help her bring up further broods.

2. SOLITARY BEES. A very common English solitary bee is the Lawn Bee (*Andrena armata*), which usually burrows in open grassy places. The female is a handsome insect with a black head and reddish velvety hair on the body. A number of females often make their burrows close together in open grassy places, and the tiny mounds of earth thrown up by the diggers in the spring are very conspicuous and often a nuisance to the owners of lawns. Many species of solitary bees make their burrows near one another often only a few centimetres apart; and these are said to be 'gregarious'.

The Leaf-cutter Bee bores long tunnels in old and rotten wood and lines them with cells made from tightly overlapping pieces of leaf cut from roses and other plants. *Anthidium manicatum*, a fairly common little black British bee, uses a fibrous down which she scrapes from the stalks and undersides of the leaves of certain plants.

There are many species of Leaf-cutter Bees all over the world, some of them very brightly coloured.

Mason Bees build their cells of cement composed of clay or fine particles of sand, made workable by saliva. The European Black Mason Bee, of which Fabre has given such a fascinating account, often builds several cells side by side on a large pebble and then covers them with a mortar of finer composition, so protecting the delicate grubs inside from extremes of heat and cold. A common British bee, *Osmia rufa*, also constructs her cells with

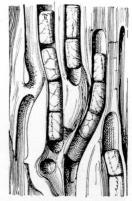

Fig. 2 *a*. NEST OF LEAF-CUTTER BEE, SHOWING TUNNELS IN WOOD AND ROWS OF CELLS

Fig. 2 *b*. CELLS OF *Osmia rufa*, SHOWING PARTITIONS AND COCOONS IN CELLS

mortar. She makes use of deserted insect burrows or other small cavities, such as the disused lock of a door, which she enters through the keyhole. Other species habitually use empty snail shells.

Some solitary bees have no means of collecting pollen, and sip nectar from flowers only for their own nourishment. They are parasites and, instead of making nests, lay eggs in other bees' cells, which have been stored with food by their rightful owners. In Europe most of these cuckoo bees belong to the genus *Nomada* and are small black-and-yellow, or black-and-red, wasplike insects. Each species of solitary bee of the genus *Andrena* usually has its own particular kind of *Nomada* dependent upon it.

3. SOCIAL BEES. The social bees of Britain are the BUMBLE-BEE (q.v.) and the Honey or Hive Bee.

The Honey Bee is the only social bee to build the familiar honeycomb with its double layer of six-sided cells. The combs built by the bees hang down vertically, with just enough space between them to allow the bees to move freely. The bees rear their brood in the middle and lower parts of the comb, and store their honey above and to the sides of the breeding

Eric Hosking

Fig. 3. A SWARM OF HONEY BEES

us to understand how she maintains her position in the colony.

The Stingless Bees (*Meliponinae*) of tropical and sub-tropical regions, particularly Central and Southern America, live in communities more elaborate than those of the Bumble-bee and not unlike those of the Honey Bee. Although the workers have only a rudimentary sting, they defend their nests with great vigour, flying at an intruder in great numbers, crawling into his eyes, ears, and hair, biting and smearing him with a sticky substance, and causing him to retreat in discomfort. The Maya Indians kept these bees for their honey long before the Spanish conquest, and their apiaries, sometimes comprising a hundred hollow logs used as hives, were among their most valued possessions.

See also Vol. VI: HONEY and BEESWAX.

BEETLES. 1. Beetles (Coleoptera) form the largest of the main divisions, or Orders, of insects. Nearly 4,000 kinds inhabit the British Islands alone, and in the whole world about a quarter of a million have been named. Many new ones are described every year, some of them from Britain.

Beetles are distinguished from other insects by the hardness of the first pair of wings. These fore-wings (or elytra) are not used for flying but as a protection to the second pair, which are folded beneath them when not in use. COCK-ROACHES and GRASSHOPPERS (qq.v.) have tough fore-wings, also used for protection, but in beetles the difference between the two pairs is greater, and the first pair fit together closely along the middle of the back. A beetle begins life, like a BUTTERFLY or MOTH (qq.v.), as an egg; from this emerges a larva, whose form varies according to its mode of life; then, after a resting stage generally passed in a cocoon, the adult beetle emerges. This transformation is called METAMORPHOSIS (q.v.).

Owing to their compact bodies, hard texture, and well-protected wings, beetles are the most thriving of all insects, and almost every land and freshwater habitat supports many species. The largest of them are as big as rats, while the smallest are almost invisible to the naked eye. Beetles have biting jaws, often very strong and sharp, but they do not directly injure man or his domestic animals. Some beetles, how-ever, are very harmful (see BEETLE PESTS, Vol. VI). The DEATH-WATCH BEETLE (q.v.) for

zone. The wax, out of which the cells are made, is produced by the workers in the form of tiny scales, which appear between the plates or segments of the underside of the abdomen. The queen Honey Bee is larger than the worker bee. She lacks the pollen baskets on the hind legs, and her tongue is shorter. In fact she is quite unfitted to live for any length of time without the attendance of her workers. These are the bees which the bee-farmer keeps (see BEE-KEEPING, Vol. VI).

In recent years many important discoveries have been made about honey-bees. The Austrian naturalist von Frisch has discovered that bees reveal to other bees the distance and position, in relation to the hive and the sun, of sources of food from which they have just returned. This they do by the movements they make in a round dance over the combs of the hive. Much more has been learnt, too, about bees' sense of time and their ability to detect the plane of polarized light coming from a patch of blue sky. It is now known that the queen secretes a substance which seems to satisfy the workers' craving—a fact which helps

E. O. Hoppé

HERCULES BEETLE OF SOUTH AMERICA—ONE OF THE LARGEST
BEETLES

Two-thirds natural size

instance, may bring old buildings to ruin by devouring the timber; and others, such as the COLORADO BEETLE and WEEVILS (qq.v.), by attacking important crops may threaten us with famine. On the other hand, there are many kinds which, by destroying harmful insects, are of very great service to mankind. LADYBIRDS (q.v.), for instance, feed upon harmful insects; many CHAFERS (q.v.) act as scavengers; STAG BEETLES (q.v.) help to clear woods and forests of dead trees. It is generally as larvae, when they are seldom seen, that beetles feed most, and are therefore of most importance.

Most adult insects have compound eyes, sometimes containing several thousands of lenses. These are extremely sensitive to changes in the light falling upon them, which give the insect instant warning of approaching danger. Beetles' eyes, however, do not function like our own; they can form clear images only of objects close at hand. Different beetles have different powers of sight, and some, for example, cave-dwelling species, are completely blind. A much more important sense than sight to most of them is that of smell, the organs of which are contained in the feelers or antennae. It is by means of these that they are able to recognize others of their kind, to find, sometimes at great distances, the proper food for themselves or their progeny, and to return, when necessary, to their own burrows. Many beetles (*see* CHAFERS) have the end joints of their antennae enlarged and placed side by side, like the leaves of a book:

this both increases their sensitivity and gives them protection. Some of these beetles spend weeks or months in providing for their young; and, like BEES, ANTS, and WASPS (qq.v.), they often perform the most delicate operations in complete darkness. Some of the little wood-boring beetles, known as Ambrosia Beetles, live in communities in extensive galleries, which they excavate in tree-stumps or logs. In their tunnels they cultivate, on specially prepared beds, a minute fungus, the so-called ambrosia, and this supplies food for themselves and for the grubs. The mould continues to grow provided that the timber is sufficiently damp, but if it should become too dry, the beetles leave the log and seek another, carrying the spores of the fungus with them.

Many beetles are able, by rubbing one part of the body against another, to produce chirping or squeaking sounds. This is generally done by scraping exceedingly fine and close ridges on one part of the body against hard ridges on some other part, as a violin bow scrapes the strings; the instrument may be played by quick movements of the head, the tail-end, the front or hind legs, or some other part. The grubs of

S. Beaufoy

GALLERIES OF BARK-BEETLES IN ELM

a group of beetles called Passalids, which live, together with their parents, in the interior of tree-stumps, appear to have only four legs: the third pair are useless for walking, but make a chirping sound when drawn across the fine ridges on the basal joint of the second pair of legs. The parent beetles also chirp by rubbing hard rough bosses against their folded wings. Perhaps parents and young communicate with each other by this means.

2. WATER BEETLES. A great many beetles spend almost all their lives in water—in rivers, streams, and even the smallest ponds. If these dry up, they either fly elsewhere or burrow in the damp mud, where they remain until the ponds fill again. The wing-covers of most beetles, besides protecting the wings, enclose a supply of air, which is used by the insects while they are below the surface of the water. This makes them so light that, when they cease to swim, they cannot stay below unless they grip some firmly anchored object. When a beetle rises to the surface it pokes the end of its body out of the water and renews the air supply. A water beetle swims with its hind legs, which are fringed with stiff hairs and act like oars to drive the beetle rapidly through the water. It uses the middle pair of legs for clinging to weeds or stones, and the front pair to grasp its prey, for most of them devour other aquatic animals. The Great Carnivorous Water Beetles, *Dytiscus*, of which six species occur in Britain and which are 2·5 cm or more in length, are very fierce, both as larvae and as adults, and destroy large numbers of aquatic insects, tadpoles, and even young fish. Other water beetles, in addition to an air supply beneath the wing-covers, carry another beneath the body, where it is retained

by fine silky hairs. The great shining black *Hydrophilus*, one of the largest British beetles, makes a remarkable silken raft for its eggs, from which the larvae escape directly into the water. These feed upon water-snails, breaking their shells by squeezing them between the head and back. The adult *Hydrophilus*, however, is a vegetarian.

The small shining black Whirligig Beetles are often seen in groups dashing about in a kind of communal dance over the surface of smooth water. Since they live on the surface, they are exposed to attack both from the air above and the water beneath. Their eyes are each divided into two, so that in effect they have four eyes; two on top of the head which enable them to detect danger from the air, and two beneath it which warn them of enemies in the water.

B.M. Nat. Hist.

A WHIRLIGIG BEETLE
About 4½ times natural size

3. LAND BEETLES. Most of the many beetles to be found running swiftly over the ground or sheltering beneath stones also feed upon other insects. The prettily decorated Tiger Beetles, for instance, often seen in sandy places, hunt flies and other insects. Their eggs are laid in holes in the ground, and the young larva, on hatching, digs a perpendicular shaft, in which it lies in wait for its prey, its head exactly fitting the mouth of the shaft. As soon as an insect appears within reach, the Tiger-larva, by a sudden spring, grips it in its sharp jaws and drags it into its lair to be devoured. In wintertime the shaft is sealed up, its occupant remaining secure until spring-time. When fully grown it again seals its burrow, casts its skin, and, after another change of skin several weeks later, becomes a winged beetle. Its life may last 4 years or more in all. The great African Tiger Beetle cannot fly, but hunts insects on the ground.

The common Ground Beetles, much more numerous than the Tiger Beetles, resemble them in their habits, some being even more voracious. In the larva-stage they generally live underground, and so are not often seen. Some of the beetles, when disturbed, are able to shoot from the hinder end of the body a drop of fluid, which

S. Beaufoy

GREAT WATER BEETLE
Left, larva; *right,* adult. Natural size

explodes on meeting the air, making a puff of vapour capable of injuring, or at least shocking, the enemy, and so giving the beetle time to escape. Most beetles with this strange habit live in Africa and Asia—the only British ones being pretty little insects, half red and half blue, generally found beneath large stones near water, and known as Bombardier Beetles.

Rove Beetles (Staphylinidae) have quite short wing-covers covering only the front of the abdomen. They feed on decaying matter, dung, and dead animals, and many also capture and eat live insects and other small animals. Most species are small, but the common British Devil's Coach-horse is 3·8 cm in length. It is black, and when disturbed has a habit of curling the tip of its body upwards and giving out an offensive smell.

Many beetles burrow into the ground, either in search of food or to store provisions for their future offspring. The Burying Beetles, handsome creatures, black with red or orange markings, bury the bodies of small animals and birds as food for their grubs. Their wonderful power of scent brings them quickly to a carcase. With their strong legs, they dig away the earth beneath the carcase until it is almost concealed in the hole. The females then lay their eggs upon it, and remain near the spot to feed the young grubs when the eggs hatch.

Most of the beetles which dig underground nests and provision them for their young are SCARABS or CHAFERS (qq.v.) of some kind. These industrious insects remove great quantities of decaying matter from the surface of the soil. According to the great naturalist FABRE (q.v. Vol. V), the horned Dor Beetle or Minotaur sometimes makes its nest as much as 1·5 metres below ground—the female digs out the earth, and the male carries it up the long shaft and ejects it. In India the stored cells made by a very large Chafer (*Helicopris*) have been found as deep as 2·5 metres.

Other beetles live in trees, depositing their eggs upon the trunks or branches, on which the grubs feed for months or years. A large group, the Longicorns (or Long-horns), have especially long antennae. The male of one species of Longicorn, sometimes found in felled pine-trees or wooden coal-mine props, has antennae four or five times as long as its body. Another common British Longicorn is called the Wasp Beetle, because it is decorated with bright

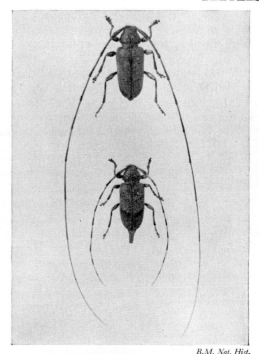

LONG-HORN BEETLES
Male (top) and female. Natural size

yellow bands. Its grubs feed inside decaying wooden posts or stumps.

A great many different kinds of beetles feed upon the leaves of plants. The common Tortoise Beetle feeds only upon thistles, and the Colorado Beetle only upon the potato and related plants. During their grub stage some members of this group live in cases, which they drag about with them and enlarge as they grow, changing to the beetle-shape before leaving the case. One of these (called *Clythra*) lives in its case within the nests of the large Wood Ant, and feeds upon the plant-fragments of which they are built. The ants will not allow the mother beetle to enter the nest, but she drops her eggs, each enclosed in a tiny capsule of excrement, near the nest, from a convenient bough. The ants carry them into the nest, probably mistaking them for the bracts on the ends of birch catkins, which they collect and which the capsules closely resemble.

Many beetles live at the expense of ants or of nest-building TERMITES (White Ants) (q.v.). Some of them have special glands which produce a sweet secretion like the 'honey-dew' of APHIDES (q.v.). This is very attractive to the ants, who treat the beetles favourably, even feeding them. One genus of these beetles, found in Britain, is called *Claviger* (Club-bearer), because the feelers are like massive clubs. These beetles are quite blind, and entirely dependent for their food upon the ants with which they live. The ants stroke them with their antennae, and they give out drops of sweet fluid, which the

B.M. Nat. Hist.

A SOUTH AFRICAN
PAUSSID BEETLE

Twice natural
size

ants immediately swallow. Ants even allow others of these parasites to devour their helpless brood, and do not drive them from the nest. Some beetles, however, are not so welcome in the ants' nest, and these protect themselves in all sorts of ways. One remarkable group called Paussids can, like the Bombardier Beetles, fire an explosive fluid in the faces of the ants.

BELL-BIRD, *see* CHATTERER; HONEY-EATER.

BERRIES, *see* FRUITS, Section 3 *a*.

BIRCH, *see* WOODLANDS, Section 5; *see also* Vol. VI: TREES, BROADLEAVED.

BIRDS OF PARADISE AND BOWER BIRDS. There are at least fifty species of these tropical birds of the very large order of Passerine or perching birds, belonging to closely related families, the Birds of Paradise to Paradisaeidae and the Bower Birds to the Ptilonorhynchidae.

1. Birds of Paradise are found mostly in the dense forests of New Guinea and the neighbouring islands, though there are a few in Australia. They vary in size from that of a starling to a large crow, and are remarkable for the adornment of the adult males, which carry plumes of eccentric shape and brilliant hues of scarlet, gold, violet, bronze, green, and many other colours. When plumes were in fashion, the Birds of Paradise were relentlessly hunted, and would have been exterminated had not a law been passed forbidding their import into America and Britain (*see* FEATHER HUNTING, Vol. VI). The birds were first brought to Europe by the survivors of Magellan's voyage round the world in 1521,

when they were given their present name. The legend grew up that the birds were legless and therefore were not inhabitants of the earth, an idea that arose presumably because the skins brought to Europe had had the feet removed.

There is a wide variety in the types of plumes. The best-known species, the Great Bird of Paradise of the Aru Islands, near New Guinea, a bird about 58 cm long, has an abundance of long, golden-yellow plumes, which do not reach their prime until the bird is 7 or 8 years old. The Red Bird of Paradise has shorter flank plumes of a rich crimson, and the two middle tail-feathers are long, slender streamers, nearly 60 cm long. The Long-tailed Bird of Paradise has tail-feathers over 60 cm long and tinted à brilliant opal-blue. The Six-plumed Bird of Paradise has a set of three small black plumes on very long quills on each side of the head. Albert's Bird of Paradise, one of the most remarkable of the family, has a long streamer, twice the length of the body, coming from the head behind each eye. Each of the streamers is made up of thirty or forty squared lobes of feathers, light blue above and dusky below.

John Warham

GREAT BOWER-BIRD DISPLAYING TO FEMALE

This wonderful plumage in the male attracts the female; and the way in which the males use their plumage in their courtship display is most interesting. The males have their regular dancing places, either on the ground or in trees, where they display their plumes to entice the female. As the breeding season approaches the excitement of the cocks increases—and the sight of a dozen or twenty fully plumaged cocks together, raising their wings, stretching their necks, spreading their plumes, calling, and flying at intervals from branch to branch, is a sight not to be forgotten. The nest is usually placed high in the tree-tops, and generally two cream-coloured eggs are laid. Some species, however, appear to nest in holes in tree-trunks.

2. BOWER-BIRDS, mainly inhabitants of Australia, though two types are found in New Guinea and the Papuan Islands, are less spectacular in appearance than Birds of Paradise, though some of them have very handsome colours. They are so called because, at the mating season, the male constructs a 'bower' as part of his display to attract the female. He then uses the bower as a sort of 'playground' in which to perform his dancing displays. The hen, however, appears to pay little attention to the bower, and builds a nest of the ordinary type in a bush or tree, often some distance away.

The Satin Bower-bird, so called because of its blue-black, shiny, satin-like plumage, constructs an elaborate bower. First he makes a twig tunnel, about 45 cm high, out of two parallel rows of twigs, their ends stuck in the ground and their tops nearly touching. All around this he places bones and coloured objects, such as shells, pebbles, feathers, and flowers—blue appearing to be a favourite colour. Then he paints the sticks of the bower blue with the blue juice crushed from a berry. The Gardener Bird of Papua builds perhaps the most remarkable bower. He makes a hut-like structure some 60 cm high, at the foot of a tree, and roofs it with orchis stems radiating from a central support, and with a mass of moss. In front of it he lays out a bed of moss, into which he fixes bright-coloured berries and flowers, which he replaces as they wither. (*See* Colour Plate opp. p. 16).

See also ANIMAL LANGUAGE.

BIRDS. This group of warm-blooded, vertebrate (backboned) animals, which usually, but not always, possesses powers of flight, has evolved in long-past ages from reptile ancestors (*see* EVOLUTION, CHART). Their anatomy more resembles that of reptiles than of mammals (which are also descended from reptiles). It is believed that the ancestor of birds was a small, tree-climbing, lizard-like creature.

The birds, with their powers of flight, have evolved skeletons distinguished at once for lightness and strength. The little Humming-bird, for instance, which is able to make a non-stop flight across the Gulf of Mexico, some 800 km, weighs less than 30 grammes. The bird's skull is in remarkable contrast to the solid, heavy skull of the mammal. It consists of a box of thin bone to accommodate the brain, deeply hollowed at the sides to give room for the large eyes, and a light and flexible scaffolding of bony splints which supports the beak, palate, and lower jaw. Most of a bird's bones are hollow, with the interior webbed across by fine girders of bone to give added strength. The bones of the spine are flexibly connected in the neck, strongly bound

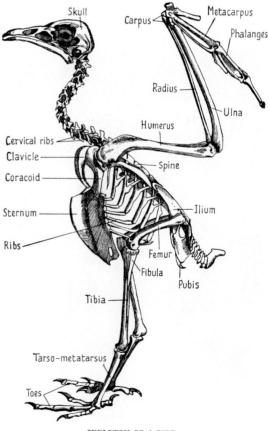

SKELETON OF A BIRD

together in the front part of the body, and united in the hinder part with the bones of the pelvis into a solid, rigid mass. The number of vertebrae in this rigid section varies in different species from ten to twenty-two. A small number of movable caudal vertebrae provide a support for the tail.

The large breast-bone or 'sternum', with its deep fore-and-aft keel, provides attachment for the powerful muscles which move the wings. The skeleton of the wings corresponds to the bones of the fore-limb (or arm) of other higher vertebrates. The number of bones in the 'wrist' and 'hand' is reduced (the fewer the moving parts, the greater the strength), and traces of only three fingers remain. The flight-feathers are carried on the bones of 'hand' and 'fore-arm'. The leg bones are comparatively little modified; the toes never number more than four, and the so-called 'knee' of a bird is a joint which somewhat resembles the ankle of a man.

The muscles which raise and lower the wings at each stroke are all attached to the lower side of the breast-bone. The down-stroke is made by a direct pull; but the wing is raised by a ten-don which passes from the upper side of the humerus, through a kind of pulley in the top of the shoulder girdle, and so downward to the muscles. The breast muscles may amount to as much as one-fifth of the total weight of the bird. The lungs of a bird are very important, for so large a mass of muscle, working at high speed, demands a good supply of oxygen. The lungs are so formed that the air is drawn into a system of air-sacs extending beyond the areas where oxygen is taken up by the blood. As a result, all the capillaries of the lung are in contact with freshly drawn air at each breath—a more efficient method of RESPIRATION (q.v.) than that of the mammals, in which the air in contact with the capillaries of the lungs is completely changed only once in several breaths.

In basic structure all birds are very much alike; but different ways of life have produced some outward differences. Beaks vary greatly with the uses to which they are put. The flesh-eating OWLS, HAWKS, and SHRIKES have beaks strongly hooked at the tip, while fish-eating AUKS and diving DUCKS have sharp-edged or serrated beaks for grasping slippery prey. The

G. K. Yeates

NEST OF RED-THROATED DIVER

beaks of Snipe and Woodcock are long for probing and sensitive at the tip for finding hidden prey by touch. Seed and fruit-eaters, such as the Finches and Nuthatch, have stout, strong beaks which enable them to tear open tough shells and crack hard stones; while many insect-eating birds, such as the Fly-catchers (qq.v.), have sharp-pointed beaks, which make neat forceps for seizing small and agile victims. The feet, too, vary considerably—from the small feet of Swifts (q.v.), with all four toes set forward and used almost entirely as a set of hooks wherewith the bird can hang itself up, to the enormously long toes of the Jacanas and Lily-trotters of tropical regions, which enable the birds to walk across floating vegetation. Most swimming birds have their toes united by a web (Cormorants, Geese, Gulls) or flanged with lobes of skin (Grebes, Coots, Phalaropes) (qq.v.).

A bird's feathers are of two kinds, the large feathers of flight—on wings called 'remiges', and on tail 'rectrices'—and the smaller contour feathers which make the general covering. In most birds the contour feathers do not grow evenly all over the body, but along certain feather tracts. All feathers are renewed by a process of moulting, in which the worn feather is dropped and replaced by a new one. The number of moults in the year, and the seasons of moulting, vary greatly between species, and sometimes between the two sexes of one species. At the moult the colours of a bird may be changed or made brighter. In some species, for example the Brambling (see Finches), certain colour-changes are effected by the wearing away of a feather tip, which is coloured differently from the rest of the feather.

The coloration of birds may serve to conceal them from their foes (see Camouflage), or to advertise them to the other members of their own species. Brilliant or conspicuous colours may be used by birds in displaying to their mates (see Animal Language), and also in making the wearer look large and terrible to his opponents in battle. Where the sexes differ in colour, the male is generally the more brilliant, for the more soberly coloured female, which performs the duties of incubation, needs to be as little conspicuous as possible. In a few species, such as the Red-necked Phalarope and Painted Snipe, the female is the brighter bird—and in these species it is the female which makes a courtship display to the male.

G. K. Yeates

NEST OF PENDULINE TIT

It used to be thought that most quarrelling between birds was for the possession of mates; but it is now known that much of the fighting between male birds (or of displays in place of fighting) is for the possession of a plot of ground in which the bird can breed (see Animal Territory). A bird without a territory, forced to lead a wandering life, is unlikely to retain a mate. The value of territory in helping to maintain the bond between the birds of a pair is undoubted. Many ornithologists believe that this habit of claiming a territory also prevents birds from crowding in upon a favourable area and over-taxing the supply of food. Song (the repetition of notes in accordance with some recognizable pattern for each species) is one of the best known of bird habits, and serves to announce the ownership of a territory—a warning to rival males and a signal to hens in search of a mate.

The building of the nest may be the duty of one or both birds of the pair. Nests may be built of a variety of materials—often depending on what is most readily available in the bird's locality. They may be placed at the top of tall trees (CROWS and HERONS); in hollows among dense vegetation (WADING BIRDS); in tunnels made by the bird in trees (WOODPECKERS); or in the ground (BEE-EATERS and KINGFISHERS) (qq.v.). Some water-birds, such as the GREBES and DIVERS (qq.v.), make no more than a mound of sodden plant material floating among reeds and rushes, and some waders scrape a shallow depression in the ground and line it with fragments of shell or bone. The African Palm Swift constructs only a little pad of down on a palm leaf—so small that it cannot support the egg, which must be glued to it by the parent bird. Some birds make bag-shaped nests with entrances at the top or on the side (GOLDCREST, Long-tailed TITS (qq.v.)). The Tailor-bird stitches together the edges of a suitable leaf with cobweb and cotton to make its hanging nest. Some species of WEAVER-BIRDS (q.v.) construct a communal nest, within which many pairs of birds have their homes. One species of Swift builds a nest of its own saliva, which is eaten as a great delicacy in the Far East.

Some birds lay only one egg a year; others, such as some of the game birds, lay up to twenty. The incubation of the eggs is sometimes undertaken by the hen alone, sometimes shared between the parents. When the male is smaller and more dully coloured than the female, he usually takes the larger part in incubating the eggs and tending the young. When the young have hatched, they are either fed in the nest with food brought by one or both parents, or (in many wading and game birds) led forth to seek their own food. In most of those species in which the young remain some time in the nest, their droppings are collected and removed by the old birds—otherwise deep and hollow nests would become terribly fouled. The BRUSH TURKEY (q.v.) buries its eggs in a heap of dead vegetation, so that they are incubated by the heat of decay. Some birds bring up only one brood in a season, others as many as three.

It has been observed from ancient times that at certain seasons some species of birds were absent from their accustomed haunts. It used to be believed that the summer residents of the British Isles spent the winter in HIBERNATION (q.v.), sleeping in safe retreats until the spring, as do many species of mammals. When, however, in the late 18th and early 19th centuries, much more came to be known about the natural history of foreign lands, the truth about bird migration was established. Birds seen in Britain in the summer months were found to be inhabiting other countries during the winter, but not during the time of their residence in Britain. Migration seemed to be the only reasonable explanation—in fact, by regular movements to and fro about the world many species were able to inhabit areas which were suited to their needs for only part of the year. The routes which birds follow and the distances which they go have been much studied in the present century by the use of bird-ringing (or banding). A very light ring bearing an address and a serial number is clipped around the leg of the bird, and by the return of these rings from other lands, where the bird has been killed or found dead, it is possible to fix at least two points in its journeyings. (*See* MIGRATION.)

Because they can fly, birds are able to make long migrations relatively easily. Some flightless birds, however, such as the PENGUINS (q.v.), perform long migrations partly by swimming and partly by walking over the ice. There was a tendency at one time to exaggerate the speeds at which birds flew, more especially when on migration; but now it is known that speeds of more than 96 km/h are rare, and that many small birds usually fly at speeds of between 32 and 48 km/h. A hunting Barn Owl may fly as slowly as 22 km/h.

Birds have acute eyesight and good hearing, but little sense of smell (*see* SENSES). Though their senses closely resemble those of man, their mental processes are probably very different. They have a curious way of concentrating upon certain features of an object which engages their attention, and apparently neglecting others— they do not seem to look at the object as a whole. For example, the red breast of a ROBIN (q.v.) is a signal for another Robin to expel the intruder from his territory by battle (a stuffed Robin being just as fiercely attacked as a live one). A stuffed Robin with the breast discoloured, however, excites little attention; yet the red breast feathers alone, although not actually carried by a bird, will excite attack. Again, one of the American woodpeckers, the Flicker, distinguishes between the sexes by the presence or absence of a black moustachial streak, worn only by the male: a male Flicker will actually attack his own mate as though she were another male if she has an artificial 'moustache' glued to her plumage. That one small visual change seems to be sufficient to prevent his recognizing her. As soon as it is removed, however, he will greet her affectionately once again. The investigation of these problems of perception in birds has been one of the most rewarding lines of ornithological research in recent years.

BIRD WATCHING, *see* Vol. IX: Bird Watching.

BIRDWING BUTTERFLIES, *see* Tropical Butterflies, Section 2 *b*.

BISON. This huge animal is a member of the Cattle family (q.v.), its main characteristics being short horns, a distinct beard under the chin, and high forequarters, which in winter are covered with a great mane of woolly hair. There are only two species, the European and the American Bison, which differ little from each other, and both of which are now protected in game preserves. In spite of their great size, bison are active animals, and can trot and gallop with great speed—they gallop with their heads close to the ground and their tails high in the air. During the breeding season they are fond of rolling in the dust, and the bulls fight fiercely amongst each other.

The European Bison or Wisent used to roam the large forests of Europe, and from fossil remains we know that it once inhabited Britain. Its numbers were gradually reduced by systematic hunting until it very nearly became extinct, and is now only to be found, protected, in eastern Europe. These bison feed mostly on the leaves, twigs, and bark of trees.

The American Bison lived in vast numbers, until comparatively recently, on the prairies of the United States and Canada. In 1871, a traveller estimated that a herd through which he had to pass covered an area of about 80 km by 40 km, and could not have numbered less than 4 million. The bison was to the Plains Indians of North America much what the camel was to the people of the Sahara, or the Yak to the people of Tibet—the provider of most of the necessities of life; and bison were hunted in every way possible (*see* American Indians, North, Vol. I). The decline in their numbers happened very quickly as the white man moved westwards, bringing horses and fire-arms with him. The massacre was completed when the building of the great railroads across the continent prevented the seasonal movements of the herds between north and south—a movement which had taken place from time immemorial. The vast armies employed on building the railway were supplied with buffalo beef ('buffalo' being the name quite inaccurately given by the European to the bison). One man, Buffalo Bill, with his troop of hunters, entered into a contract to supply the meat, and consequently played a large part in practically exterminating the animals. An unusually fine bull may measure 1·7 metres at the withers, but the average is considerably below this height. The cow does not breed till three years old, and sometimes produces two calves at a birth. American bison feed entirely on grass.

BITTERN, *see* Heron.

BIVALVE, *see* Molluscs.

BLACK ARCHES MOTH, *see* Tussock Moths.

Mondiale

BULL BISON

BLACK BEETLE, *see* COCKROACH.

BLACKBIRD, *see* THRUSH.

BLACKCOCK, *see* GROUSE.

BLENNY. Most people who have examined a rock-pool on the coast after the tide has gone out will be familiar with Blennies. They are small fishes that lie in crevices in the rocks or among the weeds, and dart quickly from place to place. They seem to be able to withstand great variations of temperature, for when the cool waters of the sea have retreated, they survive in shallow pools exposed to the sun's rays, where the water may get quite warm.

There are very many different species of Blenny found on sea-shores throughout the world. All have rather long bodies, though the tropical species are usually shorter than those in the Arctic. The pelvic fins are placed far forward on the throat, and the two dorsal fins, the first of which has many spines, are usually joined together, extending right along the back. Most of them have little flaps of skin, tentacles or filaments, above the eyes, on the nose, or on top of the head.

Several different kinds of Blenny are found on the British coast, the best-known being the Common Blenny, which has tentacles over its eyes, and the Shanny, which has none. The Butterfly Blenny is a handsome species, with a large and prettily marked first dorsal fin. Very similar kinds are found around America and Japan. All these, and many of the tropical species, have no scales; but there are also many kinds in which scales are present.

Most Blennies lay eggs, which they usually conceal carefully under stones or among seaweed; but a few, such as the Viviparous Blenny of Europe, bear their young alive. A closely related family, the Wolf-fishes, grow to quite a large size, inhabit the open sea, and are of value as food. The flesh is salted, and the skin is used for making shoes and handbags. They have large, ugly heads, with very strong teeth, including canine or biting teeth in front of the jaws, and molars or crushing teeth at the back. Housewives are unwilling to buy such ugly-looking fish, so they are usually beheaded and skinned before being brought to market, where they are sold, along with other kinds, under the name 'Rock Salmon'.

BLIND FISH. In the underground waters of limestone caves in the United States of America dwell a number of fishes, related to the ordinary freshwater fishes of that region, but having very small eyes. A prolonged existence in these dark surroundings has resulted in the complete loss of the sense of sight and the great development of special sense-organs in the skin, so that they can feel their way about the dark recesses of the caves and be aware of the presence of their prey. The best-known of these is the Kentucky Blind Fish from the famous Mammoth Cave, Kentucky.

Another group of fishes in which the eyes are very small, and which rely largely on their 'feelers' or barbels, namely, the CAT-FISHES (q.v.), have likewise found it possible to colonize caves and wells in the United States, Brazil, Trinidad, and Africa; while in the latter place, also, two or three relatives of the Barbel (*see* CARP) have taken up their abode in underground lakes.

The loss of all or most of their sight in these fishes is accompanied also by loss of colour, most of them being pale and translucent. Eyes

A. Fraser-Brunner

BUTTERFLY BLENNY

enable fish to see, and coloured patterns may make them inconspicuous, but neither of these is of value in total darkness, and they have degenerated or disappeared. It has been shown, too, that the presence of light is necessary for the development of both eyes and pigment (the colouring matter of the skin). So in the very deep sea (the sun's rays being unable to penetrate beyond a depth of about 250 fathoms), many of the fishes are almost or quite blind, and, if blind, they are usually also colourless and

A. Fraser-Brunner

THE BLIND-FISH OF THE KENTUCKY CAVES AS IT IS SEEN BY TORCH-LIGHT

provided with sensitive organs (*see* DEEP-SEA FISHES). Such are those belonging to a family called Brotulidae, to which the Cuban Blind Fishes belong. How these oceanic fishes came to be living in the underground fresh waters of Cuba is a matter of great interest: they must have been living among rocks at a time when these were raised up above the surface in a past geological age, and so have developed along with the caves, gradually becoming accustomed to living in fresh water.

The Blind Goby, found on the shores of southern California, spends its whole life under rocks or in the tunnels made by a species of burrowing shrimp. It is about 5 centimetres long, pale pink in colour, with a smooth, naked skin. When very young, the eyes, though very small, can be used; but in the adult they are minute vestiges, and the fish is quite blind. It is, however, well supplied with sensitive organs on its head.

BLOODSUCKER LIZARD, *see* AGAMA.

BLOOD SYSTEM. In all except primitive animals such as HYDRA and SPONGES (qq.v.) digested food (and in the higher animals oxygen also) is carried to the living CELLS of the body (q.v.) in a fluid called blood. In the course of evolution, as animals became larger, special organs, such as an alimentary canal and digestive system for NUTRITION (q.v.) and gills or lungs for RESPIRATION (q.v.), became necessary. Together with the development of these organs

in localized parts of the body a system was evolved for conveying the food and oxygen from the parts of the body where they were taken in to the parts where they were required, and also for carrying away waste gases such as carbon dioxide. This 'transport' system is the blood system; the transport fluid, or blood, is usually carried in tubular channels called the blood-vessels; and the movement of the blood is brought about by a pumping organ called the HEART (q.v.).

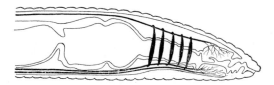

Fig. 1. BLOOD SYSTEM OF EARTHWORM

The vessels containing the blood are divided into two groups; the canals by which the blood is carried away from the heart to the tissues of the body are known as arteries, and those by which the blood returns from the tissues to the heart are called veins.

A definite blood system occurs in some worms such as the earthworm (*see* WORM). Three blood-vessels run the length of the body, and in these there are five pairs of contractile vessels which function as hearts and drive the blood round the body. In INSECTS (q.v.), above the gut there is a single closed vessel which is divisible into a pumping organ behind and a

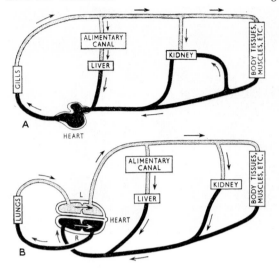

FIG. 2. A. SINGLE CIRCULATION AS IN FISHES. B. COMPLETE DOUBLE CIRCULATION AS IN MAMMALS

conducting vessel called the 'aorta' in front. Elsewhere the blood flows freely through the cavities of the body and the appendages, and there are no definite veins or arteries. A somewhat similar system also occurs in MOLLUSCS (q.v.) such as the snail; but in the OCTOPUS (q.v.) the blood is restricted to definite channels like those present in vertebrates.

In animals such as the earthworm, in insects, and in fishes there is a single circulation. In fishes the blood passes from the heart to the gills on its way to the various body organs; when it has picked up oxygen in the gills it passes straight to the tissues and not first back to the heart (fig. 1).

The blood system of FROGS and TOADS, REPTILES, BIRDS, and MAMMALS (qq.v.) consists of two separate circulations (fig. 2). In these animals the blood, after it has been passed to the lungs where it picks up oxygen, is returned to the heart before being pumped to the body tissues. This necessitates a more complicated heart than is needed for animals with a single circulation. In animals with a complete double circulation, the heart is divided into compartments which keep the oxygenated and deoxygenated blood separate; the left side and the right side of the heart are separated from each other, and both sides are divided into an auricle and a muscular ventricle. The two separate blood circulations are the body or systematic circulation and the lung or pulmonary circulation. The body or

systematic circulation carries oxygenated blood from the left ventricle to the head, toes, and other parts of the body and returns it back as deoxygenated blood to the right auricle. The lung or pulmonary circulation carries this deoxygenated blood with its carbon dioxide from the right ventricle to the lungs; there it loses its carbon dioxide and becomes charged with oxygen, returning as oxygenated blood to the left auricle. The person who first discovered how this complicated system works was Sir William HARVEY in the 17th century (q.v. Vol. V).

See also Vol. XI: BLOOD (Human); BLOOD, CIRCULATION OF (Human).

BLOOD WORM, *see* MIDGE.

BLOWFLY. There are several kinds of large Blowflies—the Bluebottles which are dull blue, the Greenbottles which are brilliant metallic green, copper, or blue, and the FLESHFLIES (q.v.). They normally breed in carrion and sometimes in dung. Bluebottles often enter houses, attracting attention by their loud buzzing noise. The females lay their eggs in batches and are the commonest cause of fly-blown meat in the kitchen. The maggots, which are like those of the HOUSE FLY (q.v.) but larger, are often used for fishing bait, and are known as 'gentles'. Their life-history is similar to that of the House Fly, but takes longer to complete—at least three weeks. Greenbottles rarely come indoors, though Fleshflies do so occasionally. All, especially Greenbottles, infest sores or wounds on living animals. An infestation by fly maggots is called 'myiasis', and one on sheep is called a 'strike'. The Sheep-maggot Fly lays its eggs on the damp wool of the sheep where it is soiled by dung or urine. The maggots, when they hatch, tunnel into the flesh and often kill the sheep. Indeed, losses from this cause are very serious in Australia, exceeding those from all other factors combined.

The maggots' habit of feeding on wounded animals was made use of in surgery during the First World War with very satisfactory results. The larvae, reared under perfectly clean conditions, were placed in the wounds, where they cleared away pus-laden tissue and stopped the growth of BACTERIA (q.v.).

See also FLY.
See also Vol. XI: HOUSEHOLD PESTS.

BLUEBIRD (Blue Robin). This very well-known and favourite bird of North America is slightly larger than the European Robin, and is related both to the WARBLERS and the THRUSHES (qq.v.) The upper surface of the male is cobalt-blue, and the throat and underparts chestnut, while the female is an indeterminate blue-brown. The Bluebird winters in the Southern States, and is one of the first birds to arrive in the Northern States in the spring, arriving as early as February or even January. The male arrives first, and greets the female on her arrival with a delicate bubbling song, to which she makes a low two-syllabled answer. They build a very simple nest of a few straws and feathers in a hole in a tree, and often in a nestbox. The hen lays four to six bluish-white eggs, and two or three broods are produced in a year. Both male and female are excellent parents, feed their young on insect or vegetable food, and keep the nesting hole scrupulously clean.

BLUEBOTTLE, *see* BLOWFLY.

BLUES (Butterflies). There are eleven species of this large family of small butterflies in Britain. The Long-tailed and Short-tailed Blues visit Britain as rare migrants. The Mazarine Blue bred here in the last century, and became extinct about 1876, only occasional migrants having since been reported. In most species the males have blue wings and the females brown, the undersides of the wings being peppered all over with various patterns of black dots. The caterpillars are shaped like wood-lice, and generally feed on leguminous plants, common on heaths and downs where Blues are usually to be found. Some species supplement their plant diet by preying on other species, and a few foreign species are entirely carnivorous.

The caterpillars of all the British species have a honey-gland on the back, which produces a sweet fluid very attractive to ants. The ants do not harm the caterpillars, but vigorously defend them against attack; so that both partners benefit from the association, one obtaining food and the other protection (*see* ANTS). The Large Blue, found only in North Cornwall, Devon, and the Cotswolds, has a very strange life-history. The eggs are laid in July on the buds of wild thyme, on the flowers of which the caterpillar feeds for about 20 days, augmenting its diet by attacking smaller individuals. Then it wanders,

eventually being found by an ant, which strokes it until it yields some of the sweet fluid from its honey-gland. After an interval the caterpillar suddenly hunches its back, a signal for the ant to carry it off to the nest; and there it remains for the rest of its caterpillar life, feeding on the ant larvae. It remains in the ants' nest as a chrysalis all winter, and emerges as a butterfly in early July. The wings of both sexes are blue, spotted with black and with white fringes.

The Small Blue is fairly well distributed over the chalk country and other regions of the British Isles, small colonies often being found in disused chalk-pits. The tiny females are dark chocolate-brown, and the males are faintly dusted with silvery-blue. Their wings are fragile, the scales coming off at the slightest touch. The caterpillars feed on kidney vetch, and generally live through the winter among the dead vetch flowers, which they exactly resemble. The butterflies emerge quite early in the summer.

The male of the Common Blue butterfly is pale violet-blue; usually the female is brown, but with some orange spots round the edges of her wings. Both sexes gather in the evening in long grass, where they rest head downwards. Two generations occur in southern England, in May and again in late August, though farther north there is only one generation, appearing during June and July. Isolation has produced distinct forms in Ireland and on one of the Scilly Islands. The caterpillars feed on bird's-foot trefoil, and hibernate when quite small, deep down in tufts of grass.

The Holly Blue is light blue, tinted with lilac, the female being distinguished by a deep border of black on the fore-wings, and a row of black dots round the edges of the hind-wings. This Blue hibernates as a chrysalis, attached by a girdle to the underside of an evergreen ivy leaf. It emerges very early in the spring, and, although a woodland species, is often seen in towns skipping over garden bushes, behaving more like a HAIRSTREAK (q.v.) than a Blue. The first brood lay their eggs chiefly on young shoots of holly. Some of these produce a more heavily marked second brood in July, while others hibernate and emerge the following spring. Occasionally there is a third brood, usually on the flower buds of ivy. The tiny, green, slug-like caterpillar eats its way into the centre of the bud as soon as it hatches, and remains hidden there until, having 'sucked' the bud dry, it moves to

another one. The butter-
flies may sometimes be seen
drinking at wet mud or
moist dung.

The Chalk Hill Blue ap-
pears in August. The male
is 'Cambridge' blue, the
female dusky, almost
coffee-coloured, with a
row of bright orange spots
on the lower wings and
fainter ones on the upper
wings. The caterpillars
feed on horseshoe vetch on
the chalk downs of southern
England, and can be found
in the evenings crawling
up out of thick grass tufts
to feed

Zoological Society of London

GREEN TREE BOA

The Adonis Blue is the most beautiful of the
family. The caterpillars, which hibernate, feed
only on horseshoe vetch. The butterflies are to
be seen by May, a second brood appearing in
late August, and in a fine autumn continuing
even late into October. The Silver-studded
Blue is fairly widely distributed in the south,
in Norfolk and Suffolk, and in Wales, colonies
often being found in rough meadows, on heaths
and commons, and less frequently on the chalk.
Distinct races occur on the mosses of north-west
England and on the limestone cliffs of Caernarvon. The caterpillars feed on gorse, as well
as on most low-growing leguminous plants,
though the Caernarvon race eats rock-rose. The
winter is spent in the egg stage, the butterflies appearing in July and early August. The
males are violet-blue with black hind margins;
the females rich brown, often dusted with
greyish-blue.

The Brown Argus is brown in both sexes, with
a row of brilliant orange spots running round
the edges of its wings. The Scottish race, possessing a white spot on the fore-wings, has only one
generation a year, while the southern race is
double-brooded. The two meet and interbreed
in northern England, producing intermediates.

BOA. The Boa family of SNAKES (q.v.) is
divided into two sub-families: the true Boas,
which are found in tropical America and Madagascar, and the Pythons and Sand Boas, which
inhabit Africa, Asia, and Australasia. The family
includes the largest snakes now living, the

Reticulated Python and the Anaconda, which
reach a length of 8·5 or 9 metres. Such gigantic
snakes have enormous strength, and can attack
and overcome powerful animals, such as leopards
and wild boars. Many Boas and Pythons are
beautifully coloured with reds, greens, yellows,
and blacks, and have a wonderful sheen on their
scales when the skin has just been shed. Among
the most beautiful are the Diamond Snake of
Australia, the Royal Python of Africa, the Indian
Python and the Reticulated Python of India,
and the Boa Constrictor of South America.

The name Tree Boa is given to several species
that live in trees. The Sand Boas inhabit the
desert regions of south-west Asia and northern
Africa, and spend much of their time buried in
the soil; they have short, blunt-ended tails and
are a dull uniform colour. The Anaconda, a
dark greyish-brown above, with large black
spots, lives in the dense forest regions of Brazil
and the Guianas. It loves the water and spends
much of its time in it. It feeds upon mammals
and birds. The Blood Python of Malaya is so
named because it is brownish-red above, with
large spots. It is a small species, not exceeding
9·7 metres in length, but it has a very thick body.

BOAR, *see* SWINE.

BOMBAY DUCK, *see* LANTERN FISH.

BONITO, *see* MACKEREL.

BOOK-LOUSE. This minute insect is not a
true LOUSE (q.v.). It belongs to the order

Psocoptera. Of the thousand known species eighty-seven occur in Britain. They usually have four wings, but many are wingless. They may be found on tree trunks and old fences, where they feed on fragments of plant and animal material and especially on the lichens, fungi, and bright green algae which cover them.

Some species have taken advantage of the many artificial habitats created by man, where they sometimes breed in enormous numbers. Some, belonging to the genus *Trogium*, are completely wingless, about a millimetre in length, and brownish or yellowish in colour. They have jerky and uncertain movements, and when they are touched dart backwards for a short distance before going forward again, either in the same or in another direction. They are commonly found in houses, especially in damp, shady rooms, where they may be seen running over mantlepieces and along the book-shelves of libraries. Their food is probably the glue and paste of book-bindings and the moulds which grow on them. They are sometimes found in great numbers in new houses, where they consume the paste fastening the paper to the wall. Another common and slightly larger house-hold species has tiny wing flaps and rows of reddish spots on a pale body. It makes a faint noise, often amplified by loose wallpaper, by rapping its abdomen against the surface on which it rests. Other book-lice are common pests of warehouses, among collections of dried plants or insects, and in stored products. In the warm, dark holds of grain-ships they some-times occur in millions, especially if the grain is slightly damp and mouldy.

Young book-lice, known as nymphs, closely resemble the adults. In one species no males exist; and the females lay fertile eggs without mating—a kind of REPRODUCTION IN ANIMALS called 'parthenogenesis' (q.v.).

Book-lice are not particularly harmful in small numbers, though they may cause further losses to goods already damaged by the moulds on which they feed. They have sometimes given rise to actions at law by being confused with true lice.

See also Vol. XI: HOUSEHOLD PESTS.

BOWER BIRD, see BIRDS OF PARADISE, Section 2; Colour Plate facing p. 16.

BRACKEN, see FERNS.

BRAIN. The brain and several important organs of sense—those of smell, sight, hearing, and taste—are at the front end of the animal, all close to each other. As most vertebrate animals move forwards, it is the head which usually makes contact with a new environment. Information about the outside world is relayed from the sense organs along nerves to the brain, which then transmits instructions to the muscles and to other organs.

Relatively simple animals such as HYDRA (q.v.) have no central nervous system and no brain; they have only scattered nerve cells linked up with one another to form a continuous nerve net. FLATWORMS (q.v.) have a nerve net, much like that of hydra, but they also have local concentrations of cells forming not only a pair of nerve cords running along the length of the body but also a thickening in front near the eyes, which acts as a primitive kind of brain. It receives impulses from neighbouring sense organs and from the longitudinal nerve cords, and exercises some control over the activities of the body as a whole.

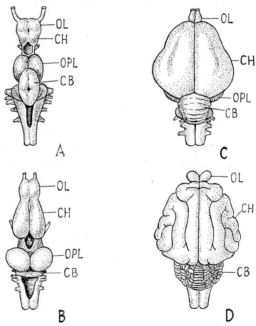

BRAINS OF (A) FISH, (B) AMPHIBIAN, (C) BIRD, (D) MAMMAL

The cerebrum or cerebral hemispheres (CH), the thinking part of the brain, develops enormously from the lower to the higher animal

CB = cerebellum (controlling sense of balance)
OL = olfactory lobes (controlling sense of smell)
OPL = optic lobes (controlling sense of sight)

Animals which are forward-moving have their brain—and also the more important sense organs of smell, sight, hearing, and taste—in the front end, or head, of the body, since this is the first to make contact with new environments. Round the brain and the sense-organs is a dense concentration of the nervous system, along which messages are received by the brain from the SENSES and necessary instructions transmitted from the brain to the MUSCLES and to other organs (qq.v.).

In all vertebrates the brain first appears in the developing animal (or embryo) as a swollen front end of the spinal chord. This is faintly divided into three parts, known respectively as the fore-brain, mid-brain, and hind-brain, each part being hollow. As the embryo grows, the brain develops in a definite pattern distinctive of the group to which it belongs. The simplest brain is found in FISHES (q.v.): here the fore-brain becomes divided into three parts: in front is a pair of olfactory or smelling lobes; behind is the cerebrum or thinking part; and the hinder part of the fore-brain bears two glands, the 'pineal' above and the 'pituitary' below, its side walls forming the optic thalami where the optic nerves emerge. The mid-brain gives rise to a pair of optic or seeing lobes; and the hind-brain becomes divided into two very important organs —the 'cerebellum', which is concerned with the control of all movements, and the 'medulla oblongata', which controls such functions as breathing, the circulation of the blood, swallowing, and feeding.

It follows that the shape and proportions of the brain vary according to the habits of the animal possessing it. Those depending largely on smell for their livelihood, as dogs and wolves do, have well-developed olfactory lobes; those depending on sight, as birds do, have large optic lobes. Intelligence is linked with the growth and size of the cerebrum, which is quite small in the fish but develops to an enormous size in human beings.

See also INTELLIGENCE.
See also Vol. XI: BRAIN (Human).

BREAM, *see* CARP.

BRILL, *see* FLATFISHES.

BRIMSTONE BUTTERFLY, *see* YELLOWS (Butterflies).

BRISTLE FLY (or Tachinid). This is a stoutly built insect, about the size of the House-fly, though some are larger, with strong bristles on its abdomen. Bristle-fly larvae are internal parasites in the grubs of butterflies, moths, and other insects, which they kill when fully grown. Usually the Bristle Fly lays its egg on the body of the caterpillar, and the newly hatched maggot burrows through the caterpillar's skin. The eggs of some species hatch immediately they are laid, and there is, therefore, little danger of their being lost when the host caterpillar sheds its skin (*see* METAMORPHOSIS). Other species lay their eggs on leaves and so are eaten and hatch inside the body of the caterpillar. The eggs are minute, and the fly lays enormous numbers of them, thereby increasing the chance that some will be eaten by a caterpillar. It must, however, be the right kind of caterpillar, for each sort of Bristle Fly is usually adapted to live on only one particular species or group of species. The egg hatches into a whitish maggot which has a small pair of spiracles, or breathing holes, in front and a larger more conspicuous pair behind. The maggots obtain air either by perforating the body wall of the host or by tapping its breathing tubes.

A caterpillar consumed by parasites will suddenly collapse with its body bent into several short, straight lengths. If its skin is slit from end to end, a number of the whitish maggots will be found within. These normally bore their way out and, after wandering about, turn into reddish-brown oval puparia, from which Bristle Flies emerge later. Practically nothing but the skin of the caterpillar remains— it is extraordinary that it should remain alive so long.

Bristle Flies and ICHNEUMON FLIES (q.v.), which have a similar mode of life, exercise a very great effect upon the numbers of other kinds of insects. One species, for example, is believed to destroy in some years four-fifths of the caterpillars of the Small Tortoiseshell Butterfly. They have therefore been used for the biological control of harmful pests (*see* PESTS AND DISEASES (*b*), Vol. VI). Sometimes the maggots of two species of Bristle Fly develop within the same caterpillar.

See also FLIES.

BRISTLE FLY

BRISTLE-WORM, *see* WORMS, Section 4.

BROWNS (Butterflies). This family is made up
of brown or yellowish-brown butterflies, usually
having somewhere on their wings black spots
with white centres, resembling eyes. Most of
them have a slow and feeble flight. There is
usually one generation a year, and the winter
is normally spent in the caterpillar state. They
do not hibernate completely, but sleep inter-
mittently, waking to nibble at grasses on warm
winter days. The HEATHS (q.v.), described
separately, also belong to this family.

The Meadow Brown, very common in the
British Isles, is perhaps the laziest of all butterflies, and will almost allow itself to be trodden
on before taking to wing. The females are
more orange-brown than the males, and have
much larger eye-spots on their fore-wings. Distinct races occur in Scotland, Ireland, and the
Scilly Islands. The caterpillars are green, with a
cream-coloured stripe above the legs. Like most
Browns, they feed on grass under cover of darkness, and crawl down among the tufts of grass
at dawn. The rich orange-brown Gatekeeper,
sometimes known as the Hedge Brown, is to be
seen commonly in country lanes, rough fields,
on heather, in woods, and on commons.

The Grayling, found on dry heaths and
downs, is the most alert and fast-flying of this
family. On alighting, it displays for an instant
the eye-spots on the underside of the fore-wings,
so diverting the attention of any watching enemies from its vulnerable body to the relatively
unimportant wings. When the danger has
passed, the conspicuous fore-wings are slid out
of sight beneath the hind-wings, which so
closely resemble the background in pattern that
the butterfly becomes indistinguishable from it.
Finally, the butterfly heels over at a steep angle
from the sun, so that not even its shadow betrays
its presence. It sits for long periods taking advantage of its perfect camouflage, but if disturbed, it is up and away in a flash. The females
are more brightly coloured than the males on
the upperside, and have cream-coloured splashes
on all four wings. The caterpillars are brownish-
grey, with darker lines running the length of
the body. They pupate beneath the surface of
the ground, making a rough cocoon, as certain
moths do—a habit unique among British butterflies.

The Wall Butterfly sits with wings wide open

S. Beaufoy

WALL BUTTERFLY

Above: Spreading its wings in the sunshine
Centre: Settling to rest, the eye-spot on the fore-wing is
  exposed
Below: The eye-spot is covered by the hind-wing

on sunny walls—the reason, presumably, for its popular name. But it also frequents exposed hedgerows and the southern sides of hills, being an extremely restless butterfly, settling only for a few moments. The females lay their eggs on various grasses. The greenish caterpillars are long and thin, tapering towards the tail, and are quite inconspicuous amongst blades of grass. There are two distinct broods, in May and again in August.

The Speckled Wood Butterfly avoids direct sunshine, frequenting shady lanes and rather overgrown woodland ridings. Numbers of them may often be seen playing 'hide-and-seek' in and out of sunlit patches and shadows. The caterpillars, a clear green with a rather round green head, are continuously brooded from April to October. Strangely enough, only some of the caterpillars go into hibernation in September: the others pass the winter as chrysalises, hanging from withered grass stems and looking like large drops of greenish oil.

The Marbled White, a black and white butterfly with markings like a chess-board, differs markedly in some of its habits from the other members of the family. It lives in colonies on the rough grassy slopes of chalk downs or un-cultivated fields and waysides, rarely straying far from its breeding-ground. Unlike most other Browns, which seem to select with the greatest care a certain blade of grass for each egg they deposit, the females drop their eggs loose amongst the grass as they fly lazily to and fro. After eating the egg-shell, a source of protein food, the caterpillars hibernate until the spring, when they crawl up at dusk every night to feed on young grasses. They are greyish, with two yellow lines running the length of the body. Two specimens, a completely white one and a com-pletely black one, were caught last century. Today we avoid killing such rare butterflies.

The Scotch Argus, though quite common in parts of Scotland, occurs in few places in Eng-land. It is a medium-sized butterfly, with rich brown wings, near the outer margin of which is a lighter band of rusty red, dotted with eye-spots. The caterpillars feed after dark on various grasses. The butterfly is on the wing throughout August, keeping to the lower slopes and valleys in mountainous districts. The Mountain Ring-let, much like the Scotch Argus but only about half the size, is the rarest of this family. Though more widely distributed in Scotland, it is found in England only above 550 metres, in little pockets in the mountainous districts of Cumberland and Westmorland. It is nowhere easy to find.

The Ringlet Butterfly, characteristic of wood-land rides, looks almost black from a distance, but at close quarters is a dark chocolate-brown. One variety has no rings round the eye-spots, and another has the spots much enlarged and almost pear-shaped. It, also, like the Marbled White, drops its eggs at random. The cater-pillars are small when they hibernate, and by the spring are brownish-grey and slightly hairy. They pupate on the ground in tufts of dead grass, and emerge in July.

BRUSH TURKEY

BRUSH TURKEY. This bird is no relative of the Turkey, though it has a superficial resem-blance to it. It belongs to an Australasian group of birds, called Megapodes, which bury their eggs in mounds of sand, earth, or decaying vegetable matter, and allow them to be hatched by the warmth of the sun or by the heat generated by fermentation. The cock Brush Turkey spends a considerable part of the year in building a great mound of dead leaves and other rubbish, which he rakes up with his large feet, always working backwards. The hen-bird places her eggs in tiers in a vertical position, the more pointed end downwards. During the period of incubation the cock-bird guards the mound against all intruders, and, when a chick is hatched, he care-fully scratches away the material to let it out. The chick emerges in a well-developed condi-tion and able to look after itself.

Closely related is the Maleo, a remarkable bird about the size of a domestic fowl, which inhabits North Celebes. It has dark brown upper plumage and salmon-pink underparts, with an almost naked head carrying a large, black, helmet-like protuberance. Several birds lay their eggs in the same place, burying them in the sand on the beach, where they are eventually hatched by the warmth of the sun.

BUDGERIGAR, *see* PARROT.

BUFFALO. These wild CATTLE (q.v.) are all heavily built animals with thick, strong limbs, moderately long tails tufted at the end, short necks, very broad muzzles, and large ears. Their hair is often very thin, and in old age leaves the skin almost entirely naked. The main species are the African Buffalo, Indian Buffalo, and the Anoa or Pigmy Buffalo of Celebes in the East Indies. The North American 'buffaloes' are not buffaloes at all, but BISON (q.v.).

The largest African Buffaloes are found living in large herds in the reedy swamps of South and East Africa. The old bulls, who often live to some 30 years of age, often wander alone or in small parties. They are usually black, with horns which vary in size, but sometimes reach

a span of up to 140 cm between the two bends. A well-grown bull will stand about 1·5 metres at the shoulder. The calves are born, apparently never more than one at a birth, from January to March. The cow hides her calf in long grass, and for about ten days separates herself from the herd, to remain within a short distance of her offspring. A smaller African buffalo, known locally as the Bush Cow, lives in the forests of West and Central Africa. It is covered with bright orange-red, longish hair, and has long fringes on its ears. The bulls stand only about a metre high at the shoulder.

The Asiatic Buffaloes have larger heads and smaller ears than the African, and their horns are longer, though less massive at the base. They are very fond of water, and generally live in swamps. Wild Indian Buffaloes are nearly always found in herds of about fifty head. The calves are born in summer, and there are often two at a birth. The Indian Buffalo has been domesticated since very early times: it is bred to provide milk and used also as a beast of

Paul Popper

A HERD OF BUFFALO ON THE PLAINS OF MOZAMBIQUE
The white birds circling over the animals are Tickbirds (cattle herons), which pick vermin off the animals' backs

Paul Popper

OLD BULL BUFFALO PUSHING HIS WAY THROUGH
THE BUSH AFTER HIS MUD BATH

burden. One of its characteristics is that it always carries its head very low.

The Anoas or Pigmy Buffaloes, which live in the forests of Celebes, are the smallest wild cattle, being just about a metre high. They have almost straight, sharp-pointed horns, about a foot long. The males are fierce little creatures, and turn their sharp horns against any animal that interferes with them. The new-born calves have a fawn coat of woolly hair; but as they grow older the hair is gradually shed, until the bulls become quite bare, their skin shining as though it were polished.

BUFF-TIP MOTH, *see* PROMINENT MOTHS.

BUG. This term should be restricted to insects having mouth-parts formed into a beak for piercing and sucking. The beak may be short or long, but it is always present, whether the insect is mature or immature. Most species have two pairs of wings, though many are wingless. This important group of insects, the Hemiptera, is often split into two divisions. In the first, the tip of the fore-wing is soft and flexible, all the rest being stiff and horny. The fore-wings protect the hind-wings, which are folded beneath them when the insect is not in flight. This division includes the SHIELD BUG, WATER-

BOATMAN, and BED-BUG (qq.v.). In the second division, though the fore-wings are often stiff, there is no flexible tip. This includes the APHIDES and FROG-HOPPERS (qq.v.). The META-MORPHOSIS (q.v.) of all bugs is incomplete, the nymph (or immature bug) resembling its parents except for the smallness of the wings. These increase in size at each moult until the adult stage is reached; only then are they of use in flight.

Bugs feed throughout life by piercing living tissues, either animal or plant, and sucking the juices. Most of them attack plants only, but others live on animal juices, and some of them cause very painful wounds.

The Assassin Bugs in most instances live on other insects, though a few attack higher animals, including man. Certain South American species transmit PROTOZOA (q.v.) which cause a fatal disease akin to sleeping sickness. The British species are harmless—indeed one of the largest frequents houses and attacks the Bed-bug. It chirps like a grasshopper, producing the sound by rubbing its beak against its body between the fore-legs.

ASSASSIN BUG
× 2

The Lace Bugs are pretty insects, so called because of the gauze-like appearance of their wings and of the thick expanded parts of the thorax. The Mirid Bugs (formerly known as Capsids) are very numerous. They are mostly soft-bodied insects with long legs. They are very active and, if disturbed, fall off their food-plant, but soon fly back again. They usually feed on plant juices, but some are predatory and one species is an important enemy of the Fruit-Tree Red Spider Mite (*see* MITE AND TICK PESTS, Vol. VI). A few have changed their

CAPSID BUG
× 5

habits in recent years: for instance, a species which originally fed on willow now attacks apple and black-currants, sometimes causing serious damage. The Tarnished Plant-bug does great harm to potatoes and is now an almost world-wide pest of cultivated plants. Other land bugs, the black and red Cotton-stainers, are serious pests to cotton-growers for they pierce the stems and bolls of the plants and suck the juices—and, worst of all, stain the cotton (*see* TROPICAL PESTS, Vol. VI). The Tea-bug of Assam and the Chinch-bug, so destructive of American wheat and other cereals, also belong to this order.

Although most bugs are found on land, some have taken to water. Among those that live on the surface of water are Pond-skaters and Water Measurers. A Pond-skater has a velvet pile on its undersurface, which prevents it from becoming wet, and very long middle and hind legs which enable it to move rapidly over the surface. In still pools they may often be found in great numbers. They are capable of jumping from the water to attack insects that have fallen in and are struggling on the surface. A Marine skater has even been reported on the surface of the sea 1600 kilometres from land. Water Measurers are slender insects with long, thin, stilt-like legs. They creep slowly over the surface of stagnant ponds.

More completely aquatic are Water-Boatmen, WATER SCORPIONS (q.v.), and Giant Water Bugs, some of which are more than 10 centimetres long, and feed upon fish and frogs. One interesting species, *Aphelocheirus*, is able to live in fast-running streams; it rarely needs to come to the surface to replenish its supply of air because it possesses a 'breast-plate' of special hairs which holds a thin film of air so firmly that it acts as a gill, and the bug obtains oxygen directly from the water, like a fish.

See also LANTERN-FLY; SCALE-INSECT.

BULBS, *see* STEMS, Section 2 *d*.

BULBUL. This bird is a little smaller than a thrush, with rather short legs and wings, and most species have crests. It is usually grey or brown, but many species have bright colours, either on the ear-coverts or under the tail-coverts. It is found in southern Asia, the East Indies, and Africa.

Green Bulbuls, or Fruit-suckers, have very much the same habits, but belong, in fact, to a different family. They have longer, stronger legs, green plumage, and no crest. They live on fruit, the nectar of flowers, and insects. The Golden-fronted Fruit-sucker is often kept as a cage-bird, and becomes extremely tame. The word Bulbul is also used in Turkey and Persia

to describe the NIGHTINGALE (q.v.), and in this connexion has found its way into English poetry.

BULLFINCH, *see* FINCHES, Section 4.

BUMBLE-BEE (*Bombus*). This belongs to the group of insects called Hymenoptera, and is a member of the Bee family. It is one of the social bees, as is the Honey Bee (*see* BEES). Bumble-bees occur almost entirely in the cooler parts of the world, one species being found as far north as Lapland; while those few which occur in the tropics seem to be confined to high mountain ranges. There are nineteen different kinds in Britain, and six very similar Cuckoo-bees, most of them black, with yellow bands and white-tipped abdomens. *Bombus lapidarius*, a very handsome bee, is closely covered with black

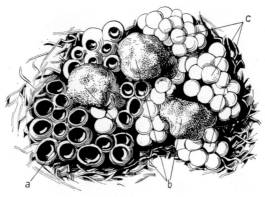

NEST OF BUMBLE-BEE

a. Empty cells used for storing honey
b. Masses of growing larvae covered with wax and pollen
c. Clumps of cocoons spun by larvae before pupating

hairs, and has a conspicuously red-tipped abdomen. A few species, among them the very common *Bombus agrorum*, are almost entirely brown.

The queen comes out of her winter sleep in the spring or early summer, and soon sets about the important business of founding her home. She finds a deserted mouse burrow, making herself snug and comfortable in the nest of grass and leaves left by the mouse. After working hard for about a month, gathering honey and pollen for her growing family, she has usually brought up a small brood of some half a dozen workers, who then take over the task of running the little community. Henceforth, the queen devotes herself to egg-laying, and, with possible rare exceptions, never leaves the nest again. Towards the end of summer, males and perfect females (like the queen-mother) are reared by the workers from eggs laid by the queen. These fly from the nest for mating. After a short life the males die; but the young queens, as soon as they have mated, hide away in the ground or among leaves, and there they remain for their winter sleep until the following year.

Some Bumble-bees nest on the surface of the ground. They are called Carder Bees, from their habit of tearing dried blades of grass into fine threads, which they weave into their dome-shaped nests. They are the brown Bumble-bees referred to above; and the commonest of them, *Bombus agrorum*, is very frequently seen in gardens and often makes its nest in rough grass. The communities of Bumble-bees are usually small, rarely containing as many as 100 workers. On the whole the bees themselves are not aggressive: most of the species do not even attack when their nest is seriously disturbed. But *Bombus terrestris*, one of the commonest of the banded kinds, will sting fiercely in defence of its home.

Of particular interest are the Cuckoo-bees (*Psithyrus*). They are not Bumble-bees, but so closely resemble the true Bumble-bees that only an expert can tell them apart. However, like the bird which gives them their name, they are unable to feed and bring up their young themselves—and the Bumble-bees do it instead. The female Cuckoo-bee (to whom we can hardly give the title of queen, since she does not produce worker bees) seeks out the nest of the Bumble-bee in early summer, and settles down in it. At first the *Bombus* workers try to drive her out; but, thanks to her thick armour plating, she is well protected against their stings, and is soon allowed to crawl about the nest unmolested. After a while she kills the *Bombus* queen, and usurps her role as head of the colony. The workers then tend and rear the brood of the Cuckoo female. Males and females eventually emerge and leave the nest for pairing, as do the *Bombus* males and females. After this the males soon die, and the females go into hibernation for the winter.

In the Bumble-bee community there is no elaborately constructed comb—the actual nest is formed merely by the accumulated mass of tough cocoons spun by the larvae before pupation. There are no sharp differences between queen and worker, except size and the inability of the worker to mate and produce offspring.

The queen is, in fact, a very capable worker, for she can collect nectar and pollen and tend her brood, just as the workers do.

See also BEES.

BUNTING, *see* FINCHES, Section 7.

BURNET AND FORESTER MOTHS. These brightly coloured, day-flying moths are sometimes mistaken for butterflies, but may be distinguished by the antennae. The Burnets have dark, metallic greenish or bluish fore-wings with crimson spots and hind-wings, while the Foresters have golden green fore-wings and grey hind-wings. They move slowly, boldly displaying themselves on flowers, often in groups, their conspicuous colours serving to remind possible enemies that, in fact, they are unpleasant to taste. (*See* PROTECTIVE COLORATION.) Over 100 species are known, of which seven Burnets and three Foresters are British. One Burnet is restricted to the mountains of Aberdeenshire, and another occurred only in the New Forest, but is now extinct. The Five and Six Spot Burnets are locally common in summer among long grasses. Several species have thinly scaled and rather transparent wings. Blackish and yellow varieties are occasionally found, and, more frequently, specimens in which the crimson spots of the fore-wings have run together.

The black and yellow spotted green caterpillars are stout and somewhat hairy, and feed, without seeking cover, chiefly on trefoils and vetches. They hibernate as caterpillars, and in May they spin tough, yellowish, spindle-shaped cocoons in which to pupate. Those of the Six Spot Burnet are sometimes found attached to such supports as twigs or fences, though more usually they spin their cocoons on grass stalks some distance above the ground—and birds find them difficult to attack and break open

S. Beaufoy

BURNET MOTHS MATING

from the slender swaying grasses. Both the caterpillar and the blackish chrysalis within the cocoon are thought to be distasteful to birds; but this fails to protect them in the breeding season, when there are numerous young birds to feed.

The Scarce Forester, attached to knapweeds, is found only on the Sussex and Kentish downs, while the Cistus Forester, which feeds on rockrose, occurs both on chalk and limestone, and extends as far as Yorkshire and Wales. The Common Forester is found locally in damp meadows and the outskirts of woods all over England, and less frequently in Wales, Scotland, and Ireland. The young caterpillar bores between the upper and lower surfaces of a sorrel leaf, soon making characteristic blotches by eating away the leaf until nothing is left but the transparent skin. After hibernation, it attaches its tough white cocoon low down on stems. The moths may be seen near the flowers of Ragged Robin in June.

See also MOTHS.

BUSTARD. This bird belongs to the same order as the CRANE (q.v.). It is a lover of open country, and the Great Bustard used to breed on Salisbury Plain and in stretches of East Anglia. Although it now occasionally migrates to Britain in the winter, more than a hundred years have passed since a nest was found. There are altogether about 30 species, all confined to the Eastern Hemisphere. The Bustard is a large, heavy bird, with stout legs and broad, rounded wings. A full-sized male may measure a metre from tip of beak to tail, and its wing-span may be more than 2 metres. It is a handsome buff and brown bird, its back being marked with russet and black bars, and its underparts and wing-coverts white or grey. It has keen eyesight and can detect an enemy from afar. Its food is mainly vegetarian, though most species also eat reptiles, mice, or any other animal food that comes their way.

During the mating season the cock Bustard performs a remarkable courtship display. To attract the hen it inflates its neck and breast feathers, throws forward its tail, and spreads its wings. The cocks fight for the hens much as turkeys do, and even after the hens are sitting on their eggs the cocks often go on sparring— apparently for pleasure. (*See* ANIMAL LANGUAGE.)

There are several other birds closely allied to

Harold Bastin
GREAT BUSTARD

Bustards, among them the Indian Floricans, very long-legged black birds with more or less white wings. They are shy and wary, and not easy to approach.

BUTCHER-BIRD, *see* SHRIKE.

BUTTERFLIES. These belong to the same order of insects as MOTHS (q.v.), the Lepidoptera (scaly wings). All Lepidoptera have their whole surface, and particularly their wings, covered with minute scales, and most possess a sucking proboscis. Butterflies are to be found in most parts of the world: there are very many different species in the tropics, but fewer species in temperate climates. The British Isles have about sixty different butterflies, and there are altogether about 10,000 species known in the world—many fewer than moths, of which there are over 2,000 in Britain alone.

The main groups of British butterflies are the SKIPPERS, WHITES, BLUES, HAIRSTREAKS, BROWNS, and the Nymphalidae (FRITILLARIES, TORTOISESHELLS, &c.) (qq.v.). The DUKE OF BURGUNDY and the SWALLOW-TAIL (qq.v.) are the only representatives of their families in

Britain. Some butterflies migrate to the British Isles every year and stay to breed there: these include the Red Admiral and the Painted Lady of the tribe Vanessinae, and the Clouded YELLOWS (qq.v.). Occasional visitors to Britain are the

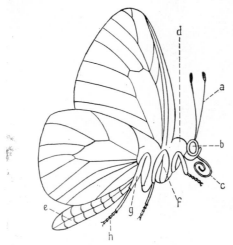

Fig. 1. DIAGRAM OF BUTTERFLY

a. Clubbed Antennae; *b.* Compound Eye; *c.* Proboscis; *d.* Thorax; *e.* Abdomen; *f.* Femur; *g.* Tibia; *h.* Tarsus

MONARCH (q.v.) from North America, the Queen of Spain Fritillary, the Bath White, the Long and Short-tailed Blues from the Continent, and the Camberwell Beauty from northern Europe.

Most butterflies inhabit a particular kind of environment. The Cabbage White haunts gardens and allotments—as most gardeners know to their cost. Small Tortoiseshells and Peacocks also frequent gardens; and most people have seen the magnificent Red Admirals settled, with wings spread out, on buddleias or Michaelmas

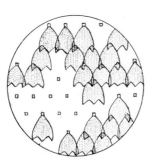

FIG. 2. PART OF THE WING OF A BUTTERFLY GREATLY ENLARGED SHOWING THE ARRANGEMENT OF SCALES

Fig. 3. DANAID BUTTERFLY: POWDER-PUFF APPARATUS

daisies, or feasting on over-ripe, fallen plums. Fritillaries, on the other hand, are to be found in the open clearings of woods, although some frequent rough, grassy uplands, where their strong, fast flight is in striking contrast to the rather slow, clumsy flight of the Browns, which are to be seen in most country lanes and fields. Blues are characteristic of chalk hills and downs. In the evening sunshine they will settle with wings outspread, looking like sapphire jewels, and then, as dusk descends, they gather, head downwards, with wings closed, several together on a grass stem or flower head. The Hairstreaks and Skippers do not belong to any particular territory—some frequent woods, others heaths and commons, while at least two of the Skippers seem particularly fond of grassy railway banks.

Butterflies can be distinguished from moths by their antennae, which are clubbed, and by the fact that, when they rest, they hold their wings vertically over their backs, exposing the underside, whereas most moths rest with wings folded down over the body It is often said that butterflies fly by day and moths by night: yet though all British butterflies certainly are day-fliers, so are a number of moths. Generally speaking, butterflies are more brilliantly coloured than moths, though some moths, especially in the tropics, have magnificent colours.

A butterfly has two pairs of wings—fore and hind. These are composed of an upper and lower membrane stretched over a framework of hollow ribs or 'veins', much as an umbrella cover is spread over the frame. The way the 'veins' are arranged is an extremely important point in CLASSIFICATION (q.v.). The patterns and colours on the wings are due to minute scales attached by short stalks to the membrane. These scales are actually broad, flattened hairs, which overlap like slates on a roof and are so close together and so tiny that, until very closely examined, they appear to be one complete surface. Looked at through a microscope, the scales are seen to be of many different shapes and sizes, often varying on different parts of the wing, as well as on the wings of different species. The colour is, for the most part, pigment laid inside the scales during the stage in the insect's life when it is confined in a chrysalis. The underside of the wings usually has a different and much less conspicuous pattern than the uppersides, so that the butterfly, when at rest with its wings folded over its back, remains hidden from

S. Beaufoy

Fig. 4. LIFE-CYCLE OF SMALL TORTOISESHELL BUTTERFLY. (A) EGGS, (B) CATERPILLAR, (C) CHRYSALIS, (D) ADULT

view. The names of the different parts of a butterfly's body can be seen from Fig. 1.

Male and female butterflies are often very different in appearance, the male usually carrying far more brilliant colours and taking the active part in courtship, though the female is often the larger. The male of a Common Blue is a beautiful violet blue; while the female is not blue at all, but a much less conspicuous reddish-brown. The female of the Orange-tip is without the gay orange tip which the male carries on its white wings. The male of the gigantic tropical Bird-wing has magnificent velvety, green, gold, purple, and black wings; but the female, often distinctly larger, is an inconspicuous brown or buff. The female's larger wing expanse no doubt enables her to carry better her heavier body

distended with eggs, while her more sombre appearance gives her greater protection. Occasionally freak specimens occur in which one side is male and the other female. In species where the colours of the two sexes differ, these freaks can easily be recognized by the contrasting colours.

The courtship of a female by a male is one of the most interesting things a butterfly hunter can see. One of the world's most common butterflies, *Danaus chrysippus*, a near relative of the Monarch, and found everywhere in tropical and sub-tropical countries in the Old World, uses a remarkable piece of apparatus in courtship. The male hovers near the female, stimulating her with scent by protruding a powder-puff from the end of his body. The scent is produced by special scales in a particular patch on the hind-wing, and the butterfly charges the powder-puff with scent by protruding it and wiping it on this patch Special scent-producing scales are also found on British butterflies: the male Green-veined White has a scent like lemon-verbena, and the male Grayling has been seen to perform antics in front of the female which bring his scent patches into contact with her antennae. British butterflies are without complicated scent-distributing apparatus, such as the powder-puff, but many British moths possess brushes which can turn inside out and evidently serve a similar function.

A female butterfly may lay less than 100 or up to 3,000 eggs, the number as well as the size and shape of the eggs varying with the species. Most butterflies lay their eggs singly, placing them on the leaves of a particular plant suitable for the food of the caterpillar when it emerges. How they select the right plant is a mystery; but one butterfly, the Painted Lady, has been observed drumming on various leaves with its front feet, presumably until it makes contact with a leaf of the right type. This contact stimulates it to cease drumming and to lay an egg. Butterflies certainly have highly sensitive taste-organs on their feet. Some species, in particular the Whites, lay large batches of eggs together on the food-plant. Most of these eggs never become adults either because they never hatch or because the caterpillars are eaten up by the caterpillars' natural enemies, such as birds, BRISTLE FLIES, and ICHNEUMON FLIES (qq.v.). The effect of these varies from season to season, but this is the way in which the number of butterflies is controlled and the reason for their fluctuations in abundance. The ordinary cycle of a butterfly's life is from egg to larva (caterpillar), then to chrysalis (pupa), and then to adult butterfly (imago), a process called a complete METAMORPHOSIS (q.v.). Its adult life is generally very short—perhaps only a few weeks; though some species, particularly the Brimstones and members of the family Nymphalidae, sometimes live in a state of complete rest, neither eating nor moving, in a sheltered place all through the winter (see HIBERNATION). Butterflies feed on nectar from flowers, over-ripe fruit, and other sweet food, which they suck up with their mouth-parts. A few imbibe juices from carrion or animal droppings. In the tropics, and occasionally in very hot summers in Britain, some species will swarm on damp patches of ground, where they drink freely. The sugars which constitute their normal food supply the necessary fuel to replace the energy expended in flight. But body-building foods are not a necessity to them in their short lives, as all growth takes place in the CATERPILLAR stage (q.v.)—in fact, some species have mouth-parts which will not open, so that they cannot feed.

See also CATERPILLAR; INSECT; METAMORPHOSIS; MIGRATION.

BUTTERFLIES AND MOTHS (Tropical).

1. 'Tropical' is a geographical term used for lands lying between the tropics of Cancer and Capricorn. But quite close to the Equator there are snow-capped mountains where, of course, no 'tropical' insects can live; and in other highlands within the tropical regions the climate is temperate, and so we find insects much like our own. A common Small COPPER (q.v.), for instance, very much like the British species, is found in the highlands of East Africa; and a form of our Large WHITE (q.v.) lives in Abyssinia. Here, however, we are concerned with butterflies and moths (Lepidoptera) living in lands with a hot climate. In the lower-lying hot lands of the tropics are found many spectacular and gaudy insects not to be seen in colder climates.

As in England, the favourite haunts of butterflies and moths are wooded lands and grass lands—clearings in forests, or openings made by roads or rivers, and the open savannahs. The insects appear in greatest numbers during or after a rainy season, and are not often seen in the dry season. Some butterflies, especially those of the African genus *Precis*, have more than one generation in a year, and specimens caught in wet and dry seasons are quite different. Most species feed chiefly on the nectar of flowers, and on fruit juices—especially rotting fruit, and an over-ripe bunch of bananas is good bait for many fine species. Decomposing animal matter or droppings attract certain species.

2. TROPICAL BUTTERFLIES. These often belong to the same families as British species; but the larger and more gaudy members of the family are to be found only in the tropics. Their brilliant colours are often a form of PROTECTIVE COLORATION (q.v.) called 'warning coloration', since they warn any insect-eating animal that this insect is unpleasant to the taste. The cater-

BUTTERFLIES AND MOTHS

1. Click-butterfly, *Ageronia februa* Hbn. (S. America). 2. Butterfly, *Heliconius doris* L. (S. America). 3. Map-wing Butterfly, *Cyrestis* sp. (Sumatra). 4. Syntomid Moth, *Napata splendida* H.-S. (S. America). 5. Moth, *Castnia zerynthia* Gray (S. America). 6. Long-tailed Blue Butterfly, *Lampides boeticus* L. (Europe). 7. Queen of Spain Fritillary, *Argynnis lathonia* L. (Europe). 8. Bird-wing Butterfly, *Ornithoptera priamus* L. (New Britain). 9. Figure-of-eight Butterfly, *Callicore neglecta*, underside (S. America). 10. Atlas Moth, *Attacus atlas* L. (India) (*Slightly over half natural size*)

pillars, also, often carry warning colours. A characteristic butterfly of the Ethiopian region (Africa), an *Acraea*, for instance, has brightly coloured wings in red, yellow, and black, which would remind any animal that this insect is better avoided.

The tropical regions of the world include the Ethiopian (Africa), the Oriental (southern Asia), the Australasian, and the tropical American regions Moths and butterflies show the same general distribution in those regions as do other animals (*see* ANIMAL DISTRIBUTION).

(*a*) Ethiopian Region. As well as the brilliant *Acraea* mentioned above, there are a great many kinds of BLUES (q.v.), many of which have caterpillars which are intimately associated with ants, as is the British Large Blue. Others have hairy caterpillars more like those of moths. One interesting African species successfully mimics a distasteful butterfly, and so acquires protection. A black and white butterfly called *Amauris*, found only in Africa, is a member of the same large family (Danaidae) as the American Milkweed Butterfly, a noteworthy migrant (*see* MIGRATION). There are a great many SWALLOW-TAILS (q.v.), and in the savannah lands the typical butterfly is the orange or purple-tipped *Colotis* of the White family.

(*b*) Oriental and Australasian Regions. These two regions have much in common, and produce the largest and most spectacular specimens. There are many lovely Swallow-tails, spangled with blue, green, and gold, one kind (*Battus*) carrying red spots. Closely related to the Swallow-tails are the magnificent *Ornithoptera*, or Bird-wings, so called because of their great size. They are the largest of all butterflies: some of them measure up to 25 cm or more from one wing-tip to the other, and the shape of their wings when outspread gives the appearance of a bird in flight. Their brilliant colours range from green and gold to the most vivid purple, generally on a background of velvety black. They are found only in the Pacific Islands and north Australia, and are not easily seen, as they usually keep to the tree-tops. The females, often larger than the males, have none of the brilliant colouring, but are dark brown, streaked with buff or cream. The family Danaidae is well represented, the most common type having pale blue wings with a black network. The large, ghost-like *Idea*, a whitish butterfly with black spots and thinly scaled transparent wings, is only

found in tropical Asia. Another whole section of the Danaidae, belonging only to these two regions, is particularly noticeable: the butterflies of this group have large velvety-black or brownish wings which in the male often carry a purple or bluish sheen. Another butterfly belonging only to Asia, particularly northern India, is the famous Dead-leaf Butterfly (*Kallima*) which, when at rest with its wings closed, looks exactly like one of the fallen leaves among which it settles (*see* Colour Plate opp. p. 336).

(*c*) Tropical America. This is a region in which Swallow-tails abound, especially the group called *Battus*, with their warning colours of red, green, and white. Other butterflies, found in greater numbers in America than elsewhere are the Riodinidae, smaller insects, many of which are so brilliantly coloured that they look like living jewels. There is a solitary representative of this family in Europe, the Duke of Burgundy Fritillary. One member of the family Danaidae, with wings marked with patterns of brownish-yellow and black, belongs exclusively to tropical America, as does also a group called Heliconiinae. These are medium-sized butterflies with elongated front-wings and rather small hind-wings, often marked beneath with flame-coloured, radiating streaks. The large metallic-blue Morphos are peculiar to the forests of tropical America: their brilliant wings are used in the manufacture of butterfly pictures and jewellery, for which industry the butterflies are bred in considerable numbers.

3. TROPICAL MOTHS. The greater number of these are little different in appearance from the common species of our gardens and woodlands, though some are much larger. The most spectacular are those which fly by day. Perhaps the most remarkable are the SILK MOTHS (q.v.) of the large family Saturnidae, the family to which the British EMPEROR MOTH (q.v.) belongs. The caterpillars are often very spiny, and some make a strong but rather coarse silk, from which the Chinese manufacture tussore silk. The long-tailed, pale green Moon Moth and the huge Atlas Moth are well-known Indian species. The Atlas Moth is the largest of all butterflies and moths, with a wing-span measuring sometimes over 30 cm from tip to tip. It has enormous, strong fore-wings of a peculiar shape, and coloured every shade of rich brown, purple, and grey. Both fore- and hind-wings are marked with large eye-like blotches, and the moth has a stout

Gordon Woods

MOON MOTH

woolly body and feathered legs and antennae. Its caterpillar is magnificent: it has a clear, rich green, velvety body, divided into well-marked segments which are marked with golden, rose-coloured, and sky-blue warts.

Some of the day-flying Uraniid moths, with their tailed hind-wings and resplendent gold and green colouring, are easily mistaken for Swallow-tails. One family of tropical moths, called Limacodidae, have caterpillars with no visible legs. They move about like slugs, and are often provided with poisoned spines, which sting severely. Two representatives of the family, the Festoon and the Triangle, occur in Britain.

Tropical moths have been both friends and foes to man. Life in the hot countries seems to proceed with greater violence, so that ravages by pests are apt to be spectacular. For instance, the copra trade in Fiji in the Pacific Isles was almost destroyed because of a moth which fed on the leaves of the coco-nut palm, and multiplied without being checked by any natural enemy. A fly, however, was introduced from the East Indies, because it was known there to destroy moths of the same family—and this saved the situation. In Australia the prickly pear which had been imported from tropical America, and was spreading with such devastating rapidity that it was ruining the farming land, was finally checked by a small Argentine moth called *Cactoblastis*. The caterpillar of this moth burrows into the fleshy leaves of the prickly pear and kills the plant (*see* CACTUS). The moth, being transplanted from its natural home, was also removed from its natural enemies; and within 5 years (1927–32) it had reached large enough numbers to destroy the cactus plague. Now, the moth and the cactus control each other, for if the cactus dies out too much, the moth dies for lack of food. This use of one living organism to control another is known as BIOLOGICAL CONTROL (q.v. Vol. VI).

BUTTERFLY-FISH, *see* SEA PERCH.

BUTTERWORT, *see* INSECTIVOROUS PLANTS, Section 2.

BUZZARD, *see* HAWKS, Section 4.

C

CABBAGE MOTH, *see* Night-flying Moths.

CABBAGE WHITE, *see* Whites (Butterflies).

CACTUS. This word was first applied by the Ancient Greeks to some prickly plant, and was later adopted by the famous Swedish botanist, Linnaeus (q.v. Vol. V), as the name for a group of curious, succulent plants, most of them prickly, some of which produce beautiful flowers. The largest number are found in the hot, dry regions of America, although some have been introduced into other hot, dry lands such as parts of Australia and Africa.

Although very varied in shape, they all have in common the complete absence of normal leaves. The work of Photosynthesis (q.v.) is carried out by the green stems, which are swollen and fleshy, and are often of quite fantastic shapes—some globular, some cylindrical, and some flattened into lobe-like divisions. Although some cactus stems are quite smooth, the surface of most of these peculiar plants is either ribbed like a melon or covered with nipple-like bulges. In addition many of them bear bunches of strong, sharp, horny spines, mixed with fine, barbed hairs, which are difficult to remove and which may cause intense irritation if they get under the skin. The plants are able to survive the very hot, dry conditions under which most cactuses live because of the rather compact shape of the plants and because the absence of leaves reduces the amount of water lost by Transpiration (q.v.). Many cactuses also have enormously wide-ranging roots, which tap as much as possible of the meagre water-supply in the soil.

The fleshy stems and branches of some kinds contain a store of water, which has, on occasion, saved the lives of travellers in the American desert regions. The juices of edible cactus fruits are sometimes used in cases of fever as a cooling drink. Probably the best known of these edible fruits is the Prickly Pear, which is also called the Indian Fig. Another cactus, a most beautiful hot-house plant, produces a purplish fruit resembling a gooseberry, which is good to eat; the fleshy part of its stem can be used as a vegetable, after the spines have been removed. The Torch Thistle of Mexico, which is probably the tallest of all the cactuses and may reach a height of 21 metres, produces edible fruits. These are 5 to 7 cm long, and contain a crimson pulp from which the Indians make an excellent preserve.

Because of their prickly character, Opuntias (Prickly Pear) and other cactuses are planted around Mexican houses as protective fences. In Australia, however, cactuses are not so popular —as the story of the spread of the Prickly Pear will explain. In 1839 and again in 1860, species of Prickly Pear were brought to New South Wales by settlers. Soon these plants escaped cultivation and began to flourish exceedingly. From 1900 onwards the spread became very rapid: by 1925 about 20 million hectares of Queensland and over 4 million hectares in New South Wales were affected. The dense growth of cactus choked all other growth and made the land unusable. Since the Australians could find no way of checking the Prickly Pear, they sent scientists to America to find some antidote. After experimenting with some 150 species of animals known to eat cactus, some of which could not thrive in Australia, while others would not restrict their attacks to cactuses, they discovered an insect,

Harold Bastin

THE STEMS AND FLOWERS OF THE PRICKLY PEAR

The stems are thickened to conserve water and are protected with spines

Ewing Galloway

CACTUSES IN THE ARIZONA DESERT

Barrel cactuses, or Bisnaga, can be seen in the foreground

a moth-borer, with the name of *Cactoblastis cactorum*, which showed promise of solving their problem. Some 3,000 million insects were released in Australia between 1928 and 1930, and in a few years vast areas of prickly pear were reduced to a decaying pulp. Indeed, by 1931 the *Cactoblastis* began to die out through lack of food and the cactus made an alarming revival. But the insect soon took charge again, and by 1934 the areas were again under control. Today, 95% of the area formerly devastated by cactus is free once more.

See also DESERT PLANTS; Colour Plate opp. p. 464.
See also Vol. VI: CACTUSES (hothouse).

CADDIS FLY. Most people know Caddis Flies better in their earlier stages than as adults. 'Caddis-worms' attract attention by the cases they live in and drag about the bottoms of ponds and streams. The head and thorax of the larva, or Caddis-worm, protrude beyond the mouth of the case, so that the legs are outside; the abdomen, meantime, grips the case by means of a pair of hooks. The head and thorax, which are thus exposed at times, are hard and horny; but the abdomen is quite soft. The Caddis-worm breathes through gills, which are supplied with water by movements of its abdomen. The water is drawn through the front of the case, and flows out at the back.

The foundation of the case is a silk secreted by the labial glands. At first these are silk-glands only; but during the pupal stage they are transformed into the adult insect's salivary glands. In addition to the silk foundation, the materials which the Caddis-worm uses to make its case vary, as a rule, with the different species: so that in some the silken foundation is covered with brown twigs, in others with stones or with small shells. However, a Caddis-worm is obliged to use only what is at hand, so that if the insect has been deprived of a case of brown twigs and then finds itself in water where grass only is available, it will be moving about next morning in a new case covered with short lengths of green grass. Most Caddis-worms are vegetarian; but some are carnivorous.

The pupa, which also breathes through gills, has a protective case attached to a solid support. To make it more secure, there are silken barriers across the ends, to which fragments of stone are often added—but never so as to exclude the free passage of water through the case. The pupa has movable jaws, by which it bites its way out when the time has come to emerge. Its legs and wings are also free, and when it has bitten its way out it either crawls or swims to the surface of the water. Those that swim have their middle legs long and oar-like, and fringed with hairs. In species living in fast-flowing rivers, the adult emerges as soon as the pupa reaches the surface.

Adult Caddis Flies are moth-like, with very hairy wings, and are generally brown. Though they live near ponds and streams, they are attracted by light at night, and so sometimes enter houses. Their jaws are either very small or absent altogether, and most species are not able to feed.

CAMBERWELL BEAUTY, *see* Vanessinae Butterfly.

CAMEL. These most valuable beasts of burden in desert country can travel long distances, carrying heavy loads, with little food or water.

This is because their bodies are specially adapted to hold large amounts of water, and because they have a reserve of fat in their humps. When a camel is in good condition and well fed, its hump is large and firm; but when food is scarce and its store of fat is getting used up, the hump becomes flabby and may hang down. On their chests, ankles, and knees, camels have pads of hard skin on which they rest when lying down. Their peculiar swaying motion—not very pleasant for anyone riding them—is due to the fact that the two legs of one side move simultaneously, instead of alternately as with most animals. Over soft, sandy ground where most animals would get stuck a camel can travel because of the cushion-like nature of the two widely spread toes of each foot, connected by a stout web of skin which prevents its feet from sinking into the sand. Besides using camels as transport animals, the Arabs (q.v. Vol. I) drink their milk, eat their flesh, weave their hair into cloth, and burn their dung as fuel—in fact, the camel supplies them with almost all the necessities of life.

Camels have been domesticated for so long that it is not known for certain where they originated, though Arabia is thought to be the most likely country. There are two distinct

A GROUP OF ARABIAN CAMELS WATERING AT ONE OF THE FEW WELLS IN THE NORTHERN SAHARA

Paul Popper

species—the Arabian or one-humped camel, found in the hot desert-lands of north Africa and south-west Asia (and later introduced into Australia), and the Bactrian or two-humped camel —a sturdier, shorter-legged animal, inhabiting the colder regions of central Asia. They both belong to the group of animals called RUMINANTS (q.v.), chewers of the cud.

There are several breeds of the Arabian camel. The lighter and swifter, known as Dromedaries, are used for riding, while the heavier breeds are used as baggage-carriers. Arabian camels are usually over 2 metres high and generally sandy-coloured, though sometimes they are white, various shades of brown, or black. They are powerful, ungainly-looking creatures, with a rather supercilious expression. They are stupid and, far from becoming attached to their masters, are often positively vicious. They have a habit, when passing a mounted man on a narrow path, of turning their heads suddenly round and trying to bite the rider's arm or shoulder. In the mating season the males have fits of almost uncontrollable rage, uttering a loud, unpleasant, bubbling noise. Arabian camels are fed mainly on grain; but they need a certain amount of green food, and to obtain it they will eat even the most thorny of branches. They dislike having to cross streams, and often have to be helped, for they are poor swimmers.

The two-humped Bactrian Camel is much better suited to rocky country than the Arabian Camel, as its shorter legs make it a better climber. In parts of central Asia droves of these animals are found living wild, and feeding chiefly on the bitter-tasting plants of the steppes, which most animals will not touch. They like salt and will drink the water of the salt lakes common in

BACTRIAN CAMEL

central Asia. When hungry they will devour almost anything—even blankets, flesh (including skin and bones), and fish. The mating season is from February to April, and one young camel is born 13 months later. The baby camel is very helpless at first, and has to be looked after with great care; but it soon gains strength, and is able to eat solid food after a week. In its third year it is ridden on short journeys, and becomes fully grown in its fifth year. Bactrian Camels are said to be useful up to the age of twenty-five.

See also Vol. IV: BEASTS OF BURDEN.

CAMOUFLAGE. This word has come to be associated with modern warfare, as well as with natural history. In modern warfare it has become necessary, not only for the men of opposing armies to conceal themselves, but also to conceal their guns, tanks, and ships, and even camps, forts, and all buildings of military importance. Camouflage in the military sense achieves the same end and is based on the same principles as that found in the animal kingdom, and has exactly the same significance—protection from the enemy, either in defence or attack. The only difference is that a man-made camouflage is, as a rule, less effective than that found in animals.

Camouflage may, then, be described as the taking on of deceptive appearances for purposes either of defence or offence and, except for a few of the very lowest forms of life, it is probably true to say that no animal is without its protective camouflage, either to conceal itself from its prey until the most favourable moment of attack, or to assist it to hide from its enemies. Since all animals either prey upon others or are preyed upon, it follows that camouflage is of prime importance and, by trial and error, it has been brought to a high pitch of perfection in the long evolutionary history. Warning colours also are a form of camouflage. Even armoured animals— such as the shelled molluscs—have their protective coating so developed and coloured that it harmonizes with its surroundings.

Animal camouflage is achieved either by having a particular colour pattern (the stripes on the tiger, or the mottled pattern on some kinds of deer); by some peculiarity of shape (such as the stick insects or Dead-leaf butterfly); or by some trick of behaviour; or all three may be found in one animal. These have been given various names, such as protective coloration, protec-

South African Railways

GIRAFFES IN KRUGER NATIONAL PARK

The broken pattern of their colouring helps to break up the outline of their bodies. In particular, the dark line on their necks is difficult to distinguish from the boughs of the trees

tive resemblance, or mimicry—but they all achieve the same results (*see* Colour Plate, opp. p. 336). Yet in spite of the many devices used, it still remains the fact that camouflage is only effective as long as the animal keeps still. Even with the most skilful disguise, movement will betray the presence of its possessor. This does not matter in the long run, for it is while the animal is at rest, that is to say, when it is not on the alert, that disguise is most needed.

Colour is used in one of the following ways: to break up the outline of the body, or to make it harmonize completely with the background, or to provide obliterative shading. A good example of a colour pattern breaking up the outline of the body is found in many of the small song-birds. A wren, for example, with its mottled plumage of browns and greys, will be inconspicuous in a green hedge because of the broken pattern caused by the shadows among the foliage. An adder, because of its banding and mottling, does not strike the eye while it is

among herbage, but becomes very conspicuous with its comparatively uniform pattern when it crosses a road.

Some animals have developed a mechanism which changes the colour pattern of the body according to the background. Certain spiders which frequent flowering plants will be red when resting on a red petal, green if on a leaf, yellow if on the centre of a daisy. The same spider will change from one colour to another as the occasion demands, the change usually taking several days to accomplish. The CHAMELEON (q.v.) is probably the best-known example of this kind of change; but FLAT-FISHES (q.v.), such as the plaice, also do the same. It should be noted that the ability to change colour in this way is found only in animals which stay motionless, or nearly so, for long periods on the same background. There is, obviously, no advantage in this for an animal moving quickly from one background to another.

Many animals have a dark colour on their backs, shading into a pale colour on the under-

Eric Hosking

WOODCOCK NESTING

The speckled plumage of the bird is much the same colour as the sticks and lichen among which it nests. The eggs, also, have the same speckled pattern

parts. This counteracts the effect of light falling from above, and produces the appearance of a flat and uniform surface, making the animal almost invisible against a background of the same tint. This type of colour concealment is seen particularly in land animals and in fishes. For fish there is an added advantage: a fish with a mottled back is almost invisible, viewed from above, against a background of weeds, mud, and stones; while viewed from below, its silvery belly tones in with the colour of the sky as seen through the water.

Reference has been made under PROTECTIVE COLORATION (Insects) (q.v.) to the *Kallima* butterfly, which closely resembles a dead leaf. There are many other such—caterpillars resembling twigs, stick insects, and the like. There is a fish, *Monocirrhus*, living in the Amazon River, which has a body like a leaf, with a short stalk protruding forward from the lower jaw, which looks just like a leaf-stalk. The Frog-fish of the SARGASSO SEA (q.v. Vol. III) has a body

covered with leafy-looking outgrowths, so that it is difficult to distinguish it from the weed. Finally, among the many examples which could be quoted, is the Sea-dragon, a relative of the well-known SEA-HORSE (q.v.), the body of which bears a number of membranous streamers giving it perfect concealment when among seaweed.

Another kind of camouflage used by a variety of animals depends on tricks of behaviour. Among the best known of these tricks is that of 'shamming dead', a well-known trick of the OPOSSUM (q.v.), which has given rise to the expression 'playing possum'—a trick used also by many insects and spiders. There are many other kinds of camouflage depending on tricks of behaviour: the Spider Crab, for instance, decorates itself with seaweeds which disguise its presence; the Slender File-fish, with slender body and tail, mottled green in colour, stands on its head among eel-grass, so that the body and tail wave gently in the current like the blades of eel-grass;

and some kinds of spiders decorate their webs with bands of silk, leaving gaps into which they themselves fit so that they look like a continuation of the bands.

CANARY, *see* FINCHES, Section 1; *see also* Vol. IX: BIRD-KEEPING.

CAPERCAILLIE, *see* GROUSE.

CAPYBARA, *see* CAVY.

CARBON IN LIVING THINGS. Every living thing contains carbon. This can be shown by taking any dead organic matter (that is, matter derived from plants or animals), and burning it. Sugar, for example, turns black and gives almost pure carbon. Wood forms almost pure carbon, as charcoal. Coal is largely made up of carbon. The presence of carbon in organic substances has been so well recognized by the chemist that the branch of chemistry called 'organic chemistry' is sometimes also called the chemistry of carbon compounds (*see* CHEMISTRY, Vol. III).

The importance of carbon in Nature is enormous. There is a constant building-up and breaking-down of carbon compounds, so that a steady circulation is kept going. The chief building-up process is PHOTOSYNTHESIS (q.v.), whereby plants make their own food (and, indirectly, food for all other living things). This cannot take place without carbon dioxide from the atmosphere. One of the breaking-down processes is RESPIRATION (q.v.), which, in plants and animals, liberates energy from food-stuffs, carbon dioxide being evolved as a waste product. If the amount of carbon dioxide taken in during photosynthesis were equal to that given out during respiration, there would be a regular and balanced circulation of carbon in nature. More carbon dioxide is taken in by photosynthesis, however, than is given out by the respiration of both plants and animals. Unless there were other processes in which carbon compounds were broken down, in time all the carbon dioxide in the atmosphere would be used up and photosynthesis would come to a stop. This would mean the end of all life in the world.

But carbon compounds are also broken down by decay. This is largely carried out by bacteria in the soil; but, usually, before they begin their work, the remains of dead animals and plants—or humus—are acted upon by FUNGI and other plants called SAPROPHYTES (qq.v.), which, instead of building up their own food-stuffs from raw materials, obtain them from the dead remains or waste products of other plants or animals. The remains of the dead plants and animals are then acted upon by bacteria which cause final decay, and eventually the carbon compounds are reconverted to carbon dioxide, which can be used again by plants.

Perhaps the clearest illustration of the way in which the carbon of plant tissues is restored to natural circulation is given by COAL (q.v. Vol. III). During the Coal Age, some 300 million years ago, before flowering plants had been evolved (*see* EVOLUTION), the common plants were large tree-ferns and horsetails. These died, and in time their remains became buried hundreds of metres under the earth's surface. By compression, by the action of bacteria, and by other means, they became converted into an almost pure form of carbon, namely, coal. When coal is burnt, it is changed mostly into carbon dioxide, thus returning to circulation carbon which has been removed from the natural cycle for 300 million years.

CARDINAL FISH, *see* SEA-PERCH.

CARIBOU, *see* REINDEER.

CARNIVORA (Flesh-eaters). To this large order belong, typically, all those mammals whose most distinctive habit is eating the flesh of other animals. Not all Carnivora, however, live entirely on animal flesh: the extent to which they are flesh-eaters varies a great deal—most bears, for instance, live mainly on a vegetable diet. Neither are the Carnivora the only flesh-eating mammals: many of the INSECTIVORA will also eat small vertebrates, and one group of MARSUPIALS (qq.v.) lives almost entirely on them.

The Carnivora have the following characteristics in common. The number of complete toes on each foot is never less than four, and is often five. All the toes have claws, which are generally sharp and curved, bearing no resemblance to nails. The first toe is never, like the human thumb, opposed to the others, and so they are not able to grasp. Most of them walk on their toes only, though not on the tips; but the bears and the badgers walk on the whole foot. The number of their teeth varies from 30, in the case of cats, to 42 in dogs; but all have strongly developed canine teeth, as weapons for seizing prey.

The order is divided into two sub-orders: (i) the Normal-footed Carnivora (Fissipedia), to which belong CATS, HYENAS, DOGS, WEASELS, BADGERS, OTTERS, RACOONS, BEARS (qq.v.), and others; and (ii) the Fin-footed Carnivora (Pinnipedia), to which belong SEALS (q.v.), whose feet have been converted into swimming flippers.

CARP. This freshwater fish was originally a native of Persia, China, and the Malay Archipelago. It was introduced into Europe at an early date, and was known to be already under cultivation in Germany by 1258, though it was not referred to in England until the end of the 15th century. Carp in this country are now generally kept as interesting additions to ornamental waters; but on the European continent, particularly in Germany, Poland, and Russia, Carp is a popular food, and great farms, with acres of breeding, rearing, and fattening ponds, supply a ready market.

Carp grow to about 60 cm long, get very tame, and live a long while—the greatest age for which we have reliable evidence is 40 years. Stories about Carp reaching the age of 200 years or more are not to be accepted. Two interesting varieties of the Common Carp are the Mirror Carp, with a row of large, silvery scales along each side, and the Leather Carp, with a few large leathery scales scattered on the body. There are also a Silver Carp and a Golden Carp, the latter not to be confused with the Goldfish, also a member of the Carp family.

The Carp and its relatives probably form the largest single family of fishes (the Cyprinidae). They include most of the freshwater fishes of Europe and Asia, and many of those of North America and Africa. In South America, however, their place is taken by the CHARACINS (q.v.). Members of the Carp family are recognized by having no teeth in the jaws (though they have special 'pharyngeal' or throat teeth attached near the gills). They have only one dorsal (back) fin, which has flexible rays, except for the first one, which is stiff; and they usually have distinct scales. They also have the air-bladder connected with the ear (see FISHES), a peculiarity they share with Characins and CATFISHES (q.v.). Most of them seem to feed on a mixed diet of small animals, such as worms, molluscs, and insect larvae, with a certain amount of vegetable matter.

The family includes many fishes familiar to the angler, such as Roach, Rudd, Dace, Chub, Gudgeon, Tench, Bream, and Barbel—also the ornamental Goldfish and Golden Orfe, and the small boy's friend, the Minnow or 'Tiddler'. The Golden Orfe is a domesticated variety of the Ide, another member of this enormous family, common in European rivers.

The Barbel is so called because of the 'barbels' or sensitive feelers on its lips, which help the fish to locate in the mud and stones the small animals on which it feeds. There are many different kinds found in freshwaters all over the Old World, especially in the tropics. Some are very prettily marked. They vary in length from 5 cm to a metre or more (as, for example the Mahseer of India). One species is found in British fresh waters, where it affords sport to fishermen.

Another small member of the Carp family, the Bitterling, some 5 cm or more long, is found wild in the freshwaters of Europe, but not of Britain. It is interesting chiefly for its habit of laying its eggs inside the shell of the freshwater mussel, where they are safe from enemies. The female has at breeding time a long tube, called an ovipositor, which she places between the two halves of the mussel-shell while it is

A. Fraser-Brunner

THE COMMON CARP

open. The breathing of the mussel helps to aerate the eggs until they hatch out, which takes about a month. In return, the mussel casts its own young ones out of the shell—to fix themselves to the parent Bitterlings, who perforce carry them until they can fend for themselves. This saves the mussels from overcrowding.

The Goldfish is the most popular of all ornamental fish (*see* AQUARIUM, Vol. IX). It is the domesticated form of a far-eastern member of the Carp family. The wild fish is an inconspicuous darkish green, and would have received little notice had it not produced an occasional 'sport' of bright reddish-gold, said to have been first noticed in China about A.D. 1200, and carefully fostered by breeding ever since. This golden variety is due simply to the absence of black colouring-matter (pigment), only the red and yellow being left. As bred by the Chinese, many fishes of curious shape and colour were evolved; but out of these, six main types have been selected for breeding. Although cultivated for so long, Goldfish still show signs of their wild ancestry. For some time after being hatched they have the natural colouring, and turn gold only when they are several years old. If left to breed for several generations in open water, they gradually revert to the wild form—a fact which caused great disappointment to a potentate from Madagascar who wished to beautify the waters of his own country by filling them with thousands of these enchanting fish. But the imported Goldfish soon reverted to their dingy wild colour—and incidentally ousted the only freshwater foodfish of the island.

A western relative of the Goldfish, which spread to Europe in remote times, is the Crucian Carp, sometimes called Prussian Carp. It is a rather deep-bodied, bronze-coloured fish with a rounded dorsal fin, and is sometimes kept in ornamental waters. Both Crucian Carp and Goldfish differ from true Carp in having no barbels, in having a saw-edge on the front ray of the dorsal fin, and in their smaller size.

CARPET-MOTH, *see* LOOPERS.

CASE-BEARER MOTHS. The small caterpillars of the family Coleophoridae are the principal makers of cases among moths. Of nearly 1,000 known species, 110 occur in the United States, and 102 in Britain. The young are usually leaf-miners, and later construct distinctive

cases of silk, leaf-hairs, scraps of leaves, dead flowers, or seeds, according to the species. The case, about 6 mm in length, is attached in such a way to a leaf or seed-vessel that the caterpillar can push its head out and feed in all directions, without leaving the safety of the case. A pale blotch on a leaf, with a round hole in the centre of one side, is a sure sign of damage by a case-bearer.

Change to the chrysalis usually takes place inside the case in May, and the moths emerge in July. When fully expanded, they are about

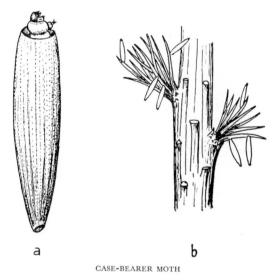

a   b

CASE-BEARER MOTH

a. Larva in case; *b.* Larch shoots showing the cases attached

1 cm across, and have dark grey fore-wings, and white, yellow, brown, brassy, or bronzy hind-wings, marked with various sprinklings and streaks.

See also CHINA-MARK MOTHS.

CASSOWARY, *see* OSTRICH, Section 2.

CATERPILLAR. This is the common name for the larva of BUTTERFLIES, MOTHS, and SAWFLIES (qq.v.). The caterpillar represents the second stage in the complex life-history of these insects from egg to adult (*see* METAMORPHOSIS). It is during this stage that eating and, consequently, growth take place, and so the main function of the caterpillar is to eat and grow. Though some are gregarious, caterpillars generally live quite solitary lives, concentrating on the task of eating. Some eat only by day, some only by night, and some all the time. They nearly always eat only one type of food plant—the Painted Lady larva, for instance, eats only thistles, the Privet Hawk Moth larva privet leaves, and the Red Admiral and Peacock larvae (qq.v.) nettles. Many of the smaller ones, such as Leaf-rollers (q.v.) and Leaf-miners, roll leaves round themselves or tunnel in them. Some Sawflies make galls. A few are carnivorous (see Blues). Some caterpillars live on, or beneath, the surface of water, breathing oxygen from the water by gills (see China-mark Moths).

Some caterpillars move very little and slowly, depending either on Camouflage (q.v.) or on bright warning colours to protect them from their natural enemies (see Protective Coloration). Others, on the other hand, will move very quickly, or drop suddenly, and take cover; while some have strange defensive movements, such as the sudden jerking up of their heads and front quarters, which a colony of caterpillars will do as a united action, when faced with danger. Sometimes they will wave unpleasant scent organs or spray poison at an approaching enemy (see Prominent Moths). Some live in protective cases which they carry about (see Bagworms, Case-bearers). Sawfly caterpillars are sometimes covered with a white powder, others are slimy and resemble slugs. During their lives they cast their skins (moulting) at regular intervals, usually four times, so allowing for growth. Caterpillars generally live about a month, though this varies a great deal, and in many species the caterpillars hibernate in a state of complete or partial rest in some sheltered place through the winter. Finally, however, they enter the pupal (chrysalid) stage, and many, especially caterpillars of moths and sawflies, prepare for this by spinning an elaborate cocoon of silk or of other materials (see Silk Moths).

The caterpillar is long and cylindrical in shape. It is made up of a head, followed by a body composed of thirteen ring-shaped segments, some of which bear legs. Its head is hard and firm, with strong jaws working sideways instead of up and down. The caterpillar of a butterfly or moth has on each side of its head six minute and very simple eyes, whereas a sawfly larva has only one. In front of these, on each side, are tiny antennae corresponding to the larger ones of the adult. It has also two tiny tubes, called spinnerets, from which comes a liquid that dries into silk. The first three segments of the body (the 'thorax') each carry a pair of legs, each leg ending in a single claw: these correspond to the three pairs of legs of the winged insect. In addition, caterpillars of butterflies and moths usually have five pairs of legs (commonly called 'prolegs') on the last segments of the abdomen, the last pair on the last segment of the body being called 'claspers'. These, unlike the thoracic legs, have fleshy soles for grasping, and are armed with many small hooks: they disappear after the larval stage. Looper caterpillars of the family Geometridae, however, have only two pairs of abdominal legs, and have therefore developed the peculiar gait from which they get their name. They hold on by their front legs while they draw up their hind legs, hitching their body into a loop. Then, holding on by the hind legs, they throw their body forward, and grasp again by the front legs (see Looper Moths).

The young caterpillars of Night-flying Moths (q.v.) often have the first two abdominal legs undeveloped, so that they, too, walk like loopers; but the older caterpillars are normal, except in a few instances, such as the Silver-Y Moth, where the looping habit persists. Sawfly larvae usually have more than five pairs of legs on the abdomen, these being without the hooks so characteristic of Lepidoptera. They sometimes rest in a peculiar fashion, grasping the foliage with the front legs and holding the abdomen in the air.

Caterpillars breathe through nine pairs of openings on each side of the body, known as 'spiracles', which lead into branching tubes to carry the air to all parts of the body. The spiracles are often surrounded by conspicuous bright-coloured spots or other markings. A straight digestive tube runs down the whole body. The caterpillar's blood is often full of green colouring. Its skin is covered with hairs, sometimes so small that the caterpillar looks smooth or naked, sometimes so long and thick that it looks like a fur coat (see Tiger Moths). The Looper caterpillars have rough skins with

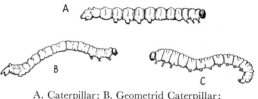

A. Caterpillar; B. Geometrid Caterpillar;
C. Sawfly larva

S. Beaufoy

LOOPER CATERPILLAR OF THE PEPPERED MOTH

S. Beaufoy

CATERPILLAR OF PRIVET HAWK MOTH

E. Syms

WOOLLY BEAR CATERPILLAR OF GARDEN TIGER
MOTH

S. Beaufoy

LOBSTER MOTH CATERPILLAR REARING ITS HEAD IN
DEFENSIVE ACTION

CATERPILLARS OF MOTHS

raised knobs or warts, which make them resemble twigs. Some species carry large horns (*see* HAWK MOTHS), or have sharp and even poisonous spikes on their skins (*see* TUSSOCK MOTHS). The very largest caterpillars are sometimes as much as 17 or 18 cm long.

CATFISH. Many different species are to be found in the Catfish family, and we can mention only a few outstanding ones here. Nearly all the Catfish are freshwater fish; but a few live in the sea. They are found over the whole world, except for a few small islands and the very cold regions. They all have barbels or 'whiskers' round the mouth, often very long teeth in the mouth, only one dorsal (back) fin, with one stiff, saw-like spine (the rest being flexible) which is followed by a low, fleshy flap called the 'adipose

A. Fraser-Brunner

THE GIANT CATFISH, THE WELS, RISING FROM THE MUD IN PURSUIT OF A WATER-FOWL

fin'. Most Catfish have no scales; but some go to the other extreme and have a heavy suit of armour, formed of bony plates. Each breast-fin has usually a strong spine, like the one on the back, sometimes with a poison-bag, which makes them dangerous to handle.

Many Catfish are quite small, but some grow to nearly 2 metres in length. Of the big ones, the best known is the Wels, which, next to the Sturgeon, is the largest river fish in Europe. It is not found in Britain, France, or Italy, but is common in the Danube. It spends a good deal of time in the mud, but will rise to the surface to seize such prey as water-birds and otters—for it is very voracious, and has been known to swallow a child whole.

Some of the little Armoured Catfish, from South America, are amusing to keep in a tropical AQUARIUM (q.v. Vol. IX), where they are useful as scavengers. A North American species, often called the Common Catfish, has been acclimatized to Europe and Britain, and is often kept in ponds and aquariums. The name Catfish is also sometimes given to one of the sea-fish called BLENNY (q.v.).

CATKINS, *see* FLOWERS.

CATS. Of all the CARNIVORA (q.v.), or flesh-eating mammals, cats are the most highly developed, and the most perfectly adapted

for a life of preying on other creatures. Their long, lithe bodies are agile as well as extremely strong, the larger cats being easily able to kill and drag away animals much larger than themselves. Other characteristics of the Cat family are their very short muzzles, their powerful canine and cutting teeth, and their strongly curved claws, which they can draw into sheaths for protection when not in use. All cats have rasp-like tongues which enable them to lick the meat from bones, and which perhaps also help in cleaning their fur.

Some member of the Cat family lives in almost every part of the world, except Australia and the Arctic regions; but the large cats are found mainly in hot climates. The largest cats are the LIONS and TIGERS, and then the JAGUARS, LEOPARDS (or Panthers), and PUMAS (qq.v.); and there are a great number of smaller cats. Their fur is usually short; but those which live in cold climates, such as the Ounce and Lynx, grow fairly long coats, while the length of the Tiger's fur varies according to the climate. With few exceptions, the cat tribe has a great dislike for water. All the cats feed upon other animals and

Paul Popper

NORTHERN LYNX

TWO CHEETAHS IN KRUGER NATIONAL PARK   *Paul Popper*

birds which they themselves have killed; a few hunt fish as well. The following are some of the more important wild cats which have not been dealt with in separate articles.

The Lynx is a wild cat about 76 cm long, with a whisker-like fringe of hair on its cheeks, and tufts of hair growing from its ears. In south-eastern Europe and Asia there are still a number of places where the smaller Lynxes live close to towns and villages. Very occasionally they make savage, unprovoked attacks on human beings; but they are generally looked upon as cowardly, timid animals, about as dangerous as a common fox or coyote. They prey on animals varying in size from a mouse to a sheep, and often kill more than they can devour. Their lairs are usually among rocks. They generally produce from two to five cubs at a birth. The Canadian Lynx is a more formidable animal, with a strange habit of trailing a human being for miles—though this is apparently more through curiosity than with any idea of harming the man. Many of these animals do on occasions, however, make most vicious attacks.

There is only one wild cat in Britain—the European Wild Cat—which is found in the wild parts of Scotland, and also in various districts of the Continent. It is about the same size as the domestic cat, and marked very much like the fireside tabby; but its tail is shorter and ends bluntly instead of tapering to a point. It is probably one of the ancestors of the domestic cat, though there is considerable division of opinion on this. It is an expert climber, and its favourite home is in the most inaccessible mountainous woods. The females usually produce four or five kittens in a litter, and they have been known to bring them up in a deserted or captured nest of a large bird, although they normally use cavities among rock-piles. Even the kittens are most fierce and savage, and they will hiss and spit vigorously at intruders. Grouse, ptarmigan, rabbits, hares, fawns, and lambs are some of the creatures they destroy.

The Cheetah is a large, spotted, cat-like animal found in central India, Persia, and throughout the greater part of Africa. An adult is about 1·5 metres long, with a longish tail. It is lightly built, and has very long legs. For 500 metres it is able to run faster than any other living animal, but after that it tires and cannot keep up its high speed. It relies, therefore, on capturing its prey in one swift rush. Cheetahs are easily tamed, and in India are trained to hunt antelopes. The Cheetah is not a typical cat; it differs mainly in having blunt claws, which are only partially retractile (able to be drawn in).

See also Vol. IX: CATS; PETS.

A MUSK OX

CATTLE, WILD. This is the name applied to all members of the Ox Tribe, to which belong the Bison, Buffaloes, Yaks (qq.v.), Gaurs, Musk Oxen, and various other wild species. These are all members of the order Artiodactyla (even-toed hoofed beasts). The Cattle, together with the Sheep, Goats, and Antelopes (qq.v.) form a group known as the Hollow-horned Ruminants (q.v.), that is to say, animals which have hollow, unbranched horns and which are true 'chewers of the cud'. Cattle are mostly large and heavily built animals, and both sexes have permanent horns—in which respect they differ from the Deer (q.v.) whose horns (antlers) are shed and replaced annually.

The Gaur, found in India, Burma, and the Malay Peninsula, is a very large species of Wild Cattle, with massive horns, sleek, dark brown coat, and whitish 'stockings'. The bulls may be nearly 2 metres high. Gaurs prefer hilly districts to plains, and generally wander about in small herds of about a dozen head, governed by one of the old bulls. This leader is in the end expelled from the herd by the younger bulls and cows, as he frequently causes trouble by objecting to any of the rising generation making advances to the cows in his herd. These solitary old bulls are extremely dangerous; but, having the finest heads and horns, they are most sought after by sportsmen (see Vol. IX, Big-game Shooting). A domesticated race of the Gaur is known as the Gayal or Mithan.

Musk Oxen are a species of cattle to be found in the Arctic regions of north-eastern Canada, Greenland, and the adjoining islands. They stand over a metre high, and have a dark brown, hairy coat, which makes them look a good deal larger than they actually are. This coat reaches a long way down their massive legs, hiding their short tails. They have a light brown undercoat of fine, soft wool. In spring they shed their long winter coat in blanket-like masses. The adult bulls have large horns, generally about 60 cm long, which are broad and flat on their forehead, and then get narrow and grow downwards before turning up in sharp points. The horns of the young bulls and cows are very much smaller. All Musk Oxen have a large growth of hair between their hoofs, which enables them to secure a sure foothold on the frozen ground. They feed upon whatever vegetation they can find in a barren land where the surface of the ground scarcely thaws. Their name is derived from the musky flavour of their flesh.

Our domestic cattle are descended from a wild species called the Aurochs, which once lived in Europe, including Great Britain, but became extinct about the 17th century. They were domesticated in ancient times, and are now one of the most useful and indispensable of all the animals man has tamed for his use.

See also Vol. VI: Cattle, Domestic.

CAVY. This South American family is a group of Rodents (q.v.), differing from each other a good deal in appearance, but all having either very short tails or none at all. The true Cavies are probably the ancestors of the domestic Guinea-pig (q.v. Vol. VI); the Patagonian Cavies look rather like hares; and the Capybaras are the largest of all the rodents.

The true Cavies are a greyish colour. Their favourite haunts are marshes, where they live in the shelter of the vegetation; but they are also found occasionally on sandhills. They feed in the early morning and evening, eating roots and plants. Unlike domestic guinea-pigs, they breed

A GAUR

only once a year, and have only one or two young. The best-known species is the Restless Cavy or Cutler's Cavy, which was domesticated by the INCAS of Peru (q.v. Vol. I), and from which it is thought the domestic guinea-pig was derived.

Patagonian Cavies, or Maras, are 76 centimetres or more long, and rather over 30 cm high. They have long legs and ears, and are covered with thick grey fur, becoming yellow on their flanks and white underneath. They are shy and timid, and take to flight at the least alarm.

The Pacas or Spotted Cavies are about 60 cm long, and have coarse, dark brown fur, with rows of white spots. The natives hunt them for their flesh at all seasons, but especially in February and March, when the Pacas become extraordinarily fat: they first smoke them out of their burrows by lighting a fire at one of the entrances, and then chase them with dogs. The Pacas invariably make for water in their efforts to escape, since they can swim very fast.

The Capybaras, or Carpinchos, are over a metre long and weigh about 44 kg. On account of their large size, bristly hair, and grunting cries, they are often called 'water hogs'. Their hind legs are a good deal longer than the front legs, and they have short webs between their toes. They love water and spend their time by the rivers and lakes, resting, or feeding on water plants and the bark of young trees. Their principal enemies are jaguars and pumas. If there is any likelihood of attack, they plunge headlong into the water, and travel for long distances below the surface. On land they trot slowly or progress by leaps.

See also AGOUTI.

CEDARS, *see* CONIFERS.

CELLS. All living things consist of small units called cells. The 'simple' forms of life, ALGAE and PROTOZOA (qq.v.), consist of a single cell, which has to carry out all the processes of life including reproduction. The bodies of more complicated plants and animals contain many kinds of cells, for instance, bone, muscle, and blood cells in animals. Special cells are set aside for reproduction. Each cell consists of a mass of jelly-like material, called protoplasm, surrounded by a membrane and containing the nucleus, a denser structure which controls the activity of the cell. In addition to this basic structure many plant cells contain the green pigment chlorophyll, and a quantity of watery sap. The cells are protected by a fairly rigid wall formed of cellulose and lignin; a large number of such hard-walled cells, packed tightly together, form the woody parts of plants, even making them, as with trees, very large and heavy, although the cells themselves are too small to be seen without a microscope.

See also ANATOMY; GROWTH OF ANIMALS.

CENTIPEDE, *see* MYRIAPODA.

CHAFER. This is a kind of beetle which includes Cockchafers, Rose-chafers, and many others. Their antennae or feelers have the end-joints flattened and arranged side by side, so that they can be opened and closed like the leaves of a book. These joints bear the organs of scent, and by their enlargement, and the protection gained by closing them when not in use, their sensitivity is much increased. In the south of France dogs and pigs are used, on account of their keen scent, to hunt for the underground edible fungi called truffles. But a little chafer, called *Bolboceras*, can find them with still greater exactitude. When it flies through the air, alights, and begins to scrape away the ground with its forelegs, a truffle is always to be found just beneath. A naturalist in Corsica, who had caught a female of another chafer, *Pachypus*, and put her into a box in his pocket, soon found himself pursued by males which had scented her from afar.

The truffle-loving beetle is closely related to another chafer of southern Europe, called the *Rebenschneider* or Vine-cutter, because it nips off tender shoots of the vine for its brood. A pair of the beetles dig a burrow in the ground, the male carrying away the soil dug by the female at the bottom of the shaft. The female then makes an oval cell opening out of the shaft, while the male goes off to collect provisions. Biting off a

S. Beaufoy

COCKCHAFER LARVA

DOR-BEETLE
S. Beaufoy
Natural size

ROSE-CHAFER BEETLE
S. C. Bisserôt
About 20 times natural size

shoot, he carries it back to the female, and returns for more. When the cell is packed full, an egg is laid in it; and then a few more cells are prepared and provisioned in the same way. Each young grub, on emerging from the egg, finds its food at hand, and by the time it has eaten it all up it has reached full size and is ready to undergo its transformation. The parents are said to guard the entrance to the nest while the grubs are growing.

The Dor-beetles of English pastures and woods are related to the Vine-cutters, and have rather similar habits. They, too, work in couples, the male carrying supplies while the female labours in the burrow. The nest is provisioned with the droppings of rabbits, sheep, or cattle, brought by the male and packed into branch-tunnels by the female—who afterwards places an egg in each. Most of the spring and summer is occupied with these labours, although the family is a small one. Winter is spent below ground, and almost before it is past work begins again.

The male of one of the Dor-beetles, which the great naturalist FABRE (q.v. Vol. V) calls

the Minotaur, has a pair of curious horns upon its back. Many other chafers carry horns of astonishing size and shape. The largest insects in the world, the Elephant-beetles, and Hercules Beetles of South America, and the Goliath Beetles of Africa, also bear remarkable horns. Large males have relatively larger horns than small males of the same species, but the females are almost always without them.

See also BEETLES.

CHAFFINCH, *see* FINCHES, Section 3.

CHALCID FLY. This is a minute insect related to the ICHNEUMON FLY and the GALL-WASP (qq.v.). Many are brilliant metallic-blue or green, and nearly all are either parasites on other insects or 'hyper-parasites'—that is to say, they live on the parasites of other insects.

The Fairy Flies, which include the smallest known insects, are Chalcids that spend their larval life inside the eggs of other insects, feeding on the contents. They make use of the eggs of Butterflies and Moths, and also sometimes of Bugs and Beetles. Most of these are black and lack the metallic brilliance of other Chalcids. One species of Fairy Fly feeds on the eggs of the aquatic bug called the WATER-BOATMAN (q.v.), and to reach them it swims under the water, using its wings as oars.

Those who grow tomatoes in glass-houses find one species of Chalcid Fly very useful, as it lives on the nymphs of the Greenhouse White Fly, a bug which has found its way here from America (*see* INSECT PESTS, Vol. VI). Fig Insects, which pollinate the flowers of the fig-tree, are also Chalcids. In one kind of fig flower the female is able to reach the ovaries, in each of which she lays one egg. After the eggs are hatched, the white footless larvae attack the tissues of the ovaries, and convert them into 'galls' or growths of tissue on the plant. After the larvae have fed and pupated in the galls the Fig Insects emerge. The males are wingless, and it seems that they never leave the fig flower in which they were hatched. The females, however, do so, and as they pass out are dusted over with pollen. They then move to younger flowers, pollinating them as they seek to lay their eggs in the ovaries.

CHALCID FLY
Greatly enlarged

CHAMELEON. The lizards of this family are highly developed for life in trees. The hands and feet are modified for clasping, the digits being opposed to one another like the human thumb and fingers. The Chameleon's hand has two digits on the outside and three on the inside; in the foot this is reversed. The tail, which is also used for gripping, is generally long. The eyes can be moved independently. The tongue, of elastic tissue, is club-shaped at

E. O. Hopp

CHAMELEON IN THE ACT OF CATCHING A FLY BY SHOOTING OUT ITS LONG TONGUE

the tip and provided with a moist secretion. It can be shot out with great speed and accuracy to catch insects and grubs on which it feeds: in fact, some species can stretch their tongues to a distance equalling their own length. With this marvellous weapon at its command, the Chameleon has no need to move quickly, and all its actions are slow and deliberate. The head is helmet-shaped, often with horns and bony out-growths—altogether, the Chameleon is a very strange-looking creature. The power which it has of changing colour is proverbial, though popular legend claims much more than is justified.

The whole family is divided into four genera, with some 80 species. One species is found in the eastern Mediterranean, one in India; the vast majority live in Africa and Madagascar. Most Chameleons, so far as we know, lay eggs; a few species bring forth their young alive. The largest species, found in East Africa, grows to a length of 60 cm; but most of them are much smaller.

See also LIZARDS.

CHAMOIS. This sturdily built animal, living in the mountains of Europe and Asia, is often called a goat-like antelope. This is because GOATS and ANTELOPES (qq.v.) are structurally so alike that it is often difficult to draw a distinction between them, and chamois are sometimes classified with the one and sometimes with the other. Like goats and antelopes, they are, of course, RUMINANTS (q.v.)—that is to say, they ruminate or 'chew the cud'.

Chamois stand about 76 cm high at the shoulders; they have thick, chestnut-brown coats, and short horns which grow straight up from the forehead, ending in a sharp backward hook. They have the most acute sense of sight, smell, and hearing, and are amazingly agile and sure-footed in moving about their mountain homes. A chamois is even able to stand with all four feet on the pinnacle of a rock hardly more than 3 centimetres in diameter. It is a shy and wary animal, and when alarmed it utters a shrill whistle, which sets the whole herd moving rapidly off. For most of the year, the herds, numbering from about fifteen to twenty head, live in the woods on the mountains, feeding on lichens and mountain grass. During the summer a few leave the herd and live for several weeks among the glaciers and snow-fields above the forests. A short spell of severe frost usually drives them back to shelter.

For most of the year the old males live apart; but during the mating season, in October and November, they join the flocks of females, driving away the young bucks and fighting fiercely amongst themselves. The fawns are born in May or June. When only a day old they can follow their dams almost anywhere. Their horns first show after 3 months, and at the age of 3 years they have attained their full size. It is believed that some chamois live to be 20 or even 25 years old.

Goral, Serows, and Takin are three other goat-like antelopes related to the chamois, which all live in the Himalayas. One of the Serows is also found as far south as Sumatra. Of the three, the Takin is the largest, standing about a metre high.

A. Fraser-Brunner

THE PIRANHA OF THE AMAZON WATERS

CHARACIN. This is the name given to the members of a large family of freshwater fishes found in South America and Africa. The fact that they are found only in these two places is one of the reasons why it is thought that these great continents were joined together a very long time ago—since these fish could never have crossed the Atlantic Ocean. Another example of this distribution is the CICHLID (q.v.).

There are a great many different kinds of Characin, most of them small and pretty, and, consequently, often kept in tropical aquariums (*see* AQUARIUM, Vol. IX). Others, however, are large and fierce, like the Dorado of South America and the Tiger-fish of Africa. The Piranha, or Piraya, is perhaps the most terrible fish found in South American rivers, for, although not very big—about 30 cm long usually—great shoals of them will attack bathers, very quickly biting away all the flesh with their sharp teeth.

Characins are related to the CARP family (q.v.), but they all have teeth in their jaws and have also a small, fleshy 'adipose fin' behind the back fin.

CHATTERER. This name is used for a group of tropical birds of Central and South America, which belong chiefly to the forests of the Amazon. They vary in size from a sparrow to a crow, and many of the males have very gaudy plumage. The Cock-of-the-rock, for instance, is a fairly large bird, coloured bright orange-red, with a large, circular crest growing from each side of

the head; and the Blue Cotinga, about the size of a lark, is bright blue, with black wings and tail. They have short, wide-opening bills, and feed principally on insects and fruits.

A remarkable-looking bird of the Chatterer family is the Umbrella Bird, a large, deep black bird, the male of which has a huge crest of feathers, which usually lies contracted, but which can be erected at will to form an umbrella-like covering to the head. He also has a long, feather-covered wattle growing from the throat. Umbrella Birds are very rarely seen, as they live in the upper branches of the dense Amazon forests; but their loud piping note is more often heard.

Another bird with a remarkable note is the Bell-bird, the two best-known species being pure white birds of south-east Brazil and the Guianas. Both are about the size of Jays, and utter frequently a series of metallic, bell-like notes. The Bell-birds of Australia and New Zealand are not Chatterers, but belong to the HONEY-EATER group (q.v.).

CHEESE-MITE, *see* MITES AND TICKS.

CHEESE-SKIPPER. This name is given to the larva of the Cheesefly, a small, shining black, two-winged fly that lays its eggs on cheese, and also upon the fat of ham and bacon. The Cheese-skipper is very like the maggot of the HOUSE-FLY (q.v.), broader at the hind end, tapering to the head, and without legs. It skips along by drawing its head and tail together until they nearly meet, and then suddenly straightening out the body. A Stilton cheese (preferably a good one, as the insect breeds in the better sorts) will sometimes give an opportunity for seeing this remarkable display. Supplied with such rich material and needing no exertion to obtain food, the maggot is fully grown in under a week. It then skips out of the cheese to a quiet place and changes into a pupa. The pupa is enclosed in a golden-brown puparium, formed from the last larval skin.

See also FLY.

CHEETAH, *see* CATS.

CHEVROTAIN (or Mouse Deer). These animals, which resemble some of the small DEER (q.v.), are structurally quite different. They are RU-MINANTS (q.v.)—that is, they 'chew the cud'; but their stomachs have only three compartments in contrast to the other groups of ruminants which have four compartments. They have no antlers, but grow long upper tusks which stick out beyond their lower lips. They walk on the tips of their hoofs, making their legs look very stiff. They are shy animals and lie concealed in the grass of the jungle during the day, feeding only in the evening and early morning.

Most Asiatic Chevrotains are only from 25 to 33 centimetres high, and have brown and red-dish coats, with white underparts. The Water Chevrotain of Africa is a little larger, and has white spots and stripes on its olive body. It has large feet with wide-spreading toes, especially adapted for life in swampy ground.

CHIMAERA, *see* SHARKS, RAYS, AND CHIMAERA.

CHIMPANZEE, *see* APES.

CHINA-MARK MOTHS. Five British moths are remarkable in having aquatic caterpillars, four of which are China-marks, and the fifth a near relation. They have white wings, delicately traced with brownish markings. There are many other species, mostly belonging to the eastern tropics. In all China-marks the caterpillar constructs a case in which it remains concealed from its enemies, water-birds and fish.

The Small China-mark, rather less than 2·5 cm across the wings, occurs commonly in the British Isles near water covered with duckweed. The moths run about on the surface of the water, and lay their eggs, several together, on the underside of the weed, on which the velvety blackish-olive caterpillars feed. The caterpillar's body is covered with a coat of short fine erect hairs, which holds a layer of air and so keeps out the water. Young ones, until they have moulted twice, are not waterproof. The caterpillar's case is made out of fragments of duckweed, and con-tains a bubble of air which makes it float. Some-times the caterpillar will go below the surface of the water, dragging the case with it, often leaving part of its velvety body protruding above the water and gleaming like silver. During the

winter months the caterpillars shut themselves into their cases, not coming out to feed until mild days in April. They pupate in May in their cases.

The Brown, Beautiful, and Ringed China-marks belong to a different genus. They are common throughout most of the British Isles, though the Ringed China-mark does not extend farther north than Yorkshire. The Brown China-mark lays its eggs in a mass of jelly on the underside of the leaves of water-plants. The caterpillars make flattish, oval cases, about 4 centimetres long and 2 cm wide. They cut out a piece from a leaf and fasten it with silk to the underside of another leaf, which is cut to match the first piece. As the leaves are concave, a space is enclosed in which the caterpillar lives, sur-rounded by air. When fully mature, it constructs a cocoon attached to a water-plant, sometimes below and sometimes above the water. The Ringed China-mark builds a case below the sur-face, and depends, not on air, but on oxygen taken in from the water by gills. Every few minutes the larva makes rapid wave-like move-ments which drive out the foul water from its case and draw in fresh water.

The False-caddis Water-veneer, related to the China-marks, is more local than the others. The female moth has only rudimentary wings and uses its legs to swim below the surface of the water. Occasionally winged females appear at the end of the season. The males, which live about 2 days only, mate with the females on the surface of the water, and are often dragged down below to drown. The eggs are laid on sub-merged leaves, the caterpillars living at depths of 1 to 3 metres. They burrow into the food plant, and later make cases like those of the China-mark.

See also CATERPILLAR; CASE-BEARER MOTH.

CHINCHILLA. This is a small, squirrel-like RODENT (q.v.), with very long ears and a longish bushy tail, found in the Andes Mountains of Chile and Bolivia. Large numbers live together in rock crevices and burrows, and are often seen during the day running like mice in the shade thrown by the rocks. When feeding upon the sparse vegetation they sit up on their hind-quarters like squirrels and grasp their food be-tween their fore-paws. Very few of them are now left, because they have been much hunted and trapped for their soft, silver-grey fur.

The Viscacha, another rodent, related to the Chinchilla, lives on the Argentine pampas. It is

CHINCHILLA

a heavily built animal, about 60 cm long. Its face is covered with mottled black and grey fur, which it combs with a bunch of stiff bristles growing on its hind foot. Viscachas usually live in parties of twenty to thirty, and form large warrens, each of which may contain from twelve to fifteen burrows, the whole covering an area of from 9 to 18 square metres. Some of these burrows open out into wide chambers from which tunnels radiate. Viscachas rarely leave their burrow before dusk, and feed upon grass, seeds, and sometimes roots. Just before they come out to feed and frolic, an old male usually mounts a mound of excavated earth heaped up outside the burrows, and takes a careful survey to see that no enemies lurk about the colony.

See also Vol. VI: Fur-farming, Section 7; Furs.

CHIPMUNK, *see* Marmot.

CHLOROPHYLL, *see* Photosynthesis.

CHOUGH, *see* Crow, Section 6.

CHRYSALIS, *see* Butterfly.

CICADA. This large bug is the noisiest of all insects. Generally, Cicadas chirrup only during bright sunlight—and the hotter the sun the greater the noise; but on hot tropical nights they may continue into the hours of darkness. Only the males are musical, and in tropical countries, where the largest and noisiest species occur, the effect is said to be deafening. They are insects of the forests and woodlands, and, like other bugs, they suck the juices from the roots and foliage of the trees. So far as is known, the nymphs always live underground, using their forelegs for digging. There is only one species in Great Britain, and this is found only in the New Forest, where it is a rarity. It is about 2 cm long, with a wing expanse of just over 5 cm.

The organs of the male which enable it to sing are in the abdomen, and consist of a pair of drums, called the 'timbals', that bulge outwards. Large and powerful muscles pull these in and then release them, in a continually repeated crackling noise. There are as well 'sounding-board' arrangements which increase the noise, air-chambers, and methods of changing the air supply—altogether the most complicated mechanism for producing a sound found in any insect. Yet the result is not to be compared with the variations of the human voice, produced by the very much simpler mechanism of our vocal cords. There are different opinions about the Cicada's music. The ancient Greeks are said to have kept the insects in cages for the pleasure of hearing them sing, and the Chinese and Japanese do so now; but the majority of people agree that the Cicada's song is a strident, monotonous noise. The important thing is, however, that the male Cicada's music is favourably received by the female, who responds as best she can by making a crackling noise with her wings.

The American insect, called the Seventeen-year Locust or Periodical Cicada, is a Cicada bug, and not a locust at all. It is remarkable for the long time it takes to grow up. The eggs are laid in the twigs of trees, and the nymphs, which hatch out in about 6 weeks, drop down and go underground. They remain below,

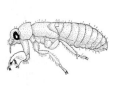

CICADA NYMPH   CICADA ADULT

sucking the juices from the roots of the trees, for 17 years, when, fully grown, they come up again and become adults. As they all emerge about the same time, great numbers of their cast-off skins are to be seen clinging to the trunks of the trees. The males appear to start their shrill music almost at once and to keep it up for a few weeks, after which they all disappear again, and silence reigns for a further period of 17 years. More than twenty distinct broods of this insect are known in the United States, each of which has its own particular year for emerging above ground, so that one or more of these broods appears somewhere in the country each year. In the south there is a brood whose period below ground is 13 instead of 17 years.

See also BUG.

A. Fraser-Brunner

THE MALE CICHLID FANS THE EGGS LAID OUT BEFORE HIM IN NEAT ROWS. THE FEMALE LOOKS FOR FOOD

CICHLID. Like the CHARACINS (q.v.), the fishes called Cichlids are found only in the fresh or brackish waters of South America and Africa, with the exception of three species in India and Ceylon. They are Perch-like fishes, the front part of the dorsal fin being supported by sharp spines (*see* PERCH). Unlike most fishes, they have only one nostril on each side. Many of them are very brightly coloured, and are favourites in the AQUARIUM (q.v. Vol. IX). In some Cichlids, when the eggs are laid, the mother takes them into her mouth and keeps them there until they hatch. Even then, should danger threaten, the baby fish will pop back into their strange hide-away, while the father swims round looking very fierce until all is safe again.

Perhaps the best-known Cichlid is the Angel-fish, found in the streams of Brazil and brought to Britain in large numbers as a favourite for the aquarium. It is silvery, with handsome dark bands, and its upper and lower fins are so long that its height is greater than its length—it is like a diamond-shape standing on one point. To add to its wonderful appearance, it has long streamers on the fins. It is so flat from side to side, that when seen in front it seems to be just an upright straight line. This is a useful protection, for if it is frightened, it darts away to a clump of weeds and, when it turns round to face the enemy, it immediately seems to disappear. The black stripes also help to make it invisible among water-plants. When it lays its eggs, it takes them in its mouth and sticks them to the leaf of a plant, or sometimes to a stone, where it fans them with its fins to aerate them until they hatch. Angel-fish are easy to keep in an aquarium if it is kept warm enough and there is a good supply of growing plants.

Another sort of Angel-fish found in tropical seas is related to the Butterfly fishes (*see* SEA PERCH).

CIVET. The Civet tribe is a group of flesh-eating mammals closely related to the CATS (q.v.), but with longer bodies, more pointed faces, and shorter legs. They are mostly from 60 to 90 centimetres long, with longish tails. The chief members of the group, the true Civets, Genets, Palm Civets, and Binturongs, are found in Asia and Africa and two species in southern Europe also.

The African and the Indian Civets are very alike: they have greyish-brown hair, with darker streaks and spots on their bodies, and dark and light rings on their tails. The Indian Civet is very destructive, eating, as well as birds and small mammals, frogs, insects, eggs, fruit, and roots. Civets are not often seen, as they hunt only at night. Certain glands at the root of the tail secrete a scent which is used by perfumers (*see* PERFUMERY, Vol. VII).

Genets are chiefly found in Africa, though the Common Genet is found also in southern Europe and south-west Asia. Genets are smaller than Civets, with shorter legs, more tapering tails, and soft, greyish or yellowish fur. When a Genet stalks its prey through the grass it presses close to the ground and stretches its long, lithe body to the utmost, so that it looks almost like a snake.

Palm Civets, except for one African species, live in Asia. They are also called Toddy Cats, because they are very fond of the palm-juice or 'toddy' which the natives in India and Ceylon collect in vessels suspended from the trees. The Indian Palm Civet, the best-known species, has blackish-grey, coarse fur. It spends most of its life in trees, and hunts for food during the night.

Binturongs or Bear Cats, which have long, blackish fur, are fairly common throughout the Malay Peninsula, East Indies, Assam, and Siam. These, in contrast to all the other members of the civet tribe, have long tufts of hair on their ears. They can support their whole weight from the branches of the trees by their prehensile tails. They hide during the day, and climb in search of food only at nightfall.

CLAM. The true Clams lead sedentary lives in pools on coral reefs, where they can be a real source of danger to the unwary. This is particularly true of the Giant Clam, for the power of its muscles is immense. Once the gaping valves of the great shell close upon the hand or foot of a man, it is practically impossible for him to free himself unaided from their vice-like grip, and, unless rescued, he will be drowned by the returning tide. There are six or seven species of Clam, the Giant Clam being the largest. In the collection of shells at the British Museum (Natural History), there are two valves of the Giant Clam weighing respectively 70 and 71 kilograms. These great shells are broadly oval in form, and extremely massive and strongly ribbed; their edges are deeply fluted, and the interior is pure white. The animal inside may weigh upwards of 9 kg, and the fleshy folds of its mantle are brilliantly coloured.

The cells of the mantle contain living green ALGAE (q.v.), which manufacture foods from the waste products of the clam and give out oxygen. Both clam and algae benefit from this association, which is called symbiosis (living

Dr. S. Manton

GIANT CLAM—ACTUAL SIZE 90 × 60 cm

together). Bivalves, or twin-shelled molluscs, filter their food and oxygen from the water as it passes over their gills. Such a system is efficient in small species, but not in large ones, and the Giant Clam could not get enough oxygen by this means alone, though it can do so easily with the help of its symbiotic algae. The algae, however, are dependent upon sunlight to manufacture their food (*see* PHOTOSYNTHESIS), and this accounts for the Clam's inverted position in the shallow pools where it lives and its freely exposed mantle.

Under the general name of Clam are included the members of another family of bivalves, the Myidae—which are quite different, however, from the true Clams. They are found on some parts of our British coasts, where they are known as 'Gapers'. They never reach the size of the true Giant Clams, and their much smaller shells, greenish or yellow in colour, gape at each end, the right valve being a little larger than the left. They live in deep burrows in the sand or mud from about low-water mark to a depth of 25 fathoms. While their shells are of a dull colour, their remarkable long siphons, which are enclosed in a wrinkled skin and project far beyond the valves of the shell, are brightly tinted with red.

See also MOLLUSCS.

CLASSIFICATION OF ANIMALS AND PLANTS. In order to make the study of living creatures, whether plant or animal, more easily intelligible, it is necessary to arrange the different kinds in some logical system. The principle adopted by LINNAEUS (q.v. Vol. V) in the 18th century, which has become the standard arrangement throughout the world, is intended to show the relationship of different species to one another.

To classify animals or plants, they are arranged in groups, and these groups are repeatedly subdivided until we reach the single species (man, salmon, red admiral butterfly, yellow waterlily). The easiest way to explain classification will be by taking, as an example, man. It is convenient to start with the widest group, the 'phylum'. Man belongs to the phylum Chordata, animals with a hollow, dorsal nervous system and jointed spinal column. Within this phylum he belongs to the 'class' Mammalia, warm-blooded animals which have hair and suckle their young. Next, the mammals are subdivided into 'orders', where man is classed in the Primates, along with lemurs and monkeys and apes. The lemurs are excluded from the 'sub-order' Anthropoidea, but here man is still classed with the monkeys and apes. Man belongs to the 'family' Hominidae, which includes fossil and modern man only. His 'genus' is *Homo*, which includes species now extinct, such as Neanderthal man (*see* FOSSIL MAN, Vol. I), and his 'species' is *sapiens*—which includes all existing men, whether Caucasian, Negroid, or Mongoloid. Thus we arrive at man's scientific name of *Homo sapiens* (*see* SCIENTIFIC NAMES). It will be seen, by working back through these groups, that we gradually discover man's different evolutionary relationships, which become wider and more numerous the farther back we go, just as in tracing the pedigree of an individual, we find two parents, four grandparents, eight great-grandparents, and so on.

In classifying plants, similar groups are arranged to show relationships in a similar manner. Thus, the common daisy is one of the 'Phanerogams', plants in which there are true flowers with stamens and pistils. (In such plants as ferns, mosses, and fungi there are no true flowers, and they are known as 'Cryptogams'.) The daisy has seeds enclosed within a fruit, and is therefore a member of the tribe of 'Angiosperms'. (The 'Gymnosperms', in which the seed is naked, include the conifers, or cone-bearing trees.) Within the seed the embryo contains two 'cotyledons' or 'seed-leaves', and the daisy therefore belongs to the great class of 'Dicotyledons'. (Among the 'Monocotyledons', with only one seed-leaf, are orchids, lilies, grasses, and sedges.) More easily observed, but less certain distinctions between these two great classes are these: that in Dicotyledons the parts of the flower are in fours, fives, or eights, and the leaves have a more or less complex system of veining; while in the Monocotyledons the parts of the flower are usually in threes, and the veins of the leaf are usually simple and parallel. The daisy belongs to the great family of the Compositae, in which each 'flower' is in fact made up of a number of small, separate flowers; it is the only British member of the genus *Bellis,* and its specific name is *perennis* (everlasting).

A SIMPLIFIED CLASSIFICATION
ANIMAL KINGDOM

Phylum: Protozoa (noncellular animals)
,, Porifera (Sponges)
,, Coelenterata (Sea-anemones, Jellyfishes, Corals)
,, Platyhelminthes (Flatworms, Tapeworms)
,, Mollusca (Snails, Mussels, Squids)
,, Annelida (Worms, Leeches)
,, Arthropoda:
Class: Crustacea (Shrimps, Crabs, Lobsters)
,, Arachnida (Spiders, Scorpions, Mites)
,, Myriapoda (Centipedes, Millipedes)
,, Insecta (Insects)
Phylum: Echinodermata (Starfish, Sea-urchins)
,, Chordata (with notochord or vertebrae):
Subphylum: Urochordata (Sea Squirts)
,, Cephalochordata (Lancelets)
,, Vertebrata (animals with vertebrae):
Class: Agnatha (Lampreys, Hagfishes)
,, Chondrichthyes (Sharks, Rays)
,, Osteichthyes (Bony Fishes)
,, Amphibia (Frogs, Toads, Newts)
,, Reptilia (Reptiles)
,, Aves (Birds)
,, Mammalia (Mammals)

VEGETABLE KINGDOM

I. Cryptogams (seedless plants):
Phylum: Thallophyta (Seaweeds, Fungi, etc.)
,, Bryophyta (Mosses, Liverworts)
,, Pteridophyta (Ferns, Horsetails, etc.)

II. Phanerogams (seed-bearing plants):
Phylum: Spermatophyta:
Subphylum: Gymnospermae (Conifers)
,, Angiospermae (Flowering Plants)

CLEARWING MOTHS. The scales that clothe the greater part of the long narrow wings of these moths are loosely attached, and, except for a few round the margins and on the veins, are lost at the first flight. Their wings then resemble the transparent wings of wasps and bees. Their likeness to wasps and bees is increased by their banded bodies and, above all, by their swift flight in hot sunshine. Many are metallic-black or blue, marked with red or yellow. Some of the fifteen British species are rare, and the moths are not easy to find. The caterpillars, however, bore into tree-trunks, stems, and roots, and either they or the chrysalises can often be found (at least, of about six species). Even the covering of hard wood does not protect them completely from woodpeckers, which open up the galleries and eat the contents.

The largest and finest British species are the two Hornet Clearwings, one being found on poplars, the other on sallows. They measure 4 cm across, and have black and yellow bands on their bodies. The caterpillar takes two years to become fully grown, and then, still within its tunnel, it spins a weak cocoon and pupates. The pupa does not have the legs sealed down against the body, as do the pupae of most moths; and it possesses rows of spines which enable it to wriggle from the cocoon and screw along the tunnel to the thin cap covering the outlet. This it breaks through, so allowing the moth to escape. The moths emerge in summer, early in the morning, but the female does not normally fly until she has mated. Males are attracted in numbers to virgin females.

HORNET CLEARWING MOTH

Its general shape and the black and yellow bands on its body make it so closely resemble a hornet that other animals leave it alone

The commonest British species is the Currant Clearwing. The eggs are laid in early summer near the tips of pruned shoots of currant bushes. The caterpillar bores down the centre of the shoot for 10 or more cm. It hibernates there, and completes its growth in the following April, often betraying its presence by pushing out brownish waste matter from the shoot. It pupates at the end of the burrow, and, just before the moth hatches, it forces its way out through the remaining thin layer of bark.

A Clearwing, known as the Peach Borer, is the most notorious peach pest in North America. The females lay several hundred eggs, either on the trunks of damaged or previously infested trees, or near them in cracks in the soil. The caterpillars burrow in the bark around the foot of the tree, where their presence is revealed by masses of waste matter embedded in gum. Often the trees die in the course of a few seasons.

CLEG, *see* HORSE-FLY.

CLIMBING PLANTS. Plants could not live if their shoots did not grow towards light. The leaves must present to the light the greatest surface possible, to assist the essential manufacture of food by PHOTOSYNTHESIS (q.v.). Most plants solve this problem fairly easily by developing stout herbaceous or woody stems which grow upwards towards the light. In others, however, the stem is so weak that the only way it can grow upwards is by making use of supports of all kinds. Many ingenious devices are used to achieve this end, and so to promote success in the struggle for existence. Sometimes their success is remarkable: pink flowers of the Blackberry have been seen forming a crown to a high Elm, for instance, while the hairy fruits of Traveller's-joy (Clematis) hang from many high trees in the autumn hedgerows.

In some cases the plant simply twines round a support. This may be a piece of string, placed by the gardener to help his Runner Beans, or the branch of a tree or post, round which the Honeysuckle can climb. Some plants, such as the French (or Kidney) Bean, Bindweed, or Gourd, climb in an anti-clockwise direction; while the Honeysuckle, Hop, and Black Bryony climb in a clockwise direction. In temperate regions climbing plants are usually herbaceous (that is, their stems do not contain much wood). In the tropics, however, the Lianas have woody stems which can twine round trunks and branches with such pressure that the limb of the tree becomes malformed. Honeysuckle will sometimes do the same in this country.

Other plants have developed special climbing organs. The Ivy, for instance, climbs by adventitious or stem Roots (q.v.), which fix themselves to the tree-trunk or wall. Traveller's-joy and the Garden Nasturtium twist their leaf-stalks round the stems of other plants. Goose-grass or Sticky Willie (Cleavers), so common in our hedgerows, climbs by means of small hooks on its stem. The Blackberry and the Rose scramble over other plants by the aid of curved woody prickles.

Probably the most important of the climbing organs, however, are tendrils. These are specialized parts of the stem, or leaves, or of portions of leaves. In the White Bryony, for instance, the twining tendrils are modified branch-stems; in the Virginia Creeper the stem-tendrils, instead of twining, develop flat, sticky disks at their tips, which stick to the walls.

John Markham

WHITE BRYONY CLIMBING BY MEANS OF TENDRILS

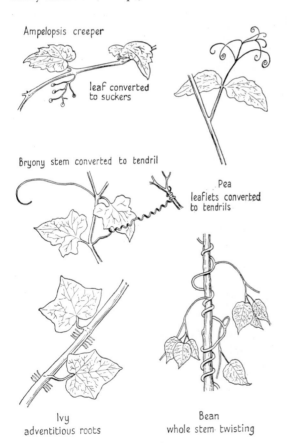

TYPES OF CLIMBING PLANTS

The tendrils of the Grape-vine are modified flower-shoots. In the Sweet Pea some of the upper leaflets of the compound leaf become modified as climbing tendrils. In the Yellow Vetchling the whole leaf is modified into a tendril, and to make up for the loss of the leaves certain outgrowths of the leaf, called 'stipules', become greatly enlarged to take over the normal food-manufacturing duties of the green leaf.

See also Stems.
See also Vol. VI: Climbing Plants, Garden.

CLUBMOSSES, *see* Ferns; *see also* evolution chart opp. p. 1.

COBRA. This name is a Portuguese word meaning simply a Snake (q.v.)—any snake. Early settlers in India saw a snake which they called *Cobra di capello*, the hooded snake, and from that the name has come to be applied to any member of the small genus of poisonous 'hooded' snakes inhabiting tropical Asia and Africa. The two best-known species in Asia are the Common Cobra and the King Cobra. The so-called hood is, of course, in no sense a covering, but is an expansible portion of the skin of the neck, moved by ribs which are elongated for that purpose. The remarkable pose, with dilated hood, which the cobra adopts when alarmed, has made it known throughout the world. (When it is crawling about the hood cannot be seen.) The spectacled form (which is often illustrated) is found only in India: the cobras inhabiting Indo-China have 'monocles', and all-black individuals, with no marking on the hood, are not uncommon in both countries.

The Common Cobra, more common in India than anywhere else, seldom exceeds 1·5 m in length. Annually many people die from its bite; but it is not an aggressive snake, and when disturbed usually makes off rapidly. It is more active at night, and will then bite more readily than in the day-time. When thoroughly roused, it will eject its poison to a distance of 1 metre or so, and with great accuracy, usually aiming at the face. On account of this habit, the term 'spitting cobra' has arisen; and one South African species, the Ringhals, is particularly given to it. The poison cannot harm unbroken skin, but if it enters the eyes it may cause blindness. The bite is generally fatal. The male and female cobra remain together after mating; the eggs are laid in a 'nest' which they make in the ground, and both parents take their turn to guard them until the young are hatched.

The King Cobra, or Hamadryad, is the largest poisonous snake known, reaching a length of about 5 metres. It is a native of India and Malaysia. The adult is dark brown all over; but the young are almost black, with distinct white cross-bars upon the body and tail. The King Cobra builds a nest of grass, twigs, and leaves; and the female (and possibly also the male) guards the eggs until they hatch out. The aggressive disposition of the King Cobra is well known, and there are many records of people having been attacked by it; but usually it makes off without delay when encountered. It feeds mainly upon other snakes.

The Crested Cobra or Crested Mamba is a legendary snake of Natal and Zululand, said to carry a crest of feathers which it spreads out like a fan when alarmed.

COCKATOO, *see* PARROT.

COCKCHAFER, *see* CHAFER.

COCKLE. If you look at a Cockle-shell endwise, you will see that the two closely fitting valves of which it is composed are rather like a heart in shape, and it is from this resemblance that the Cockles have received their scientific name of *Cardium*. On any part of the sea-shore where there is plenty of soft and rather muddy sand Cockles abound. They are collected in large quantities, some being cooked and sent to market, and some being used for bait. The Cockle is a burrowing MOLLUSC (q.v.), which uses its long and strong foot for digging. Thrusting the pointed tip into the soft sand, the Cockle pushes its foot down as far as it will go, and then, bending the end of it into a hook like an anchor, drags itself, shell and all, beneath the surface. The Cockle also uses its remarkable foot to hop along the shore, by pressing it firmly against the sand, bending it, and then suddenly letting go, so that it acts as a spring. In this way the little mollusc jumps over the sands toward the incoming tide.

There are many species of Cockle, varying in size from barely that of a finger-nail to that of a closed hand, and ranging in colour from pure white to yellow, orange, red, and brown, often marked by waving lines of a darker tint. The largest British species is the Spiny Cockle which, when full grown, measures as much as 10 cm in length and just over 7·5 cm in breadth. It has a rather solidly built shell, with prominent, beautifully fluted ribs, which radiate in regular order on both valves, and are armed with numerous sharp, polished spines. The shell has alternate concentric bands of yellowish- and reddish-brown, grading off to a creamy-white at the beaks of the two valves. The Spiny Cockle possesses a most remarkable and brilliant cardinal-red foot, which it can protrude some 10 cm beyond the edges of the valves of its shell.

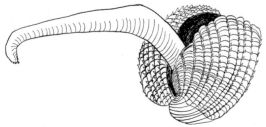

THE SPINY COCKLE PUTS OUT ITS LONG RED FOOT TO DIG IN THE SAND

COCKROACH. The Common Cockroaches, often called 'Black-beetles' although they are neither beetles nor black, came to Britain from the East. They are now found all over the world wherever there is human habitation, living in houses and bakeries. They move about only by night and frequent warm kitchens rather than other parts of the house. They have an unpleasant odour, which when there are many of them, they may impart to the whole room. What their habits were before they became domesticated we can only guess. In our houses they are scavengers, eating anything of food value, but being especially fond of sweet and starchy foods.

Cockroaches are very flat and are exceedingly swift runners. The adult male has two pairs of wings: the fore-wings are narrow and shining brown, the hind-wings small but wide, and folded fan-wise below the fore-wings. It cannot fly, though it often spins round in a circle with both pairs of wings expanded. The female has two pairs of very short and quite useless wings. Her eggs are enclosed, sixteen at a time, in a horny brown case shaped like a purse, which she usually carries sticking out of the end of her body for some time before she cements it firmly in a sheltered position, such as the space between two floor-boards. The young, known as nymphs, are much like the adults. They moult 6–12 times, the reproductive organs maturing and the size of the wing pads increasing at each moult. The whole life-history usually takes about a year.

A much larger insect, the American or Ship's Cockroach, is also an immigrant. Both sexes are winged when adult, and the hind-wings are relatively much larger than in the Common Cockroach, to which it has similar habits. It is not so widely found, but it has settled down in Britain in a number of localities. Yet a third immigrant is the German Cockroach or Steam Bug, which is much smaller and paler than the Common Cockroach. It seems to have a preference for hospitals and the galleys of ships; but it sometimes swarms in other buildings, especially about radiators. A very pretty green Cockroach, often found among bananas, is a more rare visitor that has never established itself. It is of special interest because instead of laying eggs it produces living young. Many of the tropical species are brightly coloured and live in foliage and under dead leaves. Some species feed on dead wood, digesting the cellulose with the help of living organisms in their gut.

See also INSECTS.
See also Vol. XI: HOUSEHOLD PESTS.

COD. With the exception of the Herring, the Cod is our most important food-fish. It abounds in the north Atlantic in numbers difficult to imagine: it has been estimated that about 400 million are caught each year—but these, of course, are only a small proportion of those actually swimming in the ocean. Such numbers are understandable, however, when we remember that a female Cod may lay about 6 million eggs at a time. It is true that most of these are eaten by various enemies, and that only six, on an average, grow to be adult fishes; but even at that rate the population is trebled each year. So the numbers caught are easily replenished. In the north Pacific a closely allied species, called the Alaska Cod, is probably as abundant, and would be equally important if the fishing were as well developed. A good proportion of the Cod that are brought to Britain are salted for export to European markets. The livers yield an easily digested oil, containing vitamins of great medical value.

Cod are voracious feeders; and with their strong, pointed teeth, they will eat almost anything. Among the curious things that have been found in their stomachs are a hare, various birds including a partridge, a bunch of keys, a long piece of tallow candle, and books! It is said that they feed mostly at night, guided by their sense of smell.

A close relative of the Cod is the Haddock, which when smoked is the famous 'Finnan Haddie'. Like the Cod, it has a small 'barbel' or whisker on the chin; but whereas the Cod is greenish with a white lateral line, the Haddock has a black lateral line and a dark blotch near the shoulder. A smaller relative is the Whiting, which is silvery and has no barbel. All these have a short lower jaw, so that the mouth is more or less underneath. Two other well-known species, having a long lower jaw jutting forward somewhat beyond the upper, are the Pollack and Coalfish. Like the Cod, the Coalfish has a barbel on the chin and a white lateral line; but the fish is very much darker, almost black at times. It is caught in large numbers in the Atlantic, and sometimes appears on the market. The Pollack, on the other hand, has no barbel,

COMMON LING

A. Fraser-Brunner

The Hake has much the same arrangement of the fins, but has a more Pike-like head, with much more formidable teeth. It has no barbel and is silvery in colour, reaching a large size. It is found in the Atlantic and Mediterranean, and there are related forms in the Pacific. These, too, are good food-fishes—so that, on the whole, the Cod family is of great importance to mankind.

and is bronze-coloured. It has little commercial value, but is sought after by anglers who find it a good sporting fish. All these, and a number of smaller species, are peculiar in having three dorsal and two anal fins.

Allied to them are a number of species which have only two dorsal fins—the first fin short and high, the second extending for most of the length of the body—and a single long anal fin. These species include the Rocklings, small fishes inhabiting rock-pools, and often caught in lobster-pots, and the Ling, a large fish very much valued as food, but much less common than the Cod—rather curiously, as it lays even more eggs, sometimes as many as 28 million. Similar to the Ling is the Burbot, the only freshwater member of the family. This is found in rivers of Europe and England, as well as of America, where it is known also as the Lawyer.

See also Vol. VI: COD-FISHING.

COELACANTH. This group of fishes is more closely related to LUNG-FISHES (q.v.) than to any other. Until recently, they were only known from fossils and were assumed to be extinct. Several live specimens, however, have now been caught off the east coast of Africa, and are easily recognized by their characteristic three-lobed tails and fins set on fleshy extensions.

COLORADO BEETLE. This notorious insect was originally a native of the western part of North America, where it was not known to threaten any cultivated crop, but fed upon a wild plant related to the potato. Unfortunately it soon took to eating potato leaves—and at once began to multiply at an alarming rate, spreading across America. It reached the Atlantic coast about 1874, and half a century ago was found in Europe, at first in the south of France. It now ravages potato-crops over a large part of the Continent; but, although it is found from time to time in England, it has never established itself, thanks to the careful watch which is kept for it. It is a short, round-bodied insect about the size of a large cherry-stone, and decorated with alternate stripes of black and yellow. It is avoided by birds and other insect-eating creatures as

A. Fraser-Brunner

COD-FISH

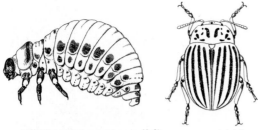

GRUB OF COLORADO BEETLE (*left*), AND ADULT (*right*)

it has a nasty taste, and its very conspicuous pattern ensures that any inexperienced young bird which tries to eat it will not do so twice. It is because birds do not normally attack it that it spreads so rapidly. The grub is equally conspicuous—a soft-bodied, reddish insect, with two rows of small black spots on each side. The orange-yellow eggs are laid on the potato leaves.

See also BEETLES.
See also Vol. VI: INSECT PESTS.

COLORATION OF ANIMALS, *see* PROTECTIVE COLORATION (Insects); CAMOUFLAGE.

COMMA BUTTERFLY, *see* VANESSINI.

CONDOR. This large bird of prey belongs to the same order of birds as the VULTURE (q.v.), which it closely resembles, although it is not, in fact, very closely related. There are ten species, all American birds, and the majority South American. They all have grotesque-shaped, naked heads, large hooked beaks, long claws, and huge wings. They are without the normal 'syrinx' or voice organ, and can utter only a kind of hiss. The largest of them is the black, grey, and white Condor of the Andes, the largest bird of prey, over a metre long, with a wing-span of up to 3 metres. This great bird extends along the whole range of the Andes, at a height of 3,000 to 5,000 metres, though some are also found on the rocky sea-coast. They breed on inaccessible mountain ledges, building no nest, but merely laying the two large white eggs on the bare rock. They feed mostly on carrion, but also frequently kill young goats and lambs, and are therefore persistently attacked by the natives, who have considerably reduced their numbers. When fully gorged, they become heavy and slow, and can often be lassoed or shot as they are roosting in trees.

The King Condor, though not so large, is brilliantly coloured, with a head and neck shading from orange to crimson and purple, cream shoulders and underparts, and black tail and wing feathers. This bird frequents forests rather than mountains, and ranges from Brazil to the southern states of the U.S.A. Another species, the Turkey-vulture, only about 76 cm long, is a black and brown bird with a red head. It has a very wide range, and is quite common in the southern and middle states of the U.S.A. The Turkey-vultures are, like other Condors, scavengers, and though most unpleasing to look at when still, they have an exceedingly easy and graceful flight.

CONDOR

CONGER EEL, *see* EELS.

CONIFERS. This group of trees includes well-known types such as the Christmas-trees (Spruces and Firs), Monkey-puzzles, Pines, Yews, Larches, Cedars, and Cypresses (*see* TREES, CONIFEROUS, Vol. VI). Only the Scots Pine, Juniper, and Yew are true natives of Britain, but many of the others are planted in gardens or State forests, and some of them have become naturalized. Conifers are often quick-growing, and are valuable for their timber (*see* SOFTWOODS, Vol. VII) and for making WOOD PULP (q.v. Vol. VII).

Conifers do not bear flowers, but produce their pollen and seeds in cones. They are the simplest seed-bearing PLANTS (q.v.) but, unlike the FLOWERING PLANTS (q.v.), their seeds are not enclosed inside an ovary, and they never produce true FRUITS (q.v.). A second broad and characteristic feature of the conifers is that their

Eric Hosking

SCOTS PINE

Eric Hosking

AUSTRIAN PINE

Eric Hosking

SPRUCE

Mustograph

CEDAR OF LEBANON

CONIFERS

leaves are always narrow and often needle-like —never broad, as are those of most flowering plants. This reduces the surface area through which TRANSPIRATION (q.v.) takes place, and enables conifers to thrive under cold or dry conditions.

Most conifers are evergreen, shedding their old leaves and growing new ones not at one season but all the year round, so that the tree is never bare of leaves. The Larch, however, is an exception in that it is deciduous, shedding its leaves completely in the autumn and growing new ones in the following spring.

Conifers are usually large, and include some of the biggest and longest-lived of all trees. The Redwoods of California, for example, are so huge that a tunnel wide enough for a motor-car to drive through has been cut through the trunk of one of them. One, with a circumference of 7 metres, is still growing on the south side of San Francisco Bay. Although its exact age is not known, records of it have been traced back to the first Spanish explorers of the 16th century.

See also FLOWERING PLANTS, Section 4; REPRODUCTION IN PLANTS, Section 4.

COOT, *see* RAILS.

COPPERS (Butterflies). The brilliant coppery-orange Small Copper is more closely related to the BLUES than to the HAIRSTREAKS (qq.v.), though all belong to the same family. It is common throughout the summer wherever its food plants, sorrel and dock, grow—that is, on un-cultivated ground, in meadows and lanes, on heaths and commons, and sometimes in gardens. Like a number of birds, it guards its own territory, and when another butterfly passes by its flower-head it will suddenly dart out and pursue it for some distance before returning to keep watch once more (*see* ANIMAL TERRITORY). It usually has three generations a year, the eggs normally being laid singly on the underside of sorrel leaves. The young caterpillars eat channels in the leaves in which they lie hidden, and after the second moult make complete holes. They grow to resemble the leaves in colour, and are exceptionally difficult to see, as their flat shape, like wood-lice, casts little shadow. The last brood remain as caterpillars through the winter. The short, stout pupa hangs from its food-plant by tail hooks, and is supported by a silken girdle.

The British race of the Large Copper, a fiery copper-coloured butterfly, became extinct by 1848. It began to decline in numbers shortly before the draining of the fens, where it used to breed extensively. As it became scarcer and more localized it was much persecuted by collectors, who reduced its numbers. Attempts to introduce the German race into the fens in 1909 and again in 1926, and also in Ireland, failed. More recently, the Dutch race, which closely resembles the extinct English one, has been established in one district in Huntingdon-shire, where it survives precariously under protection. The caterpillars feed on the great water-dock, and can withstand prolonged flooding during hibernation. They have no honey-glands, but produce a sweet substance from scattered cells in the skin. This procures them attention from ants, and consequent protection from their enemies (*see* BLUES).

CORAL. This is a small marine animal, a polyp, closely related to the SEA-ANEMONE (q.v.). So similar are the two creatures in their external appearance that a Coral might be described as an Anemone which has taken to making a skeleton of carbonate of lime. Corals differ from Sea-anemones in two ways: they cannot move about when full-grown; and they possess a stony skeleton. Like the Anemones, they have a mouth surrounded by tentacles, armed with stinging-cells, each containing a coiled tubular thread, which acts like the stinging-hair of a nettle; these threads are used in the capture of the small organisms upon which the Corals feed.

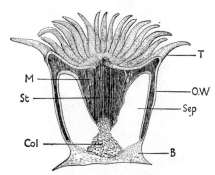

DIAGRAM OF A SOLITARY CUP CORAL ILLUSTRATING SOFT TISSUES IN RELATION TO HARD STONY SKELETON

T. Tentacle: *O.W.* Thin layer of tissue covering outer wall of skeleton; *Sep.* Thin stony plate or septum; *M.* Soft lining tissue (Mesentery); *St.* Stomach; *Col.* Columella or central stony mass; *B.* The more solid stony base of the coral

A CORAL REEF

Dr. S. Manton

The great coral reefs, so varied in form, are the work of the Reef-building Corals, which multiply chiefly by a process of budding. The bud begins life as a slight prominence on the side of the body of the parent Coral, and, as it increases in size, a mouth forms at the free end, a circle of tentacles grows out round it, and the whole bud increases until it equals its parent both in size and shape. As the young Corals formed in this way do not become entirely separated from the parent stock, repeated budding on all sides may result in the growth of a colony numbering hundreds of thousands of individuals, and measuring many metres in length, breadth, and height. No matter what size such a colony may reach, all the polyps are intimately connected to each other, so that the colony really resembles a living sheet of animal tissue, fed and nourished by countless mouths and stomachs. It is by such simple processes of division and budding that all the varied forms of reef Coral are produced. Thus, when the Coral grows upwards and more or less outwards, budding as it grows, tree-like branches are formed; or, by symmetrical budding in all directions, the massive domes of the so-called Brain Corals result.

They multiply chiefly by budding. In some species the skeleton is in the form of a shallow cup, from the centre of which thin, vertical plates radiate at regular intervals. When the Coral is alive, the central plates and sides of this cup are concealed by the mouth, the tentacles, and the outer skin of the polyp.

Besides these social or communal forms, there are many species of Corals, more particularly among those which live in colder seas than the reef-builders, which grow as solitary graceful cups or as mushroom-shaped forms such as the *Fungia*. Some of these, hardly 2 cm in diameter, live attached to the offshore rocks

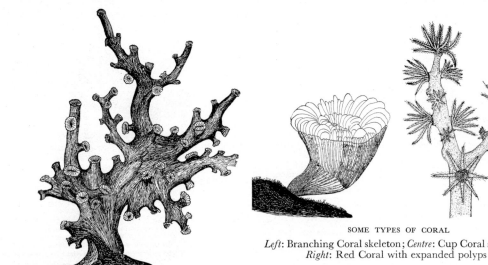

SOME TYPES OF CORAL

Left: Branching Coral skeleton; *Centre*: Cup Coral skeleton; *Right*: Red Coral with expanded polyps

and wrecks around the coasts of Devon and Cornwall. Reef-forming Corals, however, can only exist in the crystal-clear waters of tropical seas, where the mean temperature of the water for the year never falls below 21° Centigrade and there they grow at depths not exceeding 25 fathoms.

The so-called Precious or Red Coral is not a true Coral, but belongs to a closely related group of sea animals called Alcyonarians, which also include the Organ-pipe Coral and the Sea-fans. One of the outstanding differences between the true Corals and these Alcyonarians is in the number and appearance of their tentacles, those of the true Corals and Sea-anemones being simple, and usually numbering a multiple of six, whereas the Alcyonarians usually possess eight. Again, while some species of Corals live as single individuals, Alcyonarians form colonies. Many do not form a rigid stony skeleton; but their bodies are impregnated with countless spicules of lime, varying in shape and colour. The Red Precious Coral grows like a small shrub, the polyps, with their graceful, fringed tentacles, thickly covering the stem and branches, like tiny, pale bluish-white flowers. Red Coral grows on the rocky floor of the Mediterranean Sea, and its gathering used to be a small though flourishing industry.

The Organ-pipe Coral takes its name from the way it grows. It forms masses of slender, vertical tubes, which are joined at regular intervals throughout their length by thin cross-plates, giving added strength to the whole. The deep reddish-purple tubes are crowned with pale, lilac-tinted polyps, which, with their fully expanded tentacles, resemble little star-shaped flowers. It flourishes in warm and sub-tropical seas, masses of it adding to the wonderful colouring of the GREAT BARRIER REEF of Australia (q.v. Vol. III).

The Sea-fans are Alcyonarians, with horny, flexible stems growing in graceful branches covered with gaily tinted, tentacle-crowned polyps. They are found in tropical as well as colder seas. Some species inhabit the great ocean depths and are luminiscent.

See also Vol. III: CORAL ISLANDS.

CORAL SNAKE, *see* KRAIT.

CORK, *see* STEMS, Section 1 *d*.

CORMORANT. This large, fish-eating bird belongs to the same order of birds as the GANNET (q.v.), and inhabits the seas around the coasts of the greater part of the world, including the British Isles. There are many species, all of

Eric Hosking

CORMORANTS WITH NEWLY HATCHED YOUNG

which capture fish by diving, using their large webbed feet to swim beneath the surface of the water. They bring the fish to the surface, and then toss them in the air, catch, and swallow them. Young cormorants thrust their heads right down the throats of their parents to feed on the semi-digested fish in the crop.

The Common Cormorant is pitch black, glossed with bronze, with white on its cheeks and sides, and is nearly 90 cm in length. It nests in colonies, generally on sea cliffs or rocky islets, and lays its four to six bluish-white eggs in a nest consisting of a mass of seaweed, around which collect quantities of decaying fish and other refuse, producing a fearful stench. In Holland, where there are no cliffs, Cormorants nest in trees. The Shag, or Green Cormorant, a slightly smaller bird, with glossy, greenish plumage and a crest on its head, also inhabits the coasts of Britain.

In eastern Asia Cormorants are tamed and used to catch fish for their owners. They are prevented from swallowing fish above a certain size by a ring which is placed around their necks. This sport was formerly practised in Britain, the Master of the Cormorants being an officer of the Royal Household (*see* Vol. VI: FISHING INDUSTRY, Section 3).

The tropical Darters, or Snake Birds, are related to the Cormorants, but are very much more slender in build, with long, snake-like necks, small heads, and long, pointed bills. They frequent large rivers and lakes, pursuing fishes under the water and spearing them with their sword-like bills. When on the surface with the body mostly submerged, the long, slender neck looks like a snake. They build their nests in trees.

CORNCRAKE, *see* RAILS.

COURTSHIP OF ANIMALS, *see* ANIMAL LANGUAGE.

COWRY. This type of MOLLUSC (q.v.) usually lives in shallow water on rock-strewn shores, where they may be seen slowly gliding over the weed-covered rocks or in the clear pools exposed at low tide. The common British species is about 1·3 centimetres long, not unlike a split pea in shape, and the shell is a pinkish white, sometimes marked with one or two dark-brown spots. If we turn the Cowry over we shall see that it is quite unlike most univalve (or one-piece) shells,

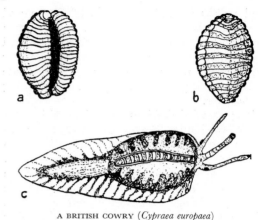

A BRITISH COWRY (*Cypraea europaea*)
a. Under surface of shell; *b.* Upper surface; *c.* The Cowry with body extended and mantle enclosing its shell

for the opening, instead of being circular, is a long, narrow slit running from end to end of the shell, and the lips of the slit are bluntly toothed and turn inwards. One would think that it must be a very thin and flat kind of animal that could comfortably pass in and out at such a door, but that is not so. When the Cowry begins to move it pushes out a long foot, which expands until it is twice as broad as the base of the shell; next appears a broad head with two long, straight tentacles; and finally, the folds of the mantle, or outer skin, project on each side and turn upwards, so that their two edges almost meet at the top of the shell. Moreover, the little animal is very gaily coloured: its large foot is golden or bright orange, marked with a long line of pale yellow; the long snout is scarlet; the tentacles light red, speckled with yellow; and the mantle a clear olive-green, splashed and dotted with black, and bordered with bright red.

Many of the Cowries living in tropical seas grow to a large size, and their shells are most beautifully coloured. The Tiger Cowry has always been a favourite with collectors on account of its brilliant markings, and it often measures a good 10 cm in length. The Orange Cowry, a good specimen of which may fetch as much as £40, is a rare tropical species, the shell being a bright orange colour, mottled with black spots, rather like a turtle-shell. The familiar little ivory-tinted Money Cowries, which come from the Indian and Pacific Oceans, were often used as money tokens in many parts of India and the Far East, and still pass as current coin among native tribes in parts of western Africa.

COYOTE, *see* WOLF.

COYPU. Also known as the Nutria or Beaver-Rat, the Coypu is a large RODENT (q.v.) which looks and behaves very much like a BEAVER (q.v.). It is found in the rivers and lakes of South America, especially in the Argentine. Its body is about 60 cm long, covered with long, dusty-looking, brownish-yellow fur, and ending in a long, rat-like tail. Coypus are bred in captivity for their valuable fur, which in the FUR TRADE (q.v. Vol. VII) is called nutria. Some have escaped from fur farms in Britain and have established colonies in East Anglia.

Coypus generally make their burrows in the banks of rivers and lakes, nearly always choosing a quiet spot. If, however, the banks are not large enough, they build a platform-like nest among the reeds. They are usually seen in pairs; but large parties often come out in the evenings to swim in the water, uttering peculiarly mournful cries. The female takes her eight or nine offspring for a swim when they are a few days old. They are reluctant to learn, and try to find a safe place on their mother's back. The mother's teats are placed on the sides of her body, so that the young ones are able to reach them as they cling to her back, and in this position they are suckled. Coypus are awkward and ungainly on land. They eat the leaves, seeds, and roots of water plants.

See also Vol. VI: FUR FARMING, Section 5.

CRAB. The true crabs make up a very large group of the CRUSTACEANS (q.v.). The majority inhabit the sea, though some species live in rivers, lakes, and swamps, and a few have established themselves on dry land, only returning to the sea for the breeding season. All are easily recognized by the broad 'carapace', or upper shell, the abdomen, which is reduced to a more or less triangular flap tucked under the body, the usually well-developed pincer-claws, and the four pairs of legs used for walking, digging, and sometimes for swimming.

The life-history of the Common Shore Crab is typical of the group. In the first stage the tiny larva has a helmet-like thorax, crowned by a long, tapering spine something like a dunce's cap, and with a second long spine sticking out in front, looking like a comical carnival nose. The eyes are large, but are not as yet carried on stalks, as they are in the full-grown crab; the abdomen is long and slender. The odd little creature swims in the sea by means of its 'maxillipedes' or jaw-feet. Gradually the larva increases in size, casting its skin from time to time, and passing through a series of changes until the second stage is reached. By now the eyes have grown out on short stalks, the ten legs have developed—the first pair as miniature claws—the dunce's cap spine has entirely disappeared, the long frontal spine has become reduced to a short triangular point between the eyes, and the slender abdomen is greatly shortened. The second-stage larva soon settles down on the floor of the sea, tucks its shortened triangular-shaped abdomen under its now-broadening carapace, and so acquires the adult form. Henceforward the crab does not change its shape, but as it grows it casts its shelly armour from time to time, and continues to do

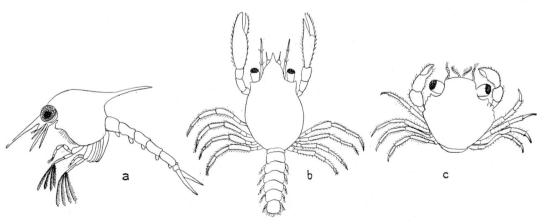

LARVAL STAGES OF THE COMMON SHORE CRAB
a. First or Zoëa stage; *b.* Megalopa stage; *c.* Young crab

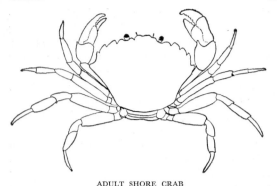

ADULT SHORE CRAB

Note the large right-hand claw used for holding and crushing food

so at ever-lengthening intervals throughout the rest of its life.

The Common Shore Crab lives mainly under the weed-covered rocks between tide-marks. The large Edible Crab lives among rocks in deeper water, though young specimens are often found in the rock pools exposed at extreme low tide. On the Tasmanian coast is found the Giant Crab, which may measure fully 30 cm across its carapace, and has one of its claws developed into a very large and massive weapon. Several species of Swimming Crabs are to be found round the British coasts, the largest of which is the Velvet Fiddler Crab, measuring some 10 cm across the carapace. It is very like the Shore Crab, except that the last pair of legs is flattened and striped with blue, while the leg-joints are bright red. The popular names 'Fiddler' or 'Swimming' crab come partly from the shape of the flattened end-joint of the hind-leg, which is shaped rather like an old-fashioned viol, and partly from the half-scrambling, half-swimming movements of the legs when the crab is in the water.

MALE CALLING CRAB

An interesting British example of the burrowing crabs is the Masked Crab, which has gained its popular name from the curious moulding of the back of its oval-shaped carapace, resembling a queer oriental mask. The body is about the size of a large walnut; the male has long and slender front legs, which terminate in small, blunt claws, while the same pair of limbs in the female are quite short and bear sharp-pointed claws. The long and stoutly haired antennae in both sexes serve as filters for the water passing down to the gills when the crab is buried in the sand. This strange-looking little crab is to be found on wide, sandy bays near low-tide mark, the only sign of its presence when the tide is out being the tips of the antennae, looking like a pair of short bristles, and just protruding from a slight hump on the surface of the wet sand.

The Spider Crabs are a particularly interesting family, not only because of their strange shapes, but also because of their curious habits. They are more or less oval in shape, with long slender legs and narrow claws, and both limbs and carapace bear a number of stout, short, curved spines. These crabs have the curious habit of dressing themselves up with pieces of living sponges, seaweeds, and other marine growths, which they gather with their claws and arrange on the carapace and legs, where they are held in position by little hooked spines. There the seaweeds and sponges continue to grow, so that the whole crab soon becomes covered by a most effective disguise. As they are slow in their movements, this method of concealment undoubtedly saves the Spider Crabs from many hungry enemies. The Giant Spider Crab of Japan is the largest of the group. Its carapace may measure nearly 40 cm in length by 30 cm in width, and its claws may have a span of more than 3 metres, when spread out. Another family of crabs which like to disguise themselves are the Sponge Crabs. They have adopted the habit of carrying a cloak, formed of a piece of living sponge, which is held in position on the back of the carapace by the last pair, or the last two pairs, of legs, these being specially modified for the purpose. Held in this fashion the living sponge continues to grow, so that the crab is completely hidden from view.

On the mud flats and salt marshes of tropical countries live the curious Calling Crabs, so named from the way in which they appear to beckon with one claw. While the females are quite normal in appearance, the males have one claw greatly developed—often larger than the crab's body, and sometimes brilliantly coloured. These gay colours probably serve to attract the female, and there is no doubt about the value of the great claws as weapons both for offence and defence, for the active and pugnacious males flourish them defiantly, and are always fighting. The Land Crabs, which have gills specially modified to serve for air-breathing, also inhabit tropical countries. Although they spend their adult life on land, their young stages are passed in the sea, so that the crabs have to go down to the shore for the breeding season. This

from his home without injury, for his body and some of his limbs are specially adapted for securing a firm grip inside the shell. His body is soft and twisted to fit the spiral shell; the pincer-claws of the first pair of legs are armoured and unequal in size, the larger of the two serving as a plug to the entrance of the shell; the next two pairs of legs are long and slender, and used for walking; while the last two pairs are short, and modified for gripping inside the shell and holding the soft-skinned defenceless body in place. House-hunting is almost an obsession in the life of the average Hermit Crab, for rarely will an unoccupied shell be passed without its possibilities as a convenient home being explored. Many

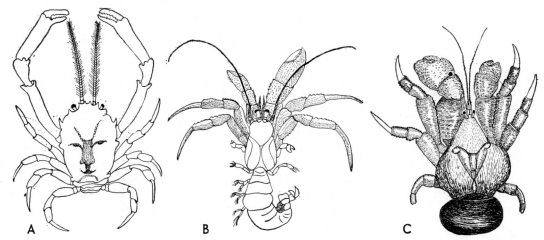

A: MALE MASKED CRAB; *B*: HERMIT CRAB. Note the soft flexible body, and the small modified limbs adapted for holding on to the interior of the whelk or other univalve shell which the crab may inhabit; *C*: COCO-NUT CRAB, a land-dwelling relation of the Common Hermit Crab

MIGRATION (q.v.) takes place annually, the crabs marching across country in great companies, and as at this time they are in prime condition, considerable numbers fall victims to the many hungry foes who waylay them.

The Hermit Crabs, on account of their shape and varied habits, are a very interesting group. Nearly all of them are soft-bodied, and so they utilize the empty shells of MOLLUSCS (q.v.), such as winkles and whelks, as temporary homes, carrying them about with them in their wanderings in search for food. Our Common Hermit Crab may often be found in the rock pools near low tide, scrambling about actively, the small ones carrying a winkle-shell, the larger a whelk-shell, into which they retreat when alarmed. It is not easy to extract a living Hermit Crab

Hermit Crabs live in close relationship with certain other marine animals—and here we have examples of that type of association between two quite different kinds of animals, in which the partners are rarely to be found separated, each benefiting more or less from the presence of the other. For example, full-grown Common Hermit Crabs, which live below low-water mark, frequently inhabit a large whelk-shell bearing a handsome Sea-anemone. The Sea-anemone benefits by sharing the fragments from the crab's meals, and the crab, while resting after the banquet, is protected by the outspread stinging tentacles of the Anemone. Sometimes a third partner is included in this curious association: a Bristle-worm may live in the upper whorls of the shell, and probably helps to keep the interior clean. It may be seen thrusting its head out at meal-times, to snatch morsels from the claws of its host. Another British Hermit Crab inhabits a spiral cavity in a living sponge. This association begins when the crab is still quite small and young, and living in a small winkle-shell on which the sponge settles. Though the winkle-shell soon becomes too small, the growth of the sponge keeps pace with that of the crab, and the latter, completely sheltered within the sponge, has no need to seek another home.

Species which may be called land Hermit Crabs, for they live almost entirely on land, are found on tropical beaches. They travel far inland and climb into low bushes in their search for food, only returning to the sea to breed. Like our British Hermits, they utilize the spiral shells of molluscs for their portable homes. The giant Coco-nut Crab, which actually climbs palm-trees to get at the young nuts, and grows to 30 cm or more in body length, although belonging to the Hermit Crab tribe, does not make use of a portable shelter. Still more difficult to recognize at first sight as members of this family are the so-called Stone Crabs, of which one species, the Northern Stone Crab, is often caught by fishermen trawling in the North Sea. It looks much like a slender Spider Crab, but is easily distinguished because it has only three instead of four pairs of walking legs behind the pair of pincer-clawed legs. The fourth pair is actually there, but they are normally folded away out of sight in the gill chambers. Both its triangular-shaped thorax and its long, slender legs are covered with many short, sharp spines, while its unsymmetrical abdomen, carried tucked up beneath the thorax, is protected by shelly plates.

See also Vol. VI: CRAB AND LOBSTER FISHING.

CRANE. This large bird is related to the BUSTARD (q.v.), and is conspicuous for its very long legs and neck, and its powerful bill, with which it digs up roots, bulbs, and worms. Superficially Cranes resemble Storks, but their structure is different, and they never perch. There are about 19 species, found in all continents except South America, and most have predominantly grey or whitish plumage. Typical Cranes can sustain long flights. They migrate in flocks, flying at great heights in a V or W shape, each with its long legs stretched out behind. A migrating flock of Cranes can be an impressive sight, as was noticed by Jeremiah (Jer. viii. 7). The birds have a loud, trumpet-like call, which can be heard 3 kilometres away. They are sometimes a menace to the farmer, for they will consume vast quantities of grain, but they are so vigilant and wary that they are difficult to shoot.

The Common Crane breeds in Europe, and winters in north and west Africa. It used to be common in Britain but has not bred here for many years. It frequents open swampy country, building a nest of dry grass and rushes on the ground. Both sexes take part in courtship dances, bowing and turning and then performing the skips and hops of the dance proper. The stately, long-legged, silvery-grey Australian Brolga also performs an elaborate courtship dance out on the plains; sometimes only a single pair, but often a large flock forms the dancing party.

The White Crane of central and northern Asia is a lovely bird, with magnificent white plumage and red legs and face. It frequents wide expanses of shallow water and feeds on rushes and aquatic plants. The large Stanley Crane of South Africa is grey-blue, with a white crown and black markings. It lives on the open plains far away from water, and is carnivorous. The widely spread Demoiselle Crane, only about 75 cm in length, is a purplish-grey, with long black breast-plumes and tufts of loose white feathers growing backwarks from each side of the head. The Crowned Cranes of Africa have a fan-shaped crest of bristle-like feathers radiating from the top of the head.

In south and central America there are several groups of birds closely related to the Cranes. The Courlans of Brazil, chocolate-brown birds some 63 centimetres long, live in swamps. The Sun-Bitterns are smaller birds, with long necks, long, pointed beaks, and a plumage marked with white, brown, and black—rather on the pattern of a butterfly's wing. They frequent the wooded banks of rivers, especially the Orinoco, and love to bask in the sun with their wings spread out, much like a butterfly. The Kagu of the island of New Caledonia is a remarkable-looking, grey-coloured bird, about the size of a domestic fowl, with a long crest of head-feathers drooping over its back. Although it has fairly well-developed wings, it seems incapable of flight, but lives on the ground, coming out at night to hunt for worms, molluscs, and insects.

CRANE-FLY (Daddy-long-legs). Crane-flies form a group of two-winged flies which must be known by sight to almost everybody. They are mostly of moderate or large size, and are easily recognized by their slender bodies and very long, fragile legs. The common Daddy-long-legs is a destructive pest. Its larva—called the 'leather-jacket' on account of its tough outer covering—lives underground, feeding on the roots of various grain crops and other grasses. The eggs are black, and are laid either on or in the ground. They hatch in about a fortnight, and the larvae feed throughout the year until the following spring, when they do their worst damage. The pupa is long and slender, usually with two horns on the forehead for breathing. It remains underground until the fly is ready to emerge, when it pushes itself partly out of the ground. The larvae of the different species have very varied habits—for while some, like the common Daddy-long-legs, are vegetarian, others are scavengers, others again are carnivorous; and while some live in the water, others live on land. The members of the Crane-fly family are sometimes called Water Spiders.

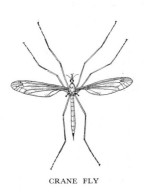

CRANE FLY

See also FLY.

CRAYFISH, *see* LOBSTER.

CRICKET. This insect can be distinguished from its near relative, the Bush Cricket (*see* GRASSHOPPER), by the way it carries its wings folded flat on its back. The outer edges of the fore-wings are bent down vertically along the sides, giving the body a flat, box-like appearance when viewed from above. The Cricket's song is made by the insect rubbing its fore-wings together, so causing them to vibrate. Crickets have hearing organs on their front legs.

Four species of Cricket—the House, Field, Wood, and Mole Crickets—have long been known in Britain; a fifth species, the Scaly Cricket, originally found in Mediterranean lands and Madeira, lives in rock crevices and under large stones on Chesil Beach in Dorset.

The House Cricket, which is common in many parts of the country, seems to keep entirely to houses and other well-heated buildings, especially bakeries. It is about 2 centimetres long, and pale brown, with darker fore-wings. Its hind-wings, used in flight, are longer than its fore-wings, and quite pale. As they enjoy throughout the year a uniform high temperature, it is not surprising that House Crickets are to be found at every season of the year in all stages of their development. They will eat anything of food-value, and may be very destructive—for instance, at night to clothes drying in front of a kitchen fire: woollen garments, especially, may be found riddled with holes next morning. They seem to be very thirsty insects—at all events they have a habit of collecting where water is stored, and water-cisterns have often been choked up with crickets that have fallen in and been drowned. In some places the House Cricket seems to be increasing greatly in numbers and becoming very much of

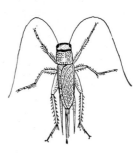

HOUSE CRICKET

a nuisance. It burrows into the walls, especially round kitchen fire-places and bakery ovens, staying in its tunnels out of sight, though not out of hearing, during the day-time, but coming out and often flying about the room at night. Its loud and not unpleasing chirruping can be distinctly heard by anyone passing a cricket-infested building at night. Their numbers, familiar haunts, and loud chirruping have caused crickets for centuries to be amongst our best-known insects. John Milton first used the phrase 'the cricket on the hearth' about 1630 in the poem *Il Penseroso*.

The Field Cricket, which is much rarer and a larger insect, is bulky and almost completely black, the male being shining black with a golden stripe across the base of each fore-wing.

MOLE CRICKET

E 2

Field Crickets live in solitary seclusion, each in its own burrow below ground. They are very shy, retiring backwards rapidly into their burrows at the sound of approaching footsteps. They need hot sunshine, and may be found throughout the summer, in wild, rough pasturage, where they sing from May to July, both by day and by night.

The Mole Cricket, which is also rare, and much larger than our other crickets, is reddish-brown, and has short fore-wings which leave the greater part of the abdomen uncovered. It lives underground, frequenting moist places such as the banks of streams and ponds. It owes its name to its burrowing habits, and to the likeness between the forelegs with which it digs and the hands of the mole. It feeds mainly on roots, and if it were common might be very destructive. It sings mostly on warm days in spring and summer. The Wood Cricket, which is very local, lives among dead leaves on dry banks in wooded districts of southern England.

The eggs of most crickets that live in the open are laid singly in holes in the ground. The ovipositor, or egg-laying tube, is slender instead of broad and sabre-shaped as in the Bush Crickets.

CROCODILES. The Crocodilians form one of the four orders into which living reptiles are divided. They are today found only in tropical regions, but in the past they were more widely distributed, far more numerous, and more varied in form. Of that original vast horde, only four groups now survive, the true Crocodiles, the Alligators, the Caimans, and the Gharials.

Crocodilians differ from all other reptiles in having a four-chambered heart, and a muscular partition, the diaphragm, which separates the heart and the lungs from the abdominal cavity. Although in having four legs and a tail they resemble the lizards, they differ from them in many structural characters, and are, in fact, only distantly related to them. All Crocodilians also have a more or less well-developed bony armour covering the back, and in some species also the belly. Many people think the crocodile and the alligator are the same creature, but they are not, slight though the differences may be. Crocodiles generally have long, narrow snouts, alligators broad and bluntly pointed ones. In the crocodile, the fourth tooth in the upper jaw fits into a socket in the lower jaw, in the alligator it fits into a groove. Moreover, the two occupy different regions of the world, and are never found living together.

All Crocodilians lay white, hard-shelled eggs, some burying them in the sand of river-banks, others building nests of reeds and grass. The female often keeps watch near her eggs until they are hatched. The home of the crocodiles is in the water; but on sunny days they will leave it to bask in the sun on the banks or upon logs. They have keen hearing and are sharp-sighted. They make a noise something between a loud bark and a bellow, but can also make a deep hissing sound. They have a well-developed tongue, which is, however, fixed to the floor of

CAIMANS

ALLIGATOR

CROCODILE

GHARIAL

TYPES OF CROCODILES

the mouth and cannot be put out.

The Crocodilians eat only flesh, and will devour anything that they can overcome. As man-eaters they have a bad reputation, but only one species, the Estuarine Crocodile, really deserves it. The discovery of human ornaments or parts of human bodies in their stomachs does not necessarily mean that they have killed humans, for they have no objection to eating corpses. Crocodiles are hunted for their skins, which make good leather, but no other part of them is of value to man.

ALLIGATORS   *Zoological Society of London*

The true Crocodiles (with one exception which is found in central America) inhabit the eastern hemisphere, living in tropical Africa, Asia, the Malay Archipelago, and northern Australia. There are some ten different species, the largest being the dangerous Estuarine Crocodile, which sometimes grows to 9 metres and more. This is the largest of all living reptiles, and, like the rest of its group, continues to grow throughout its long life. It lives in brackish waters in the lower reaches of rivers, rarely being found above the tidal limit, but it is also quite at home in salt water and has been found far out at sea. The common fresh-water species of India is the Mugger, of Africa the Nile Crocodile, and of Australia Johnston's Crocodile. All have been known to eat men, but none is so dangerous as the Estuarine Crocodile.

The Alligator was first seen by the early Spanish settlers, who called it 'el lagarto', a lizard—for it looked to them like an enormous lizard. From 'el lagarto' the English settlers produced 'alligator'. Two well-known species are the Mississippi Alligator, inhabiting the southern parts of North America, and the Chinese Alligator, living in the waters of the Chinese river, the Yangtze Kiang. In the past alligators flourished in all northern countries—indeed, the fossilized remains of one have been found in the London Clay.

The Caimans, or Jacaras, as they are called by the natives of Brazil, are the Crocodilians of Central and South America. Five species are recognized, and these differ from the true crocodiles and alligators in certain characters of the skull, and also in having a more strongly developed bony armour on both the back and belly. The largest species, the Great Caiman, grows to a length of 6 metres and has enormous bulk. On the Amazon and Orinoco rivers and their tributary waters and lakes they may be seen in huge numbers, particularly at the end of the dry season, when the receding waters confine them to certain areas. They seldom molest man and are therefore not greatly feared by the natives.

The Gharial, or Gavial, is the long-snouted crocodile of northern India, found mainly in the waters of the Indus, Ganges, and Brahmaputra, and subsisting mainly on fish. A specimen was shot some years ago in Upper Burma; but it is now very rare, if not extinct, in that part of the world. The male grows to a length of 6 metres or more and is distinguished from the female by having a large fleshy protuberance on the end of its snout. The name Gharial is said to have originated because this protuberance resembles a *ghara* or Indian earthenware pot.

Schlegel's Gharial, also known as the False Gharial, and now regarded as being closely related to the true Crocodiles, is a very rare beast and is restricted to Borneo and the Malay Peninsula.

CROSSBILL, *see* FINCHES, Section 5.

CROWS. 1. This family (Corvidae) of Passerine or perching birds includes many well-known species, such as the Rook, Magpie, Jackdaw, and Jay. They vary in size from the Raven, over 60 centimetres long and the largest of the Passerine birds, to the Jay, which is only a little more than half as big (34 cm). They are found in most parts of the world, and have, for birds, a very highly developed intelligence. Most crows pair for life, and the male shares in all the duties of parenthood. Most members of the family are disliked by the farmer or game-preserver, as they steal other birds' eggs and young, and raid the farmer's grain crops (*see* BIRD PESTS, Vol. VI). Ravens will sometimes kill a wounded sheep or attack a lamb. They do, however, eat a great many harmful grubs and insects.

2. CARRION CROW. This large, completely black bird, about 50 centimetres long, has the same build as the Raven, but is smaller. Although

Arthur Brook

RAVEN WITH YOUNG

war has been waged upon it in Britain, it is still very common, and does a good deal of damage. It builds its large, rather untidy nest on a cliff ledge on the coast, or high up in a tree. It will eat anything that comes its way, though it is a meat-eater by choice. It cracks food such as shell-fish or nuts by dropping them from a height.

The Hooded Crow, apart from its grey back and underparts, is very much like the Carrion Crow in shape and habits. In Britain, it is found in northern Scotland and Ireland, where it usually replaces the Carrion Crow, and it also migrates to the east coast in the autumn from Scandinavia, where it is common.

3. THE RAVEN, the sacred bird of the Norse god Odin and a character in many legends and traditional tales, is perhaps the most intelligent of all crows. It is a handsome bird, with its glossy black plumage and fine size, but it also has been relentlessly pursued because of its depredations. It still breeds, however, in some numbers on coastal cliffs and in mountainous districts. It nests very early in the year, starting to repair its old nest in January and producing its young by the end of February. It is a very strong flier, and during the courting season it will perform gambolling flights, diving and tumbling from great heights, dropping a pebble or twig and then diving after it, and closing its wings and rolling round in the air. It uses these tricks also to defend itself against attack by birds of prey.

4. THE ROOK can be distinguished from other crows by a bare white patch round the bill, which is more pointed than that of other crows. It is by far the most numerous of British crows, being found anywhere where there are tall trees. It is a gregarious bird, nesting in the tree-tops in great colonies, called rookeries. These colonies are very noisy, busy assemblies, especially during the period of building the large, untidy, stick nests. There is an old superstition that if the rooks desert their rookery the heir to the estate will die.

5. THE JACKDAW, the smallest true crow, has a grey patch on the nape of its neck. It is, perhaps, the most popular of the family, as it is easily tamed and makes an amusing pet. It is alternately quarrelsome, impudent, and destructive, and is a most mischievous thief, making off with and carrying to its nest any bright thing which attracts its attention. This characteristic has made it the subject of many stories, including the famous story of *The Jackdaw of Rheims*. It builds its nest in holes in trees or cliffs, or in a building—often being responsible for blocking up a chimney.

6. THE CHOUGH is the least familiar of the crow family in Britain, being represented by one species only, the Cornish or Red-billed Chough. Though now quite rare in Cornwall, it is often to be found around the cliffs of Wales, western Ireland, and the Isle of Man. It is a vivacious bird, with a bright red bill and legs, and glossy black plumage; it has a buoyant flight and very fast run. But it is shy, and rarely permits anyone to approach it. The Alpine Chough, with a yellow bill, is an inhabitant of the mountainous districts of Europe and Asia, but does not appear in Britain.

7. THE MAGPIE is well known everywhere because of its pied black-and-white plumage and long tail, and because of the superstitions which have grown round it. The old rhyme 'One for sorrow, two for joy' has various versions. In winter considerable gatherings of Magpies may be seen, but in spring and summer they are found in pairs. They build in the fork of a tree or bush, the structure of the nest differing from that of other crows. On a foundation of turf or clay is built a large nest of thorny sticks and twigs, the sides of which continue up to form a complete dome with one side open. The nest is well lined with roots and dry grass. The six or more eggs are of the usual crow type—bluish-green and mottled. Magpies also can be tamed to make amusing pets.

8. THE JAY is very different from the rest of the family in appearance, being one of the gayest of British birds, with its pinkish-brown plumage marked with white and black, and the bright blue, white, and black bars on the wing coverts. It has also a crest of upright feathers, whitish streaked with black. Most species of Jays are gaily coloured—among them the Blue Jay of North America, the Siberian Jay, grey with a bright, rust-coloured tail, to be found in the forests of northern Europe, and the crow-like Whisky-jack of Canada. Jays are noisy birds, except when near their nest, and they live in woods. They are wicked thieves of young birds and eggs, and so are shot without mercy by the game preserver. They have a very jaunty walk, including sideways hops—and this has led to the expression 'jay-walking'.

Arthur Brook

MAGPIE WITH FLEDGLINGS

CRUSTACEA. This is the division of the animal kingdom which includes the CRABS, LOBSTERS, PRAWNS and SHRIMPS, BARNACLES (qq.v.), Sand-hoppers, the Water-fleas (*Daphnia*) of the ponds, and a vast assemblage of small and less familiar creatures which are chiefly inhabitants of the sea except for a few species like the common WOODLOUSE (q.v.) of our gardens. They are extraordinarily diverse in size and shape, and many of them pass through most remarkable changes of form, or METAMORPHOSES (q.v.), before reaching the adult stage—changes as profound as those between a caterpillar and a butterfly. All, however, possess certain well-marked features by which they can be distinguished. The body and limbs are divided into segments, and are covered entirely with a tough or a hard, lime-impregnated coat, which is pliable at the joints, allowing the limbs to move in certain directions. This outer skin, the cuticle, is incapable of growth, and in fact is like a suit of clothes which, as its owner grows, becomes too small, so that it has periodically to be cast off and replaced by a new garment. It is

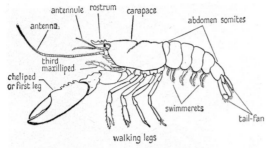

SIDE VIEW OF COMMON LOBSTER

possible to watch this curious process taking place in a shore crab in an aquarium. First the shell splits across the back at the base of what is known as the 'carapace' or upper shell, and the crab slowly extricates its body and limbs, leaving the old suit quite complete down to the smallest detail. The new suit, which has been forming beneath the old one, is at first quite soft, and the crab for a few days is in a sorry plight, quite defenceless, and moving only with difficulty. Gradually, however, the shelly armour hardens, and when its new shell is compared with the discarded one, the crab will be seen to have made a sudden increase in size. Its whole growth, in fact, takes place in the interval between its emergence from the old and the hardening of the new suit. The sexes of Crustacea are distinct; and the young, on hatching from the eggs, are usually unlike their parents.

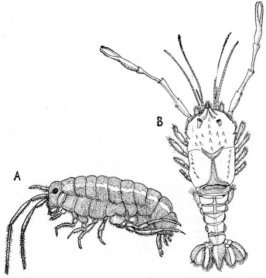

A: SANDHOPPER; *B*: POLYCHELES, A LOBSTER-LIKE DEEP-SEA CRUSTACEAN

Most Crustacea are essentially sea creatures—even the land crabs seek the sea during the breeding season. In size they range from microscopic forms to the giant lobsters and crabs. In habit they are equally varied: some act as natural scavengers, like the sand-hoppers, which help to break down and clear away the masses of sea-weed torn from the rocks and cast up on shore by the waves during heavy gales; a few species spend part of their lives as true parasites, feeding on the tissues of their unfortunate hosts. Vast numbers of small crustaceans which live in the surface-waters of the sea supply the natural food, not only of many kinds of fishes, but also of the largest living mammals, the great whale-bone whales. Crabs, lobsters, shrimps, and prawns provide a popular and valuable food for mankind.

CUCKOO. Members of the Cuckoo family are found in most parts of the world, and are more numerous in tropical than in temperate climates. The tropical varieties are gaudy birds, much larger than the European Cuckoo, with brilliantly coloured plumage. The Plantain Eaters, or Touracos, of the forests of tropical Africa, for example, are sometimes nearly a metre long, and have green and blue plumage, with crests on their heads, and long tails.

The Common Cuckoo is about 30 cm long, with bluish-grey plumage on the upper part of its body, and white plumage with dark bars on the underneath. In flight it rather resembles a hawk—a likeness which apparently deceives small birds, which often mob it as they mob a hawk. It hunts for its food both in the trees and on the ground, at first living principally on beetles, but when caterpillars become plentiful, preferring them, especially the hairy ones. The Cuckoo does not winter in this country, but reaches Britain from Africa about the middle of April, the time of its arrival in different countries being suited to the time of the foster-parents' breeding. Soon the male's familiar 'cuckoo' song, which is delivered with bowing head and fanning tail, is heard incessantly all over the country. The hen's call is a quite different, bubbling sound. The note of the male is heard until the beginning of July, when the adult birds leave to make their way to Africa, the young following two months later.

The female Cuckoo, which is much less numerous than the male and therefore polyandrous

Eric Hosking

YOUNG CUCKOO PUSHING OUT AN EGG FROM A TREE PIPIT'S NEST

Eric Hosking

MEADOW PIPIT FEEDING HER GREEDY FOSTER-CHILD

(mated to several cocks) selects the nest of a bird such as the Meadow Pipit, Wagtail, Hedge Sparrow, Reed Warbler, or Sedge Warbler, and lays one egg in it before the owner of the nest has begun to incubate her own. Each female works a particular territory, confines her attentions to a particular species of foster-parent, and lays eggs of that type only—about twelve to twenty-four in a season. The foster-parent is the more deceived by the fact that the cuckoo egg is very small for the size of the bird, and more or less resembles the eggs of the chosen host. As a rule the Cuckoo removes one of the host's own eggs from the nest and swallows it. She lays her own egg in the nest and leaves it to the care of others. The young Cuckoo is hatched out about the same time as the young of its foster-parents, and when it is only a day or two old, and still blind, unfeathered, and otherwise helpless, it instinctively throws the other nestlings or any remaining eggs out of the nest. It works its way beneath them one at a time until they rest in the small hollow conveniently present in its back; then it climbs backwards up the side of the nest, and heaves them over. In this way the baby Cuckoo secures the whole attention of its foster-parents, who still do not appear to recognize that they are fostering an interloper, and do nothing to rescue the young which the Cuckoo has thrown out. They take such good care of the baby Cuckoo that it soon grows big and fills the nest. It often becomes so large that its foster-parent has to stand upon its back in order to put food in its mouth. In about 3 weeks it is able to fly; but its foster-parents feed it for a further 4 or 5 weeks before it leaves the nest, after which it very soon migrates. As there are no parent birds to show the young Cuckoo where to go, it follows the customary route purely by instinct (see MIGRATION).

The American Cuckoo is not a parasite on other birds, but builds its own nest, rather like that of a crow. In Africa, India, and as far as Australia are found Ground Cuckoos known as Coucals, much larger than the Common Cuckoo, and these, too, rear their own young. In India the Koël lays her eggs in the nests of Crows.

CUCKOO BEE, see BUMBLE BEE; BEES, Section 2.

CUCKOO SPIT, see FROGHOPPER.

CURLEW, see WADING BIRDS, Section 2.

CUTTLEFISH AND SQUID. These belong to the same class (Cephalopoda) of MOLLUSCS as the OCTOPUS (qq.v.), though they differ from it in many ways. Their bodies are longer and more shapely, and the eight arms surrounding the mouth are covered with suckers throughout their entire length, and are much shorter than those of the Octopus. They have also two very long 'tentacles' or arms, which in some species are, when fully extended, quite three times the length of the creature's body. They are always without suckers, except at the club-shaped tips, where there are several suckers on the upper surface. These suckers have short stalks, and are surrounded by a hard, horny ring, the edge of which may be smooth or sharply toothed, making those of the larger species formidable weapons. The two long arms are used for the actual capture of prey; the short arms encircling the mouth hold the victim while it is being devoured. The Cuttlefishes have a flat, oblong shell of a chalky substance, which is

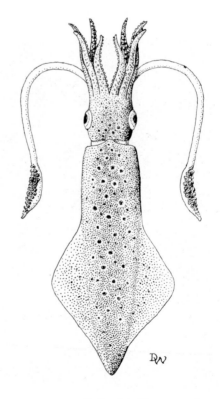

COMMON SQUID (*Loligo forbesii*), *c.* 30 cm long

entirely hidden beneath the skin of the mantle. The Squids have, instead, a slender, horny rod, often called the 'pen', embedded in the back. They are also different in shape, being more slender in build, than the Cuttlefishes.

Both the Cuttlefishes and the Squids lead a much more active life than the Octopus, some species swimming far out in the open sea in large shoals numbering several hundred. They are great hunters, and the American mackerel fisheries are sometimes ruined by them. From the ink-bags of our British Cuttlefishes—for

Zoological Society of London

A CUTTLEFISH STRANDED ON A ROCKY COAST

these creatures, like the Octopus, possess this organ of defence—the best quality of artists' sepia is manufactured.

Largest of all is the Giant Squid, which lives in the North Atlantic, and grows to a total length, including the long tentacles, of over 12 metres —a truly fearsome monster, with its great unwinking eyes, rather torpedo-shaped body, and strong, sucker-clad arms. It provides part of the food of the great toothed whales—and desperate encounters take place between these ocean giants, the whale's skin often being deeply scored by the armoured suckers of the Giant Squid.

See also Vol. VI: OCTOPUS, CUTTLEFISH, and SQUID FISHING.

D

DAB, *see* FLATFISHES.

DABCHICK, *see* GREBE.

DACE, *see* CARP.

DADDY-LONG-LEGS, *see* CRANE-FLY.

DEAD LEAF BUTTERFLY, *see* PROTECTIVE COLORATION, Section 3.

DEATH-WATCH BEETLE. In hard woods, such as oak, small round holes are sometimes found. These are the work of the Death-watch beetle, a mottled insect about 6 millimetres in length. Many ancient roofs have been brought to ruin by this pest—for its work is often unsuspected for many years. The grub continues to burrow into and feed upon the timber for about 3 years, until at last the solid oak may be reduced to a sponge-like condition. The name Death-watch is due to the beetle's habit of making ticking or tapping sounds which, to our superstitious ancestors, foretold a death. This is the beetle's method of communication. While clinging to the surface, the insect strikes its head on the wood several times in quick succession. In the spring, if we tap with the end of a pencil quickly about five or six times in some place where the Death-watch is known to be, a similar sound may be heard in reply from any beetle which happens to be sufficiently near. The beetles have no ears, but they probably feel through their feet the vibrations caused by the tapping.

The very much smaller round exit holes (worm-holes), found in furniture and articles made of deal, pine, or softwood, are the work of the common Furniture-beetle. This insect, which is seldom seen, is a small, brownish creature, covered with greyish hairs. The female lays her eggs in little crevices in the wood, and when the tiny white grub hatches, it immediately burrows inwards, feeding upon the wood for a year or often longer. When fully grown it returns to near the surface and makes a cell, in which it makes its change from grub to beetle. In the spring or early summer, the winged beetle gnaws its way out through the remaining layer of wood. Each little hole shows where a beetle has emerged, and if we can see fresh wood-dust in or near it, we know that other Furniture-beetles are still active inside the wood.

See also BEETLES.
See also Vol. XI: HOUSEHOLD PESTS.

DEEP-SEA FISHES. Sunlight does not penetrate the water-layers of the sea beyond a depth of about 250 fathoms; so in the great ocean abysses (sometimes as much as 8 km deep) the water is very cold and completely dark. At least, there would be complete darkness were it not for the fact that many of the inhabitants of these great depths carry their own lights around with them. These include various soft-bodied animals such as PRAWNS, SQUIDS (qq.v.), and fishes. This article is concerned only with the fishes.

The lamps carried by deep-sea fishes are of several kinds. Often they are arranged in rows along the sides of the fish, each kind having its own distinct number of lights, arranged in a particular way. This helps the fish to recognize another of its own species, so that shoals can keep together, and the male can find his mate. Without these 'recognition lights' they would, of course, be lost in the dark. The lamps are glands in the skin, each having a lens, behind which is a cavity where the actual light is produced; behind that, again, is a bright, silvery reflector; and finally there is a layer of black tissue that prevents any light from being lost to the rear. In fact, it is very much like a pocket-torch, except that the fish's light is produced in a different way. Two sorts of chemicals are poured into the cavity by cells—one a kind of fuel called 'luciferin', and the other an enzyme called 'luciferase' (see FERMENTATION). When the two come together, with a little oxygen from the blood, combustion takes place, and a bright light is obtained. Perhaps the most interesting thing about this light is that it is cold. Practically every sort of light we know is accompanied by heat (as, for instance, the heat of an electric lamp); but the fish's light wastes scarcely any energy on heat, and so is the most efficient light we know—indeed, could we master its secret, it might be very valuable to mankind. Fishes that have this kind of illumination naturally have large eyes, often very large, and so make use of all the light available.

A second kind of lamp is used by the weird-looking deep-sea ANGLER-FISHES (q.v.). Most of these have a sort of lamp-bracket on the nose, which they wave about in the water. Little fishes, attracted by the light, swim towards it. As the bulb is very sensitive, the Angler feels the water movement before the fish can touch the bulb, and so opens its great jaws and engulfs its prey. The Angler-fishes are nearly always black, so that they themselves are invisible; and as they live more by touch than by sight and do not swim in shoals, their eyes are very small. Yet another sort of light is found in certain deep-sea fishes known as Rat-tails. These have a gland under the body that can pour out a luminous slime. If the fish is attacked it puffs out this slime, which mixes with the water and forms a cloud of light. This dazzles the enemy, and so the Rat-tail can escape.

Other oceanic fishes get their light in a very strange way. Certain areas of their skin always contain BACTERIA (q.v.) which live and feed on the fishes' tissues. These bacteria produce substances that glow with a bright light; as fast as they use up the tissues, the fish replaces them by growing some more. It is a sort of mutual-benefit arrangement—the fish feeds the bacteria, and in return they give the fish light. Often these wonderful shining patches are found in front of the eyes, like headlamps;

RAT-TAIL FISH

A. Fraser-Brunner

A luminous 'smoke screen' dazzles its enemy while the Rat-tail makes its escape

but sometimes the whole head is lit up, or even the whole skin.

Deep-sea fishes belong to several different families, having a variety of shapes and habits; but they all have certain things in common. For example, the tissues are always soft and fragile, and the bones are thin and papery. This is believed to be due to the lack of vitamin D, which needs sunshine for its formation; but it is no disadvantage, for it helps the fish to withstand the great pressure of the water at these depths. Again, they all feed on one another; there can be no vegetarians here, for plant life cannot

LUMINOUS DEEP-SEA FISHES

A. Fraser-Brunner

Top centre is an Angler-fish that attracts prey with its luminous lure. On the right is the Gulper-eel, seen before and after swallowing a large fish. Bottom left is the Hatchet-fish, with tubular eyes always looking upward

flourish in the ocean abyss. Some of them can swallow fishes much bigger than themselves, unbelievable as it may seem. They are provided with specially elastic stomachs, and their jaws come apart at the hinges, so increasing the size of their mouths. Food is so hard to find in the darkness that they must make as big a meal as possible when the opportunity occurs. A wonderful example of this is the Gulper, an eel-like fish with a very small head but enormous jaws, and a little light on the end of its tail, perhaps used as a bait, as in the Anglers. Needless to say, nearly all deep-sea fishes have very strong teeth, and in many instances these hinge backwards, so that the prey, so difficult to obtain, may not be allowed to escape. Quite a number of species have tubular, upwardly directed eyes, so that they seem always to be gazing towards the surface.

Much remains to be learnt about the life of the deep sea, for observation is difficult. Very special apparatus is needed to catch specimens at such depths, so that collecting them is very expensive.

See also ANGLER-FISH; BLIND-FISH; LANTERN-FISH.

DEER. 1. This large family, the Cervidae, members of the order Artiodactyla (even-toed hoofed beasts), are RUMINANTS (q.v.) or chewers of the cud, like ANTELOPES, CATTLE, SHEEP, and GOATS (qq.v.). They differ from Antelopes in that instead of horns they possess antlers, which are branching and solid, and are shed and grown afresh every year. Deer are found in almost all parts of Europe, Asia, and America. There were none originally in Australasia, though the Red Deer has been imported, and in New Zealand is now a serious pest. In Africa (the principal home of antelopes) there are no deer south of the Sahara. Deer have cloven hoofs, which make them very sure-footed and able to travel on soft ground. They generally live among trees, and eat shoots and leaves of trees, grass, young heather, moss, and even sea-weed. They produce one, occasionally two, and in a few species three, young at birth. The young are always spotted, but the spots disappear, at any rate in the winter coat, in the adult, except in such species as the Spotted Deer.

The deer's antlers are of solid bone, attached to the skull only at the base. Once a year, about spring, the antlers drop off, but new ones soon sprout. At first they are covered with a substance called 'velvet', made of the skin, hair, and blood-vessels. This remains until the new antlers are fully grown, when it begins to shrivel and peel off—a process which the deer hastens by rubbing them against trees and rocks. The antlers grown by a stag in his first year are very small; but in each successive year they become larger and more branched, until their full development is reached. Some of the small deer have no antlers, but their upper canine teeth grow long and form tusks. In a few species the males have both antlers and tusks. With the exception of the REINDEER (q.v.) the females do not have antlers.

In the courting season, which takes place in the autumn, the stag uses his antlers as duelling weapons. He leaves the sheltered country in which he has been hidden, and roams boldly in the open, calling loudly to the females. Often his call is heard by another stag, who answers it with a bellowing roar of challenge. The two beasts hasten towards each other, and meet with a clash of their antlers. The struggle is furious and may last for hours, neither giving way until loss of blood or exhaustion causes one to collapse. The successful stag then proceeds to form a harem, sometimes collecting as many as a hundred females, sixty being the normal maximum, from whom he fights off any other rivals. But sooner or later, this first master-stag becomes so emaciated and exhausted that he retires before his strongest rival—who then inherits his place and herd. The second master-stag may, in turn, give way to a third. The hinds seem willing to accept whoever proves master.

There are a great many species of deer, varying considerably in size, colouring, and habitat. The Elk or Moose stands about 2 metres high, while the Muntjacs of India, China, and Borneo are only some 46 centimetres high, and the Pudu of South America are even smaller. Some species live in hot, wet climates—such as the Thamin from the swampy country of Burma and Malaya, the Chinese Water Deer from the reeds on the banks of the Yangtze River in China, and the Marsh Deer from the forests of Brazil and Argentina. Other species live in high mountains—such as the Musk Deer (again not true deer) from the Himalayas. Yet others inhabit cold, semi-arctic regions—such as the Caribou of North America and the Reindeer of Siberia, Lapland, and other parts of northern Europe and Asia. Those species which are found in the British Isles are the Red Deer, the Fallow Deer,

RED DEER IN THE HIGHLANDS OF SCOTLAND

John Markham

and the Roe Deer. Fossil remains show that the Elk and Reindeer also once lived in these islands.

2. THE RED DEER, the largest of the British deer, live wild in the Scottish Highlands, on some of the western Scottish Isles, on Exmoor, in Ireland, and in most countries on the Continent. The fully-grown stag stands over a metre high, and has antlers, often up to a metre long, with at least six points or 'tines'. A stag with twelve points is called a 'royal stag'. One stag killed in Transylvania is reported to have had 45 points. In summer the Red Deer has a reddish-brown coat; this changes to brownish-grey in the winter. The fully grown stags remain apart from the herds except during the mating season in the autumn. The stags (whose necks become swollen during these three weeks or so) then fight fiercely among themselves for the hinds, often goring their rivals to death. The white-spotted fawn, born about the end of May or June, is dropped in high heather and is subsequently visited by its mother from time to time. For about a week it is unable to stand, and lies motionless on the ground. It can gallop when it is two months old, but continues to follow its mother about for two years. The hinds can

breed in their third year. Red deer live for about 12 years, although some have been known to live to an age of 20 years. In Scotland they are stalked on foot (*see* DEERSTALKING, Vol. IX), and in Devon and Somerset they are hunted with hounds—when they frequently try to escape by taking to the water (*see* STAG-HUNTING, Vol. IX).

3. THE FALLOW DEER, natives of the Mediterranean countries, were introduced into the parks of Britain and Central Europe many years ago. They stand up to a metre high, and have small heads, large ears, and relatively long tails. Their winter coat is usually fawn or yellowish-brown, with white underparts and a dark line running down the centre of the back; their summer coat is spotted white. Fallow Deer are restless creatures, rising and lying down often during the daytime. Like other deer, they eat grass and weeds, but are especially fond of horse-chestnuts. They soon become friendly and approach man without fear.

4. THE ROE DEER, the smallest of the British deer, being only just over 60 cm high, have reddish coats in the summer, changing in the winter to greyish-brown, with a white patch on the hind quarters. They can run very fast.

Canadian National Film Board

A BULL MOOSE NEAR BANFF IN ALBERTA, CANADA

Typical antlers have three 'tines' or points, and are about 20 cm long. There are many of these deer in parts of Scotland, and they are also found in wooded areas of south and east England; but they are difficult to see, as they are timid and hide in thick cover during the day. In winter they retire into pine forests or the thickest undergrowth. The bucks, when they fight during the mating season, chase the does round and round, until they wear circular tracks in the grass.

5. THE BARKING DEER, which is about the size of a collie dog and came originally from India, has long been maintained by the Dukes of Bedford at Woburn Abbey. Recently, numbers of Barking Deer have escaped, spreading over the neighbouring countryside and doing much damage.

6. THE MOOSE or ELK, of the northerly forests of North America and parts of northern Europe and Asia, is the largest of the deer, standing about 2 metres high. The male has huge, palmated (hand-like) antlers, often with a span of from 1·5 to 2 metres, and is coated with long, coarse hair and a slight mane. Both male and female have swollen muzzles, humped backs, and thick, woolly under-fur in their winter coats. Moose feed mostly on leaves and twigs, but also on lichen, moss, and water-plants. When ruminating, they lie with their tails to windward, relying on their sense of hearing and smell to warn them of danger from that direction, while using their eyes to watch for danger from any other quarter.

In summer, Moose usually live near swamps, rivers, or lakes, and wade deep into the water to eat the water-plants. In the winter they go to higher, thickly forested ground, and stay together in small parties. The adult male sheds his antlers in January, the new ones being fully grown by August. He then comes out of his swampy retreat to fight fiercely, often to death, with his rivals for the females. The fawns (one or two, but occasionally three) are born the following May in any place likely to be free from the attacks of wolves and bears. Moose have a long, swinging trot, faster than the pace of an ordinary horse. The bull's call is either a bellowing roar or a loud, long whistle. This the Indian hunters often imitate in order to draw their quarry within shooting range. Moose flesh is regarded as excellent venison.

Another North American deer, the Wapiti, is over 1·5 m high, and is like a very large Red Deer. In the 19th century they used to roam in herds of many thousands; but now they are quite rare.

See also REINDEER; CHEVROTAIN.
See also Vol. IX: DEERSTALKING.

DESERT PLANTS. Deserts are found along the hot, dry, tropical belts of high pressure near the Equator. Here the vegetation is so scanty, and therefore so much sought after by grazing animals, that only plants which have special protections against their ravages can survive (*see* PLANT DEFENCES). The leaves and branches become modified into spiny structures: in species of the Butcher's Broom and Asparagus, which are common in deserts, the leaves are reduced to mere scales. As the development of water-storage tissue makes both leaves and stems tempting morsels, they are further protected by the development of bitter substances, disagreeable to the taste. The taller plants of desert regions are dependent on underground water, which they reach by their very long tap-roots. In places where the ground-water lies near the surface, such as depressions where a well can give a permanent supply of water, or along the banks of a river, like the Nile or the Euphrates, the vegetation shows the natural fertility of the desert soil. Here palms, especially date-palms, find congenial conditions; and, under their protection, other plants useful to human communities are cultivated.

Desert plants can be divided into two groups. First there are the annual plants, which run through the whole of their life-history very rapidly, though their seeds may remain dormant for years until some moisture reaches them. Then there are perennial plants, which adapt themselves to the peculiar conditions of the desert with its limited water-supply and great heat—the Cactuses (q.v.) being the best-known of these. Contrary to the usual opinion, there is not a month in the year when no plants are in flower in the desert; but the great spectacular show of colour comes in the spring, when the rains cause the small, quickly developing annuals and the bulbous plants to flower.

Of all the peculiar desert plants, one of the most strange is Welwitschia, which is allied to coniferous plants (*see* Conifers), and occurs only in the coastal desert of South-West Africa, especially near Walvis Bay. Welwitschia is a unique plant, and botanists place it in a group of its own. It has a short, thick, woody stem, not rising many centimetres above the rocky ground on which it grows, and narrowing below into a stout tap-root. The plant is said to live for some 2000 years—but all this time, although the

ROSE OF JERICHO
a. In flower; *b.* In fruit

stem grows thicker, it never grows longer. The top of the stem is forked, with a hollow in the centre, and from its edges spring two leathery strap-shaped leaves which continue to grow at their bases while the tips wither: one leaf of nearly 9 metres was found. The leaves are never shed and are longer-lived than those of any other plant. The flowers appear in grooves on the top of the stem, the male or pollen-bearing flowers on one plant, and the female or egg-bearing flowers on another.

In the same desert there is another peculiar plant, the Naras or Desert Melon. Unlike Welwitschia, which clings to the rocky hollows, this is a dune plant of the sand-hills. The Desert Melon obtains its water by means of a long and spreading root-system, sometimes stretching as far as 12 metres. The plant is a woody shrub, not more than 1·5 metres high, with green, well-protected branches, rudimentary leaves, and strong thorns. It produces rounded, grape-like 'Melons', which are greatly relished by the natives—and also by the jackals, which are mainly responsible for spreading the seeds.

Another peculiar desert plant is the Rose of Jericho, quite common in Palestine. The fruits mature as the dry season comes on, the leaves drop off, and the dry branches curl inwards to form a ball of tangled stems like wickerwork, protecting the pods. The ball remains in this position during the dry season until the rains come again, when it uncurls, allowing the seeds to escape. They are then washed away by the quickly flowing rivulets. But the plant has little hold on the sandy soil and is often detached by high winds and rolled away in its 'balled-up' form over the dry surface. If it reaches a moistened spot the branches uncurl and the liberated seeds have a chance to germinate.

See also Deserts, Vol. III.

DEVIL FISH, *see* Sharks and Rays.

DINGO, *see* Dog.

DIPPER (Water-Ouzel). This rather dumpy little bird, some 18 cm long, has a conspicuous white chest, and elsewhere dark plumage of chestnut-brown, with slaty-brown back, wings, and tail. It is a remarkable example of a Passerine or perching bird which has taken largely to an aquatic life. The Dipper is well known to those who frequent the hilly country of north or west Britain and is nearly always to be seen, for instance, on Highland burns or Yorkshire becks. It flits from stone to stone in a jerky manner, or stands on a rock in mid-stream, bobbing its body up and down. It does not swim at all, but sinks down under the water and walks on the stones and gravel at the bottom of the stream, hunting for food. How so light a body succeeds in keeping itself under water is difficult to understand. On coming to the surface again, it shakes the water out of its wings and is soon dry. (Another perching bird with the same habit is the Water Thrush of America.)

The Dipper nearly always builds a nest close to fast-flowing water—on a moss-grown bank just above the water, among the exposed roots of trees, under a bridge, or even on a rocky ledge under a waterfall. The covered nest is beautifully made of moss and grass, and has the entrance at the side. There are four or five white eggs, and two or three broods are reared in the same year. The bird generally returns to the same site the following year.

DIVER. Perhaps the most primitive group of birds, these belong to the order Gaviiformes. There are four species: the Red-throated Diver,

most common on British coasts, breeding on the banks of Scottish lochs and inland waters; the Black-throated Diver, a larger bird, which also breeds in small numbers in the Scottish Highlands; the Great Northern Diver (or Loon), which frequently visits British coasts in the winter, but nests in Iceland, Greenland, and also Canada; and the White-billed Northern Diver, which rarely comes to Britain. These are large birds, the Great Northern Diver being more than 76 cm long, with a strong, sharply pointed bill and long, narrow head.

Divers are generally placed rather low in the scale of bird evolution, for they are much better adapted for life in the water than in the air or on land. Some primitive fossil birds resemble Divers quite closely. They are strong fliers, but clumsy in rising and alighting and in changing direction. On land they are very awkward. In the water, however, their rather streamlined bodies cleave the water easily, and their powerfull webbed feet make them strong and agile swimmers. They feed upon fish, diving after them and capturing them by chasing and catching them below the surface. Except during the breeding season they spend much of their time out at sea, but they return to freshwater lochs

J. E. Ruxton

A PAIR OF BLACK-THROATED DIVERS

and lakes to nest. The nest is merely a heap of weeds a metre or so from the water's edge. Two eggs are laid, a rich greenish-brown, spotted and blotched, and the young take almost at once to the water. (*See* picture p. 44.)

DODO, *see* PIGEON.

DOG. Under this title are included all the animals known as WOLVES, JACKALS, FOXES (qq.v.), wild dogs, and, of course, all the domesticated breeds. It is not known for certain from which of the wild breeds the domesticated dog is descended, though it probably comes from the species *Canis lupus* (*see* DOGS, Vol. IX).

The dogs are a very distinct group of animals (the Canidae). Among their points of structural similarity, all but certain specially bred domestic dogs have long, pointed muzzles, fairly long tails, and erect, pointed ears; and all but the African Hunting Dog have five toes on their forefeet and four toes on their hindfeet. They are more widely distributed over the world than any other flesh-eating mammal: some endure the Arctic cold and live mainly on fish; others live in Africa and India. Nearly all wild dogs hunt in large packs, following their prey chiefly by scent. They make their lairs in burrows, in the clefts of rocks, in caverns, or in hollow trees. Some dig their own burrows, while others seize holes deserted by other animals; some dig solitary burrows, others dig a number close together, forming a warren. The number of young in a litter varies from three to as many as a dozen, and the pups are believed always to be born blind.

The Dingo, the wild dog of Australia, is about as large as an Airedale Terrier, tawny, with erect, pointed ears, and a white tip to its rather bushy tail. It is not, however, thought to be a native of Australia, but may have been introduced by the aborigines from Asia. When the European settlers came it was to be found throughout the whole country; but today, although there are still many Dingoes in the backwoods, their numbers have been greatly reduced. They are so destructive to sheep and poultry, killing far more than they can eat, that the Government offered a reward of 25p for each Dingo scalp. Large numbers are seldom found together, parties of a mother and her cubs being the most common. Each family is said to have a strictly defined territory, beyond which its members never venture and into which other families will

AN AUSTRALIAN DINGO   *Paul Popper*

not intrude (*see* ANIMAL TERRITORY). The young, usually from six to eight, are often born in the hollow of a tree-trunk.

The wild dogs of India and southern and central Asia, called Dholes, are pretty, fox-like animals with reddish coats. They hunt in packs at night, their prey being any animals up to the size of a deer. They run in a long, lobbing canter.

The African Hunting Dogs of South and East Africa look rather like hyaenas, for they are marked in patches of yellow, black, and white. They are about the size of small wolves, and have large ears and bushy tails. They kill cattle, sheep, and wild animals up to the size of large antelopes, but they rarely attack man.

The South American wild dogs, called Bush Dogs, have long, dark-brown bodies, with short legs and ears, and grey necks and heads. Little is known about their life, as they are very scarce and keep hidden during the day. They eat any small animals.

See also Vol. VI: DOGS, WORKING.
See also Vol. IX: DOGS.

DOG-FISH, *see* SHARKS AND RAYS.

DOLPHIN, *see* WHALE.

DONKEY, *see* ASS.

DORMOUSE. This small RODENT (q.v.) is closely related to the MOUSE (q.v.), and is distributed over most of Europe, Asia, and Africa.

A. R. Thompson

A COMMON DORMOUSE ON A WILD ROSE STEM

The Common Dormouse, famous for its drowsiness and long winter sleep, is about the size of a mouse, and has a tawny coat and very striking, large, black eyes. It lives in trees, and sleeps during the day, only coming out at night, when it moves about with great agility. Like the squirrel, it sits up to eat, holding its food between the forepaws. It eats hard nuts, acorns, corn, haws and other wild berries, insects and grubs, and probably small birds and eggs. During the summer it puts on fat, which is used up in its winter sleep (*see* HIBERNATION).

Dormice hibernate from mid-October to mid-April, curled up in a ball, sleeping so soundly and becoming so cold and rigid that they can be rolled on a table without waking. On warm winter days, however, they will wake and eat from the large stores of food they have laid up, before settling down again. They usually build their winter nests underground, but sometimes they use birds' nests. In the spring they build, for their day-time rest, small nests near the ground in a thicket or hedgerow, and larger nests for breeding. The nests are built of grass, moss, and strips of honeysuckle bark, and are lined and covered with leaves. There is a litter of two to four young ones in June. Sometimes the young are born in the autumn, but these

probably do not survive the winter. They are born blind and naked, but quickly develop, growing a first coat of grey, which does not change to tawny until they are 18 months old.

The Grey or Fat Dormouse, also known as the Edible Dormouse, is larger than the Common Dormouse. It was introduced from the Continent to Hertfordshire and Buckinghamshire, where it is now quite common.

DRAGONFLY. The brilliance of the Dragonflies' colouring and the beauty of the compound eyes of the larger species are unequalled in any other insects. Their colours fade, however, very rapidly after death, except in the case of metallic blue or green. In the sexes, the colours are sometimes so unlike that the female may appear to belong to a different species from the male.

There are three types of Dragonfly: the large species, which are very rapid in flight and have slender bodies and big eyes meeting at the back of the head; those that are somewhat smaller, with shorter and flatter bodies, but equally fast on the wing; and others, often called Demoiselles, or sometimes Damsel-flies, which flutter in a weak, delicate manner along the banks of streams and rivers. These are usually much smaller, and have very slender bodies and eyes wide apart. Most are pale blue; but two belonging to this type have brilliant metallic blue or green bodies and wings with similar colourings.

Most people know our larger Dragonflies by sight, and often compare them to miniature aeroplanes. They are often thought to be dangerous, and the name of 'Horse-stingers' is common in many places; but Dragonflies sting neither horses nor anything else, and are, in fact, quite harmless. They feed on other insects, and our larger species will kill wasps and other insects of powerful flight like the Red Admiral Butterfly. They catch their prey in the air, and neatly strip off its wings before eating its body.

The early life of a Dragonfly is spent in the water. Some Dragonflies skim over the surface and dip the tip of the abdomen below it at frequent intervals, dropping eggs at random. Others settle upon a water-plant and puncture the submerged stems, inserting an egg into each puncture. With some species, the male is in constant attendance upon the female, gripping her round the neck by the end of his abdomen, so that the pair fly 'tandem-wise'. The eggs may be dropped while they hover in this way over the water, or placed in the tissues of a water-plant while both are resting upon it, the female below with the tip of her abdomen submerged. On such occasions the colour differences between the sexes of certain species may be easily seen.

The young Dragonfly, which is called a nymph or naiad, eats different food at different ages, but is always carnivorous. It captures its food by means of an organ (called the mask, because it more or less covers the face when not in use) which has much the same movement as the human arm and forearm. In its resting position it is bent double at what corresponds to the elbow, and held between the limbs. It is broadest in front, where there are two movable hooks. When attracted to a prey, the nymph shoots out the whole organ, grips its victim, and brings it back to the mouth to be eaten. As the nymph grows, the rudimentary wings increase in size after each casting of the skin; and at about the time of change into the adult, they stand out a little from the body. The large compound eyes, hitherto dull, may now begin to gleam. Up to this stage, breathing has been carried out by means of gills—three flat gill plates at the end of the body in the smaller species, and in the larger species, internal gills. But the gills now stop working, and the nymph breathes through its 'spiracles', or breathing-holes, holding fast to some support, such as a water-plant, with the front of its body out of the water. After resting this way for a time the nymph suddenly moves forward right out of the water—some go only 10 cm or so, while others will travel some distance up a tree-trunk. The insect then remains fixed, until the nymphal skin splits along the back of the thorax. The head and thorax, legs and wings, are withdrawn from the skin, but the lower part of the abdomen remains inside. The body falls back and hangs down until the legs are strong enough to grip. A sudden movement then brings the body back again, the legs seizing either the empty skin or the support beyond it. The abdomen is now completely withdrawn, growing longer and narrower until it reaches its adult length (which is often much greater than that of the nymphal case from which it was withdrawn); the wings, which were quite small when first freed, expand to their full size. The Dragonfly is at first pale, and does not attain its full beauty until it has been on the wing for some time. The females

S. Beaufoy

ADULT DRAGONFLY (⅔ natural size)

of many of the larger kinds forsake the water, except for mating or egg-laying, and frequent woodlands, where they may be found during hot sunshine, hawking to and fro, often for long periods without a rest.

Dragonflies are among the oldest winged insects. *Meganeura*, found as a FOSSIL (q.v. Vol. III) in the coal measures, had a wing expanse of over 60 centimetres and was the largest insect that has ever existed. Damsel-flies often rest with their wings held over their backs, though most Dragonflies usually rest with wings spread out.

See also INSECTS.

DRINKER MOTH, *see* LACKEY MOTHS.

DROMEDARY, *see* CAMEL.

DRONGO. The King Crow, or Indian Black Drongo, is one of the most common birds in India, both in the hills and the plains. It is frequently to be seen perching on bare branches or telegraph-wires, and making quick, darting flights to catch insects. It has deep black plumage with a steel-blue gloss, and is about 28 centimetres in length, with a short bill and a forked tail. Other members of the family are to be found from Afghanistan to China, in Africa, and one species in Australia. The Racket-tailed

Drongo, which lives in the forests of India, has a fine crest on its head, and the outer two tail-feathers are long and wire-like, ending in large racket-shaped plumes. All Drongos eat insects only and have a fine song.

DUCKS. 1. The Ducks, with the SWANS and GEESE (qq.v.), form the family Anatidae—web-footed birds of fresh or salt-water, found throughout the world. Although we commonly divide the family into these three groups, it is not always easy to say what is a duck and what a goose. Most of the family are omnivorous, eating grass, grain, insects, and grubs; but one group, the Mergansers, live entirely on fish, while the geese eat mainly grass. Some feed on land, like the Geese; others on the surface of the water or by up-ending, like the Swans; others again by diving. Ducks are found all over the world, but are more numerous in the colder regions of the northern hemisphere. Those of the northern hemisphere migrate, often very great distances, but those of the tropics make much shorter or no MIGRATIONS (q.v.).

In most of the ducks of the northern hemisphere the sexes have very different plumage, the drakes being much more brightly coloured, and also sometimes larger, than the ducks. But soon after the breeding season the drakes put on a dull-coloured 'eclipse' plumage, closely resembling that of the females, and do not regain their full plumage until early autumn. This strange fact is explained by the way ducks moult: they lose all their quills at the same time, and until a new lot has grown are unable to fly. They would, therefore, be easily caught by their enemies until the wing feathers grow again, if they did not assume a protective inconspicuous dress. In the Sheldrakes and many of the tropical species both sexes are alike and do not have this habit.

All the ducks have much the same courtship behaviour. The drakes woo the ducks by bobbing around them in the water, flirting their tails, raising and dipping their necks, and showing off their breasts. The Sheldrake leads off his mate to the nest, talking to her softly. Teals pretend to fight, and shoot through the water, showing off in front of the ducks. Ducks make simple nests, generally near water, though some nest in holes in the ground or in trees, often at some distance from the water. They line them with down plucked from their breasts. The Tree-ducks of the tropical and sub-tropical world often nest in the fork of a large branch, and sometimes make use of a discarded crow's nest. Ten or twelve eggs are usually laid, and the ducklings, which are covered with down at hatching, are able to walk and swim as soon as they are dry.

2. The Duck family falls into two separate groups: the Surface-feeding Ducks and the Diving Ducks, including the Mergansers or Saw-billed Ducks. All Surface-feeding species have a patch of colour on the wings, known as the 'speculum', and this is often the same in the two sexes. These patterns are useful in identifying the species. Of the Surface-feeding Ducks, the best known is the Mallard, or Wild Duck, which is found in the northern hemisphere from America to Siberia, wintering as far south as Panama and India. It is the most numerous of all the ducks, and is the bird from which the many domestic kinds are derived (*see* DUCKS, Vol. VI). The handsome Sheldrake is found on the coasts, especially the sandy coasts of all temperate regions of the Old World (there is none in the Americas). One species is a resident of the British Isles. It nests in a burrow, often a rabbit-hole, making its nest sometimes 3 or 4 metres from the entrance. The Teal, another common species, is the smallest of the British ducks, about 37 centimetres long. It is found throughout Europe and Asia, and a very similar

G. K. Yeates

TUFTED DUCK

RED-BREASTED MERGANSER

EIDER DUCK NESTING

species inhabits America. Its flight is full of sudden twists and turns and is very rapid, though not so rapid as that of the Garganey, sometimes called the Summer Teal. The Wigeon breeds in the north, but visits British shores in thousands in the winter, when it can be recognized by its swift flight and high-pitched, whistling cry. Less common, but similar in distribution, is the very handsome Pintail, with its long, pointed tail and rapid flight; and the dull-coloured Gadwall may be seen at all times of the year in East Anglia and occasionally elsewhere. The Shoveler is easily recognized by the broad, ungainly bill, serrated along the edges, with which it sifts small animals from the surface of the water, in much the same way as the Baleen Whales. It is spread over the whole northern hemisphere, nesting principally within the Arctic Circle, and wintering farther south. There is also a species in South America, one in Africa, and two in Australia.

3. The Diving Ducks usually have shorter bodies and legs than the Surface-feeding Ducks, and spend almost all their time in the water. The Pochard and Tufted Duck have both increased considerably as breeding species in

Britain within the last 50 years. Larger than either of these is the Golden-eye (48 cm long), which breeds in northern Europe and visits Britain in the winter; its relative the Buffle-headed Duck of America, has occasionally strayed across the Atlantic. Many of the Diving Ducks, including the Eider, are birds of the sea-coasts. The Eider, which lives on northern coasts of Europe, including Britain, and America, is well known for the beautifully warm and elastic down which the female plucks from her breast to line her nest. In Scandinavia and Iceland, the down is carefully collected, but the birds are very strictly protected by law. The Eider Ducks become as tame as domestic ducks, and show no objection to a portion of their down being taken when they are incubating, and the rest when the ducklings are hatched. The Black Scoters are sea birds, and very gregarious, except during the nesting season. They nest far north, and in September and October migrate south-wards, often appearing on British coasts in huge black flocks. The Common Scoter (length 51 cm) breeds in small numbers in Scotland; while the Velvet Scoter, a larger bird with a white patch on its wings and head, is a visitor

Paul Popper

A GOOSANDER

from the north. An American species, the Surf Scoter, has been met with off the British coasts on a few occasions. The Scaup, not unlike the Tufted Duck, breeds in some of the Scottish islands, but is mainly a winter visitor; and the extremely handsome and graceful Long-tailed Duck is only a winter visitor.

The Mergansers or Saw-bills are a small group of Diving Ducks distinguished by the very narrow beak with a hook at the end, and by the serrations on the bill which enable them to hold fish. Two species, the Goosander and the Red-breasted Merganser, breed in Scotland; in winter, the Merganser is more often seen on salt-water, and the Goosander on fresh-water lakes and reservoirs. The small Smew is a bird of northern Europe which visits this country in small numbers in winter. Another member of this group, the Hooded Merganser, with its remarkable crest of stiff, hairlike feathers, white edged with black, has occasionally crossed the Atlantic from its native America.

DUKE OF BURGUNDY FRITILLARY. Despite the name, this small speckled brown and black butterfly is not a Fritillary, but is the only European representative of the family Riodinidae, chiefly found in South America. It looks, however, rather like a Fritillary, and so the name has stuck. The hairy caterpillars, which feed on primrose or cowslip leaves, hide during the day and only come up to feed after dark. The chrysalis is unlike that of any other butterfly, being hairy all over. It remains in this stage the whole of the winter, the butterfly emerging in May. In the British Isles it is occasionally found in clearings in woods, or on rough, uncultivated pastures where primroses grow. It rarely visits flowers, but frequently rests, after short, rapid flights, on twigs or leaves a metre or so from the ground.

DUNLIN, *see* WADING BIRDS, Section 3.

E

EAGLE. This great bird of prey belongs to the same family as the FALCON, HAWK, BUZZARD, and VULTURE (qq.v.). There are a great many different species to be found in all parts of the world. They vary in size from the Bateleur Eagle of central and southern Africa, the male of which is only 53 cm long, to the magnificent Steller's Sea Eagle of eastern Siberia, north China, and Japan, which is about a metre long. The female is generally larger than the male. The True Eagles, to which group the Golden Eagle belongs, feed on game-birds such as grouse, hares, rabbits, small mammals, and carrion, and will also attack a sickly lamb. Sea-Eagles eat fish and water-fowl also. The Buzzard-eagles and Serpent Eagles of south-east Asia feed mainly on snakes and other reptiles. The handsome Monkey-eating Eagle of the Philippines is said to live principally on the Macaque monkeys. Most Eagles, especially the magnificent Golden Eagle, contrary to the general idea, are not bold or courageous, and are often driven off their food by smaller birds or animals. A Golden Eagle has been observed to be attacked and routed by a pair of Skua Gulls. They are cowardly even in defence of their nest, and will fairly readily desert it if disturbed. They are rather lethargic birds, appearing to prefer a meal of carrion which can be obtained without effort, to making their own kill. Their flight, too, though very powerful, is generally slow, and includes much sailing and circling. The Golden Eagle is, however, capable on occasions of a faster flight than any other bird (*see* FLIGHT).

Eagles usually build their eyries or nests on

The late Arthur Brook

A GOLDEN EAGLE FEEDING HER YOUNG ON GROUSE, IN HER EYRIE ON A CRAGGY LEDGE

rocky crags or on tree-tops, though sometimes they build in low growing trees or even on the ground. They generally return each year to the same eyrie, and build on to the old nest. A White-tailed Sea Eagle, for instance, has been known to use the same nest for 20 successive years, building on to it each year until it became a very large construction, as much as 2 metres in diameter and rather less high. A Golden Eagle's nest in Colorado grew to 2 metres high. Golden Eagles as a rule nest in two places, returning to each eyrie every alternate year. Generally two eggs are laid—large, dull white, and thinly speckled with irregular markings. The parents go on feeding their young for some five months after incubation.

Two species, the Golden Eagle and the White-tailed Sea Eagle, used to breed regularly in several places in the British Isles; but they were destroyed, largely by the use of poisoned meat, because of their attacks on game birds. Now, the Golden Eagle nests in some places in the Scottish Highlands, and probably a few in the more remote mountains of Ireland, while the Sea Eagle is only an occasional visitor. They are both very fine-looking birds, with strong wings reaching nearly to the end of their tails, strong curved claws, and straight beaks ending in a deep hook. The Golden Eagle, of which the female is almost a metre long (the American species being just over a metre), is a tawny golden-brown, shading to nearly black, and has feathered legs. The Sea Eagle has a greyer head, white tail-feathers, and legs of which only the upper part is feathered. It has a loud, shrill, yelping cry.

Of the many other species, one of the most spectacular is the great Harpy Eagle of the forests of Central and South America, called by the Aztecs the 'winged wolf'. This bird will attack and kill animals much larger than itself, and can often be seen wheeling in circles high up over the forest. The much smaller African Bateleur Eagle is very different in appearance. It has a handsome maroon, black, and grey plumage, with short tail and wings, and voluminous crest. It prefers open mountainous country, and is quite common in some parts.

EARWIG. This is one of the comparatively few insects that give maternal care to their eggs and young. In the spring, having laid her eggs in a hollow in the ground, the female European

Earwig rests over them and guards the young Earwigs when they hatch out several weeks later until they are large enough to fend for themselves. Young Earwigs resemble their parents in shape, and moult four times before they become adult. Earwigs mate in the autumn before hibernating, and die in the following summer. They eat plant food, often damaging cultivated plants, but they also eat insects, and occasionally serve a useful purpose in devouring insect pests.

The 1100 species of Earwigs belong to the small Order Dermaptera. Some species are

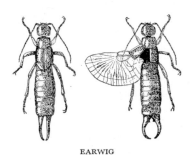

EARWIG

Left: Female; *Right*: Male

wingless; but in others the short fore-wings are hard, while the semi-circular hind-wings are large, transparent, and veined. The Lesser Earwig often flies during the day, but other species are rarely seen on the wing. All species have forceps at the end of the body, which they have been seen to use for holding their prey and for folding their hind-wings. Their true function, however, is probably defensive, for Earwigs open their forceps when they are alarmed. The females have smaller and straighter forceps than the males. Some tropical species have particularly large and curiously shaped forceps.

Earwigs are easily carried about the world in food and other goods, and often establish themselves in new countries for short periods. A few species have become world-wide; those that originated in the tropics frequent bakehouses and other warm places in cooler countries. A few species, mainly from Java and Sarawak, are external parasites of bats; another species, from Sierra Leone, lives on rats. These Earwigs are wingless, and they possess either very small, weak eyes or no eyes at all.

It is a myth that crawling into ears is a normal habit of earwigs.

See also Vol. VI: Insect Pests.

John Warham

COMMON ECHIDNA

ECHIDNA. The Spiny or Porcupine Ant-eaters, as the Echidnas are often called, together with the Duck-billed PLATYPUS (q.v.), constitute the order Monotremata, being the only mammals which lay eggs. They live in rocky districts in Australasia, subsisting almost entirely on ants. They are from 45 to 60 centimetres or more in length, and have thick spines covering their bodies, short, round heads, small, toothless mouths, and long, slender beaks for snouts. They also have the long, worm-like tongue typical of all ant-eaters. On their short, sturdy legs they have strong claws, which they use for digging and for tearing open ants' nests. During the breeding-season—usually in May, which is at the beginning of the Australian winter—the female develops a rudimentary pouch on the underside of her body, in which the single egg is incubated. The young Echidna, about 1·5 cm long, remains in the pouch and is nourished with milk which the mother ejects through pores in her skin into a hollow in her abdomen, for she has no teats. She removes her offspring from her pouch when it has grown to a certain size, but it returns to the pouch from time to time for suckling, until its spines are sprouting.

There are two species of Echidnas. The Common or Five-toed Echidna lives in Australia, Tasmania, and Papua—the Tasmanian Echidna being the largest, and exceptional because its spines are completely hidden by its fur. The Three-toed or New Guinea Echidna, found in the north-west of New Guinea, has fur almost completely concealing the spines. It is the larger of the two species, measuring 60 cm or more in length, and has fewer and shorter spines.

ECOLOGY OF PLANTS. 1. This is concerned with the study of plants in relation to their natural surroundings. Certain plants, for instance, will grow only in woods, others in marshes, and others on sand-dunes. The seed of a wild plant has no choice in the place where it settles. If it is fortunate in arriving at a suitable spot, the plant becomes established; if, on the other hand, the plant finds itself in an unfavourable place, it either perishes or develops poorly. On a sand-dune we find those plants which are adapted to grow in a shifting environment with little water; we do not expect to find these plants in marshes. In the same way we search for bluebells not on moorlands but in oak-woods. For in the course of time plants have developed special characteristics which fit them to live in some habitats, but not in others.

With cultivated plants it is possible, up to a point, to provide artificially the conditions in which the plants may flourish out of their natural homes. In the greenhouse it is possible to regulate the temperature of the atmosphere, and even to control the temperature of the soil. Thus, by controlling conditions, man has been able to make plants grow in places which would otherwise be unsuitable to them. In nature plants have become adapted to particular types of environment. In some this is so marked that it is possible to tell by looking at them the kind of habitat from which they have come. Ecology, then, is the study of plants in their natural communities, how they are affected by one another or by animal neighbours, the succession of plants according to the seasons, and so on.

2. PLANT ASSOCIATIONS. A good method of studying colonization by plants is to watch the gradual invasion of a newly exposed piece of soil. A great deal of information can be obtained by watching the newly made banks of roads and waste ground. Records should be kept over several seasons of the type of plant, the time that it arrives, the percentage of different plants, and similar facts. The first arrivals are plants which develop quickly from spores and not from seeds. These will include FUNGI, MOSSES AND LIVERWORTS, and FERNS (qq.v.). Spores, being microscopic in size, are easily carried in the air, and are always present in millions in the atmosphere. These are followed by the short-lived and annual flowering-plants which are common in the neighbourhood. And so a community of plants begins to be built up. Since the land we are observing has no established perennial plants, it is still open to new-

John Markham

A BOMBED SITE NEAR ST. PAUL'S, LONDON

The Ragwort (*Senicio squalidus*) and Rose-bay Willow Herb are quickly taking possession, springing up wherever any soil is to be found

comers, and is called an 'open community'. Then come the hardy perennials, such as grasses, thistles, plantains, and dandelions. Competition between the plants is keen: the community is in danger of becoming overcrowded, and survival goes only to the fittest. The weaker plants are choked out and die, and the hardier ones become more firmly established. Finally, only those plants which are most suited to that soil and climate remain; and the community is then said to be closed. Such a community of plants, living in harmony with each other, allowing only those new-comers which can compete with them to remain, and choking out any new-comers that are unsuited, is called a 'plant association'.

The struggle is not only for a place in the sun: there is also competition among the roots for a place in the soil. Root competition is chiefly due to the search for an adequate water-supply —and the depth to which some roots go shows the keenness of the competition.

The study of ecology need not be confined to natural vegetation. Slum-clearance areas, coal-tips, and lawns are also excellent places for observation. The effects of lime can be studied by watching the growth of plants under the lines of a marked football or hockey pitch. During the Second World War the colonization of bombed areas by such plants as the London Rocket and the Rose-bay Willow Herb was a constant source of wonder because of the rapidity with which they appeared and spread. The natural succession of plant communities was well illustrated after the eruption of the island KRAKATAU (q.v. Vol. III) in the Dutch East Indies in 1883. This tropical island was split in half, and one half disappeared into the sea, causing a gigantic tidal wave which swamped the rest and drowned 30,000 people. Practically all the plant life of the island was destroyed by hot volcanic material. Within 20 years, however, through seeds borne by wind and sea, the land had recovered, and the former tropical vegetation was practically restored.

3. DOMINANT PLANTS. No plant association is absolutely stable, since, when it appears to be settled, influences like disease epidemics, harmful animals, or the needs of man will come along and upset it. It also often happens that one or more plants tend to dominate the association. These are called the 'dominant plants'. In beech-woods, for instance, the dense foliage of

the dominant Beech lets through little light; therefore few light-loving herbs can belong to an association in which the Beech is the dominant plant. In some communities the plants are complementary to one another, each taking something different from the soil or occupying different levels in the soil and atmosphere. Thus, in an oak-wood the trees are tall and the roots go deep. The floor or carpet plants, such as Primroses and Ferns, are low-growing plants, with roots near the surface. Between these two there are shrubs, like the Hazel, which have shoots and roots between those of the tree and floor plants. This kind of complementary arrangement allows an abundant and mixed vegetation.

The study of plants in their natural surroundings is proving to be of great practical value in the planting up of newly developed areas. Fresh information about the most suitable plants for arable and grazing land is being obtained, and the ecologist is also providing the scientific knowledge to combat the grave problem of SOIL EROSION (q.v. Vol. III), which exists in so many countries. Among the more interesting plant communities found in Great Britain are those of WOODLANDS, HEATHS AND MOORLANDS, GRASSLANDS, HEDGEROWS, WATERPLANTS, and SEASHORE PLANTS (qq.v.).

EDELWEISS, see ALPINE PLANTS.

EELS. Despite their snake-like appearance, Eels are true bony FISHES (q.v.), differing from most others in that their scales are much reduced and buried in the skin and their paired fins are often much smaller. Because of their long bodies, Eels do not need a caudal fin to act as a lever; this fin, therefore, is either much smaller or else entirely absent. Like most fishes Eels swim by means of undulating S-shaped movements from side to side, but these movements are more pronounced than in typical fishes, and their longer dorsal and anal fins give Eels greater speed. Because of their shape Eels are suited to seeking their food and hiding from their enemies in soft mud, amongst plants, and in narrow crevices inaccessible to other fishes.

Most Eels live all their life in the sea, but a few, the Freshwater Eels, inhabit ponds or rivers, often very far from the sea. It is only in the last 40 years that the wonderful life-story of the European Freshwater Eels has been

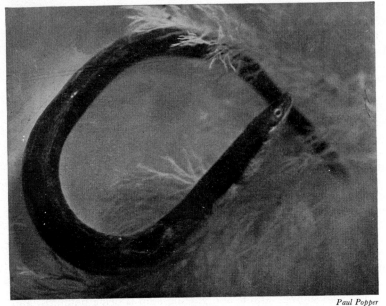

Paul Popper

A COMMON EEL

Stream. These larvae are tiny, transparent, leaf-shaped creatures with small heads and sharp needle-like teeth, with which they catch minute organisms for food. It is not surprising that, when they were first discovered, they were not recognized as Eels at all. For about $2\frac{1}{2}$ years they drift slowly with the current towards the European coasts, growing all the time, so that when they reach their destination they are nearly 8 cm long. They are now recognizable as miniature Eels, though they are still transparent; at this stage they are called Elvers, or Glass-eels.

completely known. The early naturalists were puzzled because, although fully grown Eels were to be found in fresh waters all the year round, no one ever found any eggs or young ones (larvae)—and some very queer guesses were made to account for this. But, as so often happens, the facts were stranger than the fictions. While living in fresh water, the Eels are of a dull yellowish colour, and have rather small eyes; the females grow to a much larger size than the males. When at least 8 years of age a remarkable change comes over some of these 'yellow eels': the eyes grow much larger, the snout more pointed, and the sides become silvery instead of dull yellowish—in fact, there is such a difference that at one time these 'silver eels' were thought to be a different species from the yellow. The Eels now make their way down to the sea. As they are often in small isolated ponds they have to journey overland to the nearest river, usually by wriggling through damp grass. They do not breed as soon as they get to the sea, but instead, they begin a long journey, sometimes as much as 6,400 km, to a small area in the western Atlantic, which is their breeding-ground. Here, in the deep sea, they lay their eggs and then die.

The eggs float for a while, and the young, when they hatch out in the spring, live near the surface, drifting north-eastwards with the Gulf

They now assemble in large numbers and swarm up the rivers. They reach distant ponds and marshes by wriggling through damp grass, just as their parents did on their way down to the sea. These invasions by untold millions of Elvers are known as 'Eel-fares', and have been noticed from the earliest times. It is only recently, however, that we have learnt that these Elvers are the young of parents which migrated out to sea at least 4 years earlier, and that they in their turn will undertake the return journey.

A closely allied American Freshwater Eel breeds in much the same area of sea as the European species. The larvae of both can be found together, but they never get mixed. The American species develops much more quickly, taking only a year to become an Elver; so if these moved towards Europe they would develop too quickly and die in the salt water. If the larvae of the European Eel reached America, they would either be washed up on the shore or be killed on entering fresh water. Probably some larvae do go the wrong way, but as they would not normally survive, the two species do not mix.

Something similar seems to happen in the Pacific Ocean, where there are other Freshwater Eels, but these have not yet been studied so completely.

The first leaf-like larva to be recognized as a

young Eel was that of the Conger Eel, a much larger species, that does not enter fresh water, though it may be found at river mouths. It usually lurks among rocks, or between the piles of piers, ready to dart out at likely food. When caught on hook and line, it often attacks the fisherman, like a dog, with its many strong, sharp teeth. Females grow to a length of nearly 2 metres and a weight of about 27 kg, males being much smaller. This species breeds far out at sea, but does not make such a remarkable journey as the Freshwater Eel.

Numerous kinds of Eels are found throughout the seas, some very small and wormlike, others large and fierce. The Morays are large Eels of which many elaborately coloured varieties are found in the warmer waters. They lurk among rocks or coral, and dart out to attack any suitable prey.

The snake-like appearance of Eels serves one of the tropical species in good stead. This fish, an inhabitant of the coral reefs of the East Indies, has alternate stripes of black and yellow, which give it a striking resemblance to a very poisonous sea-snake that lives in the same region. This resemblance is a protection to the Eel, for its would-be enemies doubtless mistake it for the snake (*see* PROTECTIVE COLORATION).

Perhaps the strangest Eels are those called Snipe-eels, which are found in the open ocean. Their jaws are long and slender, and curved away from each other so that it would appear that they cannot be brought together, even though they are armed with many small teeth. Yet one of these fishes has been taken with a large prawn in its stomach. Snipe-eels are exceedingly long and thin, with delicate fins, and sometimes with a sort of whip-lash on the end of the tail. They may be found swimming, with swift undulations, close to the surface of the sea, though they seem to be equally at home in the great depths.

See also Vol. VI: EEL FISHING.

EGG, *see* REPRODUCTION IN ANIMALS.

EGGAR MOTH, *see* LACKEY MOTHS.

EGRET, *see* HERON.

EIDER DUCK, *see* DUCKS, Section 3.

ELAND, *see* ANTELOPE, Section 4.

ELECTRIC FISHES. The idea of a fish being able to generate electricity strong enough to light small bulbs, or even to run an electric motor, is almost unbelievable. But several kinds of fishes are able to do this, and, curiously enough, they are not even very closely related. This strange power has been acquired, quite separately, by fishes belonging to very different families.

Perhaps the best known are the Electric Rays or Torpedoes, of which several kinds are found in warm seas. These possess, on each side of the head behind the eyes, a large organ consisting of a number of hexagonal-shaped cells, rather like a honeycomb. The cells are filled with a jelly-like substance, and contain a series of flat electric plates. One side, the negative side, of each plate is supplied with very fine nerves, connected with a main nerve coming from a special lobe of the brain. It has been shown that the current passes from the upper, or positive, side of the organ, downwards to the negative lower side. Generally it is necessary to touch the fish in two places, completing a circuit, in order to receive a shock. The strength of this shock depends, of course, on the size of the specimen, but newly born ones, only 5 centimetres across, can be made to light the bulb of a pocket torch for a few moments, while a fully grown Torpedo gives a shock capable of knocking a man down, and, if suitable wires are connected, will operate a small electric motor for several minutes.

A. Fraser-Brunner

THE TORPEDO, OR ELECTRIC RAY, OF WARM SEAS

Another famous example is the Electric Eel (which, though eel-like in shape, is more nearly related to the CHARACINS (q.v.) found in the Amazon and Orinoco regions of South America). The shock given by this fish is even more powerful, and is produced by organs on each side of the tail (which makes up most of the length of the creature). This organ differs from that of the Torpedo in that the plates run lengthways, and are supplied with nerves from the spinal cord, instead of from the brain. Consequently, the current passes along the fish from head to tail.

The electric organs of both the Torpedo and the Electric Eel are really altered muscles, and, like all muscles, are apt to tire, so they are not able to produce an electric current for very long. It is said that the natives of South America, who value the Electric Eel as food, take advantage of this fact by driving horses into the streams or ponds, against which the fishes will discharge their electricity. The horses, however, are less affected than a man would be, and when the Electric Eels have exhausted themselves they can be caught without danger. Several other fishes have these muscular electric organs to a lesser degree.

The Electric Catfish of the Nile and of other African fresh waters produces electricity in a different way. The inner layer of the skin over the whole body, with the exception of the head, serves as a generating organ, in which electric plates are scattered irregularly. These plates, as before, are supplied with nerves, but in this case the nervous side is positive, and the current passes from the tail forward to the head. The shock given by this arrangement is not so strong as in the first type, but is none the less unpleasant. The Electric Catfish is a slow, lazy fish, fond of gloomy places, and grows to about a metre long; it is eaten by the Arabs.

The power of producing electricity may serve these fishes both for defence and attack. If a large enemy attacks them it will get a shock that will drive it away; but it appears that the Catfish and the Electric Eel use the current most often against smaller fishes, stunning them so that they fall an easy prey.

ELEPHANT. This is the largest of the world's land animals. It is found in southern Asia and Africa, and is the only member of its order, the Proboscidea—all other members, such as the Mammoth, being extinct. Its unique characteristic is its proboscis or trunk—an elongated nose with nostrils at the tip. This serves as a most efficient arm and hand—picking up and conveying food to the animal's mouth, drawing up water and squirting it into its mouth, or in hot weather giving it a shower-bath. The elephant's tusks correspond to one pair of incisor teeth in other mammals. They go on growing in the upper jaw throughout the animal's life, most males and many females having them. The elephant's brain is small in comparison with the size of its skull, and is not very highly developed.

Wild elephants eat grass, leaves, wild fruits, bamboo shoots, and the twigs and bark of trees. The female gives birth to a single offspring (very rarely twins) in the autumn, after carrying it for about 640 days. The newborn calf stands nearly a metre high, weighs about 90 kilograms, and has a fairly thick woolly coat. We can tell the age of an Elephant up to 30 years by its teeth. One Indian Elephant lived in captivity to 69 years, and an African Elephant of 55 years has been recorded. There are two distinct species—the Asiatic or Indian Elephant, and the African Elephant, the larger of the two.

The Indian elephant is found over the greater part of India, and in Ceylon, Burma, Siam, Malay, and the East Indies. On an average, an adult male is

A. Fraser-Brunner

THE ELECTRIC CATFISH OF AFRICAN FRESH WATERS

Paul Popper

A HERD OF AFRICAN ELEPHANTS

These elephants in the Wankie Game Reserve, Southern Rhodesia, are coming to enjoy a mud bath in the evening

not more than **3** metres high, and weighs about 3 tonnes; but animals almost 3·5 metres tall have been reported. As a rule, only the males have tusks. Indian elephants prefer to live in districts covered with tall forest, where there are plenty of bamboos. At the beginning of the rains they venture into the open glades to eat the young, succulent grass. In cloudy and showery weather they move about a good deal, marching in single file from one forest to another. The herds generally number from thirty to fifty head (they may, however, be twice as large), all of which usually belong to one family. When fodder is scarce, the large herds break up into small parties of from ten to twelve, keeping within 15 to 30 km of each other, and joining up again when conditions are better. Although the herd may include males of all ages, a female is almost always the leader. On the march, the females with their calves are at the front, while the males bring up the rear. At times, some of the male elephants leave the herd to lead a solitary life. They are known as 'rogues', because they are fierce and quarrelsome and likely to cause a great deal of damage.

The herds roam about and feed during both the day and night, but generally rest during the heat of the day from about 9 a.m. to 3 p.m., and then again during the night from 11 p.m. to 3 a.m. They go down to the rivers to drink soon after sunset and shortly after sunrise. In hot weather they like to bathe or roll in the wet mud, and sometimes protect themselves from the scorching sun by throwing mud, leaves, or straw on their backs.

An Indian Elephant can walk for long distances at a pace of 10 to 13 km per hour, and it can increase the pace of its walk to 24 km/h, sustaining it for perhaps a couple of hundred metres; but it cannot trot, canter, or gallop. It cannot jump, but it can climb and descend steep slopes with amazing agility. It is quite at home in the water, and is an excellent swimmer. Its cry is either a shrill trumpet or a hoarse rumbling. Except for 'rogues' and females with calves, the Indian Elephant is generally fairly timid. At certain periods, however, the male becomes highly excited; he is then said to be *mast* or 'mad', and is very dangerous to his fellows as well as to human beings.

For hundreds of years the Indian Elephant has been domesticated and used as a beast of burden, but it very rarely breeds in captivity. Although not highly intelligent, it learns to obey almost any order, and can be completely trusted, even when its *mahout* or keeper is away. There are many stories of the elephant's remarkable memory for any acts of kindness or cruelty. Elephants are used in India today for a great variety of tasks. They can often be seen starting out in the morning from the village, each holding in its mouth an end of rope. When they arrive at their place of work, the other end is fastened to a log or large stone, which the elephant then half carries on its trunk, half drags to its destination. They carry all heavy things in this way, as their trunks are too delicate to bear much weight. The tamed elephants are also used to help in the capture of a fresh supply of wild elephants. The wild elephants are headed into a stockade. Then the *mahout* attaches a chain to the leg of his own elephant, rides it in among the herd, and skilfully fastens the other end of the chain to the leg of one of the wild elephants. In this way, chained together, the tame elephant brings the wild one back. Specially trained elephants are used for BIG-GAME HUNTING (q.v. Vol. IX), especially tiger shooting. The finest specimens, with mag-nificent tusks, are bought by the native princes and used in State pageants. White or albino elephants are still regarded as SACRED ANIMALS (q.v. Vol. I) in Siam and Burma.

The African Elephant is usually larger than the Indian, often standing over 3 metres high and weighing 6 tonnes. It has enormous ears, and at the tip of its trunk it has two 'fingers'—whereas the Indian Elephant has only one. Both males and females generally grow tusks. African Elephants have been so much hunted for the ivory of their tusks that their numbers have been greatly reduced, and they are now mostly found protected in Government preservations. They are as a whole more powerful and active than the Indian Elephants, bear the heat much better, and move very much faster. They feed a great deal on trees, uprooting any small tree that excites their appetite. They also dig with one particular tusk—nearly always the right one (a habit which has been compared with man's instinctive use of the right hand). The herds usually consist of young males, females, and calves, while the old bulls keep apart. The African Elephant is usually much fiercer than the Indian, the females, especially when they have calves, being really aggressive and capable of charging without any provocation.

ELK, *see* DEER, Section 5.

ELM, *see* VOL VI: TREES, BROADLEAVED.

EMPEROR MOTH. This moth is the smallest member of the family Saturniidae, and the only one found in Britain. Most members of the family are very large moths belonging to the tropics, only a few species spreading to temperate regions. The Indian Atlas Moth, with a wing-span of 25 cm, is one of the largest moths in the world; and the European Great Peacock Moth, much like our own Emperor, and found in southern Europe and western Asia, is larger than any other European butterfly or moth. All these moths have an eye-like mark or transparent window on each wing. The antennae of the females are almost thread-like; but those of the males are strongly combed, and possess delicate sense-organs which enable them to detect at a distance of 1–2 kilometres the scents given off by unmated females. The mouth-parts are usually degenerate, and the adult moths cannot feed. The females are larger than the males,

Mondiale

AN INDIAN ELEPHANT WITH CALF

A PAIR OF EMPEROR MOTHS

S. Beaufoy

The female is the larger, with fine antennae and pale grey colouring. The male has combed antennae and rich brown chestnut colouring

their greater wing-span enabling them to carry their large bodies, heavily laden with eggs. The caterpillars are smooth and stout, and have many fleshy protuberances covered with spines. They spin strong cocoons, the silk of some being of commercial value (*see* SILK MOTHS). The Emperor Moth is found locally in many parts of Britain, and can be seen in April and May flying over sunny moorlands. The female, which only flies at night, lays about 200 eggs, usually in batches of two to five. The caterpillar, which feeds on heather, blackthorn, and other plants, changes its colours as it matures, until it reaches its full adult brilliance, when it is perhaps the most beautiful caterpillar found in this country. It is bright green, ringed with black, and has rosy or yellowish warts with black bristles—a coloration which makes it difficult to detect amongst the heather. The pear-shaped cocoon has many stiff, silken bristles at the narrow end, arranged in such a way that the moth can easily push them aside to escape, but an enemy cannot penetrate through them.

EMU, see OSTRICH, Section 2.

ENZYMES, see FERMENTATION.

EVERGREENS, *see* CONIFERS; LEAVES.

EVOLUTION (literally 'unfolding', 'development'). The theory of evolution is based upon the supposition that all animals and plants have changed gradually during the history of the earth, so that those now living are descended from the extinct types that lived long ago. Many of these extinct types are found as FOSSILS (q.v. Vol. III) bearing obvious points of resemblance to other fossils and to present-day types. In some cases a family history has been worked out in such detail that there can be no reason to doubt the truth of this theory. In the case of one type of sea-urchin called *Micraster*, for instance, the examination of thousands of fossils taken from successive layers of chalk has enabled us to trace the most minute stages of change. Striking changes of features are also seen in the fossil history of the horse. The horse of today is unique among animals in walking on only one toe—or rather toe-nail—for such the hoof really is. But we are able to trace back its ancestry to a small animal which had four toes. The so-called 'splint-bones' of the horse today are evidence of these four toes. The reduction in the number of toes enabled the horse to become a swift runner and to live on plains of short grass where it could rely on speed to save it from its enemies.

Most features of living things have an obvious function in their lives, and it is natural to ask how these 'adaptations' arose in evolution. DARWIN'S theory of natural selection (q.v. Vol. V) and the Mendelian laws of inheritance (*see* HEREDITY) together provide an explanation. Put briefly, animals and plants which have characteristics likely to make them survive and produce more offspring obviously become the parents of a high proportion of the next generation. If these characteristics are inherited, they will be possessed by an increasingly high proportion of individuals in succeeding generations, until they become normal attributes of the species.

An example of this natural selection is to be seen in the Peppered Moth. This, like a number of British moths, has a black variety and also one coloured like the lichens found on tree trunks in the country. The black variety has become far more abundant in large towns than the paler variety because, when resting in the daytime on smoke-blackened surfaces, it is far

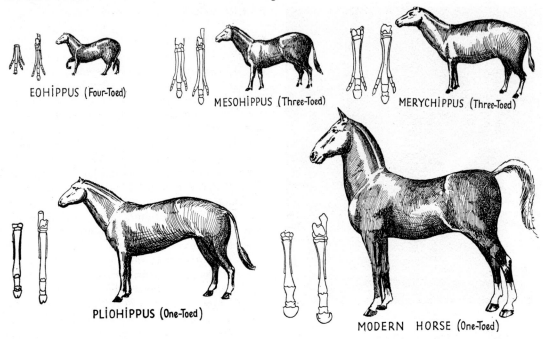

EOHIPPUS (Four-Toed)

MESOHIPPUS (Three-Toed)

MERYCHIPPUS (Three-Toed)

PLIOHIPPUS (One-Toed)

MODERN HORSE (One-Toed)

THE EVOLUTION OF THE HORSE

less conspicuous to the birds which eat Peppered Moths. Blackness has become a dominant characteristic, inherited by an increasing proportion of Peppered Moths in industrial areas in each generation. The pale variety, however, is far more common in areas where there are lichen-covered trees (*see* Camouflage). The principle of selection is made use of by farmers and gardeners in evolving improved breeds of domestic animals and plants (*see* Stock Breeding; Plant Breeding, Vol. VI).

The example of Peppered Moths helps us to understand how very much larger and more complex differences developed millions of years ago. The Chart of Evolution (*see* opposite p. 1) suggests how these and other developments in plant and animal structure may have evolved. Sometimes a fossil of a Prehistoric Animal (q.v. Vol. III) provides a 'missing-link' between one line of animals and another. The fossil, *Archaeopteryx*, for example, had many features of birds intermingled with some features of reptiles: for instance, it had teeth in its jaws as well as wings and feathers. It was, in fact, just what an intermediate between birds and reptiles would be expected to be like.

The theory of the gradual development of one type from another explains some of the likenesses which biologists and botanists have noticed between different species and which have led them to classify animals and plants into sub-kingdoms, phyla, and classes (*see* Classification of Animals and Plants). The different species, once established by the process of evolution, remain distinct because they do not interbreed.

See also Vol. I: Evolution of Man.
See also Vol. III: Earth, History of.

F

FALCON. These birds of prey belong to the same family as the HAWK and the EAGLE (qq.v.). They have long, pointed wings, in contrast to the rounded wings of Hawks, and short curved beaks. Most falcons capture their prey by overtaking them in the air and swooping on them; only the common British Kestrel hovers motionless in the air, spying for its prey on the ground and then dropping on it. In old days FALCONRY (q.v. Vol. IX) was a fashionable and exciting sport in European countries, and at the present time in Arab countries falcons are still used for taking game. In falconry, only the female is properly called the 'falcon', the male being known as the 'tiercel'. The female in most species is considerably larger than the male. Falcons vary in size from the large Saker Falcon, the female of which is over 60 cm long, to the little Pigmy Falcons or Falconets of Southern Asia, the smallest species of which is only 14 cm. These little birds of prey live on dragonflies, beetles, and butterflies, while the large falcons seize game birds even as big as a pheasant. Falcons nest in trees, among rocks or ruined buildings, or on rocky cliffs, and often make use of the deserted nests of other birds, such as Crows and Herons. The eggs generally have the predominant colour of orange-brown or brick-red.

The Peregrine (in America known as the Duck-hawk) is the largest British falcon, and is remarkable for its quite magnificent flight. It is exceedingly swift and powerful, and has also great agility. In the sport of falconry or hawking, the female Peregrine was flown at game as large as Herons or Wild Geese, while the male, the tiercel, was flown at smaller birds, such as Puffins, Grouse, Wild Duck, Pigeons, and Rooks—which now make up its normal food. It strikes down its victim by its splendid, headlong swoop, seizes it with its claws, and either forces it down to the ground or carries it away to the cliffs where it breeds. Because of its attacks on grouse, game-keepers have destroyed it whenever they could, and during the Second World War an order was made for its destruction because of the risk of its killing messenger-carrying pigeons; but young Peregrines ('eyasses') were caught and trained to catch and bring back such pigeons.

The Merlin, no bigger than a Missel-thrush, is a falcon of the moors, where it makes its nest in the heather. It preys chiefly on small birds, such as Larks and Pipits. The Hobby, about the size of a Kestrel, has a shorter tail and long, slender, scythe-shaped wings, like those of a Swift. It is one of the fastest and most graceful fliers of all European birds, and can overtake and capture even such swift fliers as Swallows and Martins. It may also be seen catching

Arthur Brook

A PEREGRINE FALCON ALIGHTING AT ITS EYRIE IN AN IVY
COVERED CLIFF

Arthur Brook

HEN KESTREL WITH YOUNG AT HER NESTING HOLE

FALSE SCORPION. This is a member of the class of animals called Arachnida, to which belong also SPIDERS, true SCORPIONS, MITES, and TICKS (qq.v.). False Scorpions owe their name to the possession of a pair of large, pincered 'pedi-palpi' or specialized feelers, like those of the Scorpions; but they lack the Scorpion's tail and sting. These pedipalpi contain poison-glands; but they are not dangerous to man, for even the largest species is less than 60 millimetres long, and cannot pierce the human skin. There are about a thousand known species, twenty-four of which can be found in Britain. False scorpions are world-wide. It is possible to find them almost everywhere by sifting fallen leaves on a sheet of newspaper, when they can be easily distinguished from other small creatures by their pedipalpi, which are usually stretched out in front, and by their ability to run forwards and backwards with equal speed.

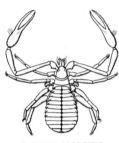

A FALSE SCORPION

They eat smaller animals; and they build 'nests' or cocoons of earth and silk (which they secrete), and within these they moult or lay their eggs. The newly hatched young are fed in a peculiar way on a fluid produced by their mother. The beauty of their small, segmented bodies, covered with incredibly fine 'hairs', is astonishing—indeed, it would be hard to find a group of animals more certain to yield interesting results when carefully and scientifically studied.

dragonflies on the wing. It nests in small numbers in some of the southern counties of Britain, to which it is a summer visitor.

The most common British falcon is the Kestrel, well known because of its habit of making a circling flight and then hanging in the air with vibrating wings and outspread tail, sometimes staying in the same place for several minutes if there is an uprising current of air to support it. From this habit it has gained the popular name of 'Windhover'. Its prey is mostly small rodents, such as mice, but it is also content to attack grasshoppers and other insects.

The Gyrfalcon, a larger, heavier bird than the Peregrine, but otherwise much like it, lives in northern Europe; and in Iceland and Greenland there are paler varieties of this species, the Greenland Falcon being almost white. The Lanner is a falcon of the Mediterranean region, which breeds in the Pyramids, and was regarded as sacred by the ancient Egyptians. Another Mediterranean falcon is the very dark Eleonora's Falcon, which breeds on the cliffs of rocky islands. Some species of falcon is to be found in almost every part of the world.

See also Vol. IX: FALCONRY.

FEATHERS. Although BIRDS (q.v.), which alone have feathers, are known to have developed from primitive reptiles, and although feathers, like SCALES (q.v.), are produced by the epidermal or outer cells of the SKIN (q.v.), just how they evolved is unknown. The plumage of a bird is made up of feathers of three kinds. The contour feathers or 'pennae' cover the body, and are specialized in the wings and tail. Down, formed of 'plumules', is characteristic of nestlings, but may also be seen under the contour feathers of fully grown birds. The third kind, the hair-like 'filoplumes', can be seen when a bird has been plucked. Some birds have bristles about the base of the beak, and a few have eyelashes; but these are modified feathers and not hairs.

Contour feathers are strong, light, elastic, and air-proof. Embedded in the skin of the bird is the hollow quill (*calamus*) from which the shaft (*rhachis*), filled with a white pith, extends. On either side of the shaft is the vane, which is made up of a great number of interlocking barbs and barbules. Down feathers are smaller, soft, and fluffy, and often have no shaft. Some birds, such as herons and parrots, have powder-down: in these, the barbs and barbules break down into a rather greasy powder, with which the birds dust their plumage, and which probably helps to keep the plumage dry and free from parasites.

Feathers help to retain the heat of the bird—an important contribution, since birds tend to

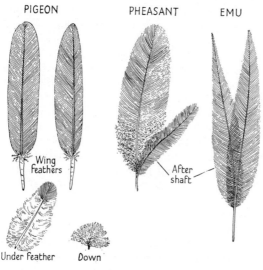

TYPICAL FEATHERS

have very high temperatures. In cold weather they may be seen fluffing out their feathers in order to trap air in the plumage to add to their insulation from the cold—following the same principle that guides travellers in cold regions to wear several layers of light clothing rather than one or two layers of thick clothing.

Flight is, of course, possible without feathers, as is shown by insects and bats; but the combination of great strength with lightness in feathers has enabled birds to excel over all other animals in FLIGHT (q.v.). Because of the lightness of their structure, feathers wear out gradually and have to be replaced. This process is called the moult.

Just as the colour of the fur protects many mammals, so too are birds protected in various ways by the colour of their plumage. (*See* CAMOUFLAGE.) But though many birds have a sombre plumage, in others there are patches of brilliant colour—and, indeed, birds surpass fishes and insects in the variety and gorgeousness of their colouring. Bright colours often form an important part of a bird's display, either to warn off an enemy, to attract a mate, or to help recognition by others of its own kind (*see* ANIMAL LANGUAGE).

See also Vol. VI: FEATHER HUNTING AND FARMING.

FERMENTATION. This is the name given to the action of substances called 'enzymes' which bring about chemical changes in the material of living plants and animals. The most familiar example of fermentation is the conversion of sugar to alcohol in the manufacture of beer and wine, the enzymes causing this conversion being produced by YEASTS and MOULDS (qq.v.), which must be added before the process can begin. All living things are dependent on these chemical changes for the processes which make life possible, for example RESPIRATION and NUTRITION (qq.v.). In fermentation energy is produced by the conversion of sugar into alcohol, and in respiration by the conversion of sugar into carbon dioxide.

Most of the changes brought about by the action of enzymes take place within living CELLS (q.v.), but sometimes, as in digestion and brewing, the enzymes pass out of the cells which produced them and mix with the substances on which they work. Their main tasks are the transformation of simple substances into the complex materials needed for the formation of new cells and, conversely, the breaking down of complex substances so that they may be excreted, or got rid of. These breaking-down processes usually involve the production of energy, necessary if growth and movement are to take place. The enzymes are quite unaffected by the action of fermentation: their mere presence is all that is required; and they are capable of working on a very large volume of material compared with their own bulk. Each enzyme is able to carry out one particular process of conversion on one particular material; but the same enzyme can often bring about this process in either direction. For instance, 'Lipase', which converts fats into substances that can be absorbed by the body, also builds up fat in the body by the reconversion of those same substances.

Other enzymes include 'Thrombase', which causes the blood to clot, and 'Pectase', which helps in building the skeletons of plants. Others, again, produce the break-up of cellulose, so essential to the carbon cycle, transform ammonia in the soil into nitrous acid and ultimately into nitrates which can be used by plants (*see* NITROGEN SUPPLY IN PLANTS), and, as a last example, cause the putrefaction of dead organic matter, so that their component materials can be used again in the cycle of life.

FERNS AND FERN ALLIES form the biggest group of PLANTS (q.v.) which do not bear seeds. There are over forty different kinds in Great Britain alone. Ferns are more complicated in structure than MOSSES AND LIVERWORTS (q.v.), and have developed roots whereby they can absorb water containing mineral salts from the soil. The life-history of a fern consists of two alternating generations, an asexual or spore-bearing generation, and a sexual generation. (*See* REPRODUCTION IN PLANTS.) The plant which represents the sexual generation and produces the sex cells is very small and difficult to find. It is known as a 'prothallus'. The fern plants which we see represent the asexual generation, and bear spores which, without any kind of sex process or fertilization, develop into the prothallus. The brown spores are usually found in large quantities on the under-surfaces of fern fronds and, when ripe, can be shaken off on to a sheet of white paper and inspected. They are very light, and are freely blown about by the wind. If they settle in warm, moist places, each bursts from its tough protective coat and undergoes rapid division to form a thin, leaf-like prothallus. After a while, male and female gametes are produced in special organs formed on the surface of the prothallus; fertilization takes place; and the normal fern grows out to bear more spores, so beginning the cycle.

Besides producing spores, some ferns propagate in a very unusual way. One New Zealand species pro-

A PROTHALLUS WITH
YOUNG PLANT

duces little buds on its leaves, which grow into small plants—so that each leaf may be responsible for dozens of new ferns. The so-called Walking-fern, of North America, bears long, tapering leaves something like our Hart's-tongue Fern. These bend over till their tips touch the ground: where they do so, a bud is produced which takes root and grows into a new plant. It is believed that the Bracken Fern rarely reproduces by means of its spores, but spreads effectively by means of the strong growing underground STEMS (q.v.), which spread out in all directions. When young, the leaves of most ferns are spirally coiled like a watch-spring. As they grow to maturity, the coils unwind. This is an important characteristic of ferns.

Ferns are found in all parts of the world, there being every possible variety of habit and size, varying from the tall tree-ferns of the tropics and New Zealand, which may reach 18 metres in height, to minute filmy ferns which are scarcely bigger than mosses. Besides the Bracken and Male Fern, well-known examples of British ferns are the Hart's-tongue Fern, the Hard Fern, and the Lady Fern. The Hart's-tongue Fern, found on dry banks and walls, grows from a tufted rootstock which rises well above the level of the ground. It has smooth, undivided leaves, like long tongues, on the back of which the spore-cases are arranged in parallel lines. The Hard Fern, found on heaths, is peculiar in that some of its leaves do not bear spore-cases. The fertile leaves, those which bear the spore-cases, are longer and narrower than the sterile green ones: both are leathery. The Lady Fern, found in wet hollows in moist oak-woods, resembles the common Male Fern of gardens, but has a more fragile appearance. Its leaves are a delicate pale green and may grow to a length of 4 feet. Probably the most distinguished-looking fern is the Royal Fern, normally 90 to 120 cm high and sometimes much more. It produces fertile and infertile leaves, the fertile ones bearing clusters of spore-cases. It grows best on the banks of rivers or streams.

Clubmosses and Horsetails, often called 'fern allies', though not very closely related, also have a prothallus stage. Clubmosses have small undivided leaves and spore-cases at the leaf bases or in spikes. Horsetails have spores in cones at the tops of the shoots. Extinct species of both plants grew as tall as trees.

See also Vol. VI: FERNS (GARDEN AND GREENHOUSE).

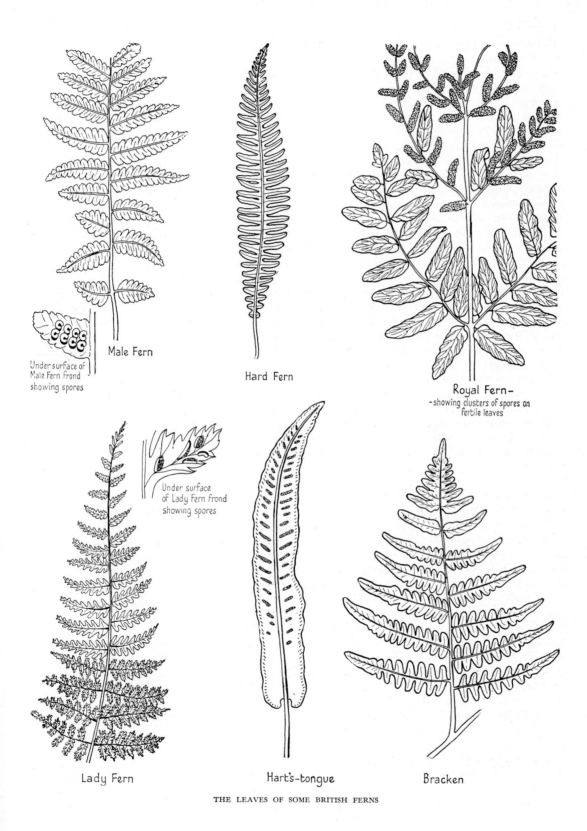

Male Fern

Under surface of Male Fern frond showing spores

Hard Fern

Royal Fern–
–showing clusters of spores on fertile leaves

Lady Fern

Under surface of Lady Fern frond showing spores

Hart's-tongue

Bracken

THE LEAVES OF SOME BRITISH FERNS

FINCHES. 1. The finches form a large family of small birds belonging to the Passerine or perching order of birds. There are altogether some 200 species, distributed over most cold or temperate regions of the world, with a few tropical species. They include some of the commonest of British birds, such as Chaffinches, Linnets, Yellow Hammers, and the common House-sparrow. They all have much the same general pattern of behaviour; but they vary greatly in plumage. Some, like the Linnet and Corn-Bunting, wear a comparatively sober dress; others, like the Goldfinch and Bullfinch, are handsomely coloured; while some of the tropical species, such as the crimson-red Cardinal Finch of Mexico and central America, and the Rose Finch of Asia, are very gaudy. They are characterized by their strong, hard beaks, specially suitable for breaking into the seeds which form their principal food—the Hawfinch has so stout a beak that it can crack cherry-stones. Finches eat other food besides seeds: in summer they catch insects, on which the fledglings are mostly fed, and the Bullfinches in particular are a nuisance to the fruit-grower by eating the buds of his fruit-trees. They search for their food mainly on the ground, where they move by hopping. Most finches have an inconspicuous and not very melodious song; but there are exceptions, such as the Goldfinch and Linnet, and the wild Canary of the Canary Isles, from which has been bred the domestic Canary with its much more varied song. Many of them build most beautifully constructed nests, those of the Chaffinch and Goldfinch being lovely little cups of moss and wool, lined with hair and feathers. They generally build in hedges, shrubs, or the low boughs of trees, though some species, particularly the Buntings, often build on the ground. From four to six eggs are most usual.

2. GREENFINCHES AND HAWFINCHES. These finches have very stout beaks, deep at the lower end. The Greenfinch or Green Linnet is a common resident of the British Isles, even as far north as the Orkneys. A great many more arrive in the autumn from colder regions to winter in the east of England. They are also found over all Europe, north-west Africa, and much of Asia, as far as China and Japan. Their near relatives, the Grosbeaks and Red Cardinals, are found in most parts of the Americas. Greenfinches differ from other finches in building rather untidy nests; the eggs are greenish-white marked with reddish-brown speckles. They have been known to mate with Goldfinches or Linnets, and to produce hybrids. In captivity they will mate with Canaries or Bullfinches. Hawfinches are easy to recognize because of their large, heavy bills and their thick-set build; but they are shy birds, and therefore not easy to see. They generally frequent the edges of woods, especially where there are hornbeams, the seeds of which are a favourite food; and they can be seen during the summer making their rapid undulating flight among the trees and bushes of gardens and orchards. They sometimes build in trees, and lay greenish-white eggs marked with spots and streaks of greyish- and greenish-brown.

3. CHAFFINCH, GOLDFINCH, AND SISKIN. The Chaffinch is one of the commonest of British birds and is a typical finch. Its numbers are increased considerably in winter by immigrants to the British Isles. In the summer the birds are seen about in pairs; but in the autumn, like many other species of finches, they become more gregarious, the sexes generally keeping to separate flocks. The eggs, laid in a beautifully constructed little nest, are a pale purplish-grey, spotted and streaked with shades of red. The Brambling is a near relative of the Chaffinch, with a nest and eggs much alike. It comes to Britain in winter, but nests farther north.

The Goldfinch is one of the loveliest of British birds, and since the trapping of them as cage-birds has been forbidden, they have become much more common. They will now quite often appear in gardens to feed on the flower seeds, especially the seeds of Michaelmas Daisies, and serve a useful purpose in eating large quantities of weed seeds, being particularly fond of thistle seeds. In full spring plumage the cock has vivid crimson cheeks and head, a white throat, and wings barred with gold and black. The female is only a little less brightly coloured. The nest, built generally in shrubs or trees not very high up from the ground, is a most perfect construction, and contains bluish-white eggs, mottled, mainly at one end, with purple-red. The Siskin is a near relative with similar habits, and is also a good songster. It nests, generally in fir-woods, freely in north Scotland and parts of Ireland, and less freely farther south.

4. THE BULLFINCH is a quite unmistakable little bird, and has been very popular as a cage-bird. The male in his full spring plumage is very

TROPICAL FISHES OF AUSTRALIAN SEAS

Above: Superb Trigger-fish
Below: Adorned Trunk-fishes, male (*left*) and female (*right*)

handsome. He has a stubby, slightly hooked beak, glossy black head and tail, black wings barred with white, a back shaded from black to blue and white, and a bright cherry-red throat, chest, and underparts. The female is inconspicuously coloured. Bullfinches almost certainly mate for life, and generally produce two broods, sometimes three, in a season. Their nest, a shallow cup of roots and hair, on a platform of twigs, is placed in a hedge or near the end of a low bough and the eggs are greenish-blue, spotted and streaked with purple, mostly at the large end.

5. THE CROSSBILL is a brightly coloured finch, not very common in England except after occasional invasions from northern Europe—though it has recently established itself in Norfolk and Suffolk. It breeds in parts of Scotland where

common on the moorlands and mountains of Scotland, Ireland, and Norway, but does not come very far south. The Lesser Redpoll is a smaller Linnet with dark plumage, a red forehead, and carmine breast. It breeds mainly in the northern part of the British Isles, but is found also in the south-eastern counties.

7. BUNTINGS. These also form a distinct group of the finches, the most typical being the Corn-Bunting, a bird rather like a Lark in appearance —though it can be quickly distinguished by its finch-like 'seed' beak. During autumn and winter it feeds almost entirely on corn, eating insects the rest of the year. It makes its nest, a loose cup of dry grass and roots, in a well-concealed hollow in the ground, and lays a typical Bunting egg, a faintly purplish-white with blotches and long streaks of purple. It has

FINCHES

A: Chaffinch   *B:* Goldfinch   *C:* Hawfinch

there are pine forests. It has a remarkable beak of which the points are elongated and crossed to make an effective 'pair of scissors', capable of dealing with the hard seeds of the conifers on which it chiefly feeds. A legend relates that the bird twisted its beak in pulling out the nails from the Cross, and that its blood-red colour is a mark of the service it rendered.

6. LINNETS AND TWITES. These form a distinct group of the finches, with different appearance and habits. In many species their otherwise inconspicuous plumage is brightened by patches of red, especially on the head. They frequent commons with gorse and broom bushes, very often building their nests in gorse bushes, usually not far from the ground. The eggs have purple and red markings on a bluish-white background. The Mountain Linnet, or Twite, is a more slender bird, which is quite

a very distinct song, a series of abrupt, hard notes, ending in a confused jumble which sounds rather like the jingling of a bunch of keys. The Reed Bunting is common in swampy, marshy country and along streams with banks overgrown with willows, alders, and reeds. It makes its nest in clumps of reeds or coarse grass, or near the roots of waterside trees.

The most common Bunting is the Yellow-hammer, a rather smaller bird, with bright yellow and brown plumage, common all over northern Europe and to be seen in almost every hedgerow in many parts of England. It has a persistent and characteristic song, consisting of a series of quick, hard notes, ending in a long drawn-out wheeze. The Cirl Bunting is comparatively rare, and very local—usually to be found in chalk districts.

There are other species of Buntings which

A GOLDFINCH

Eric Hosking

occasionally visit the British Isles, among them the Ortolan, a handsome bird, with a greenish head and 'moustaches', which used at one time to be prized as a table delicacy. There are several species of Buntings in America, the best known being the Indigo Bird, and the Bobolink, whose cheerful song is a favourite in springtime in the United States.

The House-sparrow, which is also a member of the finch family, is described under the headword SPARROW (q.v.).

See also Vol. IX: CAGE BIRDS.

FIR-CONES, *see* REPRODUCTION IN PLANTS, Section 4.

FIREBRAT, *see* SILVERFISH.

FIRE-FLY. These beetles, of which there are none in Britain, are endowed with the strange power of giving off light. They belong to two different groups. One group, belonging to the family Lampyridae, is related to the common GLOW-WORM (q.v.) and rarely shows itself in the day-time. In the adult, both sexes have luminous organs on the hind part of the abdomen, on the sixth and seventh segments in the male and on the seventh only in the female. The light, which is often brightest in the female, is usually pale yellowish-green, and is thought to serve the purpose of bringing the sexes together. A congregation of fire-flies is often seen to flash their 'lights' on and off in unison. Why and how they do this we do not know, nor have we yet discovered why the eggs and larvae of some species are also luminous.

The other group of fire-flies, the Cucujos (*Pyrophorus*), belong to the family Elateridae, and are related to the Click-beetles (*see* WIRE-WORMS). They are found in the West Indies and in Tropical and South America. The luminous organs in the adults are located, in both sexes, on either side of the thorax and at the base of the abdomen, those on the thorax giving a yellowish-green light, and those on the abdomen a reddish light; the latter is visible only when the insect is flying. The eggs and larvae in this group are also luminous. The light is produced as a result of chemical changes taking place within the insect cells.

See also BEETLES.

FIRS, *see* CONIFER.

A PAIR OF CROSSBILLS

Eric Hosking

FISHES. 1. The term 'fish' is often used quite inaccurately: people speak of shell-fish, when they mean mussels, winkles, and scallops (which are Molluscs), or crabs, lobsters, and shrimps (which are Crustaceans). Whales, dolphins, and porpoises are spoken of as fishes, whereas they are Mammals (qq.v.)—warm-blooded animals that suckle their young—and are shaped like a fish only because that is the shape most suitable for a life in the water. The term 'fish' includes several classes of cold-blooded vertebrates (animals with backbones) all of which are entirely aquatic for the whole of their life cycle.

Many millions of years ago the earliest animals—non-cellular creatures such as Amoeba (q.v.)—probably lived in the sea. In the course of Evolution (q.v.), as animals became larger and more active, some sort of framework for the attachment of muscles and for stability became necessary. Some animals, such as the ancestors of Insects, developed a hard outer covering, or external skeleton; while other animals, the ancestors of fish, Amphibia, Reptiles, Birds, and Mammals (qq.v.) developed an internal rod-like structure, known as a 'notochord'. This was the beginning of an inside framework or internal skeleton. In time small plates of cartilage (gristle) grew along the notochord and made the backbone flexible, while special plates developed at the front end to protect the brain. The study of Fossils (q.v. Vol. III) shows that the very earliest fish had a strong internal bony skeleton, and that many were also covered with heavy bony plates. The modern Lampreys (q.v.), though they have no bony covering, may well be their direct descendants. Some of these primitive fishes, which were very abundant in fresh waters, lost their bony armour and the bony quality of their skeletons probably when, at an early date, they colonized the sea. The modern descendants of these cartilaginous fishes are the Sharks and Rays (q.v.). Those primitive fishes which remained in fresh waters were the ancestors both of the Amphibia and of the bony fishes, many of which later invaded the sea. It is these bony fishes which predominate in modern waters.

2. Structure of Fish. Fishes vary greatly in structure, though the major groups each have a definite basic plan. Here, only the bony fish will be described.

Since fishes are aquatic, they are dependent for breathing on oxygen dissolved in the water in which they live. (A few specialized forms such as Lungfish and Labyrinth Fish (qq.v.) can breathe air directly as well.) Water is taken in at the mouth, passes over the gills, and is expelled through the gill openings. As the water passes over the gills, oxygen from the water is exchanged for carbon dioxide—a waste product. In bony fishes the gills are protected by a movable cover of bony plates just behind the mouth.

The Heart (q.v.) of a fish has only two chambers, an auricle and a ventricle. Blood, having passed round the body and given up its oxygen and absorbed carbon dioxide, enters the auricle; it then passes to the ventricle, which pumps it to the gills, where the opposite exchange takes place. Fishes are known as cold-blooded animals; that is, their internal temperature is much the same as their surroundings. When the water and the blood are warm, the animals are active; but in cold weather they become quiet and may not feed at all.

Though many fishes have no teeth, others are provided with an amazing array of them, not only in the jaws, but often on the roof of the mouth and the tongue as well, together with certain special ones in the throat on some of the gill-bones. The teeth differ in shape and arrangement according to the kind of food the fish requires. The digestive organs are similar to our own, though somewhat simpler.

Most fishes possess a 'swim bladder' in the middle of the body cavity at their centre of gravity. This bladder is supplied with gases which enable the fish to float easily in the water. Many fish can vary the quantity of the gases in the bladder at will, expelling some on diving, or absorbing more on rising towards the surface.

Fishes have a simple brain, sharp hearing (though of a somewhat different kind from ours), and a keen sense of smell, the majority having two nostrils on each side. The eyes are usually large and well adapted for seeing through water; but sometimes they are feeble, and a few fishes are quite blind (see Blind-fishes). Along each side of the body there is nearly always a 'lateral line', a series of special organs for detecting vibrations and changes in pressure in the water, which serves to warn the fish of the approach of other creatures or of its nearness to some solid body. It is a kind of 'sixth sense'.

A fish's muscles are fairly simple, being mostly concerned with the side to side swimming movements of the body. Most fishes have an outer covering of scales, usually small and thin and arranged in rows, but sometimes large and bony.

The great majority of fishes possess fins (each with their own special bones), which serve to propel them through the water and to maintain balance. They are thin membranes, supported by movable 'rays', so that they can be closed like a fan. These are of two kinds. The first kind, known as the vertical fins, stand upright along the back (dorsal fins), at the end of the tail (caudal fin), and underneath the tail (anal fin). The second kind are known as paired fins, as there is one on each side, one pair just behind

the gill-cover (pectoral fins), and a pair beneath the body (pelvic fins). These correspond to the limbs of higher animals, the pectoral fins corresponding to the arms, and the pelvic fins to the legs. Usually all these fins, paired and unpaired, can be seen on the same fish; but in some species one or more of them may be absent: in a very few kinds, such as certain rare eels, all the fins have been lost.

3. HABITS OF FISH. There may be about 40,000 species of fishes in the world, and new ones are being discovered each year. The variety of their forms and manner of life is almost endless, with wonderful adaptations to meet the differences of environment. There is scarcely any water on the earth's surface where they are not to be found.

Those that roam far and wide near the surface of the great oceans are called 'pelagic fishes' (from the Greek word *pelagos*, the ocean). They include swift creatures, like the MACKEREL, that swim in great shoals, feeding on the young of various other fishes, which in turn feed on the multitude of larval and invertebrate creatures forming the 'plankton' or floating life of the sea. The mackerel themselves are hunted by still larger fish, such as TUNNY and SHARKS (qq.v.). In the great depths, where the temperature is always low and no light ever penetrates, there lives a completely different set of fishes. These are often of fantastic shapes, with large jaws and a vast array of teeth (*see* DEEP-SEA FISHES).

The coasts abound with an endless variety of forms —fishes brilliantly coloured to match the coral among which they live, fishes drab and stone-like from the sombre rocky shores; some

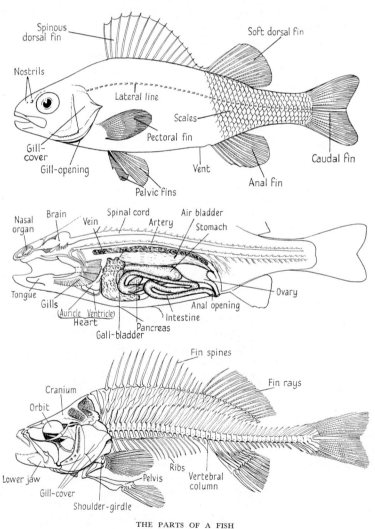

THE PARTS OF A FISH

Above: the outside parts; *Centre*: the internal; *Below*: the skeleton

long and slender, some short and deep, others with tassels and flaps resembling sea-weed—all needing to be concealed from prey or enemies (*see* CAMOUFLAGE). Many are armed against their enemies with heavy armour-plating or poison spines (*see* POISON FISH), or even by being able to puff themselves up with air as can the Porcupine Fish. Some feed on lowly plant-life which they scrape from rocks, some have powerful teeth that can crush hard mollusc-shells or crabs, some eat worms; but most devour their smaller brethren.

Similarly, the fresh waters are everywhere inhabited by fishes—great lakes, mere ditches, water-holes in the desert, even the very edges of waterfalls, where the fish have special fins to prevent them, by suction, from being swept over. Insects form a large part of the diet of fresh-water fishes, which in swampy country play a part in keeping down the mosquitoes (*see* MOSQUITO FISH).

The majority of fishes lay eggs that either lie at the bottom, or, as in many sea-fish, float at the surface. Some sea-fishes, such as the Cod and Halibut, lay and then leave to their fate millions of tiny eggs, most of which are eaten by other creatures, possibly about six from each batch reaching the adult state. On the other hand, some freshwater fishes lay very few, large eggs, and take great care of them, fanning them with their fins, driving away enemies, even in some cases keeping them in their mouths as a protection (*see* CICHLIDS). Some fishes go so far as to construct a sort of nest (*see* STICKLEBACK). There are certain fishes, both marine and freshwater, that bear their young alive (in other words, the eggs hatch inside the mother), and when they are born the young are able to swim and feed. Some kinds of fish change in the most remarkable way as they grow up, so that the connexion between young and adult is difficult to see (*see* EELS). Sometimes, too,

A. Fraser-Brunner

PORCUPINE FISH

In the background a Porcupine fish swims normally, while the one in front is puffed out, with its sharp spines raised

the female is so different from the male that in the past they have been thought to be separate species.

4. DISTRIBUTION OF FISH. No one kind of fish is to be found everywhere: generally each species can thrive well in only one particular set of conditions. Most of the freshwater fishes cannot live in the sea, and very few sea-fishes can live in fresh water. Among sea-fishes, those that live near coasts, in shallow water, are used to particular temperatures; so, with some exceptions, those in the tropics cannot move far north or south, and those of the colder seas do not travel far towards the Equator. East and west travel is hindered for most sea-fishes by the great continents, so that the same species rarely lives in both the Atlantic and Pacific Oceans; or in the Atlantic and Indian Oceans; but some of the Indian Ocean species pass into the Pacific by way of the East Indies.

The distribution of fishes is governed by several factors. We have already touched on the importance of temperature; the ocean currents also play a large part in distributing marine fishes. Although many adult shore-fishes do not travel far, in their immature stages, either as eggs or larvae, they may be carried wherever the currents take them, since they float helplessly near the surface. So, if we find West Indian fishes on the coast of West Africa, or East Indian fishes at Madagascar, the explanation lies in the great currents that move between these places. Geology also helps to explain the present-day distribution. Fishes lived in the seas long ago, when the arrangement of the land masses was quite different from what it is today. This probably explains why some North Atlantic fishes, such as Hake and certain dogfishes, have close relatives in the South Atlantic, with no connexions whatever in the vast area that lies between. It seems certain that they did inhabit the area near the Equator at a time when conditions were quite different; but as these conditions changed, the fish retreated, some to the north and some to the south, while other kinds came in to inhabit the modern equatorial waters.

Each of the great river systems of the world has its own kinds of fishes, normally isolated either by oceans or by great mountain and desert barriers. The distribution of freshwater fishes is difficult to understand if we consider things only as they now exist. For instance, there are two great families of freshwater fishes, known as CHARACINS and CICHLIDS (qq.v.), that are confined almost entirely to the rivers of South America and Africa. Since it is unlikely that they have crossed the ocean from the one continent to the other, the only explanation of their presence in these two widely separated places alone seems to be that in a past geological age South America and Africa were joined together, and were divided from the rest of the world by a great sea. Much other evidence from the distribution of animals supports the idea of a wide link between these two continents in past geological time.

FLAMINGO. The six species of Flamingoes belong to a large order of water-loving birds, which also includes the HERONS and STORKS (qq.v.). They are distributed over most of the warmer regions of the world, but not Australia. A few individuals have, from time to time, wandered as far north as Britain, while the European Flamingo breeds by the salt-marshes and lagoons at the mouth of the Rhone, in Spain,

G. K. Yeates

A FLAMINGO NESTING COLONY

Some of the eggs are already hatched out and the little fledglings are beginning to leave their flat mud nests

and in other places. Flamingoes are large birds, a full-grown adult varying from about 1·5 to 2 metres in height. They are characterized by their extremely long, thin, pinkish-red (or occasionally yellow) legs, their very graceful swan-like necks, and their peculiar heavy bills, the lower part being much heavier and larger than the upper. Their colour varies from rose-tinted white to full scarlet, with black wing quills and some black markings. One South American species is a light vermilion, with brighter wing coverts.

Flamingoes generally live in flocks. On the lakes of North India these flocks sometimes number tens of thousands, and are a wonderful sight, either massed on the water or rising in a great rosy cloud. Although they prefer wading, they can swim powerfully. When they fly, they stretch their long necks out in front and their legs behind, and generally utter a 'gaggling' cry, much like that of geese. They feed mostly on small aquatic animals. When hunting for these they turn their heads the wrong way up, so that the bent beak forms an excellent instrument for scooping up the muddy water. This they sift through the sifters on the edge of the bill, and so select the molluscs. They make nests on circular heaps of mud, fairly close to one another, near swamps or river estuaries. They generally lay one or sometimes two eggs, and these have greenish-blue shells, which are covered with a chalky covering.

FLAT-FISHES. Although many fishes are flattened in some way or another, the name Flat-fishes is reserved for a large group of bony fishes, such as Plaice and Sole. These lie on one side on the sea-bed, and have both eyes on the other uppermost side. Their eyes are somewhat raised up and often mobile, enabling them to scour the neighbourhood for food.

When first hatched, a young Flat-fish swims upright near the surface of the sea, and has an eye on each side of the head, just like a typical bony fish. When the young Flat-fish is a centimetre or more long, the skull begins to twist, one eye passing over the top of the head to the other side, and the mouth tending to move in the opposite direction. At the same time the fish sinks slowly to the sea-bed. It appears that the twisting of the skull alters the animal's balance: it is unable any longer to swim like an ordinary fish, and falls to one side.

A. Fraser-Brunner

A SOLE

Both eyes are to be seen on one side of the head

Most Flat-fishes are coloured to match the ground on which they lie; and if they move on to a different surface, say from sand to pebbles, they show a remarkable ability to change their colouring to match. This affords the fish excellent CAMOUFLAGE (q.v.). Normally only the side of the body that lies uppermost is so coloured—the other side being usually white. The colour is produced by cells in a layer of the skin called the 'dermis' (see page 193). These colour cells may contain black, red, orange, or yellow pigments, and they can contract or dilate in response to visual stimuli—in other words, what the fish sees around it. There are also cells in their skins containing crystals of a substance called 'guanine' which cause a white or silvery iridescence.

Generally, a particular kind of Flat-fish has the eyes and colour always on the same side (though reversed examples are known). Thus, the Halibut, Plaice, Dab, Flounder, and Smear Dab (or 'Lemon Sole') are right-sided, while the Turbot and Brill are left-sided. Owing to the twisting described above, the mouth comes to lie more on the blind side, and the teeth are usually better developed on that side. This is most convenient for the fish, which feeds mostly on creatures on the sea-bed, such as molluscs and small sea-urchins. When moving from one place to another Flat-fishes swim with the eyed side uppermost and are propelled by undulating movements of the body, the effects of which are increased by their elongated dorsal and anal fins.

The largest of the Flat-fishes is the Halibut, which may grow to a length of 3 metres and a weight of 270 kg. It inhabits the northern parts of the Atlantic and Pacific Oceans, and is an important food-fish. In recent times the oil from its liver has been used increasingly in medicine, as it is rich in vitamin D. Related to the Halibut is the Brill, which has smooth sides, and the Turbot, which has a number of wart-like tubercles scattered on the body.

Another well-known and important food-fish is the Plaice. This is caught by means of the trawl, the best catches being at night, since at that time the fish are feeding above the surface of the sand (*see* TRAWLING, Vol. VI). A near

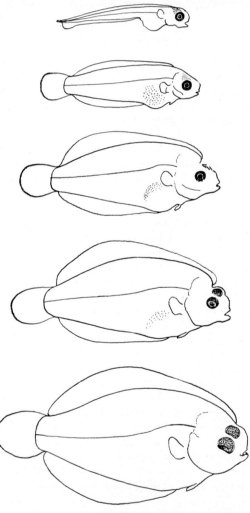

A FLAT-FISH

Sketches of Plaice, showing how, as the young fish grows, one eye moves over the top of the head to join the others. In the first two stages there is an eye on each side, like any other fish. In the last stage both eyes are on the right side, and the back fin has grown forward on the head

relative, the Flounder, is common near estuaries, and often travels a long way up rivers, being one of the few species which enter fresh waters. A smaller kind, the Dab, is found close inshore, and is the kind usually caught by anglers from the end of piers. Another of these right-sided species, the Smear Dab, is caught in large numbers by trawlers in deeper water, often being sold in shops as 'Lemon Sole', though it is not a true Sole. The common Sole, a left-sided Flat-fish, is one of the most valued food-fishes. It can always be distinguished because its snout and upper lip overhang its lower jaw, which also does not jut forward as in the other kinds; the mouth is very small, and the eyes are close together, with no bony ridge between them.

Altogether, about 450 species of Flat-fish are known, though most of them are smaller and less important than the ones mentioned; they are found in almost all seas, but rarely in fresh waters.

FLATWORM. *See* WORM, Section 6.

FLEA. There are at least forty-seven different species of fleas in Great Britain. They are all small and, when adult, are external parasites upon birds and mammals, piercing the skin and sucking the blood of the animals upon which they live. Like many other insects parasitic on higher animals they are wingless. The body of the flea, however, is deep and narrow, whereas the bodies of all other insect parasites are broad and flat.

Fleas go through all the four stages of a typical INSECT (q.v.). The eggs—oval in shape and white in colour—are laid among the fur and feathers of the animal upon which the parent feeds. They are not glued to the fur or feathers, as are those of most external parasites, and they soon drop off on to the ground. The larvae are elongate and without legs; they are not parasites, like their parents, but are scavengers, feeding on dung and other organic debris in places where their parents abound. Hen-houses, not kept properly clean, are infested with the larvae of the domestic fowl flea; those of the flea found on man will occur in cracks in the floor and under carpets; those of the rat flea are found in barns and granaries. The larva casts its skin twice during its growth period, and then spins a silken cocoon in which it changes into the pupa. In this stage they can lie dor-

FLEA (greatly enlarged)

mant for a long time. The pupae, however, are very sensitive, and as soon as they are disturbed they become active. On emerging from the cocoon, the adults have to find the particular kind of animal they live on, which, indeed, often happens to be the particular animal that had disturbed the pupa. Until they find their correct host, they cannot feed; but they seem able to live a long time before taking their first meal.

When an animal dies, any fleas upon it at once leave it and look for another animal upon which to feed. Generally speaking, each flea has its own particular preference—so that the fleas found, for example, on rat, dog, hedgehog, cat, rabbit, and man, are all different species of insect. Nevertheless, if need be, they will turn to other animals. Thus the flea common to the rabbit has been found on cats which hunt rabbits, and the rat flea is known to transfer its attention to man: in fact, bubonic plague— a rat disease—is transmitted to human beings by certain kinds of fleas which desert the dead body of the rat, carrying the disease with them.

The Jigger or Chigoe is a tropical flea of Africa, central America, and the West Indies. It attacks a number of different animals, including man. At first the Jigger lives the usual active life of a Flea; but later, the females burrow under the skin, and their abdomens become distended with eggs, swelling up to the size of a pea. On man these insects chiefly burrow into the toes, causing a serious sore, which may involve the loss of a toe or even of a leg.

See also Vol. XI: HOUSEHOLD PESTS.

FLESH FLY. This is the name given to a group of true flies belonging to the family Calliphoridae, and closely related to the BRISTLE-FLY (q.v.). They are large, grey or silvery flies, with coral-red eyes, dark longitudinal lines on their thoraxes, and dark and light draught-board markings on their abdomens. They are common insects, fond of settling on the ground in woods, in pastures, along country roads, and on moorlands. Like most two-winged flies, they are usually seen during the hours of hot sun-shine, and they often come into houses in rural districts.

All Flesh Flies look much alike, and about twenty species are found in Great Britain. So far as we know, they never lay eggs: they generally drop their larvae, usually in a not very advanced stage of development, upon decaying vegetable or animal matter, upon which the maggots then feed. One species of Flesh Fly has been seen to do this accurately from a height of over 60 cm. Flesh Flies also drop their larvae on open wounds on animals, and even on human beings, often causing much harm. Many of these larvae are internal parasites of scorpions, snails, earthworms, and insects.

See also FLY.

FLESH FLY ($\times 1\frac{1}{2}$)

FLIGHT. Flight may be of two sorts—either the passive gliding flight, seen in squirrels, lizards, and fish, or the active flapping flight, seen in birds, bats, and insects.

In passive gliding flight animals keep themselves airborne either by their own muscular efforts before 'take-off' or by breaking their fall under gravity by some sort of natural parachute device. FLYING-FISHES (q.v.) have greatly enlarged pectoral fins: having given a final muscular flip with their tails which drives them high in the air, they spread their fins and glide over the surface of the sea. Flying Squirrels, on the other hand, have a broad membrane skin stretched between the legs which acts as a parachute when they fall. Colugos, or Flying Lemurs, and some tree-haunting lizards have similar braking devices. Many gliding animals lack control over the direction of their flight. In active flight, however, the flying animal can remain airborne as a result of repeated muscular movement, and has normally complete control over the direction of flight.

The wing of a bat consists of a fold of skin stretched out on greatly lengthened fingers, and attached behind to the hind limb. In some ways bats are more efficient fliers than birds, in that they achieve as proportionately a good result with much smaller wing muscles. They also have a greater manœuvrability. (*See* BATS.)

In BIRDS (q.v.), on the other hand, the whole body is made very light by the hollowness of

WHINCHAT COMING IN TO ALIGHT ON A PERCH
The two photographs above and that on p. 155 show stages in the flight of a bird as it alights; the movement of the
tail feathers assists the bird in braking

the bones, the lightness of the feathers, and the presence of air-sacs inside the body itself. The back is rigid, and the wings, hinged against the backbone, are actuated by powerful muscles stretched over the keel or breastbone. Birds' flight, like that of bats, is normally effected by a flapping movement of the wings—that is, by movements which are apparently up and down —though, in fact, the tip of the wing describes a figure of eight, because the action is similar to that of an oar in rowing. But many birds, especially sea-birds, are able to glide for very long distances (*see* GULL, ALBATROSS, PETREL); and others can soar to great heights and for long periods (*see* HAWK, VULTURE, STORK). Gliding differs from soaring in that a gliding bird tends to lose height, and must flap to regain it, while a soaring bird does not. Birds that glide frequently have long, narrow wings, while those that soar generally have broad wings: both have larger wings than birds that merely flap. In both gliding and soaring, birds make use of air-currents (*see* GLIDING, Vol. IX). Off shore, GULLS (q.v.) will usually follow in the wake of a ship; and they are commonly to be seen passing forwards and upwards beside the ship in the strong air currents created as the ship moves forward, and then circling back, and losing height, as the calmer air astern of the ship is reached.

Some birds, such as the KESTREL (q.v.), are able to hover (or remain motionless in the air) by making use of the air-currents, holding wings

and tail meanwhile in such a way as to give buoyancy; others, such as the HUMMING BIRD (q.v.), hover by a rapid beating of the wings. Most birds, however, are unable to hover, and, consequently, below a certain speed must stall like an aeroplane, and come to earth. The stalling speed is very low in most birds, because they are provided with slots in their wings (now copied on aircraft) which guide the air smoothly round the end of the wing. These slots are plainly to be seen when rooks are in flight. Normally birds steer with their tails, and also use their tails as brakes.

The wings of INSECTS (q.v.) are not limbs, like those of bats and birds, but are extensions of the covering of the body. Insects usually have two pairs of wings, but the true FLY (q.v.) has only one pair. In all insects the method of flight is by flapping, sometimes alternated, in species with large wings, by short glides. Many insects are able to hover, and this they do by an extremely rapid beating of the wings. The fastest insect is the bee which, when it is not laden, can reach 48 km/h. The legend that the Deer-bot fly can travel at 1,300 km/h. is incorrect.

The fastest British bird is the Golden EAGLE (q.v.), with a maximum speed of 193 km/h., followed closely by swifts and swallows with 112 to 160 km/h. Ducks and geese fly at 64 to 96 km/h., crows and starlings at from 48 to 80 km/h., and the smaller birds at 32 to 56 km/h. Not only do birds excel in speed, they

WHINCHAT ALIGHTING
(See p. 154)

are also capable of great endurance in flight. The Arctic Tern, for instance, breeds in the Arctic and winters in the Antarctic, and so flies many thousands of kilometres every year; the Manx Shearwaters that breed off the coast of Britain go to the north coast of Spain to feed; and the tiny swallow winters in South Africa, doing the 8,000 km journey there and back every year of its life—no small achievement for an animal weighing barely 28 grammes.

See also MIGRATION.

FLOUNDER, *see* FLAT-FISHES.

FLOWERING PLANTS. 1. STRUCTURE. Flowering plants first appeared about one hundred million years ago (*see* CHART, opp. p. 1). Today there are at least a quarter of a million species, without counting the hybrids and varieties which have been developed by horticulturists. They have penetrated to all parts of the world, including the frozen wastes of the Arctic, the dry zones of the desert, and the hot, humid jungles of the tropics. They propagate by seeds contained in ovaries, or seed-cases—in contrast to plants such as CONIFERS (q.v.), which have naked seeds, or ALGAE, FUNGI, MOSSES AND LIVERWORTS, and FERNS (qq.v.), which reproduce by spores. The seeds of flowering plants have a double protection against unfavourable conditions, such as drought, heat, or cold, because they are protected not only by

their own tough coats, but by the seed ovaries in which they first develop.

Each seed consists of an outer protective coat containing a young plant complete with the beginnings of a root, known as the 'radicle', and a tiny shoot, the 'plumule'. Attached to this young plant are one or two special seed-leaves or 'cotyledons' containing a store of food for the young seedling, to feed it until it gets established. Some flowering plants have only one cotyledon, and are known as 'monocotyledons'; others have two, and are known as 'dicotyledons'. (*See* SEEDS.) Other differences between these two big groups are in the structure of the flowers and leaves and in the kind of foodstuffs which they build up. All flowering plants, although so different, are built to the same plan, the main features of which are the root, stem, leaves, and flowers. The extent to which each is developed, however, differs greatly from plant to plant.

The ROOTS (q.v.) serve to fix the green plant firmly in the ground, and also to take from the soil water containing the dissolved mineral salts. The main function of the STEM (q.v.) is to support the leaves and display them to the sunlight, an end achieved in many different ways. Also, the stem conducts the water from the roots to the leaves. The LEAVES (q.v.) are the food-factories, and in them food-stuffs are made up from the raw materials taken in by the roots and from the atmosphere. They contain the green colouring matter, 'chlorophyll', which has the unique property of being able to absorb radiant energy from sunlight and convert it into chemical energy, this being stored at first as food. (*See* PHOTOSYNTHESIS.) Lastly, there are the FLOWERS which produce FRUITS (qq.v.) containing the seeds.

2. HERBS, SHRUBS, AND TREES. A plant with a thick woody stem or trunk is called a tree. A small plant with a stem which contains little wood and which is usually green is called a herb Plants intermediate between the herb and the tree, with much wood but with no main trunk or bole, are called shrubs. The elm and ash are trees; the daisy and sunflower are herbs; the privet, bramble, and gorse are shrubs. There is, however, no hard-and-fast line to be drawn. The hawthorn, for example, in some places grows with a well-developed trunk, and would have to be described as a tree; in other places it has many woody branches coming straight from the ground and seems to be a typical shrub.

3. LENGTH OF LIFE. Herbs are generally much shorter-lived than shrubs or trees. In contrast to trees, some of which are reputed to be several thousands of years old, some herbs complete their life-cycles so quickly that their offspring can also complete their life histories in the same season. There may even be three or four generations within the same year. Because their lives are so short, such plants are called 'ephemerals' (from a Greek word meaning short-lived). Many weeds, such as groundsel, are ephemerals—as the gardener, who suffers from their rapid propagation, is only too well aware.

Many herbs live only for one season. In Great Britain we sow our seeds in spring; and in the autumn, when the crops are ripe, we gather in the harvest, taking good care that there are enough seeds to sow again in the following spring. These one-year plants are called ANNUALS (q.v. Vol. VI), and include all our cereals, such as wheat, and all those flowers like the marigold, sweet pea, and nasturtium, the seeds of which we have to sow afresh each spring.

Many plants, such as the carrot, seldom complete their life history, because we lift them to eat at the end of their first year of growth. If left in the soil, carrots would go into a resting condition in the winter; in the following spring they would throw up tall shoots with leaves and flowers; these would draw upon the food supply in the swollen root, and, after seeds had been produced, the whole plant would die. The carrot thus takes two years to complete its life-cycle, and is described as a BIENNIAL (q.v. Vol. VI). Many of our common 'root' vegetables, such as the swede, turnip, mangold, beetroot, and parsnip, are biennials.

Other plants, the grasses, daisies, buttercups, bluebells, crocuses, hollies, pines, oaks, and so on, live longer than annuals or biennials, their length of life ranging from a few years to many centuries. Some of these PERENNIALS (q.v. Vol. VI) are herbs, which store up food in underground parts during the growing season. In the cold season they pass into a resting condition, the delicate stem and leaves dying down. Growth is renewed in the next season at the expense of the food stored underground.

4. TREES. Trees and shrubs store up food in their shoots as well as their roots, and grow new shoots and roots each year. They can live to a very great age. The great Dragon's-blood Tree (so named because of the red resin that it yields) which was blown down in Teneriffe in 1869 was said to be over 6,000 years old. Possibly the oldest trees living today are the North American Bristlecone pines, some of which are over 4,000 years old. Another ancient tree, 1,500 years old or more, is the 'Big Tree of Tule', a bald cypress in Mexico. Its circumference a metre or so from the ground is no less than 48 metres.

We can estimate the age of a tree by counting the number of annual rings. If a tree is sawn down, the stump is seen to be made up of two kinds of wood. In the middle is wood of a darker

Ewing Galloway

THE BIG TREE OF TULE—A CYPRESS 1,500 YEARS OLD OR MORE

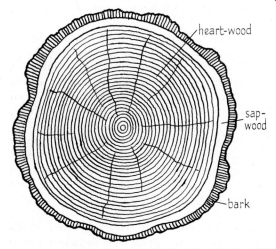

SECTION OF A TREE TRUNK SHOWING THE ANNUAL RINGS

colour called the 'heart-wood', and surrounding it lighter-coloured wood known as 'sap-wood'. Water containing dissolved mineral salts, which goes by the name of 'sap', passes through the tubes of the sap-wood to the leaves from the roots. The heart-wood is older, and dry, and contains no sap. Each year, during the growing season (which in temperate countries like Great Britain is from spring to autumn), the tree grows a thin layer of wood which is added on to the outside of the already-existing sap-wood. No new wood is formed during the winter. Because more sap rises in the spring than in the autumn, the tubes which are produced in the spring are bigger than those produced in the autumn. Then comes the winter when no tubes are produced. The following spring more big tubes grow, followed by small ones in the autumn, and so on. The difference in size between the small and big tubes causes the appearance of alternating light and dark rings, called 'annual rings', which can be counted to tell the approximate age of the tree. Experienced botanists can go even further than that and, by examining the size of the tubes, can tell us, for instance, whether it was a fine or wet autumn in the year that Queen Anne died.

See also VOL. VI: TREES, BROADLEAVED; TREES, CONIFEROUS; TIMBER.

FLOWERS. The flower is responsible for the production of the seeds, which carry the species on from one generation to another. Before one generation dies the seeds of another must be sown. Certain parts of the flower, the stamens and the carpels, are concerned only with reproduction, while other parts, the sepals and the petals, serve for protection or for attracting the insects to pollinate the flowers. Reproduction of flowers is sexual—fundamentally the same as that in most animals, including man.

The flower is really a condensed shoot in which the leaves have become modified to take on other work than manufacturing food. In a simple type of flower, such as the Buttercup, these are arranged in nearly concentric circles, called 'whorls'. The outermost are five green, leaf-like 'sepals', which protect the flower in bud. Inside the sepals are five usually heart-shaped 'petals', each with a small flap at its base making a little sac or nectary in which the sweet nectar is produced. The nectar serves to attract insects, and some of it later becomes converted into honey by bees. Both sepals and petals are attached to the swollen end of the flower-stalk, called the 'receptacle', which projects like a cone into the flower.

Above the sepals and petals come those parts of the flower which are essential in reproduction. First, there are numerous 'stamens', or male reproductive organs, each consisting of a stalk-like filament and a head, called the 'anther'. The anthers contain compartments called 'pollen sacs' which, when they are ripe, contain the yellow pollen. Each pollen grain contains one male reproductive cell. At the top of the receptacle are many kidney-shaped 'carpels', each having a projecting beak or 'stigma' at the upper end. The lower, expanded part of the carpel is called the 'ovary', and contains the 'ovule' within which the egg, or female reproductive cell, is produced.

Most flowers are built on some such plan as this; but there are wide variations, not only in

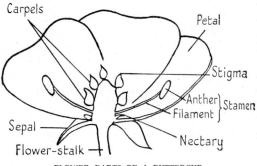

FLOWER PARTS OF A BUTTERCUP

Harold Bastin

HAZEL FLOWERS

The male catkins consist of pollen-bearing flowers. The inconspicuous, female, nut-producing flower is seen on the lower part of the stem

size, shape, and colour, but also in the numbers of the different parts. Catkins, which are clusters of the flowers of certain trees and shrubs, are unlike most flowers because they have no sepals or petals and the male and female flowers are grouped separately. In Hazels, Oaks, and Walnuts the male (stamen-bearing) flowers are grouped together on a long stalk to form dangling catkins. The insignificant female flowers are protected by scales like those covering the leaf buds, with only the stigma showing. In the Willow and Poplar the male and female catkins are very similar, and in the Sweet Chestnut there are a few female flowers at the base of each catkin, all the rest being male. Trees bearing catkins are wind pollinated, and their catkins produce enormous quantities of pollen, which even the slightest wind will shake out. Their flowers always open before the leaves

so that pollen can more easily reach the female flowers.

Variations, though less startling, are seen in other flowers. The tulip, for instance, shows no distinction between sepals and petals, but has six brightly coloured floral leaves called 'perianth leaves'. The Poppy has only two sepals, while the Lesser Celandine has three. Sometimes, instead of being free, as in the Buttercup, the petals are joined to form a tube, as in the Primrose. In other flowers, such as those of the Pea family, the petals in the same flower may take on different shapes and have different uses.

There is variation in the stamens and carpels, too. Such flowers as the Deadnettle and Wallflower, instead of having an indefinite number of stamens and carpels, have a constant number. In the Buttercup the stamens are carried on the receptacle, while in the Primrose they are joined to the petals. In many flowers, as in the Buttercup, the number of carpels is indefinite, and they are all separate; in other flowers the number is constant, and often they are fused together. The Gooseberry, for example, has two carpels which are intimately joined, and the Primrose has five which are joined in a different way.

Flowering plants are classified into families according to these many differences. The basis of all flowers is, however, that they produce male and female reproductive cells which, after fusion, develop into the seeds from which new plants grow. All other parts of the flower are incidental to this fundamental process of sexual reproduction. (*See* REPRODUCTION IN PLANTS: *see also* INDEX, p. 63).

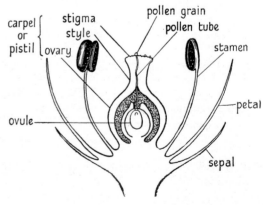

THE PARTS OF A FLOWER

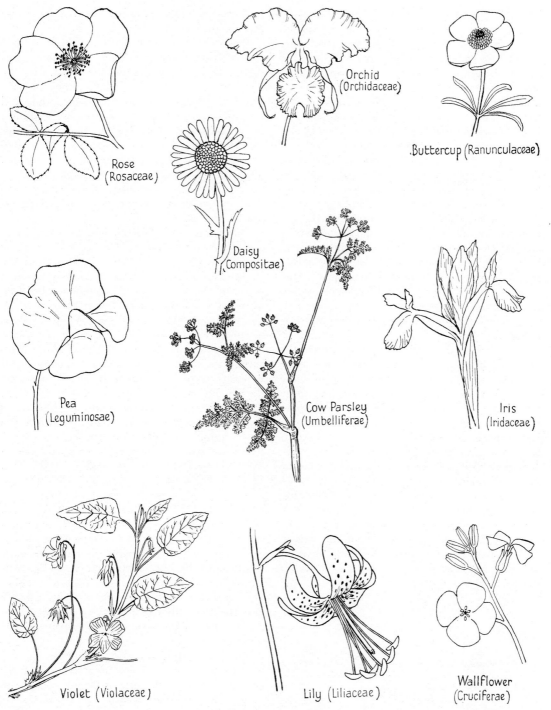

Rose
(Rosaceae)

Orchid
(Orchidaceae)

Buttercup (Ranunculaceae)

Daisy
(Compositae)

Pea
(Leguminosae)

Cow Parsley
(Umbelliferae)

Iris
(Iridaceae)

Violet (Violaceae)

Lily (Liliaceae)

Wallflower
(Cruciferae)

COMMON FLOWER FAMILIES

FLY. The true flies (Diptera) form one of the largest orders of insects; over 5,200 species occur in Great Britain. True flies have only one pair of wings, the hind pair, usual in other insects, having been reduced to a pair of club-shaped structures called 'halteres', which act as balancers. The two halteres are clearly seen in the CRANE FLY (q.v.) or Daddy-long-legs; but in flies such as the HOUSE-FLY (q.v.) they are covered over and hidden by scales.

During their long life-history flies pass through an egg, larval, and pupal stage before becoming adult (*see* METAMORPHOSIS). Flies have sucking mouthparts, usually in the form of a proboscis, which with some species is also adapted for piercing. Most flies are active by day and feed on nectar and decaying matter; but in some species, such as MOSQUITOES, HORSE FLIES, and TSETSE FLIES (qq.v.), the females suck blood, and it is blood-sucking flies that transmit TROPICAL DISEASES (q.v. Vol. XI), such as malaria, yellow fever, and sleeping sickness.

Most flies lay their eggs in places suited to the habits of their larvae, which in most cases have to look after themselves. The larvae of some species, however, hatch and are nourished inside the female, often one at a time, and in some cases do not emerge until they are fully grown and ready to pupate. The KED (q.v.), a common skin parasite of sheep, and the Tsetse Fly of tropical Africa nourish and drop their larvae in this manner.

Fly larvae, many of which are commonly called 'maggots' and 'gentles', are legless. They have a wide variety of habitats: they may live in the water, underground, or in the leaves, stems, or roots of plants; they may live as internal or external PARASITES (q.v.) of other insects or of the higher animals. Many of the fly larvae living as parasites on man can cause serious illnesses.

Pupation may take place in either of two ways. In the first way, the larval skin splits along the back, liberating the pupa. In the second, the adult larva, when it has stopped feeding, wriggles away from its food supply and becomes oval in shape, usually brown or reddish in colour, and hard in texture. Inside this outer covering, formed out of the larval skin and called a 'puparium', the pupa is generally immobile. The adult fly emerges from the pupa through a longitudinal split, and those which have also to escape from the puparium do so by forcing off its top or 'lid'.

One group of flies which pupates in a puparium has on the front of its face a narrow slit called the 'frontal suture'. This is in the shape of an inverted V or U, and passes upwards between the eyes and the antennae, bending over just above the latter. Traced into the head, this slit leads into a closed sac. When the fly is about to escape from its puparium the sac is forced inside-out through the slit by fluid pressure in the head, and it forms a balloon-shaped structure in front of the head. This presses on the top of the puparium till the latter gives way. Soon after the fly has escaped the balloon is drawn back by muscles through the slit into the head again, and is of no further use.

See also BLOWFLY; BRISTLE FLY; CHEESE-SKIPPER; FLESH FLY; HORSE-FLY; HOUSE-FLY; HOVER-FLY; HUMBLE-BEE FLY; MIDGE; MOSQUITO; STABLE FLY.

FLY-CATCHERS. These are small Passerine or perching birds, feeding principally upon flying insects, which they catch on the wing. There are a number of species distributed over most countries of the Old World, and Australia, with a separate family found only in America. There are two British species, the Spotted Fly-catcher and the Pied Fly-catcher, which arrive in late April or early May to breed, and migrate farther south in September.

The Spotted Fly-catcher, which is spotted most when young, is an inconspicuous bird, quite common in all parts of Britain except the very north, and often seen in London parks. It has favourite perches on which it waits for insects, and from which it makes sudden little dashing flights to snap up its prey. It builds a neat little nest in a crevice in a wall, tree, or building, or in a creeper or shrub, and lays four

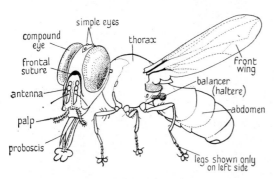

DIAGRAM OF A HOUSE-FLY

Eric Hosking

A SPOTTED FLY-CATCHER

stream. The nest, made of grass, strips of bark, and roots, is covered over with cobwebs, so that the whole thing looks like a knot of wood on the branch.

The King-bird belongs to the Tyrant Fly-catchers of Central and South America, and goes to the eastern states of the U.S.A. to breed. It is very bold in defence of its nest, fiercely attacking any other bird that comes near.

FLYING-FISHES (Exocoetidae). On any voyage across the Pacific Ocean one is almost certain to see a shoal of Flying-fishes. These fishes, shaped rather like herrings, have very large wing-like, pectoral fins, and in some kinds large pelvic wings too. They do not flap their fins in flight but are gliders (*see* FLIGHT). Generally they swim near the surface of the water with their fins close against the body. Just before they launch themselves from the water, they point slightly upwards and swim rapidly with the tail. As they leave the water they give a final flip of the tail (the lower part of the caudal fin is large for this purpose) which drives them high in the air, and then, spreading their fins wide like the wings of an aeroplane, they glide. There are many upward currents of air above the surface of the sea, due to the difference in temperature between the water and the atmosphere and these may help to keep the fishes airborne. Flying-fishes, however, seem incapable of steering themselves when gliding.

The Flying-fish makes a sort of nest. The eggs, unlike those of so many oceanic fishes, are heavier than water and would sink were they not laid in a bunch of floating weed bound together with tough white threads. Since the SARGASSO SEA (q.v. Vol. III), a part of the

to six greenish-white eggs clouded with rusty markings. The Pied Fly-catcher has black and white on the head and wings, so that it is more conspicuous; but it is far less common. It lays six to nine pale blue eggs, occasionally speckled with red.

The Fly-catchers of tropical and semi-tropical countries are much more showy. The Paradise Fly-catchers are found from Africa eastwards to Japan. The males of most of these have long central tail feathers, and for part of the year the plumage is mainly white with a glossy blue crown. These birds appear in many Chinese and Japanese paintings. In India there are the lovely blue Niltavas; and Australia has a number of Fly-catchers and also the related Fantails and Robins (not European Robins). The bold black-and-white 'Willie Wagtails' are general favourites, as are also the friendly little Scarlet Robins and the Yellow Bobs. The Australian Black Fantail Fly-catcher builds a lovely cup-shaped nest, often on a branch overhanging a

A. Fraser-Brunner

FLYING-FISHES LEAPING OVER THE WAVES

western North Atlantic, has such abundant floating weeds, it is a favourite breeding-place for Flying-fish.

Several kinds of fishes can fly. In tropical seas we find the Flying Gurnards (Triglidae)—heavy looking creatures, with enormous, gaily coloured 'wings'. A small South African river and swamp fish and a few of the South American CHARACINS (q.v.), or Hatchet-fish, are also capable of short, erratic, gliding flights. The latter are, perhaps, more bird-like than any of the others, for they can flap their 'wings'. They have, like birds, a large keel for the attachment of the huge pectoral muscles; in BIRDS (q.v.), however, the keel is on the breast-bone, while in these fishes it is part of the shoulder-girdle.

See also Vol. VI: FLYING-FISH FISHING.

FLYING FOX, *see* BAT.

FOSSILS, *see* Vol. III.

FOX. This member of the Dog family is well known to those who enjoy FOX-HUNTING (q.v. Vol. IX), or to farmers and game-preservers who have suffered from its depredations (*see* PESTS, ANIMAL, Vol. VI). Foxes are related to WOLVES, DOGS, and JACKALS (qq.v.). Native species are to be found in most parts of the world, but not in Australia and New Zealand.

The most common fox generally is the Red Fox. The English Red Fox is reddish-brown, with a white belly and throat, a white tip to the tail, and black patches behind its ears. The North American Red Fox includes two colour

A. R. Thompson
A DOG-FOX NEAR HIS LAIR

varieties: a beautiful silver, and also a cross—a reddish-black fox, both much sought after by the fur-hunter, and bred by the fur-farmer (*see* FUR FARMING, Vol. VI). Another species is the Arctic fox, some of which remain bluish-grey the whole year round, while others turn white to suit their snowy surroundings during the winter. The smallest-known fox is the beautiful little sand-coloured Fennec Fox of the Saharan Desert, which is distinguished by its large ears.

Foxes hunt mainly by night, and hide during the day in holes or burrows, called 'earths' (often taken over from rabbits or badgers), in ravines, or among thick undergrowth. They are usually silent; but on a winter night the yapping scream of the vixen or the yelping bark of a dog-fox may often be heard. They hunt hares, rabbits, ground birds (particularly partridges), and frequently make raids on poultry-yards; they will carry off young lambs, and have even been known to kill a pony foal. When food is scarce they will eat rats, worms, beetles, frogs, fish, and almost any other animal, dead or alive.

All foxes are very intelligent, as every fox-hunter knows, and their cunning is proverbial. They use a number of ingenious devices for concealing from the hunter their strong scent, which is secreted in a gland beneath the tail. They will double back on their tracks, leap sideways, climb trees, take to water, mingle with sheep, roll in muck, and even put up another fox to side-track their pursuers. They use as varied a number of devices in their own hunting. Rabbits have often been deceived by watching a fox gambolling and rolling over and over with an apparent innocence of intention. The rabbits, reassured, draw near to watch—whereupon the fox pounces. Foxes can swim well, can climb trees, and can get out of almost any enclosure.

Except for the Fennec Foxes, which are social, foxes live solitary lives, save during the breeding season. Several dog-foxes will often fight fiercely over a vixen. They breed in early spring, and generally have a litter of four to six cubs.

FRIGATE BIRD. This ocean bird belongs to the same order as the CORMORANT, GANNET, and PELICAN (qq.v.)—all lovers of water. Frigate Birds inhabit the open sea, the Great Frigate Bird ranging the warmer regions of the Atlantic, Pacific, and Indian Oceans, and the Lesser Frigate Bird confining itself mainly to the Indian

A PAIR OF FRIGATE BIRDS AT THEIR NEST
The female's scarlet pouch is enormously distended

Ocean. They come to land in order to roost in trees and to breed on inaccessible cliff ledges or on the shores of little-inhabited islands; but they spend much of their time on the wing, making long, powerful, graceful flights, soaring to such heights that they have been called 'sons of the sun'. In build they are well fitted for such a life. They have slender bodies and very short legs, but long pointed wings and a long, deeply forked tail. Their hooked beaks are long and powerful, and they have a remarkable pouch of scarlet skin beneath the throat, which they can inflate with air to a considerable size.

Frigate Birds catch fish for themselves on the surface of the sea; but they also depend largely for food on attacking other birds, such as Gannets and Terns, and making them disgorge their catch. Gannets returning from a feeding-ground in the evening will be assailed by two or three Frigate Birds, who will chase them relentlessly until the exhausted Gannets disgorge some of their fish. The Frigate Birds immediately dive for the morsel, catching it in mid-air. Sometimes they will seize their victims and shake them to make them disgorge.

FRILLED LIZARD, *see* AGAMA.

FRITILLARY, FLOWER, *see* LILIES.

FRITILLARY. BUTTERFLIES. These tawny butterflies, which generally live in woods, have black markings on the upperside of their wings, and often silver patterns on the underside. They belong, with the ADMIRALS, TORTOISESHELLS, and PURPLE EMPERORS (qq.v.), to the family Nymphalidae, which use only four legs for walking, their small forelegs being tucked up against their bodies. The larvae have small heads and long, thorn-like spines. The pupae hang by tail-hooks only, and have sharp spines supposed to protect them from injury should they strike anything as they swing in the wind. They often have silver and gold spots, on account of which the name 'chrysalis', meaning 'golden', came to be used for the pupae of all butterflies.

The Pearl-bordered, probably the commonest of all the British Fritillaries, can be seen in most southern, dry, wooded districts in May and early June. It has seven border 'pearls', and two other silver spots on the underside of its hindwings. The Small Pearl-bordered occurs more commonly in wet woods, and even marshes, in the same locality, and is the only Fritillary found in the north of Scotland. The two are often difficult to distinguish; but the underside of the smaller species is more richly coloured and has more silver spots, and the adult emerges a little later. The females of both these butterflies lay their eggs on the leaves of Dog-violet, or on pieces of trailing bracken near-by, and the black, spiny caterpillars hibernate amongst the fallen leaves.

The Silver-washed, the largest British Fritillary, has silver stripes and spots on the underside of its wings, the male usually being a lighter orange than the typical female. The variety *valezina*, restricted to females, is dark olive-green, and, though fairly frequent in the New Forest, is rare elsewhere. The females lay their eggs singly in the crevices of tree trunks, where the young caterpillars hibernate all the winter, subsisting only on their egg-shell, which they eat when they hatch. When the weather turns warm in the spring, they drop to the ground in search of violets. They are purplish-brown, with two yellowish stripes along the back—these divert attention from their real shape and make them very difficult to find. The butterflies emerge in July, and may be seen in many of the larger woods in the southern counties, as also in Wales and Ireland. They feed freely at bramble flowers.

S. Beaufoy

SILVER-WASHED FRITILLARY ON BRAMBLE FLOWERS

The Marsh Fritillary has a misleading name, as it occurs as much on hilltops as in marshy meadows. The colouring is very variable, no other British butterfly having so many distinctive forms for the localities it frequents. The females lay large batches of yellow eggs on the underside of scabious leaves, and these take much longer to hatch than most butterflies' eggs—nearly a month instead of ten days or a fortnight. The black, spiny caterpillars live together in thick webs, which they weave amongst the leaves and grass stems. They hibernate when about half-grown, and come out again in the first warm days of spring. When disturbed, they all jerk up their heads—this kind of collective movement being common among caterpillars which have a disagreeable taste, for it serves to remind would-be enemies of previous unpleasant experiences.

The Heath Fritillary is another butterfly with an even more misleading name, as it occurs only in woods, and never on heaths. It is easily distinguished from the other Fritillaries in having no silver or black dots on the underside of its wings. The tiny, black, shiny caterpillars hibernate in little groups of five or six in dead leaves on the ground. Their favourite food-plant is cow-wheat, a tiny yellow-flowered weed which grows best in the newly cut-down parts of a wood. The butterfly breeds only where its food-plant grows, and so is continually changing its headquarters. It is now restricted to Kent, Devon, and Cornwall, except for colonies in Essex and Sussex where it has recently been reintroduced.

The Glanville Fritillary breeds in the British Isles only in the Isle of Wight, where it is found mostly in sheltered spots on steep cliffs in May and June. The black, spiny caterpillars have reddish-brown heads and feed on plantain. They weave webs and live beneath them in large colonies throughout the winter, starting to feed, still in colonies, in the spring. When they have cast off several coats and are in the last skin, they begin to feed singly, nibbling the narrow-leaved plantain leaves which grow between the shingle within a few feet of high tide. They are named after a Lady Glanville, who, in the 18th century, was accused of lunacy because she collected butterflies!

The Dark Green Fritillary is a fast-flying butterfly, seen on the wing in July. Unlike most Fritillaries, it seems to prefer hill-sides and rough wild country to woods, a fine large and dark race occurring in the Hebrides. On the underside of its wings it has a regular pattern of silver spots on a greenish-brown background. The female lays her eggs on violet plants, especially those growing under bushes. The caterpillars hatch in about a fortnight, and at once go into hibernation, without feeding. The High Brown, usually found in sunny glades and ridings of woods, looks very like the Dark Green when seen on the wing. The undersides of their wings are, however, slightly different, the High Brown having a row of reddish-brown spots, with silver eyes along the edge. Like the Dark Green, the female lays her eggs amongst the leaves of violet plants, but they do not hatch until the following spring. The chrysalis of both the Dark Green and High Brown Fritillaries is sheltered in a tent made of leaves. Both the High Brown and the Silver-washed Fritillaries have the habit of resting in trees overnight and on dull days.

The Queen of Spain is a rare immigrant to this country from the Continent, where it is common. It has been known to breed in the British Isles, but it cannot survive the winter, and so dies off until fresh immigrants arrive. It has a number of large silver spots on the underside of its wings.

The DUKE OF BURGUNDY (q.v.) resembles Fritillaries in colour, but belongs to another family.

FROG. It is easy to distinguish frogs from Toads (q.v.) in England, for the frogs have a smooth, slimy skin, while the toads have a dry and warty one. But there is also a difference in the skeleton, and this distinguishes them all over the world. In frogs, the two front halves of the shoulder-girdle meet in the midline and form a firm bar; in the toads, they overlap. Strictly speaking, therefore, all those with a firm bar should be called frogs, and all the others toads —and some naturalists have tried to apply this definition. But popular names do not grow up in that way, and the terms 'frog' and 'toad' are often interchanged. For instance, the Green Tree Frog of Europe, with its smooth and slimy skin, is structurally a toad. On the other hand, there is a large genus of Tree Frogs in Asia (such as Wallace's Flying Frog) which is externally very similar to the Tree Frog of Europe, but anatomically is a frog.

The Common Frog is found throughout most of Europe and northern Asia, and its spawn and tadpoles are familiar to everyone. Most of its life is spent on land, where in fields and gardens it is most useful in destroying insects and slugs. In Spring frogs go to water to breed, often returning to the same pond year after year. In winter they hibernate in the soft mud at the bottom of ditches and ponds.

Closely related to the Common Frog is the Edible Frog, which is widely distributed over the whole of Europe. Although unlikely to be a native of Britain, it may have been introduced by French monks to add to their diet. But these introductions must all have died out. In the 19th century, however, between 1837 and 1842, a great many were brought into East Anglia and, later, to many parts of southern England, and small colonies of their descendants can still be found, even within a few miles of London. The Edible Frog is green to bronzy-brown on top, with black spots and three more or less dis-

A COMMON FROG   *S. C. Bisserôt*

tinct stripes down the back, and a green stripe flanked by two yellowish ones along the spine. The general colours, however, are very variable. In the breeding season the males can be very noisy; when croaking, they inflate sacs on either side of the head. Only the hind legs of the frog are eaten. The flesh, which is white and is served up fried, tastes like young chicken. Another well-known European frog is the Fire-bellied Frog, of which there are two species. They live in hilly districts, and are about 4 to 5 centimetres long. Their general colour is dark grey to blackish, except for the belly and the under part of the limbs, which are conspicuously marked with red in one species, and with yellow in the other. When first caught, these frogs adopt a peculiar threatening attitude, throwing back their heads and turning their limbs upwards so that the bright colours of the under parts are shown.

The name Tree Frog covers a large number of frogs and toads which live in trees. They have adhesive pads to their fingers and toes, with which they cling to the bark or leaves. Many of them are green in colour. One large family of Tree Frogs, known as the Hylidae, which in structure are really toads, are to be found all over the world, and are represented in Europe by the well-known Green Tree Frog. Another large family, the Rhacophoridae, are true frogs, and are restricted to tropical Asia and tropical Africa. Most of the Hylidae spawn in the water like ordinary frogs; but the Rhacophoridae make 'nests', whipping the gelatinous substance which surrounds the eggs into a foam so as to enclose

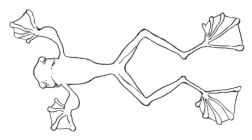

A FLYING FROG

them completely. This mass is then floated on the water. The early larval stages are passed in the foam; but after a time, the wriggling tadpoles drop into the water, and then continue their development in the usual way. The European Tree Frog has been imported into England on several occasions: one colony has now lived for over 20 years in the Isle of Wight, and breeds there.

The best-known Flying Frog, Wallace's Flying Frog, is a species of Tree Frog of the genus *Rhacophorus*. It is some 7·5 cm in length, has a green back, and large black webs between the fingers and toes. It spends the greater part of its life at the tops of high trees, where, with its webbed digits expanded, it can glide through the air from one tree to another. Wallace's Frog lives in Borneo; but there are several other species, with equally broad webs, found in other parts of the Malayan region. The Hairy Frog is a species found in West Africa. The flanks and thighs of the male are covered with blackish growths, resembling hairs, which provide an additional means of breathing during the breeding season.

The name 'Bull Frog' is applied indiscriminately to many frogs with a particularly noisy croak.

FROG-HOPPER (Cercopidae).

On the stems and leaves of many plants during summer months a white frothy substance called 'cuckoo-spit' can often be seen. In the middle of this is a little white grub, the small 'nymph' of a Frog-hopper bug. The froth, formed from a fluid issuing from the end of the abdomen, is blown into bubbles by air from a cavity below the abdomen. One species from Madagascar is said to discharge watery fluid at such a rate that it resembles fine rain. The froth is thought to protect the nymphs from drying up, and it also probably protects them from their enemies, though wasps have sometimes been seen to seize the nymphs from their froth. The adult Frog-hopper leaves the 'cuckoo-spit' and feeds on the juices of the leaves and stems of plants. When sitting on the leaves it is supposed to resemble a frog, and this, together with its habit of jumping, accounts for its common name, Frog-hopper. About ten species of this bug are found in Britain. Most of these are pale brown or yellow, but the largest species is scarlet and black.

See also BUGS.

FRUITS.

1. The botanist uses the term fruit in a different sense from the housewife or greengrocer. To a botanist, Rhubarb is simply a swollen leaf-stalk, the Strawberry is not a true fruit but a collection of fruits, whereas the Tomato and the Peapod with its peas are true fruits. The fruit is the complete structure formed by the ovary and neighbouring parts of the flower after fertilization has taken place (see REPRODUCTION IN PLANTS); and it contains the seeds, which develop from the ovules after fertilization.

The fruits of flowering plants take on many shapes and sizes, and may be formed from one carpel or from many (see FLOWERS). Each fruit may contain one or a number of seeds, which may be distributed direct from the plant or, more often, shed from the fruit after it has left the plant. Many fruits are modified in structure to ensure that they and their seeds are widely distributed (see SEEDS).

Fruits are of three kinds—simple, aggregate, and composite. Simple fruits, such as those of the Sweet Pea and Poppy, are formed from one carpel or from a number of carpels joined to form a single structure. Aggregate fruits, of which the Buttercup is a good example, are formed when each carpel gives rise to a fruitlet, and the fruit is therefore made up of a number or aggregate of fruitlets. Composite fruits, of which there are not many, are formed, not from a single flower, but from a number of flowers, as in the Fig, Pineapple, Mulberry, and Hop.

BUTTERCUP
An aggregate of fruits

It is convenient to divide simple fruits into two groups according to their condition when ripe: dry fruits, and succulent or fleshy fruits. Dry fruits can be either 'dehiscent' or 'indehiscent', according to whether they possess a mechanism allowing them to open to distribute their seeds or not. (*See* SEEDS, Section 2.)

MULBERRY
A composite fruit

2. DRY FRUITS. (*a*) 'Achenes' are fruits which are dry, indehiscent, and one-seeded. In the Buttercup, for instance, each carpel ripens after fertilization into a separate fruitlet, the whole collection of fruits being described as an

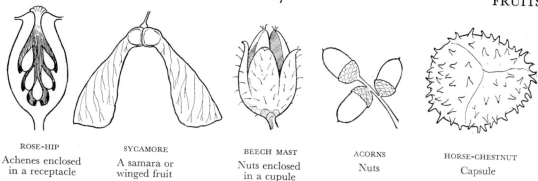

ROSE-HIP	SYCAMORE	BEECH MAST	ACORNS	HORSE-CHESTNUT
Achenes enclosed in a receptacle	A samara or winged fruit	Nuts enclosed in a cupule	Nuts	Capsule

aggregate of achenes. After fertilization, the carpellary wall undergoes no special change, so that each fruit is simply a single seed surrounded by the hardened carpellary wall; and before it can germinate, the fruit wall, or 'pericarp', must be ruptured to allow the radicle and plumule to emerge.

Other examples of achenes are found in the Dock, Sorrel, and also in the Rose-hip, where the receptacle is red and cup-shaped and encloses the achenes. The fruit of the Strawberry, whether the cultivated variety or the Common Wild Strawberry, is a greatly swollen, red, fleshy receptacle, bearing scattered achenes (the pips).

(b) 'Samaras' (Winged Fruits) are achenes in which the hardened carpellary wall grows into a long, flattened, wing-like structure, adapted for dispersal of the fruit by wind. A good example of the samara is the fruit of the Ash, which hangs from the tree in large bunches after fertilization. The fruit of the Elm might be described as a double samara, while in the Sycamore two and sometimes three samaras fuse slightly at their swollen bases.

(c) 'Nuts' are dry, indehiscent, one-seeded fruits, closely related to the achene. They may or may not be formed from one carpel. Unlike the achene, the carpellary wall of the nut becomes hard and woody. The term 'nut' is usually applied to all large or hard-coated achenes, although some are not nuts at all: for example, the Brazil-nut and Horse-chestnut are seeds; the Walnut, Almond, and Coco-nut are 'drupes'. Among true nuts are the Hazel, Oak, Beech, and Sweet Chestnut.

In the Hazel or the Filbert (which is a cultivated Hazel), the shell is the hardened carpellary wall and the kernel is the seed. The nut lies in a large green leafy cup formed from the small leaves immediately behind the flower, but which have persisted after fertilization. In the Beech and Oak the nut is formed from three carpels, but only one seed develops. In the Beech and Sweet Chestnut the nuts are completely enclosed in a cupule formed of bracts. It is easy to see that fruits, and not seeds, are enclosed, because the remains of the style and stigma can be seen on the nut. In the case of the Horse-chestnut and Sweet Chestnut, the brown-coloured bodies, which superficially resemble each other, are in the former case seeds and in the latter case fruits.

(d) 'Schizocarp' is a dry, indehiscent fruit formed from two or more carpels which, when ripe, splits into portions, each portion containing one seed. The schizocarp of the Mallow or Hollyhock is a stout ring which splits into wedge-like segments. The schizocarp of the Geranium is formed from five joined carpels, and splits at the base into five one-seeded portions.

(e) 'Caryopsis' is the characteristic grain or fruit of all grasses and cereals, such as Oats, Maize, Wheat, and Barley. It is a dry, indehiscent fruit, in which the pericarp, or fruit wall, is so closely joined to the seed-coat that the seed cannot be taken out of its case. What appears to be the 'seed' of cereals, therefore, is really the fruit. In many cases, the fruit or grain is covered by the persistent bract which forms a husk around it. Cereal grains will live in a dormant condition up to perhaps about 15 years, though claims that 'mummy wheat' grains taken from the tombs of Ancient Egypt are still alive have been proved to be without foundation.

(f) 'Follicles', such as the fruits of the Marsh Marigold, Monkshood, and Larkspur, are one of the simplest kinds of dry, dehiscent or splitting fruit. Each follicle is formed from a single, free carpel, containing several ovules. When the

PEA

A pod or
legume

WALLFLOWER

A siliqua

POPPY

A capsule

SCARLET
PIMPERNEL

A pyxidium

seeds are ripe the follicle splits along the whole length of the inner seam which bears the seeds, so that the seeds are exposed for distribution. The aggregate fruits of many members of the Buttercup family consist of collections of follicles.

(g) 'Pods' or legumes are dry, dehiscent fruits, like follicles in that they are formed from a single, free carpel, containing several ovules which later become the seeds; but unlike follicles, the pod, when ripe, splits, not only along the inside seam, but also along the outside seam or midrib. The pod is the characteristic fruit of the Pea family.

(h) 'Siliquas', the characteristic fruit of the Wallflower family, are dry, dehiscent fruits, which are formed from two carpels. The siliqua appears to be two-chambered, because of the growth of a false partition between the two carpels. The fruit is long and cylindrical, and when ripe, the two parts split from the bottom upwards, exposing the seeds, which are attached to the false partition. In some members of the Wallflower family—Honesty, for instance—the fruit is short and flat. When the fruit splits the seeds are left exposed on the oval, flattened, false partition, which looks like silvery parchment.

(i) 'Capsules' are a form of dry, dehiscent fruit, which show many variations. They are many-seeded, formed from two or more carpels, and may be one-valved or many-valved. Although they vary greatly in the way they split, most of them split the whole length of the capsule, the number of splits corresponding to the number of carpels that formed the 'valves' or segments. The Iris, for ex-

ample, splits along the midribs into three valves; the capsules of Willow and Poplar split into two valves, and the Willow-herb into four. Many capsules which split lengthwise split down only a little way, and are said to open by teeth. These teeth are only open in dry weather, remaining closed on wet days. The number of teeth is either the same, or twice as many, as the number of carpels. The Primrose capsule, for instance, opens by five teeth and the Campion by ten, both fruits being formed from five carpels.

Capsules sometimes open by pores. This is seen in the Poppy and Snapdragon, where a number of pores are formed by a breaking away and bending back of tissues at the top of the ripe fruit. In the capsule of the Canterbury Bell and other Campanulas, however, large pores are formed at the base of the fruit. Some capsules split crossways—a good example of this being the fruit of the Scarlet Pimpernel, which looks like a little box and is called a 'pyxidium'. The whole top of the capsule comes off readily, like a little lid, exposing the seeds attached to the central core. The cone-shaped fruit of the Plantain is also a pyxidium.

3. FLESHY FRUITS. (a) 'Berries' are one of the simplest types of fleshy or succulent fruits, in which the whole of the fruit wall is pulpy or fleshy. The seeds, which are usually hard, are embedded in the pulp. Common berries are the Tomato, Grape, Currant, Banana, Orange, Lemon, Grape-fruit, Gooseberry, Pomegranate, and Cucumber.

The Tomato is formed by the union of two carpels. When ripe, the fruit wall, a mass of tissue with a thin tough skin, becomes thick and juicy, and a sticky fluid is given off into the ovary cavity. The Tomato is a native of South America, first brought to Europe by the Spaniards, and originally called the 'love-apple'. As a vegetable, it has only been popular in Great Britain for about a century. The Grape is also a berry, formed from two joined carpels, in which the fruit wall becomes fleshy. Dried currants, raisins, sultanas, and muscatels are all dried forms of Grapes and are, therefore, berries. True Currants, black, white, and red, are the berries of small deciduous shrubs. The Banana is also a berry, though highly cultivated Bananas, which are now successfully propagated by cuttings, do not develop seeds, the only sign of them being a brown dustiness sometimes to be seen in the centre of the fruit.

Oranges, Lemons, and Grape-fruit, all closely related tropical plants, produce berries, each of which is composed of six or more fused carpels, in which the fruit wall is divided into a tough outer skin containing many oil-glands, and a fleshy inner part. In the Gooseberry and Pomegranate, the pulp or edible portion of the berry is derived largely (in the case of the Gooseberry) or entirely (in the Pomegranate) from the outer coats of the seeds. The Date is a most interesting berry, easily mistaken for a drupe. The stone or seed of a Date has no kernel, as has the stone of a drupe, but is hard all through, because the reserve food is stored up as cellulose. This seed is completely surrounded by the fleshy fruit wall.

GOOSEBERRY CROSS-SECTION

A berry

BLACKBERRY

A collection of drupes

(b) 'Drupes' (Stone fruits) are succulent, one-seeded fruits, examples of which are the Plum, Cherry, Peach, Apricot, Coco-nut, Walnut, and Almond. In the drupe the fruit is formed from either one carpel or three joined carpels. Whereas in the berry the whole fruit wall or pericarp becomes fleshy, in the drupe the fruit wall swells and becomes divided into three distinct layers—the 'epicarp' or outer skin; the 'mesocarp' or middle region, usually a thick, fleshy and often edible portion; and the 'endocarp', the hard inner part or 'stone', which encloses and protects the seed.

The Walnut is not easily recognizable as a drupe, because what we crack to eat is the stone only. In green pickled walnuts, however, the drupe-like character of the fruit is clear. The fruit is formed from two fused carpels, and consists of a thin epicarp, a fleshy, green mesocarp, and a woody endocarp (or stone) containing the seed. As it ripens, the two large seed-leaves or cotyledons, which form the mass of the kernel, become divided by a thin partition, and sometimes also by thin cross-partitions. The Almond is another example of a fruit of which the portion used for food is only the seed. The actual drupe is composed of a fruit wall divided into three layers—an epicarp, which is green and velvety, a tough, downy mesocarp, and the stony shell or endocarp. The bitterness of some

almonds is due to the presence of a complex organic chemical. The Coco-nut, too, has its epicarp and mesocarp removed before it is offered for sale in the shops, and we see only the woody endocarp with the contained seeds—though traces of the mesocarp occasionally remain as fibrous tufts, for here the mesocarp is not fleshy but fibrous.

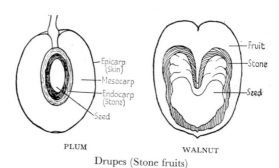

PLUM

WALNUT

Drupes (Stone fruits)

(c) 'Pomes'. In the Apple, the Pear, and other fruits derived from some members of the Rose family, the succulent 'fruit' called a Pome is formed, not from the ovary, but from the greatly swollen stem or receptacle. The true fruit is the membranous core. The ovary of the flower is formed from five fused carpels, and is

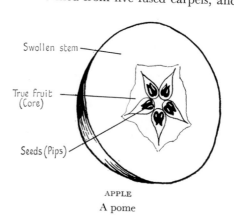

APPLE

A pome

intimately fused with the surrounding receptacle. After fertilization of the flower, this receptacle swells greatly to form the fleshy part of the fruit. The carpels themselves become tough and form the core, which contains the small brown pips or seeds. Among other pomes are the Quince, Medlar, Rowan (Mountain Ash), Cotoneaster, and Hawthorn.

(d) Pineapple. This is an interesting 'fruit' because it is not really a fruit at all. It is a swollen stem, where the fleshy axis and the flowers have all fused together. In the ripened 'fruit' the diamond-shaped areas on the surface mark the remains of the fertilized flowers. Seeds are rarely formed. At the top of the stem is a tuft of green foliage leaves. The name 'pine-apple' was given by Spanish explorers, who found it in America and thought the 'fruit' resembled a pine-cone.

FUNGI. There are 80,000 known kinds of fungi. These plants vary in size from tiny mildews to large bracket fungi, such as the Dryad's Saddle, which may measure as much as 35 centimetres across. Though fungi differ in size and in their place of growth, they all have one characteristic in common. Unlike most other plants, they lack green-colouring matter, or chlorophyll, and, in consequence, cannot manu-facture food for themselves by PHOTOSYNTHESIS (q.v.). Instead they get their nutrition either from dead organic matter, such as leather, stale bread, damp floor boards, rotting leaves, and manure (see SAPROPHYTES), or from living plants and animals (see PARASITES). Among saprophytic fungi are the MOULDS and YEASTS (qq.v.), dry-rot, the common MUSHROOM (q.v. Vol. VI), and the inedible fungi commonly known as 'toadstools'. Among parasitic fungi are the Jew's Ear Fungus, which grows on the trunks of trees, and the Rust of Antirrhinums and many crops. Some parasitic fungi live on animals and even on human beings; Ringworm, for example, is a fungus disease.

The structure of a fungus is quite different from that of a FLOWERING PLANT (q.v.), for it cannot be divided up into root, stem, leaves, and flowers. A fungus is made up of a mass of fine threads, forming what is called a 'mycelium'. In the simpler fungi, such as the moulds, this mass of threads is not arranged in a definite shape but simply grows over and through what-ever the fungus is living on. For part of their life the larger fungi take this form also, but, when the time comes for them to reproduce, some of the threads grow together to form the 'fruiting bodies', namely, the cap and stem with which mushroom-seekers are familiar.

In many of the larger fungi—for example, the Death Cap and the common Mushroom—the mycelium mats together into tiny knobs inside which, covered by a membrane, the cap and stalk develop. As these two mature the mem-brane slits, often leaving remnants at the base of the stem, called the 'volva'. The gill cavities on the underside of the cap are also covered in the early stages by a membrane which also splits as the cap grows, and leaves a ring on the upper part of the stem.

Fungi reproduce themselves, not by flowers and seeds, but by single-celled spores. In gill-fungi these spores are produced in the gills, and when ripe drop downwards between the gills and are scattered by the wind. If the stem of a young fungus is cut close up under the cap and the cap laid gill downwards on coloured paper, a beautiful spore pattern will appear within 12 hours. The Boletus family of mushrooms, instead of having gills, has a layer of tubes whose openings resemble fine pores.

Fungi also reproduce by 'vegetative propaga-tion'—in other words, part of the white fibrous matter, called the 'spawn', breaks off from the mycelium and forms an independent plant (see REPRODUCTION IN PLANTS). The mycelium has a tendency to grow outwards in rings: this can be seen in the growth of round patches of mould; it accounts also for the well-known fairy rings made by Champignons and other fungi. The rings are formed by the outward growth of the fungal threads, which spread rather as ripples spread when a stone is thrown into a pond. The deeper colour of the grass inside the ring is due to the fertilizing effect on the soil of the decaying fungal threads. In the autumn, the young threads at the edge of the rings throw up the fruiting bodies (the mushrooms) to form a circle. Some fairy rings are said to be 300 or 400 years old.

The fruiting bodies of fungi grow very rapidly, appearing overnight and, in the case of the smaller and more fragile toadstool, disappearing within a few hours. Mushrooms, however, sur-vive several days, and certain brackets, grow-ing on birch stumps, may last several years.

Fungi are often repellent in appearance and smell, and unpleasant to the touch. Many parasitic fungi cause serious diseases in the plants and animals upon which they live, resulting in great loss to farmers. For example, almost as much as 227 tonnes of oranges imported from Israel to England used to be lost every year because of the attacks of a mould fungus. The failure of the potato crop in Ireland in 1846, which brought about a devastating famine, was due to a fungus disease called potato blight. All

Jew's Ear Fungus

Eric Hosking

Stinkhorn Fungus

A. R. Thompson

A Puff-ball

Harry Meyer

Amanita mappa, a Fungus of the Death Cap type

Harry Meyer

SPECIES OF BRITISH FUNGI

the main foods of the world, such as rice, wheat, oats, barley, and millet, are subject to attacks by fungal diseases, and so also are crops such as fruit and timber. These diseases are so serious that almost every country has laws dealing with the introduction of plants from other countries, and with the notification and treatment of disease (*see* PLANT DISEASES, Section 2, Vol. VI).

Other fungi grow in or on the roots of many forest trees and especially also plants of the orchid and heather families. The fungi obtain food from the roots, while the presence of the fungi helps or is even necessary to the absorption of water and mineral salts by the roots. This close association between fungus and root is called 'mycorrhiza'.

Though some are so harmful, many fungi perform a useful function in nature. The saprophytic fungi, by causing decay, rid the world of the useless remains of dead animals and plants, which would otherwise accumulate and would in course of time interfere seriously with the life of succeeding generations.

Man, too, has found uses for many fungi. The valuable drug penicillin is produced from a mould fungus, and the common fungus, yeast, plays an essential part in making bread rise and in the brewing of beer. Many fungi, besides mushrooms, are edible and have an excellent flavour—for example, the Champignons, Truffles, and Morels (*see* FUNGI, Vol. XI).

Truffles grow only in a few localities in Great Britain and are consequently expensive; but in Europe they are cultivated and are a popular food. A curious feature of Truffles is that the edible part, as well as the rest of the plant, grows underground. To know where to dig for them, farmers who cultivate truffles keep pigs, who can smell them and root them out with their snouts. Years ago, a certain variety of dog was bred for the same purpose, even in Britain.

Morels, used for food for thousands of years and now usually dried and used for flavouring, have, when they are fresh, brownish-yellow caps and short white stems, grooved at the base. The commonest morels are found in springtime in hedges or garden borders. They seem to like ground which has been disturbed or burnt, and flourished especially on bombed or shelled areas in France. At one time in Germany, country-women had to be stopped from burning land in order to encourage the growth of morels. The

morel is the only fungus which the Indian Muslims will eat, all others being considered impure food.

Among other edible fungi are the Chantarelle, the Blewit, the Shaggy Ink Cap, the Giant and Common Puff-Ball, and some kinds of Boletus. The latter are much prized in Russia, and were always to be bought at the great fungus market which used to be held in Moscow during the first three days of Lent, and which was attended by dealers from all parts of Europe. All these edible fungi are quite distinct in appearance, and not at all likely to be confused with poisonous species. It is wise, however, to get expert advice before trying out an unfamiliar fungus.

Many fungi are mildly poisonous, but only one British species, the Death Cap, is deadly poisonous. This fungus is common in woods and adjoining pastures in late summer and early autumn. In its earliest stages it looks much like an egg half-buried in the soil; but as the cap emerges, it flattens out and takes on a characteristic olive or yellowish-green, with a darker centre. The white stem is often tinged with green and has a well-marked, large, white or greenish ring. When fresh, the flesh is practically tasteless and without smell, but becomes fetid as it decays. The Death Cap is responsible for over 90% of the recorded cases of fungus poisoning, more than 50% of them being fatal.

Closely related to the Death Cap, but not nearly so poisonous, is the beautiful Fly Agaric, the typical 'toadstool' of children's stories and pictures. The sticky cap of the Fly Agaric is scarlet or orange-red, shiny, and dotted with thick white or yellowish wart-like patches. It is common in woodlands in autumn, especially under birches and pines. When chopped up in sugar or milk, the fungus is used as a trap for flies, and is still commonly used for this purpose in Eastern European countries. There are other poisonous fungi in Britain, including the mildly poisonous yellow staining mushroom which is easily mistaken for the edible mushroom. When bruised, its skin turns a brownish-yellow. Many fungi, poisonous to man, can be safely eaten by animals. Rabbits, for example, are not usually affected even by the Death Cap, while slugs actually thrive on it.

See also COLOUR PLATE, opp. p. 224.
See also Vol. VI: MUSHROOM (Culture).

G

GADFLY, *see* HORSE-FLY.

GALLS. During the summer months, curious growths are often to be found on many plants, but most conspicuously on oak-trees and rose-bushes. These are known as galls, and are really abnormal growths of the plant caused by the presence of some animal (or sometimes plant) within the plant tissue. One of the commonest of these galls is the so-called oak-apple. This is a soft, often brightly coloured gall, to be found on the young oak twigs in early summer. This looks like a fruit, but anyone who has tasted it has found it 'bitter as gall'. If an oak-apple is cut open it will be found to consist of a central mass of separate cells, in each of which is a small white larva. From these larvae, small insects emerge in the middle and late summer. These vary in kind, but are usually pale brown and about 25 to 32 millimetres long. They are the adult Gall-wasps, insects belonging to the same group (Hymenoptera) as the ICHNEUMON and the CHALCID FLIES (qq.v.). Chalcid Flies nearly always emerge from the galls as well as Gall-wasps, for Chalcid Flies lay their eggs in galls, and their larvae, when they hatch, feed on the larvae of Gall-wasps.

The female Gall-wasp is wingless. After mating, she makes her way down the tree trunk, burrows into the ground, and lays her eggs in the roots by means of an ovipostor, an egg-depositing organ in her body which, when not in use, is hidden in the abdomen. When these eggs hatch in the autumn and the larvae develop, a woody gall, quite unlike an oak-apple, is formed on the roots. The larvae then finish feeding and pupate quite quickly, and the adults emerge during the middle of the winter. These are quite different from their parents, for they are bigger, wingless, and always female. They make their way to the surface and crawl up the nearest trunk. When they reach the young twigs, they lay their eggs in the buds. During the following spring, these buds develop into oak-apples, and the life-cycle begins again. This is only one species of gall-wasp; but there are more than forty others to be found on oak-trees in the British Isles alone. One species forms the common spangle galls on the leaves in late summer, and another forms the woody marble galls on the twigs. Most of these species have two generations a year, each, like the oak-apple wasps, making quite different galls.

In Britain, besides the oak-tree gall-wasps, there are over thirty other species of gall-wasps which attack other plants such as Wild Rose, Poppy, Knapweed, Bramble, and a number of others, mostly of the Daisy and Dandelion family. None of these have more than one generation a year, and thus only one form. Perhaps the most familiar of these is the Robin's Pincushion, a large, red, fluffy gall, commonly found on Wild Rose bushes. This is caused by another Gall-wasp, a species of a group all of which make their galls on the rose. Another of these is responsible for the pea-like galls to be found usually on the underside of the Rose leaves.

Though many galls are caused by Gall-wasps, there are a number of other animals, mainly insects, which produce similar growths on their food plants. Some species of a certain group of Chalcid flies, which live in grasses during their larval period, produce conspicuous galls on the stems. Some of these are major pests of wheat, barley, and other cereal crops, particularly in America.

Some species of true FLY (q.v.), for example,

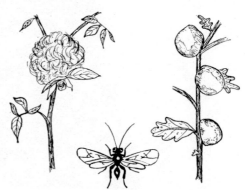

Left: PINCUSHION GALL; *Centre*: GALL-WASP; *Right*: OAK-APPLE GALL

Gall-midges and Gall-flies, also form galls; some of these are responsible for the large woody growths on Willows and for the galls in the flower heads of Knapweed and Thistle.

See also INSECTS.
See also Vol. VI: INSECT PESTS

GANNET (Solan Goose). These are large, somewhat goose-like, white sea-birds with straight, sharp-pointed bills, long wings with black wing-quills, and wedge-shaped tails. They belong to the same order as the CORMORANT, PELICAN, and FRIGATE BIRD (qq.v.). The Common or Northern Gannet is found in great numbers, especially on the west coasts of Ireland and Scotland, in the Orkneys and Hebrides, and on the shores of North America. They sometimes range as far south as the tropics in the winter, but breed farther north. The Gannets on the Bass Rock at the mouth of the Firth of Forth have often been described. The Boobies, the Gannets of the southern seas, also breed in vast numbers on rocky islands.

The Common or Northern Gannet is the largest and most powerful flier of all British sea-birds. All round our coasts, the Gannet may be watched in spring, summer, and autumn, patrolling the seas. It is most at home on the sea or in the air, rarely coming to land except during the nesting season. It can often be seen dropping like a stone from a height to dive after a fish, which it catches with its beak. The Gannet is equipped for diving with air-sacs on either side of its neck, which are inflated before the dive. Also it has no external nostrils. The bird rests for a few seconds after the dive, then shakes itself, and flies off low above the surface, mounting gradually and gracefully into the air, ready to dive again. Gannets feed almost entirely on fish, and cause great devastation on the shoals of herrings.

The Gannets breed in colonies on islands off the coast, sometimes on ledges and precipitous cliffs. The nests are made of seaweed and any rubbish available, and usually only one egg is laid—a pale blue with a whitish, chalky cover-

Eric Hosking

A NESTING COMMUNITY OF GANNETS ON THE ISLAND OF GRASSHOLM, OFF THE PEMBROKESHIRE COAST OF WALES

Paul Popper

A GANNET IN FULL FLIGHT

ing. At birth the young are naked, but they soon grow a covering of white down. This is replaced by a dark brown plumage with white-spotted feathers. The adult white plumage is not fully assumed until the birds are 4 or 5 years old. Young Gannets grow slowly, being nearly 3 months old before they take their first flight, to which they are forced by hunger—for their parents have by then deserted them.

GARFISH. These form a group of bony fishes, some of which may be nearly 2 metres long. They are chiefly distinguished by having both jaws lengthened to form a slender beak, which is armed with strong teeth. They are all voracious species, hunting usually in shoals and preying on the smaller fish which abound in the surface waters of tropical and temperate seas. They are quite good to eat, although the housewife is sometimes put off because their bones are bright green.

Related to these is the much smaller Skipper of British waters, which preys on Pilchards, but is itself eaten by larger fish. The curious tropical Half-beak is also a relation, though it is a vegetarian, and has only the lower jaw prolonged. All these fishes are closely related to the FLYING-FISH (q.v.), having the habit of leaping from the water when attacked by enemies from below.

GAUR, *see* CATTLE.

GAZELLE, *see* ANTELOPE.

GECKO. This is a lizard of the family Gekkonidae, of which there are more than 300 species.

Geckos inhabit tropical and sub-tropical regions, and the species best known to us are those which live in houses and can be seen after dark running up and down the walls and even across the ceiling in search of food. They are able to do this because they carry special plates (*lamellae*), with adhesive powers, on the under-surfaces of the fingers and toes. Some species have not this adaptation, and live on the ground. The main classification of the family is based upon the way their fingers and toes are formed. The eye is usually large, and in most species is covered with a transparent membrane, as in snakes; but a few species have well-developed eyelids. The skin is usually soft, and covered with tubercles or small grain-like projections: only a few species have scales. The tail is fragile and very variable in shape. All the Geckos have voices. Usually they make a soft chirruping or clucking sound, such as we can make with our tongue; but some of the large Malayan species (Tookays) have a loud cry that can be heard a long way off. Many of them squawk when caught. They feed chiefly on insects; but some of the larger species will devour small mammals. The House Geckos are frequently transported in ships' cargoes, and

Paul Popper

A GREEN GECKO FROM NEW ZEALAND

A TOOKAY

the wide distribution over the world of some of the species is due to this. Nearly all the Geckos lay eggs, usually two in number; one species inhabiting New Zealand produces living young.

The Tookay, or Tuktoo, is one of the largest of the Geckos. It is a native of Malaya, but has been introduced into Calcutta and into Indonesia. It is common in the towns, and is well known to the people of southern Indo-China and Malaya on account of its loud call—from which comes its name. For a Gecko, it is a handsome creature, being pale grey above with large pinkish or reddish spots. It bites fiercely when caught.

See also LIZARD.

GEESE. These large, web-footed birds belong to the same family as the SWANS and DUCKS (qq.v.), though most of them are land-birds and grass-feeders. There are many species, most of which belong to America; but some species of both Grey and Black Geese visit the British Isles, and the Grey Lag Goose breeds in decreasing numbers in Scotland. Geese mate for life, and tend to return year after year to the same breeding

area. They have a strong but rather heavy flight, many species making long migratory journeys.

The Grey Lag Goose is the species from which domestic GEESE (q.v. Vol. VI) are derived. They live in flocks during the winter, frequenting marshes, lakes, and open country near water, and often going to the coasts in hard weather. They have a harsh, discordant cry, well known to all keepers of domestic geese. Other grey geese which visit Britain are the White-fronted Goose, a rather smaller bird with a white patch on the forehead; the Pink-foot Goose, which breeds in Spitzbergen and Iceland; and, much less common, the Bean Goose, which breeds far north and winters over much of Europe and Asia.

Paul Popper
SNOW GEESE

Paul Popper
BARNACLE GOOSE

Paul Popper
BRENT GEESE

Most Black Geese are smaller and more marine in their habits. The Brent Goose inhabits the coasts of Arctic Europe and northern Asia, and visits chiefly the east coasts of England and Ireland in the winter. Those of America nest in Greenland and winter sometimes as far south as Texas. The Barnacle Goose, a visitor to the west coast of Scotland and north Ireland, was so called because, according to the old legend, it was supposed to have developed from a BARNACLE (q.v.). Other wanderers to Britain are the strange-looking Red-breasted Goose from the tundras of Siberia, and the white snow Geese from Arctic America. The Canada Goose and the Egyptian Goose have both been introduced into Britain, and breed in the wild state in some parts, the former even more freely than the Grey Lag. Other exotic species, such as the Chinese Goose, may be seen on ornamental waters.

An extinct flightless goose is known to have existed formerly in New Zealand. This was related to the Australian Cape Barren Goose—a large, stoutly built goose, with a short neck and a large greenish swelling at the base of its short beak—which lives almost entirely on land.

GENTIAN, *see* ALPINE PLANTS.

GERMINATION, *see* REPRODUCTION IN PLANTS, Section 7.

GHOST MOTH, *see* SWIFT MOTH.

GIBBON, *see* APE.

GIPSY MOTH, *see* TUSSOCK MOTH.

GIRAFFE. These, with the OKAPI (q.v.), are the only existing members of a family which is intermediate between the DEER and CATTLE families (qq.v.). With their immensely long necks and legs, giraffes are by far the tallest of all the mammals, the largest of them being 5·5 m high. But despite its size, a giraffe, standing motionless among trees, is almost invisible, its orange-red skin, mottled with darker spots, blending perfectly with the patches of sunlight and dense shadows of leaves. On its long, delicately shaped head are small blunt horns, covered with skin and surmounted by tufts of black hair. Some species have a second pair of rudimentary horns, merely bony lumps, at the back of the

South African Railways

GIRAFFES IN THE KRUGER NATIONAL PARK, TRANSVAAL, STANDING IN A CHARACTERISTIC POSITION

head; others have a single third horn on the forehead between the eyes. The body is proportionately short, and slants towards the tail. In its long tail, ending in a tuft of long hair, the giraffe has an invaluable fly-wisk, an essential weapon against the poisonous flies and stinging insects of central Africa.

Giraffes are found only in Africa, in dry regions south of the Sahara. They are most numerous to the north of the Kalahari Desert, in very dry country. It is a curious sight to see giraffes drinking water, for in spite of their long necks they cannot reach the water without straddling their legs wide apart. They have the same difficulty if they want to pick up a leaf from the ground, or when they graze, which they rarely do. They normally feed on leaves from trees, especially mimosa or acacia, and with their long tongues they can strip branches as much as 6 metres from the ground. Herds of giraffe vary in number from fifteen to as many as eighty. Their acute sight and hearing are useful means of defence, and with their great height they can see their enemies from a long distance. They defend themselves with their very powerful kick—the female defends her calf in this way against any attacks by flesh-eating foes, while the males kick fiercely when they fight in the mating season. Giraffe fawns are born singly in May or June, and after three days can trot by the side of their mothers.

Giraffes have great speed and endurance: big-game hunters say that it takes a good horse to run them down, and if the wind is favourable they will carry on for great distances. They run with a peculiar gait like an awkward gallop, carrying their tails twisted like corkscrews over their backs.

GLASS SNAKE, *see* SLOW WORM.

GLOW-WORM. The Glow-worm is the British relative of the FIRE-FLIES (q.v.) of warmer climates and belongs to the same family of beetles—the Lampyridae. Only the female insect deserves the name; for the male, which flies about at night and sometimes enters houses, attracted by the lights, is often only very slightly luminous. The female seen by day is an inconspicuous, flat, crawling, grub-like creature, found in the hedgerows or near the ground; after dark, when she displays her pale green light, she becomes very obvious. The light sometimes shines brightly and sometimes fades or goes out, to return again in all its beauty. It is produced by an organ on the lower surface of the body, a little in front of the hinder end. The light is best seen when the insect climbs

S. C. Bisserôt

A GLOW-WORM

above the ground on bank or herbage. Both males and females in the grub stage closely resemble the mature female and are found in the same places, where they feed upon snails, entering their shells and not leaving until the occupant has been entirely devoured.

In tropical America there are insects, related to the Glow-worm, which carry a row of lamps along each side of the body. These give a beautiful green light, while the head glows with a fiery red. Only the female is capable of this wonderful display, which she can control in the same way as the Glow-worm. She is even more sluggish than the Glow-worm, while the male is an active winged insect, but not luminous.

See also BEETLES.

GNAT, *see* MOSQUITO.

GNU, *see* ANTELOPE.

GOAT. There are about ten species of wild goats, often called Ibexes, living in Europe, central Asia, Egypt, and Ethiopia. It is not always easy to distinguish between wild sheep, antelopes, and goats; but male goats always have a strong smell, and generally a beard on their chins. Both sexes have horns, those of the males being much the larger. They curve upwards and backwards, and are twisted in various shapes. Like the sheep, they are mountain animals, usually living in the most rugged districts. They are among the most sure-footed of animals, running up and down rocks and cliffs with the greatest ease. As well as grass, they eat any young shoots and leaves of trees and shrubs within their reach. They masticate this food when resting, by ruminating or 'chewing the cud' (*see* RUMINANTS). Nearly all wild goats live in herds, only some of the males leading a solitary life.

The Markhor, a goat living in Afghanistan and the western Himalayas, is 112 cm high, and has horns twisted like a corkscrew. Markhors are wary animals, greatly prized by sportsmen. The Persian wild goats or Pasangs, found in south-west Asia, are very active animals, about 90 cm high. They often appear near roads, but always take care to post a sentinel to warn the herd of danger. The Spanish wild goats are smaller still, about 65 cm high. As a rule the old bucks stay all the year round on the highest and most exposed peaks of the mountains,

Paul Popper
A GRECIAN IBEX WITH YOUNG KID

regardless of the snow and cold. The does, however, live on the southern slopes, and in the depths of winter approach close to the villages. The kids, by the time they are a few days old, are able to follow their mothers over the roughest ground; but while they are still young, the mothers keep to the southern slopes and warmer parts of the mountains, carefully shielding them from cutting winds.

Domestic goats are descended from the Persian wild goat. They were domesticated by the prehistoric inhabitants of the Swiss lake-dwellings, and were also kept by the ancient Egyptians.

See also Vol. VI: GOATS.

GOAT AND LEOPARD MOTHS. These primitive moths, belonging to the small family Cossidae, range in size from 3 to over 25 cm. They are found all over the world, but especially in temperate deciduous forests; three species occur in Britain.

The Goat Moth is so called because the caterpillar has a strong goat-like smell, coming from a yellow oil secreted by glands in the head. The full-grown caterpillar, 7 to 10 centimetres long, is brownish-red above and yellowish-pink at the sides, with a shiny black head and black marks on the next segment. It is found in Britain much more commonly than the large brownish moth, and usually when wandering about before constructing its cocoon. The cocoon is made of tough silk, plastered with numerous particles, and the caterpillar overwinters within, not

pupating until the following spring. The night-flying moth emerges in the summer and, like many other moths, is attracted to sugar. Groups of eggs are laid on tree trunks, and the young caterpillars on hatching begin to tunnel between the bark and the wood, later boring deeply into the heart wood. They can digest only the sugar and starch in the wood, of which there is so little that they have to remain sometimes as much as 4 years in the caterpillar stage, eating great quantities of wood, before they have grown enough to pupate. In captivity, however, beetroot will supply all they need in a single season. The fermenting sap given off from trees wounded by these caterpillars attracts many insects, including Red Admirals and wasps.

The Leopard Moth, common in southern England, is 6 to 7 cm across, and has thinly scaled whitish wings with bluish-black spots. The antennae of the female are thread-like, but those of the male are combed at the base. The female lays her eggs singly from June to August in cracks on the stems or branches of young trees, including fruit trees. The yellowish-white caterpillar has a brown head and is spotted with black. It tunnels in the wood for 2 or 3 years, causing the leaves of infested branches to wither, turn yellow, and be liable to break in the wind. The caterpillar pupates within a cocoon strengthened with particles of wood. The adult moth is attracted to light. The brownish and smaller Reed Leopard is restricted in Britain to the Cambridgeshire fens and to Dorset, where the caterpillar burrows in the stems of reeds, feeding for 2 years upon the pith.

GOBY. Round sea-shores practically throughout the world, in rock-pools and coral-reefs, Gobies swarm in great abundance and variety; and many are found also in fresh waters. They are small fishes, rarely longer than 15 cm, and usually very much less. One of them, found in the Philippine Islands, is the smallest vertebrate animal in the world, the adult being little more than a centimetre long.

Gobies are distinguished by having two dorsal fins, no lateral line, eyes placed near the top of the head, and, in most species, pelvic fins joined together at the base to form a sucking disc on the breast, by which they can attach themselves to the rocks. Some Gobies can live out of water for some time, the most interesting of these being the so-called Mud-skipper, or Walking-fish,

A. Fraser-Brunner

THE WALKING GOBY OR MUD-SKIPPER IN A MANGROVE SWAMP

which lives on mud flats in the East Indies, using its fins like legs and skipping about in pursuit of its insect prey. This fish has even been observed to climb about over the roots of mangrove trees.

Male Gobies often fight fiercely in the breeding season, the winner displaying his colours before the female. Even in northern waters they are often brightly coloured, while in the tropics they are frequently brilliant; a few, however, such as the Transparent Goby of British seas, are colourless and glass-like. Generally, they take some care to protect the eggs by hiding them under stones or among seaweeds; and sometimes the male will make a sort of nest by turning over an empty shell and digging a pit underneath it.

A few Gobies live inside sponges and occasionally have been found in the gill chambers of larger fish, such as the Shad. One kind lives in the tunnels of burrowing shrimps, and is quite blind (see BLIND FISHES).

See also FISHES.

GODWIT, see WADING BIRDS, Section 3.

GOLD AND PURPLE MOTHS. These brilliant, metallic, day-flying insects, formerly classified together in one family, measure only about a centimetre across the wings. They have attracted much attention as being by far the most primitive of all Lepidoptera, and as throwing much light on the evolution of the Order. About a hundred species are known, most occurring in Europe and New Zealand, but some

belonging to South Africa, Indo-Malaya, Australia, and North America—such world-wide distribution being characteristic of ancient groups. Gold moths have jaws and feed on pollen, but they have no 'proboscis' or sucking organ. In Purple Moths, however, a short proboscis has evolved, and the jaws are correspondingly reduced.

Purple Moths, of which nine species occur in Britain, lay their eggs in a slit in a leaf, usually birch, sometimes hazel, oak, or chestnut. The legless caterpillar feeds on the inner tissues of the leaf, making a characteristic blotch, and when mature pupates in a tough cocoon in the ground. The pupa is remarkable for its comparatively large, toothed jaws, with which it bites its way out of the cocoon through the soil to the surface.

One of the six British species of Gold Moth occurs commonly in May and June in buttercups, often many individuals being together in one flower. The caterpillar, which probably feeds on mosses, has eight pairs of jointed abdominal legs, conspicuous antennae, and eight rows of peculiar globular appendages. The pupa has movable legs and jaws.

There are so many differences between Gold and Purple Moths that it is best to consider the Purple Moths as the most primitive Lepidoptera, and place the Gold Moths in the separate Order Zeugloptera, more ancient in origin than the Lepidoptera.

GOLDCREST (Golden-crested Wren). The name Wren—given, presumably, because of the bird's tiny size—is quite inaccurate: the Goldcrest is related to the WARBLERS (q.v.), the smallest European bird. It is very gaily coloured, with olive-green plumage and a bright yellow and black crest. It is resident in the British Isles, frequenting plantations of conifers. Sometimes in autumn great flocks of immigrants from Scandinavia are to be seen, while in other years they are less noticeable.

Goldcrests are sociable little birds, often hunting for their insect food in company with

Tits and Creepers. The nest is generally built on the underside of a conifer branch. It is a beautiful little bag, made of moss, wool, spiders' webs, and such material, and lined with feathers. The eight or more eggs are tiny, barely a centimetre long, and white with reddish specks.

The Firecrest is very much like the Goldcrest, but the crest is redder and there are whitish streaks round the eye. It is common in many parts of Europe and sometimes visits Britain in autumn and winter. The American species is called the Rubycrest.

GOLDFINCH, *see* FINCHES, Section 3.

GOLDFISH, *see* CARP.

GOPHER, *see* RODENT.

GORILLA, *see* APE.

GOSSAMER, *see* SPIDERS.

GRASSES. This group of flowering plants is one of the largest and most valuable, since it includes the cereals. Both man and the hoofed animals are dependent on them for their staple foods (*see* GRASSLANDS, Vol. VI). There are over 8,000 different species of grasses. Indeed, wherever flowering plants can exist, grasses of some sort will be found.

Most grasses are herbs (*see* FLOWERING PLANTS), and have fibrous root-systems (*see* ROOTS, Section 2); but some tropical forms, such as BAMBOOS (q.v. Vol. VI), grow to more than 30 metres in height. Although most cereals and some grasses are annuals, a few cereals and the majority of grasses are perennials, and reproduce by the spread of underground stems, as with the Couchgrass, or with runners, as with the Common Bent (*see* STEMS). In most cases the stems are hollow, but in the Maize they are solid. The leaves are characteristically long and narrow, and are arranged along the stem alternately in two ranks. Few grasses have stalked leaves, but each leaf has a sheathing base that surrounds the stem and more or less conceals it. The stem, with the leaf-sheaths, is known as the 'culm'. The leaves are usually smooth and often glossy, the outer cells containing a certain amount of silica (a hard white mineral, which, when the grass leaves are burnt, is usually enough to leave a distinct skeleton of the leaves).

In several of the tropical bamboos a white opal-like substance called 'tabasheer', mainly composed of silica, and much prized by the natives as an ornament, is found in the joints. In one East Indian aquatic grass the wide leaf-sheaths are much dilated and serve as floats.

The grasses of temperate regions rarely branch at the upper parts of the culm, but bamboos and many tropical grasses branch freely. In many bamboos these upper branches are long and spreading, or drooping and much-branched; in others they are merely hooked spines. One bamboo, a native of Malay, climbs over trees which are 30 metres or more in height. Grass-culms, especially bamboo culms, grow rapidly: a bamboo sometimes grows as much as 30 metres in 2 or 3 months. Some grass-culms can grow a metre or even more in 24 hours. In cool countries grasses are able to form turf, and they can do this because they produce in shallow soil a great mass of fibrous roots.

The flowers are borne in groups called 'spikelets', which are enclosed in leaf-like structures called 'glumes'. There are no petals or sepals in the flowers. The stamens are usually conspicuous,

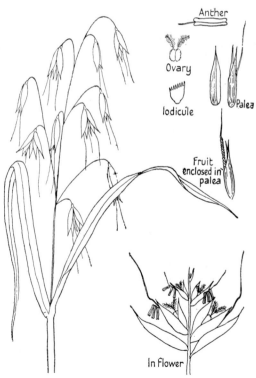

DETAILS OF STRUCTURE OF GRASS FLOWERS

FOREST OF GIANT BAMBOO GRASSES GROWING ALONG A RIVER BANK IN BURMA

and there are generally three of them. Each anther is carried on a long stalk. There is one carpel, with two feathery styles, and after fertilization the single-chambered ovary develops into the typical fruit or grain. In some bamboos, however, the fruit is thick and fleshy, forming a berry, often as large as an apple. The appearance of grasses when fruiting varies according to whether the stalks of the spikelets are long and spreading outwards from the stem, as in the Oat or Quaking Grass, short, as in the Meadow Fescue, or absent, as in Wheat or in Perennial Rye Grass. Each flower in the spikelet is protected by two structures (palea) of which the outer, in some cases, bears a long bristle (awn). This is very prominent in some grasses, especially in the cereals Oat, Barley, and Bearded Wheat.

In most cases grasses are pollinated by wind, though in the majority of cereals self-pollination takes place. The fruit is also usually light enough to be disseminated by wind. The awn helps in the distribution of the fruits by making them stick to animals or birds (see SEEDS 2(b), Animal Dispersal). The awn is also of use in burying the fruit in the soil; in the Oat, for instance, and other grasses, at the base of the glume is a sharp point, which easily penetrates the ground and cannot easily be withdrawn, because of the short, stiff, upwardly pointing hairs above. The long awn, which is bent and

closely twisted below the bend, reacts strongly to moisture in the atmosphere, the coils untwisting when damp and twisting up again when dry. When the upper part of the awn has become fixed in the earth, or caught in the surrounding vegetation, the repeated twisting and untwisting drives the point deeper into the ground. Such grasses often cause harm to sheep by catching in the wool and boring into the skin.

Of the British wild grasses, some of the most common are the Fescues. The Meadow Fescue grows about half a metre high, and bears its flowered spikelets in close nodding clusters 20 to 25 cm long. It is a good pasture grass. The Tall Fescue grows along river banks and in wet places, and is nearly a metre tall. The clusters or spikelets are only 7 to 15 cm in length. Some Fescues, especially when growing on mountains, reproduce themselves in a curious way. Instead of the usual flower spikelets, there are small, leafy shoots. These develop adventitious roots at their bases, and eventually fall off and take root in the soil (see ROOTS, Section 5).

The Quaking or Quake Grass grows in dry pastures, especially among taller grasses, and comes into flower during June and July. The many-flowered spikelets, which shiver at the end of long thin stalks, have given the grass the popular name of 'Shivery-shakes'. Cocksfoot, a valuable pasture grass, bears groups of flowers which are distinctly branched and form dense tufts. Yorkshire Fog, a perennial grass, common in meadows, pastures, and waste places throughout Britain, has a short awn, and the flowers are pinkish-grey. Marram Grass grows in tufts on sea-shores, especially on sand-dunes (see SEA-SHORE PLANTS). It has long, ridged leaves, covered with a pale green bloom. This grass is often deliberately planted on dunes and elsewhere in order to bind the wind-swept sand. Couch-grass is an abominable weed in gardens and on farmlands, because it spreads by long, tenacious, underground stems which are difficult to eradicate. A small portion of such a stem, if left in the ground, will send up shoots and begin to spread.

Besides the cereals and the Sugar-cane, the most interesting foreign grasses are the tropical Bamboos, which grow in large clumps and spread rapidly by means of underground stems. Some Bamboos flower annually, others at longer intervals, and others once only before they die. The Pampas Grass, with its long, dark, arching leaves and its enormous white plumes carried at the end of long, straight stalks, is a native of Argentina and Brazil, but it is often seen in this country in our larger gardens and parks.

See also Vol. III: GRASSLANDS.
See also Vol. VI: GRASSES; GRASSLANDS.
See also INDEX, p. 71.

GRASSHOPPER AND LOCUST. Three closely related insects—the grasshopper, locust, and CRICKET (q.v.)—are similar in general appearance. Their mouth-parts are used for biting; they have hardened, elongated fore-wings, with the hind-wings folded fanwise beneath them; the hind legs are very long, with enlarged femurs; the males, and sometimes the females, are provided with sound-producing organs, and in both sexes there are organs for the reception of sound. The METAMORPHOSIS (q.v.) is incomplete, the immature insects or nymphs resembling the adults, except that their wings are rudimentary.

Grasshoppers can be separated into two distinct groups—the Short-horn Grasshoppers and the Long-horn or Bush Crickets. The first, which are common in Britain, have short antennae, and are vegetarians. Bush Crickets have long antennae, and many are carnivorous.

Two very obvious characteristics of all these insects are their sound-producing capacity and their powers of movement by leaping. In the Short-horn Grasshoppers the sound is made by rubbing the hind femur, that has a row of pegs, against a thickened rib of the wing. The sound-receiving organs are two tightly stretched membranes, each surrounded by a horny ring, situated one on each side of the first segment of the abdomen. In both the Bush Crickets and the Crickets sound is produced by the friction of one fore-wing upon the other. A pair of similar sound-receivers is situated on the surface of the tibia of each fore-leg. These membranes vibrate in response to the sound from a neigh-

bouring insect, and the vibrations are interpreted as sounds by means of the nervous system. The production of these various sounds by insects is called 'stridulation' from a Latin word meaning 'creaking'. Grasshoppers and Crickets may 'sing' for various reasons. The males 'sing' to attract the females' attention during courtship, and also in rivalry with each other. One of the most insistent chirrupers is a North American Long-horn Grasshopper, which has brilliant green leaf-like fore-wings, and is called the Katydid because its notes suggest that it is constantly repeating 'Katy did, she did'.

If we look at the hind legs of these insects from the side, the enlarged femur is very obvious. Above is the big muscle which straightens the leg. If it contracts quickly, the insect will jump. Below it is a much narrower muscle which bends the leg again. Large Grasshoppers do not jump nearly so well as the small insects, the best performers of which have been known to jump a length of nearly 2 metres.

Short-horn Grasshoppers have very short ovipositors or egg-laying tubes. The female digs a hole, usually in the ground, with her ovipositor, and extends her abdomen to twice its normal length in order to deepen the hole. The number of eggs laid at any one time varies with the species but may be as high as 120. The female pours upon them a fluid, which

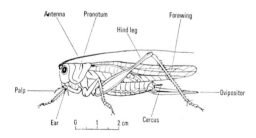

FIG. I. A GREAT GREEN GRASSHOPPER
A Bush Cricket, found in southern England

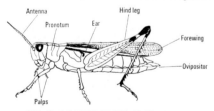

FIG. 2. A LARGE MARSH GRASSHOPPER
A Short-horn Grasshopper,
found in English and Irish bogs

hardens into a protective covering, a means of protecting the eggs resembling that used by her relatives, the COCKROACHES (q.v.). She may be capable of egg-laying for as long as two months, during which time she deposits several batches of eggs. The nymphs cast their skins from five to eight times during growth, and there may be either one or two generations in a year. The Bush Crickets (Long-horns) have stout, curved ovipositors, sometimes as long as the rest of the body. Because of the shape of these organs, the insects are often called the Sabre-tailed Grass-hoppers. Sometimes the eggs are laid in the ground, but more often in the tissues of plants. The eggs of British Grasshoppers are laid in summer and hatch in spring. The adults die when the cold weather of winter starts.

There are many kinds of grasshoppers. Some resemble their background and look like leaves, grass-blades, or pebbles, and many can change their colour to a certain extent to match a new habitat (see CAMOUFLAGE). Other species are wingless, and a few are adapted for swimming in water.

LOCUSTS (q.v. Vol. VI) are Short-horn Grass-hoppers. Unlike other Grasshoppers they like to live in crowds. The nymphs or 'hoppers' get together in tens of thousands to form bands which move about the countryside as much as a kilometre a day; adults collect into swarms and fly several kilometres a day (see MIGRATION). Occasionally odd Locusts fly to Britain, although they are normally found only in the tropics and sub-tropics. Locusts do considerable damage to crops, as do some other Grasshoppers, especially in North America.

GRASS SNAKE. (Sometimes also called the Ring-necked Snake.) This is the commonest of the three British snakes, being found all over England, Wales, and south-eastern Scotland, as well as throughout Europe. There are several colour varieties, each with its own geographical range. In England it is normally greyish, olive, or brownish above, usually with black spots or narrow cross-bars on the back and vertical ones on the flanks; it has a yellow or orange collar on the neck, bordered behind with black; the belly is chequered with black and grey or white, or may be entirely black. In old females the orange collar and the black markings on the back have sometimes disappeared. Males sel-dom exceed a metre in length; females grow

J. J. Ward

COMMON GRASS SNAKE, ABOUT A METRE LONG

larger, and a specimen measuring 1·7 metres has been recorded. Such a size, however, is most unusual in Britain, although in southern Europe it is not uncommon.

The Grass Snake lives in hedgerows and open woodland country. It is fond of water and can swim well. When caught, it does not bite, but gives out a nauseous-smelling fluid from the vent. In captivity it soon becomes tame, and if properly cared for will live for several years. Its main food is frogs, but it will also eat toads, newts, and fish. Eggs are laid in June, July, and early August, manure heaps being favourite places for them, or they may be hidden under dried leaves or in holes in walls. The young emerge some two months later.

Closely allied to the English Grass Snake, and much like it in general appearance, though it is without the yellow collar, is the Tessellated Water-snake. It has a wide range in Europe, and is sometimes sold in England as a pet.

See also SNAKES.

GRASS-VENEER MOTHS. These small, brownish, yellowish, or whitish moths, some-times streaked with silver, are very abundant almost everywhere in summer in long grasses—thirty-seven species occurring in Britain. They rest with their long 'palpi' or feelers projecting forwards and their long, narrow wings so folded that they appear cylindrical, their form and colour making them difficult to distinguish among the dry grass stems. They fly at twilight or by night, and, when disturbed during the day by anyone walking in the grass, they soon settle again. The eggs are either scattered freely or attached to grasses, and the caterpillars either bore into the stems or crowns of grasses or cereals, or live about the roots. Many construct silken galleries, a habit which has earned them the American name Webworm. Several species are serious pests—notably the Oriental Rice Borer, which causes enormous losses in southern and eastern Asia, and the Sugar-cane Borer of the West Indies and United States. Much remains to be discovered about the biology even of British species.

GRAYLING BUTTERFLY, *see* BROWNS.

GREBE. The Grebes are water-birds, which are more inclined to frequent fresh water than DIVERS (q.v.) are. They are found over much of the world in temperate or sub-tropical climates, and are fairly familiar British birds. They have legs placed very far back, close thick plumage, and lobes on the toes, all fitting them for an aquatic rather than a terrestrial life. Some species fly well, with their necks stretched out before them; but all prefer water to air, and the Dab-chicks, in particular, are unwilling to fly, always escaping from an enemy, if they can, by diving, rather than by flight. They are expert divers, and swim long distances under water. They seek concealment often by sinking under the water and staying with only the tip of the beak showing. How so light a body can keep itself submerged without exerting great force is a mystery—like that of the DIPPER (q.v.), which can walk underwater on the floor of a stream. Grebes breed on freshwater lakes, ponds, and broads, and construct a floating nest, often at the edge of a reed bed. When the bird leaves the nest, it covers the 3–5 whitish eggs with pieces of water weed, which conceals them from predators, such as CROWS (q.v.). After hatching, the chicks take to the water almost at once, and when they are small often sit on their parents' backs; this protects them from enemies, such as the PIKE (q.v.). They feed on frogs, small fish, molluscs, and water-insects.

The largest and most handsome of the Grebes is the **Great Crested Grebe**, about 53 cm long. It has a grey, chestnut-brown, and white plumage, darker in the summer than winter, with large tufts of feathers making a frill round its neck, and with a double crest. (In fact, the word 'grebe' comes from a Celtic word for a comb, though most of the family are without anything like a 'comb'—and even this species loses its crest in the winter.) The smallest member of the family, and the most familiar, is the Dabchick or Little Grebe, found on streams, ponds, and lakes throughout the British Isles, though less commonly farther north. Other species which breed occasionally in Britain or are winter visitors are the Red-necked Grebe, the Slavonian Grebe, and the Black-necked Grebe.

GREENFINCH, *see* FINCHES, Section 2.

GREENFLY, *see* APHIS.

GREENSHANK, *see* WADING BIRDS, Section 3.

GROUSE. There are some thirty species of this family of game-birds of the order Galliformes, which are found for the most part in the northern half of the northern hemisphere. They have, in general, stout, compact bodies and strong legs with curved claws, with which they can run quickly and scratch efficiently. The legs, and often also the toes, are feathered. The males are generally larger and more brightly coloured than the females. Most of them have a loud cry, in some species produced by the inflating and deflating of air-sacs on the side of the neck. Grouse build nests on the ground, generally in hollows in heather or grass or under cover of a bush, lining them scantily with grass or moss. Even those species, such as the Blackcock and Hazel-hens,

G. K. *Yeates*

GREAT CRESTED GREBE ON NEST

Eric Hosking

RED GROUSE AND NEWLY HATCHED FLEDGLINGS

cock and their relatives, the Capercaillies, both of which are polygamous, perform excited courtship dances, the Capercaillie in its favourite pine-tree, and the Blackcock on its display grounds, in which a number of cocks gather and display against each other. Two Blackcocks will approach each other in a crouching attitude, their throats vibrating with their bubbling cries. They will go forwards and backwards several times, and then suddenly rush at each other and, almost interlocked, rise a little way into the air, striking at each other with their feet and uttering a high, hissing note. The Prairie-hens of America assemble in the early morning on high, dry hillocks and, inflating their orange air-sacs and raising their long neck-tufts, they utter their loud courting-cry.

which prefer woods to open moorland, nest on the ground. Most species lay seven to twelve eggs or even more, the Prairie-hens of the Mississippi valley reaching, not infrequently, as many as twenty. The chicks are hatched well developed and covered with thick down, and become fully grown in a few weeks. Grouse are sedentary birds, rarely wandering from their breeding area.

Many species of Grouse make elaborate courtship displays (*see* ANIMAL LANGUAGE). The Red Grouse cocks fight in the spring, the victor often rising to a height of some 6 metres in the air and crowing before descending to claim the hen. Red Grouse and their near relatives, the Ptarmigans, have one mate only. The Black-

The Red Grouse, the game-bird of British moorlands, is the best known of the family. This is the only bird which is found in the British Isles and nowhere else, though it has a relative very much like it, the Willow Grouse, which is found in Europe and North America. The Red Grouse, unlike the Willow Grouse, never turns white in winter. It has, however, remarkable colour variations, ranging from phases of entirely black (which is rare) to chestnut-red, and to spotted white. Its main food is heather, but it also eats bilberry, crowberry, various seeds, and caterpillars and insects. Grouse are subject to serious epidemics of grouse-disease, the first recorded outbreak being in 1815. The hen generally sits very close on her nest in the heather, relying on the good camouflage of her plumage to protect her.

The Ptarmigan is a mountain bird, found at high altitudes over a wide area of

Eric Hosking

CAPERCAILLIE NESTING ON HEATHER ON THE EDGE OF A PINE FOREST

northern Europe, Asia, and America, including the Scottish Highlands. In summer it has a grey-brown plumage, with a red comb over the eye, while in winter the plumage becomes almost purely white—a perfect camouflage when the Ptarmigan is roosting in the snow. It has the strongest flight of any game-bird, and the chicks are able to fly when they are only 10 days old.

Blackcock, the hens of which are called Grey-hens, inhabit woods near moors or rough land, and perch in trees. The cock is bluish-black, with some white on the wings and under the tail, and the hen is brown and grey. They are most common in Scotland, but are found locally in Wales and north and south-west England.

The Capercaillie, a near relative of the Black-cock, is like it in many ways, but is much larger. It is the largest of the Grouse, the cock being nearly as large as a turkey. The females are much smaller. Capercaillies inhabit the pine forests of northern Europe, north and central Asia, and the Pyrenees, Alps, and Carpathian mountains. They became extinct in Scotland about 1770, but were reintroduced successfully in 1837, and are now thriving.

GROWTH IN ANIMALS. Young animals are born much smaller than their parents, and reach adult size by growth as a result of NUTRITION (q.v.). After fertilization of the egg, many complex changes take place in the animal before birth or hatching occurs.

After birth, growth is usually gradual and often ceases when maturity is reached; fish and some other animals, however, may grow continuously, though progressively more slowly with age. Human height actually declines in old age, and this growth in reverse (or degrowth) is more striking still in some other animals. Starvation of flat worms, for example, results in overall degrowth, and very tiny worms can be produced from initially large specimens. They grow large again in time if fed.

A very interesting type of growth called regeneration occurs with any of the brown or black species of flatworms called Planerians (see WORMS, Section 6). Any part lost by injury can be regrown, and a flatworm cut in half in either direction grows into two worms. The ability to regenerate lost parts varies enormously in the animal kingdom. SPONGES (q.v.) can be passed through a sieve, and very small parts will reorganize into small sponges and

start growing again. By contrast, birds and mammals have little power of regeneration; they can, for example, grow a new skin over small wounds only. LIZARDS (q.v.) cast their tails when in danger and grow new ones; but they do not regenerate lost limbs. NEWTS and SALAMANDERS (qq.v.) are vertebrates with exceptionally good powers of regeneration; they can eventually even regrow lost legs.

Growth in Arthropods—INSECTS, CRUSTACEA, MYRIAPODA, SPIDERS, SCORPIONS (qq.v.)—presents special problems. These animals are encased in a rigid cuticle, or skeleton, which has to be shed and replaced at intervals by a larger one. This process is called 'the moult'. Increase in the external dimensions of most arthropods occurs immediately after a moult, through the swallowing of air or water and the stretching of the new soft cuticle which has been previously formed under the old one. The space provided is then filled up by the growth of the internal organs. Some insects have larvae with soft cuticles over most of their bodies which can stretch with growth, so that moulting is less frequent.

Rate of growth and adult size are both inherited (see HEREDITY), but can be altered by environment. Starvation obviously must stop growth, but lack of essential substances may stunt animals, even if the total bulk of food is normal. Proteins are essential for life and are therefore essential constituents of food if growth, that is increase of living material, is to take place. Even when adult size is reached, continual replacement is necessary. Hair, claws, and skin are continually, or periodically, growing and continually being worn away on the outside. Blood-cells are continually being produced, each red corpuscle in a mammal being used only for a few weeks. The constituents of all cells are, in fact, being continually replaced while animals are living active lives.

As well as large quantities of proteins, a number of other substances are needed in small quantities which the animals cannot make for themselves. These are called VITAMINS (q.v. Vol. XI), and lack of them can cause striking abnormalities of growth. Rickets, for example, are produced by insufficient vitamin D (see DEFICIENCY DISEASES, Vol. XI).

Hormones are important in the internal regulation of growth. These are substances secreted straight into the blood by special 'ductless' or ENDOCRINE GLANDS (q.v. Vol. XI). The pituitary gland of vertebrates lies under the brain and inside the skull; its hormones control growth directly, and also control other endocrine glands, which in turn affect growth. Dwarfs and giants can result from rare pituitary abnormalities; extreme stunting, for example, is caused by the lack of a hormone secreted by the thyroid gland in the neck. A pituitary hormone controls thyroid secretion.

The growth rates of different parts of the body may be different, and the shapes of animals are partially controlled in this way. EARWIGS (q.v.) provide a simple example. The forceps of earwigs grow faster than the rest of the body, and large earwigs have disproportionately large ones compared with smaller individuals. In man the proportion of leg-length to trunk-length increases from babyhood to maturity, while head-size does not increase so fast as the trunk. The resulting changes of shape are striking, although familiar.

The strength of the bones and muscles that support an animal do not increase in proportion to an increase in length. This places a limit on the size of land mammals, but WHALES (q.v.) whose weight is supported by water, can become much larger. The Blue Whale, which reaches nearly 150 tonnes and 30 metres in length, is the heaviest known animal. Some of the extinct REPTILES (q.v.) were more than 24 metres long and may have weighed 50 tonnes, but these were probably aquatic and seldom had to support their full weight.

The length of life of animals is just as variable as their size; in the case of mammals and birds the larger the species the longer it is likely to be able to live. We have very little knowledge of the length of life of animals under natural conditions, with the exception of fish and animals with shells. Fish scales and shells usually show annual increases in growth, not unlike the rings seen in the cross-section of a tree trunk. The Herring, because of its economic importance, has been studied thoroughly, a small bone, the otolith, from the inner ear being used to determine its age.

Unfortunately, the time animals can live when protected in captivity bears very little relation to their usual length of life under natural conditions, for in the wild they are readily preyed upon or, once they pass their prime, fall victims to disease. The Robin appears to have a maximum age of about 20 years in a cage, but the average length of life of wild Robins is only about one year, although one exceptional wild Robin was recorded to have lived for 11 years (see THE LIFE-CYCLE OF ANIMALS, INDEX, p. 144).

GROWTH IN PLANTS. If a living cell were placed in circumstances where growth could proceed without interruption, the cell would grow evenly in every direction and eventually form a sphere. Plants and animals are seldom spherical, because growth takes place more at some points than at others. The term 'growth' means a permanent increase in size and shape. Temporary increase in either size or shape can take place for reasons other than growth. When a root-hair absorbs water from the soil it increases in size, an increase due to a swelling of the cell with extra water. Similarly, when a plant absorbs water rapidly, much of it may enter the leaf-cells and make them swell so much that the leaf area is increased, and the general shape altered; but later the leaf will return to its original shape—so no growth has occurred. A plant can only be said to have grown when it has permanently increased in size, and consequently in bulk. In plants, growth takes place by the use of energy which has been released from food by respiration; and growth is, therefore, one of the important results of NUTRITION (q.v.).

Growth is the product of two sets of opposed forces which go on in the plant. Some processes, of which PHOTOSYNTHESIS (q.v.)—the production of foodstuffs by green leaves in the presence of sunlight—is the most important, build up new tissues for the plant. Other processes, of which RESPIRATION (q.v.) is the most important, break down the built-up food substances to release energy, and this is again used in the building-up processes. So the two apparently opposed forces are really interdependent, and if the building-up process predominates, growth takes place. When the breaking-down process takes place faster than the building-up process, growth ceases. The sum of the two processes is known as 'metabolism'.

Active growth takes place in young plants at the extreme tip of the shoot and also just behind the tip of the root. In the root the tip itself consists of a root-cap, a layer of cells which bears the brunt of the friction caused as the root forces its way through the earth. Although the outer layers are constantly being worn away by this friction, new cells are as constantly being formed, and the delicate growing-point is permanently protected. The growing-point itself consists of a number of active cells, regularly and rapidly dividing to produce new cells, and so increasing the length of the root.

The rates of growth in differing plants vary considerably. In most FLOWERING PLANTS (q.v.) in Britain, the growth is usually so small each day that it is scarcely noticeable; but in Ceylon certain Bamboo stems normally grow 40 cm in a day. The most rapid growth in plants, however, takes place in small structures like fungal threads, flower-stamens, and pollen-tubes. These grow 40, 60, and even 150 times faster than bamboo shoots. The fruiting body of the Stinkhorn fungus, for example, will grow from beneath the soil to its full height of about 15 cm in just over an hour. The force produced by growing plants is often considerable. Some shoots have been found to exert a quite powerful upward pressure, and growing roots have often forced rocks and banks apart, and even caused houses to tumble down.

It is very difficult to measure growth in plants accurately, since they spread in three directions, and growth in length may not be accompanied by a corresponding growth in thickness. In some trees the shoot ceases to grow in length by early summer, but continues to grow in girth. If increase in weight were taken as a test of growth, this would be considerably affected by the amount of water present in the plant, and therefore by whether or not the roots had been recently absorbing water, and whether the leaves had been giving off water by TRANSPIRATION (q.v.). Generally, growth in plants is measured by their increase in dry weight; but to do this the plant has to be killed, and so cannot be used to compare dry weight at different times. There is no one way of measuring growth, and different methods have to be used in different circumstances.

Since the growth of a plant depends upon the combined effects of the various processes which nourish it, such as food-manufacture, absorption of water, and loss of water, and since these are all influenced by external conditions, growth, too, will be dependent on conditions such as temperature, light, and the available water-supply. As with respiration and other plant processes, there are two extremes of temperature above and below which no growth takes place. A plant will go on respiring at a much lower temperature than it will go on growing. Generally, the rate of growth is doubled for each 10 degrees rise of temperature, falling off at about 30° C. and ceasing altogether at about 35° C. The effect of temperature on growth is seen when plants are grown in hot-houses. In this way flowers and vegetables of all kinds can be given an artificially made temperature, and so be 'forced' to grow out of season.

Light affects growth in many ways. For instance, the shoot and root of a green plant grow more rapidly in length at night than during the day, whereas growth in area of the leaf-blade is much reduced by the absence of light. This effect of darkness in developing stems is made use of by gardeners in growing Rhubarb, Celery, and Sea-kale. If plants like the House-leek, which normally has a rosette habit of growth, are grown in the dark, the stem lengthens considerably, so that each leaf has a well-marked piece of stem between it and the next. The rate at which a stem grows in length is not the same throughout the whole period of development: at first its rate of lengthening is small, then it increases to a maximum, and finally slows down before it ceases altogether.

During the last 40 years crop-breeders have been experimenting on the effect of varying periods of light on certain plants. It was noticed that a certain tobacco plant in America, called Maryland Mammoth, produced no flowers at certain latitudes; but at other latitudes, where the days were shorter and the nights longer, it blossomed. It was then found that some plants produce flowers and fruit of better quality more quickly if they are illuminated for periods of less than 12 hours daily. These are called 'short-day' plants. Others have been found to do better with light-periods of more than 12 hours, and have been called 'long-day' plants. A considerable amount of experimental work, especially in Russia and America, is proceeding along these lines, particularly in the introduction of new crops in new territories. Chrysanthemums are short-day plants: that is why they thrive during the autumn.

PLANT HORMONES. Plants need the correct external conditions—water, light, warmth, for example—for normal growth. In addition to these, however, growth is also influenced by internal factors. The shoot of a plant, for instance, will bend upwards towards the light, and the root will bend downwards; but if the tip of the shoot or root is cut off, then these movements will not take place. This is because the tips are producing a substance, called an 'auxin' or 'plant hormone', which affects the growth of the regions below them. This substance, when extracted from stem or root tips, always seems to be the same; and so, strangely enough, the same auxin makes roots turn downwards towards gravity, and stems turn upwards away from gravity. This auxin has a very important effect on the life of the plant, for it ensures that roots grow down into the soil and that stems grow up towards the light.

Other substances have been found recently which also have an effect on the growth or development of plants. Some varieties of apple-trees, for example, have caused great anxiety to fruit growers because most of the fruit tends to drop off long before it is ripe. A hormone has been found which, if sprayed on the trees at the right time, prevents the fruit from falling until it is ripe. Other substances, extracts of which can now be bought by gardeners, encourage cuttings to grow roots. Hormone weed killers, if used on lawns, make the broad-leaved plants, such as plantains, dandelions, and daisies, grow so fast that eventually they outgrow their strength and die.

See also MOVEMENT IN PLANTS.

GUILLEMOT, *see* AUK, Section 3.

GUINEA-FOWL. This African group, named after the Guinea Lands of West Africa, belongs to the order of game-birds. There are several species, the predominant colours being black, pale blue, and white, and some species carrying handsome crests. They are gregarious birds, and collect in large flocks in grass-covered plains near forests. But they are very shy, and make their escape by running at great speed through the grass. They were already domesticated in the days of the ancient Greeks, our domesticated Guinea-fowl coming from one of the West African species (*see* GUINEA-FOWL, Vol. VI).

GUINEA-PIG, *see* CAVY.

GULLS. 1. Sea-birds of the order Charadriiformes include the typical Gulls and the Terns, Skimmers, Kittiwakes, and Skuas. Although they are all essentially sea-birds, some gulls often come a long way inland and will breed on inland waters. The Herring Gull, for instance, can often be seen following the plough on an inland farm, in search of worms. Gulls are to be found over much of the world, though in fact no gulls proper inhabit the great area lying between South America and Australia—only Terns. They are mostly gregarious, noisy birds, powerful fliers and good swimmers, though few of them dive to catch fish. Their food is principally fish and refuse, though they will eat almost anything. Their plumage, except for the Skuas, is predominantly white, their wings are long, and their feet webbed. They have long bills, the upper half being longer than the lower, and bent over at the tip. They generally nest in colonies, some species choosing ledges on cliffs, others inland swamps, sand-dunes, or coarse grass. The order also includes several families dealt with in this book under the heading WADING BIRDS (q.v.).

There are between forty and fifty species of typical gulls, the smallest being the Little Gull, common in Mediterranean countries and a visitor to the British Isles, and the largest the Glaucous or Greater White-winged Gull, an Arctic bird measuring fully 80 centimetres, which comes farther south only in winter. The comparatively small Black-headed Gulls are the most common in Britain, preferring flat shores in winter and breeding in marshes. They are, in fact, nearly as much inland as sea birds. The Common or Mew Gull visits England mainly in winter, breeding throughout northern Europe and Asia, and in Ireland and Scotland and locally in England. The Herring Gull, a larger bird, measuring 58 cm or more, frequents all British coasts and those of northern Europe and North America, reaching as far as North Africa in the winter. It nests on broad cliff-ledges, the eggs varying widely in colour. Herring Gulls are so named because they follow the shoals of herrings, hovering above them before plunging for their catch. They are magnificent fliers, gliding, soaring, and riding on the gusts of wind. Another resident in Britain is the Black-backed Gull, though that and the Great Black-backed Gull are found more often in the north. The Great Black-backed Gull, the 'vulture of the seas', preys on other birds, and will even attack a young lamb or wounded animal, killing it after first pecking out its eyes. Perhaps the most

Eric Hosking

A PAIR OF BLACK-HEADED GULLS AT THEIR NEST

Eric Hosking

GREAT BLACK-BACKED GULLS WITH THEIR CHICKS

beautiful of the gulls is the snowy-white Ivory Gull, which breeds in Spitzbergen and other far-northern regions.

2. TERNS (or Sea Swallows) have long, pointed wings, deeply forked tails, slender bodies, and short legs. They rarely rest on the water, but fly skimming over it, generally with their bills pointed downwards, scanning the surface for small fish on which to plunge. Most Terns are spring and summer migrants to Britain, returning farther south for the winter.

ARCTIC TERN IN FLIGHT

L. Hugh Newman

COMMON NODDIES NESTING

John Warham

A HERRING GULL

Eric Hosking

They make practically no nest, but lay their two to three eggs on shingle beds or in sand-dunes or dry grass. They generally breed in large communities. They will defend their nests with great boldness, flying in the face of intruders and even killing other birds or animals. There are several species, ranging from the Little Tern, which is 23 cm long, to the Sandwich Tern, which is 41 cm. The Arctic Tern is famous for the tremendous range of its migratory flights (*see* MIGRATION). The tropical Noddy, a dusky black tern, nests in vast quantities in islands off the coast of Florida and many other tropical lands.

3. KITTIWAKES, close relatives of the Gulls, breed on cliff ledges, often only a little way above the water, and are altogether more completely sea-birds than the Gulls. Unlike other members of the family they are expert fishers, diving skilfully after their prey. There are only two species, the North Atlantic and North Pacific Kittiwakes. They are very strong fliers, being known regularly to cross the Atlantic.

4. SKIMMERS. These close relatives of the Terns are like them in most respects; but they have very remarkable beaks, which have led to their being called 'Scissor-bills'. The beak is elongated and compressed to a knife-like shape, with the upper half much shorter and more flexible than the lower. There are three species, belonging to India, the Red Sea and Nile, and North America respectively. The North American bird has been observed skimming over the water with the long lower half of its bill beneath the surface—doubtless catching food.

5. SKUAS. These residents of north Scotland, the Scottish Isles, and other northern regions, have strong, hooked claws and sharp, hooked beaks. They are the pirates of northern waters, rarely fishing for themselves but attacking other birds and making them disgorge their catch. The Skua then swoops after the falling morsel so swiftly that it generally recovers it in mid-air. Two species breed within the limits of the British Isles, the Great Skua, a bird some 63 cm long, which leads a solitary life, generally out at sea, and the Arctic Skua, a more common and gregarious bird. Three species are found in the southern hemisphere, dispersed widely from the coasts of South America to those of New Zealand and the Indian Ocean.

GURNARD, *see* SCORPION FISH.

H

HABITAT, *see* Animal Distribution; Plant Distribution; Ecology of Plants.

HADDOCK, *see* Cod.

HAG-FISHES, *see* Lamprey.

HAIR. All mammals except the whales, porpoises, and dolphins have a covering of hair—and even whales, when they are young, have a few bristles on the snout, though these disappear later. A hair grows from a small depression or tube in the skin called a 'hair follicle'. This is formed by the 'epidermis' (or outer skin) growing down into the 'dermis' (or true skin). A tiny 'papilla' or outgrowth appears at the bottom of the follicle, and the cells of this then divide and grow rapidly, until the young hair projects beyond the surface of the skin.

Each hair has a fibrous interior and an outer horny coat. A blood-vessel at the root supplies food material, and a gland opening on the side of the follicle supplies a kind of oil or fat to keep the hair soft and pliable. The follicle is in a slanting position, so that the hair usually lies down one way. At the root of the hair is a tiny muscle, and when this contracts it pulls the hair upright. Cats, dogs, and animals with manes are able to use this muscle to make themselves look bigger and more ferocious; but in man the muscle has practically ceased to function, so that fright no longer causes the hair to stand on end. Colour granules give the hair its tint; but in people who are in ill health or who are elderly, tiny air-bubbles take the place of the granules and the hair becomes white or grey.

Hair may be fine, coarse, straight, curly, long, or short. The wool of sheep, the fur of seals, the manes of lions, and the spines of hedgehogs or porcupines are all different kinds of hair. The horns of the rhinoceros and the armour-like skin of the armadillo are just cemented masses of hair.

Nails and Claws, as well as Hoofs (qq.v.), are produced in the same way as hairs. Instead of a small follicle we find a mass of cells making a nail-bed, so that a wide horny outgrowth comes from the broad root. Feathers (q.v.), which are peculiar to birds, are produced in just the same way as hairs.

HAIRSTREAKS. These butterflies, members of the same family as the Blues and Coppers (qq.v.), are called 'Hairstreak' because of the delicate white lines on the undersides of their wings. The males have special scales which distribute alluring scents during courtship. These are grouped into bands on the front wings, whereas the Blues and Coppers have them scattered. Four of the five British species are named after their distinguishing colours: green, purple, brown, and black. All but the Green Hairstreak have at the angle of each hind-wing a tiny, slender tail, which may deflect the attention of enemies away from the vulnerable head. The caterpillars are shaped like woodlice, and lie flat, casting little shadow.

The Green Hairstreak, the most common species, is seen in May and June almost everywhere in the British Isles where dogwood grows. The caterpillars eat a variety of other plants, such as broom, bramble, rock-rose, and whortleberry, and also are carnivorous. The stout pupa, which is capable of making a creaking sound, lies under a few silken threads at the foot of its food plant from July until the following May. The butterfly has entirely green under-

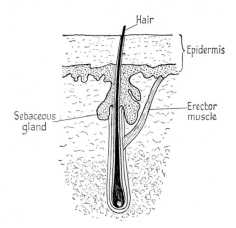

SECTION OF SKIN SHOWING HAIR FOLLICLE

Hair

Epidermis

Erector muscle

Sebaceous gland

S. Beaufoy

FEMALE PURPLE HAIRSTREAK BUTTERFLY RESTING ON AN
OAK TWIG

sides, the colour being due to the structure of the scales and not to pigment. Since this colouring is such good camouflage when the butterfly rests with wings closed on the green leaves, it is strange that it is not more common.

The White Letter Hairstreak, restricted to midland and southern counties, has white hairstreaks forming a definite letter 'W' on the hindwings. The female lays her eggs only on elm twigs. Generation after generation will breed on one large tree in a group of elms, nothing short of the felling of their tree inducing them to move to another. The butterflies are sometimes found in great abundance in July and August at the flowers of privet and bramble.

The Purple Hairstreak has an ashy-grey underside; the upper side of the male has a purplish gloss, while that of the female has a patch on the fore-wing of about as brilliant a purple as that of the male PURPLE EMPEROR (q.v.). These Hairstreaks can often be seen flitting round the outer branches of old oak trees during July and early August, but usually well out of reach. The larvae, descending from the oak to pupate in late May, may be found in the litter beneath the trees.

Brown Hairstreaks, not uncommon in many southern, western, and midland counties, fly high over tree-tops during August and September, but can sometimes be seen when they descend to suck nectar from flowers or to lay eggs on the twigs of low-growing blackthorn saplings. The caterpillar hatches in the following spring, and pupates in June on the underside of a leaf, the old larva-skin holding the pupa in place, for it has no tail hooks.

The Black Hairstreak, a very rare resident butterfly in Britain, is restricted to blackthorn thickets in the woods of Huntingdonshire, Northamptonshire, and the Oxfordshire–Buckinghamshire border. The females fly in June and July, and select the highest spikes of old blackthorn bushes on which to lay their eggs. The caterpillar emerges in the spring, and in June changes into a pupa easily mistaken for a bird-dropping.

HAKE, *see* COD.

HAMSTER, *see* MOUSE.

HARE. Hares belong to the same order as RABBITS (q.v.). They are natives of Britain, and also of most parts of Europe, Asia, Africa, and North America, and have been introduced into Australia and New Zealand, where they are not so much a pest as the rabbit. Like the rodents, their two upper and two lower incisor teeth are especially adapted for gnawing. They have divided upper lips, which has led to the expression 'hare-lipped'.

The common Brown Hare is a great enemy to the farmer and gardener (*see* VERMIN, Section 8, Vol. VI), and would probably have been exterminated were it not preserved for sport (*see* HARE HUNTING, Vol. IX). It lives on grass, young corn, roots, and bark. The hare is an unsociable animal. It does not live in burrows, but in the open, and selects convenient places, called 'forms', where it lies crouched and concealed during most of the day and night. Hares will sometimes allow themselves to be almost trodden on before stirring. When forced to move, they will run to a safe distance and then sit up on their hind legs, with ears erect to listen. They have a very acute sense of hearing and smell, but, because of the position of the eyes, it is thought that their forward vision is limited. This weakness of sight, as well as their habit of following regular runs, make them easy to snare or net.

Hares show much cunning in escaping from

pursuers and in laying a baffling scent. They will elude a faster pursuer by 'jinking', or swerving at high speed. When hunted, they use most of the same tricks as the Fox (q.v.): in particular, they double back on their tracks and then make a series of long, sideways leaps before continuing their run. It is said that, when coming to or from their form, they will take two very long leaps (nearly 5 metres) to break the scent. They move by a series of jumps with their long hind legs and skip with their fore legs: the faster they go the longer are the jumps. They can jump up on to a high wall, and can swim well.

The main courting season is February and March. The jacks (as male hares are called) in their pursuit of does get very excited, and run about, kicking, bucking, and jumping—from which has come the expression 'mad as a March hare'. The doe has two litters in a year, producing at a birth two to five young 'leverets', which she cares for very well and in whose protection she will fight fiercely. The leverets are born in the open, and soon after their birth the mother finds separate 'forms' for each leveret, visiting each in turn by night to suckle it. The tiny leverets, therefore, go a remarkably long time without food, much longer than most large animals. In about a month's time they are able to fend entirely for themselves.

The Brown Hare is rarely found on hills and moors, or far north, where the Blue Mountain or Alpine Hare takes its place. This hare is rather smaller, and is bluish-grey in the summer, gradually changing in the autumn and winter to white. It is duller in colour than the brown hare, and its flesh is much poorer in flavour. The Scottish Mountain Hare belongs to this group. The Irish Hare, much like the Blue Hare in most ways, is rather larger, and much more gregarious: as many as 200–300 have been seen in droves. The American Prairie Hare is most usually called the Jack Rabbit (a shortening of Jackass Rabbit). It is a large hare, with very long ears and legs, and it makes enormous, kangaroo-like bounds. In Arctic regions, the American hare, which is white in winter, is known also as the Snowshoe Rabbit, from the thickly furred soles of its feet that enable it to move on soft snow.

HARRIER, *see* HAWK, Section 5.

HARTEBEEST, *see* ANTELOPE.

HARVESTMAN. This is a member of the same class of animals as SPIDERS (q.v.)—the Arachnida. It is distinguished by the absence of the narrow waist (which in spiders separates the two portions of the body), by the great length of its legs, and by the possession of two glands in the head, which secrete an evil-smelling fluid. There are about three thousand known species, twenty of which can be found in Britain, the rest being distributed all over the world, except in the polar regions.

In this country Harvestmen are most conspicuous in the autumn, to which fact they doubtless owe their popular name. Although a few species are frequently active in the sunshine, most of them come out by night. Using the long, second pair of legs as sense-organs, they detect their prey by touch, and seize it in their pincer-like jaws. They do not possess venom-glands. Many Harvestmen live near water or in moist surroundings: they have a constant thirst for water, and die in a short time if they cannot get it. Harvestmen very often shed their legs if they are grasped; but, unlike all other Arachnida, they are unable to grow them again. Since they have four pairs of legs, they do not seem to be seriously inconvenienced by the loss of one or two. If, however, they lose both legs of the second pair, they are seriously handicapped and usually do not live long.

The female lays her eggs underground in the autumn in clumps of twenty or more. They hatch in the spring, and the young ones, which resemble their parents except in size, grow during the summer, with periodic castings of the skin. A few exceptional species are to be found as adults at all times of the year.

Harvestmen normally feed on insects and other small creatures; but they will also eat a variety of other foods. They have been seen feeding on dead moles, on the patches of 'sugar' used by moth-collectors, and on the marmalade of a picnic party. Only in rare circumstances are they cannibals—in which they differ from most other members of their class. They are easy to keep under observation in captivity, and there is still much to be learnt about their habits.

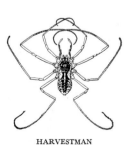

HARVESTMAN

HAWFINCH, *see* FINCHES, Section 2.

HAWK. 1. The Hawk tribe forms a very large group of the Birds of Prey, to which also belong the FALCONS and EAGLES (qq.v.). Its members are distributed throughout the world. The common Sparrow-hawk of Britain is a typical Hawk. The larger Goshawk is now only a rare visitor to the east coast, though it used to be much more common in Britain, and was a great favourite with falconers (*see* FALCONRY, Vol. IX). The Hawk Tribe also includes the Kites, the Buzzards, and their near relatives, the Harriers.

2. The SPARROW-HAWK, one of the smaller members of the family, is distinguished from a Falcon, to which it is closely related, by its shorter, rounded wings and its long tail, which it holds at a downward angle when in flight. It is an elegant-looking bird, about 33 cm long, with very sharp eyes and a hooked beak. It is a bold robber. Its flight is swift and dashing rather than long-sustained, and it attacks its prey by a sudden rush, generally from behind, instead of (as with a Kestrel) from above. Sparrow-hawks build nests of sticks in trees, and lay five or six handsome eggs, with orange and brick-red markings on a whitish ground—typical of the family.

3. KITES are larger birds, about 60 cm long with long narrow wings. They used to be common, and were often to be seen flying in circles or hanging in the air above the streets of London and other European cities, where they acted as scavengers. They were consistently attacked by sportsmen, farmers, and gamekeepers, because of their depredations on young birds, until by 1895 they were practically extinct. Now, a few pairs of Red Kites have been successfully re-established in the mountains of South Wales. They are magnificent fliers, appearing to hang in the air for long periods, with hardly any movement of the wings. They feed on carrion and garbage of any sort, and although they will attack young or weakling birds, they are not bold robbers. The Honey-buzzards (Bee-hawks), relatives of the Kites (not the Buzzards), are now practically extinct in Britain. These large, rather un-hawklike birds, so called because they will dig out the nests of bees and wasps with their claws to feed on the grubs, are found over northern Europe and much of Asia.

4. BUZZARDS are rather more like lesser Eagles than Hawks, being some 60 cm in length

The late Arthur Brook

COCK SPARROW-HAWK AT NEST

and lacking the dash of Hawks and Falcons. They are not a danger to gamekeepers, for they feed mainly on insects, young rabbits, mice, voles, and worms. They are found in remote districts in Wales, the Lake District, the Scottish Highlands, and elsewhere, and make bulky nests

The late Arthur Brook

THE MALE BUZZARD (RIGHT) ARRIVES WITH FOOD FOR THE FAMILY

The late Arthur Brook

MONTAGU'S HARRIER AND YOUNG

of sticks in high trees or on craggy ledges. At times, especially in the breeding season, Buzzards will soar in circles high in the air, uttering at intervals their shrill, whistle-like cry. Species of Buzzards are to be found over most of the world.

5. HARRIERS, relatives of the Buzzards, used to be more common in Britain than they are now. The Hen-harrier breeds on the wilder moors of Wales and Scotland, the Marsh Harrier in East Anglia, and the Montagu's Harrier very locally in southern and eastern England. They are slender birds, with long legs, tails, and wings, and they feed mainly on field-mice, lizards, frogs, birds, eggs, and larger insects. They have a characteristic flight when hunting. They quarter the ground very carefully, flying low over it with alternate flapping and gliding. When gliding, they hold their wings tilted up, instead of horizontally like most birds. The male passes the prey in mid-air to the female, who catches it in her talons and takes it to the nest.

HAWK MOTHS. These rather large moths, belonging to the family Sphingidae, are very powerful flyers. They occur in most parts of the world. Of 900 known species, 17 occur in Britain, though only 9 of them habitually breed, the others being immigrants of greater or lesser frequency. They have long fore-wings, smaller hind-wings, and hooked antennae. The proboscis or sucking organ varies greatly in length: in some species it is very small and almost useless;

but in others it is much lengthened, notably in those which hover on the wing and, without alighting, probe the depths of long tubular flowers for nectar. The Convolvulus Hawk, which occurs throughout the Old World and in many Pacific Islands, and is an immigrant to Britain, has a proboscis about 12 centimetres long, more than the wing expanse; while there is a tropical American species with a proboscis twice this length. Many of these moths fly at night or at twilight, and the flowers dependent upon them for pollination are often white and therefore conspicuous in the dark. Humming-bird Hawk Moths fly in the sunshine, their size (over 4 cm in expanse), colour (greyish-brown forewings, and orange hind-wings), and behaviour so strongly suggesting HUMMING-BIRDS (q.v.) that experienced travellers are often deceived. Bee Hawks also fly by day. The colour of their hairy bodies and their transparent wings give them a mimetic resemblance to humble bees (see PROTECTIVE COLORATION).

The Death's Head Hawk, a robust insect with a wing spread of 12 cm, has dark fore-wings, brownish-yellow hind-wings with two black bands, and a yellowish blotch suggesting a skull and crossbones on the thorax. Its range extends across Europe to North Africa, through Central and Southern Asia to Japan. It is a migrant to Britain, where it occasionally breeds. It enters bee-hives for the honey, and squeaks like the queen bee, the sound being made by forcing air from the gut over a vibrating fold in the mouth. The full-grown caterpillar, which usually feeds on potatoes or nightshade, measures over 12 centimetres long. It may be brown, yellow-green, yellow-purple, green-blue, or yellow-blue. The seven oblique side-stripes, so characteristic of Hawk Moth larvae, are bluish or purplish, and the horn near the rear end, also characteristic of the family, is short, rough, and bent back at the tip. When about to pupate, the caterpillar first wanders, and then burrows a few centimetres into the earth, where it constructs a cell made of particles of soil held together by a gummy liquid which it secretes, and a little silk. Caterpillars in this stage grind their jaws together, making a noise resembling the winding of a watch. The caterpillar changes to a dark-brown pupa usually in July and August, about 10 days after it has ceased to feed.

Other species found commonly in Britain are the greenish Lime Hawk, the greyish Poplar

E. Syms

S. Beaufoy

EYED HAWK MOTH CATERPILLAR AND ADULT MOTH

The Moth is showing his eyes because he has been disturbed

S. Beaufoy

POPLAR HAWK MOTH

S. Beaufoy

ELEPHANT HAWK MOTH ON ROSEBAY WILLOW-HERB

Hawk recognized by the rusty red patch on the hind-wing, the black, grey, and pink Privet Hawk, the brownish Eyed Hawk which has an eye-like spot on each hind-wing, and the rosy-pink Elephants, Large and Small. The caterpillars of the first three feed on the plants from which they take their names. The magnificent larva of the Privet Hawk is bright green with seven pairs of oblique white and lilac stripes. The Eyed Hawk caterpillar, also green, but with only white stripes, is sometimes a pest in apple orchards. The Elephant Hawk caterpillar, found on willow-herb, bedstraw, or fuchsia, is normally blackish or brownish and bears several eye-like markings in front which the insect displays if molested. When full grown and fully extended, it is nearly 8 cm long and tapers strongly towards the head, reminding one of an elephant's trunk. The large green caterpillar of the Convolvulus Hawk may be found occasionally on bindweed in cultivated fields on the coast. It changes to a chrysalis in which the proboscis stands out from the body as does a handle from a jug. The Pine Hawk, formerly found mainly in Suffolk and Dorset, is now more abundant and more widely spread. The Oleander, Spurge, Bedstraw, and Striped Hawks are migrants apparently unable to complete their life-cycle in Britain in the open. In America Hawk Moth caterpillars are known as Hornworms. One of the most injurious pests of tobacco plants is the green and white striped Tobacco Hornworm.

See also MOTH.

HAZEL, *see* FRUITS, Section 2 c.

HEARING, *see* SENSES, Section 3.

HEART. The lowest animals in the evolutionary scale, such as HYDRA (q.v.), obtain food and oxygen from the water in which they live. As animals became larger and required more food than can be supplied by this method, a BLOOD SYSTEM (q.v.) has evolved for supplying the CELLS (q.v.) with food, and a pump in the form of a heart is necessary for the transport of the blood. In the higher animals the blood system and the heart are more complex, because the blood carries oxygen as well as food to the cells, and brings back the waste product—carbon dioxide. The heart has to be so constructed that, when it pumps the blood, the oxygenated and deoxygenated blood are kept separate.

The hearts of the lower animals, such as the earthworm (*see* WORM), are formed by the five blood-vessels surrounding the gullet or food passage; these, having valves, expand and contract and thus force the blood along. INSECTS (q.v.) have similar tubular hearts. Since air reaches the various parts of an insect's body direct from openings in its sides, the blood system does not need to carry much oxygen, and therefore only a single circulation and a simple heart are needed.

FISH (q.v.) have a two-chambered heart (Fig. 1), with an 'auricle' or upper chamber, a 'ventricle' or lower chamber, and valves to control the flow of blood. The blood is pumped from the heart to the gills, and then passes direct with

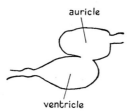

FIG. 1. TWO-CHAMBERED HEART OF FISH (SIDE VIEW)

its oxygen to the body, before returning with its carbon dioxide to the heart. The fish's blood system, therefore, different from that of most vertebrates, has a single circulation.

In MAMMALS and FROGS (qq.v.) the blood, once it has received oxygen in the lungs, is returned to the heart before being pumped to the

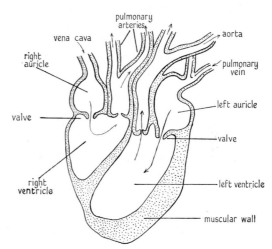

FIG. 2. FOUR-CHAMBERED HEART OF MAMMAL

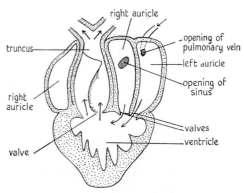

FIG. 3. THREE-CHAMBERED HEART OF FROG (FRONT VIEW)

other parts of the body. The heart is more complicated because the blood carrying oxygen has to be kept apart, as much as possible, from the deoxygenated blood returning with its carbon dioxide. Mammals, including man, therefore, have a four-chambered heart, which is really two pumps in one, operating two blood circuits. One circuit, from the left ventricle, sends oxygenated blood around the body and back to the right auricle. The other circuit, from the right ventricle, sends deoxygenated blood to the lungs for fresh oxygen. Having received this, the oxygenated blood returns to the left auricle, ready to repeat the journey round the body (as shown in Fig. 2).

The frog's heart (Fig. 3) is only three-chambered. The oxygenated blood is partially mixed with the deoxygenated blood in the undivided ventricle; but as the frog can respire through its skin, there is less need to supply all the oxygen through the blood, and so the mixing does not matter. The frog's blood system, like that of mammals, has a double circulation.

See also Vol. XI: HEART (Human).

HEATH (Butterfly). The Small Heath, which belongs to the same family as the BROWNS (q.v.), is one of the commonest butterflies in the British Isles, and is a familiar sight on commons and heaths in all parts except the Scillies, Orkneys, and Shetlands. It is normally tawny, but may be deeper or lighter in tint, and very rarely creamy-white. Some forms have a large, clear eye-spot on the upper side of the fore-wing, but in others this is either faint or entirely absent. The Heath is an inactive butterfly, generally flying only when disturbed. The female lays her eggs in early summer singly on blades of grass, on which the striped green caterpillars feed. They either hibernate or yield a second brood in the autumn, of which the larvae always overwinter.

The rarer Large Heath resembles the Small Heath, except that it is about half as big again; but it is a more active butterfly. The green-and-white striped caterpillars are well camouflaged on the food plant, white beak-sedge, and live

Gordon Woods

LARGE HEATH BUTTERFLY

up to an altitude of 600 metres. They hibernate during the winter. The Large Heath does not breed in southern England, but has been found on rough pastures, bogs, and mosses, in the Lake District, parts of Yorkshire, Lancashire, Cheshire, and Shropshire, in Wales, Scotland, the Hebrides, Orkneys, and even the Shetlands, where it is the only indigenous butterfly. It is also common in parts of Ireland. This distribution suggests that the Large Heath established itself in Britain before the separation from the mainland of Ireland and the smaller island groups. The Mountain Ringlet (*see* BROWNS) also occurs in Ireland. These two northern species are represented by distinct British forms and are probably the butterflies longest resident there. The Large Heath shows a continuous gradation from dark, heavily ringed specimens in England, through intermediates in Cumberland, to light, indistinctly spotted forms in Scotland. Intermediates also occur in Wales. This gradation in the characteristics of a species, through a range involving considerable change in climatic or other factors, is called a 'cline', and is typical of animals tending to remain in the districts in which they were born.

HEATHER, *see* HEATHS AND MOORLANDS.

HEATHS AND MOORLANDS. These occur on gently undulating land which is exposed at higher altitudes to sun and wind. Moorland is characterized by wet peat, which is brown in colour, acid in reaction, and often of considerable depth, whereas heaths are found on shallow soils which are generally sandy or gravelly.

Heath soils do not retain water, and in the course of time the soluble mineral salts have been washed out from them. They are therefore poor, dry, and unsuitable for the growth of most plants, those that do grow there having special characteristics which enable them to survive. Among the heath-plants are the Ling, Bilberry, Bell-heather, and Broom. In all these the leaves are greatly reduced and have thickened surfaces, and the 'stomata' or pores through which water-loss or TRANSPIRATION (q.v.) takes place are especially well protected, so that the plants can conserve as much as possible of the water which has been absorbed by the roots. Bracken is found also on heaths—and it is significant that the leaves of these heath brackens are much thicker and stouter-looking than those of the graceful brackens found in woods. Besides the sandy soils and the lack of water and of mineral salts, other difficulties against which heath plants must contend are exposure to high winds, the recurrence of fires (caused by people's carelessness), and interference by animals.

The peat of moorlands is due to the accumulation of plant remains over long periods under conditions which were unfavourable to decay. Peat, which usually contains much humic acid, when once established, becomes independent of the underlying rocks. In places it may be as thick as 9 metres.

There is great variation in the amount of water to be found in different moorlands, and this accounts for the wide range of plant populations. Dry moors usually occur on high ground, and may extend over the summits of hills. Ling is the dominant plant here, while the Bilberry, common Mat Grass, and Bell-heather also occur. Other plants found in the dry peat areas are the orange-berried Cloudberry and the Crowberry. Cotton-grass also occurs on these moors and, where the peat is wetter, it becomes the dominant plant. On the uplands of Wales, north England, and Scotland, the soil is composed of glacial clays left by the retreating glaciers of the ICE-AGE (q.v. Vol. III). The peat, about 15 cm in depth, overlies the water-holding clay, making the soil sour and sometimes waterlogged, although in summer the surface layers may become dry. Because the water drains more readily here than on the moors where the peat is very thick, there is more oxygen dissolved in it; and in consequence, the Purple Moor Grass, which demands more oxygen than the Cotton Grass, is often the dominant plant. The Purple Moor Grass has a great many roots, some penetrating quite deeply and others remaining short, by which the plant absorbs water readily. The roots are invaded also by fungal threads, called 'Mycorrhiza', which break down the decaying humus and pass on the nitrogen compounds to the plant, so making up for the deficiency of nitrates in the soil. In summer the leaves of the Purple Moor Grass are withered at the tips, and in winter the withered leaves bend before the wind, giving the appearance of waves. Since this grass grows in situations where the supply of oxygen is limited, it gets what it needs from the air passing through numerous air-canals which extend throughout the plant.

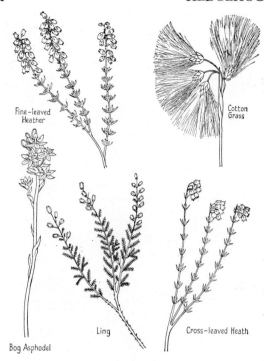

Fine-leaved Heather

Cotton Grass

Bog Asphodel

Ling

Cross-leaved Heath

HEATH AND MOORLAND PLANTS

Various rushes and sedges also grow on grass moors, as well as the lovely Bog Asphodel, Cross-leaved Heath, and Sweet Gale.

See also Vol. III: MOORLAND AND MARSH.

HEDGEHOG. This very common little member of the INSECTIVORA (q.v.), or insect-eating mammals, is found throughout the whole of Europe, in Asia, and in Africa. He is about the size of a large guinea-pig, and has a pig-like snout and extremely short legs. His protective coat of sharp spines grows only on the upper part and sides of his body, the rest being covered with coarse hair which offers little protection against the sharp teeth of his natural enemies, such as the fox or badger. But when the hedgehog rolls himself up, the unprotected parts of his body are tucked away, together with his head and feet, inside the prickly ball, leaving sharp spines sticking out in all directions. The hedgehog has a most acute sense of smell and hearing. On sensing danger, he stops and listens, then drops his head between his forefeet, erects his spines, and if, further alarmed, rolls himself up into a tight ball. The badger sometimes manages to tear open the prickly ball with his long, strong claws, and the fox is said

A. R. Thompson

HEDGEHOG AND FAMILY

to have many clever tricks to make a hedgehog unroll.

Hedgehogs are usually seen waddling slowly along the ground; but they can run quite fast. Down steep slopes they either roll, or drop like a ball, landing on their spines, and in water they are very good swimmers. The adults occasionally emit a subdued grunt or cough-like snort, and the young have a shrill squeak. They spend most of the day hidden in hedges and shrubberies, or in holes, and hunt for food during the night—though in summer and autumn they quite often venture out before dusk. Besides insects, they eat a great deal of animal food, such as slugs, frogs, young birds, rats, and mice, and they will taste almost anything. A hungry hedgehog will sometimes make a meal of a snake —even a poisonous viper or adder. He makes a swift snap at the snake's back to break the backbone and cripple his enemy. Then instantly he rolls himself up into a prickly ball, at which the snake strikes in vain, inflicting severe injury on itself. When at last the reptile lies dead, the hedgehog crushes its bones and, beginning at the tail, devours it all.

During the summer and autumn the hedge-hog eats as much as he can to put on fat. Then, late in November or December, he retires to hibernate in a warm bed of mossy leaves. He sinks into a deep sleep, his heart almost ceases to beat, and he scarcely breathes. During his hibernation he uses up the fat he has stored in his body, so that when he wakes up in the spring, he is quite thin and very hungry (*see* HIBERNATION).

The sow has two litters a year, of from four to seven young. They are born blind, with tiny soft spines which take about three weeks to harden, during which time the babies are defenceless.

HEDGEROWS. Although these are artificial barriers introduced by man, and not natural features of the vegetation of a country, hedge-rows are interesting plant associations (*see* ECOLOGY OF PLANTS), because they show so many communities. Usually a hedge includes three things: the hedge itself, the bank, and the ditch at the bottom. The plants in these different positions have their own characteristics, and vary according to the nature of the soil, its dampness, and their exposure to the sun. The direction in which the hedge runs has a strong effect upon the vegetation, a hedge extending from north to south, thus presenting east and west aspects, having a much richer plant population than one running from west to east. The plants on the two sides also differ from one another, particularly in the case of a hedge running from west to east, and can be broadly divided into shade-loving and light-loving plants.

The vegetation of the ditch at the bottom of the hedge depends upon the water-supply. In a dry ditch, plants like Silverweed, Colts-foot, and Red and White Dead-nettles are typical. If the ditch is damp, even for part of the year, tall plants like Stinging-nettles, Horsetails, and Hogweed occur. In a ditch where fresh water is standing most of the year, the characteristic plants are Brooklime, Figwort, Meadowsweet, Wild Celery, and various Mints.

The bank of the hedge shows many variations, but the soil is generally dry. The typical plants are Thale-cress, Ivy-leaved Speedwell, and Chickweed. These are annual plants which flower early in the spring, when moisture is still present, and set their seeds before the drought of summer. Other plants germinate in the autumn, and spend the winter as seedlings, before completing their development in the spring. Seedlings which can be seen in the winter include Cleavers (Goosegrass, Sticky Willie, or Bobby-buttons), Garlic-mustard (Jack-by-the-hedge), and Shepherd's Purse. Many plants of dry hedgebanks have a rosette habit, the leaves spreading close to the ground and keeping the soil moist. Among these are the Daisy, Dandelion, Plantain, and Cat's Ear and Mouse Ear Hawkweed. On the light side of the banks are prostrate plants, like the Creeping Buttercup and Wild Strawberry; while the non-climbing shade plants, such as Woodsage, Yarrow, and Heath Stitchwort, usually have long, narrow, and much-divided leaves, adapted to making the most of the rays of light which penetrate the hedge. The shade plants proper include the Wood-violet, Primrose, Ground-ivy, and Cuckoo-pint, and, if the atmosphere is moist enough, ferns such as the Harts-tongue.

The hedge proper consists of shrubs and bushes, such as Hawthorn, Hazel, Elder, Maple, and Sloe, together with small trees of Elm, Oak, Ash, and Willow. Sometimes a hedge is formed wholly of trees which are kept cut—Beech and Hornbeam being often used. To thicken a hedge, the shrubs are cut back regularly, as this causes dormant buds at the base to grow into branches, which can be 'laid' into position by the farmer (see HEDGING, DITCHING, and WALL-ING, Vol. VI). The original planted hedge soon becomes colonized by other species, most of them being climbers or scramblers, using any available means of support to grow up to the light. (See CLIMBING PLANTS.) Some of these, such as the Bindweed, Black Bryony, and Honeysuckle, have twining stems. Clematis has twining leaf-stalks, while the White Bryony and Vetches have tendrils. The Ivy has adventitious roots, which adhere firmly to the bark of shrubs or trees. Of the scramblers the most common are Cleavers, the Rose, and the Bramble, which scramble by means of hooks or thorns. Besides exposing their leaves to light, climbing plants also display their flowers for pollination and their fruits for dispersal by wind. Many of these hedge-top plants, such as the Hawthorn, Rose, Bramble, Elder, Ivy, and Bryony, have juicy fruits attractive to birds—who thus help to disperse their seeds. (See also ECOLOGY OF PLANTS.)

HEDGE SPARROW, *see* THRUSHES, Section 5.

HERBS, *see* FLOWERING PLANTS.

See also Vol. VI: HERBS, GARDEN.

HEREDITY. It is a matter of common observation that the offspring resembles the parents. We do not expect a cat to have a litter of puppies or a cow to throw a foal. In all species, young are produced which, even though they may differ markedly from the parents at first, will eventually grow to resemble them. This is expressed in the well-known saying that 'like begets like'. The process of heredity goes farther than this, however, for if a pair of tabby cats mate, we expect to see tabby kittens; and from black parent cats we shall expect black kittens, and so on. Sometimes, however, a pair of pure black cats will have one kitten or more not pure black. Obviously there is some mechanism by which the uniformity of the species is maintained, and by which the individual characteristics of the parents are passed on to the offspring. This mechanism has been very extensively investigated during the last hundred years, and although there are many questions still unsolved, considerable progress has been made in understanding it. Heredity, however, is a difficult thing to understand, and the subject is best approached historically.

A 19th-century Bohemian monk, Gregor MENDEL (q.v. Vol. V), experimented in the middle of the century with garden peas. So that he would know the identity and characters of both parents of the seeds produced, he transferred pollen artificially from one plant to another. When he crossed tall pea plants with short pea plants and sowed the seeds which were produced, he found that the offspring were all tall. This result was unexpected; at that time it was generally assumed that crossing resulted in the blending of the parents' characters, and so it was expected that plants of medium height would spring up. Mendel's later experiments showed even more clearly that this idea of blending was wrong, for when he self-pollinated the offspring of the first cross and sowed the resulting seeds, both tall plants and short plants sprang up, the tall ones outnumbering the short by three to one.

The character which completely excludes the other alternative in the first generation is called a dominant character—in this case, tallness is dominant to shortness. The character which appears in the second generation, but not in the first, is called the recessive—in this case, shortness. In the same way Mendel discovered that yellowness and smoothness of seeds are dominant characters, therefore, pea plants producing green seeds are recessive to those producing yellow seeds, and those producing wrinkled seeds are recessive to those producing smooth seeds.

Since the rediscovery of Mendel's work at the beginning of the 20th century, breeding experiments have been carried out on a very wide range of living things, and this same pattern of heredity has been found to be general in plants and animals that reproduce sexually. The quality of whiteness in albino animals, for example, has usually been found to be recessive. Pink-eyed, white, pet mice are albinos. If they are crossed with pure-bred mice of any colour, all the offspring will be coloured. However, if these cross-breeds or hybrids intermarry, a quarter of their offspring will be albinos (see Diagram). In the same way short-eared mice are recessive to those with ears of normal length.

The most obvious example of this pattern of heredity in human beings is the inheritance of eye-colour. Blue eyes are recessive to brown eyes. In consequence only marriages in which both parents have blue eyes may be expected to produce blue-eyed children. If both parents have brown eyes, they will have blue-eyed children only if they are both brown-eyed hybrids, and even then the chances are three to one against their children being blue-eyed.

Very occasionally intermediates are produced in the first generation, but the second generation shows that the apparent blending is the result of lack of dominance. A good example of this is shown when red and white Snapdragons are crossed. Pink flowers are produced by all the offspring in the first generation, but the second generation of plants produces some with red flowers, some with pink flowers, and some with white flowers, in the ratio of $1:2:1$.

Mendel's experiments also show what happens when the parents differ in several contrasted characters. If peas producing yellow, wrinkled seeds are crossed with peas producing green, smooth seeds, all the first generation produce yellow smooth seeds. Each of the two pairs of alternative characters behaves just as if it were the only difference present, and all four possible types—yellow-smooth, yellow-wrinkled, green-smooth, and green-wrinkled—are produced in the second generation, in the ratio of $9:3:3:1$. The same 'independent assortment' of characters would result if coloured mice with short ears were crossed with albinos having normal ears.

We are now faced with the problem of what it is in the animal or plant which is passed on from one generation to the next and causes these characters and the other features of a species to be copied in the offspring. In animals which reproduce sexually the only continuity between parents and young are the gametes—the male sperm and the female ovum (see REPRODUCTION). The sperm, although very different from the ovum, must contribute the same type of material to the fertilized egg, because in the above examples it does not matter which parent has the dominant, and which the recessive, character. Almost all CELLS (q.v.), including gametes, contain a central body known as the nucleus which has the same structure in both male and female gametes. In higher plants a nucleus, apparently by itself, passes from the pollen grain into the ovule to unite with one of the nuclei there. This nucleus must, therefore, contain hereditary material. During cell division, structures, called chromosomes, which are found in all nuclei, behave in precisely the manner in which they would have to behave if they were responsible for the pattern of inheritance discovered by Mendel. In normal nuclei there are several pairs of chromosomes, all of similar thickness but of various lengths. The number of chromosomes is, as a rule, constant for each species. Man has twenty-four pairs of chromosomes in each cell nucleus throughout the body; other species such as Protozoa may have over a hundred pairs, and others, for example, parasitic roundworms, have only one or two pairs of chromosomes.

We can illustrate the mechanism of heredity very simply with the Snapdragon example already referred to. Imagine for simplicity that one pair of chromosomes in each cell is concerned with making red pigment. In red-flowered plants both members of the pair can do this, in pink plants only one member of each pair, and in white plants none can make red pigment. When a plant is growing normally, every chromosome divides lengthwise each time a cell divides, and the two cells produced have identical nuclei. The nuclei of gametes are unusual because they have only one member of each pair of chromosomes and, therefore, only half the usual number for the species. One gamete from each parent fuses to form the fertilized egg, which then has a pair of each sort of chromosome, one member from each parent, and the usual total number is reached again. When red and white Snapdragons are crossed, one red-producing chromosome and one which cannot produce red are found together in each cell of the offspring, which are pink because only half the quantity of red is produced. When these hybrid pinks reproduce, they produce two sorts of gametes: those containing red-producing chromosomes and those not. If these pair off at random, it is easy to see that all three sorts of flowers are produced. We have seen that dominance of one character over the other is more usual; therefore, if white and coloured mice are crossed, the hybrids cannot be distinguished from the pure-bred coloured parent except by breeding from them. Obviously in such cases one colour-producing chromosome per cell is enough to produce the maximum coloration.

There are far more possible character differences than there are pairs of chromosomes, so each chromosome must be responsible for a large

number of effects. We saw how two characters behaved when parents differed in both of them, but we were lucky in choosing two characters produced by different pairs of chromosomes. Characters which appear distinct do tend to be inherited together and are said to be 'linked' by being caused by the same chromosome. The number of chromosome pairs of the species concerned corresponds with the number of groups of linked characters; and this confirms our view that chromosomes are the material basis of heredity. Haemophilia, the tendency to bleed profusely and uncontrollably from even a small

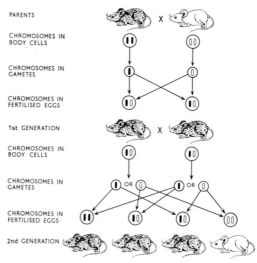

PARENTS

CHROMOSOMES IN BODY CELLS

CHROMOSOMES IN GAMETES

CHROMOSOMES IN FERTILISED EGGS

1st GENERATION

CHROMOSOMES IN BODY CELLS

CHROMOSOMES IN GAMETES

CHROMOSOMES IN FERTILISED EGGS

2nd GENERATION

DIAGRAM SHOWING HOW THE PARENTAL CHARACTERS ARE INHERITED IN THE OFFSPRING IN A REGULAR ARITHMETICAL PROPORTION

cut, is a disease which usually manifests itself in the males, but is passed on by the females.

A number of things, including irritant chemicals, X-rays, and the radiations produced by atomic bombs, damage chromosomes, and the effects on the organism have been observed. For example, when the chromosomes in the gametes of Fruit flies are damaged by X-rays, freaks are produced in the offspring which result from these gametes. Fruit flies have very large chromosomes in their salivary glands, and some types of chromosome injury can be seen under the microscope.

The changes produced by damage to chromosomes are called 'mutations'. Such changes can occur normally in the wild, though not frequently. Albino animals, for example, such as white blackbirds, are the result of mutations, though albinoism being generally a disadvantage to animals is usually recessive. Most mutations are crippling and many result in death before birth. Occasionally, however, mutations become widespread and established in the species as a result of natural selection, and the result is a small step in EVOLUTION (q.v.).

The effect of heredity may be changed by environment, but, unlike mutations, environmental effects are usually beneficial. The calluses on a gardener's hands are a good example of the effect of environment, being produced by hard manual work as a protection against further damage.

Many interesting comparisons of the effect of environment can be made in identical twins. Identical twins, unlike dissimilar twins, are produced from a single fertilized egg which divides to produce two children of identical hereditary make-up. As they grow older identical twins develop slight differences as a result of differences in environment, these being more marked if the twins are separated at an early age and brought up in very different surroundings. Yet it is remarkable how slight these differences produced by the effects of environment really are. The control exercised by heredity is overwhelming. Besides the similarity in appearance, identical twins have a similar resistance or susceptibility to particular diseases, and the difference in intelligence is less than half that between dissimilar twins.

See also Vol. VI: PLANT BREEDING; STOCK BREEDING.

HERMIT CRAB, *see* CRAB.

HERON. This group of birds includes the typical Herons, Egrets, and Bitterns, and also the STORKS (q.v.). There are about 70 species, found in most parts of the world, but not in the extreme north, the majority preferring warm or hot climates.

The common Heron stands over a metre high, with a wing-span of just under 2 metres. Most of its height is made up by its very long neck and legs, its total weight being only between 1 and 2 kilograms. Its grey plumage shades to pale bluish-white down the front. It is a powerful flier, but neither very fast nor skilful in manœuvring. In consequence it is rather defenceless against the attacks of birds such as Rooks and Terns, which often set upon it if it flies too near their nests. Herons always live near

G. K. Yeates

THE COMMON GREY HERON AT ITS LARGE UNTIDY STICK-NEST IN A TALL TREE

water—inland lakes and marshes or quiet sea-lochs—and feed on fish or any kind of small water-animal. They fish principally in the early morning and evening, standing for long periods in the fishing-ground, and making no movement at all until some prey comes within reach. Then, one quick movement of the long neck—and the prey is caught in the sharp bill. A Heron will swim from one fishing-ground to another to avoid the trouble of flight.

Herons nest in heronries on the tops of tall trees, building large, flat nests of sticks, in which they lay three or four bluish-green eggs, and often produce two broods in a season. They return year after year to the same heronry, adding to the nests, which often become very large constructions. In olden days, when Herons were protected, because they were popular game for the sport of FALCONRY (q.v. Vol. IX), there were many great heronries in Britain, especially in southern Lincolnshire. In that county, the famous heronry of Cressy Hall had as many as eighty nests. Even now, 4,000 pairs nest regularly in England and Wales, the largest heronries containing 100 nests. In Britain Herons generally choose tall oaks or elms for nesting; in North India they select the magnificent plane trees, in which they nest in great numbers. Closely related to the Grey Heron are the Purple Heron, common in many parts of Europe, and the Giant or Goliath Heron, a much larger bird, found mostly in Africa.

The Egrets, smaller birds, some 63 centimetres long, and the larger White Herons are found in Mediterranean countries and through southern Asia, and also a rather different form in Australia and New Zealand. They have beautiful pure white plumage and black legs and beaks. Egret plumes, much sought after by feather-hunters, are often marketed as 'ospreys', though their correct name is 'aigrette' (*see* FEATHER HUNTING, Vol. VI).

The Bitterns, shorter-legged relatives of the Herons, are occasional breeders in eastern Britain, and spread over most of the warmer countries of the world. They are essentially birds of the swamps, their mottled buff, brown, and black plumage harmonizing with the reeds and flags among which they live and nest. They often stand erect and still among the reeds, looking very much like a pointed stump. They have a booming cry, especially in the mating season.

HERRING. Of all fishes, the Herring family (Clupeidae) are probably the most important as food for man, for not only do they appear with almost unfailing regularity in vast shoals, but also the flesh contains more nourishment than that of any other fish except Salmon. The common Herring is found in great schools, often numbering millions of individuals, throughout the North Atlantic—though the schools do not travel the immense distances they were once supposed to do. They are divided into a number of local races, which inhabit definite limited regions and always spawn in the same area. The eggs are 'demersal'—that is, they lie on the bed of the sea, among gravel and rocks, unlike those of most other sea fishes, which float near the surface. The Herring and some of its American relatives, such as the Alewife, may sometimes enter rivers, and when they get cut off from the sea adapt themselves to life in fresh water; while the Shads, belonging to the same family, swim up rivers to lay their demersal eggs in fresh water. The Herring family is characterized by its very typical 'fish-shape', and its silvery scales that come off very easily. None of the fins has any stiff sharp spines. There is but a single short dorsal fin on the back, while the pelvic fins are far behind the pectoral fins; and there is usually a sharp edge along the middle of the lower surface, which is often made saw-like by the scales.

Closely related to the Herring is the Sprat, a smaller species, with a stronger 'saw' on the belly, and no teeth on the roof of the mouth. This fish lays eggs of the floating type. It is common off Norway, where it is caught in large numbers and canned as 'brisling', after the manner of 'sardines'. (The real 'sardine', however, is the young of the Pilchard, a more southern fish, which is the subject of an important industry in Portugal and southern France. Other species are found round America and Japan.) An easy way to tell the difference between a Herring, a Sprat, and a Pilchard is to hold them up by the dorsal fin. A Herring will balance evenly; a Sprat will hang head downwards, because the fin is nearer the tail; while the Pilchard will tilt with tail downwards, as the fin is nearer the head.

Other near relatives of the Herrings are the Anchovies, which often abound in warm seas. These are small fishes, with rather long snouts jutting forward over the mouth. They have a very strong flavour, and when salted are greatly valued for savoury dishes. Other interesting relatives of the Herring family are the Gizzard-shads of American rivers, which have small mouths with no teeth, and feed mainly on mud. The stomach forms a strong muscular gizzard

A. Fraser-Brunner

THE TARPON, A GIANT FISH, CLOSELY ALLIED TO THE HERRING FAMILY, LEAPING FROM THE WATER

something like that of a fowl. The last ray of the dorsal fin is elongate and whip-like, similar to that of the Tarpon, a giant fish, closely allied to the herring family. Tarpons live in tropical waters and afford great sport to anglers by taking great leaps out of the water, especially when caught by a hook and line (*see* Big-Game Fishing, Vol. IX).

See also Fishes.
See also Vol. VI: Herring Fishing.

HIBERNATION (from the Latin word meaning 'winter'). When the days become cold, many smaller wild animals are no longer to be seen. Some, such as the field-mice, have gone to warmer nesting sites in barns and hay-ricks, where they continue to be active and even to breed. But many other animals, such as Frogs, Newts, Toads, Lizards, Dormice, Bats, Snails, and many Insects (qq.v.), have gone into the long, deep sleep which is known as hibernation. In this condition the animal appears to be lifeless and is very hard to waken. Breathing almost stops: bats, for instance, normally take 200 breaths a minute, but a hibernating bat breaths only twenty times a minute. The heart-beat is also slow, and the body temperature of warmblooded animals is much colder than normal, although the blood in their hearts does not grow nearly so cold. Many animals take no food for several days before they begin their long winter sleep and, of course, they take no food once hibernation has begun. The very little energy that they expend while dormant is supplied by sugars stored in the liver and by the fat that has been built up during the summer. Mild winters are bad for hibernating animals, because they wake up during warm spells, use energy in moving about, but do not eat sufficient for their needs; and for this reason by the end of the winter they are very thin.

Some animals, such as the Hedgehog (q.v.), always wake in mild spells. Squirrels (q.v.) seldom hibernate in Britain, though they do so in colder countries or during severe weather. Many bats awaken in mild weather and feed on the hibernating insects that generally share their cave or tree. At such times the Whiskered and Pipistrelle Bats often fly about outside during the day. A few animals, such as Bears (q.v.), are very lethargic during winter, sleeping a large part of the time, but they do not really hibernate.

Animals hibernate in sheltered places, either underground or at the base of trees; bats retreat into caves or buildings. Frequently they make nests of leaves to keep out the cold, for if the animals are frozen they die. Frogs, toads, newts, lizards, and snakes often hibernate with

Harold Bastin

DORMOUSE'S WINTER SLEEPING-NEST, BUILT IN THE BOTTOM OF A HEDGE

Harold Bastin

DORMOUSE JUST WAKING

others of the same species and, as they cannot burrow, they have to make use of natural cracks and holes. Some snakes have been known to return to the same crack year after year.

Many species of insects survive the winter as eggs, but in others the larvae or adults hibernate during the winter—for example, Earwigs, Flies, Tortoiseshell Butterflies, and Hawk Moths. An American butterfly, the MONARCH (q.v.), is found in Canada during the summer. In the autumn this species migrates to Florida and California where the butterflies hibernate on certain trees, which they use year after year. In the spring they fly north again. Animals such as Snails creep into cracks during the winter and close the opening of their shells with a tough 'skin'.

Just as some animals in cold climates escape severe weather by hibernating, so some animals of the tropics, frogs, toads, and rodents in particular, avoid hot, dry spells by retiring underground to sleep. This is known as aestivation (from a Latin word meaning 'heat'). The LUNG-FISH of Africa (q.v.), which can breathe air, often aestivates for 6 months at a time in the dried up mud of river beds. Even in Britain, snails and worms aestivate during dry summer spells.

HIPPOPOTAMUS (River-horse). This huge African animal is a distant relative of the SWINE (q.v.), and no relation at all to the horse: it would, therefore, be more accurately called 'Suopotamus' or River-pig.

There are two species, the Common Hippo and the Pigmy Hippo. The Common Hippo used to be very common in all the large rivers and lakes of Africa; but its numbers have been greatly reduced by sportsmen and farmers, to whose crops it is a serious menace. It is nearly 1·5 metres high, 3 or 4 metres long, and weighs nearly 4 tonnes. Its ugly head seems to be too large and heavy for its body, since the animal is often seen resting its muzzle on the ground, as if to relieve its neck of the weight. Its upper and lower incisors grow into long tusks. It has short legs, and feet with pad-like soles and four well-developed toes encased in rounded black hoofs. Its skin is naked, rough, and warty, and enormously thick.

Hippos spend the greater part of their life in the water, where they move more naturally and faster than on land. Although they can run with ease at the bottom of a river or lake, they do not normally stay under water for more than five minutes at a time. On coming to the surface they spout up columns of water by violently

Radio Times Hulton Picture Library

A HIPPOPOTAMUS WITH HER YOUNG

blowing out air through their nostrils. Hippos usually dive hindquarters first, instead of going into the water head first. However, when on a high bank and suddenly frightened, they will not hesitate to plunge headlong into the water. They spend most of the day in a drowsy, yawning state, taking very little notice of their surroundings. But an hour after sunset, they set out on food-gathering excursions overland, and do not return until dawn. During the night they utter loud snorts and grunts, which can be heard a kilometre or more away. Their enormous stomachs (3 metres long when extended) give an idea of the huge amounts of food they require. In uncultivated districts they eat grass and water plants; but where there is neighbouring land under cultivation, they cause great damage by trampling down, as well as eating, the crops.

The dam gives birth to a single offspring at any season of the year, having carried it for 8 months. She looks after it carefully, letting it stand on her back, and protecting it from the male, who is often evilly disposed towards it. Though the males are quarrelsome and bad-tempered with each other, even attacking a wounded comrade, hippos are as a rule fairly timid towards human beings. If, however, a boat should run unexpectedly into the middle of a sleeping herd, or close to a solitary hippo at night, there is little chance of escape. Hippos used to be hunted for the ivory of their tusks; but now they are sought only for their hide, fat, and flesh. Their hide is used for making whips, and their feet make an excellent stew.

The Pigmy Hippo, which lives in parts of West Africa only, is a very much smaller animal, about 0·75 metres high, 1·7 m long, and weighing only about 180 kg. It spends less time in the water, but is extremely fond of a mud bath. It wanders for great distances in the woods, moving amazingly quietly considering its bulky body.

HOATZIN. This pheasant-like bird, sometimes called the Stink-pheasant because of its strong odour, is found near the Amazon and other rivers or lakes of north-western South America. It spends its life almost entirely in trees, eating an enormous quantity of leaves. Although it has long wings, it has a very poor flight. Its plumage is olive with white markings above, and dull red below. Its long, loose crest and the tips of its long, rather square tail are yellowish. Its

skeleton is peculiar, the lower part of the breast-bone, on which the bird often supports itself when resting, being broad and flattened.

The Hoatzin builds a nest of sticks in bushes or low boughs overhanging the water. When the nestlings are hatched, they immediately begin to climb about actively, like little reptiles, among the branches, holding on not only by their beaks and clawed feet, but also by their wings. If they fall or dive into the water, which they often do, they can swim to the side and soon climb back safely to their branches. The wings of these nestlings are an interesting survival of an earlier form of limb belonging to ancestors of birds which lived entirely in trees, and used their wings (or arms) for climbing rather than for flying. The 'hand' part of the wing is relatively long, and is provided with finger-like ends and long claws. Before the nestling grows feathers, the wing-quills begin to develop, and these grow in such an order that they do not impede the use of the wing as a hand until the wing-feathers are grown enough to be able to carry the weight of the body. The adult Hoatzin uses its wings, though not very effectively, as other birds do.

See also BIRDS.

HOBBY, *see* FALCON.

HOLLY, *see* PLANT DEFENCES.

HONEY BEE, *see* BEES.

Australian News & Information Bureau

SPINEBILL HONEY-EATER OF AUSTRALIA

HONEY-EATERS. This group of birds belongs to Australia, New Zealand, and the islands of the South Pacific. They are distinguished by their long tongues, which have brush-like tips and can be formed into a tube for sucking honey from flowers, especially from the various species of Eucalyptus. They vary considerably in colour, some being plain brown or greenish, while others are more brightly coloured, and one, the Blood Honey-eater or Soldier Bird of Australia, is deep black and brilliant scarlet.

The Parson Bird or Tui is a common bird in New Zealand, and well known for its lovely and varied song, in which the sound 'tui' is frequent. The male is a shining greenish-black, with white spots on the wings and two tufts of white feathers at the throat. The Stitch Bird, also named because of its note, carries bright, canary-yellow wing feathers, which were so much sought after for decorating the robes of Maori chiefs that the bird has been almost exterminated. Another Honey-eater is popularly called 'Four o'clock', and the Hawaiian species is called by the natives the 'O-o'—in both cases because of the cry. The now rather uncommon New Zealand Bell-bird is well known in that country because of its bell-like note.

HOOF. This is the horny cap, corresponding to a finger- or toe-nail, on one or two toes in the hoofed animals, or 'ungulates'. In these animals the limbs are used only for running and walking, and the fingers have become unusually long and reduced in number. In cloven-hoofed ungulates there are two functional toes to each foot; but in horses there is only one, although remains of the others are seen in the splint bones. The way the horse's hoof has evolved is shown on page 138.

See also NAILS AND CLAWS.

HOOPOE. This bird is so called because of its cry. It is a little larger than a thrush, and has sandy-coloured plumage, with vivid markings of black and white bands, and on its head a striking long crest, which it can open like a fan. It has a long, slender, and slightly curved bill, and broad wings. There are six species of Hoopoe, three of which are confined to Africa and Madagascar, and a fourth to India and Burma. The typical Hoopoe spreads over most of Asia, and central and southern Europe, wintering in Africa and India. It sometimes visits Great Britain and does occasionally also breed here.

Eric Hosking

HOOPOE AT ITS NESTING HOLE

It feeds on insects, grubs, and worms, which it collects mainly from the ground. It has an apparently weak fluttering flight, yet when attacked by hawks is often able to escape without much difficulty. Hoopoes generally nest in hollow trees. The female sits very closely during the period of incubation, being fed regularly by the male, and leaving the nest for very short periods only. The nest gets very dirty and acquires a most unpleasant smell.

The Wood Hoopoes of Africa, a different family, are shy and wary birds, living in trees and seldom coming to the ground. They are rather larger, darker in colour, and have no crest.

HORMONES, PLANT, *see* PLANT GROWTH.

HORNBILL. This tropical bird of the Old World, of which there are some sixty species, is mainly conspicuous for its fantastic beak—as its name suggests. Hornbills vary in size from that of a pigeon to the Great Pied Hornbill of Asia, which measures over 1·5 metres in length. They generally have mainly black and white plumage, with fairly long tails. The majority of species have enormously developed, long beaks, along

Paul Popper

HORNBILL

the top of which is a casque or helmet of a light, spongy, but very strong, texture. Most Hornbills are forest birds, living in trees and feeding on fruit and small animals caught among the trees. The African Ground Hornbills, however, live mainly in the open plains, hunting for food, such as reptiles, on the ground. Groups of them will attack and kill snakes.

Hornbills are particularly interesting because of their nesting habits. They nest in hollows in tree-trunks. When the period of incubation starts, the male shuts the female into the nesting-chamber by building a clay wall over the entrance, leaving open only a slit through which he can provide her with food. The female makes use of this period of imprisonment for completing her moult. When the eggs hatch, the male breaks down the wall with his powerful beak, and releases his family. By the end of the incubation period the nests are generally filthy and give forth a fearful stench, and the female is wasted and dirty, being for a time hardly able to fly. Hornbills have an odd habit of tossing up into the air and catching again in their bills every piece of food which they pick up. They

are noisy birds, noisy in their heavy flight, and in their characteristic cry, which is somewhere between a bray and a shriek.

HORNET, *see* WASPS, Section 3.

HORNS AND ANTLERS. Many mammals carry on their heads more or less conspicuous weapons, usually in pairs—for the UNICORN (q.v. Vol. I) is a mythical beast—which are generally referred to as horns. Those of cattle, sheep, goats, giraffes, and other RUMINANTS (q.v.), except deer, are produced by the skin, and are, therefore, the same kind of growth as HAIR (q.v.). They are made of a nitrogenous compound called 'keratin', and the animal that possesses them carries them throughout its life. (In the newly born animal they are normally not present.) These hollow, unbranched horns cover a solid, bony core. The antlers of the deer family, on the other hand, are branching bony extensions from the skull of the animal, and are usually shed each year and regrown. The horn of the rhinoceros consists of matted hair. The 'horn' of the narwhal is made of ivory and is, therefore, a kind of TUSK (q.v.).

Horns and antlers are primarily used as weapons; the female reindeer, who retains her antlers throughout the winter, after the male has shed his, protects her young with them. Some animals also use them as tools; cattle, for instance, will tear up turf with their horns.

HORSE. Horses belong to the order Perissodactyla (odd-toed hoofed beasts); they differ from CATTLE, SHEEP, and DEER (qq.v.) in being one-toed and in not chewing the cud. The genus *Equus*, includes also the DONKEYS and ZEBRAS (qq.v.). In prehistoric times, wild horses roamed all over Europe and Asia. Today, however, the only real wild horses are those living in Mongolia. These are small, dun-coloured animals with a single dark stripe along the back. The so-called wild horses of America and the Brumbies of Australia are both descendants of imported domestic horses which have run wild. The evolution of the horse has been an interesting study for zoologists. The present horse has evolved in a series of gradual transformations, lasting for 50 million years, from a quite small, four-toed animal (*see* EVOLUTION). Horses have been domesticated since very early times, but not so early as the dogs, oxen, or asses. They were not known at all in America until the Europeans came in the 16th century, and not until two centuries later in Australasia.

See also Vol. IV: HORSE TRANSPORT.
See also Vol. VI: HORSES, FARM.
See also Vol. IX: HORSES; RIDING.

HORSE-FLY (Tabanidae). Twenty-eight species of these rather large flies (also called Gad-flies, Stouts, and Breeze-flies) are found in Great Britain. They have very large eyes, iridescent when the insect is alive, which extend outwards so as to make the head wider than the front of the thorax. The abdomen is flat, and usually has more or less parallel sides. Most species are dark in colour, with grey or yellowish mottlings, but some are yellow-banded, looking like Hover-flies. Some species are among the biggest of British flies. During hot summer weather they can be very troublesome to horses and cattle in fields, and to ourselves. Only the females suck blood, the males suck only water, honey-dew, or the nectar of flowers.

The small species called Clegs (genus *Haematopota*) are dark grey-brown and have mottled wings. They do not make the humming noise in flight that most Horse-flies do, and so their attack is unannounced. Clegs are usually more common, and therefore more of a nuisance, in wet pastures.

Although Horse-flies may be found in woods and dry pastures, they lay their eggs on plants growing in water or wet places. The larvae are carnivorous, feeding on insect larvae and other small creatures they find about them.

HORSE-FLY
Natural size

See also FLIES.

HOUSE-FLY. The House-fly and the Lesser House-fly, belonging to the family Muscidae, are familiar to everybody. The larger species is found wherever there is human habitation, and seems to be able to adapt itself to all sorts of climates and temperatures. The higher the temperature, however, the better it flourishes and the greater its numbers.

The eggs are laid in batches of anything up to 150, a single female laying as many as 1,000 in its short lifetime of about a month. (Individual

House-flies may live for two months in the adult state.) The eggs are usually laid in stable manure, but may also be laid in an uncovered dustbin or on meat. They hatch in about 19 hours; the first casting of the larval skin takes place about 24 hours later; the second occurs after another 24 hours; and the third and last 3 or 4 days later still—when the pupal stage begins. After about 4 days as a pupa, the adult fly emerges. These times may be lengthened during cold weather, or speeded up during very hot spells. In an ordinary summer, an average of 10 to 11 days from egg-laying to the emergence of the adult fly is usual. The larva is a typical fly maggot, with a long, soft, whitish body, very narrow at the head and thick at the back. The pupa is contained within

LARVA. × 2

a typical brown, horny puparium, consisting of the last larval skin.

Because of their feeding habits, House-flies are carriers of disease. In nearly all our two-winged flies the gullet is divided into two tubes as it passes back through the neck into the thorax. The upper tube is the intestine, and the lower leads to a blind sac, the food reservoir, in the lower part of the abdomen. On taking a meal, the fly fills this reservoir, and later sends its contents back into the intestine for digestion. In the House-fly, however, when the reservoir is emptied, the food is actually passed out of the mouth to be re-eaten. In this way it makes vomit-spots, which disfigure our window-panes in the summer, and may infect all kinds of food.

The Lesser House-fly is not really very closely related to the House-fly, nor very like it in appearance. It is the insect with a queer jerky flight that loves to fly in little groups, preferably just below the light in the middle of a room. It appears earlier in the year than the House-fly, and disappears when it arrives. The larva of the Lesser House-fly is flat, with a double row of spines along each side and along the back. It grows up in much the same places as the larva of House-flies.

See also FLIES.
See also Vol. XI: HOUSEHOLD PESTS.

HOVER-FLY. This is the common name given to the family Syrphidae, true flies capable of hovering for long periods in one place. Their movements are very quick as they dart from one place of hovering to another. These flies, which are often seen in the summer months around flowers, especially round Cow Parsley, are very varied in shape, size, and colour. The abdomen may be broad and flat or rather long and thin. Hover-flies are usually brightly coloured, but may also be dull brown and furry. They may be striped, spotted, banded with blue or yellow, or metallic blue-green and brown; they may have red abdomens with black tips. The striped and banded species resemble wasps not only in pattern but also in their humming flight; some of

BRAMBLE HOVER-FLY
About natural size

the furry brown ones mimic hive-bees. Many of the Syrphids which mimic bees and wasps have larvae that live in the nests of the particular species they resemble. They usually live on the organic debris at the base of the nests, but some feed on liquids excreted by the bee or wasp larvae. Other species of hover-fly larvae feed on plants, including fungi; yet others on decaying organic matter, dung, liquid mud, or water. One group preys on other insects, especially APHIDES (q.v.), which they suck dry but do not eat entirely. Another group lives as scavengers in the nests of ants. Many of the larvae living in water, mud, or decaying matter are known as 'rat-tailed maggots', because they possess long flexible 'tails' at the end of their bodies which enable them to breathe from the air while still submerged far below the surface.

Hover-flies are said to be the chief pollinators of the little blue speedwells. Very few are harmful: two species, known as Narcissus Flies, are, however, destructive during their larval life to various kinds of bulbs.

See also FLIES.

HUMBLE-BEE FLY (Bee Fly). This beautiful insect should be looked for on the brightest and hottest days of spring and early summer. It is a true fly, a member of the family Bombyliidae. It is densely covered with brown and golden fur, and its long slender legs and often its long proboscis stretch straight out in front. Its wings, which remain outspread when the insect is resting, are spotted or bordered with brown. When visiting low-growing tubular flowers, such as those of ground-ivy, Humble-Bee Flies do not settle but hover over them, inserting their tongues into the flower-tubes, much as a tropical Humming-Bird does; but when visiting such flowers as primroses, they hover with some of their legs just touching the petals.

Some species of Humble-Bee Flies lay their eggs on the ground, and the larvae find their way into the nests of solitary bees. At first they feed upon the pollen stored there for the larva of the bee; but later they devour the larva itself. Other species feed on the larvae of other insects.

Of about 2,000 species of Humble-Bee Fly, only 12 occur in Britain; they are very numerous in South Africa.

See also FLIES.

HUMMING-BIRD. There are a great many species of these little birds, inhabitants of South and central America and the West Indies. Some of them migrate northwards as far as Canada in the summer. The majority are very small, the largest, the Great Humming-bird of the Andes, being about 20 cm long, and the smallest little larger than a bumble-bee. They mostly have brilliant plumage of metallic green, purple, cinnamon, black, and other colours. Some carry crests on their heads, others have long, fantastically shaped tails. They have long, slender bills, some straight and others curved, and they all possess long, tubular tongues, which they thrust down into flowers to suck up the nectar on which they feed.

Booth Steamship Co.

TINY HUMMING-BIRD IN ITS NEST BUILT ON A LARGE
TROPICAL LEAF

Humming-birds, which are related to the SWIFTS (q.v.), have long wings, with very strong wing-muscles which enable them to sustain for long periods the extremely rapid wing-beats necessary for their hovering flight. The little birds do not settle on flowers while extracting the nectar, but hover over them with such a rapid wing-motion that the wings become almost invisible, and produce a distinct 'hum'. Slow-motion films have shown that the wings move almost horizontally, and for the backstroke the wing is turned almost upside-down. When not hovering they make very quick darting flights, and perform strange contortions in the air as they catch the tiny insects which also form part of their diet. The beautiful, long tail-feathers of the Long-tailed Humming-bird are fascinating to watch during these rapid evolutions.

During the courting season, Humming-birds are vicious fighters, flying at each other with such violence that they sometimes blind each other with their beaks. The nests are beautifully constructed, fairly deep, little cups, some being less than 3 centimetres across, woven out of soft materials such as vegetable down and spiders' webs. Two eggs are laid, white, and oval in shape.

Humming-birds are found only in America; but other birds of the same type, though unrelated, which suck nectar from flowers inhabit the Old World. The HONEY-EATERS (q.v.) belong to Australasia; and in Africa and tropical Asia the Sunbirds form a large group of brilliantly coloured, small, elegantly shaped birds, which feed upon the sweet juices of flowers and small flying insects. Neither of these groups, however, hover while they feed.

HYAENA. This carrion-feeding beast represents a type of CARNIVORA which appears to link the CATS and the CIVETS (qq.v.). It is found in countries ranging from India, westward through Arabia, to Africa, and fossil remains show that it once also inhabited Europe, even as far north as Britain. It is entirely absent, however, from America and Australasia. There are three species now existing, the Striped, the Spotted, and the Brown Hyaena. They are all about the size of a wolf, and have greyish or yellowish-brown, coarse, shaggy coats, marked with darker stripes or spots. Their disproportionately short hind legs give them an ungainly appearance. They are extremely strong, especially in

Paul Popper
HYAENAS SCAVENGING FOR FOOD

their jaws and teeth, which are powerful enough to crack open the bones of the largest animals. Their necks also are strong; and it has been claimed that they can carry off a full-sized ass, though this has not been proved.

Hyaenas are mainly scavengers, eating dead animals in any stage of decomposition; but they also kill and devour dogs, sheep, and goats, which they hunt in packs. They will cripple other creatures, it seems out of sheer cruelty, and they will lie in wait and pounce on young kids and lambs even when they are not hungry. They live wherever there is suitable cover, spending the daytime in dark caves or ruins, or occasionally in burrows, and coming out at nightfall to hunt for food. They are greatly dreaded in inhabited districts, as they often enter villages and camps to raid the domestic animals, occasionally attacking even human beings. They have been known to rob graves, eating a part of the corpse on the spot, and dragging the rest to their den. When out hunting, hyaenas utter uncanny, maniacal laughter and hair-raising howls. Strangely enough, in captivity they often become quite docile, and both in India and Africa they have been tamed and used as dogs.

HYDRA. This small animal, from 30 to 60 mm long, lives in not too stagnant freshwater ponds. It is a close relative of CORALS, JELLY-FISH, and SEA-ANEMONES (qq.v.)—among the simplest of multicellular animals. The body consists of a hollow cylinder with a closed end, the basal disk with which it clings to stones, sticks, or water plants. At the opposite, free end are up to ten fine tentacles surrounding a conical mouth. The walls of the body and the tentacles consist of two layers of cells, an outer one and an inner digestive layer.

Hydra feed on minute water-animals. When these come in contact with the tentacles, they are paralysed and held by the stinging cells, which are scattered over the surface, especially on the tentacles. Later they are pushed into the mouth by the tentacles, the mouth often stretching considerably to receive them. In the hollow cavity of the body the prey is digested, the indigestible parts being ejected, again through the mouth.

Living actually inside some of the Hydra cells are some small green ALGAE. These make food by PHOTOSYNTHESIS (qq.v.), using the carbon dioxide produced by the respiration of the Hydra. In return for the supply of carbon dioxide, and also protection, the Algae supply oxygen and some carbohydrates to the Hydra cells in which they live. This association of two organisms for the benefit of both is called 'symbiosis'.

Hydra reproduce both asexually and sexually. By the former method a bud appears on the side of the parent body. It grows, and produces a mouth and tentacles. Eventually it becomes detached and starts an independent life. If food is plentiful, a Hydra produces several buds, and these may grow secondary buds, forming a temporary colony. Hydra are 'hermaphrodite'— one individual producing both male and female cells. The sperm is liberated into the water, where it swims freely until it reaches a Hydra with a mature ovum, which it then fertilizes. After a number of cell divisions, a small resistant cyst is formed, which is shed from the ovary and eventually falls to the bottom of the pond. Here it remains until the weather is warm enough, usually in the following spring. Then a two-layered embryo emerges from the cyst, develops a mouth and tentacles, and becomes a young Hydra.

See also Diagram on p. 9.

A ROCK HYRAX

HYRAX. This small, rabbit-like animal, an inhabitant of Africa and south-west Asia, has puzzled zoologists. It is in no way related to the rabbit or any other rodent. Its molar teeth and much of its skeleton show likeness to the rhinoceros, its lower incisor teeth to the hippopotamus; the structure of its feet resembles the elephant; and it has more pairs of ribs than any animal except the sloth. Professor Huxley finally placed it in an order of its own, the Hyracoidea. The Hyraxes are active little creatures, about 30 to 45 cm long, with blunt muzzles, small round ears, and thick, soft, greyish-brown fur. They feed on leaves and young shoots.

There are two kinds of Hyraxes: the Rock Hyraxes, which live in colonies among rocks and on cliffs, and the Tree Hyraxes, which use hollow trees for shelter and are sometimes called Tree Bears. Although they have hoof-like claws, which cannot grasp like the hands of a monkey, and have no prehensile tails, yet they climb up the smooth trunks of trees and over rocks. Apparently the naked soles of their feet, like those of the GECKO (q.v.), adhere to smooth surfaces. They are very timid—and with good reason, for they are favourite food for leopards and large birds of prey; but they are gentle and can easily be tamed. When feeding, they are said to place one of their number, usually an old male, to keep guard, and he gives notice of danger by uttering shrill squeaks, which send the whole colony to shelter.

I

IBEX, *see* GOAT.

IBIS, *see* STORKS.

ICHNEUMON, *see* MONGOOSE.

ICHNEUMON FLY. If cabbages in a garden have been attacked by caterpillars of the Large White Butterfly, it is most likely that, late in summer, one will find on the palings, walls of the tool-shed, or similar places, masses of about a hundred or more small golden-yellow cases, and perhaps amongst them the dead body of one of these caterpillars. If these are kept under observation, it will be found that, in about a month's time, one end of each case will be neatly removed from the inside, and out will come a very lively little black fly, with four wings and long slender antennae. This is an Ichneumon Fly.

Adult Ichneumon Flies seek out their 'hosts', usually caterpillars, in which they lay their eggs. Large species may insert only one egg in the body of each host insect, small species as many as 100 or more. The young larvae, hatching

from these eggs, begin to feed on the fat of the host, but avoid its vital organs. A caterpillar which has been 'ichneumonized' goes on feeding and moving about as usual until nearly full grown. At this point it becomes lethargic and suddenly collapses; then the larvae of the Ichneumon escape by boring through its skin, and each spin a silken cocoon.

Ichneumon Flies belong to a large group of insects related to the BEES and WASPS (qq.v.). As larvae they are all internal parasites, most of them in the caterpillars of butterflies and moths, though other insects and also spiders are attacked. The attacks of such parasitic flies are often devastating. Thus, on one occasion, of a batch of 100 caterpillars of the Large White Butterfly, only four survived to enter the chrysalis state. All Ichneumon Flies have slender bodies, rounded heads with long antennae, a very narrow 'waist', and, in the female, a slender ovipositor, by means of which the eggs are laid within the body of the creature attacked. The majority are either black or amber-brown; but they vary greatly in size. Some of our British species are as much as 2.5 or 3 centimetres long, whereas others are very small indeed. One handsome species, black with small yellow spots, is actually longer than the Giant WOOD-WASP (q.v.), the insect that it parasitizes, and is remarkable for the way it seeks out its victims. The larva of the Wood-wasp burrows through the timber of pine-trees; but even here the Ichneumon Fly succeeds in locating it, and then drills through the wood until it reaches its victim.

Ichneumon Flies are very active insects, taking readily to flight; they may often be seen running over the window-panes in houses. It seems that their antennae play an important part in selecting the victims for egg-laying, as they are perpetually a-quiver, apparently testing everything they approach.

There are other insects which have similar habits to the Ichneumon Fly—such as the BRISTLE-FLY, CHALCID-WASP, and FLESH-FLY (qq.v.).

IGUANA. This lizard of the family Iguanidae is found in tropical America, Madagascar, and Fiji. The Iguanas of the Galapagos Islands are the only lizards today with marine habits, but the majority of Iguanas usually live in trees. They are, however, good swimmers, taking

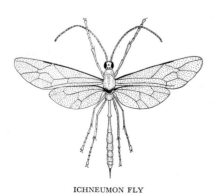

ICHNEUMON FLY

Paul Popper

TUBERCULATED IGUANA, A TREE-LIVING LIZARD OF TROPICAL AMERICA

of them have long, sensitive snouts, with which they forage in the ground for food. The African Elephant Shrews, for instance, are so named because of the length of their flexible snouts. Their teeth are excellently adapted for crushing the hard cases of insects, being armed with numerous sharp cusps. They differ from CARNIVORA (q.v.) in having very small canine teeth. Most, but not all, insect-eating mammals come out only at night-time to hunt for food.

See also MAMMALS.

readily to water. Although they will devour insects, they feed mainly upon young leaves, flowers, and fruit. *Iguana delicatissima* is hunted for its flesh, which is said to taste like the breast of a chicken. Its eggs also are eaten. It grows to a length of a metre or more, two-thirds of which is the tail.

Another large group of this family are the American Anoles, some of which, like the GECKOS (q.v.), have developed adhesive pads upon the under-surfaces of their fingers and toes. However, they rely mainly upon their claws for climbing. Many of them are beautifully coloured, particularly the males in the breeding season. Like their relatives, the AGAMAS and the CHAMELEONS (qq.v.), they have the power of rapidly changing their colour.

See also LIZARDS.

INSECTIVORA (Insect-eaters). Representatives of this large group of mammals are found all over the world, except in Australia and almost all South America. They may live on the ground, under the ground, in trees, or in water; and are usually small, though they differ greatly in appearance and form. The British mammals belonging to this Order are HEDGEHOGS, MOLES, and SHREWS (qq.v.).

Although they are called insect-eaters, they by no means restrict themselves to a diet of insects. The British Insectivora eat any small creatures they can lay hold of, alive or dead, and in some cases they also eat vegetable food. Most

INSECTIVOROUS PLANTS (Insect-consuming plants). **1.** These comparatively rare plants are interesting because of the wonderful methods they have adopted for catching their small animal prey. Some of them, such as the Butterwort, Sundew, and Bladderwort, can be found growing wild in Great Britain; while others, such as Venus's Fly-trap and Pitcher-plants, are found only in the tropics.

Much of our knowledge of insectivorous plants is derived from the field observations of the great naturalist CHARLES DARWIN (q.v. Vol. V), who, in a book published in 1875, drew attention to these peculiar plants. Although they trap insects and other small animals, and actually consume certain digestible parts of their victims' bodies, insects never form more than a very small fraction of the food of insectivorous plants, all of which possess green leaves and obtain their main food supply in the normal way by PHOTO-SYNTHESIS (q.v.).

Why, therefore, do such plants trap insects at all? This can be easily explained. Most insectivorous plants are found in swampy and boggy places, where there are few plants and animals. The almost waterlogged soil, therefore, contains comparatively little humus, and so the nitrogen content of the soil is very low. Further, the nitrates that are present in the soil are quickly washed away by the abnormal amount of water present. Insects and small aquatic animals have a high protein content in their bodies, and so the insectivorous plants make up for deficiencies of nitrogen, and especially of protein, in the soil by digesting the bodies of the animals. It is, however, quite possible for them to live healthily without these animal supplements to their food.

2. THE BUTTERWORT grows wild in temperate countries, and is found in wet places in Great Britain, especially in hilly districts, on the Somerset Plain, and in Yorkshire and Scotland. It is a small herb, with leaves about 4 cm long arranged in a rosette. It is called Butterwort because the upper surface of the leaves is covered with a pale-yellow, sticky substance which looks like a thin layer of butter. An unwary insect, alighting on this sticky surface, gets caught like a fly on a flypaper. The margins of the leaves are incurved, and when an insect is caught, they curve over still farther so as to hold it. On the surface of the leaves are certain microscopic structures, called glands, which give off a juice containing enzymes. These ferments help in splitting up the proteins of the insect body to make them digestible. The digested proteins are absorbed by the surface of the leaf, which then unrolls to await another victim.

3. THE SUNDEW has a more complicated trapping mechanism than the Butterwort. The long-stalked leaves, which are green with patches of red on them, are arranged in rosettes, the edges and upper surfaces being covered with long hair-like growths called 'tentacles'. Each of these ends in a club-shaped swelling, which is covered with a sticky fluid. This little blob of fluid, which glistens in the sun like dew, has given the plant its name. Small insects are attracted and held by the sticky tentacles, which then begin to bend towards the middle of the leaf until the insect is firmly pressed against its surface. The ends of the tentacles then give out a protein-digesting enzyme, and the insect is digested and absorbed. After the process is finished the leaf reassumes its normal shape, and the indigestible parts of the insect are exposed and blown away by the wind. The tentacles are then ready to capture another insect. Two species of Sundew are commonly found in boggy places in Great Britain, one having rounded leaf-blades and the other oval.

4. THE BLADDERWORT, a common British insectivorous plant, shows a yet more ingenious method of trapping small insects and animals than either the Sundew or the Butterwort. The Bladderwort is chiefly found in stagnant water. Its leaves are very finely divided, and cer-

tain of them develop into the bladder-like structures from which the plant takes its name. Each bladder has one opening, which is protected by a valve. The valve, as efficient as any valve contrived by an experienced mechanic, will open only inwards. Some books state that small aquatic animals, such as water-mites and water-fleas, willingly enter the bladder—possibly in an attempt to escape pursuing enemies; but this is not true. If by chance a water animal touches the sensitive hairs on the valve of the Bladderwort, this stimulates the bladder to swell quickly —thus sucking in the animal. Then the valve closes, and the victim is trapped. The inside surface of the bladder is covered with glands, which give out protein-digesting enzymes. These digest the proteins of the insect, and the soluble nitrogenous matter is absorbed through the surface of the bladder. The bladder 'resets' itself by means of little glands inside, which draw out the water, leaving a vacuum; the resetting takes about 15–30 minutes. Three species of Bladderwort are found in Great Britain.

5. VENUS'S FLY-TRAP is common in the peat bogs of North and South Carolina, and is often cultivated in hot-houses in Great Britain. Like

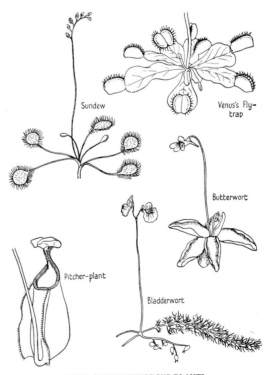

TYPES OF INSECTIVOROUS PLANTS

Harold Bastin

PITCHER-PLANT (*Nepenthes*) WITH INSECT-CATCHING LEAF-
BLADES

the Butterwort, Sundew, and Bladderwort, it catches insects with its leaves, and the mechanism is equally fascinating. The leaves, which are arranged in a rosette, have two lobes on either side of the midrib. On the margins of each lobe are long, firm spikes. The surface is covered with glands, and each lobe has three bristles which are sensitive to touch. When an insect alights on the surface, it cannot help touching one or all of these sensitive bristles. In less than a second, the lobes move towards each other, using the midrib as a hinge. When the margins of the lobe meet, the strong spikes intertwine and prevent the lobes being pushed apart. The insect is thus trapped. Then the glands begin to give off their digestive enzymes, the proteins of the captured insect are absorbed, and the plant gets its extra nitrogen. It is interesting to note that if the closing of the lobes is caused by, say, a pencil, they do not close completely, and in a short time the leaf opens again.

6. PITCHER-PLANTS, the most remarkable of the insectivorous plants, are found in tropical and subtropical regions, especially in Asia,

North Australia, and Madagascar: northern Borneo is particularly rich in them. Several types of plants have developed the pitcher mechanism for trapping insects, but the best-known example is *Nepenthes*. Pitcher-plants are herbaceous, in which the whole or part of the leaf-blade is modified to form a pitcher, while the leaf-stalk is flattened, and carries on the process of food-manufacture normally done by the leaf-blade in ordinary green plants.

The pitcher itself is tubular, and often has two wing-like structures running down its outer surface. The rim of the mouth has an incurved margin, with a firm, shining surface. There is a definite lid, like that of a coffee-pot or hot-water jug, which, when the pitcher is young, covers the opening. As the pitcher grows, the lid opens, taking up a fixed oblique position which probably helps to keep rain-water out. The size of the pitcher varies with the species, from the size of a thimble to that of a quart mug. Its outside is often brightly coloured, varying from bright red to yellow, and these colours, as in flowers, serve to attract insects. Also, a sweet substance is given off by the stems of the plant, right up the leaf-stalk to the lid of the pitcher. Still more honey-like liquid is given off inside the pitcher, just below the margin.

The insect, attracted by the bright colours, crawls up to the margin of the pitcher and tries to get the sweet food material just inside. In doing so, it often slips on the shining surface of the rim and tumbles down inside the pitcher, falling at the bottom into a liquid which has been given off by glands. When the bedraggled insect tries to climb out of the pitcher, it is trapped at the top by a ring of hairs all pointing downwards, and at last, tired out, it falls again into the liquid and is finally drowned. The liquid contains protein-digesting enzymes, and the insect body becomes digested and finally absorbed.

Harold Bastin

THE *Nepenthes* PITCHER IN
THE PROCESS OF CATCHING
FLIES

This fascinating mechanism is generally a most efficient means of trapping insects. Some pitcher-plants, however, are sometimes so inefficient that they catch nothing: mosquitoes have been known to enter the pitchers, to lay their eggs, from which the young have hatched out and escaped. Other pitcher-plants belong to the kind known as *Sarracenia*, which differ from *Nepenthes* in that no enzymes are produced, the bodies of the insects being decomposed by the action of BACTERIA (q.v.), and the soluble products then absorbed.

See also NITROGEN SUPPLY IN PLANTS.

INSECTS. Insects form one class of the largest group of animals, known as the Arthropoda, to which also belong centipedes and millipedes, crabs and lobsters, scorpions, spiders, and mites. These all resemble each other in three ways: (i) each has a body made up of a number of segments arranged in order, one behind the other; (ii) some or all of these segments carry pairs of jointed limbs, called 'appendages', some of which are used as legs, others as jaws, others as 'antennae' or feelers; (iii) the body has a horny covering or outer skeleton, which, however, allows movement in at least some of the joints through which the segments are united.

The insects, of which there are more than a million species in the world, are constructed as follows: (*a*) a head, bearing as appendages one pair of antennae and three pairs of mouth-parts; (*b*) a thorax, bearing three pairs of legs; and (*c*) an abdomen, the most flexible part of the body, without limbs. Usually the thorax carries two pairs of wings. The antennae are usually long, slender, and flexible, and are undoubtedly organs of sense—though whether the sense is that of smell, hearing, touch, or even some sense we do not ourselves possess, is not easy to decide. Many insects seem to feel with them—hence the name feelers.

In an insect that bites, the first pair of mouth-parts is its 'mandibles', the second its 'maxillae', and the third pair is united into a single 'labium' or lower lip. In other insects, the mouthparts are all modified to form piercing and sucking organs, like the 'beak' or rostrum of a BUG, or sucking organs only, like the proboscis of a MOTH or HOUSE-FLY (qq.v.).

In addition to its appendages, the head has usually a pair of large, compound eyes, one on each side, and often three very much smaller,

simple eyes between them. The compound eye is divided into a very large number of small compartments, usually six-sided and fitting together like the cells of a honeycomb. Each compartment acts as a single small eye and sees one small part of the whole picture. When all these small pictures are fitted together, the whole picture is formed. Any movement, either of the insect itself or in its surroundings, makes at least some of these separate eyes see something different from what they saw before—a change which the insect at once perceives. Compound eyes seem, therefore, especially useful for appreciating quick movements. Very slow movements, which bring about gradual changes in what each eye can see, appear much less alarming. This explains why alert insects such as Dragonflies, usually so hard to catch, can be approached quite closely by slow stalking.

Three segments make up the thorax, and each bears a pair of legs. Each leg has five parts—the 'coxa', 'trochanter', 'femur', 'tibia', and 'tarsus'. The tarsus may be many-jointed. If there are wings, the two pairs are carried on the second and third segments of the thorax; they may be large or small, broad or narrow. In the true flies, the hind pair is reduced. In many insects, for example, beetles, bugs, and cockroaches, the fore-wings are hardened and serve as covers to the hind-wings, these often being folded beneath them when not in use. Such fore-wings are called 'elytra'.

The horny covering of an insect's body is brown or amber and is firm and inelastic, except at the joints where movement is allowed. Because of this inelastic covering, made of a substance called 'chitin', an insect can grow only by casting off the skeleton from time to time, a process called the 'moult'. After each moult, when the new skeleton is soft, the insect can expand. Once the skeleton has hardened, there

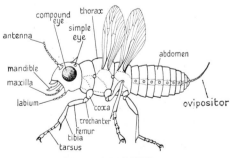

PARTS OF AN INSECT

follows a period of very slow growth, till the time comes for another moult.

Insects breathe differently from other animals. Along the sides of the body are paired openings called 'spiracles', which lead into branching tubes called 'tracheae'. Air passes direct to all parts of the body along these tubes, and so the oxygen needed for the body does not have to be carried by the blood (*see* RESPIRATION). The throbbing of the body, by which the circulation of the air is kept up, can easily be seen in Wasps and Dragonflies. The heart is a long, pulsating tube, lying just under the skin along the back. The alimentary canal is placed centrally, and usually has two 'salivary glands' (which in many insects are really digestive glands) lying on either side of it in the thorax; these discharge into the mouth. In the case of blood-sucking insects, these pump into the wound of the victim a juice which keeps the drawn blood fluid; otherwise the insect's mouth would be clogged with clotted blood. In larvae that spin silk, it is these glands which produce the silk. An insect's nervous system, consisting of a double nerve-chord, lies below the alimentary canal. The two chords separate in front to enclose the gullet, meeting again above to form what may be called the insect's BRAIN (q.v.).

The reproductive organs lie in the abdomen and open near the end of the body. The females of some species possess a long, rather pointed, ovipositor for egg-laying, the same structure serving as the sting in bees. Insects usually produce sexually and lay eggs. But some insects, such as the APHIS (q.v.), have no males in one generation, and the eggs hatch inside the female (*see* REPRODUCTION IN ANIMALS).

When hatched, some insects are like their parents, except in size; but the majority are unlike, and the changes they undergo to gain their adult appearance are called collectively the METAMORPHOSIS (q.v.). Insects which go through the four stages of egg, larva, pupa, and adult, in which there are marked changes between each, are said to undergo a complete metamorphosis.

See also ANTS; BEES; BEETLES; BUGS; BUTTERFLIES; DRAGONFLIES; EARWIG; FLY; GRASSHOPPER; LICE; MAYFLY; MOTHS; TERMITES; WASPS.

INSTINCT, *see* INTELLIGENCE.

INTELLIGENCE. It is very difficult to say exactly what we mean by intelligence. Broadly speaking, it suggests the ability to reason a thing out for oneself, or to understand the cause of a thing. Very often a person is looked upon as intelligent when the chief thing he possesses is a very good memory. Another person may appear intelligent because he responds quickly to changed circumstances. Another may be quick at learning, as a result of being able to imitate. Another is very observant. Probably intelligence consists of all these things. When, therefore, we say that an animal, such as a cat, a dog, or an elephant, is an intelligent animal, we need to inquire a little more closely into what precisely we mean by the word.

There is general agreement that no animal is as intelligent as a human being, although the larger apes, such as the chimpanzee and the gorilla, can behave in some ways very like human beings. Even so, there is a big gulf between man and even the most intelligent ape; and as we go down the animal scale, intelligent behaviour grows less and less obvious. We can say, therefore, that as animals become more and more complicated in the structure of their bodies—and, especially, as the brain becomes more highly organized—so intelligence becomes more marked.

Animal behaviour is built up in four stages. In the very lowest animals (the simple microscopic forms in which the body consists of one cell only), all behaviour is governed by 'taxis' —in other words, the whole body of the animal moves automatically in response to an external stimulus, such as light or heat. If such an animal moves always away from the light, it is said to be 'negatively phototactic'; if it moves towards the light whenever possible, it is said to be 'positively phototactic'. Even complicated animals often show taxis. Ticks move towards the light and so are positively phototactic. The larvae of meal worms on the other hand are negatively phototactic and move away from the light. Captured bees and blue-bottles become positively phototactic and fly to the window of a room. Another form of taxis is seen when an earthworm, with its head protruding from the burrow, quickly withdraws as we walk towards it. It is reacting to the vibrations in the earth, and is said to be 'vibrato-tactic'. In the same way, when a fly becomes entangled in the silk of a web, the spider runs out to it in response to the vibrations caused by its struggles. (*See also* SPIDERS.)

Although most moths come out only at night, shunning the light, because they are negatively phototactic, it is well known that they will fly into a candle-flame or circle round an electric-light bulb. This action, however, results from a different cause: it is said to be due to a 'reflex' —which means that a part of the body involuntarily moves in response to a stimulus. When a bright light falls on the left eye of a moth, the left wing beats more feebly than the right, causing the moth to fly in decreasing circles round the source of the light, whether it be candle-flame or electric bulb. Or if the light falls more strongly on the right eye, the right wing beats less

Above right: INSTINCTIVE BEHAVIOUR
The Spider constructs a trap which catches its prey
J. J. Ward

Centre: CONDITIONED REFLEX
Two Sheepdogs have learnt to pen the sheep as a result of careful training
Radio Times Hulton Picture Library

Below right: DAWNING REASONING POWER
The Chimpanzee puts one box on top of another in order to reach the bananas. From Yerkes & Yerkes, *The Great Apes* (Yale University Press)

strongly than the left. If someone sticks a pin into your leg, you jump; if a spark flies towards your face, your eyelids automatically close quickly to protect the eyes—these and many others are reflex actions: they are automatic, and we do them without thinking.

Just as HEREDITY (q.v.) ensures that animals look like their parents, so it may also ensure that they behave in a similar way. Some very complicated behaviour patterns are inherited, and this is what we mean by instinct. Under certain conditions the animal behaves in an automatic way. A spider's web, for instance, is wonderfully intricate, but each spider is born with the knowledge of how to make a web. It does not have to learn. All spiders of the same species make similar webs. Song Thrushes know how to sing their song by instinct. Other birds, such as the Pipit and Skylark, have to learn theirs from their parents. Yet other birds, such as the Chaffinch, the Linnet, and the Greenfinch, know how to sing the basis of their song by instinct, but have to learn its finer variations. Normally, instinct allows the animal to behave in what we might call a 'sensible' way, but by playing tricks on the animal we can soon see that his instinctive behaviour is automatic and not the result of 'sensible' thought. The little hunting wasp digs a series of holes in the ground. In each hole it places a store of caterpillars and grasshoppers, paralysed by a special poison, for food for the hatching larva. It then lays an egg on top. Digging the hole, capturing the prey, laying the egg, and closing the hole are all instinctive acts, each following the last automatically. If, however, we take away the egg and the paralysed insects when the wasp has just begun to close up the hole, the female after inspecting the hole, continues to close it up as though nothing were amiss. Insects and birds show the most highly developed instinctive behaviour, although they do, of course, show other kinds of behaviour as well. Human beings have practically no instinctive behaviour, but, since we have great powers of learning, we are much better able to fit our behaviour to changing circumstances (see INTELLIGENCE (human) Vol. XI).

There is another form of behaviour which sometimes passes for intelligence. A chaffinch one day alights on the sill of a window and, because it sees its own reflection in the glass, or for some other trivial reason, it pecks at the window-pane. The people in the room think this clever, and respond by putting some crumbs on the window-sill. At first this causes the chaffinch to fly away; but it quickly learns to associate tapping the window-pane with food—it learns, we say, to come and 'ask' for its food. The peck on the window-pane has become a 'conditioned reflex' associated with food. Pigs soon learn to associate the rattle of the bucket with feeding-time; chickens will run towards anyone who approaches them at about the hour for feeding-time; all animals respond in some such way if the same, or similar, actions are regularly associated with pleasurable sensations—usually the sight of food. Domesticated animals, especially circus animals, are often trained to do amazing tricks by having punishment—or, preferably, reward—associated with the performance of these actions or tricks. We are apt to speak of their intelligence; but, rather, we should speak of their conditioned reflexes.

Finally, we come to consider reasoning power, the ability to work a thing out, to understand why a thing is done or what shall be done about it. Reason is found in very few animals apart from man. The monkey at the zoo who, when a banana is dangled from the top of the cage, fetches a box to stand on in order to reach it, or uses a stick to pull it down, is using reason. When we study animals closely, we find that reason enters very little into their behaviour. Even the best human beings use reason, or pure thinking, for only a small percentage of their daily actions. If by intelligence we mean reason or understanding, then only man has intelligence, and a few of the higher animals have a dawning intelligence. If, on the other hand, we accept as its meaning the sum total of behaviour which enables an animal to live successfully, then we must regard intelligence as a mixture of taxes, reflexes, instincts, conditioned reflexes, and, where it is present, reason. In that case, we can say that intelligence, roughly speaking, increases as the animal becomes more highly developed and, especially, as the BRAIN and NERVOUS SYSTEM (qq.v.) become more extensive.

SOME FUNGI FOUND IN BRITAIN

1. Common or Field Mushroom, *Psalliota campestris*. 2. Shaggy caps, *Coprinus comatus*. 3. Ceps or Edible Boletus, *Boletus edulis*. 4. Parasol Mushroom, *Lepiota procera*. 5. Common Morel. *Morchella esculenta*. 6. Blewits, *Tricholoma personatum*. 7. Yellow-staining Mushroom, *Psalliota xanthoderma*. 8. Fly Agaric, *Amanita muscaria*. 9. Death Cap, *Amanita phalloides*. 1–6 are edible, 7–9 are poisonous

J

JACKAL. This carrion-feeding and cowardly Dog is a near relative to the Wolf (qq.v.), but is much smaller and lives only in the warm regions of Asia and Africa. Like the fox, it has an offensive smell, which comes from a gland at the base of the tail.

Jackals prey on smaller mammals and poultry, and also eat birds' eggs, maize, sugar-cane, and fruit: in vineyards they are often a serious pest as they steal the grapes. They are carrion-eaters, and sometimes follow lions and tigers, to feed on their leavings. They hunt mostly by night, sometimes singly or in pairs, and occasionally in packs. When hunting or being hunted, they show the same kind of cunning as a fox. The whole pack, when hunting an antelope, will carry out a carefully laid plan to surround their victim and drive it into an ambush. According to the natives, the African jackals actually help lions to find their prey—and it is well known that lions do not seem to resent the presence of jackals when they are having a meal. The jackals wait until the lion has finished, and then help themselves to what remains. A jackal's cry is a long, wailing, blood-curdling howl. A cry from one member of the pack is enough to set the whole pack shrieking, a chorus which is kept up through most of the night.

The cubs are generally born, three to five at a time, in a hole in the ground; but shelters such as an old drain are sometimes used.

JAGUAR. This is the largest of the great Cats (q.v.) of South America, a typical adult being more than a metre long, with a very long tail. It has rich, reddish-yellow fur, marked all over with black rosettes. It lives chiefly in the forests, but sometimes ventures out on to the plains.

The jaguar is, for its size, the most powerful beast of prey in existence—able to kill a man

with a blow of its paw, to pull down and kill animals much larger than itself, and to drag away a carcass which would take three strong men to move. It cannot run any great distance, but ranges and hunts in the trees, springing noiselessly from one to another, and dropping upon its quarry from an overhanging branch. It rarely exposes itself to view or takes any risk which can possibly be avoided. It preys on deer, great ant-eaters, agoutis, and, in fact, on every native mammal except its rival, the Puma (q.v.). It also attacks monkeys and birds in the trees, turtles, fishes, and even alligators. When it fishes, the jaguar lies along a jutting rock or an overhanging branch, watching the water; when a fish appears, it kills it with a blow of its paw.

Paul Popper

THE SOUTH AMERICAN JAGUAR

Jaguars frequently make attacks on domestic cattle.

In the mating season, jaguars utter wailing cries and yells, like those of the domestic cat, but much more powerful. Two young are born about every 2 years.

JAY, *see* Crow, Section 8.

JELLYFISH. The true Jellyfishes belong to a group of marine invertebrate animals called the Scyphozoa—literally cup-animals. These have a remarkable life history. The Common Jellyfish of British shores may be taken as a typical example. In the adult Jellyfish, the circular, semi-transparent, gelatinous body is fringed with a row of delicate tentacles; while embedded near the centre of the body are four red or purplish horseshoe-shaped bodies, which are the reproductive organs. The mouth, in the centre of the under-surface of the body, is a four-sided opening, surrounded by four long and delicate tentacles, and leads into a capacious stomach

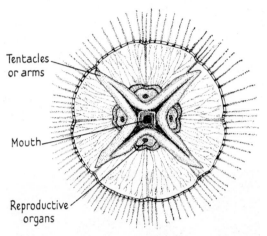

Tentacles or arms

Mouth

Reproductive organs

FIG. I. UNDER-SURFACE OF ADULT JELLYFISH

(*see* Fig. 1). The eggs, when ripe, are discharged through the mouth into the sea, where they are fertilized. Each egg then develops into a hollow, oval larva, covered with hair-like organs by means of which it swims through the water. On coming to rest on a suitable rock or weed, it

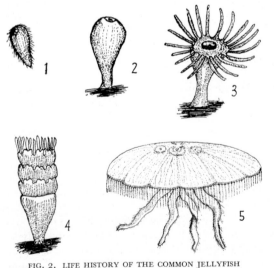

FIG. 2. LIFE HISTORY OF THE COMMON JELLYFISH

1. Free-swimming larva. 2. Larva, fixed to rock or weed, develops into a small polyp. 3. Polyp develops a mouth surrounded with tentacles. 4. Polyp divides transversely. 5. Full-grown Jellyfish

becomes attached, and the lower half of its body becomes rather slender. It then gradually acquires the cup-shaped form of a small polyp, with a stomach and mouth encircled by waving tentacles used for capturing food. In this stage it is very similar to a small HYDRA (q.v.). After a time, the little polyp, which has increased slightly in height, begins to show a series of transverse divisions, and the creature grows to look like a pile of miniature saucers. In time these saucers detach themselves, turn over, swim away, and become full-grown jellyfishes, whose offspring again will develop into cup-shaped, anchored polyps. Thus, in the life history of the Common Jellyfish (*see* Fig. 2) we have an example of the phenomenon called the 'alternation of generations', or the alternate occurrence of two different forms in one life history—the fixed polyp, and the free-swimming jellyfish which develops from it. In the plant world the same phenomenon occurs in the life history of FERNS (q.v.).

Although milky-blue is the dominant colour, some tropical species are brightly tinted, and grow to a great size. Shoals are sometimes to be seen during calm summer weather, drifting with the tide or slowly moving up and down in the water by rhythmic contractions of their bodies. On a calm, dark, summer night, from the deck of a ship, jellyfishes can often be seen, faintly illumined by their own light, passing in an endless procession. Their food consists of small crustacea, fish, and the like, which are rendered helpless by the stinging cells in the tentacles. Nevertheless, some young fishes, such as young whiting and horse-mackerel, find safe temporary shelter inside the umbrella-shaped bodies of certain species—though whether the association is in all cases of entirely mutual benefit has yet to be proved.

See also CORALS; HYDRA; SEA-ANEMONES.

JERBOA. This RODENT (q.v.), often called the Jumping Mouse, lives in the deserts of Asia and North Africa, where its sandy colouring makes it difficult to detect. It has long hind legs, but very short front ones—the disproportion being greater even than in Kangaroos. Like Kangaroos, it makes enormous bounds, using its long muscular tail to help it, and sometimes making jumps in such rapid succession that it appears to be flying. Jerboas live together in large numbers, often in company with sand-grouse, desert larks, and lizards. They use their fore feet to dig burrows in the hard ground. Just before sundown, they come out to eat seeds, and insects, and quite often sit near the mouth of their holes during the day, though at the slightest sound they dive down their burrows. In hot weather they become very torpid, and fall into a long sleep.

Widely distributed over North America is a close relative of the Jerboa family, the Labrador Jumping Mouse. It is the smallest of the family, measuring nearly 13 cm, and its tail is much longer than its body. It lives near woods and shrubby places. In winter, having acquired a thick layer of fat, so that its weight is more than half as much again, it hibernates in its burrow, rolling itself into a tight ball to sleep (*see* HIBERNATION).

A. Fraser-Brunner

THE JOHN DORY SURPRISES ITS PREY BY STRETCHING FORWARD ITS JAWS LIKE A TELESCOPE

JOHN DORY. This fish, common in the Mediterranean and found in most temperate seas, is a useful food fish, sometimes to be seen in fish shops in Britain. According to legend, the large black spots on each side of its body are the marks made by St. Peter's finger and thumb when he took a piece of money from the fish's mouth (Matt. xxvii. 24–27).

As the John Dory is very flat from side to side, it is scarcely visible when seen from the front. This allows it to approach quite close to its prey without causing alarm. Having got within striking distance, it suddenly shoots its jaws forward, like a telescope, and sucks the unfortunate victim down.

JUNGLE FOWL, *see* PHEASANT.

JUNGLES, *see* TROPICAL JUNGLES.

KANGAROO WITH HER YOUNG IN HER POUCH

K

KANGAROO. This, the best known of the MARSUPIALS (q.v.) or pouched animals, is to be found only in Australia, Tasmania, and New Guinea. There are many different species, the smaller ones being known as Wallabies. Their general appearance—their long, strong, hind legs, with peculiar elongated feet, their short front legs, thick, muscular, tapering tails, and small heads—is well known to everyone. When the Kangaroo is not moving, it sits up on its hind legs, supported by its tail, with its short fore legs hanging like arms in front. It uses its fore legs only when moving slowly to graze; when travelling at speed, it moves by enormous leaps, propelled by its hind legs and balanced by its tail.

Young kangaroos are born one at a time, and, like all marsupials, are very small and un-developed at birth, those of the larger species being only about 2·5 cm long. As soon as it is born, the tiny creature works its way with its front claws into its mother's pouch, where it becomes firmly attached to her nipple; and, as it has not the power to suck, milk is pumped into its body by the mother. When developed enough to move by itself, it becomes detached from the teat, but remains in the pouch until it can run by its mother's side. At the approach of danger, however, the mother will pick up her young and thrust it into her pouch for safety.

The larger kangaroos are as tall as a man, while some of the smaller are no bigger than a rabbit. The two largest species are the Great Grey Kangaroo, which lives in forest country, and the Red Kangaroo, of the open plains. When travelling at full speed, these animals can leap 7 metres at a bound, and clear objects 2 metres high. In the mating season the males fight one another, striking forward with their hind legs and inflicting serious injury with their formidable claws. Another well-known species is the stout, heavily built Wallaroo, which has long, thick, grey fur.

Kangaroos are vegetarians, feeding mainly on grass, young heather, and other green plants. They are timid creatures, with acute sight, hearing, and sense of smell. Like those of hares, kangaroos' eyes seem to be set in such a way that their forward vision is limited, so that the animals may blunder into something directly in their path. Kangaroos always go about in droves, following a leader. The various droves keep to their own districts and have their own particular feeding-grounds. They feed in the early morning, at twilight, and during the night, and lie up by day in damp, scrubby gullies in summer, or on dry, sandy ridges in winter.

Quite distinct from the typical Kangaroos are the Tree Kangaroos found in the dense tropical forests of New Guinea and northern Australia. These have front legs very nearly equal in length to their hind legs, and they spend most of their time climbing among trees, aided by their strong claws, and using their long furry tails to balance them.

The Rat Kangaroos are little larger than rabbits. They have small, rounded ears and long, furry tails, which are generally prehensile at the tips. Some of them use their tails to carry grass and other materials for their nest-building, curving the tip of the tail down below the bundle. They lie hidden in their nests in the grass during the day, and go out only at night.

KEA, see PARROTS.

KED. This insect, sometimes wrongly called the 'sheep-tick', is a very common skin parasite on sheep, and may be found clinging to the wool with its claws. It sucks blood, and has a very hairy, reddish or grey-brown body with a flat abdomen. It has no wings. Keds belong to the section of flies called the Pupipara or Louse Flies, all of which (with one exception, the Bee Louse) are parasites on birds and mammals, produce their young alive in an advanced stage of larval development, and pupate in a 'puparium' (the last larval skin).

Like so many external parasites, the Ked is spread by contact, and so passes from sheep to sheep; but it may occasionally be found crawling about the ground near sheep pasturage. Sometimes it finds its way upon sheep-dogs or other animals. The larvae are born one at a time, at intervals of several weeks. They are dropped in the sheep's wool, and then burrow deep down amongst it. In about twelve hours they change into pupae, the pupal state lasting for about three weeks.

Some Louse Flies, such as the Forest Fly, a parasite on the horse, are fully winged, others have imperfectly developed wings, and others, like the Ked, have no wings. Some cast off their wings after they have arrived upon their hosts. The female of one of this last kind (a parasite on bats, found in Queensland and in some of the East Indies) embeds herself in the skin under a bat's ear, and then casts off both wings and legs. The Bee Louse, which is very minute, and has neither eyes nor wings, is found clinging to the thorax of the queen or of drones. Unlike the members of the Pupipara, the female Bee Louse lays eggs; and the larvae, which are typical fly-maggots, feed in the brood-cells of the honeycomb upon the material stored there. They pupate in the honeycomb, and, when adult, make their own way on to the bees.

See also FLIES.

KENTISH GLORY MOTH. This moth, the only European representative of the family Endromididae, is a near relative of the domestic Silk Moth. Its name dates from the 18th century, when in England it was known only in

FEMALE KENTISH GLORY MOTH

Gordon Woods

Kent. Now, it is most abundant in Scotland and Wyre Forest, Worcestershire, where it frequents moors and woods containing young birches. The male, recognized by its combed antennae, has a wing-span of quite 5 cm, the fore-wings being brown, the hind-wings orange. The pale smoky-white female is even larger. Both sexes have white streaks and spots, two black lines edged with white across the fore-wings, and a single line on the hind-wings.

Freshly emerged unmated females give off scents which are attractive to the day-flying males: indeed, in Sussex, 118 males were once known to assemble to a single female. The somewhat cylindrical eggs are laid on birch twigs in double rows. The black young larvae congregate together near the tip of the twig, and, clinging by the abdominal legs, hold up their heads and fore parts so that they closely resemble little stumps on the twig. They become green on moulting, and then so closely resemble a group of birch catkins as almost to defy detection. As they grow larger, their resemblance to catkins is less striking, and they gradually become more leaf-like in colour and attitude. The mature caterpillar lives alone and is mainly green, with a dark central line. In June or July, shortly before pupation, it becomes reddish-brown, and so is not very conspicuous when it abandons the birches to spin its blackish-brown silk cocoon among moss and leaves on the ground, or just below the surface. The pupae, which often spend 2 years in this stage, work their way out of their cocoons in March or April, a week or so before they hatch

KESTREL, *see* FALCON.

KING CROW, *see* DRONGO.

KINGFISHER. These brilliant birds are to be found all over the world, the majority of species belonging to tropical countries. We could divide them into those which feed entirely on fish and live near rivers and lakes, and those, often living some way from water, which have a mixed diet including fish.

The common Kingfisher, a resident of the British Isles, is the most brilliantly coloured of European birds. It has a stocky body and short tail, and an unmistakable, long, dagger-shaped bill. Its back and wings are a dazzling blue-green, its throat and underparts salmon-pink

Ardea Photographics
KINGFISHER SITTING BY ENTRANCE TO ITS NEST

ing habit is very different from that described in the Greek legend of the Halcyon (or Kingfisher), which was supposed to build a floating nest on the surface of the sea. According to the legend, Alcyone, the daughter of Aeolus, King of the Winds, was changed into a Kingfisher. She was granted two weeks' calm weather at the winter solstice, so that she might brood in peace. For this reason all sailors on the Mediterranean enjoyed a period of tranquillity during the 'Halcyon Days'.

The other group, the tree Kingfishers, which eat reptiles, crabs, and various insects, are often found in forest or bush country. The largest group is that of the Wood Kingfishers, of which there are about seventy species, the best known being the White-breasted Kingfisher, a bird found over all southern Asia and the greater part of Africa. Another well-known and larger species is the Kookaburra or Laughing Jackass of Australia.

KITE, *see* Hawk, Section 3.

KITTEN MOTH, *see* Prominents.

KITTIWAKE, *see* Gulls, Section 3.

KIWI. This bird belongs to New Zealand only. It is a member of the section of flightless birds, to which also belongs the Ostrich (q.v.). The

and chestnut, and its feet bright red. It is a comparatively common bird where conditions are suitable, and is becoming more common now that it is no longer pursued for its feathers. It can be seen skimming over the surface of the water like a blue flash, or perching upon some branch, post, or rock over the water, watching for a fish or water-insect. On sighting its prey, it plunges headlong, and on securing its fish, it returns to its post, beats its victim on the perch until it is dead, and then swallows it head-first.

The Kingfisher makes a burrow for itself in the bank of a stream, digging out the earth with its strong beak, and making a tunnel horizontally into the bank for a distance of a half to one metre. The tunnel ends in a circular chamber where the six or seven round, glossy, white eggs are laid in a nest consisting of no more than a few half-digested fish-bones. By the end of the incubation period the nest is fouled with disgorged fish bones and other refuse. This nest-

The New Zealand Herald
A FAMILY OF NEW ZEALAND KIWIS

bones of the wings are very small and slender, the whole wing being entirely concealed by the plumage of the back. But though Kiwis cannot fly, they can run very fast. They are robustly built, and have strong legs and feet, with which they scratch up the worms and insects on which they feed. They have long slender bills, useful for probing into soft ground and under leaves or moss. Their feathers are long and rather hair-like, reddish or grey in colour, streaked with a darker shade. They have no tails. They are little larger than a domestic hen.

Kiwis are night-birds, spending the day hidden in burrows or hollow logs, or under thick vegetation. They nest in some such hidden spot, laying one or two whitish eggs, remarkably large for the size of the bird. The incubation and care of the chicks is carried out almost entirely by the male, who generally will not allow the female to come near the nest after she has laid the eggs. Kiwis are now very scarce, and are carefully protected by the New Zealand government.

KOALA (Australian Bear). This animal is not a bear, but belongs to the same order of MAR-SUPIALS as the KANGAROO (qq.v.). Its tubby shape and soft, greyish-brown, woolly coat has made it popular as a model for 'Teddy-bear' toys. It is about the size of a large poodle-dog, and has large, rounded ears and a prominent, black, india-rubber-like nose. In its cheeks it has pouches for storing food, like many monkeys.

Koalas live entirely in the trees, climbing by means of the long claws on their feet. They are rather sluggish creatures, and move awkwardly on the ground, always making for a tree if pursued. They are not seen very often, as they stir very little until nightfall. They feed entirely on the leaves of certain kinds of gum-trees, and do not thrive on other food.

One young Koala is born at a time, and, like all young marsupials, it is reared in its mother's pouch, which, unlike that of a kangaroo, opens backwards. When it is a few months old, the mother carries it on her back. Koalas used to be common in eastern Australia, but they have been so much hunted for the sake of their fur that they are now scarce in most districts. They are rarely kept in zoos outside Australia because of the difficulty of supplying them with their natural food.

KRAIT. This genus of poisonous snakes, found in India and Indo-China, is most nearly related to the COBRAS (q.v.), but it differs from them in having no hood. Kraits have highly polished scales, with an enlarged series down the middle of the back. They are particularly abundant in India, where many people die every year as a result of their bite. There are thirteen species, the two best known being the Indian Krait, which is black with white cross-bands and grows to well over a metre in length, and the Banded Krait, which has broad yellow bands and has been known to reach 2 metres in length. Other species are the Ceylon Krait, the Black Krait of Assam, and the Yellow-headed Krait of the Malayan Region.

Another group of poisonous snakes closely related to the Kraits is the Coral Snakes, remarkable for the beauty of their colour. They may be red, pink, yellow, brown, black, or purple, and banded, spotted, or striped, with an equal variety of colours. Their scales are highly iridescent, but they are without the enlarged series down the back. They inhabit the tropical regions of America, India, and Australia.

See also SNAKES.

E. O. Hoppé

THE KOALA, OR NATIVE BEAR OF AUSTRALIA

L

LABYRINTH-FISHES. Many kinds of fishes are able to breathe air, as well as the oxygen dissolved in water. Outstanding among these are members of the Anabantidae family called Labyrinth-fishes. These are so named because they have a special breathing-chamber, which is sometimes very complicated and like a labyrinth. The Labyrinth-fishes are inhabitants of the fresh waters of Asia and Africa. To the group belong the Climbing Perch, the Fighting Fish, the Paradise Fish, and the Gouramies. Some of these fishes are so dependent on dry air that they cannot live without it, and will drown if forced to stay below water all the time. They inhale air in gulps at the surface, and this passes into the complicated labyrinth organs, which are richly supplied with blood-vessels for the absorption of the oxygen, the used air then passing out through the gill-openings.

Most Labyrinth-fishes have very interesting breeding habits, in particular the species known as Fighting Fish. The male first builds a nest of bubbles at the surface, often amongst water plants, which are stuck together with a sticky secretion, and form a dense floating mass. After completing the nest he finds a mate. This often involves a long mating display, but eventually he persuades the female to remain under the nest. There she begins to lay her very small eggs, which drop towards the bottom. The male, swimming underneath, catches the falling eggs and blows them up into the nest amongst the bubbles. Then, the egg-laying being finished, he drives off his mate and stands guard over the nest, adding more bubbles as needed and rescuing any eggs which may drop. When the eggs hatch, the minute larvae hang from the bottom of the nest as just visible specks. As they grow, they begin to leave the nest, but are immediately blown back again by the male. After about a week, however, they are so active that the male is unable to catch them all. He soon gives up, and the young fish, now big enough to fend for themselves, leave the nest for good. The other Labyrinth-fishes have similar habits, most of them building bubble nests.

The Climbing Perch of India often come out of the water, moving from one pond to another at night, and after a heavy shower of rain, sometimes entering gardens in search of small animal food. They travel over the ground by means of mobile, sharp-prickled gill-covers, assisted by a row of spines at the anal fin. From the earliest times this fish has been credited with the habit of climbing trees, its discoverer in 1797 having actually found one in a cleft in the bark of a palm near a pond. It seems unlikely that, in fact, they normally do this, but probably when travelling over land, some fishes are seized by birds, such as crows or kites, which place them

A. Fraser-Brunner

CLIMBING PERCH OF INDIA

The fish moves over land by using alternately the spiny gill-cover and anal fin

in the trees to be eaten later. It is certainly difficult to guess why a fish should want to climb trees in any case.

In India and Malaya Climbing Perch are used as food, and are stored alive for days in damp clay pots to be eaten fresh when required.

The Fighting-fishes are native to Siam. Long ago it was discovered that if two males were put in the same small tank together, they would immediately become angry and fight to the death. Since then, they have been carefully bred and selected for their fighting prowess, much like fighting cocks. In Bangkok, the capital, at least a thousand people breed them for contests, on the results of which large sums are wagered. Males are kept separately, in special glass jars, until the time for the fight arrives; then they are placed together in a bowl or jar. They at once approach each other, spreading their fins and gill-membranes. Then, with great rapidity, they attack again and again, with short intervals between the sallies. Gradually their fins are torn, or their gills are injured, until at last one of them gives up the fight and tries to escape. The other is then judged the winner. A wild fish will rarely fight for more than about 10 minutes, whereas a pedigree champion has been known to attack for 6 hours!

Many Labyrinth-fishes are popular as ornamental fish for the AQUARIUM (q.v. Vol. IX). Male Fighting-fish for this purpose have been bred in a variety of brilliant colours, with long, graceful fins. The females are smaller and much less brightly coloured.

LACE BUG, *see* BUG.

LACEWING. The Lacewings belong to the order of insects known as Neuroptera and are of two kinds—Green Lacewings, 14 of the 800 species of which occur in Britain, and Brown Lacewings of which there are about 40 British species, the Giant Lacewing being the largest. They have two pairs of large elongate, usually almost identical wings, transparent, except for the network of veins (to which the insect owes its name); these are the same colour as the slender body. The Green Lacewings are also known either as 'Golden-eyes' because of the metallic glitter of their eyes, or as 'stink-flies' because they often emit a very unpleasant smell.

The Green Lacewings lay their eggs in a peculiar manner. Before laying an egg, the

S. C. Bisserôt

GIANT LACEWING

female Lacewing deposits a drop of fluid on a leaf; then she raises her body so as to draw the fluid out into a sticky thread, on the top of which she places her egg. The thread hardens, so that the egg is attached to the leaf by a long, slender stalk. The Brown Lacewings do not produce these stalks.

The Lacewings have a complete META-MORPHOSIS (q.v.). The larvae are whitish and spindle-shaped, with long slender legs and powerful jaws. They feed on aphides, leaf-hoppers, mites, &c. One Lacewing is said to be able to destroy up to 400 aphides during its period of growth. They force their long sickle-shaped jaws into their prey and suck them dry. The larvae of the Green Lacewings cover themselves with the skins of their victims, keeping them in position by hooked hairs on the back of their bodies. When it is ready to pupate, the larva spins a dense silken cocoon on the underside of a leaf.

LACKEY MOTH. Lackeys, Eggars, Lappets, the December, Fox, and Drinker Moths all belong to the family Lasiocampidae, of which about 1,400 species are known, chiefly from tropical forests of Asia, Africa, and South America. The moths have heavy bodies, and are various shades of brown, with lighter or darker bands crossing the wings. Both sexes have combed antennae, and a very small proboscis. The large, hairy caterpillars of some species attract attention by their bright colours, and by their habit of living together in groups. Some spin webs—indeed, those of the destructive Tent Caterpillars of North American forests may cover whole trees. One species, the Syrian silk-moth, used to be reared by the Greeks, especially on the Island of Cos, for the sake of the silk produced by the caterpillar. It was still bred in Italy up to the 19th century, but is now replaced by the Chinese Mulberry Silkworm, a species closely allied to the KENTISH GLORY (q.v.) (*see* SILKWORMS: Vol. VI).

The small Common Lackey lays its grey-brown eggs in July and August, in a ring-like cluster of 100–250, completely encircling a twig, often of hawthorn. The bluish caterpillars, with white and orange stripes along their backs, and brown hairs, hatch in April or May. They make conspicuous tents, in which they live in colonies, completely stripping the leaves from neighbouring shoots. After moulting, they move on to construct another and more elaborate tent elsewhere. In June they pupate within a double oval cocoon. The Ground Lackey is found only locally in Britain, on salt marshes. The Pale Oak Eggar, attached to hawthorn and sloe, and the Small Eggar, with its tent-making caterpillar, are common in woods in southern England, and less common farther north. The rather transparent greyish December Moth is frequently attracted to light in November and December, and sometimes in October. The caterpillar rests by day in cracks in the bark of trees, which it closely resembles, climbing the tree at night to eat the leaves. The magnificent yellowish-brown female Oak Eggar, with a wing-expanse of nearly 8 cm, and the smaller rich chocolate-brown male, are common in July and August along the margins of woods and hedgerows. The dark moorland form, characteristic of Scotland and northern England, takes two years to complete its life-cycle. The males, flying by day in bright sunshine, are attracted in large numbers to the scent given off by an unmated female. The eggs, scattered freely over the food-plants as the female flies in circles, hatch in late summer, and the caterpillars over-

S. C. Bisserôt

OAK EGGAR

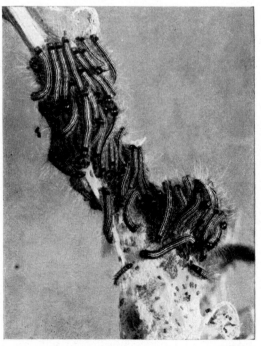

S. Beaufoy

A CLUSTER OF LACKEY MOTH LARVAE ROUND A HAWTHORN TWIG. (×2)

winter when still small. The full-grown caterpillar, which curls up when disturbed, is brown, with deep velvet-black rings and a white stripe at the sides. It pupates in a hard, yellowish-brown silk cocoon suggestive of an egg, hence the common name Eggar. The smaller Grass Eggar, a local species flying in August, is best known from sandhills on the coast, its caterpillar usually feeding on grasses.

Fox Moths, named from their reddish-brown colour, are nearly 5·5 cm in expanse, and have two pale lines crossing the fore-wings. The males can be commonly seen flying wildly over heaths in May and June sunshine. The brown eggs are laid in groups on stems, and the caterpillars feed until October, when they hibernate, coming out on fine days to bask in the sun, and not pupating until March or April. They are magnificent insects, 9 cm in length, and velvety-black with golden-brown hairs.

The Drinker, so called because the caterpillar was observed as early as the 17th century to drink dew, is a common moth, measuring 5 or 6 cm across, the female being yellowish and the male reddish-brown, both sexes having two white spots on each fore-wing. The caterpillar is slaty-grey, with two rows of yellowish spots on the back, orange spots and tufts of white hairs at the sides, and a pointed tuft of black hairs at each end. It feeds on reeds or coarse grasses by rivers, ditches, and marshes. The yellowish cocoon, nearly 4 cm in length, is attached to stems about 30 cm from the ground.

The Lappet is so called because the caterpillar has fleshy flaps at the sides, effective in reducing shadow as it rests on a branch of sloe, hawthorn, or apple. The whitish eggs are laid, a few at a time, on the undersides of leaves in July and August, and the caterpillars hibernate when about 2 or 3 cm in length, resuming feeding in the spring. A full-grown female reaches about 10 cm in length, though the males are smaller. Their actual colour-pattern depends upon that of their surroundings during growth—the general colouring being dark grey or brown with some white markings suggesting lichen. The beautiful reddish-brown moth has scalloped outer margins to the wings, and rests with its hind-wings projecting in front of the fore-wings so that it closely resembles a bunch of dead leaves.

The Small Lappet, attached to bilberry, is very rare in Britain.

See also MOTHS.

E. O. Hoppé

FEMALE LADYBIRD LAYING HER EGGS ON A PLANT INFESTED BY GREENFLY

LADYBIRDS (Coccinellidae). Because of their bright colours and patterns Ladybirds are amongst the best known of all the BEETLES (q.v.). There are about 5,000 species in the world, of which 45 live in Britain, probably the most familiar being the Two-spot and Seven-spot. Many species vary greatly in colour and pattern. The majority of Ladybirds prey on Aphides, Scale Insects, and other small insects; but some feed on plants, and a few live in association with ANTS (q.v.). Ladybirds are very useful to man because they help to control INSECT PESTS (q.v. Vol. VI). One species from Australia, for example, was imported into California to control a Scale Insect pest on the citrus fruit.

Like other beetles, Ladybirds have a complete METAMORPHOSIS (q.v.). The female lays her yellow eggs in batches, those that eat insects laying theirs on plants close to the colonies of insects on which their young will feed. The larvae, which are soft-bodied, spiny, and usually greyish in colour, with yellow or white markings, have long legs and sickle-shaped mandibles. They usually moult four times before they pupate, which they do by anchoring themselves to plants, fences, &c., by their back end and then by casting their skin, which remains attached to the pupa at the base.

Many Ladybirds produce a brownish, rather bitter liquid when disturbed, and this, together with their bright warning colour and pattern, helps to protect them from being eaten by other animals, such as birds (*see* PROTECTIVE COLORATION). Ladybirds are sometimes seen in vast swarms, especially just before hibernation.

LAMPREY. Lampreys and their relatives, the Hag-fishes, are probably the lowest living type of vertebrate (back-boned) animal possessing anything that can truly be called a skull. The skull consists of a number of plates of cartilage (gristle), which do not form a complete box for the brain; there are no jaws; a complicated arrangement of rods of cartilage forms a basket-shaped structure for the protection and support of the gills, which are in pouch-like gill-chambers; and the spinal column consists only of the primitive 'notochord' (or rod of gristle) and a series of isolated pieces of cartilage on each side of the spinal chord. These creatures are so distinct as to be placed in a separate class, the Agnatha, the earliest vertebrates, which have no jaws.

The Hag-fishes seem to be more primitive than the Lampreys, the mouth being simply an opening, in front of which are four pairs of short tentacles. The single 'nostril' is connected with the back of the mouth. The eyes are very small and feeble. A strong, rasp-like tongue is set with horny teeth, by which the Hag-fish bores its way into the bodies of larger animals, such as injured or dead sharks or other big fish, eating away the flesh and leaving only the skin and bones. The catches made by fishermen are often ruined by the attacks of Hag-fishes. When not feeding, these creatures live in the mud at the bottom of the sea, in rather deep water, and are capable of very rapid movement. They can exude an amazing amount of slime from special pores along their sides, and if placed in a bucket will fill it with slime

in a few minutes. Hag-fishes are found in most temperate seas of the world.

Lampreys have a somewhat stronger 'skeleton' than Hag-fishes, a better developed brain, more useful eyes, and other features that approach more nearly to typical fishes. There are seven gills, each with its own outer opening, and the 'nostril' is not connected with the mouth. The mouth is surrounded by a disk capable of powerful suction, and is armed with horny rasping teeth (in addition to those on the tongue). By means of this disk, Lampreys attach themselves to the body of a larger fish and rasp away the flesh with the horny teeth, while the victim, in its attempts to escape, carries them about.

Young Lampreys are so different from their parents that they were once thought to be different animals, and were named *Ammocoetes*. This young stage, still referred to as the *Ammocoete* larva, lasts for about 3 years, during which time the creature, being blind and without teeth, lives and feeds in the mud. The larva may well resemble the ancestors of the true fishes. Its method of feeding on small animals by filtering them through the gills is similar to that of the LANCELET (q.v.). It then undergoes a change, or METAMORPHOSIS (q.v.), and after about 3 weeks reaches the adult stage.

Several species of Lamprey are known. The Sea Lamprey, large, with a marbled colour-pattern, spends its *Ammocoete* stage in rivers, migrating to the sea in order to become adult.

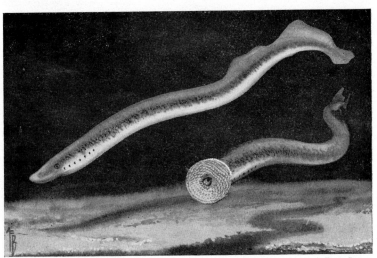

A. Fraser-Brunner

SEA LAMPREYS SEEN IN AN AQUARIUM

One of them has attached itself to the glass by its suckerlike mouth, showing its many horny teeth

The Lampern is sometimes called the River Lamprey, although it seems to spend most of its time in the sea, moving up the rivers only in order to spawn. It is smaller than the Sea Lamprey, and was at one time abundant in the River Thames. Still smaller is the Brook Lamprey, which spends all its time in fresh water.

Lampreys were at one time much sought after as food, and still are in some parts of the world; but in Britain at least they are no longer of any commercial importance. They are not as common as they were, probably owing to the pollution of rivers by industry.

LANCELET. These are small animals, up to 10 cm long, which live buried, except for their mouths, in coarse gravel on the sea bed. One species occurs off the south coast of Britain. Though Lancelets lack many features possessed

A. Fraser-Brunner
THE LANCELET, RESEMBLING THE EARLY ANCESTOR OF FISHES

by vertebrates, such as skull, jaws, heart, eyes, and scales, they are nevertheless classified as chordates; they are not unlike the *Ammocoete* larvae of LAMPREYS and the tadpole larvae of SEA SQUIRTS (qq.v.).

A rod of stiff but bendable supporting substance, similar in effect to the gristle of vertebrates, passes along the length of the Lancelet's body above the gut. This 'notochord', as it is called, does not develop the separate vertebrae which form the backbones of vertebrates, but along its top passes a nerve chord, similar in position and form to the nerve chords of vertebrates. The Lancelet has a row of gill slits along its throat, and water currents pass into the mouth and out of its gill slits, as in a fish. It uses its gills, however, for feeding, for these filter off minute plants and animals from the water.

Through its transparent skin muscles can be

seen, arranged in a series along its sides, rather like those of a fish. These enable the Lancelet to swim by wriggling its body from side to side.

LANTERN-FISH. This name is given to the many species of little oceanic fishes, usually about 5 centimetres long, belonging to the family Myctophidae, related to the SALMON (q.v.). They all have large mouths, rather large eyes, and a small 'adipose fin' behind the dorsal fin on the back. Their most interesting feature is the series of luminous organs arranged in definite patterns on the body and head. About two hundred species of Lantern-fish are known, and each one has its own special arrangement of these 'lamps', probably enabling members of the species to recognize each other in the darkness of the deep ocean. Lantern-fishes, indeed, spend most of their time in darkness. During the day they remain in the deep waters of the ocean, beyond reach of the sun's rays, which would injure their large, sensitive eyes. At night, however, they often come nearer the surface, and, curiously enough, may be attracted by a bright light put over the side of a ship. Many have been caught in this way; for, although they are darkness-loving creatures, they seem to be fascinated by the light, just like moths round a lamp, and are easily netted. The eyes of Lantern-fishes are large in order to take advantage of every ray of light given out by the luminous creatures in the gloomy waters they inhabit; for only in this way are they able to keep together in shoals, to distinguish sexes in order to mate, and to find food, which consists for the most part of small luminous prawns that swarm in the deeper waters.

The so-called Bombay-duck, found in the Indian Ocean, and used, after drying and salting, as an accompaniment to curry, is related to the Lantern-fishes.

See also DEEP-SEA FISHES.

LANTERN FLY. As long ago as 1705 the name Lantern Fly was given to bugs belonging to the family Fulgoridae, because it was thought that these insects had luminous heads. This belief is now known to be unfounded. Some of these insects possess BACTERIA (q.v.) in their alimentary canals, and it has been suggested that some of these under certain conditions may be luminous and shine through the body.

Many Lantern Flies have projections on the

front of their heads, which are often hollow, bladder-like structures. Viewed sideways these projections look like the head of a prehistoric reptile, and black markings on them often produce the illusion of eyes and nostrils. It is thought that this illusion may serve to keep away the insect's enemies.

The Chinese Candle Fly was also assumed, without foundation, to be luminous. Certain other species of bugs secrete a white feathery, waxy substance, which streams behind them when they fly. The Chinese collect this material and use it to make candles.

See also Bugs.

LAPWING, see Wading Birds, Section 5.

LARCH, see Conifers.

LARK. This brown or sand-coloured bird is a ground bird, nesting on the ground and very seldom perching on trees. It runs along instead of hopping. It is conspicuous for its song, the European Skylark being one of the best songsters in the family. There are a great many species, found especially in deserts and open plains of Asia, Africa, and Australia. Europe has several species, two of which breed in the British Isles and others being occasional visitors.

The Skylark is a common bird in most parts of Europe. Large numbers, breeding in northern Europe, migrate to Britain in the autumn, while others, which have bred in Britain, emigrate to warmer climates for the winter. The Skylark is well known for its habit of circling high in the air with rapid wing-beats, singing all the while. It makes a simple nest in a tussock of coarse grass, and three to five speckled grey and brown eggs are laid.

The Woodlark, somewhat smaller than the Skylark, is more common in most of Europe than in Britain, where it is confined to certain districts in the south. It is an exception to the rest of its family in that it perches on the upper branches of trees to sing. Its song is rich and sweet, though less sustained than that of the Skylark.

The Crested Lark, so called from its small pointed crest, is common on the Continent, where it usually becomes very tame. The Shore Lark, a yellowish buff and black bird, which might well be called the Mountain Lark, for it breeds high in the mountains of Scandinavia

and North America, sometimes visits the east coast of Britain on migration. Other species, including the Black Lark from Russia and the large-billed Calandra Lark from the Mediterranean, are very occasional visitors to Britain.

LEAF-INSECT, see Stick Insect.

LEAF-ROLLERS (Tortricoidea). This very large group of small, wide-winged moths produces caterpillars which live concealed in their food-plant. Some live in the roots, fruits, or stems on which they feed; others, which are leaf-feeders, roll an edge of the leaf into a tube. Many are serious agricultural pests—such as the world-known Codling Moth, the larva of which lives in the core of the apple, the Peach Moth, and another species which attacks grapes (see Insect Pests, Vol. VI). Others attack trees, such as pines, larches, and oak-trees.

One of the most spectacular is the Green Oak-roller or Oak Tortrix. The moth is bright green with grey hind-wings. The caterpillars, lengthy for their size, and slightly hairy, attack the leaves of oak-trees in such numbers that, in dry years, whole forests of trees may be stripped of leaves even to the point of being killed. The caterpillars spin strands of thread across the part of the leaf to be rolled. As the silk threads dry, they shrink, drawing over the leaf-edges. This process is continued until a complete tube has been formed. These caterpillars, if disturbed, will drop out of their leaf-tubes and hang by a silk thread. Anyone passing through an oak wood in a dry May will soon find himself walking into them, as they hang all round him on their long threads. When ready to pupate, they either remain in the folded leaf, or drop by their threads to a chink in the bark or other suitable crevice.

The foxy-red Larch Tortrix moth lays eggs on the tip of a young larch shoot. The Pine-gall Tortrix larvae feed within the stem of a pine leaf-bud. As they tunnel into the stem, a drop of resin is exuded, and this forms a gall-like bulge on the twig, which increases in size as the caterpillar tunnels. The insect passes its pupal stage within this 'gall'. This excrescence should not be confused with the real Gall made by the Gall-fly (q.v.). The Light Brown Apple Moth is a serious defoliator of apple-trees in Australia and New Zealand.

See also Moths.

ER-JACKET, *see* CRANE-FLY.

. 1. FUNCTION. The main function of
.... leaves is that of PHOTOSYNTHESIS (q.v.),
by means of which the green leaf is able to take
raw materials and, in the presence of sunlight,
convert them into food materials to nourish all
parts of the plant. The work done by the green
leaf, therefore, is responsible, directly or indirectly, for all life in the world. Since photosynthesis in the leaves depends upon sunlight,
the stems that bear them grow in such a way
as to present the greatest possible surface of

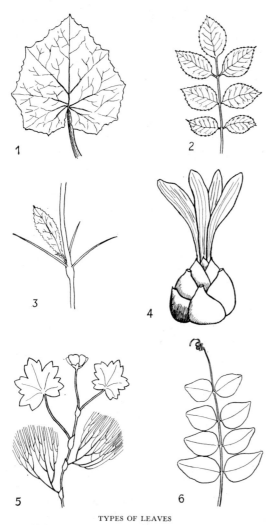

TYPES OF LEAVES

1. Simple leaf (Coltsfoot); 2. Compound leaf (Rose);
3. Leaf converted to spines (Barberry); 4. Simple leaves
and swollen food-storing leaves (Lily); 5. Submerged and
floating leaves (Water Buttercup); 6. Climbing leaf with
part converted to tendril (Vetch)

leaf-blade to the light. Most leaves have their
blades almost parallel to the ground, and it is
interesting to see, in creeping and climbing
plants, as well as in trees, how little overlapping
there is. The leaves are so arranged that those
growing below fit into the spaces left by those
above, making not only a beautiful pattern, but
also an efficient sun-trap. This leaf-pattern,
or leaf-mosaic as it is called, is especially pronounced in trees with a dense canopy, and in
smaller plants growing in the shade. It can be
seen by standing under a Beech or Elm, and
looking upwards, and is well demonstrated by
the young branches of Ivy and Sycamore.

2. LEAF STRUCTURE. Although there is a
large number of different types of leaves, each
plant has its own typical leaf-shape. The Privet,
for example, has one of the simplest of leaves—
a leaf-blade in one piece, and a simple leaf-
stalk. The Banana plant has also a simple leaf,
but a very great deal larger—anything from 1 to
3 metres long, though this frequently becomes
broken up. The leaf-blade of the Horse-chestnut is divided into many leaflets, and is far
from simple; but, like the Privet and the Banana
and all other leaves, it is typical of its species.
Between the simple leaf of the Privet and the
compound leaf of the Horse-chestnut, there are
leaves of intermediate kinds, ranging from those
with jagged or serrated edges, like that of the
Elm, to those with a deeply indented edge, like
the Oak leaf. Leaf-shape, therefore, affords a
good way of identifying a plant.

Most leaves are composed of a leaf-stalk and
a leaf-blade. The leaf-stalk widens at the base,
where it joins the stem into what is called the
leaf-base. Sometimes this is merely a thicker
structure, as in the Horse-chestnut, sometimes
it is elongated into a sheath, as in the Buttercup.
The flattened portion of the leaf—the leaf-
blade—is sometimes joined to the leaf-base
without the intermediate leaf-stalk. The thicker
lines on the leaf-blade are veins or channels for
conducting water to, and food from, the leaf.
From the main vein, or midrib, side veins are
given off, and these go on branching until the
tiny vein-endings cover the whole leaf-blade.
Most leaves have this net-veined lace-work; but
the blade-like leaves, such as those of Grasses,
Lilies, Irises, and Daffodils, have several main
veins running parallel to one another instead
of a mid-rib.

Compound leaves are easy to confuse with

stems bearing several simple leaves. But there is usually a leaf-bud in the angle which a leaf-stalk makes with the stem. This angle is called the axil of the leaf. No matter how many leaflets there are in the compound leaf, there is only one leaf-bud; whereas, when several separate leaves are attached to a stem, there will be several leaf-buds (*see* STEMS). In the type of compound leaf to which the Horse-chestnut and Lupin belong, the leaflets stretch out somewhat like fingers spread out, and the leaf is described as 'palmate'. Another type of compound leaf is the 'pinnate' (feathered) leaf, such as the Rose and the Vetch, where the leaflets are arranged in pairs along the midrib of the leaf.

3. LEAF MODIFICATIONS. Leaves develop special modifications to suit different circumstances, just as do roots and stems. The sharp spines of the Barberry, for example, represent foliage leaves which have become reduced, presumably as a means of protection against browsing animals (*see* PLANT DEFENCES). Here the whole leaf has become reduced to a spine; but in the Holly only the leaf-margin forms a series of spines. However, the belief that most holly trees bear more spines on the lower leaves within easy reach of animals, and less on the upper branches, can be disproved by anyone who uses his eyes. In a young Gorse plant it is possible to see all the stages between the whole leaf with its three leaflets and the spines into which it becomes modified. Some branch stems of the Gorse produce spines, too. Since buds grow in the axils of leaves, we thus get long 'stem' spines growing out of the axils of shorter 'leaf' spines.

Leaves also become modified for storage purposes, sometimes as water-reservoirs and sometimes as food reserves. Those that store water are generally found in plants growing in dry regions, so that the water-supply in the leaves makes up for the scarcity in the soil (*see* DESERT PLANTS). The House-leeks and Stone-crops, which grow on rocks and walls, are good examples of this, and so are the succulent Samphires, which grow on cliffs. The Ice-plant, too, which, though not a native, grows freely by the sea in the south of England, stores water in its swollen leaves. In the fleshy leaves which form bulbs (*see* STEMS, Section 2(*d*)) food is stored. Leaves are also modified as tendrils for climbing purposes (*see* CLIMBING PLANTS); while, in some very peculiar plants, the leaves are modified as bladders and pitchers to trap insects (*see* INSECTIVOROUS PLANTS).

The Australian Acacias and Myrtles show an extraordinary kind of leaf modification: the blade often disappears completely, and the stalk becomes flattened to carry out the normal work of the leaf. The probable explanation of this is that it saves the leaves from over-exposure to the excessive light and heat of a tropical climate. Whereas the normal leaf-blade is arranged horizontally to face the sun, these flattened leaf-stalks grow vertically, exposing only their edges to the sun, and thus avoiding direct contact with its rays. Such flattened leaf-stalks are called 'phyllodes'. Among British plants, the Grass Vetch possesses well-developed phyllodes.

4. LEAF-FALL. One of the vital problems which plants, like human beings and all other living things, have to solve is how to obtain an adequate supply of water. The plant normally absorbs all the water it needs from the soil through its roots. In a tropical country, where there is little difference in climate between the seasons, absorption through the roots takes place as readily in winter as in summer. In temperate countries like Great Britain, however, plants are most active during the warm summer, and practically come to a standstill, carrying on only essential processes, during the winter. The slowing-down of plant activities is due, not so much to the cold itself, as to the plant's inability to absorb water from the cold winter soil. Plants, therefore, must conserve water as much as possible during the winter. As plants give off water chiefly by TRANSPIRATION (q.v.) through the leaves, it is natural that some trees with thin, delicate leaves get rid of their leaves in the autumn. These trees are called deciduous. The few evergreen trees that occur naturally in Britain have their leaves specially thickened and modified to prevent their losing water, as happens in the leaves of deciduous trees. In herbaceous plants, the problem scarcely arises, because the shoot itself dies down before winter.

The autumn leaf-fall of deciduous trees is by no means haphazard. Before it begins, the green leaves gradually lose their colour and take on the characteristic shades of yellow, brown, and red, which we associate with the autumn. These colour changes are partly due to a chemical breaking-down of the green colouring matter, chlorophyll, revealing other pigments present in the cells (*see* PHOTOSYNTHESIS). At this time, layers of cells at the base of the leaf-stalk become separated from one another and form a point of weakness, leaving the leaf-stalk attached to the twig only by a vein. By the weight of the leaf, or by the action of wind and frost, the vein is broken and the leaf falls. If this were the only process that had been taking place, the stem, of course, would be left with an open wound, which might soon be infected. A row of cells, however, underneath those at the base of the leaf-stalk, has been forming cork, and, by the time the leaf falls, this has spread right across the wound, sealing it off and leaving a healthy scar.

Leaf-fall, therefore, is an active process carried out by deciduous trees to get rid of structures which might otherwise cause them to loose too much water. Some experts say also that waste products are passed into the leaf before it falls, and that the tree uses this as one way of getting rid of waste matter formed during its life-processes. It is interesting to note that if a branch dies, or hangs broken from a tree, its leaves wither and curl up, but do not fall: this makes it still more evident that leaf-fall is a living process.

LEECH, *see* WORMS, Section 5.

LEMMING, *see* VOLES.

LEMUR. These are smallish, monkey-like animals, with pointed, fox-like faces, thick, woolly fur, and, as a rule, long, bushy tails. They belong to a sub-order of the Primates,

the highest order in the animal kingdom, to which belongs man himself; but they are less highly developed—in the brain, for instance— than APES and MONKEYS (qq.v.). Some species of Lemurs are found in south and central Africa, in southern Asia, and in the East Indies; but by far the majority belong to Madagascar, where they are very common indeed.

Lemurs live in trees, very rarely coming to the ground. Some species are active only during the night; but others start hunting for food at dusk, uttering loud cries which resound through the forest. They feed on fruit, leaves, birds' eggs or small birds, reptiles, and insects.

The Mouse Lemurs of Madagascar are the smallest of the family, some being no larger than a mouse. They have large eyes and ears, and hunt at night, stalking moths and beetles, and making long jumps from branch to branch. During the very dry, hot season, when food is scarce, they lie asleep in their nests in the hollows of tree-trunks, living on the great amount of fat which is stored in their tails.

The Galagos, popularly known as Bush Babies, are a group of small Lemurs living in tropical Africa. Some are as large as a rabbit, others as small as a dormouse. They are night-hunters, taking enormous leaps from one tree to another. They have huge, naked ears which are extremely sensitive, and which they can fold up close to their heads so that they are not injured when they are hunting through thick foliage or going to sleep in wet surroundings.

The Lorises of Asia, about the size of a

Paul Popper

SLENDER LORIS OF ASIA

Paul Popper

THE TARSIER OF THE EAST INDIES

A RING-TAILED AND A RED-FRONTED LEMUR

squirrel, have thick coats of very close, woolly fur, large round eyes, and either a short tail or no tail at all. They are unable to leap, but move about the forest trees slowly and deliberately, grasping the branches with their feet and hands. They are generally silent; but when angry, and especially when about to bite, they give a fierce growl.

The Aye-aye is a strange Lemur, about the size of a cat, which lives in the Madagascar forests. It differs from other Lemurs in having teeth like a RODENT (q.v.), which it uses, together with its peculiar, long middle finger, for digging out grubs from under the bark of trees or in decaying wood. Its large ears enable it to detect the grubs by listening. Since it has such strong teeth it can tear away the wood to reach its food.

The Tarsiers of the East Indies also belong to the Lemur group, though they are in some ways more like monkeys. They are especially interesting to zoologists, being regarded by some as the most closely related of all living animals to the stock from which man is descended. They are weird-looking creatures, about the size of a small rat, with enormous eyes, very long ankle-bones, and fingers and toes equipped with sucker-like disks which enable them to cling firmly to the branches of trees. Like OWLS (q.v.), they can turn their heads round to face backwards without moving their bodies. They hunt insects and small reptiles, and take enormous leaps from bough to bough among the trees.

The Colugos or Flying Lemurs are not now regarded as members of the Lemur family, but as a separate group of the order INSECTIVORA (q.v.). They are about the size of small cats, and have a very effective parachute made by a membrane of skin stretching between the neck and forelimbs and beyond to the hind legs and tail. When they stretch out their legs, this enables them to glide from one tree to another. One kind lives in the Philippines and another in the Malay States, Siam, and Borneo.

LEOPARD (Panther). Although not as powerful, these big cats are in many ways more dangerous than tigers, for they are easily provoked. They are found throughout southern Asia, Ceylon, Java, and Africa. In India they are usually called 'Panthers'. The average leopard is 1·2 metres long, with a tail nearly a metre; it stands 0·6 m at the shoulder, though some are much larger or much smaller. Their coat is usually a tawny-yellow, marked with black spots arranged in rosettes; but black leopards are common in the hills of southern India, Asia, and the Malay Peninsula. They are very active, agile beasts, able to make tremendous leaps and bounds and to climb trees with the ease of a monkey.

The leopards' favourite strongholds are on rocky, scrub-covered hills, from which they can watch the surrounding country. Keeping to the cover of the rocks, they descend at sunset to cut off stragglers from the herds and flocks returning to some neighbouring village. During the night they climb over walls and native huts, and raid goat-folds and calf-pens. They will eat any flesh, but bullocks are about the largest animal they can kill. They seize their prey by the throat, and cling with tenacious claws to its neck until they succeed in breaking its spine or, if the bones are too strong, in strangling their victim. They have a peculiar liking for dog-flesh, and leopards in hill-stations have on occasion swooped down in broad daylight and carried off

A LEOPARD

Harold Bastin

dogs from before their owners' eyes. There are very few man-eating leopards; but they frequently make attacks on children. There are usually from two to four cubs in a litter. Young leopards are generally more difficult to tame than young lions and tigers, and the adults are uncertain and morose in captivity.

The Snow Leopard or Ounce, which lives in the Himalayas, has long grey fur, marked with black rosettes. It is smaller and less powerful than the common leopard, and hunts comparatively small animals. As a rule it does not thrive in captivity, although it becomes very tame.

The Clouded Leopard of south-western Asia is greyish-brown, beautifully marked with darker blotches bordered with black. It is much smaller than the leopard, and has an exceptionally long tail. Most of its life is spent in the trees, where it preys on birds and tree-climbing animals.

See also Cats.

LEOPARD MOTHS, *see* Goat and Leopard Moths.

LEOPARD SNAKE, *see* Smooth Snake.

LEPIDOPTERA, *see* Butterflies; Moths.

LICHENS. These are unlike other plants in that they are 'compound' plants, being made up of cells of Algae and threads of Fungi (qq.v.) so closely interwoven that they form compact, and often beautiful, shapes, which differ according to the species. The algae provides food by Photosynthesis (q.v.), while the fungi absorb water vapour from the air and minute quantities of mineral salts from the rocks on which they grow. Lichens are found in all extremes of climate and at almost any altitude—in many places, in fact, where the algae and fungi would be unable to survive were they not living together in such close association.

Many lichens are edible. The kind known as 'reindeer moss' grows abundantly in the tundra lands of the Arctic, and, besides providing food for wild reindeer, is harvested as fodder for cattle. The manna which saved the children of Israel in the wilderness is reputed to have been an edible mountain lichen.

Dyes made from lichens were commonly used in ancient times and are still used in the dyeing of Harris Tweeds.

LILIES. True lilies are bulbous plants belonging to the flower family Liliaceae. A typical lily has its flower parts in threes or groups of three, with its sepals and petals alike, and usually coloured. It has six stamens and an ovary, which is raised above the other parts of the flower; and it carries its fruit either in a capsule or a berry (*see* Index, p. 69). Many plants, which do not have these characteristics, are incorrectly called 'lilies'. Neither Arum Lilies nor Water-Lilies, for instance, belong to this family; and it is almost certain that the New Testament 'lilies of the field', which surpassed 'Solomon in all his glory', were really red anemones, a common flower in Galilee in the springtime.

Lilies are popular as garden and hothouse plants (*see* Lilies, Vol. VI), but very few members of the lily family grow wild in Great Britain. The Bluebell is probably the most familiar; rarer species include the Bog Asphodel,

Fritillary, Meadow Saffron, Solomon's Seal, Grape Hyacinth, Yellow Gagea, and Herb Paris. The handsome Purple Martagon Lily has become naturalized in a number of counties (*see* Colour Plate, opp. p. 272).

The Bluebell produces a typical lily bulb; it also propagates by seeds—though it takes 3 years from the time of germination before the bulbs are large enough to develop flowering shoots. The leaves are characteristic of those plants which have only one cotyledon in the SEED (q.v.): they are long and narrow, pointed at the tips, with parallel veins, and sometimes reach a length of 45 centimetres. The bell-like, blue flowers grow in pendulous clusters, so that all the flowers seem to be hanging from one side of the flower-shoot.

The little Bog Asphodel grows on wet moors and in bogs, with thick underground stems and rigid, ribbed leaves ending in a sharp point. The star-like, golden-yellow flowers appear in June, July, and August, and although they are conspicuous they contain no nectar to attract insects and are frequently self-pollinated.

The Lily of the Valley grows wild in Britain, but it is not common. It is shade-loving and grows in woods, where it spreads by means of a thick, underground stem, each branch of which produces a few scales and one pair of foliage leaves each year. Thus a well-established plant, which has been spreading for some years, produces a mass of broad, lance-shaped leaves. The white flowers, appearing in May and June, are carried in clusters of six to twelve, and are frequently hidden behind the canopy of leaves. In structure, the flower is similar to the bluebell; but the fruit is a spherical red berry.

Solomon's Seal is sometimes found growing wild in woods. Its name comes from the fact that the annual shoots, when they die away, leave curious, seal-like markings on the thick underground stem. The leaves, oblong and pointed, grow alternately on arched stems, 60 to 90 cm long, and the groups of greenish-white flowers hang from the stem at intervals of about 30 cm. The fruit, a black berry, is rarely seen.

The Meadow Saffron resembles the Autumn Crocus and the ordinary cultivated Crocus (which belong to the Iris family and have only three stamens) in forming a similar underground storage organ or 'corm'. In the early summer, the corm of the Meadow Saffron produces smooth, lance-shaped, bright green leaves and

Paul Popper

GLORIOSA VIRESCENS A SCARLET AND YELLOW CLIMBING LILY WHICH GROWS WILD IN KENYA

Paul Popper

WHITE SPIDER LILY (*HYMENOCALLIS TUBIFLORA*)
Native to America

Paul Popper

A

Paul Popper

B

Paul Popper

C

Paul Popper

D

A. RAIN LILIES FROM TROPICAL AMERICA
B. TIGER LILIES FROM MEXICO
C. PYJAMA LILY FROM KENYA
D. BLOOD LILIES FOUND ALL OVER AFRICA

long-stalked egg-shaped fruits. These are followed in the autumn by a large, solitary, rosy-mauve flower, which forces it way through the soil above, remaining attached to the corm without an intervening stalk. Although comparatively rare in England, these Meadow Saffron flowers are sometimes found locally in meadows in purple masses. The leaves contain a chemical substance called colchicine, which is poisonous to animals and can cause damage to the cells of other plants.

Others of the less common British flowers belonging to the family of lilies are the white and yellow Star of Bethlehem, the Snakeshead or Fritillary, and the strong-smelling Garlic or Ramsons. One British member of this family,

the Butcher's-broom, which has flattened, leaf-like shoots, and grows in shady places in the south of England, is an evergreen shrub.

It is in tropical countries that wild lilies reach their real magnificence. The Tiger-lily of China and Japan, for example, has several varieties, one with orange, trumpet-shaped flowers, and another with scarlet flowers marked with black spots. The Golden-rayed Lily, also of Japan, bears large, white trumpets in bunches at the end of long leafy stems. Another beautiful flower is the Orange Lily, a native of several semi-tropical countries. This lily produces in the axils of its leaves tiny bulblets, from which the plant can reproduce itself. The Turk's-cap Lily of the eastern Mediterranean countries has vivid scarlet flowers; the Meadow Lily of the U.S.A. has brilliant yellow and orange flowers; *Lilium grayi*, also found in North America, has flowers which are deep crimson outside and yellow, blotched with purple, inside. Our garden tulips, of which there was once a wild British species, belong to the lily family. They are natives of north temperate regions, and are found wild in great profusion on the steppes of central Asia.

A few members of the lily family grow like trees, the most notable being the Dragon's-blood Tree of Mexico, so called because of the red resin it yields, and the Aloe of South Africa, which yields the purgative juice called aloes. Yucca or Adam's Needle, another Mexican tree-like lily, has a short, thickened stem crowned with a tuft of long, thick, sword-like leaves, and large, hanging, creamy, bell-shaped flowers, growing in a bunch on a stem which sometimes rises a metre or so above the tops of the leaves. This plant can be pollinated by one insect only, the night-flying Yucca Moth (q.v.).

A well-known member of the lily family is the Asparagus, quite a common wild plant in the drier, warmer parts of Europe and Asia. One wild variety is sometimes found in western England. The plant spreads by means of thick, creeping, underground stems, which send up the erect shoots used as a vegetable.

The Aspidistra is also a member of the lily family, hailing from eastern Asia. It rarely blooms under cultivation, and, when it does, the flower grows so close to the ground and is so insignificant, that it is often overlooked.

LIMPET. The familiar conical shell of the Common Limpet varies a good deal in colour and ruggedness with the age of the animal: old shells usually have a more rounded contour and a less roughened surface, while the colour may be greyish, olive-green, or yellow, obscurely marked with narrow rays of dark grey or chocolate-brown.

Limpets adhere strongly to rocks by a strong muscular foot. When seen from the underside, this foot is a central, almost circular, structure. In front of the foot can be seen a distinct head, with a small mouth and two small, horn-like tentacles, each with an eye at its base; while around the whole of the body is the edge of the pale coloured mantle, and between the mantle and the foot a frill of gill-plates. The Limpet's most remarkable organ is its long 'radula' or

tongue, which is armed with row upon row of minute teeth, estimated to number 1,920 or more. By means of this rasp-like tongue, the Limpet scrapes from the surface of the rocks the delicate seaweeds upon which it feeds. Some South African Limpets have their own 'gardens' of seaweed growing on the shell and around them. The Limpet has a remarkable homing instinct, and after its excursions in search of food it returns regularly to its own particular resting-place on the rock. This home-spot is a shallow depression which the Limpet has worn in the surface of the rock, and into which the margin of its shell exactly fits. A perfect fit is of prime importance, for any space between the rock and the base of the shell would render impossible that firm grip upon which the animal's safety depends. No two Limpet shells are so exactly alike that they would fit into the same depression.

The several British varieties of the Common Limpet differ chiefly in size, shape, or colour, and are now regarded not as different species but rather as interesting examples of adaptation to local conditions. Large quantities of Limpets are used as bait in line-fishing, and they used to be a popular food.

Limpets are closely related to the Ormer (*Haliotis*), a Mollusc that many people regard as a great delicacy to eat. It lives very low down on the shore, lower than most other Limpets, and occurs as far north as the Channel Islands. The mantle has a slit which runs to the top of the rather flat shell where it opens through a row of holes. These serve for the escape of water. The closely related Keyhole Limpet is so called because of the single hole in the apex of the shell.

See also Molluscs.

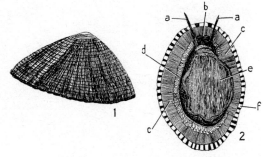

LIMPET: I. SIDE VIEW; 2. UNDER SURFACE
(*a*) Tentacles; (*b*) Mouth; (*c*) Mantle; (*d*) Gills; (*e*) Foot; (*f*) Shell edge

LING, *see* COD.

LINNET, *see* FINCHES, Section 6.

LIONS. Lions are the largest of the great CATS (q.v.). They are found today in many parts of Africa south of the Sahara, but have practically disappeared from Asia. In India, they are now found only in one large game reserve in Gujerat. The various forms of the African lion differ to some extent in size and appearance: the Somali race is particularly small, and the Senegal lions grow practically no mane; while the now extinct lions of the Cape and Algeria grew particularly fine manes. Indian lions, generally, do not have such fine manes as the African lions.

African lions live in nearly all districts where there are large numbers of their natural prey— antelopes, zebras, and wild swine. Like most of the large cats, they hunt at night, lying asleep during the day in thick beds of reeds or among thickets and bushes in dry districts. Their colouring blends extraordinarily well with their surroundings. At sundown they begin their nightly prowl, being most active on dark and stormy nights, and very cautious in bright moonlight, especially when going to their drinking-place. As a rule, they begin to roar at nightfall and continue all through the night, reaching a climax when several troops approach the watering-place at the same time, and roar defiance at each other. The vibrating sound of the roar is often intensified by the habit they have of putting their mouths close to the ground.

African lions may be met alone or in pairs; but they very often, especially in the interior, hunt in companies numbering anything from four to twelve. They frequently join company in order to attack large animals, such as buffaloes, which would be difficult to overcome single-handed. Unlike TIGERS (q.v.), which always kill large prey by dislocating their necks, lions seem to have many methods of attack. They have been seen to kill antelopes by biting their throats, and horses and zebras by a bite on the back of the neck. It is said that a lion sometimes breaks the neck of a buffalo by springing on its shoulder, seizing its nose with one paw, and giving the neck a sudden wrench. No matter how plentiful game may be, lions will almost always feed on any dead animal left by a hunter. They frequently eat carcasses in a very advanced state of decomposition, although it would be little trouble to make a fresh kill.

Paul Popper

LIONESSES AND CUBS IN THE KAFUE NATIONAL PARK, NORTHERN RHODESIA, MAKING A MEAL OF A ZEBRA CARCASS

When lions get old and feeble, and less successful in the chase, they will eat any small animal they can catch, and even grass. Such beasts often become a menace to farmers, attacking domestic animals and frequently becoming man-eaters. In many districts, if a man is killed, the whole neighbouring population is roused and hunting parties immediately go out. Even if the lion escapes, it is so scared that it quickly leaves the district. Young lions, and particularly lionesses with cubs, will also become man-eaters if food is very scarce. Any lion if roused is a formidable foe, and a wounded animal is especially dangerous. The lion will conceal itself amazingly well in the long grass or thick cover, and will then rush upon its pursuer with lightning speed, uttering a coughing roar. Many a sportsman has taken refuge in a tree—for the lion, unlike other cats, does not normally climb. He will wait below the tree, however, ready to pounce should his prey try to descend or fall from exhaustion.

When a male lion has selected his mate, they stay together for most, if not all, of their lives. Wild lionesses never have litters of more than two or three cubs, but in captivity there may be up to six. The lioness is a very devoted mother. She guards her cubs carefully while they are still helpless, hiding them when she goes out to hunt for food. She will brave any danger to satisfy their hunger. When they get a little older, she brings back small live animals, and with these she begins to teach them to hunt for themselves. The young lion cubs are marked with dark stripes and faint spots. Their mane begins to grow at the age of 3, and stops growing when they are 6 years old. Lions in captivity often live to be 20 years old. If caught young, they are easily tamed, and are much more reliable in captivity than tigers.

See also Vol. VI: BIG-GAME HUNTING.

LIVER FLUKES, *see* Vol. VI: PARASITIC WORMS.

LIVERWORTS, *see* MOSSES AND LIVERWORTS.

LIZARDS (Sauria or Lacertilia). These are reptiles of the same order as SNAKES (q.v.), from which they differ in having four well-developed limbs, eyes with movable eyelids, and a broad fleshy tongue. This short list of differences will cover the vast majority of lizards; but there are many exceptions. Some, like the SLOW-WORM (q.v.), have lost their limbs and have acquired an elongated body; others, like the GECKOS (q.v.) and certain of the Skinks, are without eye-lids; and the MONITORS (q.v.) have a snake-like tongue. In their bodily structure the lizards show enormous variation. The CHAMELEONS (q.v.), and the Flying Lizards, each in their own particular way, are built for living in trees; many of the Skinks have lost their limbs and live a subterranean life; the Geckos have developed adhesive pads to their digits, with which they can climb trees and the walls of houses; and the Sea Lizards of the Galapagos Islands live on rocky shores, feeding on sea-weeds, and dashing into the waves in time of danger.

The skin of lizards is normally covered with scales, the outer layer of which is shed periodically. It usually comes off in flakes; but in those species which have a greatly elongated body it may be shed in one piece, as with snakes. In some families there are small, bony plates in the skin. Most lizards lay eggs; but some produce their young alive. The egg-shell of the Geckos contains lime and is brittle; of other lizards it is parchment-like, as in snakes' eggs. The tail may or may not be fragile; a broken tail is always regrown, but can usually be recognized by its stumpier appearance. Young lizards are usually more brilliantly coloured than their parents, and sometimes their colour-pattern is so different that they have been regarded as different species. The brilliant colours which the IGUANAS and AGAMAS (qq.v.) develop in the breeding season are of quite a different nature: they are dependent upon stimuli of various kinds, and in moments of intense excitement may sweep over the creature like a wave. The sight of an enemy— for in the breeding season many lizards fight for their own particular territory—may produce quite as brilliant a colouring as the sight of a mate (*see* ANIMAL TERRITORY). These colours are always most vivid in the males.

Some 2,500 species of lizards are known. They are divided into many families, the best-known of which, apart from the Lacertids or typical lizards, are the Geckos, the Agamas, the Iguanas, the Chameleons, and the Monitors (all of which are described in separate articles). Another important family are the Skinks— rather small, harmless lizards, of which some

S. C. Bisserôt

A SAND LIZARD

600 species are known, distributed over the tropical and sub-tropical regions of the world. The majority of these are ground lizards, common in the compounds and cultivated areas of the tropics; but a few species live in trees, and some live underground, having lost their limbs and developed long, snake-like bodies.

Two species of lizard are found in England: the Viviparous or Common Lizard, and the Sand Lizard. The Viviparous Lizard is common all over the British Isles and Europe. It lives on heaths and commons, in wooded areas, and in hedgerows. In colour it is variable, being brownish, greyish, or reddish above, with lighter or darker spots, and sometimes with dark lines down the back and sides. The underparts of the male are orange or red with black spots, in the female yellower and with the spots less distinctly marked. It grows to 15 cm in length, of which the tail forms one-half. As its name implies, its young, from six to twelve in number, are born alive. When born, they are enclosed in a more or less transparent membrane, which they break through at once. The Viviparous Lizard is one of the hardiest of reptiles: in Europe, it ranges farther north and at greater altitudes than any other species, having been found in latitude 63 N. in Russia, and in the Alps at a height of 3,000 metres.

The Sand Lizard is not uncommon in the heather country of Hampshire, Dorset, and Surrey, and is found also in the sandy parts of Lancashire, border-ing the sea. It is bigger than the Viviparous Lizard, reaching 20 cm in length, of which the tail forms nearly one-half. Its upper parts are greenish or greyish in colour, with rows of black and white-eyed spots along the sides of its back and tail. In the breeding season, the male takes on a brilliant green hue, when it is sometimes mistaken for the Green Lizard (not found in the wild state in Great Britain except in Jersey). The Sand Lizard does well in captivity, and if properly looked after and given the right place in which to hibernate, will live for several years. It quickly becomes tame and learns to feed from the hand. Mating takes place in May and June, and the eggs, five to eight in number, are hatched in July and August. The Sand Lizard is found all over Europe and in western Asia.

The common Green Lizard of Europe is one of the largest of the European species, the male being about 40 or 43 centimetres long, of which about one-half is the tail. It is most common in countries on the eastern and northern shores of the Mediterranean. It is bright green above (with or without black specks), greenish-yellow on the flanks, and yellow on the belly. In the breeding season, the throat of the male is blue. The young are marked above with one or two longitudinal yellowish stripes. This beautiful lizard is often kept in captivity in England; but although it feeds well, it does not usually live long. Attempts have been made to get it to live in a wild state in North Wales and the Isle of Wight; but after some years the colonies have always disappeared. Closely allied to the Green Lizard is the Eyed Lizard, an inhabitant of western Europe. It differs in colour, for the sides of the body are adorned with some two dozen blue, black-edged spots or 'eyes', the intensity of the blue and of the green of its body varying with the sex and with the time of year.

A FLYING LIZARD

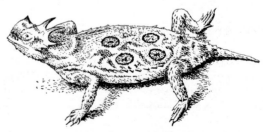

HORNED TOAD, A MEXICAN LIZARD

It is a voracious creature, and will devour other lizards, or even snakes and mice.

Another Lacertid lizard, the commonest of all the lizards in southern Europe and the islands of the Mediterranean, is the Wall Lizard, a small creature, not more than 18 cm in length. The upper parts of its body are brown or grey, sometimes with a bronzy sheen, and with black spots and streaks that vary greatly in size, intensity, and arrangement. Each particular region, sometimes each island, has its own special form, its main interest to naturalists being the great number of races and sub-species which can be recognized. No other lizard in Europe is so variable.

Some lizards (of the genus *Draco*) are known as Flying Lizards, because they can glide from one tree to another by means of a wing-like, membranous expansion from the side of the body, supported on extensions on the ribs. The distance travelled depends upon the height from which they have started; but they have been seen to cover between 36 to 45 metres. They live entirely among trees, and for that reason are not often seen, although in some places in the East they are common. When they are resting or climbing about in search of food, their wing-membrane is folded back along the sides of the body and is hardly visible. In many species it is beautifully coloured with red or yellow, and barred or spotted with black. The throat of the male has a membranous pouch (the female also has one, but much smaller) and in courtship this is often blown out like a paper bag. Some forty species of *Draco* are known. They are found mainly in Indo-China and Malaya; but one species inhabits India.

The only poisonous lizard known is the Gila Monster, which is a native of Mexico and the neighbouring countries, and lives in the desert. It is a thick, heavily-built creature, nearly 60 cm long, with a bulbous tail. It is barred and mottled with dark brown, pink, and orange. Its poison gland is in the lower jaw, and this

Paul Popper

THE BEARDED LIZARD OF SOUTHERN AUSTRALIA

carries a venom powerful enough to produce severe symptoms in man—though death from the bite is very rare. When in captivity, which it stands well, it is very fond of eggs.

Certain lizards of North America, called Horned Toads, have the remarkable habit, when caught, of spurting little jets of blood from the eyes. The blood, which comes from the veins of the eyelids, and is ejected by a sudden contraction of the muscles covering them, can be thrown for a distance of 38 cm, often several times in succession. Horned Toads are about 12 or 13 cm long, the head, back, and tail being covered with horny spines. They live mainly in sandy regions.

Among the burrowing lizards is the Amphisbaena family, which includes some 70 species of degenerate, worm-like creatures, inhabiting northern and central Africa and tropical America. Most of them live in burrows, but some inhabit ant-holes. In form and structure they are well adapted for underground life: their eyes are concealed under the skin; they have small mouths, no ears, and, except for one species, no limbs; their skins are covered with squared plates arranged in regular rings; and their tails are short. They can move both backwards and forwards (their name, from the Greek, means one who can go in either direction). They feed on small insects and worms.

The Basilisk is a harmless lizard of tropical America, distinguished by a pointed casque on the back of its head, and a high crest of skin along its back to the base of the tail. It lives in trees, generally near water, into which it

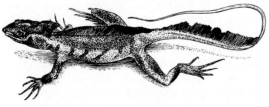

A BASILISK LIZARD

plunges when frightened. It feeds mainly on leaves, fruit, and flowers. The fabulous basilisk of the ancients was a reptile with a withering gaze, hatched by a serpent from a cock's egg (*see* FABULOUS CREATURES, Vol. I).

LLAMA. These animals, inhabitants of South America only, are RUMINANTS (q.v.), or chewers of the cud. They are related to the CAMEL (q.v.), but are far smaller and lighter in build, and have no humps. Llamas are found only in captivity, their domestication dating back to very early times, when the ancient Peruvians used them not only for transport, but also for their wool, milk, and flesh. They have very thick, woolly coats. Like camels, they have an expression of supercilious aloofness and calm contempt. They are extremely sure-footed, and their soft, padded, almost claw-like toes seem to adhere like suckers to the rocks. It is a common sight to see a herd of Llamas grazing on the precipitous side of a mountain so steep that the native Indians can hardly find a foothold. They are most useful transport animals, able to carry loads in high altitudes, in extreme cold, but they are not very strong, and will refuse to carry a load too heavy for them. (*See* BEASTS OF BURDEN, Vol. IV.)

The Alpaca—the other domestic member of the Llama family—is smaller than the Llama, and is specially bred for its wool, which is very fine and long, sometimes reaching almost to the ground. Alpacas are kept in herds on the high plateaux of Bolivia and southern Peru, and are driven down to the villages only once a year, at the shearing season. The flesh both of the Llama and the Alpaca is excellent to eat.

There are two wild relatives of the Llama: the Vicuña, and the larger Huanaco (or Guanaco), from which both the domestic Llama and the Alpaca are believed to be descended. The Huanaco is swift of foot, but not nearly so fast as the lightning-like Vicuña. Herds of these wild Llamas, sometimes numbering several hundred, live on the arid deserts, high plateaux, and mountain defiles of the Andes, and feed on the sparse vegetation. They have the curious habit of spitting at any intruder who goes near them. The Vicuñas can often be seen at play, racing around in circles, playing leap-frog, and even turning somersaults; but at the first sign of danger, they vanish in a cloud of dust. Strangely enough, nothing will induce them to cross, leap over, or push through a barrier, no matter how flimsy it may be. The Vicuña fawns are born singly in February, and from the beginning are remarkably swift and strong. Young males remain with their flock until they are full grown, when they are expelled by the dams. They then band themselves together in groups of twenty to thirty. Incessant fights take place between these male flocks in the mating season, when they utter a peculiar neighing sound which can be heard from a very long distance. The victorious males become leaders of flocks numbering from six to fifteen females. The male always remains a few paces behind his flock. If he sees danger, he utters a shrill warning whistle, whereupon the flock collects, and gallops off swiftly, with the male at the rear, stopping now and then to observe the foe.

LOBSTER. The Common Lobster is a CRUSTACEAN (q.v.), living in the shallow off-shore waters all round the coasts of Britain and western Europe. It shelters in crevices in the rocks, crawling forth at night in search of food, and, when alarmed, shooting swiftly backwards through the water by powerful strokes of its broad tail-fan. The two great claws differ in size and shape, the larger having the blades armed with blunt knobs for crushing, while the smaller has saw-edged blades for holding and

Zoological Society of London

ALPACA

tearing its prey. When alive, the Lobster is dark blue or nearly black on the back, with a good deal of red or orange on the underside of the body and limb-joints. The female Lobster produces immense numbers of eggs, which are attached to limbs, called 'swimmerets', on the under surface of her body, and are carried in that position during the whole period of incubation—some ten months. The young, on escaping

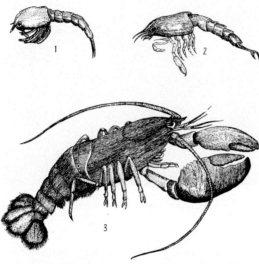

THREE STAGES IN GROWTH OF THE LOBSTER
(1) Early larval stage; (2) Late larval stage; (3) Adult

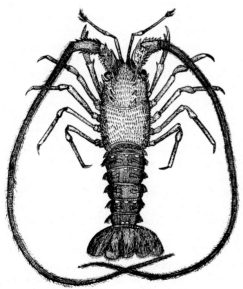

CRAWFISH OR SPINY ROCK LOBSTER

from the eggs, are transparent, quite unlike their parents in appearance, and can swim actively in the surface waters of the sea by means of the swimming-branches attached to their legs. They pass through three larval stages and moult many times before they are adult. Lobsters, like most of the larger Crustaceans, readily throw off a limb that is grasped by a foe or injured in the course of a fight. The relinquished limb parts company at a special fracture-point near the base, and later is replaced by a new one, which, after a series of moults, may attain almost the size of the original.

Closely related to the Common Lobster is the so-called Dublin Prawn or Norway Lobster, now chiefly caught in the North Sea. It is much smaller than the Common Lobster, from which it is easily distinguished by its long, slender claws, kidney-shaped eyes, and, when alive, by its beautiful orange colour marked with red and white. The little Freshwater Crayfish is closely related to the Lobster, but does not pass through a free-swimming larval stage; the young Crayfish hatches from the egg in a form differing very little from that of the adult, and remains clinging to its mother's swimmerets until sufficiently developed to fend for itself. In general appearance the Freshwater Crayfish resembles a lobster in miniature, measuring some 7 to 10 centimetres long, and is usually of a brownish-green or olive colour. It digs holes in the earth, or hides in crevices in rocks along the edge of streams, and appears to be more active at night, when it goes out in search of food.

The large Spiny Rock Lobster or Crawfish is easily distinguished from the Common Lobster by its spiny carapace or upper shell, by the antennae (the second pair being stout and stiff, and the first pair having very thick basal joints), and by the total absence of the great claws. The pincer-claw of the lobster is replaced by a single short hooked claw, working against a knob or blunt spine—an arrangement very like that of the SHRIMP (q.v.). The larvae of the Spiny Rock Lobster have oval, flattened bodies, and are almost transparent—being popularly known as glass-crabs. They have long spidery legs, and large black eyes mounted on stalks. Crawfish live in rock clefts in offshore water and are almost world-wide.

See also Vol. VI: CRAB AND LOBSTER FISHING.

LOBSTER MOTH, *see* PROMINENT MOTHS.

LOCUSTS, *see* GRASSHOPPER; MIGRATION; *see also* Vol. VI: LOCUSTS.

LONG-HORN MOTHS. Over 200 species are known of these small, often brilliant, metallic, day-flying moths belonging to the family Adelidae, fourteen occurring in Britain. They are conspicuous for their extremely long, thread-like antennae, which in males are sometimes four times the length of the body. The males of some species also have enlarged eyes. The Green Long-horn, one of the commonest British woodland species, is a beautiful coppery-green moth, with a wing-span of nearly 1·5 cm. On sunny days in May and June, the males, in swarms of twenty to thirty, dance above the leafy branch of an oak some distance from the ground, resting at intervals, and then resuming the dance. The females sit about on neighbouring leaves and enter the swarms to mate. The eggs are laid in the midribs of leaves, and the caterpillars of most species mine in the leaves or flower-heads, and then make flattish cases from leaf fragments attached to fallen leaves. British species occur on Black Hore-hound, Scabious, Privet, Lady's-smock, Germander Speedwell, and other plants.

S. Beaufoy

LARGE THORN MOTH CATERPILLARS RESEMBLING TWIGS OF AN OAK SPRAY

LOOPERS. These caterpillars, of which there are some 3,000 species in the northern regions of the Old World, lack abdominal legs, except on the 6th and 10th abdominal segments (*see* CATERPILLAR, Fig. 1 B). They walk by gripping an object with their front legs, arching their bodies to bring up their hind legs, and then holding on with these, extending themselves to the fullest extent to obtain a new grip with the front legs. The scientific name of the family of moths, Geometridae, to which they belong, and the common American names, 'measuring worms' or 'span-worms', refer to this habit of matching their length against the ground. The slender, hairless caterpillars often resemble brown or green twigs, and not only have rough processes suggesting buds or leaf scars, but assist this deception by resting on real twigs, which they grip with the hind legs, while their bodies, sometimes supported by a silken thread, are held out rigidly at an angle (*see* CAMOUFLAGE).

Geometrid moths have slender bodies and relatively large wings. They have conspicuous openings in the sides of the first abdominal segment, which leads to well-developed, sound-detecting organs, to be compared with the ears of vertebrates. Most of them fly by night, but they will take to the wing in daylight when disturbed. Most species rest with the wings flat on either side of the body; but occasionally the wings stand erect, as in butterflies, or slope roofwise. Many rest by day on tree-trunks, where their general resemblance to lichen-covered bark is enhanced by their habit of resting so that they cast no shadow, and so that the dark lines on their wings fit in with the vertical cracks in the bark. Some kinds of Carpet Moths seek safety by resembling bird-droppings, and Thorn Moths resemble dead leaves. A few, such as the Magpie Moth, have bold warning colours, in this instance, white with black and yellow spots (*see* PROTECTIVE COLORATION).

Several Geometrid Moths have names reminiscent of butterflies—for instance, the pale-yellow Swallow-tailed Moth, with a wing-expanse of 4·5 to 5·5 cm, and with a caterpillar which feeds on ivy; the smaller, bright-yellow Brimstone Moth, common in hawthorn hedges; and the still smaller and local, brownish-white Peacock Moth. The Yellow Shell, with its many

S. *Beaufoy*

A WAVED UMBER CATERPILLAR IN TYPICAL LOOPING
POSITION

narrow brown markings, is one of the commonest
summer moths among bushes and hedgerows.
The robust Peppered Moth is light coloured,
speckled with black; but recently it has been
completely replaced in the smoky industrial
areas of northern England by a black variety—
less conspicuous in these sooty surroundings.
The Emeralds are delicate shades of green, a
rare colour in butterflies and moths. The caterpillar of the Essex Emerald achieves camouflage
by covering itself with pieces of its food-plant,
the sea wormwood. There are many species of
Waves, whitish, yellowish, or brownish moths,
with darker, wave-like patterns crossing the
wings. The Pugs, easily recognized by their
small size and long, rounded forewings, are
brownish, greyish, or greenish. The Seraphims
have glandular flaps on the hind-wings, suggesting an extra pair of wings. Though the male
Winter Moth is on the wing from October to
February, often to be seen in the beams of car
head-lamps, the almost wingless female is unable
to fly, but climbs the trunks of trees to lay her
bright green eggs singly on buds and spurs or
in cracks in the bark, where they soon turn
brick red. The green-striped caterpillars hatch

out in March and April, and start to feed on
the opening buds, doing much damage to fruit
trees. Other fruit pests with wingless females
are the March Moth, Mottled Umber, and the
Early Moth. The Vestal, a small, pale-yellow
moth, with a pink or brown stripe on the fore-
wings, is ordinarily only an occasional visitor
to Britain from the Mediterranean region; but
in 1947 it reached the south coast in great
numbers, and successfully bred there.

See also MOTHS.

LOUSE. Lice are insects and are external parasites on birds and mammals. They have very
powerful claws, by which they cling tightly to
feathers or hair. Some lice are eyeless, but others
have well-developed compound eyes. All are
wingless, and have very short antennae. There
are two groups, Biting Lice (*Mallophaga*) and
Sucking Lice (*Anoplura*), both of which have
small, flat bodies. Biting Lice, of which we know
about 2,000 species, over 500 of which occur in
Britain, use their mouthparts for chewing, and
feed on feathers, hair, and similar dry material.
As they are much more often found on birds
than mammals, they are often called Bird Lice.
All birds seem to be affected by these lice, and
the habit birds have of taking dust baths is
probably for the purpose of ridding themselves
of them. Pigeons are almost always infested
with a very slender louse, which looks to the
naked eye like a dark line on
the feather. It clings so tightly
to the feathers that it is very
difficult to remove without tearing off the claws. Sucking Lice,
which puncture the skin and
suck the blood flowing from the
wound, are found only on mammals. There are about 35
species in Britain, and some 250
species altogether have been
identified. Two species are
found on man, about a dozen
on his domestic animals, and
the remainder have been found
on wild mammals.

Lice have an incomplete
METAMORPHOSIS (q.v.), the immature insects being like their
parent, except in size. The eggs
are called 'nits'. The female of
the Human Louse is able to lay

SUCKING LOUSE
× 15

BITING LOUSE
× 10

some 300 eggs in the course of a month. Those of Biting Lice are cemented to the feather, and soon hatch out. There are several moults during growth, which lasts 5 weeks. The whole life of the insect is spent upon the warm-blooded animal it parasitizes, and it soon dies if removed.

NITS ON PIG BRISTLE
Magnified

Infection of one animal from another takes place very easily by contact. Lice of any particular species confine themselves to one particular species of animal, and will not remove themselves to another species. But this does not mean that one animal can be attacked by only one species of Louse: ducks, for example, are attacked by several different kinds of Biting Louse, and there are two different species to be found on the dog.

See also INSECTS.
See also Vol. VI: INSECT PESTS.
See also Vol. XI: HOUSEHOLD PESTS.

LUMPSUCKER. Known also as the Sea-hen, this rather curious-looking fish of the North Atlantic is quite common on some parts of the British coast. The pelvic fins form a sucking disk beneath the body, by which the fish attaches itself firmly to rocks. (*See* GOBY.) The eggs are laid in spring, between tide-marks on the shore, in great masses averaging 100,000. The male, which is smaller and more brightly coloured than the female, guards the eggs faithfully, fanning them with his large pectoral fins to aerate them. Both fish and eggs are likely to fall prey to numerous enemies, for when the

A LUMPSUCKER DEFIES THE SWIRL OF THE TIDE BY ATTACHING
ITSELF TO A ROCK

tide is out, they are exposed to attacks from sea-gulls, rooks, and rats, and when they are under water various other fishes feed on them. Nevertheless, the male will suffer death rather than leave his eggs. The Lumpsuckers grow to a length of about 45 centimetres. They are not much used for food.

LUNG-FISH. The three living species of Lung-fish are the only survivors of a group of fishes that were numerous in an earlier period of the world's history, and are believed to have been the near ancestors of the Amphibia (Frogs,

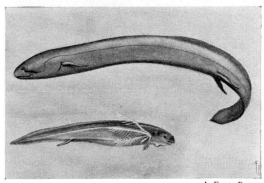

A. Fraser-Brunner

THE SOUTH AMERICAN LUNG-FISH AND ITS TADPOLE-LIKE
LARVA

Newts, and Salamanders). The air-bladder in these fishes is connected to the back of the mouth cavity below, and is used in the same way as the lungs of higher animals. Breathing was probably the original function of the air-bladder in the early fishes, but in the later bony fish it has lost this use, and often also its connexion with the mouth cavity. The Lung-fish also have paired fins of a peculiar kind, which are borne on a fleshy lobe supported by bones in some respects similar to the leg-bones of higher vertebrates.

One species of Lung-fish valued as food is found in Queensland, Australia, where it is known as the Barramunda. Since its flesh is pink, it is often referred to as 'salmon'. It comes to the surface of the water to take air into its (single) lung, and when the used air is forced out through the gullet it produces a loud grunting noise that can be heard for some distance. The Barramunda is a large, clumsy-looking fish, with big scales.

The two other living species of Lung-fish

come one from tropical Africa and the other from South America, and in some ways look remarkably like SALAMANDERS (q.v.). Young ones have large, feathery, external gills, like those of tadpoles, which shrink as the animal grows up. The adult, therefore, has small gills, which are not sufficient to meet its needs, so that it has to breathe air by means of its lungs. These fishes are sluggish, moving slowly about at the bottom of swamps, using their paired fins like legs, to climb among the roots of vegetation. They burrow a great deal, their shape being well adapted for this. During the rainy season, when food is abundant, they feed heartily; but when the dry season comes, and the water begins to dry up, they burrow into the soft mud to await the return of the rains. Presently, the mud dries up quite hard, and the fish is then in a sort of earthenware cocoon. Fossils of such cocoons have been found in America many millions of years old. The cocoons are often used as food—and lung-fishes have been sent long distances in this condition, afterwards to be liberated in water and exhibited in aquariums. Lung-fishes lay their eggs in underground burrows, the male remaining in the 'nest' to guard the eggs and aerate them.

See also COELACANTH.

LYNX, *see* CATS.

LYRE-BIRD. This Australian bird, slaty-brown in colour and nearly as large as a pheasant, is conspicuous for the development of the tail-feathers of the cock. These rise in a spectacular fan over the bird's back, the middle pair of feathers being narrow and curved, and the outer pair very broad, banded with chestnut, and shaped like the sides of a lyre. The inner plumes are lighter in colour, and very fine and hair-like. Lyre-birds have long legs and large, strong feet, well adapted for scratching up the grubs on which they feed. In the forests of south-eastern Australia these birds used to be common; but the clearing of the forests, bush fires, and the depredations of foxes, who attack the nests, have reduced their numbers considerably.

Lyre-birds carry out a remarkable courtship display in the mating season. The cock-bird makes a mound in the forest; and there, throwing his wonderful tail forward over his head, he sings vigorously and performs a display dance.

Australian News & Information Bureau
LYRE-BIRD OF AUSTRALIA DISPLAYING HIS MAGNIFICENT TAIL

The Lyre-bird is a fine songster with rich and powerful notes. Young birds do not sing until they have grown their full tails—which is not, apparently, until they are 4 years old. Both cocks and hens are remarkable mimics of other birds' songs, their power of mimicry being greater, perhaps, than that of any other bird. During the mating season each cock has his own territory, and rarely infringes on that of another bird (*see* ANIMAL TERRITORY). He is accompanied by two or three females—though it seems likely that only one hen in each party lays in one year. The nest, placed on the ground, is made of small sticks interwoven with moss and roots; it is roofed over, the entrance being at the side. Only one egg is laid, a dark, blotched purple. The birds often build on the outskirts of a dense covert, where the nest can be clearly seen from the road. The birds themselves can also be seen roosting high up, generally in a gum-tree.

See also Colour Plate opp. p. 16.
See also ANIMAL LANGUAGE.

M

MACAW, *see* PARROT.

MACKEREL. Among the loveliest fishes that swim in the oceans are the Mackerels (Scombridae). They are beautifully streamlined, with a widely forked caudal (tail) fin, and many are handsomely coloured. The rich, oily flesh of most of the species is excellent food.

The common Mackerel has a glittering green back with black cross-stripes; the two dorsal fins, the first with slender spines, are set far apart; and above and below the tail is a row of little extra fins. Mackerel run in vast shoals, feeding, as they swim at great speed through the surface water, on small crustaceans and other animals of the 'plankton' or floating ocean life. Spawning takes place not far from land, each female laying about half a million eggs per year. These are minute, and each is provided with an oil globule, which enables it to float for a time. Schools of Mackerel 32 kilometres long and 800 metres wide have been seen off the American coast, where the Mackerel is more numerous than in European waters—the American fishery for them being enormous (*see* FISHING METHODS, Section 1 *c*, Vol. VI).

The true Mackerels (there are other species in the East Indian and Australian regions) are quite small, rarely more than 30 cm in length; but some of their relatives are much larger. The so-called Spanish Mackerel of American coasts, for instance, grows to 5 kg or more in weight, and is much sought after by anglers, to whom it affords great sport and good food. The Seer of India, one of the most esteemed food-fishes of that country, grows to a length of over a metre.

The giants of the family, however, are the Tunnies, or Tuna, which have a band or 'corselet' of large scales round the shoulders, but are otherwise very much like overgrown Mackerel. Some of these grow to over 2 metres in length, and may weigh 400 kilograms. The Atlantic Tunny, though a fish of the warm seas, follows the Gulf Stream from America in summer to feed on herring in the North Sea, where it has been caught by anglers off Denmark and the English coast. Others are said to reach Cornwall from the Mediterranean. The blood of Tunnies is generally warmer than that of other fishes, and the flesh is red in colour. There is a regular fishery for them in the Mediterranean, where the flesh is canned as 'Thon rouge'.

Similar to the Tunny, but not so large, and with longer pectoral fins and white flesh, are the Albacores, which are also canned, under the name 'Thon blanc'. Smaller still are the Bonito, which are usually about 4·5 kg in weight. These beautiful fish move in immense schools at great speed—they are said to be the swiftest of all fishes. They are the 'tuna' of the canning industries in America and Japan (*see* BONITO FISHING, Vol. VI).

Nearly related to the Mackerel family are two families of giant fishes, which have the upper jaw prolonged into a sword or 'rostrum': the Swordfishes, and the Spearfishes and Sailfishes. The most famous of these is the Swordfish, which has a flattened rostrum and no pelvic fins. It has a habit of attacking things larger than itself, such as big sharks, whales, and ships—for what purpose is not understood. There are many records of its sword having been driven right through the side of a wooden boat. It is much sought after by anglers, especially round New Zealand, and when hooked it takes great leaps from the water (*see* BIG-GAME FISHING, Vol. IX). Much the same may be said of the Spearfishes and Sailfishes which have a rounded rostrum

A. Fraser-Brunner

THE COMMON MACKEREL

A. Fraser-Brunner

SWORDFISH

and possess pelvic fins. The Sailfish gets its name from the high, sail-like dorsal fin, the use of which is not known.

Finally, mention should be made of another family, the Gempylidae, the members of which although related to the Mackerel do not look at all similar. These are long, flattened fishes, with large mouths full of very strong teeth, a fin along the whole length of the back, and the tail ending in a fine point. These are all voracious fishes living near the shore. They include the Cutlass-fish, which can grow up to 1–5 metres in length, and the Snoek, an important food-fish in southern seas.

MAGPIE, *see* CROW, Section 7.

MAGPIE MOTH, *see* LOOPERS.

MALLARD, *see* DUCK, Section 2.

MAMBA. This poisonous snake of southern and central Africa is greatly feared on account of its vindictive nature and deadly bite. The common belief that there are two species, a black and a green mamba, is not correct: they are colour phases of the same species, and many specimens that are green when young turn darker with age. The Mamba grows to about 2 metres long. It is without doubt the fastest snake we know of: there is good evidence to show that on suitable ground it can travel at perhaps 32 km/h, and can keep it up for 90 metres or so. The fastest snakes in America are called the Racers, but experiments with them have shown that they do not travel more than 10 kilometres an hour.

See also SNAKES.

MAMMALS. The Subphylum of Vertebrate animals is divided into seven classes, of which the mammals are the most highly developed. The term 'mammal' was introduced by LINNAEUS (q.v. Vol. V), and means an animal which has 'mammae', or milk-secreting organs, for suckling its young. Mammals first arose during the Age of Reptiles—as did Birds, which are also descended from Reptiles. Man, the most highly organized of all animals, is a mammal (*see* EVOLUTION CHART, opp. p. 1).

The two main characteristics are the growth of hair and the secretion of milk. The purpose of HAIR, as of FEATHERS (qq.v.), is to keep up a constant body-temperature in the varying conditions of a mammal's environment. The velvety fur of a mole, the wool of a sheep, the spines of a hedgehog, or the bristles of a pig are all forms of hair. All mammals carry some hair, though Whales and Hippopotami have very little. Milk is the ideal food for the young, who, while they are suckling, remain dependent on their mothers for protection and generally, also, for training.

Mammals normally have two pairs of limbs, both in the majority of species being used for walking. In the Sea-cows and Whales the front limbs are modified for swimming, the hind legs being lost, and in the Bats the arms have been modified for flying. All mammals have tails, though in some species, such as Man, the tail is undeveloped, while in others it is prehensile and can be used as a fifth limb. The brain is more highly developed in this class than in any other, the higher mammals being better able than any other animals to condition instinctive behaviour as the result of experience, and so to change their behaviour patterns. Some, such as the Apes, show the beginning of the power of reason, which guides Man's intelligent behaviour (*see* INTELLIGENCE).

There are three sub-classes of mammals, the primitive egg-laying mammals, such as the DUCK-BILLED PLATYPUS and the ECHIDNAS (qq.v.); the MARSUPIALS (q.v.) or pouched mammals; and the placental mammals, in which the young remain within the womb of the mother until it has reached a comparatively advanced stage of development. This last group, which is much the largest, has proved the most successful in the struggle for existence —the first two groups being mostly found in regions, such as Australia and New Guinea, where members of the last group are not indigenous. The last group, the placental mammals, is subdivided into sixteen main orders, of which the Edentata, or mammals with few or no teeth, are the most primitive, and the Primates, including Man, the most developed. Two of the orders, the Sirenia or Sea-cows, and Cetacea or Whales (qq.v.), Dolphins, and Porpoises, contain mammals adapted for life in the sea. The hoofed mammals include the Artiodactyla, with two main toes as in Cattle and Sheep, and the Perissodactyla, with one or three toes as in the Horse and Rhinoceros (qq.v.). The Rodentia have special teeth for gnawing (see Rodents), and the Carnivora (q.v.) for tearing flesh. The Insectivora (q.v.) feed mainly on insects. The Chiroptera (see Bats) contain the only mammals able to fly.

MANATEE, see Sea-cow.

MANDRILL, see Baboon.

MARMOSET, see Monkey.

MARMOT. This small, stout rodent, related to the Squirrel (q.v.), is found in the northern parts of Europe, Asia, and North America. It is generally about 50 centimetres long, and is covered with fairly long, coarse, reddish-brown fur, with tail, and short legs, and small ears.

Marmots live in large colonies in burrows, which they dig in open spaces. On fine days they sit on the observation-mound at the entrance of the burrow, or go for short distances in search of food—roots, leaves, and seeds. At the least alarm they rush back to the entrance of their burrow, where they sit up on their hindquarters surveying the scene and trying to detect the danger. If the enemy comes at all near, a loud, whistling scream from one of the party is a signal for all to dive headlong into their burrows. After a short time they put their heads out to see if the coast is clear.

In the autumn, marmots carry large quantities of hay into their burrows to make snug beds for their long winter hibernation. As they lay up no store of winter food, it is likely that their sleep is unbroken throughout the whole winter. The young are born in the early spring, and on warm days in early summer are to be seen outside their burrows in numbers.

The American Marmot, or Woodchuck, differs from the other species in occasionally climbing trees. The reddish-brown Prairie Marmot, or Prairie Dog, lives on the open

Paul Popper

PRAIRIE MARMOTS ON THE LOOK-OUT FOR POSSIBLE DANGER NEAR THEIR BURROW

plains east of the Rocky Mountains. The American Chipmunks, often called Ground-Squirrels, are not, however, true squirrels, but are related to the Woodchucks and Prairie Dogs. They make themselves most comfortable three-roomed burrows, consisting of a living compartment, a food-store, and sleeping quarters. Realizing that he would be cornered were an enemy to find his way in, the Chipmunk provides a safety-exit by making a second burrow leading from his apartment to a back door, which is cleverly hidden under, for instance, a stone or log.

MARSH PLANT, *see* WATER PLANTS.

MARSUPIALS (Lat. *marsupium*, a pouch). This is the name for the Pouched Mammals, which are found only in Australasia and the Americas. Among the best known are the KANGAROOS, KOALAS, and OPOSSUMS (qq.v.).

The chief difference between the marsupials and other mammals is that young marsupials are born very undeveloped and extremely small. The only parts at all well developed at birth are the front feet and claws; and with these the tiny creature instinctively crawls through its mother's fur to her pouch, where it becomes firmly fixed to her nipple. It has no power to suck, but the mother injects milk into it by a muscular action. Some of the marsupials have no actual pouch, but the young, when clinging to their mother's breast, are hidden by her fur. Most of the Australasian marsupials are pouched; some, like the Kangaroos, Wallabies, and Wombats, are vegetarians; others are flesh-eaters; while others, including the Pouched Mice and the Banded Ant-eaters, feed on insects. The American marsupials are known as OPOSSUMS (q.v.), and are both flesh and insect-eaters. All, except the Water Opossum, live among the trees, most of them being excellent climbers, making use of their prehensile tails, which they can twine round the branches.

The name 'possum' is also commonly used in Australia for a group of Australian marsupials, though it is perhaps more correct to call these Phalangers. The group is made up of many small and medium-sized animals, including the KOALA (q.v.). Some are vegetarian, while others also eat flesh. They live in trees, have thick woolly coats, and all except the Koala have long tails, which in most cases are

prehensile. The Flying Phalangers (or Flying Possums) have a membrane joining the fore and hind limbs, by means of which they can glide for great distances from branch to branch. One of these, popularly known as the 'Flying Squirrel', or 'Sugar Squirrel', is often kept as a pet in Australia.

The Wombats are a distinct group of Australian marsupials, which can gnaw like rodents and burrow with their feet. They are thick-set, about the size of badgers, and look rather like small bears. They sleep during the day in burrows, feeding at night on grass, leaves, bark, and roots. They walk in a peculiar shuffling way, and when irritated utter either a hissing sound or a short grunt. They are normally shy and gentle, but can bite savagely in self-defence.

Members of the Bandicoot family vary in size from that of a rat to that of a rabbit. These Australian marsupials eat both animal and vegetable food, and are detested by the farmer because of the great damage they do to crops. They are nocturnal, hiding by day in holes in the ground or in thick vegetation. The most distinctive member of the group is the Rabbit Bandicoot, which has long ears like a rabbit's, a fairly long tail, and long hind legs like a kangaroo's, and looks something like a cross between a rabbit and a rat.

Of the Australian flesh-eating marsupials the largest is the Tasmanian Wolf. It is very like a European wolf, though smaller, and it has dark bands across the hinder part of its greyish-brown body. It is now rare, as its night-time ravages among sheep and lambs have led to its extermination, except in the wild mountainous parts of Tasmania. The Tasmanian Devil, about the size of a badger, has a short body, short legs, and a very large head. It has thick, black fur, with a white stripe across the chest. It hunts its prey at night, attacking any creature it can overcome, including sheep and wallabies.

The Native Cats of the mainland of Australia are about the size of a small ordinary cat—but are, of course, no relation to the real cats. They are either black or pale brown, spotted with white. They eat birds and small animals, and are extremely troublesome to poultry-keepers. They live in trees, behaving very much like MARTENS (q.v.).

Among the insect-feeding marsupials are the

Australian News & Information Bureau
TASMANIAN DEVIL
A nocturnal killer of sheep and poultry

Pouched Mice, which vary greatly in size, some being about the size of a small squirrel, while the tiny Common Pouched Mouse is only 9 centimetres long. Most of them keep to the ground, living in rocky caves or hollow banks; but some of them climb trees. As many as ten young may be born at a time, and are brought up in the pouch of their mother. Another insect-eater, the Banded Ant-eater, is one of the few marsupials in which the female has no pouch. It is about the size of a squirrel, with bands of white across the hinder part of its body, the ground colour of which is dark chestnut-red above and white below. It feeds chiefly on ants and termites.

See also MAMMALS.

Paul Popper
SHORT-HEADED FLYING PHALANGER

MARTEN, *see* WEASEL, Section 4.

MARTIN, *see* SWALLOWS.

MAYFLY. On warm summer evenings large numbers of male Mayflies appear suddenly over the surfaces of rivers and lakes, and perform an aerial wedding dance, in which they fly swiftly upwards and then sink slowly downwards again, wings and tails sloping upwards. Other peculiarities which make these insects particularly interesting are the facts that adult life in many species is very short, and that the adults do not feed. About 46 species are found in Britain.

Mayflies have two pairs of triangular wings, the fore-wings being large, the hind-wings very small, and both showing an intricate network of cross-veining. When the Mayfly is at rest, it holds its wings vertically over its body, like a butterfly. At the tip of its abdomen are three, sometimes two, long, slender tails. Its mouth-parts are minute and useless because the adult (imago) does not feed. Most species live for only 4 or 5 hours as adults, though some live for several days.

The eggs of the Mayfly are often very numerous—as many as 4,000 having been counted from one mother. The nymph lives entirely in the water, under stones, buried in mud, or freely swimming in swiftly flowing streams, for three or more years. Along its abdomen are plate-like gills. It is thought to cast its skin at least twenty-three times during its pre-adult life. Most are vegetarians. When it is fully developed, the nymph floats to the surface of the water, the skin cracks along the back, the Mayfly emerges, and almost at once flies away. It looks exactly like the imago, but is softer and duller than the adult and is called the 'sub-imago'. The whole body, including the wings, is enclosed in an extremely thin, transparent sheath, which must be cast off for the true imago to emerge. The Mayflies are the only insects which cast their skin after they are fully winged. The empty skins may often be found on tree-trunks, on the banks of rivers and lakes, or floating on the surface of the water. Once the skin is shed they begin their wedding dance, the females flying straight up into the swarm of rising and falling males. In one species it has been observed that, when the male has found a mate, he flies beneath her and takes hold of her with his long fore-legs. Grasping her

S. C. Bisserôt

A MAYFLY

or that the magnificent sapphire DRAGONFLY (q.v.) was once a drab, inconspicuous, aquatic larva.

All Arthropods—that is to say, LOBSTERS, CRABS, WOOD-LICE, SPIDERS, CENTIPEDES, and INSECTS (qq.v.)—have their skeletons on the outside, and in growing cast off one skeleton and then, after an interval, harden another, larger one—a process called the 'moult'. But many arthropods make a change in shape and appearance, also, at the time of these moults: this change is called a metamorphosis (or change of form). In a few insects such as the SILVERFISH (q.v.), although each moult brings about a slow development of the sexual organs, the change of outward form is so slight that the insect is said to undergo no metamorphosis. Other insects, such as BUGS, GRASSHOPPERS, LOCUSTS, DRAGON-FLIES, and MAYFLIES (qq.v.), have an incomplete metamorphosis. The young (or larvae) on hatching from the egg resemble the adult insect (or imago) in shape, possession of compound eyes, and in the type of mouth-part, and differ primarily from the adult in lacking well-developed wings and sexual organs. Each moult brings about the gradual development of these in the immature insect (or 'nymph') until the adult stage is reached. The nymphs of dragonflies and mayflies appear to differ strikingly from the adult, but this is because the nymphs are adapted to living under the water.

Other insects, such as BEETLES, BUTTERFLIES AND MOTHS, WASPS, and BEES (qq.v.), have a complete metamorphosis—that is, they make the changes from egg to larva (caterpillar, maggot, or grub); from larva to pupa (chrysalis); and from pupa to adult insect (imago). On hatching from the egg, the larva does not usually have compound eyes, and the shape of its body and its type of mouth-part are unlike those of the adult; in consequence their food is often different. The caterpillars of Butterflies, for example, have biting mouth-parts and feed on plants, whereas Butterflies have sucking mouth-parts and feed on nectar. Instead of changing gradually to the adult structure after each moult, the larva at the end of the larval stage 'pupates'—that is to say, it changes to a pupa or chrysalis. Pupation and the final emergence of the adult insect from the chrysalis shell are most easily observed among the Lepidoptera (Butterflies and Moths).

Caterpillars pupate in different places accord-

body from below with a short pair of claspers, which (in males only) are at the base of his tails, he passes his outer tails between the hind and fore-wings of the female. The instant they separate the female returns to the water to lay her eggs. Then, their short life as 'spinners' over, they fall dead into the stream.

MERGANSER, *see* DUCKS, Section 3.

MERLIN, *see* FALCON.

METAMORPHOSIS. This is the scientific name used to describe the very striking changes in structure which occur in the life history of some animals. Until we understand the process of metamorphosis we can hardly credit the extraordinary fact that the gaily-coloured Peacock BUTTERFLY (q.v.) which we see flying over the flower-border is in reality the same individual as the black prickly CATERPILLAR (q.v.) which was feeding on the nettles a few weeks back. Almost as unbelievable is it that the long-legged FROG (q.v.), which hops out of the wet grass, is the same individual as the little black tadpole, seen a short time back in the pond;

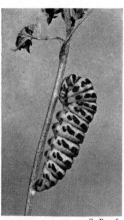

S. Beaufoy

FIG. I. SWALLOW-TAIL CATERPILLAR CASTING ITS SKIN AS IT PUPATES. *Natural size*

ing to their kind, some in the earth, some in the plants upon which they have fed, while others attach pieces of bark or other material with silk or with a sticky substance to form a rough case. To become a chrysalis, the caterpillar must cast off its skin—and this requires a series of muscular feats. The caterpillar's skin splits along the back from the head, and the pupa gradually draws out of it (*see* Fig. 1), sometimes leaving the cast skin clinging to the tail end of the chrysalis. The newly formed chrysalis has a soft outer shell, which hardens and darkens in a few hours. An immobile period, apparently for rest, then follows, and lasts for about 10 days—though some butterflies and moths will hibernate in this condition and not emerge till the following spring. Some moths will remain as pupae for a year—and have even been known to persist as long as 5 years in the chrysalis stage. Indeed, the 'Seventeen-year Locust' sometimes remains as a pupa for 17 years before it emerges as an adult.

Although during this period the insect inside the chrysalis appears to be quite inactive, in fact immense biological changes are going on to prepare for the transformation that follows. The internal organs of the insect are broken down and then rebuilt within the chrysalis case. The strong jaws of the caterpillar are no longer wanted by the butterfly, and so a different mouth-part is built up, with a sucking organ, called a 'proboscis', to enable the insect to suck nectar from flowers. The rudimentary antennae of the caterpillar develop into the important sense-organs of the butterfly, and a pair of large compound eyes provide it with a wide range of vision for its new life. The thirteen segments of

the caterpillar's body are retained in the butterfly's body; but the three segments of the thorax become separated from the ten segments of the abdomen by a slender waist. The embryo wing-buds, on the second and third segments of the thorax in the caterpillar, develop within the chrysalis into closely packed wings, ready to expand when the butterfly emerges. The three pairs of short front legs of the caterpillar develop, while the five pairs of abdominal legs disappear. The male and female sex-organs, entirely embryo in the caterpillar, develop in the butterfly, so that mating can take place, and the female lays eggs to produce the next generation.

When the insect finally breaks out of the chrysalis shell (*see* Fig. 2), it expands its wings and dries them, and within about an hour, after opening and closing its wings as if to test them out, it launches forth into the air to begin a new life. All insects which pass through a complete metamorphosis follow much the same pattern described here for butterflies, though different species vary the procedure in some minor respects.

Many invertebrate animals, particularly marine invertebrates such as SEA URCHINS, SEA ANEMONES, JELLY FISH, and MOLLUSCS (qq.v.), undergo metamorphosis. Most species of these animals develop from free-swimming larvae living in surface waters and totally different in appearance.

Metamorphosis is found in some vertebrates—for example, EELS and SALMON, and also in some AMPHIBIA, notably in FROGS and TOADS (qq.v.). The adult frog lays eggs from which,

S. Beaufoy

FIG. 2. YELLOW BRIMSTONE BUTTERFLY EMERGING FROM THE CHRYSALIS SHELL. *Natural size*

after about 10 to 12 weeks, hatch tadpoles, the frog's larvae. The newly hatched tadpole appears to consist mainly of a round head with a tail. As it lives entirely in the water, it is provided with gills. After a period of growth, the tadpole gradually develops legs, its gills are replaced by the lungs of the adult frog, and it loses its tail. From now on it can breathe air, and can live on land or in water. The life history of the toad follows much the same pattern.

Metamorphosis is often found in those animals which, during the course of their development, change the element in which they live, or materially alter their habitat within a single element, for such animals have, naturally, to undergo structural alterations to adapt them to their new environments.

MIDGE. The two families, biting and non-biting Midges, resemble the Mosquito (q.v.) but have no wing scales. Of the 530 British species, the females of some 30 are bloodsuckers, but others are harmless, as they take no food at all in adult life. They are among the most irritating of all insects, as they usually emerge in the evenings in considerable swarms, which dance up and down in the air at about head height. In early life, midges are usually aquatic. Often the larvae are red, and are then called 'bloodworms'. The red colour is due to haemoglobin, the pigment that colours our own blood. It is usually considered that this red pigment greatly increases their breathing capacity below water—and, certainly, the haemoglobin is not present in those species whose larvae feed at the surface of the water. The pupae may be active

and swim about, or they may stay at the bottom. At the end of the pupal stage, they come up to the surface, their skin splits open, and the adult emerges and flies off.

See also Flies.
See also Vol. VI: Fly Pests.

MIGRATION. Many kinds of animals—mammals, birds, fish, crustaceans, insects, and others—move from one place to another at certain seasons of the year, returning at other seasons. These periodical movements are known as migrations. The term should not be used for those movements which are made in one direction only, without any return (usually spoken of as 'emigration'), since these are generally prompted by some abnormal external circumstances, such as bad weather, lack of food, or destruction of normal habitat. True migrations take place in accordance with some inner need (physiological or psychological) of the animal—although the stimulus may depend upon some external condition, such as temperature.

Migration is often connected with the breeding cycle of the animal. Thus Turtles, which live most of the year in the sea, must come to land to lay their eggs on the beach—afterwards returning to the sea. In contrast with this, Eels breed in the Sargasso Sea, but migrate as small elvers to the fresh water of European rivers. Some years later, when mature, they return to breed in the depths of the Sargasso Sea—and are seen no more. Salmon (qq.v.) follow the opposite course, coming up the rivers to breed, but passing down to the sea to feed and grow.

Many animals, and especially birds, breed in

the cooler parts of their range, generally in the north. (The number of species which breed in the southern hemisphere and move to the south of their range to breed is far smaller; but a glance at a map of the world will show that there is far more land towards the north than towards the south.) In Newfoundland, the Caribou move south in winter, but in summer return to the north again. In mountainous country, many animals move to lower ground for the winter, returning to the heights in spring to breed.

A great many butterflies and moths, including several common British species, are regular migrants, and depend wholly or partly on migration to keep up their numbers. Both the Large and Small WHITES (q.v.), though able to winter in Britain, have their numbers increased by enormous migrations from Europe. Darwin, when he once witnessed their arrival, described it with the phrase 'snowing butterflies'—an apt description of their irregular flight, which resembles falling snowflakes. A record migration, seen at Dover in 1846, was said to have completely obscured the sun for hundreds of yards over the Channel. The RED ADMIRAL and the PAINTED LADY (qq.v.) cannot survive the British winter, and they arrive in spring in large numbers from the Continent. The Painted Lady, a large, delicately coloured, pink and brown butterfly, is very widely travelled. It is believed that it originally starts from the regions of the Atlas Mountains in north Africa. In 1869, a naturalist in the Sudan, on a sunny morning in March, watched thousands of Painted Ladies emerge from their chrysalises and almost at once take to the air to move off northwards in a mighty company. They usually reach the Mediterranean coast in April, continuing their journey through Europe to arrive in England in late May or June. Individuals have been known to reach north Scotland and even Iceland and the Arctic Circle—a journey of over 1600 kilometres. Among moths, the Death's Head Hawk, the SILVER-Y MOTH, and the Humming-bird HAWK MOTH (qq.v.) are notable migrants.

The migrations of butterflies and moths are not as regular as are those of birds, and until recently there was little evidence of any return south in autumn—which is not surprising in such short-lived creatures. Hordes of them will set out on apparently pointless journeys across the sea, only to fall, exhausted, into the water. Their movements are, therefore, strictly speak-

Eric Hosking

DUNLINS GATHERING ON THE SHORE PREPARATORY TO MIGRATING

KNOTS IN MIGRATORY FLIGHT

ing, emigrations. The movements of the huge, reddish-brown American butterfly, the MON-ARCH (q.v.) or Milkweed, are, however, true migrations, for they are observed in both directions regularly. The insects fly about singly until the autumn, when they begin to congregate, like swallows, and gradually move southwards in an ever-growing army of tens of thousands. They normally fly up to 5 metres above ground, and when they settle for the night they appear to change the colour of the vegetation. When they reach warmer lands they cluster on the limbs of trees for the winter. In the spring, the multitudes break up and travel north again, setting off in ones or twos to re-colonize their old haunts. The Monarch is a regular migrant to and from Canada, and has also quite often crossed the Atlantic and reached Britain.

Still more spectacular are the migrations of many species of birds. The SWALLOW (q.v.), which breeds so commonly in the British Isles, and as far north as the Arctic circle, winters in South Africa. The huge flocks of STARLINGS (q.v.) that feed on our fields in winter are drawn from Russia and the Baltic countries, vastly augmenting the numbers of our own native Starlings, which, oddly enough, do not migrate south, but remain all winter. Some of

the shore birds breed in the tundra of Europe and in autumn pass our coasts on the way south. The Sanderling, for instance, flies south to South Africa, Patagonia, or New Zealand (*see* WADING BIRDS). These birds travel for the most part along the coasts, though they must also cross great stretches of open ocean. The North American Golden Plover, which breeds in the Canadian Arctic, flies direct from Nova Scotia across 3,000 kilometres of the Atlantic to the coasts of South America; while the birds of the same species on the Pacific coast fly an even greater distance from Alaska to their wintering grounds in Hawaii. Even the tiny Ruby-throated HUM-MING-BIRD (q.v.) flies across the Gulf of Mexico, a non-stop flight of 800 kilometres.

Many birds migrate in large flocks, sometimes composed of several species flying together—and there is surely no more remarkable sight in the world to watch than the resolute progress of such a flock. Many birds migrate by day; but others, such as the small WARBLERS (q.v.), Duck, Snipe, and Woodcock, migrate at night, when the calls by which they keep in company are the only indication of their passing.

The birds which fly at night are often those which are most active during the day, and it is difficult to understand how they avoid hills, trees, and buildings in their way. It is puzzling how birds find their way thousands of kilometres across land and sea to their summer or winter home. Many birds follow coastlines and are able to recognize landmarks, for they have keen eyesight. Scientists suspect that some birds, for example, Manx Shearwater, Pigeons, and Gulls use the sun as a compass on long trips, but there is still much that we do not understand about how or why these migrations take place. It is, of course, absurd to say that a Swallow needs to go all the way to South Africa to find the food it requires: even if there is not enough in England in winter, it need go no farther than the Mediterranean. It is no less absurd to suggest that a Sanderling cannot find enough food on any shores till it reaches Patagonia, or that an Arctic TERN (q.v.) has any physical need (that we can discover) to winter in the Antarctic. Neither is it an adequate explanation to say that a Swallow, or a Sanderling, or an Arctic Tern must return north in the spring to find a suitable nesting-place. We believe that it must somehow benefit the birds to undertake these arduous and perilous journeys—and that is all we can say.

Perhaps the most extraordinary and inexpli-

Anti-Locust Research Centre
A SWARM OF LOCUSTS DESCENDING ON A PLANTATION IN
NIGERIA

cable of so-called migrations is that of the Lemmings (see VOLES), yellowish-brown rodents, about 13 cm long, which normally live in the mountains of Norway and other Arctic countries. Since this migration has no return, it should be called an emigration. It is probably caused in the first place by scarcity of food, though search for food is clearly not its purpose. In certain years there is an exceptional increase in the Lemming population, which is soon followed by a food shortage. Countless swarms of these little creatures make their way in a straight line across country. They climb mountains, swim rivers and lakes, eat their way through fields of corn and grass, perhaps taking up to 3 years to reach the sea. On that journey they are accompanied by great numbers of birds and animals who harass them continually, so that in all probability only a small proportion ever complete the journey. Even when they reach the sea, as they eventually must, they plunge in and continue their journey, swimming on till all are drowned. Why they do this no one knows.

An emigration of the same kind is carried out by certain kinds of hairy caterpillars which, for no apparent reason, will start to walk towards a lake. They progress at a slow pace, often covering considerable distances—only at the end to drown themselves in the water. Perhaps these strange emigrations originated when physical conditions were different, and some benefit was to be gained. Now the impulse remains though the results are disastrous.

Locusts regularly carry out migrations from one breeding place to another (see GRASSHOPPERS). These flights are made at night. The Desert Locust, for instance, breeds in North Africa in the winter. In the spring the adults fly south to the summer rains of the Southern Sahara, and their offspring make the return journey north again in the autumn. When locust populations increase, the adults form swarms and emigrate to new breeding grounds. Swarms fly by day and, helped by the wind, may fly thousands of kilometres before they lay their eggs. In the air, swarms look like clouds and may blot out the sun. A medium-sized swarm contains about a million Locusts and eats about 20 tonnes of food a day (see LOCUSTS, Vol. VI).

The recording of the facts of migration, by the marking of individual animals, whether fish, or mammals, or birds, is a fascinating study.

It is possible to discover what happens on migration—the speeds and heights at which the birds travel, the sort of weather and wind they prefer, the routes they take, and so on. Much is already known about these matters, and also about the astonishing ability of birds to find their way home to their nests, perhaps hundreds of kilometres away, and from a district where neither they nor any of their kind have ever been. But the more information that is gathered, the less possible does it seem to account for the how and why of it all. It is likely that scientists will never discover these things, and that men will continue to wonder at the migrant birds that 'observe the time of their coming', as they have done since the days of Jeremiah.

See also Vol. I: MIGRATION OF PEOPLES.

MISTLETOE

Eric Hosking

MILKWEED BUTTERFLY, *see* MONARCH.

MILLIPEDES, *see* MYRIAPODA.

MIMICRY, *see* PROTECTIVE COLORATION, Section 4.

MINK, *see* WEASEL, Section 6.

MISTLETOE. This is perhaps the best known among semi-parasitic plants. It is an evergreen plant, which grows on the boughs of many trees, although it prefers Apples, Oaks, Hawthorns, and Poplars. It rarely grows on the Beech, Birch, and Plane, probably because their smooth bark is unsuitable for the lodgement of the seeds. The white berries of the Mistletoe develop from yellowish flowers, which the plant produces in February and March. These berries contain a sticky liquid. Birds (particularly the thrush —hence Missel-thrush) are attracted to the white fruits; and in cleaning the sticky liquid off their beaks on the branches, they rub off seeds which become lodged in crevices in the bark. These germinate, and send out a sucker which

penetrates the branch as far as the wood-vessels. From these vessels are obtained water and mineral salts, which are carried to the green leaves of the Mistletoe. There, by the process of PHOTOSYNTHESIS (q.v.), they are made up into sugars and starch—the plant's food. The sucker of the Mistletoe thus performs the functions of the root of a normal plant in the soil.

The Mistletoe was treated as a sacred plant by the Druids (*see* RELIGION, PREHISTORIC, Vol. I), and even today it is supposed to be lucky. In NORSE MYTHS (q.v. Vol. I) it was supposed to be the plant whereby the god Baldur was killed.

See also PARASITIC PLANTS.

MITES AND TICKS. These belong to the same class of animals as SPIDERS (q.v.)—the Arachnida. The most familiar include the Cheese Mite, the Sheep-tick, and the Red Spider. Most

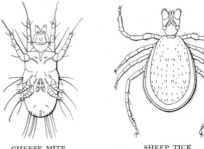
CHEESE MITE   SHEEP TICK

species of mites are microscopic in size, but they often occur in enormous numbers. A cubic metre of soil may contain many thousands. Both aquatic and land species exist, most of which are not parasitic. Many mites and ticks, however, are parasites; many help to spread diseases; and many injure our domestic animals (such as the tiny mite which causes mange in dogs), or spoil our crops (such as the mite which causes 'big bud' in currants). Because of their parasitic habits, they are rather different in structure from other arachnids—for example, they often have elaborate mouth-parts, which enable them to fix themselves to their victims. The bites of the 'Harvest-bug', which in the summer cause so much irritation to some people, are the work of mite larvae which have forced their probosces into the skin. Mites also produce galls on trees and other plants—as, for example, the 'witches' brooms' often seen on the birch.

See also Vol. VI: INSECT PESTS.

MOA, *see* OSTRICH.

MOCKING-BIRD. In the southern States of North America, this friendly, quiet-looking bird is well known for its power of mimicking the song of other birds, the cries of animals, or any other familiar sound which has attracted its attention. One species, known as the Cat Bird, utters screams and whistling cries like a tom-cat —though it has also a quite pleasant natural song. Another species makes a peculiar mewing kind of cry. Mocking-birds are very common in the southern States, where they frequent human dwellings. They build their thrush-like nests in vines, shrubberies, or piles of brush-wood, and will defend their young with great courage. The Mocking-bird is about 25 cm long, with a long tail, and plumage which is dove-grey underneath and brownish-grey above.

MOLE. This little, soft, velvety-furred, burrowing animal belongs to the order INSECTIVORA, as do HEDGEHOGS (qq.v.); but it eats insect larvae only occasionally, living principally on earth-worms. The Common Mole is found over most of Europe. It is about 15 cm in length, and is usually covered with grey-black velvety fur. Its eyes are small, and deeply buried in its fur, thus being protected from the dust and grit thrown up when the animal is burrowing. Sight is not important to the mole: with

A. R. Thompson

THE COMMON MOLE
It has strong digging claws, and a long sensitive nose

its very sensitive nose it smells out its prey, and its small, sharp, teeth crush it to pulp as soon as it is seized. Its forelimbs are armed with very strong claws which act as shovels, scooping out the soil with almost incredible speed.

Everyone is familiar with the mounds and ridges which moles make by burrowing under fields and gardens. The mole is a highly skilled engineer, making a carefully planned underground home from which several burrows radiate, and which is reached by one main and many side passages. The main run is rather wider than the animal's body. The usual way of catching a mole is to put a trap across this run. The many side tunnels are made in the search for worms and grubs. The mole needs constant supplies of food, being unable to do without it for much more than 4 hours on end. Wisely, therefore, it stores away any food which it does not need at the time. When it gathers earthworms, it bites off their heads and places them in its larder beneath its fortress home. The worms remain alive, but without their heads they are unable to dig into the earth and escape.

The females make extremely clever nest chambers. To provide against being flooded out, the nest chamber is higher than the tunnels leading to it, and has, as well, a small drainage tunnel. A gutter is made between the roof of the chamber and the surface of the earth to prevent the earthen roof from leaking or becoming so water-soaked that it might cave in. In the mating season, the males, who up till then have lived apart, fight fiercely amongst themselves for possession of a female. About May, from two to seven naked, pink-skinned young are born. Their skins darken and become hairy in about 10 days, and they leave home when they are about 5 weeks old.

See also Vol. VI: Wild Animals on the Farm.
See also Vol. VII: Fur Trade.

MOLLUSCS. These include the Cuttlefish, Octopus, Pearly Nautilus, Snails, Cockles, Mussels, Oysters, and other less familiar forms, with soft bodies usually enclosed in a shell. They are divided into five classes. First of the three most important classes is the Gastropoda —literally stomach-footed—all the members of which possess a broad, flat 'foot' on the underside of the body, by means of which they move about. Some, for instance most land and sea Slugs (q.v.), do not possess a shell, though many of these are thought to be descended from shell-bearing ancestors. Those that are shell-bearers always have a single shell, more or less distinctly spiral and cone-shaped, and, because of this characteristic one-piece shell, they are called 'univalves': the Snails, Whelks, and Limpets (qq.v.) are familiar examples. Another remarkable organ possessed by all Gastropods is a rasp-like tongue, or 'radula', which consists of a long, flexible, horny ribbon, bearing on its upper surface numerous minute and variously shaped teeth, arranged in close-set, transverse rows. The teeth are used to break up the food into small fragments, or in some species, to file neat round holes through the shells of bivalves so that the occupants may be eaten. The radula is moved backwards and forwards over a firm, fleshy cushion on the floor of the mouth by special muscles (if you watch a pond snail crawling up the glass side of an aquarium, you may sometimes see the radula at work). The shape and number of the teeth vary enormously in the different species—for instance, while one of the sea-slugs has only 17, the common garden snail can boast of no fewer than 135 rows, each consisting of 105 teeth, making a total of some 14,175 teeth.

The second great class all possess shells divided into two halves or valves, and are known as 'bivalves'. (The scientific name of this class, the Lamellibranchia, refers to the arrangement of their breathing gills.) All the bivalve molluscs feed on microscopic organisms and particles of plant and animal matter floating in the surrounding water. They have no radula, no distinct head, and in many of the most sedentary species the foot is absent or but poorly developed. In the more active species, however, the foot is well developed—for instance, in the freshwater swan-mussel it is a ploughshare-like organ, by means of which the animal ploughs its way slowly through the mud; in the cockles it is rather like a flexible finger, which enables its owner to take short jumps over the sandy shore. To this class belong such familiar species as the

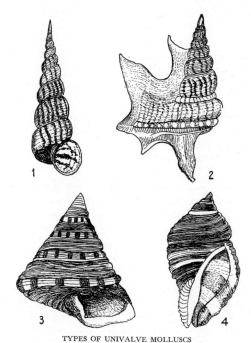

TYPES OF UNIVALVE MOLLUSCS

1. Auger Shell; 2. Pelican's Foot Shell; 3. Top Shell;
4. Dog Whelk

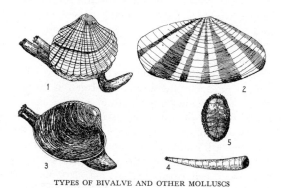

TYPES OF BIVALVE AND OTHER MOLLUSCS

1. Common Cockle; 2. Sunset Shell; 3. Smooth Venus;
4. Elephant's-tusk Shell; 5. Chiton

OYSTERS, CLAMS, MUSSELS, COCKLES, and PIDDOCKS (qq.v.).

The third important class, the Cephalopoda, includes the OCTOPUS, the CUTTLEFISHES AND SQUIDS, and the PEARLY NAUTILUS (qq.v.)—the Giant Squids being the largest living invertebrate animals. In some of these, for example, the cuttlefish, the shell has become internal and is a rather substantial plate which acts as an internal skeleton. In others, such as the Pearly Nautilus, the shell is an external one, divided into compartments. The name Cephalopoda literally means head-footed, for in these molluscs the flat foot of the Gastropoda is thought to have become converted into a circle of long-sucker-clad arms or tentacles surrounding the head. The Cephalopoda are very active, very powerful swimmers and capture their prey with their tentacles. They often creep about head downwards on the floor of the sea, and are capable of changing their colour to match their background.

The two remaining classes are smaller, and include less familiar creatures. They are the class Amphineura, containing the primitive Coat-of-mail shells or Chitons, and the class Scaphopoda, to which belong the Tusk-shells, molluscs that form a tubular shell open at both ends, and slightly curved and tapering, like an elephant's tusk.

Most molluscs possess eyes, ranging from the simplest eyespots, capable merely of responding to changing degrees of light and shadow, to the large, well-developed eyes of the Octopus and Cuttlefish. A very large proportion of the univalves or Gastropods possess a pair of fairly well-developed, though rather short-sighted, eyes, and these may be placed on the top of the longer pair of 'horns' or on the head near their base. The bivalve molluscs, on account of their more sedentary habits, usually possess eyespots only, though in the SCALLOPS (q.v.), which are very active creatures, they are more highly developed.

In all molluscs, the shell, which consists chiefly of carbonate of lime, is formed by certain fleshy folds, called the 'mantle', containing the special shell-glands, and secreting also the exquisite colours with which many shells are tinted. All molluscs lay eggs; but out of the vast numbers produced by some species, only a very small proportion reaches maturity, for they are the food of many other animals. The land snails generally lay fewer eggs, and their young emerge completely formed, differing from their parents only in size. The majority of the marine and some of the freshwater species pass through a free-swimming, larval stage before they reach the adult form; and in these early stages of their life they are totally unlike their parents in appearance. They are little oval or oblong creatures, possessing a girdle of 'cilia', or hair-like organs, by the rhythmical movements of which they propel themselves through the water. At certain seasons of the year, these larvae appear in countless myriads in the surface waters of the sea. There is a METAMORPHOSIS (q.v.) in the Molluscs, and the larva undergoes a marked change to attain the adult form.

Molluscs are an ancient group, the oldest fossil-bearing rocks being full of beautifully preserved shells which closely resemble in shape those seen on any sea-shore today. Very conservative in habit, only one group, the Gastropods, has ventured on land, the rest having kept to an aquatic life—the majority to their ancestral home in the sea. However, those which have established themselves on land have flourished to such a degree that the land snails today constitute one of the largest and most widely distributed groups of land animals.

MONARCH. This huge tropical butterfly, with a wing-span of nearly 10 centimetres, is tawny with black veins and black and white margins to the wings. It is the only member of its family, the Danaidae, to reach Britain, which it does only occasionally; since 1876, about 300 Monarchs have been reported—mainly from coastal areas. Its home is in tropical America and in the southern states of the U.S.A., where it lays its eggs singly on Milkweed plants, on which the caterpillar feeds. To reach Europe it must cross the Atlantic, since, there being no Milkweed, it cannot breed there. Whether it really crosses the Atlantic on the wing, perhaps helped by favourable winds, or whether it comes as a stowaway on a ship, or by both methods, we do not yet know. As it has occurred in Britain mainly since the development of the transatlantic fruit trade, the likelihood of its coming by ship seems great (*see* MIGRATION).

In America, the Monarch migrates northwards, and produces a succession of broods, some butterflies penetrating far into Canada. In the autumn, there is a return migration, after which large swarms hibernate along the

WILD FLOWERS OF THE LILY AND RELATED FAMILIES FOUND IN BRITAIN

(*Left side from the top*) Solomon's Seal, *Polygonatum multiflorum;* Asparagus, *A. officinalis;* Grape Hyacinth, *Muscari atlanticum;* Ramsons, *Allium ursinum;* Yellow Gagea, *G. lutea;* Autumn Crocus, *Colchicum autumnale;* Chives, *Allium Schoenoprasum;* (*centre*) Martagon Lily, *Lilium martagon;* (*right side from the top*) Star of Bethlehem, *Ornithogalum umbellatum;* Fritillary, *Fritillaria meleagris;* Herb Paris, *P. quadrifolia;* Bog Asphodel, *Narthecium ossifragum;* Bluebell, *Endymion nonscriptus;* Butcher's Broom, *Ruscus aculeatus;* Lily of the Valley, *Convallaria majalis*

Californian coasts. The large, yellowish-green caterpillar has black bands and a pair of black filaments at each end of its body, which twitch when it is disturbed. The exquisite green chrysalis, ornamented with black and gold, hangs suspended head downwards. Both caterpillar and butterfly are unpleasant in taste, and their distinctive colour patterns serve as warnings to would-be enemies to leave them alone (*see* PROTECTIVE COLORATION).

MONGOOSE. This is, strictly speaking, the Indian member of the Viverridae family—a small, carnivorous, weasel-like animal, with short legs and a bushy tail. In this article all the better-known Ichneumons are described under the headword, Mongoose. The largest of them are as big as cats; their heads have pointed muzzles with rather long noses, and

Harold Bastin

A MEERKAT—AN AFRICAN MONGOOSE
The Meerkat uses its tail as a prop when it stands erect watching for enemies

their ears are small and round. They live in Asia and in Africa.

The best-known species is the Grey Mongoose of India (Kipling's 'Ricki-Ticki'), which is about 45 cm long, with a tail almost as long again, and a coat of fairly long, grey or reddish-grey hair. It lives in hedgerows, thickets, fields, and near streams, and feeds on rats, mice, snakes, lizards, birds' eggs, and insects. It is a fierce little animal, quite ready to attack large poisonous snakes. By its quick movements, thick skin, and long, thick hair, it manages to protect itself from the snake's fangs until it is able to fix its teeth into the back of the reptile's neck. When captured young, it becomes tame, like a cat, and is often kept as a pet and as a protection against vermin.

One of the larger species is the Egyptian Mongoose of north-east Africa. This is said to dig crocodile eggs out of the sand, and its alleged usefulness in checking the increase of crocodiles led the Ancient Egyptians to consider it as a SACRED ANIMAL (q.v. Vol. I). Consequently it has gained its popular name, 'Pharaoh's Mouse'.

The Meerkat or Suricate is a small Mongoose found only in the Cape Colony, where it lives in colonies, burrowing into the sandy soil. It feeds on bulbs, which it scratches up with its long claws; and it loves to sit in the sun 'begging' like a small dog. It is a popular pet in South Africa.

MONITOR—the common name for the lizards of the family Varanidae. They are often called IGUANAS (q.v.), but should never be confused with them, as they are not closely related and live in different hemispheres—there are no Iguanas in the Old World, except in Madagascar; there are no Monitors in the New World. They are the largest of all lizards: the Common Asiatic Monitor may reach a length of 3 metres; the Komodo Dragon, although not quite so long, is a heavier beast, weighing as much as 45 kilograms. With one exception, the Monitors are fond of water and are strong swimmers; some of them live by the sea. In spite of their bulk and somewhat clumsy form, they climb well. They are flesh-eaters, and are prepared to devour anything that they can overcome; some of them like carrion. Altogether there are some thirty species, ranging over the tropical parts of Africa, Asia, and Australia.

Paul Popper

THE LACE MONITOR—A VERY LARGE LIZARD

The Desert Monitor—the only species found in dry country—inhabits the sandy regions of south-west Asia and north Africa.

See also LIZARDS.

MONKEYS. These belong to the highest order in the animal kingdom, the Primates, to which belong also the APES and LEMURS (qq.v.), as well as man himself. Monkeys are the only mammals which, like human beings, have a good stereoscopic vision—that is, they can see objects in the solid, not merely flat, their two eyes being in the front of their heads, both looking forward. The chief difference between Monkeys and the man-like apes, such as the Chimpanzee and Gorilla, is that the apes have no tails. Most monkeys live in warm climates or at least in climates with a very warm summer. Some of them can endure severe cold, and are found among the snows of the Himalayas, Tibet, and north-west China. There is only one species of monkey in Europe—the Gibraltar or Barbary ape, and in Australia none at all. Strangely enough, there are no monkeys in Madagascar, New Guinea, and the West Indies. Whilst most monkeys live in forests trees, the African BABOONS (q.v.) are an exception, as they spend most of their time on the ground, moving in troops from one place to another.

Monkeys show a great affection for each other —indeed very few sportsmen like to kill them because of the grief the rest of the troop show over their dead comrade. They all make excellent parents, nursing and fondling their babies with great care, and defending them with courage. So devoted are they to their babies that when one dies, it is often carried about by its mother for days, the bereaved parent making pathetic attempts to induce it to feed and play.

Sometimes the mother steals another baby to take the place of the lost one. Young monkeys ride like jockeys on the backs of their mothers. Almost all monkeys can be tamed, but they never seem to lose their sense of mischief. Although they can be taught many amusing performing tricks, their intelligence is generally thought to be not as great as that of a dog (*see* PERFORMING ANIMALS, Vol. IX).

The Asiatic or African monkeys are different in several particulars from South American monkeys. None of the monkeys of the Old World, the Simiidae, can swing from a branch by its tail, as can many of the South American monkeys, the Cebidae. Only the monkeys and baboons of the Old World have the peculiar patches of hard, naked skin on their buttocks, on which the monkey can rest completely when it is sitting upright. Another feature peculiar to the Old World monkeys, although by no means common to all of them, is the presence of cheek pouches in which the monkey stows away its food to be eaten at leisure in some safer place. The space between the nostrils of the American monkeys is much wider than that between the nostrils of the Asiatic and African monkeys.

One of the main groups of Old World monkeys is the Macaque genus. Most of these monkeys

Paul Popper

BLACK MACAQUES OF TROPICAL ASIA

live in troops in the forests of tropical Asia. When a party is on the move, the leader, usually an old male, stations himself at the head of the vanguard and marches majestically in front of his followers. If the younger members attempt to stray, the leader is at once among them, dealing disciplinary blows and bites. If the troop is attacked, the females and young ones are at once surrounded by the males, who attack the enemy with tooth and nail, fighting furiously. The Barbary or Gibraltar ape, the only monkey living in Europe, is also a Macaque. It is not clear how this monkey came to be on the Rock: it may possibly have arrived at a time in the distant past when Africa and Spain were connected by dry land, or it may have been brought over later by man. According to the legend, if ever these monkeys die out, Gibraltar will no longer belong to the British. There are many other species of Old World monkeys, from the Proboscis Monkey of Borneo, with its long, drooping nose, to the slender, long-tailed, and attractive-looking Diana Monkeys of Africa.

In the New World, most species of monkeys are to be found in the forest regions of Brazil. There are many species in central America, as far north as Mexico. The most docile and easily taught of the American monkeys are the Sapajous or Capuchins; and as they bear confinement and the European climate quite well, this is the kind of monkey which organ-grinders used to carry about with them. The Douroucolis, or Night Apes, are a group of small monkeys which are extremely active after dark. They have round, flattish faces, with very large eyes, and long, bushy tails. During the day they remain asleep in the hollows of tree-trunks, waiting till dark to hunt for insects and small birds. The Howlers differ from the other South American monkeys in having a large, hollow sound-box at the upper end of the windpipe, enabling them to produce a loud, discordant, howling cry from their homes in the tree-tops. The Capuchins are small monkeys with soft, woolly coats and high-pitched, trilling voices, like a bird.

The Marmosets, elegant little monkeys about the size of a squirrel, also live in the forests of central and South America. Unlike the more typical monkeys, Marmosets have claws, not nails, on their fingers and toes, which enable them to get a firm hold on tree trunks. Their tails are not prehensile. Whereas other monkeys

Paul Popper

SPIDER MONKEY OF BRAZIL

usually give birth to a single baby, Marmosets have litters of two or three. They are often kept as pets, but they are delicate, and do not keep healthy if they cannot get enough insects to eat.

Paul Popper

MARMOSET OF CENTRAL AMERICA

MONK-FISH, *see* SHARKS AND RAYS.

MOORHEN, *see* RAILS.

MOORLAND PLANTS, *see* HEATHS AND MOORLANDS.

MOOSE, *see* DEER, Section 5.

MOSQUITO (Gnat). This is a small, slender-bodied, long-legged, two-winged fly, with antennae which are plume-like in the male and hairy in the female. Along the edge of the wings, and usually also along each vein, is a row of scales. Many Mosquitoes, but by no means all, are blood-suckers, and of these not all attack man, some preferring other mammals, and others birds. In blood-sucking Mosquitoes, it is only the females that 'bite'; the males, not being able to pierce the skin, feed on the nectar of flowers or the juices of ripe fruits.

The eggs are laid either upon the surface of or near to water. The common Gnat deposits them side by side in floating egg-rafts, and may lay up to 300 eggs or more. Others lay them singly, each with a float on either side. The larva has a large head and thorax and a narrow abdomen, and has a thick tuft of bristles on each side of the mouth. The last segment but one of the abdomen carries a breathing tube, and the resting larvae hang head downwards in the water with the opening of this tube at the surface. They are to be found in lakes and streams, in small pools left after showers, in rain-barrels, and even in flower vases. Many feed on vegetable matter, but some are carnivorous and even cannibalistic.

The pupae are very active, though, of course, they take in no food. They are to be found, often in great numbers, in the same places as the larvae. The head and thorax together form a large globular front body, which carries a pair of breathing trumpets, and the pupa rests with the mouths of these trumpets at the surface of the water. The length of time required for a Mosquito or Gnat to go through all its changes varies with the temperature; it may be as short as 11 days. Thus, the rain-water in a discarded tin may be all that is necessary for development from egg to insect.

A few kinds of Mosquito are often exceedingly common within the Arctic Circle, but the greatest number of different species occurs in tropical countries. For a long time most people were interested in them only because of their blood-sucking habits. Some species attack silently; others fly with a high-pitched hum. Some attack only by day; others only by night. Some Mosquitoes are now known to carry organisms which cause certain deadly diseases: a spotted-wing Mosquito, for instance, is chiefly responsible for carrying Malaria, and the Tiger Mosquito is the carrier of Yellow Fever, the disease which nearly prevented the construction of the Panama Canal.

Compared with many other insects, Mosquitoes are easily controlled. Mosquito-infested districts have been successfully cleared by draining swamps, by pouring oil on the surface of standing water so that the breathing tubes of the larvae and pupae are choked, by the removal of likely breeding-places, and even by the importation of fish that will eat the larvae and pupae (*see* MOSQUITO-FISH). The Pontine Marshes south of Rome were for many centuries malaria-infested; but when, under Mussolini, the Italians drained the marshes, the malaria disappeared.

See also FLIES; INSECTS.

MOSQUITO-FISH. It is curious to think that the construction of the PANAMA CANAL (q.v. Vol. IV), one of the most valuable waterways in the world, was greatly assisted by small fishes. Yet it is a fact that the Panama region was so infested with fever-carrying MOSQUITOES (q.v.) that the cost in human lives would have been too high to make the canal a practical proposition had not large numbers of small fishes been liberated in the stagnant waters to feed on the mosquito larvae.

Many different kinds of fishes include these larvae in their diet; but those found most useful to man, owing to their hardiness and the rate at

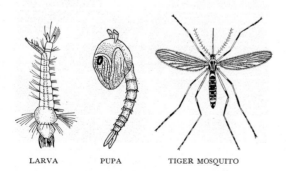

LARVA   PUPA   TIGER MOSQUITO

which they breed, belong to the family of fishes referred to in America as Killifishes or Top-minnows (Poeciliidae). Particularly valuable is the little Millions-fish, or Guppy, a native of Barbados in the West Indies, which has been introduced into many fever-stricken areas. The young of this species and its relatives are born alive. The male fish is very brilliantly coloured, though only 2·5 cm long and much smaller 'than the female. Guppies and the related Swordtails and Platys are great favourites in the home Aquarium (q.v. Vol. IX) where they will live and breed quite freely. Other species of the same family, as well as a variety of others, including Goldfish, Carp, Eels, and Gobies, are used to combat disease in Africa and Asia.

MOSSES AND LIVERWORTS are among the simplest plants, and are common throughout the world wherever there is an adequate supply of water. It is believed by most students of Evolution (q.v.) that plant life originated in water, and that the Algae (q.v.), which still live in water, Liverworts, and Mosses, all of them simple in form, were among the first living things. At a later period, it is believed, as land appeared above the surface of the ancient seas, more complicated plants began to appear, and slowly to colonize the land.

spore capsule

MOSS
(enlarged)

Liverworts—so called because, in former times, a 'wort' or brew made from the plants was used to treat complaints of the liver—often form green growths, like pancakes, on wet surfaces, such as shady banks, the sides of cuttings and ditches, neglected walls and fences, and the trunks of trees. Liverworts do not generally show divisions into true leaves, stems, and roots, like flowering plants, although they sometimes develop fine, hair-like, absorbing structures on their lower surfaces, and some kinds appear to have both stems and tiny leaves. These lowly plants propagate by means of spores (*see* Reproduction in Plants), which are produced in rounded boxes or capsules at the ends of erect stalks. When these capsules are ripe, they burst, and the light spores are set free and carried away by the wind. Most of the spores die, but a few settle down and germinate.

Mosses are more complicated in structure than Liverworts, most of them showing simple divisions into stem, leaves, and root-like structures. They are generally small, though there is one Australian moss which grows to 30 cm or more in height. Although some mosses grow in dry places and withstand long periods of drought, recovering their activity when wetted, the majority prefer damp conditions, and are chiefly found on moist tree-trunks, banks and rocks, and on the floors of shady woods. Mosses reproduce themselves in the same way as Liverworts by means of spores. Some mosses actually grow in water, either entirely or partially submerged. One of the most common of these aquatic mosses in Great Britain is the Bog- or Peat-moss, called Sphagnum, which forms enormous areas of deep peat in moist, temperate, and cool regions. The Bog-moss is spongy in texture and absorbs water; it is therefore used for packing living plants to send by post and, in war-time, is also used for making surgical pads.

See also Vol. III: Moorland and Marsh.

MOTHS. The insect order Lepidoptera is divided into about twenty super-families, one including the Butterflies (q.v.) and all the others

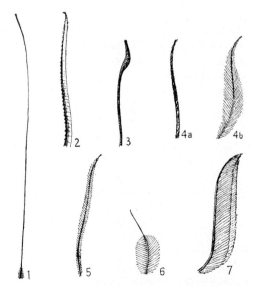

FIG. I. DIFFERENT TYPES OF MOTHS' ANTENNAE (MALE). × 3
1. Green Longhorn; 2. Elephant Hawk Moth; 3. Five-spot Burnet; 4. Brindled Beauty (*a*) female, (*b*) male; 5. Garden Tiger; 6. Leopard Moth; 7. Drinker Moth

the Moths. It is impossible to make a hard and fast distinction between the two. The moths are very much the larger group—for instance, there are about 60 species of butterflies in Britain and over 2,000 species of moths. In the world altogether there are nearly 200,000 species of moths. The most obvious distinction, which is true at least of British species, is that the antennae of butterflies are clubbed, while those of moths are not. The antennae of some species of moths, such as the Burnets, widen at the end, but they do so gradually. Moths have a variety of antennae, including many feathered types (*see* Fig. 1). In most moths, though not all, there is a curious kind of hook-and-eye arrangement for fastening the wings together, which is never present in a butterfly. The bodies of most moths tend to be stouter and more hairy than those of most butterflies, and to be without any waist between thorax and abdomen. Most moths fly by night rather than by day, and these generally are duller coloured than butter-flies. But, on the other hand, there are many brilliant-coloured, day-flying moths in Britain as well as in tropical countries.

The night-flying moths are obviously not so easy to find or to study as the day-fliers. Some species, however, can be located by searching in their day sleeping-places—the cracks and crevices of tree-trunks, old walls, or fences, lichen-covered rocks or stones, underneath loose bark on dead trees, or in poorly lighted barns or out-houses. Sometimes they can be persuaded to fly out of hedges or bushes if these are shaken or tapped with a stick. At night, they can be seen round street-lamps, or can be attracted to a strong light shone on to a white sheet spread in a woodland clearing or on a hill-top (*see* Butterfly and Moth Collecting, Vol. IX).

Moths vary greatly in size. The largest of all the Lepidoptera is the great Atlas Moth of the Himalayas, which may have a wing-span of up to 30 cm (*see* Colour Plate opp. p. 64); the smallest is the Midget Spotkin, one of the tiny leaf-borers, which has a wing-span of little more than 2 mm. The main groups of moths are dealt with in separate articles under the head-words Emperor, Hawks, Prominents, Tussocks, Lackeys and Eggars, Tigers, Night-fliers (Owl Moths), Loopers, Burnets and Foresters, Goats and Leopards, Clearwings, Swifts and Ghosts, Bagworm Moths, Gold and Purple Moths, China Marks, Leaf-rollers, and Silk Moths.

Like butterflies, moths have a complete Metamorphosis (q.v.)—that is, they go through the stages of egg, caterpillar, and pupa, to reach the adult stage. This life-cycle is generally completed within the year—one month in the egg, two months as a caterpillar, two months as a pupa, and one month as an adult moth. The winter is spent in hibernation in one or other of these four stages, which is accordingly prolonged. Moths may produce three or four generations during the summer, all but the last being short-lived. In some species, such as the Clearwings, the caterpillars take much more than 2 months, sometimes 2 or 3 years, to make their necessary growth. In others, a year or more is spent in a resting condition as egg or pupa—this dormant stage having been known to last for 5 years or more.

The female moth lays her eggs generally in small or large batches on the plant on which the caterpillars will feed. They are often stuck to the leaves with a gummy substance. The eggs of different species vary in shape, size, and colour. They are generally a plain colour, though those of the Lappet Moth are patterned with stripes of green and white. The Satin Moth lays eggs with a curious covering like candy sugar; and the pale green egg masses of the Small Emerald give off a pleasant scent—though what effect this has we do not know. A female moth lays anything from 100 to nearly 3,000 eggs; but only a very small proportion ever reaches maturity—for they have many enemies during their life-cycle. Once they have laid their eggs, moths are no longer concerned with them, though some species do, in fact, protect them by covering their egg batches with fluff from their tails.

When the caterpillars hatch, they make their first meal from the egg-shell, before turning to their food-plant. Most moth larvae eat leaves or flowers, some feeding on dead leaves. Some bore into timber, making a tunnel which widens as the caterpillar grows; some small species feed on woollen clothing, hair, or skins (*see* Butterfly and Moth Pests, Vol. VI). Many moth larvae spin a cocoon in which to pupate, either with silk only, or with wood or some other hard substance, held together with sticky liquid secreted from silk glands. Except for Plume Moths (q.v.), the pupae never hang from their tails as do those of many butterflies. They usually lie in protected crevices or on the

S. *Beaufoy*

FIG. 2. LIFE-CYCLE OF DRINKER MOTH FROM (A) EGGS, (B) LARVA, (C) PUPA, TO (D) ADULT

ground, covered by dead leaves or some such protection. Growth is completed entirely in the larval stage. The adult moth has no jaws, and can only suck with its 'proboscis' or tongue. In many species the proboscis is reduced. The GOLD MOTH (q.v.), however, has no proboscis at all but jaws instead. Some species, such as the Convolvulus Hawk Moth, have a proboscis long enough to reach down the long tubes of such flowers as the sweet-scented Tobacco Plant.

See also BUTTERFLIES AND MOTHS, TROPICAL; INSECTS; PROTECTIVE COLORATION (insects); MIGRATION; HIBERNA-TION.

MOULDS. Many organic substances (such as bread, jam, cheese, and leather), if left for some

time, become covered with a dense network of threads called a 'mould'. This is a fungus, a SAPROPHYTE (q.v.), which obtains its food from dead organic matter. Some moulds, such as *Penicillium*, from which penicillin is obtained, are blue-green in colour; others are brown or black; while yet others are white. The bread mould, called *Mucor*, is a typical mould, a description of which will serve to illustrate the main feature of all moulds.

Mucor can be easily obtained if damp bread is kept under cover at a moderate temperature for 4 or 5 days. The body of the plant, known as the 'mycelium', consists of long branching threads, each a continuous tube of fungus-cellulose, lined with protoplasm, in which smaller bodies called 'nuclei' are embedded. The mycelium penetrates the food material on which the fungus is living, and absorbs organic matter through its surface.

The mould reproduces itself in two ways, one a sexual and the other a non-sexual process. When *Mucor* reproduces non-sexually, it gives off upright branches about 3 mm long. The top of each branch swells into a small black sphere, within which develop hundreds of spores. Each branch looks like a small pin—and so the plant is commonly called Pin Mould. The wall of each sphere eventually breaks, and the millions of ripe spores are shed into the atmosphere—minute, one-celled, reproductive bodies, having no reserve food material, but capable of withstanding a certain amount of dryness or change of temperature. Under favourable conditions on the right food material, a spore germinates to form a new mycelium.

Non-sexual reproduction in fungi takes place when food is plentiful; but when food becomes scarce, the plants reproduce sexually. In sexual reproduction, two young, actively growing threads approach each other and come into contact, either side by side or at their tips. When the branches are in close contact, small protuberances are put out, in which exchange and fusion of nuclei take place. Eventually a structure with a greatly thickened dark wall is produced. This can resist adverse conditions and remain dormant for several months. Under favourable conditions it germinates, and the life-cycle of *Mucor* begins again.

One species of mould is used in making the famous Gorgonzola and Stilton cheeses and produces the characteristic blue veins in the cheese (see CHEESES, Vol. XI). Many others are important in helping in the breakdown of decaying matter in the soil.

See also FUNGI.

MOUSE. The name 'mouse' is loosely applied to any or all of the members of the mouse family, which includes Mice, RATS, VOLES (qq.v.), and Lemmings. It is by far the largest group of RODENTS (q.v.), with representatives in nearly every part of the world. The true mice and rats always have long, scaly, and generally naked tails, bright, prominent eyes, and sharply pointed muzzles, and their movements are quick and active. The most common mice in Great Britain are the House Mouse, and the Long-tailed Field or Wood Mouse.

House Mice are grey-brown, weighing only 15 grammes. They probably originated from central Asia; but they are now found all over the world in or near human dwellings and stores of food. They live only where there are human beings, as they depend for food entirely on man (see HOUSEHOLD PESTS, Vol. XI). They will eat practically anything; but their main food is grain and scraps of human food. They make their holes everywhere in houses—in the wainscoting, panelling, and floor. Their nests, which they place for preference in the wall nearest to stores of food, are made of chewed-up soft materials, such as wool, paper, linen, or straw. As a rule, House Mice are timid, only venturing out at night; but sometimes they become very bold and come out to nibble food in broad daylight, scuttling back to their holes only when someone approaches. They sit up to eat, holding their food between their forepaws. They can jump quite high, and can climb vertical wooden surfaces. When they run at full speed, they move like a cat by bounds of the hind legs and skips of the forelegs. In country villages, they take to the cornfields in the summer and to the stacks in the winter, riddling them with runways. House Mice usually have four or five litters a year, of from five to seven young, or more if there is plenty of food. The young mice can themselves

Spore capsules
(a) developing
(b) ripe
(c) shedding spores

(a)
(b)
(c)
hypha or thread

1

2

PIN MOULD

1. As seen under a microscope; 2. As seen under a magnifying glass

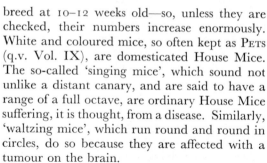

A. R. Thompson

HARVEST MICE USING THEIR TAILS TO CLIMB WHEAT STEMS

A. R. Thompson

HARVEST MOUSE ON HER NEST

breed at 10–12 weeks old—so, unless they are checked, their numbers increase enormously. White and coloured mice, so often kept as Pets (q.v. Vol. IX), are domesticated House Mice. The so-called 'singing mice', which sound not unlike a distant canary, and are said to have a range of a full octave, are ordinary House Mice suffering, it is thought, from a disease. Similarly, 'waltzing mice', which run round and round in circles, do so because they are affected with a tumour on the brain.

Harvest Mice are, together with Pigmy Shrews (q.v.), the smallest of British mammals: they weigh only 5 grammes. Their colouring is bright chestnut above and white below. In summer they are found among growing corncrops, on which they feed. They move gracefully and actively from stalk to stalk with the help of their tails, which coil round anything they touch. They are playful animals, and may be seen swinging from the stalks and performing gymnastic feats. Their summer breeding-nests are compact balls of grass, corn blades, or reed leaves, about the size of an orange, interwoven among the stalks quite close to the ground and lined with chewed grass. The entrance, which is at the side, is closed when the mother goes out. During the winter, Harvest Mice sleep fitfully in moss nests inside ricks, or sometimes in nests attached to reeds above water. Besides eating grain, they like to eat flies and other insects, which they dig out of the ground or catch with their forepaws or mouth.

Long-tailed Field Mice or Wood Mice are a little larger than House Mice, and are reddish above and white below. They are by far the most numerous of British mammals, being found in almost every garden, hedgerow, and cornfield from sea-level to mountain top. They usually make their nests in burrows in hedgerows and fields; but they also nest in the open, sometimes high up in trees. They eat almost everything, and are probably even cannibals. They store corn, nuts, and seeds for the winter in their holes and burrows, and sometimes in an old nest of a thrush or blackbird. Although they very rarely nest in human dwellings, they frequently invade country houses for shelter. They are timid, only venturing abroad in daylight if they are ill. When they are frightened, they sit up and wash thoroughly all over.

The Common Hamster, a rodent related to the mice, is found in Europe and Asia, but not in Britain. It is a stout animal, about 30 cm long, with thick, glossy fur, and a short tail. The male, female, and young Hamsters all have separate burrows. Each burrow consists of a dwelling chamber with smooth walls and a straw-covered floor, and a long gallery leading to a granary, where corn is stored for the winter. Young Hamsters have only one granary, but the old males often have several, and they spend the whole summer stocking them with corn. The burrows are kept scrupulously clean —in fact, the presence of any rubbish in a burrow shows that it is uninhabited. About October, the Hamsters close up their entrances and exits with earth, and feed for the next few months on their stores of corn. They venture out again about the middle of March, and soon build their summer burrows. Towards the end of April, the male visits the female, fiercely fighting any rival he may meet on the way. In May, there is a litter of from six to eighteen young, and yet another in July. The numbers of the Hamsters would increase, therefore, very rapidly were it not that they have a number of enemies to thin their ranks—buzzards, owls, ravens, polecats, and stoats, as well as man. Even as it is, swarms of Hamsters often damage the harvest. A very much smaller Syrian species, the Golden Hamster, has recently become a popular PET in Britain (q.v. Vol. IX).

See also Vol. VI: VERMIN.

MOVEMENT IN ANIMALS. In a biological sense the word movement has a slightly different meaning from that associated with it in everyday speech. So far as animals are concerned, we can distinguish three main types of movement, which are often related to each other, yet which belong to different aspects of life. To begin with, protoplasm itself exhibits a streaming movement. That is to say, under the microscope the substance of a living cell can be seen moving in a particular direction. If the cell is naked, as in Amoeba, or a white blood corpuscle, this streaming results in the pushing out of 'pseudopodia', or foot-like excrescences; and the streaming of

the protoplasm becomes translated into a movement of the whole cell from one place to another —or in other words, it is translated into locomotion. In plants, where the cell wall is a rigid coat of cellulose (see MOVEMENT IN PLANTS), the streaming of the protoplasm does not result in locomotion, and the streaming itself is to some degree restrained. The same is the case in animal cells where the cell wall is itself rigid, or where the cell forms part of a tissue. The streaming of the protoplasm is an essential movement in the internal economy of cells, and assists in nutrition, respiration, and excretion.

The other two types of movement are those which affect parts of the body only, and those which affect the body as a whole, among the latter being included those that result in locomotion. Both are the result of activity on the part of special cells, known as MUSCLE cells (q.v.), which have the power of rapid relaxation and contraction.

Locomotion is the sum total of movement by means of which an animal travels from one place to another. In Amoeba and its relatives, this takes the form of a rolling movement, initiated by the streaming movement of the protoplasm. In other unicellular organisms, locomotion is due either to 'cilia', delicate hairs which beat rhythmically and in so doing push against the surrounding fluid, or to 'flagella', long single hairs which, by a lashing movement, create a vortex and so pull the organism forward. Locomotion depends, therefore, upon pushing or pulling movements, the majority of locomotory movements involving a push.

A few other examples of locomotion will illustrate how the push or the pull operates in animal movements. A worm makes first a push and then a pull. Along the belly of a worm each segment is provided with four pairs of bristles, or 'setae', which can be pushed out or

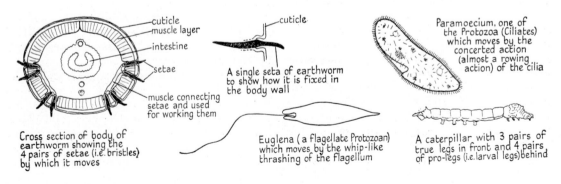

Cross section of body of earthworm showing the 4 pairs of setae (i.e. bristles) by which it moves

A single seta of earthworm to show how it is fixed in the body wall

Euglena (a flagellate Protozoan) which moves by the whip-like thrashing of the flagellum

Paramoecium, one of the Protozoa (Ciliates) which moves by the concerted action (almost a rowing action) of the cilia

A caterpillar with 3 pairs of true legs in front and 4 pairs of pro-legs (i.e. larval legs) behind

withdrawn into the body. Two sets of muscles run the length of the body—circular muscles to make it fat or thin, and longitudinal muscles to make it long or short. The bristles at the tail end get a grip whilst the worm lengthens and stretches forward. Then the bristles in the front of the body get a grip, the hind ones are released, and the body is pulled up or hauled up, becoming short and fat, ready for the next extension.

Caterpillars have three pairs of jointed walking legs near the head, ending in curved claws. A varying number of claspers, provided with tiny hooks, is situated at the other end of the body. The legs pull and grip as the body goes forward, and the claspers push to prevent any slipping backwards. Looper caterpillars push their bodies forward by getting a grip with the two pairs of claspers at the end of the abdomen, the body being then hauled up into a loop ready for the next push.

When a snail comes out of its shell, its foot spreads out along the ground. Rhythmic movements of the muscles pass along its whole length and carry the snail forward. To ensure a good grip, a gland under the mouth secretes a slime, which is left behind as the familiar slimy trail.

A starfish uses suction in order to move itself from place to place. On the under-surface of its arms there are rows of tiny tube-feet. These are distended with water, which is drawn in through a perforated plate on the upper surface of the animal. When the starfish is moving forward, the foremost tube-feet are extended and pressed on to the solid surface to get a grip by suction. The body of the animal is then pulled forward. Then the hindmost tube-feet hold fast, while the front ones are released and advanced ready for the next pull. A leech moves in much the same way; but here it is a muscular mouth that grips whilst the body is hauled forward. An adhesive sucker on the tail prevents it from slipping back.

Snakes almost 'row' themselves along on dry land. The scales of the back and sides are replaced on the belly by broad horny bands, each band attached to a pair of ribs that come down from the jointed backbone. The ribs are swung forward, the edges of the horny bands grip the ground, and as the ribs move backwards, the bands hold firm, and the snake advances. The movement of the ribs is so rapid that the snake appears to glide along.

There are a few animals that can make an emergency movement by means of an explosive recoil. The clumsy larva of the dragonfly crawls lazily at the bottom of a pond. In its tail it has a respiratory siphon which, during normal breathing, is filled and emptied quietly; but when it is emptied suddenly and quickly, the larva is shot forward to catch an unsuspecting victim. The cuttlefish also has a siphon through which water can be ejected with some force, and by changing the direction in which the siphon points, the animal can propel itself in the contrary direction. When in rapid movement, it always travels backwards.

Generally speaking, the larger the animal the more slowly it moves in proportion to its size. This is also true to some extent of different parts of the body. It is possible to move fingers or an arm about 10 times per second, but eyelids can move much faster. The wings of a dragonfly beat 28 times per second, those of a bee 190 times, and those of a housefly 300 times. The reason for this is that, generally speaking, long muscles cannot stand up to rapid movements as well as short ones. Muscle fibres, tendons, and bones, being delicate things, snap if overstrained, and the limit of safety depends to a great extent upon the length of the muscle.

See also FLIGHT; MUSCLES.
See also Vol. XI: BONES AND JOINTS; MUSCLES (Human).

MOVEMENT IN PLANTS. 1. The common belief that plants are fixed, while animals can move, is not strictly true. Some plants, such as the green scum, which often appears so mysteriously in water-butts, are not fixed to one spot. On the other hand, some animals, such as the CORALS (q.v.), are stationary. And, even in plants such as shrubs and trees, the different organs often make movements in response to changes in their surroundings, although the plant as a whole remains fixed to one spot. For instance, many plants, when kept indoors, will in time turn their flower-heads or shoots towards the light.

Movement of living things is of two kinds. The movement of the whole organism itself (as of the dog towards the bone) is called a 'taxis' (Greek word meaning 'arrangement'). In the plant world this only occurs in the lowliest, such as the unicellular ALGAE (q.v.), which react to stimuli such as light, or to the presence of dissolved salts and gases in the water in which they live. In higher plants, these taxis movements occur only in certain reproductive cells. The other type of movement is that in which the living organism moves only a part of itself, as a response to a change in the external conditions. The stem of a potted house-plant turns towards the light; and a root curls round towards its water-supply. This movement of a single organ is called a 'tropism' (Greek *tropos*, a turn).

Taxis movements are not easy to demonstrate in plants; but it has been shown how various reproductive cells will react to certain chemical substances. In ferns, for example, the male reproductive cells or sperms will swim towards a drop of malic acid added to the water in which they are living. This is because the organs in the fern plant which bear the female reproductive cells or eggs also give off malic acid when the eggs are ripe. The sperms, therefore, swim towards the eggs, and fertilization is ensured. With certain seaweeds, too, ripe sperms and eggs are shed quite freely into the sea, with no obvious means of bringing them together. But the passive eggs give off a chemical substance which causes the sperms to swim towards them, and fertilization takes place (*see* REPRODUCTION IN PLANTS).

Tropisms in plants are much easier to demonstrate. They are caused by reactions of different plant organs to various influences, such as light, gravity, or moisture. These may result in change of direction and, sometimes, in rate of growth. Most shoots bend towards the light, in order to present the maximum amount of leaf-surface to the sun; but many roots are repelled by light. Most roots, however, since they normally grow in complete darkness, are not affected by light at all. If a Mustard seedling is fixed in a hole in a piece of cork and floated on water in an upright position in a vessel from which all light is excluded, except for one slit on the side, the root of the seedling is found to bend away from the light, and the shoot towards it.

The effect of gravity can be shown by placing a potted Geranium on its side in the dark for a few days. In due course the shoot will be observed to bend upwards, while the roots will turn downwards. This reaction to gravity explains why the young shoots grow upwards through the dark soil where, until they reach the surface, they are not being influenced by light at all. Some shoots arrange themselves naturally at right angles to the pull of gravity, and grow in a horizontal position. This is seen

in the 'rhizomes' or underground STEMS (q.v.) of grasses, and in the runners of strawberries. Roots tend to grow towards moisture, even growing upwards to do so, if necessary.

Since tropisms are really growth-movements, the parts of the plant directly affected are the growing-points—that is, the tips of shoots and the parts just behind the tips in roots. If the tips of roots and shoots are removed, the plant will no longer respond to the influence of light, gravity, and moisture. In shoots, the response to gravity gets less the farther down the shoot until, beyond the growing region, it no longer exists. It is probable that the production of the growth-promoting plant hormones is in some way connected with outside stimuli, and that these hormones, in turn, affect the rate and direction of growth (*see* GROWTH IN PLANTS).

The value of these tropisms is clear. When the seed germinates, gravity draws the young root towards a greater supply of moisture and to strong anchorage; while the young shoot is drawn towards the light—a process which is continued later by the placing of its leaves in the best position for carrying out their work of food-manufacturing by PHOTOSYNTHESIS (q.v.). The Ivy-leaved Toadflax shows the importance of light-reactions particularly well: at first the flower-stalks grow out towards the light from the walls in which they live, and become prominently displayed; but later, when the fruit-capsule splits, the direction of growth is reversed—the stalks now turn away from the light, so that the seeds may be 'sown' in the crevices of the walls.

Gravity, light, and moisture are not the only causes of tropic movements in plants. The climbing organs or tendrils of some plants respond to mere contact. If the young tendril of the Passion-flower, for example, is rubbed or touched by a solid body—particularly one with a rough surface—the tendril will bend towards the stimulated side. As the tendril bends, it makes further contacts—and so the stimulus is continued until the tendril is coiled round its support. The tendril of a certain tropical Marrow will respond to the touch stimulus in less than a minute (*see* CLIMBING PLANTS).

2. SLEEP MOVEMENTS. Plants make other movements, as well as taxis and tropisms. Many flowers and leaves take up different positions by day and night. This is called 'sleep movement' —though it has nothing to do with the sleep-

Harold Bastin

SENSITIVE PLANT (*Mimosa pudica*) SHOWING 'SLEEP' MOVEMENT
Left, Plant before being touched; *Right*, Plant after being touched

ing habits of animals, of course. Night and day movements are well seen in the flowers of the Daisy, the Water-lily, and the Lesser Celandine, which close up at night; while in the Evening Primrose, Salsify (popularly called John-go-to-bed-at-noon), the Bladder Campion, and some species of the Tobacco Plant, the flowers close in the day and open at night (as we know by their scent). These flowers react mainly to changes in the intensity of light; but the Tulip, which closes at night and opens in the day, responds mainly to changes in temperature—as can easily be shown by experiment.

The reason for these night and day movements is far from clear, but may be associated with the way in which the plants are pollinated by insects. Those that open during the day are pollinated by day-flying insects such as bees and butterflies; while those that open at night are generally pollinated by night-flying insects, especially moths. The flowers of the Scarlet Pimpernel (or Poor-man's-weatherglass) close when the air gets damp: the petals close together, and the flower-stalk twists so that the

flower hangs downwards. This may be a device to keep the pollen dry. Other flowers which close as a response to moisture are Poppies, Anemones, Rock Roses, and Herb Roberts.

Certain leaves also open and close in response to changes of light and darkness. The three leaflets of the Wood Sorrel leaf close together at night so that the three under-surfaces are flattened against one another. The leaflets of the White Clover, on the other hand, close so that the upper surfaces are brought together. Since the stomata, through which the leaf gives off water during the day by TRANSPIRATION (q.v.), are found on the under-surfaces in the Wood Sorrel and on the upper-surface in the White Clover, the value of closing may be that it reduces transpiration at a time when it might do more harm than good to the plant; or perhaps, by preventing the stomata from being blocked by dew, it enables transpiration to begin as soon as the leaves unfold.

The most remarkable case of a sleep movement is that of the Sensitive Plant, a common tropical weed of the Mimosa family. In the 'sleep' position the leaflets are folded together and the whole leaf hangs down. This position is usually taken up in the evening; but it can be brought on at any time by striking or shaking the plant. If the touch is gentle, only the nearest leaflets will close at first; but if the stimulus is continued, the movement will spread downwards until all the leaflets are asleep and the plant looks almost dead. The mechanism that controls the natural closing-up at night is complicated and not yet fully understood.

See also GROWTH IN PLANTS; MOVEMENT IN ANIMALS.

MUD PUPPY, *see* SALAMANDER.

MULLET. This name is given to two very different kinds of fish, the Red and the Grey Mullets. The Red Mullets (Mullidae) (sometimes called Goatfish) are sea-fishes, mostly small. They have on their chins a pair of stiff 'barbels' or feelers, with which they explore the bed of the sea for their food. When not in use, these barbels are packed away in a groove along the lower jaw. Freshly caught Red Mullet are brilliantly red, but the colour soon fades unless the scales are removed immediately. For this reason, the ancient Romans, who valued the Mediterranean species both for its beauty and its excellent flavour, had it brought to their tables alive, so that they could admire its colour before eating it. This particular species also reaches the coasts of Britain. The Grey Mullets (Mugilidae), which are not at all nearly related to the Red Mullets, are much duller in appearance. They are found on the coasts in all temperate and tropical seas, where they grow to a length of nearly a metre, feeding principally upon mud and algae (lowly aquatic plants), which they suck up by means of their thick lips. Grey Mullet are provided with a sort of gizzard, something like that of the fowl, and the eyes are partly covered with folds of skin, called 'adipose eyelids'.

MUSCLE. In all animals except the PROTOZOA and most of the SPONGES (qq.v.), certain cells take on the function of muscle-cells. These are responsible for movements within the animal's body, and also for the movements which carry the animal from place to place. Lean meat is a good example of muscle tissue. A special feature of muscle-cells is their ability to relax and contract, being long and spindle-shaped when relaxed, but short and thick when contracted. Under the microscope, their protoplasm shows numbers of fine threads, like strands of elastic, which help them to contract. The cells themselves are very small; but where great numbers are grouped together, they may form conspicuous bands of muscle.

There are two types of muscles—those that are under conscious control, and those that continue to work without any effort on the part of the owner. When a dog wags its tail, or a man gets up from his chair, or a bird moves its wings to fly, 'voluntary' muscles are brought into action, and the movement can be brought to an end by an effort of will. Those movements of the digestive system, breathing, the pumping of the heart, and all those actions which continue even during sleep, when the voluntary muscles are still, are controlled by involuntary muscles. The voluntary muscle cells, which are controlled by the brain, can be distinguished under the microscope by the dark and light bands or 'striations', which run transversely across the cells. The cells of the involuntary muscles, however, have no striations, and are said to be 'unstriated'. In all the lower groups of invertebrate animals most of the muscle is of the unstriated type. The higher the animal is in the evolutionary scale and the greater the activity of which it is capable the more striped muscle it possesses.

Muscles are attached at both ends to various structures. The voluntary or striped muscles in vertebrates are usually attached to bones by tendons (or chords of tissues), and in Arthropods they are attached to the external skeleton. The skeletal parts can usually move only as a result of the contraction of these muscles. Muscles are usually arranged in pairs with opposing actions.

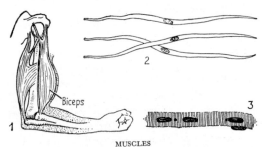

MUSCLES

1. Biceps contracting to raise fore-arm; 2. Involuntary muscles; 3. Striped or voluntary muscles

In the arm, for instance, when the biceps contract to raise the fore-arm, the triceps on the opposite side of the arm relax. When the triceps contract to pull down the fore-arm, the biceps relax.

Without oxygen a muscle soon ceases to work properly; so, in all animals that use blood for the supply of oxygen, a regular flow of blood is needed. The muscle contains a sugar, 'glycogen', from which energy is liberated by 'oxidation', or uniting with oxygen. A by-product of this oxidation is lactic acid, the presence and accumulation of which bring on fatigue, so that it must be removed. It may be reconverted into glycogen by the addition of more oxygen, and this in turn is used up producing energy (in the form of work and heat), carbon dioxide, and water. The carbon dioxide and water are removed by the blood through the veins.

It sometimes happens that muscles remain contracted and cannot be relaxed, causing cramp and pain. (Stitch in the side is a kind of cramp.) An unaccustomed amount of violent exercise or a continued muscular strain in an unnatural position will cause a lack of oxygen and, consequently, an accumulation of lactic acid in the muscle tissue, bringing on cramp. A swimmer sometimes gets cramp because the cold water causes the capillary blood-vessels to contract, thereby conserving the heat of the body, but as a result the supply of oxygen and blood to the muscles is cut down to danger-point (*see* Blood System).

Stiffness and soreness are usually the result of the tearing of some of the delicate fibres and membranes of the muscles. These fibres are very efficient; but to stand extra strain they have to be toned up gradually. Certain muscles are sometimes over-developed, while others may be seldom used. A professional cyclist, for example, with over-developed leg muscles, is not likely to be a good swimmer; because when he tries to bring the seldom-used muscles of his arms into action, they do not work efficiently, and he may become muscle-bound.

Plants have no muscles, and their movements are brought about in a different way (*see* Movement in Plants).

See also Movement in Animals.
See also Vol. XI: Muscles (Human).

MUSHROOMS, *see* Fungi. *See also* Mushrooms, Vol. VI.

MUSK OX, *see* Cattle.

MUSK RAT, *see* Vole.

MUSSEL. This is the common name for several species of bivalve Molluscs (q.v.), some of which live in the sea, others in lakes and rivers. The Edible Mussel is one of the most familiar, large numbers being found closely packed on rocks and pier piles, each mussel firmly anchored by a tuft of tough threads, called the 'byssus', spun from special glands on the short, dark-brown foot. The mussel is not necessarily permanently fixed to one spot, for it has the power to cast off the byssus threads and change its surroundings. Large numbers of eggs are produced annually. The young are quite unlike their parents, emerging from the egg as tiny oblong-bodied larvae, furnished with a band of 'cilia', or hair-like organs, by means of which they can swim actively. Partly by their own efforts, partly by the ebb and flow of the tide, they are carried away to fresh unoccupied grounds, where they settle down, undergo a Metamorphosis (q.v.), and are transformed into miniature mussels, very small indeed, but with the familiar deep purple shell.

EDIBLE SEA MUSSEL
ATTACHED BY BYSSUS
THREADS TO TIMBER

Much more remarkable is the life-history of the Freshwater Mussels, of which the River Mussel and the large Swan Mussel are common British species, and which also include the Pearl Mussel. These Freshwater Mussels live half-buried in the mud, through which they slowly plough their way by rhythmic movements of their large muscular foot. The spawning season starts in May or June, large numbers of eggs being produced. These are kept within the shelter of the parent's shell. By October a minute mussel, which has formed inside the

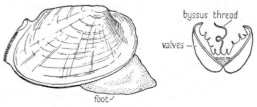

SWAN MUSSEL AND LARVA

egg, emerges. It has a toothed beak at the tip of each triangular valve, and also a single, sticky, byssus thread, by which it glues itself to the mantle-folds of its parent, and there safely shelters throughout the winter months. In the following spring, in late February and March if conditions are suitable, the parent mussel discharges its numerous offspring in tangled wisps. The young mussels swim by clapping their valves vigorously. Should a fish pass within range, they attach themselves by their byssus threads to its skin. The instant that the toothed valves of the shell touch, they take a firm hold. The flesh of the fish, irritated by their presence, swells up round them so that the young mussel is entirely covered over. It is carried about as a parasite on the fish for 3 months, during which time it absorbs food from the tissues of its host, and undergoes further important changes. Finally, its development completed, the young mussel drops from its host into the mud, perhaps a long way from the place where it first took grip. Only certain fishes, such as sticklebacks and minnows, can serve as hosts; and if none of these is present at the right time, this strange life-history cannot be completed, and the mussel spawn will perish. The Pearl Mussel has an oval shell, which, in full-grown specimens, is about 10 centimetres long by 5 across, and pitchy black in colour. This mussel occasionally forms very perfect pearls in the folds of its mantle. The Swan Mussel is the largest of the river species, a fine specimen measuring about 15 by 8 centimetres. The valves of the shell are covered by a thin, yellowish-green skin, adorned with two or three broad bands of darker green. The soft body is grey, tinged with red or yellow, with the edges of the mantle tinged with brown, and the large muscular foot a yellowish-orange colour.

See also Vol. VI: SHELL-FISH FISHING.

MUTTON BIRD, *see* PETREL, Section 6.

MYRIAPODA (many-footed). This class of jointed-limbed animals includes the Centipedes and Millipedes, animals related to INSECTS (q.v.), but differing from them in having elongated bodies composed of many segments, each of which bears one or two pairs of walking legs. Myriapoda have distinct heads and one pair of antennae. The several thousand species found throughout the world are all land-dwellers, though a few live on the shore between tide-marks. Most species feed by night, generally spending the day under such cover as stones or pieces of wood. They hatch from eggs, the young Centipedes having only six pairs of legs and the young Millipedes only three pairs. They add pairs of legs each time they shed their skin to make growth; but even when fully grown, many species do not have as many legs as their names suggest. There is, for example, the House Centipede of North America which has no more than fifteen pairs of legs altogether, though these are very long, so that the animal looks rather like a many-legged spider.

Centipedes have one pair of legs on each segment, whereas Millipedes have two pairs from the fifth segment backwards. Centipedes have flattened bodies, move quickly, and carry poison-fangs with which they attack their prey —for they are carnivorous. One tropical species, which reaches about 30 centimetres long, has a poison-fang strong enough to kill small birds. Millipedes, on the other hand, have rounded bodies and no poison-fangs, move slowly, and feed on vegetable matter. One quite common English species, the Pill Millipede, defends itself by rolling into a ball, exposing only its outer shell. It resembles the Pill WOODLOUSE (q.v.) very closely, but is distinguished by having two pairs of legs on many of its segments. Another, *Iulus sabulosus*, makes a tight coil when disturbed.

The female Millipede constructs a tiny mud hut in which she lays her eggs, finally sealing its entrance with a daub of mud. The female Centipede coats her eggs with a sticky fluid, and rolls them in the earth until they are camouflaged to look like pellets of soil. This she does to prevent the male from eating them.

See also Vol. VI: ANIMAL PESTS.

S. C. Bisserôt

A MILLIPEDE

N

NAILS AND CLAWS—the horny sheaths at the end of the fingers and toes. If they are broad and flat, as in a man or elephant, they are generally known as nails; if they are sharp-pointed, as in a lion, sparrow, or lizard, they are called claws. In birds of prey they are called talons. Nails or claws assist in grasping objects more firmly, in walking, perching, or seizing prey or food. They are used also in scratching and cleaning the body, and as weapons of defence.

Many mammals have Hoofs (q.v.) instead of nails; but in the majority nails are present on all four limbs. Birds have claws on the hind limbs (feet), but very seldom on the fore limbs (wings). In a few species, however, the nail is present on the thumb and first finger, as in some Geese and Birds

FOOT OF OSPREY (BIRD OF PREY)

of Prey—though it seems to serve no useful purpose. The only bird to use these wing-claws is the South American Hoatzin (q.v.). The spur, or nail, at the back of the leg of many members of the Pheasant family (q.v.) is used solely as a weapon.

The term 'nail' is used also for the horny sheath at the tip of the beak of some birds, especially Geese (q.v.).

NARWHAL, *see* Whale.

NATTERJACK, *see* Toad.

NERVOUS SYSTEM. In the lowest forms of animal there are no nerve-cells, the protoplasm of each cell being to some extent capable of nervous response. As the body grows more complex, so the need for an elaborate nervous system increases—just as in a small village there is no need for telephones because the inhabitants live close together, whereas in a large town an extensive network of telephone lines is needed. The nervous system is a means of communication between the sense organs (*see* Senses), which receive messages (or stimuli) from the outside world, and the Muscles (q.v.), which must carry out the appropriate action.

The nervous system consists of a central nerve cord (called, in vertebrates, the spinal chord), which runs from one end of the body to the

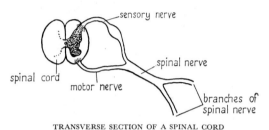

TRANSVERSE SECTION OF A SPINAL CORD

other, and a number of main nerves running from it to the sense-organs, the limbs, muscles, and other internal organs. The ends of the main nerve split into finer and finer branches until all tissues are supplied with nerve fibres. The main nerves are divided into two groups: the sensory nerves, responsible for conveying the impulses (messages) from the sense organs; and the motor nerves, carrying the impulses to the motor organs (the muscles).

In the invertebrates, the central nervous system is ventral—that is to say, it lies under the gut, in the lower half of the body. In vertebrates it is dorsal, and lies within and is protected by the skull and spine.

See also Vol. XI: Nervous System (Human).

NETTLES, *see* Plant Defences, Section 5.

NEWT. This is a Salamander (q.v.) of the genus *Triturus*, of which there are some twenty species—mostly found in Europe, although some of them inhabit Asia. North Africa has two species, and there are two in North America. Britain has three newts, the Crested or Warty Newt, the Common or Smooth Newt, and the Palmate Newt. The first is easily recognized by its large size, black, warty skin, and orange belly with black markings. It grows to a length of nearly 15 cm. The other two species seldom exceed 8 cm in length; their skin is smooth, and usually spotted or marbled with black or dark brown. These two species are much alike; but in the breeding season the males can easily be distinguished, for then the hind feet of the Palmate Newt have broad black webs, and the end of the tail is cut off abruptly and ends in a black thread. The males of all three species develop a high crest of skin on the back and tail at this time. In the Crested Newt this is deeply notched. The female also has a crest, though hers is less conspicuous than the male's. At the

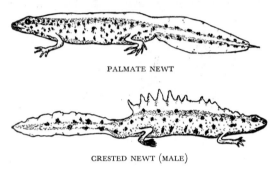

PALMATE NEWT

CRESTED NEWT (MALE)

end of the breeding season the crest disappears, and both males and females leave the water. Newts that are kept as pets should be allowed to leave the water as soon as the breeding season is over. The eggs are laid singly and carefully wrapped in the leaves of water-plants.

Other well-known species of newt, often seen in captivity, are the Marbled Newt from the south of France and Spain, and the Alpine Newt.

NIGHT-FLYING MOTHS (Owlets). This is the common name given to members of the families Noctuidae and Plusiidae, which include over 6,000 known species, nearly 400 of which occur in Britain. As all moths that fly by night do not belong to these two families, the name Night-flying Moth is rather confusing, and the name Owlet is preferable.

The average wing-span of Owlets is nearly 4 cm—the largest British species, the Old Lady, being nearly double this, and the Black Witch of America about 4 times. Owlets usually rest by day on tree-trunks, walls, or in dark places, where their brownish, greyish, or blackish colour makes them difficult to detect. The Wainscots have little-marked, yellowish fore-wings—much the colour of the dead marsh reeds among which they live. The majority of Owlets, however, have a pattern of circular and kidney-shaped spots with five cross lines, the innermost being short and the outermost zig-zagging. While resting, the moth holds its fore-wings roof-like over its stout body, so concealing the pale greyish or whitish hind-wings. Some—for example, the Yellow and Red Underwings—have brightly coloured conspicuous hind-wings, which are hidden beneath the sombre fore-wings when the insect alights. Such colours, temporarily displayed and serving to distract the attention of enemies, are known as 'flash colours' (see Protective Coloration). The moths are attracted to light and to 'sugar'; a mixture of treacle, beer, rum, and such things painted on trees will catch moths. The mercury-vapour and ultra-violet light traps are the most efficient traps for capturing these and most other moths that fly by night.

The eggs are usually spherical, slightly flattened, and fluted or netted. The caterpillars feed mainly on leaves, but also on flowers, seeds, and roots. Many species show considerable variation in their selection of food plants: the Wainscots tunnel in reeds; the Marbled Beauty, found commonly in towns on old walls, is a lichen feeder; and the local Waved Black feeds on fungi.

Caterpillars of Owlets are usually night-feeders, hiding by day, often on the ground under dead leaves, their coloration of green or brown with longitudinal stripes assisting concealment. When disturbed, they curl up into a ring and drop, remaining motionless in the herbage until danger has passed. Many have one or more pairs of abdominal legs reduced or missing, and are known as semi-loopers from their method of crawling (see Loopers). The majority are smooth, but a few, such as the scarce Merveille du Jour, are hairy. The Alder Moth caterpillar has long clubbed hairs and conspicuous warning coloration—though when young it resembles a bird-dropping. Although the moths are almost identical, the caterpillar of the Grey Dagger is easily distinguished from that of the Dark Dagger by the yellow instead of reddish stripe along the back, and a longer and thinner hump on the first abdominal segment.

The pupae of Owlets are usually shining mahogany-brown or black, and are generally formed in cells underground; though some spin cocoons among leaves or in crevices in bark.

One of the earliest British Owlets to emerge from HIBERNATION (q.v.) is the Herald; and one of the commonest in the autumn, often seen on the wing by day, is the migratory Silver-Y. Among other moths of this group are the Darts, Rustics, Brocades, Coronets, Gothics, Minors, Ears, Quakers, Drabs, Sallows, Chestnuts, Sharks, and Clovers.

Many species of this group are serious pests (*see* BUTTERFLY AND MOTH PESTS, Vol. VI). The moths of some Asiatic and Australian species damage oranges and bananas by piercing the skins with their strong tongues. The larvae of many species are pests of corn, vines, and vegetable crops, particularly in America where they are known as Cutworms. In America, too, the Army Worm sometimes swarms over hundreds of square kilometres, devastating corn-fields. In Britain, plagues of caterpillars of the Antler Moth occasionally occur in hilly parts, denuding whole districts of grass. The caterpillars of the Cabbage Moth are probably even more destructive than those of the WHITE BUTTERFLIES (q.v.), as they eat into the cabbage itself instead of confining their attacks to the outer leaves. In Australia, swarms of the Bugong Moth were formerly used by the Aborigines for food. Other common pests belonging to this group are the Turnip Moth, the Bright-line Brown-eye (known to market-gardeners as the Tomato Moth), and the withered leaf-like Angle Shades, which eats many plants, especially chrysanthemums and geraniums. The Owlets are preyed upon by Bats, which eat only the body of the moths and leave behind them, in their resting places, accumulations of wings.

NIGHTINGALE. This rather insignificant, brown bird, not unlike a small thrush, has been the subject of more poetry, perhaps, than any other creature. According to the Greek legend, its breast is pierced by a thorn as it sings, and this is the cause of the famous melancholy note which occurs in its song. In fact, the song of the Nightingale might not have been noticed above some other British songsters, including its close relation, the Thrush, were it not that the bird sings by night, when there are fewer other sounds to distract our attention. It sings also by day, when it is by no means so easily distinguished.

Nightingales winter in Africa, migrating in April to Europe where they breed. The males

Eric Hosking
NIGHTINGALE PREPARING TO SING

arrive first, and each establishes himself in a territory, making his presence known to the females by his song. The main purpose of the song is to announce to other nightingales his right over the territory in which he and his mate will breed and find food (*see* ANIMAL TERRITORY). Nightingales frequent woods and thickets, never breeding north of Yorkshire, and being found most freely in certain localities in south-east England. They build their nests in undergrowth close to the ground, and lay four or five olive-brown eggs. They cease to sing after the eggs are hatched in mid-June, and by August they are migrating to Africa for the winter. They feed mostly on the ground on worms, grubs, and insects.

There are several species of Nightingale. The Thrush Nightingale, which reaches eastern Europe, is a rather larger bird, with a more powerful, but less perfect, song. The Persian Nightingale, sometimes called the Bulbul, is distributed over central and western Asia; and there are two species in Africa.

NIGHTJAR (GOATSUCKER). There used to be an old country superstition that Nightjars

Eric Hosking

NIGHTJAR

birds are covered in thick, oily, yellow fat, which the native Indians value, and collect in clay pots, calling it Guacharo butter. In tropical Asia and Australia are other relatives of the Nightjars, called Frogmouths because of their wide mouths. They are rather owl-like in appearance, and spend their days roosting on some dead tree-stump, their mottled brown plumage making them so like the tree that they are difficult to distinguish.

See also CAMOUFLAGE.

NITROGEN SUPPLY IN PLANTS. Next to water, the chief substance which a plant requires from the soil is nitrogen. This is necessary for the manufacture of proteins, which help to build up and maintain in good health the tissues of both plants and animals. Most plants obtain their nitrogen in the form of nitrates. Obviously, if all green plants were to continue absorbing nitrates from the soil, and there were no means of replacement, the soil would soon become impoverished and the plants would die of nitrogen starvation. In nature, however, nitrogen is constantly being restored to the soil, either as animal droppings, or by the decay of dead animals and plants. The nitrogen in this dead organic matter, or 'humus', cannot be used by plants until it has undergone various changes which turn it into nitrates able to be absorbed by the root-hairs. First, the proteins in the humus are broken down into ammonium compounds; and these are then acted upon by various bacteria in the soil, until they are built up into the nitrates which the plant can absorb. In this way nitrogen is constantly kept circulating. The farmer, however, who often cannot wait for these natural processes, replaces the nitrates which his plants remove by adding nitrates in the form of artificial manures, or by returning the proteins themselves to the soil in natural manures, such as dung, humus, or leaf-mould.

ROOT NODULES. Not all plants are dependent on soil nitrates for their supply of nitrogen. Leguminous

sucked milk from goats—hence their name. The American Nightjar is often called Whip-poor-Will because of its call-note. Nightjars are to be found in most parts of the world. They are characterized by their nocturnal habits, and by their flat heads, small bills, but wide mouths with bristles at the sides, large eyes, and short legs. Both the birds and their eggs (which are laid on the bare ground with no nest) have a speckled coloration which makes them difficult to distinguish from their surroundings. Night-jars feed always at night, eating such insects as moths and cockchafers, which they catch on the wing. The European Nightjar, a bird about 27 centimetres long, winters in Africa, reaching its summer quarters during May. It may be seen in Britain, especially in dry, heathy country and open woodland, hawking for insects at dusk. Its note is a sustained churring trill, with an occasional 'coo-ic' as it flies.

In northern South America there is a relative of the Nightjar, the Guacharo or Oil-bird, a much larger bird, some 50 centimetres long, which spends its days and makes its nest in caves, coming out only at night. The nestlings of these

ROOT OF A BEAN SHOWING NODULES

plants, which include Peas, Beans, Clovers, and Vetches, possess certain swellings or nodules on their roots, which contain many thousands of a certain bacterium normally found in the soil. These bacteria infect the roots of a leguminous plant through the root-hairs, and pass to the cells underneath the skin of the root, where they multiply so much that the nodules are produced. The cells themselves enlarge to accommodate the bacteria, and even divide to produce new cells. These bacteria are able to act on nitrogen gas in the air spaces of the soil, and convert it into nitrogen compounds, such as nitrates suitable for absorption by the green plant. This 'nitrogen fixation', as it is called, cannot be performed by the green plant itself, and its importance to a plant growing in a soil deficient in nitrates is obvious. In return for the nitrogen compounds, the plant supplies the bacteria with sugar and similar compounds needed by them. This convenient arrangement, by which the bacteria and leguminous plants live on terms of mutual benefit to one another, is known as 'symbiosis'. The bacteria, of which there are several varieties, appear to be most particular: the bacteria from clover will not develop nodules in peas, nor vice versa. If a farmer has not cultivated a special kind of leguminous plant in a field for some time, he may take soil from a field where the plant has been growing recently to obtain the bacteria he needs. When crops of clover or other legumes are ploughed into the soil, they do so much to enrich the nitrate supply that the operation is called 'green manuring'.

There are other bacteria with this same power of converting nitrogen from the air into the nitrates which the plant can absorb. These live freely in the soil, and do not enter into close relations with plants.

See also BACTERIA; NUTRITION OF PLANTS.
See also Vol. VI: MANURES.

NODULES, ROOT, *see* NITROGEN SUPPLY IN PLANTS.

NOTORNIS, *see* RAILS.

NUTHATCH. This small, plump, woodpecker-like bird has a short tail and long sharp beak. It has bluish-grey plumage on its back, a white throat shading to pinkish-buff underneath, and a black stripe under its eye. Nuthatches are

Eric Hosking

NUTHATCH CARRYING INSECT FOOD TO THE YOUNG IN ITS NEST

found in many parts of the world, and are not uncommon in wooded districts of central and southeast England. They move easily up and down trunks and limbs of trees, making short hops in any direction as they tap the bark, probing the crevices for hidden grubs and insects. In the autumn they eat nuts, especially hazel-nuts, wedging them into crevices of the bark and smashing them open with powerful strokes of their bills, clapping their wings in time with each stroke. They make their nests of dry leaves in a hole in a tree, or in a nesting-box, carefully plastering the entrance with clay to ensure that it is exactly the right size. Their song has varied notes, especially in the spring, but their usual call is 'chwit-it-it'—which sounds rather like the sound of a stone being thrown across an ice-covered pond. They fly with a slow and dipping motion, quite unlike that of any other British bird.

NUTRIA, *see* COYPU.

NUTRITION OF ANIMALS. All living things, whether plants or animals, need food in order to replace the matter used up by them in the process of living. Foods are classed as proteins, carbohydrates, and fats; and in some form or other these are all required by every living thing. Unlike plants, animals cannot make their food from raw materials—carbon dioxide, water, and mineral salts: they are dependent on the conversion of these into suitable forms by plants, largely through PHOTOSYNTHESIS (q.v.). Even a carnivorous animal, such as a cat or a lion, derives its food ultimately from plants, by eating a mouse that has fed on grain, or a zebra that has fed on grass. Without the power of green plants, therefore, to use light, life of any kind would be impossible.

An animal needs proteins, carbohydrates, fats, salts, and water in order to replenish the protoplasm, the living matter of the CELLS (q.v.). When an animal feeds, the pieces of animal or vegetable matter it takes into its body are too large to be absorbed at once into the blood (which carries the food to the cells). These pieces must, therefore, be broken up and made soluble by the process of digestion, so that they may be built up again into the proteins, carbohydrates, and fats characteristic of the animal. Digestion is set in action by 'enzymes' or ferments (see FERMENTATION), which are manufactured by many of the cells in the walls of the alimentary canal, especially in the stomach and intestines. There are also glands, such as the pancreas or 'sweet-bread' of mammals, which pour into the small intestine secretions which continue the process, assisted by the warmth of the body.

When the food is seized by the animal in its mouth or beak, it may be chewed (if the animal has teeth), or it may pass at once into a gizzard, where it is milled by the small stones and grit which the animal (bird, crab, or worm) swallows from time to time. Before passing into the gizzard, the food is softened in the crop, where some birds also store food to bring home to feed their chicks. A snail has a tongue with thousands of teeth, the 'radula', which it uses as a rasp, working it against the horny roof of the mouth. Insects have a number of methods of seizing their food. Bees have no chewing apparatus, their jaws being adapted for sucking nectar, but Greenfly and many true flies and bugs have mouth parts that can pierce plant or animal cells and suck up juices. Water-beetle larva and spiders pour 'ferments' into their prey and then suck up the partly digested liquid remains. Many

sea creatures, such as mussels and Fan Sabellas (see WORMS), have thousands of tiny hair-like 'cilia' on their gills or tentacles, which they beat to produce water currents. In this way they filter tiny food particles from the water which pass into their mouths. Some of the wood-eating TERMITES cannot digest cellulose unaided, but they have pouches in their stomachs containing PROTOZOA (qq.v.), which break down the wood into substances that the termites can digest.

Mammals, also, cannot digest cellulose without the aid of internal organisms. Grass-eating mammals have BACTERIA (q.v.) in the food tract, which break down some of the cellulose into substances that can be absorbed. In RUMINANTS (q.v.) the bacteria live mainly in the rumen, whilst in horses and rabbits the bacteria live in an outgrowth of the intestine called the caecum. Human beings have colonies of bacteria in the large intestine (see DIGESTIVE SYSTEM, Vol. XI).

The value of food to the body is measured in calories, a calorie being the unit of measurement of the heat required to raise the temperature of one gramme of water one degree Centigrade. The number of calories needed to make up a satisfactory diet depends on the activity of the creature: the more active it is the more are needed. When too few calories are provided, the body begins to use up the stores of protein and fat contained in its tissues, until starvation takes place. If an animal over-eats, it has difficulty in getting rid of the excess of food, and the body suffers accordingly. In addition to the main food, animals need small amounts of other substances such as VITAMINS (q.v. Vol. XI), if they are to keep healthy.

See also GROWTH IN ANIMALS; RESPIRATION IN ANIMALS. See also Vol. XI: NUTRITION (Human).

NUTRITION OF PLANTS. The real difference between the nutrition of plants and animals is that, whereas plants can take inorganic materials and build up their own food substances, animals cannot, but must make use either directly or indirectly of the food which has already been made up by plants. Plants, like animals, need for good nutrition an adequate supply of water, carbohydrates (starch and sugar), mineral salts, fats, and proteins. To be well nourished, animals must have an adequate supply of the particular foodstuffs they require, whereas plants must have a supply of the raw materials from which the foodstuffs can be built up. And just as the mere supply of foodstuffs to animals is not enough to promote healthy nutrition and living, so in plants the conditions under which the raw materials are absorbed are of prime importance also.

Adequate supplies of water are, of course, essential to the plant, and water is always present in living plant-tissue. In many fruits it makes up 90 per cent. or more of the total weight; in green foliage leaves the content of water may be as high as 80 per cent., and even dry seeds may contain 10 to 12 per cent. In most green plants the bulk of water is taken in by the roots, and, together with the mineral salts it contains, is carried right through the plant to the green leaves. There, in the presence of sunlight, and by the addition of carbon dioxide from the atmosphere, complicated food substances are built up by the process of PHOTOSYNTHESIS (q.v.). These made-up food substances, which provide the plant with its carbohydrate and protein foods, are then conveyed to those parts of the plant—root, stems, leaves, flowers, or fruits—where they may be needed. The entire tissues of the growing plant are thus bathed in a water-flow, either taking raw materials to the leaves, or made-up food substances from the leaves to wherever they are required.

Since the plant system is covered by an outer skin, it would seem that loss of water would occur only through evaporation, and would not, therefore, be very important. As in human beings, however, the solution of one problem in plants raises another. The carbon dioxide which is used in the leaves is known to be taken from the atmosphere in the form of gas. This enters through tiny pores on the leaf-surfaces, which are able to open and close. Since much of the water in the leaf is in the form of water-vapour, the opening of the pores to admit carbon dioxide simultaneously allows water-vapour to escape in considerable quantity. The loss of water-vapour is known as TRANSPIRATION (q.v.).

The protoplasm of the plant seems to exercise a considerable degree of discrimination, rejecting some salts and taking in others (*see* ROOTS, Section 2). It is easy to understand how water with the dissolved salts passes from the absorbing hairs of the roots to the nearby plant tissues. But how does a watery liquid get from roots many yards deep in the soil to the top of a tall beech tree? Several forces are involved, the most important being suction from the leaves, which are constantly losing water. Some water is probably also pushed up by ROOT PRESSURE (q.v.). Substances are carried round the plant dissolved in this water; insoluble ones such as starch and proteins are first acted upon by enzymes and thus changed to soluble forms.

Finally, in considering the feeding of plants, its inseparable connexion with the process of RESPIRATION (q.v.) must be taken into account. In animals, we see the end-stage of a process in which food, which has been built up originally by plants, is acted upon by oxygen to release the stored energy necessary for all animal activities. This energy, which is derived from the sun, was in the first place built up into food in the plant's leaves. But the plant, also, needs energy for its successful working; so that besides the building-up process of photosynthesis, there is the breaking-down process of respiration, when complicated foodstuffs are oxidized to release their contained energy. The waste products of plants are given off in various ways by processes not fully understood.

See also NUTRITION OF ANIMALS; NITROGEN SUPPLY IN PLANTS.

NUTS, *see* FRUITS, Section 2(*c*); *See also* Vol. VI: NUTS.

O

OAK, *see* WOODLANDS, Section 2.

OCTOPUS. This strange, sinister-looking creature, with its large eyes, grotesquely shaped body, and long sucker-clad arms, belongs to the same division of the animal kingdom, the MOLLUSCS (q.v.), as the familiar oyster and snail. However, the Octopus, together with the CUTTLEFISH AND SQUID, and the PEARLY NAUTILUS (qq.v.), differ enough from all other molluscs to be placed in a class by themselves—the Cephalopoda, literally head-footed, so called from the fact that all are distinguished from other molluscs by having in the place of a foot a circle of sucker-clad arms growing out from the head. With the help of these arms, the Octopus both captures its prey, and literally walks head downwards on the floor of the sea. The Octopus swims by ejecting with great force a stream of water from a short siphon-tube which forms part of the mantle on the underside of its body, and this makes it shoot rapidly backwards through the sea. Moreover, when excited or alarmed, the Octopus discharges through the same tube an inky fluid right into the face of its astonished foe, and, under cover of this effective 'smoke-screen', makes good its escape. The inky fluid is secreted within a special glandular organ, the 'ink-sac'. In the centre of the circle formed by the formidable sucker-clad arms is the mouth, with its stout pair of horny jaws shaped like a parrot's beak; while behind the jaws, the mouth has a long armoured tongue or radula, used for grating the food into fragments small enough for swallowing.

The Octopus spends most of the day-time quietly resting in some cranny among the rocks on the floor of the sea; as darkness falls, it becomes active and wanders in search of prey, returning to its favourite hiding-place at dawn. It has remarkable powers of adjusting the colour of its body and arms to harmonize with its immediate surroundings, and this chameleon-like

Paul Popper

AN OCTOPUS DISCHARGING ITS 'SMOKE SCREEN' FROM ITS 'INK SAC'

Prof. J. Z. Young

X-RAY OF ARGONAUT SHELL

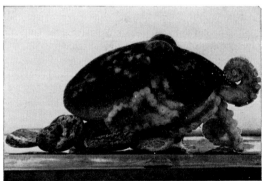

Zoological Society of London

THE LESSER OCTOPUS

ability helps it to avoid the notice of large Dog-fish, giant Conger-eels, and other hungry foes. Much information concerning the habits of the Octopus has been obtained from specimens kept under observation in marine aquaria. It seems that the female is a model mother, watching over her rather grape-like masses of eggs with devotion, and furiously attacking any prowling creature that may venture near. On hatching, the young octopods are less than 6 mm in length, with their future arms showing as a circle of budding outgrowths round the tiny head.

With few exceptions, the different species of Octopus live on or near the bottom of the sea, the majority being active, powerful animals. The Giant Octopus of the Pacific reaches a span of 9 metres across the outstretched arms; while our own British species, the Common Octopus, occasionally spans as much as 3 metres, though most specimens measure only about a metre.

Quite different in appearance from all other members of the Octopus family is the Argonaut or Paper Nautilus. The female of this smallish creature possesses a most beautiful, slightly corrugated, fragile shell, which is held in position by the two uppermost arms. These not only clasp the shell, but are expanded and provided with glands that secrete the substance of which the delicate shell is composed. This shell is also used as a receptacle for the developing eggs, and there the baby Argonauts remain until they leave their mother. The male is very much smaller than the female, and has no shell. The Argonaut is found in nearly all warm and sub-tropical seas. It was well known to the ancient Greeks, who called it the Nautilus, or Sailor, because they thought that it used its shell as a boat and hoisted its expanded front arms as sails. Actually, the Argonaut swims backwards near the surface of the sea by ejecting water from its siphon like the Octopus, and it crawls about on the floor of the sea in as prosaic a fashion as any winkle.

See also Vol. VI: Octopus, Cuttlefish, and Squid Fishing.

OKAPI. This is a very shy creature living in the densest and least-explored forests of tropical Africa—in fact its very existence was not confirmed until as recently as 1901. Though closely related to the Giraffe (q.v.), it is unlike it in its habits and differs greatly in appearance, being much smaller—about the size of a large mule.

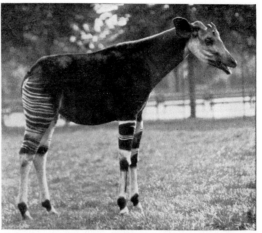

Paul Popper

OKAPI

It has a short body, rather long legs and neck (though not nearly so long in proportion as the Giraffe's), and very large ears, which are sensitive to the slightest sound. It has large eyes, hairy nostrils, and a fairly long tail, with a small black tuft of hair at the tip. Full-grown males have short horns about 7 or 8 cm long. The Okapi's colouring and marking are peculiar: it has white stripes on its hindquarters and the upper part of its legs, while the rest of its body and neck is dark chocolate-brown, its face whitish, and the lower part of its legs mostly white. This colouring makes a perfect camouflage in the subdued light of its native forests.

Like the Giraffe, it feeds on the leaves of trees, stripping them off the branches with its long tongue and flexible upper lip. Okapis are rarely seen in the wild; but a few have been kept, and even bred, in Bristol Zoo. An Okapi was first brought to the Antwerp Zoo in 1919.

OPOSSUM. This is the only Marsupial (or pouched mammal) (q.v.) found in the Americas, all others belonging to Australasia. There are several different species: in some the female has a fully formed pouch, while in others there is no pouch, or only a rudimentary one consisting of two folds in the skin of the abdomen. Opossums are rather like rats to look at (though some species are much bigger); but they have longer snouts, with quite naked muzzles. Their tails are very long, partially naked, and prehensile at the tips. Except for the Water Opossum they all live in trees, and are nocturnal, sleeping during

W. J. Hamilton, Jnr.

COMMON OPOSSUM

the day among the leaves or in hollow trunks. Nearly all Opossums are expert climbers, helping themselves with their prehensile tails, which they can twine round the branches. Most of them eat every sort of food—flesh, insect, or vegetable. In those species in which the female has no pouch, the young, after leaving their mother's teats, are carried on her back, holding on by curling their tails round her tail, which she bends back for the purpose.

The best known, and much the largest of the Opossums, is the Common or Virginian Opossum—the only species found in North America, all the others belonging to Central and South America. It is about the size of a cat, and has a tail some 35 cm in length, and a coat of long, bristle-like grey hairs with very soft black and white under-fur. These Virginian Opossums are most destructive to poultry and game, for they eat birds and their eggs, as well as the usual food of Opossums. Six to sixteen young are born in a litter. The mother shows great devotion to her offspring, and will use every means in her power to prevent her pouch from being opened. When the little creatures become too big for their mother's pouch, they cling to her body,

hanging on to her fur, legs, or tail, and are carried about with her wherever she goes. When caught, the Virginian Opossum invariably pretends to be dead—from which has originated the expression 'to play possum'.

The Water Opossum or Yapock, found from Guatemala to Brazil, has webbed hind toes, and spends much of its time in the water. It is about 35 cm long, with a tail longer than its body. Its short, close, light-grey coat has a much darker stripe, expanding into blotches down its back. It is very like an otter in its habits, and feeds on crustaceans and small fishes. The female has a complete pouch.

ORANGE-TIP BUTTERFLIES, *see* WHITES.

ORANG-UTAN, *see* APE.

ORCHIDS. Though orchids are generally thought of as exotic hot-house flowers, there are about fifty different members of the orchid family growing wild in this country. The vast majority, however, grow in warmer climates; and the remarkable flowers seen in hot-houses in this country grow equally luxuriantly and in great profusion in TROPICAL JUNGLES (q.v.), of which they are characteristic.

All orchids are perennial herbs. In the hot, steamy jungles, they grow perched in crevices in trees, sending down twining roots which cling to the branches for support. Such plants are called 'epiphytes'. They do not absorb their food or water from the tree itself—for then they would be PARASITIC PLANTS (q.v.)—but from the humus, chiefly dead leaves, which collects around them. Besides the food-absorbing roots, many orchids have long aerial roots, which hang suspended in the humid jungle atmosphere. The outside layer of these roots is spongy, offering a large surface on which moisture from the surrounding air condenses, perhaps providing the orchid with water-supply. There are a great many species of tropical orchids, many of them very richly coloured and beautiful.

The flowers of most orchids have only one stamen. There are no true sepals or petals; but the petalloid structures are arranged in two sets of three, of which the three outer are usually equal in size and comparatively small. The three inner 'petals' are very unequal, both in size and form, those in some of the tropical flowers being large and highly coloured. The lower

Harold Bastin

Heath Spotted Orchid

Harold Bastin

Butterfly Orchid

Harold Bastin

Fragrant Orchid

Eric Hosking

Pyramid Orchid

John Markham

Twayblade

Harold Bastin

Bee Orchid

NATIVE BRITISH ORCHIDS

front 'petal', called the 'labellum', is the largest, and is extended forwards to form a platform with drooping wings, and backwards to form a spur. The two inner 'petals' form an upright hood, which is fused with the style. Orchids have one of the most efficient and ingenious methods of cross-pollination in the whole plant kingdom. An insect, after alighting on the platform of the labellum, tries to force its mouth-parts down the spur, and so brings its head in contact with the contents of the anther-lobes, which are called 'pollinia'. In withdrawing, it pulls with it these pollinia (really masses of pollen), which then stand erect, like two Indian clubs, on the insect's head. They soon curve forwards and downwards, however; and when carried to the next flower, they strike against the stigma, so causing cross-pollination to take place.

Most British orchids are normal, green ground-plants; but three of them have no green parts, and obtain their food from decaying organic matter (*see* SAPROPHYTES). One is the Bird's Nest Orchid, usually found in the decaying leaf-mould of beech woods. Its underground stem bears roots, forming a tangled mass surrounded by myriads of threads of a fungus, which help the plant to absorb foodstuffs from the humus—the whole looking very much like a bird's-nest. The upright stem grows about 30 cm high, and

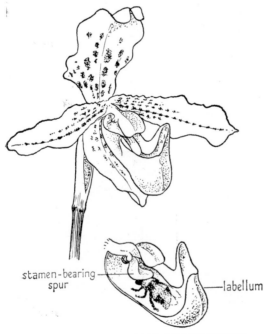

stamen-bearing spur — —labellum

FLOWER SHOWING METHOD OF CROSS-POLLINATION

bears leaves which are no more than tiny, brown scales, and dull-brown flowers crowded together in a dense spike at the top. Another saprophytic orchid is the Common Coral Root, a smaller yellowish plant, found rarely in the sandy woods of eastern Scotland. The third, the Spurred Coral Root or Ghost Orchid, is one of the rarest of British wild plants. It has been found in parts of Oxfordshire, Shropshire, and Herefordshire in only ten of the last hundred years. It has two or three flowers with yellowish sepals and petals and a large pink lip with pink markings. Its stem is also pinkish, and it has very tiny scaly leaves.

One of the most common British orchids is the Early Purple Orchid, often seen growing among bluebells and cowslips in open pastures. The long green leaves are blotched with brown, and the reddish-purple flowers grow in loose spikes. Its food is stored in tubers which, in Shakespeare's day, gave the plant the name of Dead Men's Fingers. Another common orchid is the Spotted Orchid which, with its spikes of pink-purple flowers and spotted leaves, is common in moist meadows and marshes throughout Britain, flowering in June and July.

The Twayblade, a not uncommon orchid, flowers in moist pastures and woods from May to July. This is easy to identify, because its stem, which grows up to 60 cm high, bears two large, oval, strongly ribbed leaves about half-way up. The small flowers are greenish-yellow. When touched by insect visitors, they rupture violently at one point, giving off a sticky fluid, which helps to bind the pollinia to the insect's head.

Three less common and beautiful orchids are the Bee Orchid, Fly Orchid, and Spider Orchid. They are local rather than rare, being confined to restricted areas in southern England. Many botanists have tried to find a reason for the remarkable resemblance of these flowers to the insects after which they have been named. One French scientist notes that the Fly Orchid resembles very closely the female of a particular insect, of which the male hatches some days before the female. He suggests that the male flies round looking for his mate, and finds the Fly Orchid instead. Before he can discover his mistake, his work of pollination is completed. But, in fact, most of these orchids are seldom visited by insects, and are usually self-pollinated.

The Autumn Tresses is a fairly common orchid, flowering during August and September in dry pastures. Each plant has four or five leaves, borne in a spreading tuft; while the small, white flowers, which smell like almonds, appear as a spirally twisted spike. Another rare orchid is the Musk Orchid, which has slender spikes of green flowers, smelling of musk. It is pollinated by small flies and beetles.

See also Vol. VI: ORCHIDS.
See also INDEX, p. 69.

ORIOLE.

Most Orioles, about the size of a thrush, are brilliantly coloured, yellow, green, and black predominating, though some species have crimson underparts. They are found in most tropical and temperate climates. The Golden Oriole belongs to Europe, Africa, and Asia, the Green Oriole to Australia, and the Mango Bird to India.

The Golden Oriole winters in central and southern Africa, but comes north to breed, visiting most parts of Europe and occasionally the southern counties of England. The male is a brilliant yellow and black bird, but is very shy and hides among the foliage, only revealing himself when he flies from one clump of trees to another. His loud, musical, flute-like whistle, however, often proclaims his presence. The

Eric Hosking

GOLDEN ORIOLE FEEDING ITS YOUNG

female is of a much less showy greenish-yellow. Orioles build nests which are generally suspended like a hammock from the bough of a tree.

OSMOSIS, *see* ROOTS, Section 2.

OSPREY.

This bird of prey—often called the Fishing Hawk in America—is related to the HAWKS and EAGLES (qq.v.), and is found throughout the greater part of the world, especially in northern America. It used to breed in Scotland, and one pair has done so since 1959. Ospreys are about 60 centimetres long, with very long wings and large, powerful claws covered with rough spiny scales. Their plumage is brown, the underparts white streaked with brown, and the head white.

Ospreys frequent large lakes or rivers in the neighbourhood of woods, and the sea-coast near cliffs. They feed on sea or freshwater fish, and can be seen sailing high above the water waiting for a catch. On sighting a fish, the Osprey drops suddenly and seizes the prey in its claws. It will then sometimes sail round and round for a long time, holding the fish in its claws before devouring it. It builds a large nest of sticks either in a tree or on a ledge of rock, and returns to the same nest year after year, adding to it till it becomes a bulky structure. It lays three or four eggs, and will protect the nest from attack with considerable ferocity.

OSTRICH.

The Ratites or flightless birds include not only the Ostriches proper, of Africa and south-west Asia, but also the Emus and Cassowaries of Australasia, the KIWIS (q.v.) of New Zealand, and the American Rheas, as well as several birds now extinct, such as the Moas.

1. OSTRICH. This is the largest of living birds; a male may stand over 2 metres high to the top of its head, weighing perhaps 136 kg. It is unique among birds in having only two toes, one long, strong toe on which the whole weight rests, and one much smaller and almost useless. The male has magnificent, glossy black plumage with white tail-feathers; while the female, a rather smaller bird, is dusky grey. The Ostrich has a small and flattened head, with a short beak, a very long, powerful neck, and long, stout, muscular legs, able to deliver very powerful defensive kicks, and to carry the bird at a great pace. Ostriches can, in fact, run even faster than Antelopes.

Australian News & Information Bureau

AUSTRALIAN EMU

Australian News & Information Bureau

AUSTRALIAN CASSOWARY

There are four species of Ostrich: one found in north Africa, Syria, and Arabia, and the other three in central and South Africa. Wild Ostriches are becoming scarcer; but the birds are now bred for their plumage on farms in Africa, America, and Australia. In the wild state they generally live in parties of 10 or 20, often moving about in company with Antelopes or Zebras, and depending on their very keen sight and great speed for defence. They feed on grass, leaves, and fruit, as well as on small animals and insects. They will, in fact, eat almost anything, 'the digestion of an ostrich' being proverbial. They need a certain amount of salt and a good deal to drink, though they can travel through the desert for long periods without water. As the breeding season approaches, they break up into small parties, each cock having three or four hens. The cock Ostrich makes a very elaborate display during the courtship season. He dances with his neck upright and his feathers fluffed out, and then suddenly drops to the ground and fans his mate with his rudimentary wings, blowing out his neck and making a sound rather like the roar of a lion (*see* ANIMAL LANGUAGE). The hens generally have a com-

munal nest in a hollow in the sand, in which they lay as many as twenty eggs. The cock incubates the eggs at night; during the day either the hens take charge or the eggs are covered with sand and incubated by the sun. The young chicks are guarded carefully (and often savagely) by their parents.

Ostrich-hunting has been a favourite sport of African natives, many devices for catching them being used. Generally, parties of Ostriches are surrounded by huntsmen on horseback; some times they are run down by relays of mounted huntsmen; sometimes they are driven into pitfalls; the BUSHMEN (q.v. Vol. I) used to dress up in Ostrich-skins and, keeping on the leeward side, would mix with a party of the birds. The habit proverbially attributed to the Ostrich of burying its head in the sand when faced with danger is less absurd than it sounds, for the Ostrich's skull is very weak, the most vulnerable part of its body.

2. EMU AND CASSOWARY. Both these birds, rather smaller than Ostriches, belong to Australasia, the Emus in open country and the Cassowaries in dense forests. Emus have light, mottled grey and brown plumage, with black

Mansell Coll.

MALE AND FEMALE OSTRICHES WITH THEIR NEST OF EGGS

up at the mating season into small parties of one cock and five to seven hens. The birds are fond of water and are bold swimmers. The hens lay from 20 to 30 eggs, only a proportion of which are hatched. Rhea hunting is a skilled sport, generally consisting of throwing the 'bola' (a kind of ball on a rope) at the birds.

4. MOA. This was a very large flightless bird, which used to be common in New Zealand until it was exterminated by the MAORIS (q.v. Vol. I) some time before the white man appeared there. There were several species of Moa, some as small as turkeys, and one as high as 3·6 metres. The largest egg of which the remains have been found measured about 25 by 18 centimetres.

tips to the feathers. They live in small parties, except in the breeding season, when they pair off. The female is often mistaken for the male, for she is the larger bird—and the cock incubates the eggs and broods the chicks. Emus protect their young fiercely by kicking at any enemy, both outwards and backwards. They are unpopular with farmers, since they eat the crops, and their numbers have been very much reduced in consequence.

Cassowaries have blue-black plumage, and carry on their heads helmet-like prominences of bone covered with blue-green and red skin. These and the wattles on their necks are protections to the birds as they push through the thick undergrowth of the forests. Cassowaries live in parties of seven or eight, except in the breeding season, when they pair. They are shy birds and difficult to watch.

3. RHEA. The 'Ostrich' of the plains of South America is a much smaller bird than the real Ostrich, and has three toes instead of two, a longer beak, and no apparent tail. Its blue-grey-brown plumage makes an excellent camouflage in the grassy plains. Rheas live in large companies of as many as sixty or more, and break

OTTER. This carnivorous water-animal belongs to the WEASEL family (q.v.), and is found in most parts of the world, but not in Australia. The various species do not differ very greatly from each other, though albino, cream-coloured, and spotted varieties are known, as well as the common brown. The wild Otter, if captured young, is easily tamed and will follow its owner about like a dog. In India and China, Otters are often trained to catch fish. In Britain, OTTER HUNTING (q.v. Vol. IX) used to be, and in places still is, a popular sport—a special type of hound being bred for the purpose.

The Common Otter, widely distributed throughout Europe and Asia, is a metre long, with webbed feet, thick, brown, waterproof fur, a long, tapering tail, and broad, flattened face. Both its nostrils and ears can be closed under water. It dives perfectly, and swims very fast, with muscular twists of its body and tail, and paddling with its fore-feet only. On coming out of the water, it shakes itself dry before lying up. On land it travels at a swift trot or gallop, frequently making journeys up to 24 kilometres. When excited, it utters a yelping bark, and gives a sort of whistle as an alarm note to its fellows.

Oliver Pike

OTTER ON THE LOOK-OUT

Most Otters spend the year by streams or tarns, going to the sea in dry summers and returning up-stream for the breeding season in autumn. Some, however, spend all the year by the sea-coast, only going up-stream during storms.

Otters live mainly on fish, but also eat rabbits, frogs, ducks, moorhens, snakes, worms, grouse— and they have even been known to kill sheep. They delight in hunting fish; and can chase, tire, and kill salmon larger than themselves. They often hunt in couples and, by working in circles from the centre of a pool, drive the fish to the shores. Their cheek-teeth can hold slippery fishes and at the same time pierce their hard scales. They kill their prey by biting the back-bone, and then take it on land to eat. They are shy, elusive animals, hunting only at night. They spend the day in permanent resting and breeding places, known as 'holts', in the banks of streams or in old hollow trees with an underwater en-trance. One chamber is normally used as an earth closet. On the Norfolk Broads, Otters build large nests of dry reeds; in other places, of dry grass and leaves. The female, or bitch, generally produces one to three whelps in the spring. The young are born with fine, silky coats, and are blind for 35 days. Before their eyes open, the mother carries them under water. At 8 weeks old, they reluctantly learn to swim and, gradually, to hunt for themselves.

The Sea Otter is quite unlike other members of the Otter family, and looks more like a Sea Bear (*see* SEALS). It is a larger and more massive animal than other otters, and has huge, webbed hind-feet. It used to be very common on the coasts of the North Pacific, but was very nearly exterminated by fur-hunters because of its soft, woolly, brown fur. Since 1910 it has been pro-tected, and is now becoming re-established in its old haunts. It is a playful animal, and lies on its back for hours tossing bits of seaweed up in the air. Its quick hearing and acute smell are unequalled in any other creature, and it is so timid that it will not go anywhere near where man has been.

OUNCE, *see* LEOPARD.

OVEN BIRD. The Red Oven Bird, or Hornero, of Central and South America is about the size of a thrush, with red-brown plumage above, shading to nearly white underneath, and with a bright, red-brown tail. It is most often to be found in the open country, parks, and gardens of Paraguay and Argentina. It is remarkable for its unusual nest, a large globular structure of clay, about 30 cm in diameter, and often weigh-ing as much as 4 kg, which is shaped like a baker's oven—hence the bird's name. The nest is placed conspicuously on a bare branch or post, often facing a road, or on the roof or beam of a building. It consists of an outer vestibule, with a small entrance into the central chamber, where there is a soft lining on which the four or five white eggs are laid. This nest takes a long time to build, and the birds often start building in the autumn, resuming work in open spells through the winter.

OWLETS, *see* NIGHT-FLYING MOTHS.

OWLS. These birds of prey, of which there are some 200 species distributed over almost the whole world, form an order of their own. They all have the characteristic 'owl-face', due to the forward direction of their large eyes and to the circular disk of radiating feathers round each. As the eyes can move in their sockets to a very small extent only, the owl has to turn its head when following any wide movement. This it can do so far, that it can look over its own back. Owls have well-developed ears, and a keen sense of hearing as well as of sight. They have strong, hooked beaks, feathered legs, and toes with sharp, curved claws; the outer claw can be directed backwards or forwards. Many species carry small erect tufts of feathers on their heads. The plumage, usually a mottled blending of browns and greys, is very soft; and this enables the birds to make a practically noiseless, ghost-like flight, very useful in hunting prey by night.

Owls range in size from the Pigmy Owlet, no larger than a thrush, to the Great Eagle-owl, larger than a buzzard. Most species hunt only by night and sleep all day; some hunt by either day or night; while the Hawk-owls prefer the bright sunlight for hunting. All are carnivorous,

eating small mammals, reptiles, birds, insects, worms, and snails. The large Fish-owls of India and Africa catch fish, crabs, and other water creatures. Most owls are beneficial to farmers, for they feed so largely on rats, mice, and other vermin; but the Eagle-owls, which will attack game-birds, hares, and rabbits, are more harmful. Many species are arboreal, often using the discarded nests of crows in which to lay their nearly round, white eggs. Some species roost and nest in clefts of rock or in buildings, especially barns, church towers, or ruins. They swallow most of their food whole, and throw up the indigestible parts in the form of pellets. Ornithologists, by examining these pellets, can tell exactly what the bird's diet has been.

The Barn-owls form a separate family in the Order. They are quite small—little over 30 cm long; but have larger eyes than any other bird. They are sometimes called White Owls, because their faces are white and their general plumage paler than the typical colouring. They are also called Screech-owls, because of the weird shriek which they make through the night, especially early in the year. They prefer to live close to human habitations, and their loud 'snores' have an almost human sound. Barn Owls, and other owls, lay their eggs at intervals of two or more days. The young, therefore, hatch at intervals, and birds at different stages are in the same nest. In years when food is scarce, the smaller ones cannot compete with their larger brothers, and so die of starvation. When there is plenty of food, all the young are raised. Both parents incubate, and have been found sitting side by side, each incubating some of the eggs.

The Tawny, Brown, or Wood Owl, a rather

Zoological Society of London

SNOWY OWL

Eric Hosking

BARN OWL

Arthur Brook

TAWNY OWL USING THE DISCARDED NEST OF A BUZZARD
This owl has turned her head right round so that she is
looking over her back

larger bird, lives chiefly in woods. It continually utters its cry, 'too-whit, too-whoo'; and in the breeding season, when it is very noisy, it also utters a laughter-like cry. The Long-eared and Short-eared Owls carry tufts of feathers, not really ears, on their heads. They are nocturnal in their habits, and are shy, avoiding human habitation. If attacked, they are fierce and spit like cats. If caught in the open in the daylight, they are often mobbed by the small birds who by night fly in terror of them. The Little Owl, only about 19 cm long, is a bold and savage hunter, sometimes attacking by day as well as by night, and flying rather like a bat. There are many other interesting species, including the handsome Snowy Owls of the Arctic with their white, slightly spotted plumage, and the large Horned Owls or Eagle-owls, found all over the world, except Australasia.

OX, *see* CATTLE.

OYSTER. If an unopened Oyster is carefully examined, it will be seen to have unequal shell-valves, the left or lower valve being more saucer-like in shape, stouter in build, and convex externally; while the right or uppermost valve is flatter and lighter, and therefore easier for the Oyster to raise when it gapes. It will also be seen that the surface of the valves shows many irregular narrow lines, which may be grouped into a few larger zones. These wavy lines are a record of the changes in the life of the Oyster, each zone indicating fairly accurately a year's growth; whereas the lines indicate the rhythmic seasonal alternation of periods of active growth and of inactivity, their distinctness being due to the fact that the Oyster practically ceases to feed during the winter, from about the end of November to the middle of March. As there can be no shell growth while the Oyster is fasting, what has already been formed during the spring and summer becomes slightly weathered and corroded, and this results in a distinct boundary-line showing where each new spring growth starts. Although the Common Oyster produces many thousands of eggs each year, only a very small number of the young Oysters survive, most of them being eaten by other animals. Even in later life, the growing Oyster, now settled on the sea-floor, has many enemies such as Starfishes and Dog-whelks.

What the fisherman calls 'white-sick' and 'black-sick' Oysters are not really 'sick' at all: the terms simply indicate two natural stages in the development of the young within the safe shelter of their parent's shell. When the young are ready, the parent Oyster slightly opens the valves of her shell and blows out the 'spat' (or young Oysters) in jets, looking like miniature clouds, into the surrounding water. The young Oyster must then find some suitable ground on which to anchor itself, and unless it does so within 48 hours of its expulsion from the parent shell it will perish. Once attached to some solid object, such as a piece of rock, growth is rapid, the young Oyster increasing from about 1 millimetre across to about 9 mm in the first 5 or 6 months, and in a year to about 2·5 cm. Thereafter, its age may be roughly told by the number of centimetres it measures across its shell. If left undisturbed on their natural breeding ground, Oysters become full grown in about 4 years.

See also PEARL OYSTER.
See also Vol. VI: OYSTER FISHING.

OYSTER-CATCHER, *see* WADING BIRDS, Section 6.

P

PAINTED LADY BUTTERFLY, *see* VANES-SINAE.

PALMS, *see* DESERT PLANTS. *See also* Vol. VI: PALM TREES.

PANDA. Pandas are related both to RACCOONS and to BEARS (qq.v.), and are to be found principally in north-eastern India and western China. There are two kinds—the Red or True Panda, sometimes popularly known as the Cat Bear, and the Giant Panda, or Parti-coloured Bear, which was first shown at the London Zoo in 1939, and has since become very popular in Britain.

Red Pandas, which are about the size of large

Mondiale

GIANT PANDA AND YOUNG

domestic cats, live in the south-eastern Himalayas and south-west China. Their long, thick fur is usually dark red on top of the body, and black below, including the legs; their faces are white with red stripes running from the eyes to the corners of the mouth; and their tails are marked with light and dark red rings. They move awkwardly on the ground, but spend most of their life in trees, using their sharp, curved claws for climbing. During the day they sleep in hollow trunks or between the branches. They normally sleep curled up sideways with their heads hidden by their tails; but they frequently rest by sitting down on their haunches with their heads tucked in between their forepaws. They generally eat in the early morning and evening, their food being various fruits, acorns, bamboo shoots, and sometimes eggs. They make their nests in hollow tree-trunks or in rock crevices, in which two young are born in the spring. The Red Panda is a stupid, sluggish animal, which can be captured easily. Although it will hiss and spit like a cat, and growl like a young bear when angry, it seldom uses its strong claws in its defence. It is easily tamed at whatever age it is captured; but is sensitive to the cold, and needs great care when kept in Zoos in Europe.

Giant Pandas live in the large bamboo forests of western China. They are not at all like Red Pandas, but look more like bears, and have very short tails and large, broad feet. Their colouring is remarkable—mainly white, but with black ears, legs, and feet, black patches round their eyes, and a broad black band passing round the body from the front legs over the shoulders. They sleep during the day in hollow tree-trunks or in other secluded places, and come out at night to eat roots and bamboo shoots, or small mammals and fish, which they hold between their forepaws and chew with their very powerful jaws.

PANGOLIN (or SCALY ANT-EATER). This mammal belongs to the order of animals called the Pholidota. At one time it was included with the ANT-EATERS and ARMADILLOS (qq.v.) in the order Edentata, simply because it, like the Anteaters, is toothless. In addition there is a superficial resemblance between the armour of the Pangolin and that of the Armadillo. Pangolins are found in various parts of Asia and Africa. They are covered all over with large, overlapping, horny scales, which make them look much like elongated fir-cones with a head, legs, and,

Harold Bastin

THE SCALY ANT-EATER OR PANGOLIN OF CHINA

usually, a long tail. Like the Ant-eaters, they have powerful legs and claws, and long, elastic, sticky tongues, which they use to lick up the ants and termites on which they live. The largest species live on the ground and dig themselves burrows; the smaller species live in trees, using their long tails to support themselves in climbing, the sharp points of the scales being pressed against the trunk. All roll themselves up into balls when attacked, relying for their safety upon their hard, scaly covering and on a nauseous-smelling secretion which they can give out. The young Pangolins are carried around seated on their mother's tail.

PANTHER, *see* LEOPARD.

PAPER NAUTILUS, *see* OCTOPUS.

PARASITES. These are animals or plants which derive their nourishment from the living bodies of other animals or plants. They generally weaken and sometimes even kill their 'hosts'.

1. ANIMAL PARASITES. Some animals are parasites at all stages of their existence; others, such as the ICHNEUMON FLY (q.v.), are parasites in their early stage of life but not when adult; others again, such as FLEAS (q.v.), are parasites only when adult. Many parasites, such as Liver Flukes, have different hosts at different stages in their lives. A parasite that lives upon the surface of its host, as does a BED BUG (q.v.), is an 'ectoparasite'; one that lives inside its host, as a tapeworm does, is an 'endoparasite'. External

or Ectoparasites are small animals such as FLEAS, BUGS, LICE, or MITES AND TICKS (qq.v.), most of which suck the blood of warm-blooded animals, such as birds and mammals. Internal or Endoparasites consist principally of PARASITIC WORMS (q.v. Vol. VI) and the larvae of certain flies.

Some insects that make GALLS (q.v.) live as parasites in the stems of plants and trees.

2. PARASITIC PLANTS. Most plants derive their nourishment by PHOTOSYNTHESIS (q.v.), but Parasitic plants get their food, in varying degrees, from the living cells of other plants or animals.

'Complete parasites' are totally devoid of the green colouring matter (chlorophyll) which is necessary for photosynthesis and are, therefore, entirely dependent on their hosts for food. Many FUNGI, some BACTERIA (qq.v.), and a few flowering plants, such as the Dodder, Broomrape, and Toothwort, are complete parasites. Other parasites contain some chlorophyll and nourish themselves partly by photosynthesis and partly from the bodies of other plants or animals. An example of these 'semi-parasites', which are generally flowering plants, is the MISTLETOE (q.v.). Other semi-parasites are partial root-parasites, of which the Yellow Rattle, Lousewort, Eyebright, and Cow-wheat, all members of the Foxglove family, are typical examples. Most of them live in pastures and meadows, and send out suckers from their roots to penetrate the roots of grasses, from which they absorb some of their food. The Lousewort can grow independently, but the others cannot grow apart from the grasses.

In many cases, parasitic plants kill the host plant or animal on which they live. In others, the parasites cause disease, so that the host plant becomes deformed, or has a reduced growth or production of fruit. They are a terrible pest to farmers and gardeners, and, in tropical countries, cause losses of many thousands of tonnes of valuable crops each year. Yet some plant parasites scarcely affect their hosts at all.

The Dodder is a flowering plant which is

completely dependent for food on its host plants, Clover, Gorse, Hop, Thyme, Heather, Flax, or Nettles. The Dodder seed germinates late in the spring when the host plants have already developed their shoots. The seedling is a delicate yellow thread, capable of standing erect, which sways in ever-widening circles as it grows. If, as it sways, it meets with a suitable host, it twines round the stem, and sends out suckers. These penetrate the tissues of the host until they reach the wood and bast tubes, and thus obtain supplies of organic food, as well as water and mineral salts. Once the parasite is established, its root dies. The yellowish stem branches a great deal and produces minute scale leaves and numerous small clusters of pink flowers. Dodder is common in meadows, especially in Clover fields. It seldom kills its host, which generally manages to produce enough food to supply both itself and the parasite.

Broomrapes, of which there are several species, are also complete parasites, obtaining their food from the roots of other plants. The Great Broomrape grows chiefly on the roots of Broom and Gorse, and the Lesser Broomrape grows on various plants, but more particularly on Clover. All the Broomrapes have colourless stems, bearing whitish-yellow, scale leaves. The flowers are conspicuous, being borne at the top of the stem, and vary from brown to yellow and red, but never green.

The Toothwort is parasitic on the roots of Beech, Hazel, and other trees, and is therefore found chiefly in woods. It has a creeping underground stem or rhizome, bearing crowded fleshy leaves; and the erect stem carries a spike of purplish flowers. Like the Dodder, the Toothwort obtains its food by sending out suckers into the tissues of the host plant. The hollow leaves on the underground shoots were thought to be traps for insects (*see* INSECTIVOROUS PLANTS); but they probably serve to absorb water from the host plant.

PARROTS. This group of birds, which forms a separate order containing six families, includes Parrots, Macaws, Love-birds, Cockatoos, and Budgerigars. There are altogether more than 500 species, found mostly in tropical and subtropical regions. There are not many in India, and still fewer in Africa; while in Malaya, Australasia, and South America there are great numbers of very varied types. One species is found in the southern states of the U.S.A.; but there is none in Europe.

The most characteristic features of the Parrots are their feet and beaks, both of which are adapted for their life in trees, where they need to climb more than to fly. In the feet, the first and fourth toes are directed backwards, and the second and third forwards. The feet are covered with rough scales, and the legs are short—in some species extremely short. The beak is short, stout, and strongly hooked, the upper part having a hinged top which can be lifted at will. Parrots climb as much with their beaks as with their feet, clinging with them to the branches of trees—or to the bars of a cage. In the larger species, the beak is enormously strong—the Blue Macaw of Brazil, for instance, crushes to pulp in its beak palm-nuts which a man could break open only with a heavy hammer. They use their beaks also for hollowing out a suitable nesting chamber in a tree-trunk.

Parrots lay white eggs, the larger species producing only two or three in a season. Both parents generally take part in the incubation, and the young are fed by half-digested food disgorged from the parents' crops. Parrots are vegetarians, feeding on various fruits and nuts. They generally feed in large and extremely noisy parties, and love to congregate in open, sunny gardens and orchards. One species, however, the Kea or Mountain Kaka of New Zealand, has gained a reputation for killing sheep in order to feed on the fat round the kidneys. The Keas have developed their carnivorous habits during the comparatively short period since sheep were introduced to New Zealand. Now they are a

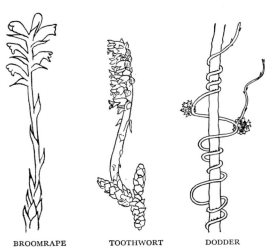

BROOMRAPE   TOOTHWORT   DODDER

considerable menace to farmers. These birds are also unlike other Parrots in that they nest in mid-winter, high up among the glaciers and snowfields of the mountains.

Parrots vary greatly in size. The Great Black Cockatoo of New Guinea is a heavy bird, about 76 centimetres long; while the Macaws of America are even longer, the brilliant Red-and-blue Macaw of Central America being 90 cm long, nearly 60 cm of which is tail. On the other hand, the green and blue Parrotlets of Central America and the vivid little Love-birds of Africa are only about 13 cm long, while the Pigmy Parrots of New Guinea are smaller than a sparrow—just over 7·5 cm. The best known of all Parrots, the African Grey Parrot, has grey plumage with a bright red tail. The prevalent colour, however, as is natural for arboreal, fruit-eating birds, is green, though many species have brilliant hues of blue, yellow, crimson, white, and occasionally black. Perhaps the Macaws are the most showy, as well as being the most noisy, of the group; though the Purple-capped Lory of Australasia is gorgeous—a scarlet bird with a golden throat, blue and green wings, and a deep purple cap on the head.

Cockatoos are characteristic of all Australasia, except New Zealand and the eastern islands. They bear a crest of feathers on the head; their skulls differ from those of other Parrots; and they

Booth Steamship Co.
A PAIR OF SOUTH AMERICAN MACAWS

have short legs, and short, deep beaks. The predominant colour, instead of green, is white, generally tinged with red or yellow, especially on the crest and tail. In one species the whole breast is red and the back is grey; another species is entirely grey except for its red head. The Raven Cockatoos are black, one species having a vermilion band across the tail. The Great Black Cockatoo, one of the largest of all Parrots, is slaty-black, with pale-red cheeks. This bird uses its enormously powerful beak for breaking open the very hard shell of its favourite food, the Kanary-nut. The most gorgeous of all Cockatoos is Leadbeater's Cockatoo of South Australia, a magnificent bird with white plumage, shading to rose-colour on cheeks, breast, and under-wings, and a very showy crest with bands of vermilion and yellow.

One of the prettiest and best known of the Parakeets is the Budgerigar of Australia. It has a complicated colour-pattern of grass-green, blue, pale yellow, and black, and has a long tail, taking up more than half its length of 19 cm. It is to be seen in large flocks in the neighbourhood of Adelaide, perching on the gum trees, or hunting for the seeds on which it lives.

Parrots, as is well known, live very well in captivity, and become extremely tame and friendly. Their great powers of mimicry and their excellent memories enable them to repeat words and phrases taught to them (see CAGE BIRDS: Vol. IX). Parrots live to a great age, many of the larger species being known to have lived 60 to 80 years in captivity.

PARTRIDGE. This game-bird (see GAME SHOOTING, Vol. IX) is a relative of the PHEASANT and GROUSE (qq.v.). The common Grey or Brown Partridge is found throughout Europe and much of Asia; and its close relative, the Spur-legged Partridge, or Francolin, belongs to Africa. The Snow-partridge lives in the high mountain ranges of central Asia; and from there to south-east Asia are found the Tree-partridges, which, unlike typical Partridges, perch in trees. Wood-partridges rarely leave the jungle, where they live in parties of six to a dozen; some of them are glossy black, while others carry fan-shaped, maroon crests of hairy feathers.

The common Partridges are stocky birds about 32 centimetres long, with the well-known horseshoe marking on their chests, the male and female birds being very much alike. They are

Eric Hosking

RED-LEGGED PARTRIDGE AND NEST

netted in vast numbers on the Mediterranean coasts, until they were nearly exterminated. Attempts are now made to protect them. There are several other species of Quails in India, tropical Africa, and Australia. The American Quail, although belonging to the same family, is a rather distant relative. There are several species, both in North and South America, one of which carries a handsome crest of black, club-shaped feathers.

See also Vol. IX: GAME SHOOTING.

PEACH-BLOSSOM MOTH. This medium-sized moth has olive-brown fore-wings with five pinkish patches clouded with brown. This coloration suggests peach-blossom—though the pink patches, in fact, make the moth resemble the fallen petals of its food-plant, bramble. The Peach-blossom Moth is common in many wooded districts in England and Ireland. The velvety reddish-brown and grey caterpillar has a series of humps on its back, and usually rests with its hind part raised. It pupates in September in a frail cocoon among dead leaves on the ground.

Other British moths of this small family are the Buff Arches, Figure of Eight, Poplar and Lesser Lutestrings, Lesser Satin, Satin Carpet, Yellow Horned, and Frosted Green. They superficially resemble Caradrinidae (*see* NIGHT-ING MOTHS), though they are not related to them, and differ from them structurally in many ways. The caterpillars usually hide by day among leaves held together with silk, and, like the Peach-blossom, frequently adopt curious resting positions. Their food-plants are bramble, poplar, birch, alder, and oak.

PEACOCK. Pea-fowl are game-birds, belonging to the same order as PHEASANTS and PART-RIDGES (qq.v.). They have the upper tail-coverts developed into a long train, which the cock can spread out into a magnificent fan. These long feathers are decorated with the well-known 'eyes'. The Peahen resembles the cock except for the train, which the cock himself does not develop fully until the third year. Pea-fowl also carry delicate, fan-like, erect crests. Peacocks are found wild from India to the East Indies, preferring jungle-land near water, and not reaching to the high altitudes inhabited by many pheasants. They have been domesticated since very early times, the Romans keeping them both

found chiefly on arable land, and are useful to the farmer as, besides being valuable food themselves, they destroy insect pests. After the breeding season, they congregate in coveys generally composed of parents and young, two or more families sometimes joining together. At night, the covey 'jugs'—that is, they form a circle, nestling closely together in grass or growing crops. In the spring, the party breaks up with a good deal of quarrelling into pairs, and these remain together, nesting at the end of April or in May. The hen lays ten to twenty olive-brown eggs in a nest in the grass. The male has a loud, hoarse cry, 'caer-wit, caer-wit', which in still weather can be heard from a great distance. In the 18th century, the Red-legged or French Partridge was introduced into Britain, and is established in many places, though it never consorts with the common Partridge. The hen French Partridge frequently lays two clutches of her yellowish-white, red-spotted eggs in separate nests, each parent incubating one clutch, and the two groups joining up when the young are hatched.

Quails are small, stout, partridge-like birds, which winter in Africa and southern Asia. In spring they migrate northwards in large flocks, the cocks generally arriving first. They breed in Europe, and occasionally in southern England and Ireland, among rough pasture and arable. The birds, which are good food, used to be

for ornament and for food. A Peacock served whole in all its plumage was a characteristic dish for a medieval banquet.

Another pheasant, rather like a Peacock in appearance, and also decorated with the characteristic 'eye-spots', is the Argus-pheasant, the most spectacular of which is the Rheinhardt's Argus of Indo-China, which measures about 2 metres from head to tail. Argus-pheasants live in the depth of the evergreen forests, each male selecting for his own territory an open, level spot, which he clears of debris and undoubtedly uses as a dancing-ground. In his courtship he makes a magnificent display of his tail and spectacular wing-feathers (*see* ANIMAL LANGUAGE).

PEACOCK BUTTERFLY, *see* VANESSINAE.

PEACOCK MOTH, *see* EMPEROR MOTH.

PEARL OYSTER. The so-called Pearl Oyster, which produces the finest pearls and most valuable mother-of-pearl, is not an oyster at all, but belongs to another family of MOLLUSCS allied to the SCALLOPS (qq.v.). It is widely distributed in tropical seas, where the different varieties have received local names, such as the Black-edged Banda-shell from the seas of the Malay Archipelago, and the giant Silver-lip Shell, highly prized for its mother-of-pearl, from Australia and New Guinea.

In outline the shell somewhat resembles that of a Scallop, the upper valve being flat, and the lower slightly convex externally. Inside the valves there is a lining of nacre, commonly known as mother-of-pearl, which is the same substance as that from which pearls are formed. Pearl growth is started by the presence of some minute foreign body, frequently the tiny dead body of a parasitic worm, a grain of sand, or a fragment of shell, which has got lodged in the mantle tissues of the mollusc, and around which the nacre or pearl secretion has been deposited. The beautiful lustre is due to extremely minute wavy lines, which break up the light falling upon the surface of the pearl, and, in mother-of-pearl, produce delicate rainbow tints.

A perfectly spherical or 'orient' pearl as it is called is one that has remained throughout its growth enfolded in the fleshy tissues or mantle of the mollusc. Very often, however, the pearl in its early stages becomes cemented at one end to the inside of the shell, so that, when ultimately cut from the shell, it presents the appearance of a sphere that has been cut in half. The perfect pearl must be of fine texture, free from any visible speck or blemish, and of a clear, almost transparent white colour, showing a soft iridescent sheen; in shape it must be either perfectly spherical or symmetrically pear-shaped. Such a specimen, flawless and perfect in shape, is rare indeed and, when found, is literally 'a pearl of great price'. What are known as 'blister pearls', hollow bodies of irregular shape formed on the inner surface of the shell, are caused by the pearl oyster protecting itself from an external boring foe by depositing nacreous material beneath the point where the enemy has started tunnelling inwards.

The Pearl Oyster is not the only mollusc capable of producing pearls: our British freshwater Pearl Mussel, the common marine Edible Mussel, the West Indian Great Conch or Fountain-shell, and the large Chink-shell all at times form pearls, while black pearls are chiefly obtained from a species of Pearl Oyster that lives in the waters of the Gulf of Mexico.

See also OYSTER; MUSSEL.
See also Vol. VI: PEARL FISHING.

PEARLY NAUTILUS. This MOLLUSC (q.v.) lives in the seas of the Far East, in the shallow waters round the Philippines, Moluccas, New Britain, New Guinea, and Fiji. It is of particular interest, because it belongs to the only surviving genus of an ancient and extinct race of Cephalopods (*see* MOLLUSCS) which flourished in the seas of past geological ages. It must not be confused

Zoological Society of London

SHELL OF PEARLY NAUTILUS

with the Argonaut or Paper Nautilus (*see* OCTOPUS), to which it is only distantly related. The Pearly Nautilus has a large and handsome cream-coloured shell, the interior of which is divided by curved partitions into a number of chambers, each a little larger than the first. These compartments have been added one by one to accommodate the Nautilus as it increased in size, the last-formed and largest chamber being its final abode. The smaller, empty and shut-off compartments are air-tight, and contain a gas rich in nitrogen, secreted by the Nautilus, which helps to make the large and solidly built shell more buoyant.

The Pearly Nautilus, like the Octopus, swims by the rhythmic expulsion of water from its siphon-tube, and crawls head downward on the floor of the sea. The visible part of the animal is brownish, mottled with white. Round the top of the head, which has the mouth in the centre, is a large number of small, short tentacles, which take the place of the sucker-clad arms of the Octopus and Cuttlefishes. When the tentacles are extended beyond the mouth of the shell, the Nautilus resembles a queer kind of Sea-anemone.

John Warham

AUSTRALIAN PELICANS

PELICAN. This large bird, which is found in most tropical and warm regions of the world, belongs to the same order as the CORMORANTS and GANNETS (qq.v.). There are about ten species, which do not vary very much from each other. They have small heads, short legs, massive bodies, long necks, and thick, harsh plumage —generally dishevelled-looking. The most conspicuous feature is the Pelican's beak, which is enormous. It is very long, flattened, and deeply furrowed, and the lower half has a great pouch. The whole beak acts like a fishing-net with a lid.

The European Pelican, which is typical of the family, has white plumage tinged with pink, with some black wing-feathers and yellow neck-feathers. The great beak is pale red, shading to yellow, with a crimson line along the middle. The pouch and feet are flesh-coloured. The birds are about 1·5 metres long. They live in very large flocks near swamps, estuaries, or rivers, feeding on fish, which they catch by diving and by systematic fishing in companies in the shallow water. They appear to keep regular periods of fishing and resting. They nest generally in small groups, making flat, sometimes large, nests of sticks, and laying two or three eggs

with thick, bluish-white shells. The female feeds the young by allowing them to thrust their beaks into her pouch, where fish is ready for them. Although Pelicans are clumsy birds, they dive gracefully and fly powerfully—a flock of them flying in a long line with their great necks bent back over their bodies is a very striking sight.

PENGUINS. These flightless birds, adapted for life in the sea rather than the air, form a separate order, which includes about seventeen species. Their wings, which are paddle-like and used for swimming instead of flying, are small and stiff from the shoulder, with no elbow-joint —so that Penguins cannot fold up their wings as other birds can. They have no quills, but are covered with small, scale-like feathers. Their legs are short and very thick, and are set very far back so that they can walk in an upright position. Their beaks are strong and pointed. They are much more agile and graceful in the water than on land, swimming and diving so well that they have been mistaken for dolphins or porpoises. They eat fish and other sea animals, which they catch (and sometimes swallow) under water, and also some weed. On land they have a quaint, waddling walk, and when frightened they help themselves along by flapping their little wings.

Penguins belong entirely to the southern hemisphere, though they range from the Antarctic to islands almost on the Equator. They breed in great numbers on most of the lonely islands of the southern seas. They are, in general, dark or even black on the back and white on the front. The Blue Penguin has a pale-blue back, with a black line down each feather. Some species have yellowish crests as well. Penguins vary in size from the great Emperor Penguin of the Antarctic, which stands about a metre high and weighs as much as 40 kg, to the little Blue Penguin of New Zealand, which is only 48 centimetres tall.

Their breeding habits vary a good deal. The Emperor Penguins and the King Penguins of the lonely islands in the Southern Ocean breed at the beginning of the winter. They make no nest, but protect the single egg by placing it in a sort of fold or pouch of skin in front of the body, where it keeps warm in the down feathers and rests on the bird's feet. The chick remains within this protection until it is developed enough to

stand the cold. In spite of this arrangement, however, a great many chicks do die of cold. The Jackass Penguins of the Falkland Isles make tunnels, sometimes 2 or 3 metres long, for their nests, burrowing into a sandy cliff or under thick bushes. While on shore, these birds keep up a strange donkey-like braying the whole day. Most Penguins breed in 'rookeries', thousands of them together, and lay their eggs in a slight hollow in the ground, both parents taking part in the incubation. They have well-beaten paths from the sea to their nesting colonies, along which they walk in solemn procession. The Black-throated or Adélie Penguins always make their nests up high cliffs reached by steep slopes, up which the birds must toil slowly every time they return from the sea—perhaps several times a day. The journey up is laborious for birds which cannot fly; but they make the return journey quickly by tobogganing down the slope on their chests. These birds carry out an amusing courtship. When they first come to the 'rookeries' in October, the sexes keep apart, the females seeking last year's nest, repairing it, and then sitting on it. After a time the males begin to get excited, fighting among themselves by pushing their chests against each other and striking with their tiny wings. Then, after much bowing and curtseying, they finally pair off. As is the case with many birds, the females appear to pay little attention to the males' display.

PERCH. Perch is a name widely applied to members of a very large group of bony fishes, the Percomorphi, which possess spiny dorsal fins. Most of these are marine and are treated under SEA PERCH (q.v.). The common Perch of the freshwaters of Europe and America is olive-brown or yellowish in colour, with dark cross-bands on the back, and bright red lower fins and tail-fin. The back-fin consists of two parts, the front portion being supported by strong, sharp spines, the hind part by soft, jointed, and branched rays. Perch generally move in shoals, and are very voracious, feeding on such small fish as Bleak or Roach—and even on smaller specimens of their own kind, difficult though these are to swallow because of the spiny fin on the back. Spawning takes place in April and May, the eggs being laid in long strings among weeds on the bed of the river. Very much like the Perch, and with similar habits, but much smaller, is the Pope or Ruffe of European and English rivers.

C. A. Gibson-Hill

A PENGUIN BRAYING

The egg is resting on the bird's feet, and is kept warm in the thick down

A. Fraser-Brunner

FRESHWATER SUNFISH AND YOUNG OF NORTH AMERICA

Among other freshwater Perch-like fishes there are the Darters, of which there are about fifty small, brightly coloured species living in American rivers, sheltering under stones in clear running water, feeding on the larvae of flies, and darting rapidly when disturbed. Much larger are the Pike-perches, found in Europe and America, some of which are popular as food and game fishes. The Common Perch has been used to illustrate the anatomy of fishes in the article on FISHES (q.v.).

The Sunfishes of North American freshwaters are very closely related to the Perch. Most of them are small, deep-bodied, and handsomely coloured. Some have breeding habits similar to those of the CICHLIDS (q.v.) of South America. Some of the prettier kinds have been introduced into Europe as pond and aquarium fishes, notably the Common Sunfish, Diamond Bass, Long-eared Sunfish, Blue-green Sunfish, and the dainty little Black-banded Sunfish, which thrives well in a tropical AQUARIUM (q.v. Vol. IX).

Much larger and longer in the body are the so-called Black Bass, celebrated as sporting-fishes, which have been introduced into various parts of the world, though not always success-fully.

PEREGRINE, *see* FALCON.

PERIWINKLE, *see* SNAIL, Section 4.

PETRELS. 1. These, and their relatives, the Albatrosses and Shearwaters, form the order of Tube-nosed birds, which contains a great many species of sea-birds, inhabiting most parts of the world, but especially belonging to the southern hemisphere. The distinguishing feature of these birds is that their nostrils grow out as tubes along the surface of the beak, the tip of which is sharply hooked. The three front toes are webbed, and the back toe is either very small or absent. Petrels have long wings and are capable of strong and sustained flight. They are swimmers rather than divers. They are carnivorous, feeding on carrion, cuttlefish, and crustaceans, and any available refuse. Some petrels, especially the Fulmars, look much like gulls, having the typical gull colouring of grey and white. They are, however, quite different structurally, and differ also in being comparatively silent.

2. ALBATROSS. This is the largest member of the order, forming a separate family, and distinguished by the fact that the nostril tubes lie along the sides instead of on the top of the beak. Albatrosses inhabit the southern seas, spending the greater part of their lives in the air. They have extremely long, narrow wings, with a wing-span of 3 metres or more—an enormous stretch for a bird weighing only some 8 kg. The Wandering Albatross is the largest of ocean birds, having a wing-span of over 3 metres. The plumage is yellowish-white, with blackish bars on the wings. The young birds are brownish, with white faces. The smaller Sooty Albatross has a dark ashy-grey plumage. Albatrosses will follow ships for hundreds of kilometres for food, a few strokes of their enormous wings carrying them great distances. They take every advantage of the wind, gliding, soaring, and making small quick movements with their wings. They only come to land at the breeding season, when they nest in colonies on lonely Pacific islands. They build a neat, conical nest of turf and clay, and lay one round white egg with a few reddish spots, as large as a swan's egg. In the Island of Laysan, the collecting of Albatrosses's eggs for the sake of their oil is an important industry.

3. STORMY PETREL. These are the smallest of the web-footed birds. No larger than skylarks, they are dingy blackish birds, with a white patch over the tail. Sailors often call them 'Mother Carey's chickens', and believe that they foretell stormy weather. When hunting for food on the surface of the water they have a habit of gliding over the waves with feet dangling, looking as though they were walking on the water—hence the name 'Petrel' (or little St. Peter). Stormy Petrels breed in the islands off British coasts. They lay their single egg in holes in walls, or in burrows, the nesting bird entering or leaving the nest only after dark. The egg takes 5 weeks

Eric Hosking
FULMAR NESTING ON A LEDGE IN THE CLIFF-SIDE

to incubate, and the nestling is fed by its parents for another two months, until it is extremely fat. When fully feathered, it is abandoned, and after a week or so of starvation, it finally leaves its burrow, and flies out to sea to look for a living.

4. FULMAR. This white and grey bird is much larger, being about 48 centimetres long. It is a superb flier, sweeping in huge arcs and, like other petrels, gliding for long distances with its wings held stiff and straight. It is very common round Pacific and North Atlantic coasts, and often follows ships for food. Its name means 'foul gull', and it is so called because, like most petrels, it has a habit of squirting stinking oil from its mouth at any intruder to its nesting ledge. The people of the St. Kilda Islands, where the Fulmar nests in great numbers, used to catch the birds for the sake of this oil, which they used for lamps. They also ate its flesh.

5. SHEARWATER. The commonest member of this species in European waters is the Manx Shearwater, a bird about the size of a pigeon, dingy black above and white below. It is so called because of its habit of shearing the wave-tops with rapid gliding flight, tilting first to one

side and then to the other. Like the Stormy Petrel, Shearwaters nest in colonies of burrows on lonely islands, and visit the nests only after dark. Then, the cries of thousands of birds, all calling at a slightly different pitch and rhythm, make a most weird din. The birds probably recognize their mates in the dark by the cry. The Great Shearwater from Tristan da Cunha, and the Sooty Shearwater from near New Zealand, often visit European seas in the summer.

6. MUTTON BIRD. This is the Australian and New Zealand name for the Short-tailed or Sooty Petrel, which inhabits the seas round those countries, nesting in vast colonies on the islands. They nest in burrows, sometimes as much as 2 metres long, and so numerous that the ground is completely honeycombed with them. Many of the nesting islands belong by tradition to the MAORIS (q.v. Vol. I), who run a flourishing trade both in the eggs and young birds for food. The young birds, just before they leave the nest, are extremely fat, and have a flesh of much the same texture as mutton, with a flavour rather like that of a kipper. The birds are not seen during the day-time, but after dark the air is filled with their weird cries.

PHALANGER, *see* MARSUPIALS.

PHEASANT. This game-bird belongs to an order containing many species, mostly belonging to the Old World. It includes the GROUSE, PARTRIDGES, GUINEA-FOWL, PEACOCKS, and TURKEYS (qq.v.), as well as the Pheasants. Most species have naked legs and feet, and carry one or more pairs of spurs on their legs.

Pheasants belong essentially to southern Asia, especially to the Himalayas, Tibet, and the mountains of north Burma, north-west China, and Manchuria. The Common Pheasant is a native of central Asia and south-eastern Europe, and was probably first introduced to Britain by the Romans. It has been a common resident ever since. It is a magnificent bird, nearly a metre long, with brilliant metallic plumage and a long tapering tail. A cock-pheasant in full spring plumage, flying out of a cover in the spring sunshine, is a sight of startling brilliance. As with most game-birds, the female is smaller and carries much more sober plumage. Pheasants roost in trees, but otherwise are ground birds, feeding on roots, grain, berries, and insects. In the spring the cocks fight fiercely for their mates.

They fluff out their feathers and fly at each other, leaping in the air and striking with foot and beak. The hen lays about ten to fourteen eggs in a hollow on the ground. The chicks, which are covered with down, run out after the hen as soon as they are hatched.

Some of the Pheasants of south-eastern Asia are brilliantly coloured birds, living at very high altitudes in the mountains, and coming down to the lower forests in great numbers in the winter. The green, crimson, and grey Blood Pheasants are to be seen in packs of seventy to a hundred birds in the forests during December. Among the most gorgeous is the Monal Pheasant, which has a long tail of chestnut-red, and long, green crest-feathers above a head and body of metallic green, blue, and purple. In the mountains of eastern Tibet and in western and southern China are found the Golden Pheasants, with scarlet and orange-yellow bodies and crests, and chestnut-brown tails twice as long as their bodies. The Amherst's Pheasant of the same regions has a dark bronze-green body, a blood-red crest, a mantle over neck and shoulders of white and blue, and an enormously long white tail, barred with black and tipped with scarlet.

The Jungle-fowl, a close relative of the Pheasant, which is common in well-watered jungle country in parts of India, Ceylon, Malaya, and the East Indies, is the only pheasant-like bird to produce a comb, a high fleshy protuberance, running from the base of the beak along the top of the head. The Red Jungle-fowl is the species from which domestic poultry have been derived (*see* POULTRY, Vol. VI), and itself resembles the Black-red Bantam.

See also Vol. IX: GAME SHOOTING.

PHOTOSYNTHESIS.

PHOTOSYNTHESIS. This word means 'building up by means of light'. In photosynthesis, the carbon dioxide which green plants absorb through their LEAVES and the water which they take in through their ROOTS (qq.v.) are 'built up' into sugars and starch. This building up can take place only in living CELLS (q.v.) which contain the green colouring matter called 'chlorophyll' and which are exposed to the radiant energy provided by light.

Chlorophyll has two forms, one blue-green and one pure green, which are found in tiny granules called 'chloroplasts' in plant cells, together with a yellow pigment (xanthophyll), which gives many flowers their colour, and an orange one (carotin), which gives carro many red fruits and autumn leaves their

Carbon-dioxide gas enters the leaf th tiny pores (stomata) in the surface and dissolves in the cell sap. The entrance to each pore is guarded by cells which, by swelling or shrinking, control the movement of carbon dioxide into and water vapour out of the leaf.

Part of the light energy absorbed by the chlorophyll splits water into oxygen, which moves out of the leaf through the stomata, and hydrogen, which attaches to a substance in the chloroplasts. The carbon dioxide combines with a sugar-like compound present in the cell, and the resulting substance, during various changes, reacts with the hydrogen released from the water. The final products are sugars and more of the simple, sugar-like compound, which is ready for continuing the cycle. During this process of sugar formation, the light energy absorbed from the sun is transformed into chemical energy, which can be released later for other purposes when the sugars are broken down in plant respiration.

The amount of oxygen produced equals the

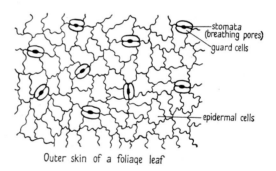

stomata (breathing pores)
guard cells
epidermal cells

Outer skin of a foliage leaf

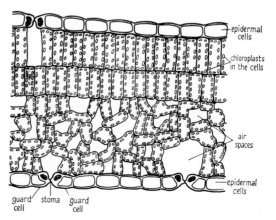

epidermal cells
chloroplasts in the cells
air spaces
epidermal cells
guard cell   stoma   guard cell

TRANSVERSE SECTION OF A FOLIAGE LEAF

amount of carbon dioxide used up. The release of oxygen during photosynthesis is very useful in preserving the balance of the gases in the atmosphere. Both animals and plants in RESPIRATION (q.v.) use up oxygen and produce carbon dioxide; photosynthesis, by using carbon dioxide and producing oxygen, restores to the atmosphere the oxygen so essential to the respiration of all living things.

The sugars, which are the first substances to be built up in the plant leaf, are immediately converted into starch. This starch is insoluble, and it is therefore converted back to soluble sugar during the night, so that it can be moved into the stems or roots, where it is reconverted into starch and stored. A potato tuber, for example, is packed with starch which is the product of photosynthesis in the leaves. The plant can also build up more complicated food substances, such as fats and proteins, but the energy for these processes comes from respiration and not from light.

The essential requirements to make photosynthesis possible, then, are the raw materials, carbon dioxide and water, together with chlorophyll and light. A plant grown entirely in the dark cannot produce chlorophyll, and therefore, because photosynthesis cannot take place and the plant has no source of food, it will grow spindly and weak until it finally dies. Plants with variegated leaves have chlorophyll only in the green streaks. In plants with red leaves, such as the Copper Beech or Red Cabbage, the leaves contain chlorophyll but the green colour of chlorophyll is masked by the red pigment. The only plants that can live without photosynthesis are PARASITES or SAPROPHYTES (qq.v.), which do not make their own food but draw it from the 'hosts' or dead matter on which they live.

Photosynthesis is one of the most important processes carried out by living things. If green plants ceased to photosynthesize, all living things —plant, animal, and man—would die, and so life on earth would cease. Life cannot continue without food; and the feeding of all other living things depends upon the green plant's ability to build up foodstuffs. Even flesh-eating animals, such as lions, are dependent upon photosynthesis, since the antelopes and zebras on which they prey are grass-eaters. When human beings eat mutton or beef or drink milk, they are eating grass—several stages removed (see NUTRITION OF ANIMALS).

See also NUTRITION OF PLANTS.

PIDDOCK. This mollusc is chiefly interesting for the ravages it makes on rocks and buildings on the sea-shore. Wherever limestone, sandstone, or other relatively soft rocks occur between tide-marks, their surfaces are likely to be pitted by its excavations. Those of the Rugose Stone-borer, a mollusc of the same type, are shallow, never exceeding 15 centimetres deep, while those of the Piddock, particularly in the softer rocks, are much larger and deeper, for it is the larger animal. The breaking up of large blocks of weathered stone which have fallen from the cliffs on to the shore is often largely effected by the activity of these molluscs.

A full-grown Piddock often measures 15 centimetres in length, and the surface of each valve of its creamy-white shell is covered with row upon row of short, sharp-pointed spines, which are thickened around the broad base. The shell, though a good deal harder than the rock attacked, does in time show signs of wear, the rows of rasping spines becoming blunted in old specimens. The Piddock has a very strong foot, with which it adheres firmly to the bottom of the burrow it is excavating. While carrying out tunnelling operations, it adopts a rocking, twisting motion, ejecting the rock debris by the help of jets of water from its outbreathing siphon. Once the burrow has been driven to a sufficient depth to hide it completely from view, the Piddock ceases operations, confining itself in the future to such occasional deepening of the burrow as may be sufficient to meet increase in growth. Like many other marine animals, the Piddock is luminescent at night, particularly

Zoological Society of London

PIDDOCK JUST VISIBLE INSIDE A HOLE WHICH IT HAS BORED IN THE ROCK

during the summer months, when its long respiratory siphons glow brightly.

The Rugose Stone-borer is much smaller, and the valves of its stout, coarsely wrinkled shell are generally oval in shape, whitish in colour, and rather opaque, the complete shell rarely exceeding 2·5 cm in length by about 1·3 cm in breadth. The front part of the body and the siphons are often bright orange-red in colour, on account of which fishermen, who use them for bait, call them 'Red-noses'.

See also MOLLUSCS; SHIPWORMS.

G. K. Yeates

TURTLE-DOVE BROODING

PIG, *see* SWINE.

PIGEON. This group, of which there are a great many species, including the Doves and the now-extinct flightless Dodo and Solitaire, are found all over the world, often in great numbers. They have rather large heads and stout, compact bodies; and most species are strong fliers. They have large crops, into which they can cram an enormous amount of food—a Wood Pigeon's crop can hold as many as sixty acorns, and the bird can consume at one time a quantity of food amounting to more than its own weight. Their principal food is grain and seeds, berries, acorns, beech-mast, peas, beans, clover, and turnip-tops—it is not surprising that they are un-popular with the farmer (*see* VERMIN, Sect. 8, Vol. VI). After an elaborate courtship, including much bowing and hopping, cooing, and flying in circles, pigeons mate for life. Both sexes take part in building the nest, generally a loosely constructed platform of twigs, and in incubating the two pure-white eggs. The young are fed on 'pigeon-milk', which they get from the parent's bill, pumped up from the crop. Later, this is mixed with half-digested food. Generally two or even three broods are reared each season.

Wood Pigeons (or Ring Doves) are very common in most wooded districts in Europe, western Asia, and north-west Africa, their numbers having increased since the larger birds of prey, their enemies, have become more scarce. They are, however, often reduced by a strange epidemic, a kind of diphtheria, which occurs in certain years in certain regions. Pigeon-shooting kills quite a number of birds—though their erratic and swift flight makes them not easy to hit (*see* GAME SHOOTING: Vol. IX).

Eric Hosking

WOOD PIGEON AND NESTLINGS

Doves are rather smaller than pigeons, but have much the same habits. Stock Doves are to be found over most of the British Isles; they nest in holes in trees or rocks, or in deserted rabbit-burrows or squirrels' nests. Rock Doves are the species from which most of the domestic breeds, such as Pouters, Tumblers, and Fan-tails, have been bred. In the wild state they reside chiefly on cliff coasts, nesting on rock ledges or in caves. The Turtle Dove, often referred to in poetry as the 'turtle', is the smallest and most slenderly built of the group. It is a summer visitor to south-east England, preferring open woodland and plantations, and nesting in trees.

The Passenger Pigeons of Central and North America, birds with much longer tails than the British species, were found in large numbers, but are now extinct. Many of the pigeons and doves in tropical regions are brilliantly coloured. In Indonesia and Australia are the Crested and Bronze-winged Doves, with golden-green wings and black crests. In New Guinea are the largest of the pigeons, the Crowned Pigeons, splendid birds with erect, fan-shaped crests. The Tooth-billed Pigeon of Samoa forms a separate family from the rest of the pigeons, being in some ways more like the extinct Dodo. It has a remarkably strong, hooked beak. These rare birds used to live chiefly on the ground, where they fell victim to wild cats and other marauders; but they now appear to have taken to an arboreal life, and their numbers are again on the increase.

The Dodo of Mauritius and Réunion, and the Solitaire of Rodriguez Island, were very large birds, as big as swans, with large, hooked beaks and short, stout legs, the Solitaire having the smaller body, but longer legs and neck. They were still fairly numerous in the early 17th century; but the Dodo had become extinct by the end of the century, and the Solitaire disappeared soon afterwards.

See also Vol. IV: PIGEON POST.
See also Vol. IX: PIGEON RACING.

PIGMY MOTHS.

PIGMY MOTHS. These tiny, very primitive moths, including the smallest of all moths, range in size from 3 to 10 mm. Their family, Nepti-culidae, is rather isolated from other moths, though perhaps most nearly related to the GOLD or LONGHORN MOTHS (qq.v.). They have a world-wide distribution, ninety species occurring in Britain. The narrow, pointed fore-wings are covered with fixed hairs and rather large scales, and have a peculiar arrangement of veins. They are usually dark and metallic, the fore-wings often tinged with purple, and sometimes with a silvery or golden band or pale spots. The hind-wings are generally grey. They fly erratically in sunshine, and hide on cold days, some species occasionally being found in great numbers in cracks in tree-trunks. The eggs are generally laid on leaves or leaf-stalks, the British species largely favouring birch, oak, hawthorn, apple, and willows, though others are attached to rose, bramble, or agrimony. The young larva eats its way out of the egg-shell directly into the leaf, and then constructs a characteristic mine near the upper surface, which may be straight, curved, twisted, wide, or narrow, or, in some types, a blotch. In autumn the part of a leaf surround-ing a mine retains its green colour long after the rest has changed, even when it has fallen to the ground. The little flattened larva, as is often the case in leaf miners, has only rudimentary legs, or in some species none at all. The larva leaves the mine to pupate in a tough cocoon among litter or in the soil.

PIKE. Of all fishes, the Pike has undoubtedly the greatest reputation for greed and destructive-ness, and has been called the 'river wolf'. It is rare to find more than one Pike in any stretch of water, for there would not be enough food to supply more—and, in any case, the larger one soon devours the smaller ones. There are records of Pike attacking and swallowing fishes as large as themselves. A good account describes how a small specimen seized a Salmon about its own size, and held on in a fierce tussle for two hours, at the end of which the Salmon was so exhausted that the Pike began to swallow it head-foremost. It was three days before the meal was finished, and then the Pike, looking very swollen, lay still for a week, almost unable to move, until the meal was digested.

The common Pike, which is found in fresh-waters throughout Europe and in North America, reaches a length of about 1·5 metres and weighs over 23 kg. There is a legend in Germany about a specimen that was supposed to have been 5·7 metres long, weighed 227 kg, and to have been hundreds of years old. Imaginative paint-ings of this monster exist, and what was sup-posed to be its skeleton is preserved in Mannheim Cathedral; but a German scientist, who examined the bones, found that there were far too many vertebrae in the backbone for any one fish—so the skeleton had apparently been enlarged to fit the legend!

Pike spawn in the early months of the year, laying about half a million tiny eggs. These lie on the bed of the stream, where most of them are eaten by other fishes long before they can hatch out. Young Pike are usually called 'pickerel' in England. A fine account of the life of a Pike is to be found in a Scandinavian book (published in English) called *Grim*.

In America there is a larger species called the Muskallunge, which is greatly sought after by anglers, and has been compared to the Salmon as a sporting fish. It inhabits the Great Lakes region, and may weigh as much as 36 kg. A number of smaller kinds, known as Pickerel, are also found in the United States. All the Pike make very good eating.

See also Vol. IX: ANGLING, FRESHWATER.

PILOT-FISH, *see* SEA PERCH.

PINES, *see* CONIFERS.

PIPIT, *see* WAGTAIL and PIPIT.

PITCHER-PLANTS, *see* INSECTIVOROUS PLANTS, Section 6.

PLAICE, *see* FLAT-FISHES.

PLANKTON. This is a term used to describe the minute plant and animal life that lives in the surface waters of oceans and fresh waters. Among the marine planktonic animals are the larvae of FISH and CORALS, many CRUSTACEA, MOLLUSCS (qq.v.), and Foraminifera (*see* PROTOZOA). They feed on the marine planktonic plants such as diatoms, which are ALGAE (q.v.), and they provide rich food for fish and the giant whalebone WHALES (q.v.). Plankton is generally more abundant in polar and temperate seas than in tropical ones. The bony remains of the dead plankton fall to the floor of the sea where they

COMMON PIKE   *Paul Popper*

form OOZES (q.v. Vol. III), which under suitable conditions are transformed into chalk or limestone.

PLANT. From a casual glance at the vegetation of a garden or meadow, it is clear that plants vary a great deal in size and form. Most people have little idea of the number of plant forms which do exist, and use the word 'plant' only for flowers, herbs, and, sometimes, for shrubs. Yet trees are plants, many of them flowering plants; and ferns, mosses, moulds, yeasts, and even the green scum which sometimes grows in water-butts, are all plants.

Perhaps the best way of grouping plants is into those which bear seeds and those which do not. The seed-bearing plants include CONIFERS (that is, cone-bearing trees) and FLOWERING PLANTS (qq.v.). Seed-bearing plants are made up of ROOTS, STEMS, and LEAVES, and they produce FRUITS which contain the SEEDS (qq.v.). In the case of flowering plants, the FLOWERS (q.v.) are responsible for producing the seeds.

Those plants which do not reproduce by seeds are FERNS, MOSSES, and LIVERWORTS, FUNGI, ALGAE, and LICHENS (qq.v.). (Algae are very simple plants such as seaweeds and the green threads which grow in ponds.) The non-seed-bearing plants are much simpler in form than the seed-bearing plants. With this type of plant, new plants will often spring up from bits of the old ones which have become detached or broken off. The usual way in which non-seed-bearing plants propagate, however, is by the production of spores—delicate, one-celled structures which, unless they quickly find conditions favourable for germination, die. On the other hand, the SEEDS (q.v.) produced by the seed-bearing plants are tougher, many-celled structures, and often contain large reserves of food on which the young seedling can draw for its first supplies before the plant has become capable of making its own food. Plants which bear seeds have, therefore, a better chance of survival in the struggle for existence. All the most complicated plants, such as Pines, Spruces, Larches, Buttercups, Dandelions, Grasses, Elms, Limes, and Oaks, are seed-bearing.

See also NUTRITION IN PLANTS; GROWTH IN PLANTS; REPRODUCTION IN PLANTS; RESPIRATION IN PLANTS.

PLANT DEFENCES. 1. When we think of grazing herds, fruit-eating and seed-eating birds, leaf-eating insects, root-eating grubs, and all the other pests which prey upon plants, the question naturally arises: how do plants hold their own? Animals, like the field vole and the locust, often turn a green and pleasant land into a frowning desert. Why does this not happen more often? How is it that animals do not devour all the plants, and so sign their own death-warrant?

The main answer is that most plants can multiply so abundantly that they can stand a good deal of thinning out. Moreover, when herbivorous animals have eaten up the bulk of available plants, their numbers are automatically reduced by starvation. Also, few animals eat the whole plant and, even when they eat the fruit, this often results in scattering the seeds more widely (see SEEDS 2(b) Animal Dispersal). Yet, while the survival of plants depends mainly upon their abundant multiplication and on their almost inexhaustible food-supplies of air and soil-water, they are not without their defences also. Venus's Fly-trap, the Sundew, and other INSECTIVOROUS PLANTS (q.v.) are actually on the offensive in their attempts to capture insects.

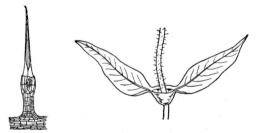

STINGING HAIR   'CISTERN' OF TEASEL—A PROTECTIVE
OF NETTLE   STRUCTURE

Most plants, however, rely on defensive mechanisms for protection.

2. PRICKLES, SPIKES, AND THORNS. A Rose-bush is covered with triangular-shaped prickles, which break off neatly when pressed sideways, showing that they are very superficial growths from the outer skin of the plant. In the Barberry, a whole leaf becomes hardened to form a spine; in the Holly, only parts of the leaf form spines; while in some Acacias, the spine is formed from a 'stipule', the name given to a small structure occurring at the base of a leaf-stalk. Plants such as the Hawthorn have hard, pointed thorns, which are formed from reduced and toughened shoots. That they are modified shoots is clear, because some thorns bear leaves—and only shoots can bear leaves. Gorse has both spines and thorns.

Spines, thorns, and prickles may have other and more primary purposes than defence. For instance, many sharp-spined plants, such as CACTUSES (q.v.), which grow in dry places, have soft leaves and shoot-tissues reduced in size in order to avoid excessive loss of water (see TRANSPIRATION). It has been found that young spiny and thorny plants, such as Gorse and Holly, if planted in a damp atmosphere and in the shade, produce fewer spines or thorns than those planted on dry soil, where there is much sun and wind. But it is probable that these defences do, to some extent, prevent the plant from being devoured by animals; and the position they occupy on the plant sometimes seems to indicate a defensive purpose. The spines on the under surface of the huge leaves of the Giant Water Lily, for example, apparently ward off the attacks of aquatic animals; and the thorns guarding the entrance to pitcher plants, such as Nepenthes (see INSECTIVOROUS PLANTS, Section 6), may baulk some insectivorous birds. Donkeys, however, enjoy thistles, and a goat will nibble off leaf after leaf from a thorny plant without once scratching its nose.

3. PROTECTIVE CHEMICAL SUBSTANCES. The Cuckoo-pint or, as it is sometimes called, Lords and Ladies—a common plant of shady places —has a different kind of defence. If a piece of one of the glossy, green leaves is broken off and nibbled, it causes a painful irritation on the lips and tongue. This is due to crystals of oxalate of lime, a waste product of the food-manufacturing process of plants, which serve to protect the plant from the attacks of snails and slugs. Indeed, if

John Markham   *John Markham*

CUCKOO-PINT   DEADLY NIGHTSHADE

Both these plants contain protective chemical substances

the crystals are washed away with hydrochloric acid, and the leaves then well washed, snails find them very attractive to eat. These crystals occur in many other plants, notably the Wood-sorrel and the Docks. Other protective chemical substances found in plants are formic acid, tannins, oils such as eucalyptus and turpentine, and strong alkaloid poisons such as those in Hemlock and Deadly Nightshade.

4. PROTECTIVE STRUCTURE. Some plants develop exceptional hardness of the leaves and shoots for the sake of protection: the hard envelopes of some seeds, for instance, save them from injury, since they pass right through the bodies of birds and animals which have eaten the fruits, and are then excreted.

In warm countries, it is often the custom to put the feet of table-legs into tiny jars of paraffin in order to trap white ants which come out of the floor and try to tunnel in the wood. In the same way, the 'cisterns' of the Teasel, formed where the leaf-bases embrace the stem, serve as moats to prevent the ascent of unwelcome insect visitors, and are often found to have trapped a number of insects. Some wild plants have defences on the same principle as the grease-

bands placed around fruit-trees to prevent the ascent of injurious grubs. The Campion, for instance, has sticky rings on its stem which act as defensive moats. Ants, however, are sometimes known to make bridges over such moats, even using the bodies of their companions to make a living (but very soon a dead) ant-bridge. The Sensitive Plant (*see* MOVEMENT IN PLANTS, Section 2) also uses what appears to be a kind of plant protection. Although this plant grows freely in tropical countries, grazing animals will not eat it, presumably because, when they touch it, it collapses—an unexpected form of behaviour, which scares off the animals.

5. STING AND POISON. One of the best-known and most effective means of plant protection is the sting. On the Common Stinging-nettle, which grows densely in waste places along road-sides and in fields, the heart-shaped leaves and the younger parts of the ridged stems are covered with stinging-hairs. These hairs are single, superficial cells, which have become elongated and tapering, and possess a bulbous base. The tip contains silica, and is so brittle that, when touched, it breaks off, the sharp point entering the skin. The pressure set up causes the poisonous liquid in the bulbous part to be ejected into the puncture. The poison which causes the irritation is not, as was once thought, formic acid, but is a protein of undetermined composition. If the leaf is firmly grasped, the nettle cannot sting, because the tips of the hairs break off, and the rest of the long hairs are bent over and crushed before they are able to make a puncture. Unlike Stinging-nettles, Dead-nettles, have no stinging-hairs. It may possibly be more than coincidence that the Dead-nettles, which so much resemble the Stinging-nettles, are nearly always found growing near them. Their likeness to Stinging-nettles, and the fact that they grow in the same places, suggest that, by deception alone, the Dead-nettles may have acquired an effective means of defence.

The scientific counterpart to the Upas Tree of Java, which, according to the fable, is said to have had a fatal influence on people who came within its spell, is the Poison Vine or Ivy of sub-tropical regions. This plant, which looks like the Virginia Creeper, often has a harmful effect on susceptible people. It is not even necessary that they should touch the plant; for the poison, which is found in a milky juice, seems to be carried through the air on floating particles. A certain Primula, originally from China, called *obconica*, also carries in the hairs of its leaves a poison, to which some people are so susceptible that they can be made seriously ill by touching the plant.

It is well to remember, however, that no matter how well a plant may be protected, some animal will always get the better of it. And those devices which we suppose to be defensive may have been produced for quite different reasons, their use in defence being only secondary.

PLANT DISTRIBUTION.

By 'the distribution of a plant' we mean the areas of the earth's surface where a plant grows naturally, but not those where it has been introduced by man, either intentionally or by accident. Although many plants are confined to certain soils, temperature and rainfall are the chief factors which determine where a plant grows. Botanists have found it convenient, therefore, to divide the world according to temperature into five main regions, each bearing a more or less distinct type of plant covering. These are arctic, sub-arctic, temperate, sub-tropical, and tropical. It is not possible to draw a very sharp dividing line between these regions, since there is no sharp climatic change from one to the next. In some cases the regions overlap: for instance, the conditions in the higher parts of mountain ranges are very similar to those in arctic or sub-arctic regions, and many of the same plants are to be found in both places. Such plants are said to have an arctic-alpine type of distribution.

In general, the arctic and sub-arctic regions tend to bear low-growing and very hardy plants, which can survive long periods entirely buried by snow. Such vegetation is called tundra vegetation. In the temperate regions conditions are less severe, and a greater variety of plants can flourish. If there is sufficient rainfall, WOODLANDS (q.v.) and FORESTS (q.v. Vol. III) will develop; where conditions are drier, enormous areas are covered by HEATHS (q.v.) and GRASSLANDS (q.v. Vol. III). Intensive farming in wide areas of the temperate regions has destroyed much of the original natural vegetation. The sub-tropical and tropical regions of the world bear two characteristic, but very different, types of vegetation, again depending on the amount of rainfall. Where there is sufficient rainfall, dense TROPICAL JUNGLES are found. In marked contrast to this, where rainfall is sparse, there are deserts which have a thin covering of highly specialized DESERT PLANTS, such as CACTUSES (qq.v.).

PLATYPUS.

The Duck-bill (or Duck-billed Platypus) is a very curious animal. It lays eggs, like a bird or reptile; yet it is a mammal, because the female suckles its young from milk secreted in its body. The only other mammal which lays eggs is the ECHIDNA (q.v.) or Porcupine Anteater; and these two together constitute the order Monotremata. The Platypus is found only in Australia and Tasmania. It is the most primitive of all mammals, its brain being of relatively low, simple type. Its jaws, which are the shape of a duck's bill, are also unique amongst mammals.

It frequents fresh waters in southern and eastern Australia and Tasmania; but being a shy animal, it is not very often seen. Its body is oval-shaped, covered with dark brown, mole-like fur, and from the tip of its beak to the tip of its short, flattened tail measures about 50 centimetres. It has short legs, and its feet, each with five toes and strong nails, are webbed for

outline of the body, makes it difficult to recognize the caterpillar in its natural surroundings. When disturbed it assumes a threatening attitude, raising up the front of its body and inflating a fold of red skin bearing two black eye-like spots, suggesting a terrifying face. If further disturbed, it sprays formic acid from a gland, and bends the hindpart of its body over its back, lashing at the enemy with two flexible red threads, which shoot out from its tail-like hind claspers. The caterpillar pupates within a very well camouflaged cocoon fastened to the bark of its food-tree. This cocoon is as hard as a nut, for the silk is toughened by treatment with the same acid secretion that the caterpillar uses in defence. The adult moth breaks through the cocoon by moistening a thin window in the wall with caustic potash from its mouth. When the silk is softened, the moth breaks it with the head-end of the pupa-case, and emerges.

The Alder, Poplar, and Sallow Kittens, named after the typical food-plants, are about half the size of the Puss Moth, and all have a distinct band across their fore-wings. Their caterpillars resemble those of Puss Moths.

The caterpillars of the Chocolate-tips hide by day among leaves fastened together with silk. The small Chocolate-tip may be found commonly during the summer on dwarf sallow in boggy places. The downy caterpillar of the Buff-tip is 5 centimetres long when full grown, and yellow with interrupted black stripes. It feeds in groups on trees, stripping bare whole branches, and is frequently found in the autumn crawling on paths beneath lime-trees, seeking a suitable place to pupate in the soil. The moth emerges in June and July, and when resting folds its silvery buff-tipped wings close to its body, so that it closely resembles a broken lichen-covered stick.

PRONG-BUCK (PRONG-HORN). This animal lives in the temperate regions of North America, where it is known by the name of 'Antelope'. It is not a true ANTELOPE (q.v.), however, because its hollow horns are branched, and because it sheds the sheaths every year, leaving a pair of hair-covered knobs on which the new horns grow. It stands nearly a metre high, and has a chestnut coat with white markings, and a brownish-black face. Usually only the males grow horns, and these increase in size year by year, reaching their full extent (30 to 43 centimetres) at 5 years old. Until the middle of the 19th century Prong-bucks were numerous; but they have been hunted so much that now they are rare. They are shy, timid animals, very fast runners, but poor jumpers.

Sometimes, when the female is about to give birth to her young, she makes her way to the middle of a patch of cactus (prickly pear), in the centre of which, so it is said, she clears a space by a series of jumps and by means of her sharp hoofs. Here the young are born, and remain protected for some time from the wolves, which cannot easily penetrate the prickly cactus fence. Eagles, however, often attack the fawns, and the mother shows great courage in protecting them.

PROTECTIVE COLORATION (INSECTS).
1. Travellers to foreign countries, especially tropical countries, often bring back with them insects which are remarkable either because they attract notice by their conspicuous colours and displays, or for the opposite reason, that they are seldom seen because their colours, form, and behaviour make them extremely like their surroundings, of earth, bark, sticks, or leaves. The result of such coloration is the same in both cases—neither is devoured by insect-eating animals. In the first case, 'warning coloration', the insect is easily recognized by possible enemies as having proved harmful or unpleasant to taste; in the second, 'cryptic coloration', the insect is protected because it is not discovered. A third type of protective coloration, 'mimicry', is achieved when the insect by its colouring deceives the enemy into mistaking it for an insect of a different kind, which is unsuitable for food, and so avoiding it.

2. WARNING COLORATION. Conspicuous colours are displayed as clearly as possible. The great naturalist, Wallace, explained the significance of this display when Darwin asked him why caterpillars were often so conspicuous. He replied that the body of a caterpillar was a thin-walled tube, containing fluids under pressure. If the skin were punctured by a peck from a bird, the juices would ooze out, and the insect would bleed to death. Even though the bird found it distasteful and did not eat it, the caterpillar would die. The bird might remember the association of the conspicuous colours of the caterpillar with its unpleasant taste, and the next caterpillar of the same kind might be left alone, at any rate so long as better food could be found.

Left, the bush-cricket of Brazil, which mimics both in colour and behaviour the burrowing wasp on the right (Pompilidae, *Pepsis*)

So the more conspicuous and easily recognized the insect is, the more likely the enemy is to remember what the bright colours mean. The insects, therefore, display their colours as well as they can. They fly or walk slowly, and sit about in conspicuous places. They make little effort to get away, for if they did so, the enemy, not recognizing them, might pursue and kill them to find out what they were. Such insects can be easily captured, and can put up with a fair amount of rough handling. A brightly coloured tropical grasshopper, for example, when handled, does not lose its hind-legs in the distressing way that an ordinary green grasshopper does.

The commonest warning colours are red and yellow; blue is rarely used, although tropical *Euploea* butterflies often have a lovely blue or purplish sheen. Black and white is common, as is shown by *Amauris* butterflies and large Carabid beetles.

Two quite different kinds of insects, both unpleasing in some way, may have the same warning colours, each reminding the enemy of the other, and both gaining in consequence. Indeed, many insects with the same warning colours, so long as each is relatively nasty, may join in such an association for the benefit of all. A good example of such common warning colours is the simple orange-brown and black colouring of the Lycid beetles, closely allied to the GLOW-WORM (q.v.), which are found in all warm countries. The Lycid coloration (*see* Colour Plate opp. p. 336) is shared by hosts of other beetles, bugs, wasps—and even flies and moths—all of which are themselves objectionable; and all, therefore, benefit by their similar coloration.

Warning colours can be found in most of the higher groups of insects, including many tropical butterflies and moths. Many tropical grasshoppers show red or purple wings when disturbed, and emit bubbles of a bitter yellow froth. The BOMBARDIER BEETLE (q.v.), and others of the family Carabidae, have the power to eject a bitter fluid (capable of burning the skin) which blows off like a puff of smoke. LADYBIRDS (q.v.) have typical warning colours—red or yellow with black spots—and they, also, give off an unpleasant-smelling juice. Everyone is afraid of touching an insect with black and yellow rings, because of the mental association with wasps.

Warning colours, it must be remembered, are only a safeguard to an insect so long as the enemy can find other, pleasanter food; when food is very short, the display colours are only a danger. So warning coloration is not seen very much in winter, or in the tropical dry season, when insects are few: it is best shown in the teeming life of the tropical jungle (*see* TROPICAL BUTTERFLIES AND MOTHS).

3. CRYPTIC COLORATION. The word 'cryptic' means secret or hidden. In this case the animal escapes being seen—and in consequence eaten—because its colours resemble its surroundings, and, so long as it keeps motionless, it appears to be part of them. Those creatures with cryptic coloration have, by the process of natural selection, tended to survive and grow more common—for it is safer not to be seen at all than to run the risk of being captured, examined, and partly eaten. All experiments so far show that a highly cryptic animal is good food. Insects, particularly, being generally small and

Left, a two-winged fly (Asilidae, *Mallophora fascipennis*), which mimics the bee on the right (*Euglossa fasciata*) from the same part of British Guiana

defenceless, have developed cryptic coloration, together with special habits and attitudes which increase their likeness to their surroundings.

This likeness may be general, as in a green grasshopper, or special, when some particular leaf, stick, seed, or other object is resembled. The famous 'Dead Leaf Butterfly' (*Kallima*) of Asia is not only like a dead leaf in shape and colour when it settles, but it also reproduces the minutest peculiarities of the dead leaf, such as the marks made by tiny fungi, even the fungus growth itself, and the holes and cracks which let light through (*see* Colour Plate, opp. p. 336). The writer well remembers catching what seemed to be a bit of thistle-down drifting by, only to find it was a small thin bug, with many fine prolongations of its skin. The 'Stick Caterpillars' of the Geometrid moths have projections on their bodies, which are very much like those on the bark of twigs (*see* LOOPERS). Wallace tells of a stick insect brought to him by the natives of Borneo, who assured him it was covered with moss—and only by very careful examination could he discover that the 'moss' was part of the insect. There are some caterpillars, like those of the rare Essex Emerald Moth, which cut off pieces of their food-plant and attach them to their spines. The grubs of the Tortoise Beetles on thistles wear their discarded skins on their backs, and look like little bits of dead leaf.

In cryptic coloration, as in warning coloration, we find that the insects have developed habits and take up positions which add to the effectiveness of their disguise. The wonderful 'Stick Caterpillars' are able to fix themselves like a twig at an angle with a branch, and to stay there during long resting periods. A moth settles on the bark of a tree in such a way that the main dark lines of the pattern on its wings fit in with the lines on the bark. It would be of little use for a caterpillar which resembles a bird-dropping to move about restlessly—and, in fact, such caterpillars are sluggish. On the other hand, some insects which resemble dead leaves have been described as moving gently with a peculiar swaying motion, like that of a wind-stirred leaf.

Another feature of cryptic coloration is what is known as 'counter shading'. Most animals tend to be darker on the upper surface (or back) and paler beneath. When the animal is seen in the open air, its upper surface is more brightly illuminated than its under parts, and so appears

Top. The male Swallowtail (*Papilio dardanus*) from Lagos, West Africa, has black and yellow colours; but the female (*centre*) mimics the black and white pattern of the distasteful Danaid butterfly (*Amauris niavius*) from the same locality

lighter, and the under parts darker, than they really are. This reduction of the contrast makes the animal less conspicuous. In some caterpillars which normally rest upside-down the contrast is reduced by the belly having a darker coloration than the back, an effect known as inverted counter shading. Some caterpillars, for example, that of the Puss Moth (*see* PROMINENT MOTH), have a conspicuous white line running along the sides of the body, which is also counter shaded. The white line, by breaking up the outlines of the body, still further aids concealment; this more complicated arrangement of colours is called double inverted counter shading.

4. FLASH COLORATION. This is a device by which some insects, in particular some species of European GRASSHOPPERS (q.v.), mislead their enemies. Bright 'flashes' of colour (usually red, yellow, or blue and generally on their wings) are visible only when the insects are in flight. On coming to rest they hide the flashes, usually by closing their wings, and thus confuse their enemies, who continue to search for a brightly coloured prey.

5. MIMICRY. This term is used for an insect which achieves some degree of safety by resembling another, better-protected insect. This is in principle quite different from the resemblance which occurs when two or more insects make use of the same warning coloration. The mimicking insect is not protected by sting, spines, or unpleasant taste, but deceives its enemy into mistaking it for another insect with these protections, whose warning coloration serves to keep the enemy at a distance. Were the enemy to investigate closer, it would find that the 'mimic', in fact, did not resemble its 'model' in structure, but only in deceptive coloration. This form of protective coloration is found chiefly among insects.

The naturalist Bates studied mimicry very thoroughly among butterflies in South America. He suggested that the resemblance which, of course, is unconscious on the part of the mimic, must have grown up gradually through the working of the law of natural selection. One insect, perhaps, differs slightly from its parents, and by this difference happened to resemble slightly some common, well-defended insect in the locality. An insect-eating animal, looking for the nicest food when choice was plentiful, might leave the doubtful specimen in favour of another which did not suggest an unpleasant taste. The insect, therefore, would survive, and some of its offspring might inherit to a greater degree this variation from the normal. This process, continued through many generations of successful survival, would produce a 'mimetic' resemblance. The mimic now looks different from its relations (although it remains like them in other ways), but so much like another unrelated insect, whose unpleasant qualities are advertised by its warning colours, that the enemy is deceived into avoiding it.

Mimetic resemblance is produced in different ways. The characteristic narrow waist of ants and other stinging insects is often mimicked: the thicker body of the mimic is made to look narrow by a 'painting out' of part of the body by white, so that a narrow dark stalk shows up, and the white part looks like white light in the herbage. Many insects, such as the Wasp-beetle, mimic ants, bees, and wasps. Beetles mimic other beetles, and some Cockroaches mimic Ladybirds. Large caterpillars of Hawk-moths wonderfully resemble small snakes, having false eyes on the swollen front part of their bodies to mimic the snake's head.

As in the case of warning and cryptic coloration, the mimicking insect develops habits which help in the deception. This is clearly shown by certain spiders which mimic ants. A spider is very different in structure from an ant. It has, for instance, four pairs of legs, but no antennae; whereas the ant has only three pairs of legs. Now an ant-like spider, when active, does not use its front pair of legs for walking, but waves them in the air in front, so that they look like the always-moving antennae of the ant. Many spiders, such as the Zebra spider, catch their prey by jumping on it. Now, if a mimetic spider jumped, the deception would be found out, for ants do not jump. Therefore ant-like spiders suppress the jumping habit, except as a last resort. The writer, in Africa, seeing some ants on a branch, put some in a box; but to his astonishment, one leapt out—and proved to be a mimetic spider. The bush-cricket shown in the picture on page 332, which is mimicking a wasp, does not fold its wings along its body when on the ground, as grasshoppers usually do, but keeps them spread out, as a wasp would carry them.

For successful mimicry, the mimic must occur with a model which is more common than itself: if an edible mimic were as common as the distasteful model, the enemy might find it worth while to catch and examine every one; but if only one out of a hundred were edible, the enemy would not investigate. Therefore, true mimics wearing false warning colours are generally among the rarer insects only, their models being among the more common.

Mimicry has been most thoroughly studied in butterflies and moths; but it occurs in many of the main groups of insects, and all over the warm parts of the world.

See also INSECTS; BUTTERFLIES; MOTHS; CATERPILLARS; CAMOUFLAGE.

PROTOCOCCUS, *see* ALGAE.

PROTOZOA—or 'first animals' (from the Greek words *protos*, first or original, *zoon*, animal). This is the name of a group or phylum of animals consisting of several thousand different species, the bodies of which are not divided into cells. They are all similar in structure to AMOEBA (q.v.), and the differences in them are best explained by describing the four classes into which they are divided. Like Amoeba, they are all found in moist or wet places, in fresh water or in the sea, and some live in the bodies of larger animals.

The first class is the Rhizopoda, or root-footed animals, with a body consisting of the usual living cell, with its central nucleus. When the animal moves, parts of its body flow out into finger-shaped, thread-like, or root-shaped 'pseudopodia', or false feet. Many of the Rhizopoda have, like Amoeba, completely naked bodies; but some make small houses of minute sand-grains or other materials. Some, such as *Entamoeba*, live in the bodies of other animals—one species living in the human intestine is responsible for the disease known as dysentery.

One order of the Rhizopoda, the Radiolaria, take up silica from the sea-water and lay it down around their bodies in the form of glassy shells of exquisite beauty. The shell of a Radiolarian is usually spherical or helmet-shaped, perforated with numerous holes, through which the pseudopodia (or false feet) protrude, and usually ornamented with radiating spines. The animals swim in the sea in myriads, and the shells of dead Radiolaria have sunk to the sea bottom over millions of square kilometres to form the mud on the ocean bed (*see* OOZES: Vol. III).

Another order, the Foraminifera, also manufacture shells for the protection of their bodies; but these are made of lime. Although these are not so intricate in design as those of the Radiolaria, they, also, are very beautiful. Foraminifera shells can often be seen in the sand of the sea-shore—but a hand-lens is needed, as they are no bigger than the sand-grains. Often the sand is made up mainly, and in some places exclusively, of Foraminifera. The shells are usually rounded, flask-shaped, or oval; sometimes they are multiple, consisting of several rounded or oval shells joined together. In some cases, the walls of the shells are pierced with numerous minute holes, or 'foramina', through which the pseudopodia project; in others, there is a single opening at one end. Fossil Foraminifera and

Radiolaria are commonly found in rocks, and there is no doubt that they have contributed largely to the formation of certain kinds of rock, especially LIMESTONE (q.v., Vol. III).

The next class of Protozoa is called the Mastigophora, or Flagellata, both words meaning 'whip-bearers'. The animal's body, which is usually oval, carries at one end one or more protoplasmic threads, like the lash of a whip, called 'flagella'. By the lashing movements of

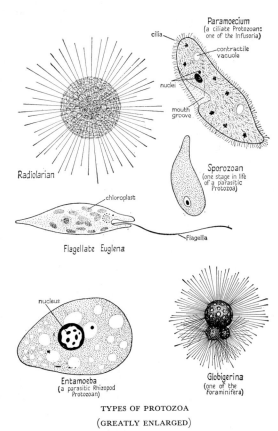

TYPES OF PROTOZOA
(GREATLY ENLARGED)

the flagella the animals are drawn through the water. The Flagellates may be found in fresh water and in the sea. Some are parasites in the bodies of other animals, and are responsible for certain diseases—for instance, for the African sleeping-sickness in man.

The next class, the Sporozoa, are all parasitic. Like all internal parasites, they have degenerated, and feed by absorbing fluid from the body in which they live. Sporozoa have a life-cycle which consists of three stages. In the first stage, the animal feeds and grows. In the second stage, two of the animals come together and join, or conjugate. The body formed by the conjugation then divides into numerous small spores, each with its nucleus, and each protected with a tough coat. In the third stage, the spores pass from the body of their host, and have to await the chance of being picked up by another host. They may be transferred to the second host by being accidentally swallowed in its food; or they may be swallowed by an intermediate host and transmitted when the intermediate bites the real host. Malaria is passed on in this way. A particular species of mosquito bites a person who has had malaria, and takes into its body the blood containing the spores which cause the disease. The insect then bites another person, and, along with its own saliva, injects the parasite into the blood of the new victim.

The next and last class is the Ciliophora, or Ciliates, both of which words mean cilia-bearers —for the body of these animals is covered with short protoplasmic hairs or 'cilia'. The Ciliates used to be called Infusoria, because they were found in infusions of water containing much decayed vegetable matter. The Ciliates show a considerable advance in organization on the rest of the Protozoa. They are still microscopic, or nearly so; but instead of the simple body with a changeable shape, and organs which arise as wanted, they have a definite shape, and a number of permanent organs. Two types of Ciliates, found in ponds and streams, either on water-plants or swimming freely in water containing dead vegetation, will illustrate what the members of this order are like.

The Slipper Animalcule, or *Paramoecium*, is shaped like the sole of a slipper. The surface of the body is coated with a great many short cilia, which propel it through the water. On one side of the body there is a groove leading into a mouth, from which a gullet runs into the body. Food, caught in this groove, is passed on through the mouth into the gullet, from which it passes round the body, being digested as it goes, the undigested remains being passed out just behind the groove. *Paramoecium*, in common with other ciliates, has two sorts of nuclei. There is one large one and one or more much smaller ones, depending on the species.

The Bell Animalcule, or *Vorticella*, has a bell-shaped body on a long stalk. It has a few cilia, but these are long and bristle-like, and are arranged round the mouth of the bell. The beat-ing of these produces a current towards the mouth which brings in food particles. The Bell has the same physical features as the Slipper Animalcule; but its most remarkable feature is that it is fixed by its stalk. If disturbed, it pulls itself back rapidly in a spiral on its stalk, until it looks like a tightly coiled spring; and after a time slowly stretches out again to its full length. Bell Animalcules are unusual in that they grow bunched together, looking, when fully expanded, like microscopic and very delicate flowers.

One unusual group of Ciliates, the Suctoria, have the cilia converted into suckers for catching their prey—usually other Ciliates.

PTARMIGAN, *see* GROUSE.

PUFFIN, *see* AUK, Section 4.

PUMA. The Puma and the JAGUAR (q.v.) are the two great CATS (q.v.) of America. The Puma is generally smaller and slimmer than the Jaguar. It has a far greater range, being found over a vast area stretching from Canada to Patagonia. In North America, where the Puma is known as the Mountain Lion, it is sometimes nearly as big as a small lioness; but in the forests of tropical South America it is very much smaller. The adult is usually a uniform tawny-brown; but the cubs, until they are 6 months old, are heavily spotted with black.

Pumas are most destructive beasts of prey, and frequently kill horses, cattle, and sheep by springing on their shoulders and dislocating their necks. In the wilder parts of South America, where there are no domesticated animals, they eat Guanacos (wild Llamas) and deer; and in the dense forests of the Amazon and Orinoco, they hunt in the trees, chasing monkeys from bough to bough. If they are very hungry, Pumas will eat almost any flesh, but they have hardly ever been known, even in self-defence, to attack a human being: even in places where they are very numerous, it is considered perfectly safe for a child to wander alone. Many sportsmen have said that they would never again kill a Puma because of its unwillingness to defend itself, and the distress it shows—it is even said to weep tears, though this we can doubt. Pumas can leap amazing distances—indeed, when pursued by dogs, they have been known to spring upwards to reach a bough 6 metres from the ground, and they can leap down from a height of about

PROTECTIVE COLORATION IN INSECTS

a. Cryptic coloration. 1. Asiatic Leaf Insect (*Phyllium*). 2. Asiatic Dead Leaf Butterfly (*Kallima*).
b. Warning coloration. 3. Asiatic Swallowtail Butterfly (*Atrophaneura*). 4, 5. British Cinnabar Moth (*Callimorpha*)
and its caterpillar. 6. African Lycid Beetle (*Lycus*). 7. Tropical American Syntomid Moth (*Histiaca*).
c. Flash coloration. 8, 9. European grasshoppers (*Oedipoda*). The patches of red or blue colour are visible only when
the insect is flying (*About three-quarters natural size*)

11 metres. In the breeding season their penetrating, screaming 'yowl' has often scared travellers.

PUPA, *see* METAMORPHOSIS.

PURPLE EMPEROR BUTTERFLY. The Emperor butterflies of the family Nymphalidae are found in nearly all parts of the world except Africa. The only British species is the brilliant Purple Emperor, so called because of the iridescent flush of imperial purple on the wings of the male. It has a wing-expanse of about 7 or 8 cm, and is sometimes called the 'King of the Forest', as it flies round the highest oak-trees in the woodlands of the south and midlands, to which it is restricted. The females, which are brown and white with no purple sheen on their wings, frequent the undergrowth, and lay their eggs singly on sallow bushes.

Paul Popper

A PUMA WITH KITTEN

The green caterpillars look rather like slugs, and in contrast to other Nymphalids are solitary in their habits, and have no spines—though they have two horns on their heads. In the autumn they spin a pad of silk in the fork of a branch, where they retire into hibernation, gradually changing to an olive colour to complete their camouflage. Sometimes they hibernate on a leaf, in which case they fasten the leaf securely to the stem with silk. In the spring their colour changes to brighter green to match the young sallow leaves on which they feed. The pupa is attached by its tail to a leaf secured by silk to the stem. It closely resembles a sallow leaf in shape and colour, its bulk being disguised by numerous small white spots which break up the dark shadows. The butterflies emerge in July and frequent the tree-tops; but they can sometimes be attracted near the ground by a flashing mirror, a bright piece of cloth, or a sheet of newspaper spread out in a clearing where they occur. They are also attracted by rotten fruit and decaying animal substances.

PUSS MOTH, *see* PROMINENT MOTHS.

S. Beaufoy

PURPLE EMPEROR BUTTERFLY

PYTHON, *see* BOA (picture, p. 398).

Q R

QUAIL, *see* PARTRIDGE.

QUETZAL, *see* TROGON.

RABBIT. This well-known British mammal belongs, like the HARE (q.v.), to the order Lagomorpha. It is found all over Europe, except in the extreme north and east, and in many other parts of the world, generally having been originally introduced by man. As rabbits eat almost any vegetable matter and have an alarming rate of breeding, they are a serious menace to farmers, who seek to exterminate them as VERMIN (q.v. Vol. VI). The doe (female) produces four to six litters of five to eight young in a year. These are blind, helpless, and nearly naked at birth; but in 2 weeks' time they are able to run, and by a month can fend for themselves. At the age of 6 months they are themselves able to breed. Given favourable circumstances, it is reckoned that a single pair of rabbits would in 3 years have a progeny numbering 13,718,000.

Oliver Pike

YOUNG RABBITS AT THE ENTRANCE OF THEIR BURROW

Three pairs of rabbits were introduced in the 18th century into Australia, and in a few years had multiplied and, with the addition of others similarly introduced, have spread over most of the continent. Since then, in spite of all attempts to exterminate them, they have caused damage costing millions of pounds each year to farmers. Export of the skins has, however, proved very profitable.

Unlike hares, rabbits live together in large numbers in burrows under the ground. The burrows are often connected by long passages, so forming a warren. Rabbits generally come out at dusk and in the early morning to feed and play, rushing out in a line, after first peering cautiously round to see if the coast is clear. They are less fleet of foot than hares, and tire easily after about 65 metres. When chased, the rabbit runs very fast, with its ears back and its scut (tail) up.

Just before breeding, the doe leaves her burrow and digs a new hole, in which she makes a nest 60 cm long, lining it with leaves, fern fronds, and fur plucked from her own body. The buck (male) sometimes helps with these preparations. When the doe leaves her young in the nest, she covers over the entrance with earth. After man, the wild rabbit's chief enemies are foxes, stoats, cats, buzzards, weasels, and polecats. Rabbits become paralysed with fear when hunted by any of these animals—so much so that they are unable to run more than a few metres before they stop and await death, screaming with terror. Recently, the virus disease myxomatosis, transmitted by insect bites, has greatly reduced their numbers in Australia and Britain.

Tame RABBITS (q.v. Vol. VI) are all descended from the wild rabbit. They are bred for their fur and meat, and also as PETS (q.v. Vol. IX); and a large variety of breeds has resulted.

RACCOON. This thick-set, carnivorous (flesh-eating) mammal, found only in the North and South American forests, is closely related to the BEAR and DOG (qq.v.). It looks more like a dog, but it walks like a bear on its soles, and eats much of the same kind of food. Raccoons spend most of their life high up in trees, but they hunt their prey on the ground. There are few wild animals so expert at concealing their presence. During the day they lie curled up in a hollow tree or in a hole among rocks, out of sight. Again, there are few animals which can use their front paws so skilfully as Raccoons: not only do they use their paws when eating, but they can pick up very small objects, and can lift a cup just like a human being. When taken young, they make interesting and, usually, gentle pets. They are very inquisitive creatures, for ever investigating anything new or strange.

The North American Raccoons are about 60 cm long, covered with soft, grey fur, and with thick, short tails, marked with black rings. Their faces are white, with large black patches under the eyes. They are excellent climbers, and also good swimmers. After dusk, they climb down from their resting-places in the trees and go in search of food. In order that their tracks may not betray their presence, they will follow cattle trails, well-trodden pathways, or even a paved road, in the course of their hunting. Birds, small mammals, reptiles, aquatic animals, and insects are all welcome food. Like the bears, they will sometimes capture fish by scooping them out of a pool or stream with a quick sweep of their paws. Before putting their food in their mouths, Raccoons have a curious habit of moistening it in some water. They sometimes use the deserted nests of large birds for shelters; but the young, usually four to six in a litter, are born in hollow trees or holes in rocks. In the Adirondack region in north-east U.S.A., where they are fairly numerous, Raccoons hibernate during the severest part of the winter; but elsewhere they usually remain active the whole year round. They are hunted a great deal for the sake of their fur.

The Crab-eating Raccoon, found in South America, is smaller and lighter in colour than the North American species; but its habits are very similar. The Coatis are related to the Raccoons, and very like them, except for their long, bushy, pointed tails, and peculiar, rubber-like snouts. Unlike Raccoons, which are usually unsociable, Coatis go about in troops of from eight to twenty strong. Frequently, when they are hunting the large lizards known as Iguanas, they divide the troop into two sections, one of which makes its way through the branches, while the other hunts on the ground, so that any prey which falls from the trees has a poor chance of escape. The Cacomistle or 'Cunning Cat Squirrel', of the forests of Mexico, Texas, Nevada, and Oregon, is another relative of the Raccoon. It is about the size of a domestic cat, with soft, yellowish-brown fur; and, although

E. O. Hopp

THE RINGTAIL, A NORTH AMERICAN RACCOON

bold and ferocious for its size, it is easily tamed and sometimes kept as a pet.

Kinkajous are the only members of the family which have prehensile tails. The tip curls round the branches of the trees, holding so firmly that it is able to support the whole weight of the animal. Kinkajous have small, round heads with flat faces and large eyes, giving them an owlish expression. Their tongues are enormously long and flexible, enabling them to lick honey from the comb, or termites and ants from holes and crevices. The Kinkajou is the most 'handy' of all the Raccoons, even using its tail to hold things, or inserting it into deep holes to grasp birds' eggs or young birds in their nests.

RAILS. This group of birds includes Water Rails, Land Rails or Corncrakes, Moorhens, and Coots, species of which are found all over the world. The greater number of them live in wet and marshy localities. They are characterized generally by having long legs and toes suitable for walking on marshy land, by their loose, hairy plumage, feeble wings, and short tails. Many species migrate considerable distances, usually flying by night. Some species, such as the Weka Rails of New Zealand, have lost the use of their wings altogether, and some, in consequence, have become, or are becoming, extinct. Even such species as the Moorhen, which can fly strongly, do not take readily to the air. Rails generally fly with their legs dangling down. Most Rails have narrow bodies, convenient for threading their way quickly through long grass and reeds. They do, in fact, tend to take cover

Eric Hosking

CORNCRAKE ON HER NEST, IN THE REEDS

Eric Hosking

THE COOT NESTS IN A REED-BED NEAR THE WATER

as soon as anyone approaches, many species, such as the Corncrake, being known better by their cry, 'crek-crek', than by their appearance. Most species have rather small heads, longish necks, and long beaks. The majority build deep, cup-shaped nests of grass and reeds—often substantial and very firmly woven. The Clapper-rail of North America, an inhabitant of salt-marsh country near the Atlantic coast, lays up to fifteen eggs; but most other species generally lay seven or eight. The large Weka Rail breeds in burrows in the ground, and lays only two or three eggs. This bird, unlike most Rails, is fearless and sometimes very pugnacious, being known even to attack fully grown rats. One species of New Zealand flightless Rails, *Notornis*, believed to have been extinct since 1898, has reappeared lately, a colony of at least 100 birds having been found near Lake Te Anau, in the South Island.

The Moorhen, easily recognized by its yellow and red beak and green legs, is a common bird throughout Europe, Asia, and Africa, living on 'meres' or marshy lakes rather than moors. It is a strong swimmer, the nestlings taking to the water as soon as they are hatched. It feeds on weed and on small water animals, and in the breeding season is an unscrupulous robber of other birds' eggs or even nestlings. It often produces as many as three broods in a season,

the young of the first brood often helping to rear the last. The Coot, a sooty-black, rather larger and heavier bird, with a bald white patch on its forehead, lives on large stretches of reed-encircled, fresh water, and often goes to the sea-coast in very frosty weather. It has lobed toes, and swims and dives like a duck. Like most of the Rails, it has a harsh cry.

RAT. This very unpopular animal is a RODENT, of the same family as the MOUSE (qq.v.). Rats are found in most parts of the world, especially near human dwellings, as they eat all kinds of human food, including grain and potato stores, and young game and poultry. Indeed, when really hungry, they will eat almost anything—their strong teeth being able to gnaw through the toughest fibre. Not only are they a menace for what they eat, but also they carry diseases, such as bubonic plague, by means of parasitic fleas. Every effort, therefore, is made to exterminate them with traps and poisons. The modern version of the rat-catcher is the local rodent officer. Rats, unfortunately, breed very prolifically indeed: the female can have a litter every six weeks, and she produces usually eight, but sometimes as many as twenty, at a birth.

Rats are difficult to trap, and, if caught, will frequently bite off a limb so as to escape. They run away from human beings unless they are cornered or starving, when they will attack fiercely. If driven from their homes by fire or shortage of food, they migrate in hordes. They need a lot of water, and have been known to gnaw through a 5-cm lead pipe to get it. They come out mainly at night for their food, much of which they take back to their nests to be eaten. In Great Britain there are two species, the Black or Old English Rat, and the Brown or Sewer Rat, sometimes called the Norwegian Rat from a mistaken belief that it originally came from Norway.

Black Rats are about 22 centimetres long, with an equally long tail. They are believed to have been brought unintentionally to this country during the 11th century by ships returning from the East, and for 500 or 600 years they were the only rats in Britain. They ran riot in the old wooden buildings, carrying the germs of the plague from one house to another. Brown Rats are thought to have arrived in the same way from the East in about 1728. They are larger and more powerful than Black Rats, which they soon began to oust from their haunts, until they became the more numerous of the two and are now the common rats of the country generally. Black Rats still infest ships and dockyards, being much more active climbers than Brown Rats. In cities they frequent sewers, docks, warehouses, and old houses, and in the country hedgerows, ricks, and coverts.

See also Vol. VI: Vermin.
See also Vol. XI: Household Pests.

RATTLESNAKE, *see* Vipers, Section 3.

RAVEN, *see* Crow, Section 3.

RAYS, *see* Sharks and Rays, Section 3.

RAZOR-BILL, *see* Auk, Section 2.

RAZOR-SHELL. The Razor-shells, of which there are four British species, are some of the most interesting of the sand-burrowing Molluscs (q.v.). The two valves of the shell are often 16 or 17 centimetres long and are either quite straight or slightly curved; it is their resemblance in shape to the protecting handle of a 'cutthroat' razor that has given them their popular name. When perfect, the valves of the shell are covered externally with an olive-green skin, mottled with bright orange; but this skin is so thin that it peels off very easily, leaving a whitish surface beneath, streaked with purple, pink, yellow, or brown. The Razor-shell lives in a vertical tunnel, which it usually makes low down on sandy shores, the entrance, something like a keyhole in shape, being only uncovered for a short time at low tide. Just before the tide begins to flow in again, the Razor-shells may often be seen sticking up a few centimetres above the surface of the damp sand—but they are very wary and any nearby movement, or the passing shadow of a low-flying gull, is quite enough to make them disappear instantly from view. They have good cause to be on the alert, for hungry gulls and shore-frequenting crows are only too ready to pounce on and eagerly devour any loiterer. It is possible, however, by the exercise of a little patience and caution, to grab one and pull it out of its burrow. The Razor-shell may be so alarmed as to contract altogether within its shell for a time; but, if placed on the damp sand, it will, if uninjured, and after a little delay, set to work to rebury itself—a process well worth watching. First, the mollusc will cautiously push out its foot, and feel about for a soft spot; then the foot is lengthened, and the pointed tip thrust into the sand. In a few seconds, the shell is pulled forward gradually into an upright position. A series of rhythmic jerks follows in quick succession, and with each jerk the shell is drawn down, until it finally disappears from view. The way in which the Razor-shell uses its foot to do this is really very remarkable. When first pushed into the sand, it is tapered to a sharp point; then, when it has stretched down as far as it will go, the mobile tip is turned to form a hook with which to anchor, while the shell is hauled into the upright position. The foot is again tapered and thrust still deeper into the yielding sand, and then, suddenly, its base swells out until it looks like the clapper of a bell, which wedges tightly against the sides of the shaft, while the upper part contracts and drags the shell downwards with a jerk. This process is repeated again and again, until the Razor-shell feels itself sunk to a depth well out of reach of danger.

RAZOR-SHELL WITH FOOT EXTENDED

RED ADMIRAL, *see* Vanessinae.

REDSHANK, *see* Wading Birds, Section 3.

REDSTART (or Redtail). This small migrant bird, which visits Europe in the summer months, is a member of the Thrush family (q.v.). It has a bright orange-chestnut tail, which is constantly quivering from side to side. Of the two species which visit Britain, the male Common Redstart has a bright orange breast and tail and a white forehead, contrasting with black cheeks, while the male Black Redstart has a black breast and throat and an orange tail. The females of both species have the orange tail, but are otherwise brownish and very similar to each other.

The Common Redstart frequents old woods and parklands, well-timbered gardens and orchards, as well as stone walls, quarries, and ruins. Its song is a high warble, ending rather abruptly, as if the singer had been surprised and stopped short. The female lays her delicate, pale-blue eggs in a hollow in a tree or hole in a wall. When the nestlings are hatched, both parents guard them anxiously, often uttering their alarm note, a hurried 'Whee-tic-tic'.

The Black Redstart is a common Continental bird, generally frequenting the neighbourhood of buildings. It used to be chiefly a winter visitor to Britain; but since the 1940s it has

Eric Hosking

THE REDSTART BRINGING A FLY TO HIS NEST

visited and even bred in the south of England, especially in bomb-damaged areas in large cities. The males are very pugnacious in the mating season, though they are not such fighters as the Robins. Black Redstarts like fine weather, and tend to mope with their feathers puffed out when it is wet.

The Blue-throat, a relative of the Redstart, is a fairly regular passage migrant in the autumn to the east coast of Britain. It breeds in central and western Europe, but winters in Africa. It has a russet tail, a whitish stomach, and a large patch of azure blue with a white spot in the middle on its throat. Another race, the Red-Spotted Blue-throat, breeds in the mountains of Norway. Both birds have a very striking song, which sounds like the tinkling of silver bells.

REDWING, *see* Thrush.

REINDEER. These are members of the Deer family (q.v.), especially adapted for living in cold climates. They are to be found in northern Europe, Asia, and America; but fossil remains show that they were once more widely distributed, and were common in the British Isles. As a protection against the Arctic climate, their noses and small ears are covered with soft hair, and their entire bodies with a woolly under-fur. They have very broad hoofs, which spread out sideways, enabling them to travel at great speed over the snow. They eat leaves, grass, water-plants, and lichens (reindeer moss) on the mountains, using their hoofs and noses to clear away the snow. Reindeer are unique amongst the deer in that both male and female have antlers. They shed them annually, the hind keeping hers longer than the buck, so as to be able to protect her calf against the attacks of wolves. The different races vary in size: the large American stags are, for instance, about 1·3 metres high, with antlers often from 1·2 to 1·5 metres long; whereas the Swedish reindeer are only about 1 metre high.

In Spitzbergen, although they have been much hunted, reindeer are still fairly numerous. During the summer they live on the grassy plains in the ice-free valleys; in the autumn they frequently go to the coast in order to eat the sea-weed thrown up on the beach. In the winter they return to the lichen-covered mountains in the interior. When the snow freezes, they find it almost impossible to get anything to eat, and

Norway House

A HERD OF REINDEER
These animals are nosing aside the snow to reach the lichen underneath

so grow very thin; but they soon fatten up again during the summer. In Siberia, the reindeer migrate in huge herds in the autumn from the hills to the forests, where they spend the winter. The wild reindeer of America, called Caribou, live as far north as the borders of the Arctic Ocean, and they, too, migrate south in the autumn to regions where food can be found.

Reindeer have been domesticated for a very long time, and various Siberian Peoples and many of the Lapps (qq.v. Vol. I) still rely on them almost entirely for their food (milk, cheese, and meat), transport, and clothing. The breed kept by the Lapps is much smaller than the wild race, and is used chiefly for pulling sleighs; but in Siberia the tame reindeer are large enough for riding. At the end of the last century the Siberian domesticated reindeer were introduced into Alaska, and have proved invaluable to the Eskimos (q.v. Vol. I), now that whales, seals, and bears have become more scarce.

See also Vol. IV: Beasts of Burden.

REMORA. From the earliest times the Remoras, or Sucking Fishes, have excited interest and wonder for their power of attaching themselves to sharks, large fishes, turtles, or even to ships. The ancients believed that the Remora could act as an anchor and stop a ship—indeed the defeat of the Emperor Caligula was said to have been due to one of these fishes holding his galley. The natives of several tropical countries have for centuries employed the sucking powers of the Remora for the purpose of catching turtles. They tie a strong cord to the Remora's tail, and when the Remora attaches itself to a turtle, the fisherman hauls in the cord, bringing both Remora and turtle ashore. This method of fishing, when described by the son of Christopher Columbus, was thought to be just a traveller's tale; but now it is known to be in fact practised (*see* Turtle Fishing: Vol. VI).

The sucking apparatus consists of a disk on the top of the head—really the first dorsal fin, the spines of which are split into halves, as it were, each half being laid sideways on the flat top of the skull. By the slight raising of these rays, a series of vacuum spaces is created, producing a suction so powerful that the fish cannot be removed by pulling it backwards. It is said that it will allow its tail to be torn off rather than release its hold; but a slight sliding movement forwards will loosen the grip. Usually one or more of these fishes may be found accompanying large sharks in the tropics, or sometimes attached inside the mouths or gill-cavities of large fishes.

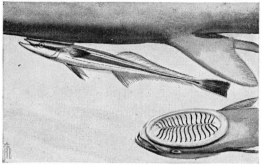

A. Fraser-Brunner

REMORAS ATTACHING THEMSELVES BENEATH A SHARK

The sucker-like fin on top of the head shows clearly in the
Remora which has not yet attached itself

They gain by this habit in two ways, firstly by
being carried from place to place without effort,
secondly by securing scraps of food left from the
meals of their large host.

REPRODUCTION IN ANIMALS. In animals there are two methods of reproduction:
without sexual cells (asexually), or with sexual
cells. In the lowest animals, which reproduce
asexually, parts of the parent are separated off
and begin an independent existence. In some,
such as the AMOEBA (q.v.), the animal simply
splits in half. In others, such as HYDRA or the
SEA-ANEMONE (qq.v.), buds are formed which,
when large enough, detach themselves as separate animals. It is obvious that in all these
creatures there is a continuity of life between
parent and offspring; and this continuity exists
even where more complex methods of reproduction tend to hide it.

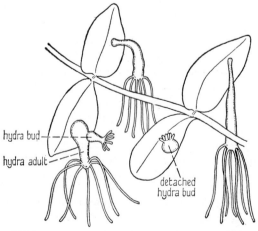

hydra bud

hydra adult

detached
hydra bud

HYDRA ATTACHED TO A WATER PLANT AND BUDDING

Those animals which reproduce sexually develop special cells (gametes) at the stage known
as maturity—a stage reached by some animals a
few hours after birth, and in others not for many
years. Generally speaking, the larger the animal
the longer it takes to reach maturity. These reproductive cells are of two kinds—the egg
(ovum) or female gamete, and the sperm
(spermatozoon) or male gamete. To enable a
new life to begin, union must take place between
one gamete of each kind—and this usually
involves the union of two adult individuals.
Even in the lower animals, such as SPONGES,
JELLYFISH, WORMS, and most MOLLUSCS (qq.v.),
which are hermaphrodite (that is, both kinds of
gametes are contained in the one individual),
self-fertilization is rarely possible. In a few
animals (for example, some aphides and sawflies) development of the eggs into new individuals may occur even if they are not fertilized.
This method of reproduction is known as parthenogenesis (virgin birth). In the higher animals, including most of the vertebrates, and
most of the higher invertebrates, such as CRUSTA-
CEANS, SPIDERS, and INSECTS (qq.v.), the sexes
are separate, which means that two individuals,
usually unlike and known as male and female,
must contribute. Often union of the two cells,
known as fertilization, takes place outside the
body of the female. This is the case with most
fishes, the unfertilized eggs being shed into the
water, where the male then pours on to them
his 'milt' (sperms contained in a fluid). In the
case of the SEA-HORSE (q.v.), the female injects
the eggs into a pouch in the underside of the body
of the male, where they are fertilized. As they
remain there till they hatch, it appears to be the
male who finally gives birth to the young. In
many REPTILES, and in BIRDS (qq.v.), the egg is
fertilized within the body of the female, afterwards being deposited and incubated—in other
words, developed through the warmth of the
parent's body, of the sand, of the sun, or in some
other way.

In MAMMALS (q.v.), except for the Duck-billed
PLATYPUS and the Spiny Ant-eater or ECHIDNA
of Australia (qq.v.), the egg, after fertilization,
remains in the body of the female, and develops
there during the period of gestation or preg-
nancy. This period may last 3 weeks (in a
mouse), 2 months (in a dog), 9 months (in a
human being), or nearly 2 years (in an elephant)
(*see* THE LIFE CYCLES OF ANIMALS, INDEX, p. 144).

The young animal is then born, more or less well developed, to be fed with milk by the mother for a further period. The foal or calf is able to stand and walk almost as soon as it is born; but puppies, kittens, and other animals are born blind and helpless—though they develop quickly. The human baby is intermediate between these extremes, but develops very slowly.

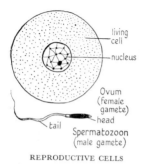

living cell
nucleus
Ovum (female gamete)
head
tail
Spermatozoon (male gamete)

REPRODUCTIVE CELLS

The MARSUPIALS (q.v.) are mammals in which the young animal is retained within the body of the mother for only a short time. When born it crawls into a pouch, where it is carried and suckled until ready to live an independent life.

See also REPRODUCTION IN PLANTS; HEREDITY.
See also Vol. XI: REPRODUCTIVE SYSTEM (Human).

REPRODUCTION IN PLANTS. 1. This may occur in three ways: by vegetative, asexual, or sexual propagation. In the vegetative form, part of the parent plant becomes detached and grows into a new plant. In lower plants, like algae or fungi, this may happen with any part of the plant; but in the higher flowering plants, the agent for vegetative propagation is usually a special part of the plant—the tuber of the potato being a typical example. In the asexual process, separate reproductive cells, usually known as spores, are formed, and these develop into new plants without sexual union. In the sexual process, special male and female reproductive cells are formed, which fuse together to form a new young plant or embryo. Asexual reproduction by spores enables the plant to spread very quickly in favourable conditions, since spores are produced in large quantities and are light enough to be disseminated widely by the wind. However, these spores are not able to resist adverse conditions, such as lack of moisture, and low or high temperature, for more than quite short periods. Seeds produced by flowering plants by sexual reproduction usually have hard protective coats which enable them to live through difficult times. Some seeds have been known to remain dormant for many years, protected by their hard coat.

2. VEGETATIVE PROPAGATION takes place in many ways. With seaweeds, new plants may be budded off from the parent near the base; while in the green pond-scums, short pieces, consisting of a few cells, may break off and rapidly grow into fresh filaments. YEASTS (q.v.) are propa-

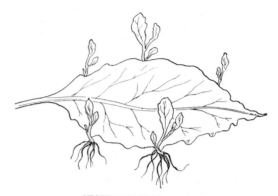

VEGETATIVE PROPAGATION

Leaf of 'Life-plant' (*Bryophyllum*) with young plants growing direct from it

gated vegetatively by a process known as budding: small protuberances or buds grow out from the parent plant, and eventually break off to form independent plants. Vegetative propagation occurs in mushrooms every time a cake of spawn is grown in a mushroom bed. The cake of spawn is made of numerous threads of mycelium of the plant, and these, under the right conditions, soon grow out and branch to form new threads. New moss and liverwort plants may be grown either from detached pieces or from separate buds on the old plant. In some ferns and some other plants (see picture), little buds may be produced on the leaves, and these grow out into small rooted plants. In higher plants, vegetative propagation may take place by the production of underground stems, such as rhizomes and tubers, or when buddings, cuttings, or graftings are made (*see* FRUIT PROPAGATION, Vol. VI).

3. ASEXUAL REPRODUCTION by means of spores occurs only in the lower plants, such as algae, fungi, mosses and liverworts, and ferns, and not in flowering plants. In the algae, spores formed by rapid divisions of the cells are shed freely into the water, to begin life as new plants. In fungi, the spores are borne on fruiting bodies, such as mushrooms, toadstools, and puff-balls. The clouds of spores which come from a dry puff-ball show what prolific numbers are produced. In mosses and liverworts the spores are carried in little boxes or capsules; while in ferns the brown lines or clusters on the under-surfaces of the leaves are collections of spores.

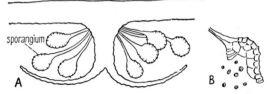

A. Section through fern frond showing sporangia (spore cases) on underside; B. Single sporangium splitting to release spores

4. SEXUAL REPRODUCTION occurs in almost all types of plants, but becomes more complicated and efficient in the higher flowering plants. As in animals, the climax of sexual reproduction occurs when the male reproductive cell or sperm fuses with the female reproductive cell or egg. In passing from the lower to the higher plants, we see the development of devices to ensure that the sperm is brought to the egg. In algae, such as the seaweeds, the sperms and eggs are shed freely into the water, and whether or not they meet with one another is largely a matter of chance—although in many instances the eggs give off some chemical substance which attracts the sperms (*see* MOVEMENT IN PLANTS). The pin-moulds (*see* MOULDS) have a form of sexual reproduction in which two threads grow together and fuse at their tips; while in some fungi no form of sexual reproduction appears to occur. In mosses, liverworts, and ferns, the eggs are not shed freely as in seaweeds, but are protected in fixed organs, which grow near to the structures containing the mobile sperm. Here, too, the eggs give off a chemical substance which attracts the sperms. In all lower plants the product of the sexual union between sperm and egg is a one-celled structure which has no reserves of food, and so is unable to withstand adverse conditions.

The most efficient form of sexual reproduction occurs in the seed-bearing plants. SEEDS (q.v.) are many-celled structures, usually with thick, toughened coats, containing food reserves, such as starch and oil, to give the seedlings a good start in life. The sperms are cells within the pollen grains, which are produced in great profusion. These are transferred to the ovules in various ways, there always being tremendous wastage. In CONIFERS (q.v.), the least specialized of the seed-bearing plants, sperms and eggs are produced in cones, and the seeds are not protected by a fruit-wall, but remain naked. In FLOWERING PLANTS (q.v.), the seed produced after union of the sperm and egg becomes protected by the growth of part of the flower to form a fruit-wall, within which the seed may remain protected for many years (*see* FRUITS).

5. POLLINATION. This is the process in flowering plants whereby the pollen, containing the male reproductive cells, and the ovules, containing the female reproductive cells, are brought together to make the eggs fertile. As in most kinds of sexual reproduction, this happens by the movement of the male cell, the pollen being transferred from the stamens to the tip of the carpels or stigma of the stationary female. Generally, pollination is dependent upon pollen from another flower (cross-pollination), though sometimes pollen may reach the ovule from the stamen of the same flower (self-pollination). Both self- and cross-pollination may be brought about by the wind or by insects; and sometimes birds or even water may cause pollination. Wind-pollination is a purely chance process, the dry pollen being caught up in currents of air, and some of it happening to alight on the stigma of a similar flower. Wind-pollinated flowers, therefore, produce large quantities of pollen to allow for the wastage. Wind-pollination is found in many British trees and most grasses, but few of the smaller flowering plants could survive by so haphazard a method.

In self-pollinated flowers such as the Chickweed, the exposed pollen merely passes to the stigma of the same flower, sometimes being carried there by the wind. Some flowers rely on self-pollination when cross-pollination has failed. In the Sweet Violet, for example, cross-pollination usually takes place; but certain of the flowers do not open, and in these, when the pollen is ripe and the anther becomes ruptured, self-pollination takes place. If the Scarlet Pimpernel has not been cross-pollinated, the flower closes up and remains closed for 2 or 3 days, while self-pollination takes place. The petals of the Garden Pea flower are so firmly interlocked that no insect can

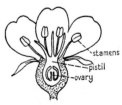

CROSS-SECTION OF FLOWER

force an entry, and self-pollination must take place.

Insects visit flowers for food or shelter, or to lay eggs. The food they seek is pollen and 'nectar' (a solution of sugars produced in little sacs called 'nectaries'). When insects, such as bees, visit flowers in search of nectar, parts of their hairy bodies become dusted with pollen, and this easily rubs off on the stigmas of that flower or the next one they visit. Insects seem to be strongly attracted by certain colours, but to pay little attention to others—though scents probably attract them more surely than do bright colours. In fact, some flowers—e.g. Meadow Sweet—are so strongly scented that insects are attracted to them though they have no nectar to offer.

Most insect-pollinated flowers have wonderful devices for guiding the movements of the insect and turning them to the best account. Sometimes, as in Dead-nettles and some members of the Pea family, and particularly in the Sage, the insect can enter the flower in one way only, and in consequence must push against special outgrowths which move the stamens and dust the pollen over its body. The Primrose has two types of flowers—the pin-eyed, in which the stigma is above the stamens, and the thrum-eyed, in which the stigma is below the stamens. When a bee alights on a thrum-eyed flower, it pushes its proboscis down to the bottom of the petal tube to obtain nectar, and in doing so the top of its head touches the ripe anthers and is dusted with pollen. This part of the bee's head later comes into contact with the stigma of the pin-eyed flower, so ensuring cross-pollination.

6. FERTILIZATION. The union of the male and female reproductive cells, after the transfer of pollen from the stamens to the stigmas of the carpels, is known as fertilization. After pollination, the pollen grain containing the male reproductive cell is held on the stigma, which is often sticky. There it absorbs moisture, swells, and its outer coat bursts, allowing the more delicate inner one to protrude. A pollen tube then grows down through the tissue between the stigma and the ovary, and through a minute hole in the ovule to reach the female cell. The two then fuse, and the process of fertilization is completed. This union of male and female reproductive cells is essential to sexual reproduction, and, when it has taken place in flowers, the SEEDS (q.v.) develop. The seed contains a minute plant packed in a small space, usually

Harold Bastin

FLOWERS OF HOLLY

Left, Male flower with stamens. *Right*, Female flower with pistil

with enough stored food to nourish it until the seedling is established. Within each carpel there are as many seeds as there were fertilized ovules. During the development of the seeds, the walls of the carpels also change in various ways, the completed structure with its enclosed seeds forming the FRUIT (q.v.).

7. GERMINATION. Seeds need moisture, oxygen, and warmth to germinate; so they remain dormant in winter, becoming active in spring. The majority of seeds do not appear to be much affected by the presence or absence of light. The seeds of some plants, however, such as Purple Loosestrife, Rhododendrons, Mistletoe, and certain of the Speedwells, are 'light-sensitive'—that is, they will not germinate until they have been exposed to the light. The seeds of other plants, such as the Tomato and cultivated plants such as Phlox and Love-lies-bleeding, are 'light-hard'—that is, they will germinate only in the dark.

Some seeds must germinate immediately they are shed from the fruit, or they will die; in others, germination can be delayed from a few days to several weeks or longer. Packets of garden seeds can be kept for several years, the seeds remaining in a resting state until conditions suitable for germination arise—though the longer they are kept the fewer will germinate. Species of Clover have remained in this resting state for 50 years, and the Indian Lotus for 250 years. Seeds can be made to germinate more quickly by being soaked in water for a day or so before sowing, or, in the case of large seeds like the bean, by having their seed-coat pierced to allow the water to enter.

See also FLOWERS; REPRODUCTION IN ANIMALS.

REPTILES

REPTILES. It is most probable that reptiles first appeared on the earth at a time subsequent to the Carboniferous Period when the climate of the world was growing warmer and drier. When water was becoming scarcer, animals not dependent on life in water were at an advantage. It is not always easy to distinguish the first reptiles from the AMPHIBIA (q.v.); but during the Mesozoic Period, 65 to 225 million years ago, before the appearance of birds and mammals, the reptiles were the dominant vertebrates on land. Some were gigantic animals, the largest being the *Diplodocus*, which reached a length of 26 metres (*see* PREHISTORIC ANIMALS, Vol. III).

Reptiles are cold-blooded animals; that is, their blood takes on the same temperature as their surroundings. When this temperature falls, they become less active, until in very cold temperatures they become torpid; and so they are never found in arctic regions. They flourish best in tropical conditions, where they can be active enough to compete successfully with other animals. In temperate climates such as Britain, they spend about half their time in HIBERNATION (q.v.). The skin of reptiles has protective horny scales and often bony plates as well. The female lays an egg which is encased in a porous shell of a rather leathery consistency, and this in most species is incubated by the heat of the sun or the warmth generated by decaying vegetation. In some species of lizards the eggs are retained in the mother's body until the young are ready to hatch.

There are four surviving groups of reptiles, and these differ considerably from each other. The first group is now represented by only one species, the TUATARA (q.v.) of New Zealand. The next group consists of the TURTLES AND TORTOISES (q.v.), reptiles well protected by bony shells. The LIZARDS and SNAKES (qq.v.) form a third group, containing most of the surviving species of reptiles; and the last group, the CROCODILES (q.v.), includes the largest living reptiles. The Crocodiles and the Birds (*see* EVOLUTION) are probably the only survivors of the largest group of reptiles in the Mesozoic Period, the rest having branched off earlier.

RESPIRATION IN ANIMALS

RESPIRATION IN ANIMALS. After food has been digested, it is transported to all the living cells of the body (*see* NUTRITION OF ANIMALS). To use the energy locked up in this material oxygen is needed. Respiration in animals can be divided into three processes: (1) the bringing of air into contact with an appropriate surface (skin, gills, lungs) for exchange of oxygen and carbon dioxide—a process known as breathing; (2) the uptake and transport of oxygen from this surface to the body tissues and the return of carbon dioxide to the surface by the BLOOD SYSTEM (q.v.); and (3) the break-down of digested food by the use of the oxygen, the release of energy, and the production of carbon dioxide as a waste product. This article deals only with the first process, breathing.

Not all animals breathe in the same way as man and the vertebrates. WORMS (q.v.) breathe through the skin, which is very thin and moist, rather like the membrane lining our lungs. INSECTS (q.v.) breathe through tracheal tubes, which run throughout their bodies from external openings or 'spiracles'. SPIDERS (q.v.) breathe through very thin sheets of skin on the underside of the body, arranged like the leaves of a book, and hence known as the 'lung-book': the air passes over these leaves, and thus exchange takes place. FISHES, CRABS, water SNAILS (qq.v.), and other aquatic animals breathe through gills, which are areas of skin rich in blood-vessels. A fish takes in water through its mouth, and passes it out at the side of the head through the gills, the covers of which may be seen opening and closing with a regular rhythm, showing, when open, the very red, thin skin of the gill openings. In CRABS and LOBSTERS (qq.v.), which have the gills at the bases of the legs, and in many other water animals, the gills are fine and hair-like. The gills of Tadpoles (*see* FROGS) and other young

DIPLODOCUS CARNEGII, THE LARGEST OF THE EXTINCT GIANT REPTILES, 26 METRES LONG

amphibians are on the sides of the head; they are then replaced by internal gills, like those of a fish; and finally by lungs when the animals emerge for their life on land.

On land, provision must be made for keeping moist the surface of the skin through which respiration takes place. In some of the more lowly animals, such as the earthworm, this is done by the secretion of slime all over the body; most animals, however, possess lungs, which are kept moist inside the body. Air is brought to the lungs from the nose or mouth through the windpipe (trachea), which is kept permanently open by means of rings of cartilage (gristle). The windpipe divides into two smaller tubes (bronchi), one of which goes to each lung. In the lung, these tubes divide and re-divide many times, thus conveying the air to the thin, moist skin of the lung's surface. The air sacs, in which this exchange of oxygen for carbon dioxide takes place, are so designed as to present as large a surface as possible to the air. A man's lungs have normally a capacity of about 4·5 litres of air; but athletes and men engaged in heavy manual work develop larger lungs, so that the blood may be oxygenated more quickly. When we get 'out of breath', it is because we are unable to take in air as quickly as the body requires for the strenuous work we are doing. The additional air sacs and actual strokes of the wings during flight are two features which help to prevent BIRDS (q.v.) from becoming out of breath. The air sacs present in some species of insects serve the same purpose.

In those animals which have no blood, such as SPONGES, JELLY-FISH, and SEA-ANEMONES (qq.v.), the sea-water circulates, carrying with it the needed oxygen, and removing the waste carbon dioxide. Most animals, however, are supplied with a BLOOD SYSTEM (q.v.). In these the blood usually contains a respiratory pigment (red in mammals, blue-green in many Crustacea), which combines loosely with oxygen. When the blood reaches the respiring tissues, the oxygen is released, and carbon dioxide is picked up.

See also Vol. XI: RESPIRATION (Human).

RESPIRATION IN PLANTS. 1. Growth in both plants and animals depends upon two things: (i) a liberal supply of building materials, such as sugars, starches, fats, and proteins; (ii) enough oxygen to release energy from these

materials. Plants make their building material by PHOTOSYNTHESIS (q.v.), which takes place in the green leaves. The release of energy, seen in animals in the forms of heat and movement, is not so obvious in plants. Respiration in both plants and animals, however, releases energy in the same way as the combustion of coal releases heat. And respiration gives rise to carbon dioxide as a waste product, just as in the burning of coal. It is an old custom to remove plants from the wards of hospitals at night, because the plants were thought to take from the atmosphere oxygen needed by the patients, and at the same time return to the atmosphere carbon dioxide, making the room stuffy. But the effect is far too small to make it worth while.

In plants, photosynthesis and respiration are often going on at the same time. In photosynthesis, carbon dioxide is taken in and oxygen given off; whereas in respiration, oxygen is taken in and carbon dioxide given off. Photosynthesis usually takes place in daylight only; but respiration proceeds at all times, oxygen being taken

Albert Steiner

ALPINE SOLDANELLA

The flowers have melted their way through the remaining ice with the heat given off during respiration

in to react with the made-up foodstuffs to release energy. It is not easy to demonstrate the process of respiration, because photosynthesis uses much more carbon dioxide than is released by respiration—and, consequently, it releases much more oxygen than respiration uses. To demonstrate respiration, we have either to use active parts of the plant which have not yet begun to photosynthesize, such as growing seeds, or else to make our experiments with green plants under conditions in which photosynthesis cannot take place, such as in complete darkness. Thus, if some germinating seeds, opening flower-heads, or ripening fruit are put, with a thermometer, into a vacuum flask (which prevents radiation of heat), the temperature within the flask will be seen to rise—showing that some energy has been liberated as heat. Or if some peas are put into water to soak for about 24 hours, the temperature of the water will increase perceptibly—absorption of water by the peas will have increased the active processes in them, and heat will have been set free by respiration.

An exceptional but most interesting example of excessive respiration producing heat is shown by a plant, *Soldanella alpina*, which is common in the Swiss Alps. In the autumn this plant develops thick, leathery leaves, which build up reserves of starch. During the winter the plant becomes covered with snow and ice to a depth of a metre or so. When spring comes, the sun melts all the snow and some of the ice, and water trickles down to the roots. The plant revives, and food is passed to the flower-buds—which therefore respire so actively that they give off enough heat to melt the remaining ice around them. The developing flowers thus actually melt their way through, and violet patches of them may be seen, as if they were growing on and in ice. By the time the flowers have forced their way out of the ice the leaves have used up so much of their stored food in this great respiratory activity that they have become as thin as paper (*see* ALPINE PLANTS).

The rate of respiration in plants, as in animals, varies greatly according to the activities of the cells. A deciduous tree, for example, grows more rapidly, and therefore respires more, during the summer than during the winter, when it is mainly resting. In dry seeds, living processes are reduced to a minimum, and respiration is very low; but when they germinate, the living processes quicken, and the rate of respiration is speeded up accordingly. Respiration is affected by temperature also—a rise in temperature of 10° approximately doubles its rate. At 35° C., however, the living processes of plants begin to fall off, as does the rate of respiration, also.

2. ANAEROBIC RESPIRATION. Although the release of energy from foodstuffs is nearly always dependent on a regular supply of oxygen (aerobic respiration), there are cases where respiration goes on in the absence of gaseous oxygen (anaerobic or 'without air' respiration). If germinating seeds, for example, are kept under conditions in which they can get no free oxygen, respiration will still occur, and carbon dioxide be released. In respiration of this kind, the chemical reactions which take place are different: instead of being completely broken down to carbon dioxide, the foodstuffs form other breakdown products, one of which is alcohol. This is made use of in the formation of beer from malt by the fungus yeast, this process of FERMENTATION (q.v.) being really an example of anaerobic respiration. Some bacteria and fungi are able to live and grow only in situations where oxygen is completely absent, and die when they are exposed to oxygen. One of these is the soil bacterium called tetanus, which, when it gets into open wounds, may cause the disease known as lock-jaw. If the existence of tetanus in a flesh wound is suspected, therefore, the doctor at once uses an antiseptic with strong oxidizing properties, such as hydrogen peroxide.

RHEA, *see* OSTRICH, Section 3.

RHINOCEROS (from a Greek word meaning nose-horn). This huge, ungainly beast can claim to be the largest of the land mammals after the Elephant, with the Hippopotamus only a very little smaller. Rhinoceroses belong to the same order, Perissodactyla (odd-toed hoofed beasts), as do HORSES and TAPIRS (qq.v.). There are five distinct species, three of which are found in Asia and the other two in Africa. They became extinct in America in very early times, and are becoming much scarcer in the Old World. They are all enormous creatures, with bulky bodies on comparatively short legs. Their heads are large and elongated, and their erect, oval ears are set very far back. They have small eyes and weak sight, and their upper lips generally protrude beyond the lower. Some of them have prominent canine teeth in their lower jaw. The horns

WHITE RHINOCEROSES IN UGANDA

Mansell Coll.

are composed of matted and compressed hair: some species have one, others two, usually of unequal length.

Rhinoceroses are found both in open plains and in grassy jungles and swamps. They feed chiefly at night, and eat only vegetable food, some species living almost entirely on grass, others eating mainly twigs and small boughs of trees. They are harmless, even timorous creatures; but their short-sightedness makes them inclined to charge blindly at anything arousing their suspicion. The African species rely entirely on their horns as weapons of defence, whereas the Asiatic kinds, having smaller horns, defend themselves mainly with their canine teeth, which can inflict enormous gashes.

The great Indian Rhinoceros is the largest of the Asiatic species, its height at the shoulder being from 1·5 to 1·7 metres, its length from its nose to the root of its tail about 3·2 metres, and its girth about 2·9 metres. It has a single horn on its nose usually up to 30 cm long, and two long canine teeth in its lower jaw. Its thick hide is hairless, except at the ears and tail, and it is studded all over with large tubercles, looking rather like rivet-heads on an iron boiler. At the joints are huge folds of skin, which divide up the body into shield-like sections, and form great rolls at the neck. The animal generally moves at a long, swinging trot; but if disturbed it breaks into a rapid but awkward gallop. When excited it makes a curious grunting noise. It is generally solitary, feeding mainly on grass, and preferring swampy districts, where it likes to wallow in the mud. In captivity it often loses its horn by rubbing it away against the brickwork of its house.

The names of the two African species, the Black and the White Rhinoceros, are misleading, for, in fact, they differ very slightly in colour, both being a slaty grey. The White Rhinoceros is the largest of all the species, being about 2 metres high. Both species have two horns. The front horns of Black Rhinoceroses can be well over a metre long; while the record for those of a White Rhinoceros is 1·59 metres. African Rhinoceroses have no protruding canine teeth, and no folds of skin like the Indian Rhinoceros. The Black Rhinoceros inhabits river valleys and thick jungles, feeding on young shoots and branches of trees. The White Rhinoceros keeps to the open plains, where it feeds only on grass; it walks with its head close to the ground. The mother always follows her calf, guiding it, apparently, with her long horns.

RHIZOME, an underground rooting stem, *see* STEMS, Section 2(*b*).

RIBBON-FISH. These oceanic fishes are very long, flattened from side to side, and very fragile. Except when washed ashore in a much-damaged condition, they are seldom observed clearly; so that, when seen from ships, they have usually been mistaken for the mythical SEA SERPENT (q.v.). They are quite inoffensive. They inhabit the open sea, usually swimming close to the surface with a side-to-side movement of the long, flexible body. There is no anal fin, and the caudal (tail) fin is either bent upwards at a sharp angle, as in the Deal-fish, or is absent, as in the Oar-fishes. The jaws slide forward by means of a very curious arrangement of the bones.

The great Oar-fish, which may grow to a length of nearly 8 metres, was long known to the Norwegians as the 'king of the herrings'; and they believed that, if harm was done to the Oar-fish, the herring would move away to some other coast. Its body is semi-transparent, and light blue in colour; the dorsal fin rises like a crest on the head, bearing tufts of bright red; and the pelvic fins are long filaments, thickened at the tips.

The so-called Deal-fish, sometimes called Vaagmaar, are very similar. These have a long, streamer-like fin above the head, and the tail fin is developed and turned upwards. In the young, the crest on the head is composed of about six long filaments, with shining tassels at intervals along them. Deal-fishes do not grow so large as the Oar-fish, and more species are known. They are said to be strong and swift swimmers, in spite of their flimsy appearance.

Quite closely related to the ribbon fishes, despite its very different appearance, is the Opah or Moonfish, which has the same curious sliding arrangement of the jaws. This beautiful fish reaches a large size, sometimes weighing 225 kg or more. The sides are tinted with lilac, shading to rich blue on the back, and are scattered with silver spots, each surrounded by a golden ring; the jaws and fins are bright scarlet. The Opah is rather rare, but is very widely distributed through the seas of the world, odd specimens turning up every now and then at widely separated places. The flesh is firm and pink, and is said to be very good to eat.

RINGLET, *see* BROWNS (Butterflies).

RING-OUZEL, *see* THRUSH, Section 3.

ROACH, *see* CARP.

ROBIN (REDBREAST). Common over the greater part of Europe, this member of the large THRUSH family (q.v.) is among the best known and favourite of British birds. Some are resident all the year round, some migrate farther south for the winter, and a number come to winter in Britain from northern Europe. Some frequent human habitations, breeding in gardens and orchards, others breed in lonely woods.

Although so friendly to man, the Robin is among the most aggressive and pugnacious of small birds. In the spring the cock lays claim to a definite estate, singing boldly and displaying his red breast as a warning to other Robins to keep away. He will attack and fight with great ferocity any rival to his territory or mate. Unlike other birds, however, the Robin continues to hold his territory after the breeding season, and in the winter the female also claims a territory and sings to maintain it (*see* ANIMAL TERRITORY). In the spring, during the courting season, the cock Robin's breast is a brilliant colour. He puffs out his feathers, sways and bobs his head, and flirts his tail in his courtship (*see* ANIMAL LANGUAGE). The hen also has a red breast, though not so brilliant; but the young birds do not show red in their first season. The Continental Robin is paler in colour; but the Ruby Throat, a species of Robin which breeds in the

Eric Hosking

THE ROBIN WITH YOUNG IN ITS NEST BUILT IN AN OLD BARREL

arctic tundras of Siberia, and winters in southern Asia, has vivid red colouring.

The name 'Robin' is used for several foreign birds with only a superficial resemblance to the Redbreast, such as the American Robin, a larger, heavier bird, and the New Zealand Robin. The American Robin, which is also a Thrush, has a ruddy breast and has also the same friendly fearlessness with human beings. It must have reminded the early settlers of the Redbreast at home. The Indian Dhyal Bird and Shama, found in most parts of south-eastern Asia, are like Robins in structure, but are distinguished by long black and white tails. The Dhyal Bird, in particular, is much like the Robin also in behaviour, being confident and friendly with humans, and exceedingly pugnacious in the breeding season. Both birds have a charming song, with an even greater compass than the European bird.

'ROCK-SALMON.' There is no living fish to which this name is properly applied: the name is given by the fish trade to any kind of fish that is not easily sold under its real identity. Wolf-fish, Monk-fish, and Dog-fish, which are too large and ugly to display complete on the fish-monger's slab, are beheaded and skinned, and the flesh, cut up into suitable sizes, is labelled 'Rock-salmon'.

RODENT. The order of Rodents (gnawing animals) is the largest group of mammals, and also the most extensive, rodents being found all over the world except in the extreme polar regions.

Members of the order all have characteristic teeth. There are two front teeth, the incisors or biters, in both the upper and lower jaws. These are large and prominent, and grow continuously throughout the animal's life. They have a hard enamel surface on the front, and little or no enamel on the sides and back, so that with use each constantly wears the other sharp. To keep them in condition, all rodents must gnaw. If one of these teeth is broken or lost, the opposite one continues to grow unopposed, finally killing the animal, either by preventing it from feeding, or by turning a full circle and piercing the brain. There are no canine teeth, a wide gap separating the incisors from the cheek teeth. The cheeks close into this gap, forming two hairy packs which help to keep such things as earth and

Harold Bastin

THE HOUSE MOUSE USING ITS INCISORS

other matter out of the mouth when the animal is gnawing or burrowing. The cheek teeth crush and grind food, but do not have cutting edges. The cheek teeth of some rodents, VOLES (q.v.), for instance, are also permanently growing and rootless, like the incisors.

Rodents nearly all live on dry land; but some, such as the BEAVER and MUSK RAT (qq.v.), live mostly in water, and others, such as the SQUIRRELS (q.v.), spend most of their life in trees. Most rodents are vegetarian, and they do much damage, especially by eating grain and stripping bark off trees. Because they have an enormous birth-rate, they are able to hold their own in the face of countless enemies which prey on them. They also show great wariness and skill in hiding. Most are timid, but some—as, for example, rats—attack fiercely if they are cornered.

The Cape Jumping Hare or Spring Haas, a South African rodent, which looks like a hare, measures about 30 centimetres long, with a bushy tail of about the same length. It progresses by a series of leaps of some 6 to 9 metres. Large colonies of these animals live on the rocky plateaux of South Africa.

The Gophers of America, burrowing, mole-like rodents about the size of a squirrel, with very short tails, live in holes in the ground. The Pocket Gophers have large pouches in their cheeks, which they use for carrying food to their underground store-rooms. They have great, sharp, digging claws, and can travel with ease and speed either backwards or forwards, their short, sensitive tails guiding them when running in reverse. They are vicious, surly beasts, and fight savagely with each other.

ROOK, *see* CROW, Section 4.

ROOT PRESSURE. When young saplings are felled or pruned in the spring and early summer, a liquid collects at the cut ends, and the 'bleeding' goes on for some time, especially in plants such as the young vine, suggesting that water is being forced up from below. This force, known as root pressure, varies with the season of the year, being much more vigorous in the spring, when the plant's water requirements are at their highest, and falling to a minimum in the autumn and winter, when its water requirements are lower. It also varies on different days, and is less by day than by night, suggesting that it is affected in some way both by the intensity of light and by the temperature. The cause of root pressure is far from clear. It results partly from water being forced under considerable pressure from the absorbing cells of the root into the woody vessels, up which sap is carried to the leaves to take part in the food-manufacturing process known as PHOTOSYNTHESIS (q.v.). Root pressure varies greatly, as can be seen in the amount by which different plants 'bleed' when their stems are cut. In conifers, such as Pine and Larch, root pressure hardly exists.

In some plants, root pressure exerts a considerable force. A cut Stinging-nettle was found to give off 9·6 litres of water in 40 hours; a potted Fuchsia produced a pressure so great that it would have been able to force a column of water to a height of 7·6 metres. As root pressure has never been found to raise water higher than about 9 metres, it seems clear that this would be incapable of raising water to the top of the tallest trees; though it may account for the upward movement of water to the leaves of some herbaceous plants. How water is raised to the top of a tall tree is a mystery yet to be solved: but probably it is due to the combined effects of many forces, mainly TRANSPIRATION (q.v.), or water-loss through the leaves.

The drops of 'dew' to be seen on grass and other plants early in the morning, especially on 'steamy' spring days, are often due to root pressure. (DEW (q.v. Vol. III) is, of course, also caused by condensation of water vapour in the atmosphere.) Since the air in the early morning is usually saturated with water vapour, transpiration from the leaves does not occur. But absorption of water continues through the roots, and the water continues to be forced upwards, where it appears as liquid drops at certain points on the leaves. This giving off of water occurs particularly in the Garden Nasturtium and in certain Saxifrages. Some Saxifrages give off water containing calcium salts in solution, and, when the water evaporates, the salts are left as a white coating on the margins of the leaf. In humid tropical forests, the oozing of water from the leaves is common, some plants giving a constant drip. One leaf has been known to exude 190 drops a minute.

Root pressure is made use of commercially in Canada, where incisions are made into the trunks of Sugar Maple in the spring before the leaves are fully formed, and the liquid, a sugary syrup, oozes out and is collected (see MAPLE TREE, Vol. VI).

ROOTS. The two main functions of roots are to anchor the plant firmly in the soil, and to absorb water containing dissolved mineral salts, which form the raw materials of plant foodstuffs. They may also serve as a food storage. Plants of the Legume family have root nodules, housing BACTERIA (q.v.), which hold nitrogen to be used by the plant (see NITROGEN SUPPLY IN PLANTS).

1. ANCHORAGE. Roots have to resist a pulling strain from above, caused perhaps by the wind or by the tugging of an animal. This is particularly true of the long, firm, main roots known as tap-roots, and the deeper these grow, the more (other things being equal) they can resist such pulling strains. Plants with stout tap-roots, such as Dandelions and Parsnips, will often resist a tug until the root tears, usually near the base of the shoot.

The other type, the fibrous root, is equally efficient for anchorage. Fibrous roots are much too branched for a main root to be distinguishable; they cover a surprising amount of space in the soil. When a plant with a fibrous root is pulled up, a large amount of root is usually left behind. The roots of oak-trees, for example, often penetrate as far down as the tree is high. The roots of wheat go down 1·5 metres, or even farther. If the soil is rocky, however, and the roots cannot go down, they spread out sideways.

2. WATER ABSORPTION. This is the most important function of the root. Soil is made up of tiny particles of various shapes which, although close together, have many air spaces between them. The water in the soil forms a film round each soil particle, and in order to get at this water film a plant has special absorbing structures, called root-hairs, which generally grow near the tip of the root. Each root-hair is composed of one cell with a very thin cell-wall, a thick lining of protoplasm, and a space in the middle filled with fluid. Water is absorbed from the soil by 'osmosis'. When a living cell is surrounded by water, or by a solution less concentrated than its own sap, water is drawn into the cell, which then swells until its walls are fully extended, its cell-sap meanwhile becoming diluted by the addition of water. Dried prunes or currants put to soak take up water by this same osmosis. We can also demonstrate it for ourselves by taking half a peeled potato, scooping a hole in the middle, putting a lump of sugar in the hole, and standing the potato in water. The sugar soon becomes dissolved by water drawn in through the tissues of the potato. Sugars and other substances in the currant, the prune, and the root-hair behave in the same way. From the root-hair, the water containing mineral salts passes into the roots, and thence up the shoot to the leaves, where the plant's food is made.

It is useless to look for root-hairs on an uprooted plant. They have either been destroyed during the pulling up, are hidden by the clinging particles of soil, or have shrivelled in the dry air. They can easily be seen, however, by allowing some seeds to germinate on paper in a damp atmosphere. The number of root-hairs varies greatly on different roots and under different conditions of humidity. In a maize plant grown in a moist chamber, 400 to the square millimetre were counted under a microscope. Water-plants do not need them.

When root-hairs are in contact with soil particles, the wall of the hair becomes soft and gummy and sticks fast to the particles. That is why roots cling so tenaciously to the soil, and why so much soil comes away with an uprooted plant.

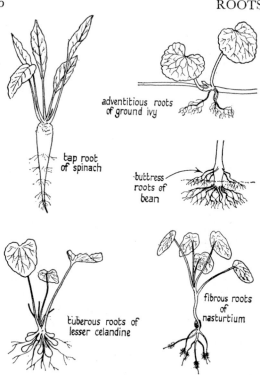

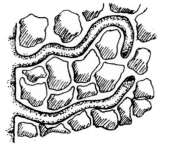

ROOT-HAIRS

Left: Pushing through particles of soil. *Right*: on a pea seedling

TYPES OF ROOTS

adventitious roots of ground ivy

tap root of spinach

buttress roots of bean

tuberous roots of lesser celandine

fibrous roots of nasturtium

There is a close connexion between the way the roots of a plant spread and the arrangement of its leaves. This is especially obvious in trees. After rain, the soil beneath the outer edge of the tree is wet, while that under the crown remains comparatively dry. The branches of the roots extend in the soil as far as the leaf-branches overhead, so that, as the water from the dripping leaves passes downwards to the soil, the root-hairs at the tips of the root-branches can absorb it. This co-ordination between leaves and root occurs in other plants besides trees. In the Arum Lily, for example, the tips of the downwardly pointing leaves are directly over the ends of the spreading roots. In the Rhubarb, however, where there is a tap-root with few branches, the water travels towards it by way of the groove in the leaf-stalk. All plants have some such arrangement for conducting rain or dew towards the root-hairs.

3. FOOD STORAGE. The third function which some roots perform is to store food which the plants have manufactured in excess of their immediate needs. Thus, in the Lesser Celandine, and various Orchids, some of the roots, which have become very thick, are found to

contain stored-up starch; these are called Root-tubers. In Carrots and Beets, the swollen tap-root stores up sugar; in other root-crops, such as the Parsnip and Turnip, it stores starch. Some of these underground storage organs, however, such as Potato tubers, Iris rhizomes, and bulbs, are not roots, but underground stems (*see* STEMS, Section 2).

4. ADVENTITIOUS ROOTS. Some roots have other special functions. It is difficult to tear Ivy from a wall or tree because of the presence of hundreds of tiny roots which fix the plant securely to its support. Because they grow from the stem, these roots are called 'adventitious roots'. In the case of the Ivy, they are also called 'climbing roots'. The root-tubers of the Dahlia, Lesser Celandine, and Orchids are also, in fact, adventitious; for they, too, grow from the stem at about ground level. Some orchids and other tropical plants, which grow on the branches of trees and never come into contact with the soil, have 'aerial roots' which remain suspended in the air, and are said to supply the plant with moisture absorbed from the saturated atmosphere of the forests. These are supplemented by similar adventitious roots. Their outer surfaces are of a spongy texture, and consist of specially modified cells. In Maize and Bamboo, where the plant is large and has only a comparatively thin stem to support it, adventitious roots, called 'buttress' or 'stilt roots', grow out from the bottom of the stem to prevent the plant from being blown over. They are not unlike the flying buttresses seen in some churches and cathedrals.

5. RESPIRATORY OR BREATHING ROOTS. Like other living structures, roots must breathe. This they can usually do by absorbing the air trapped in the small spaces between the soil particles, unless the soil becomes waterlogged. In the waterlogged mangrove swamps of the tropics, many of the mangrove trees have special modified roots which grow upwards into the air, in addition to their normal anchoring roots. Those parts of the roots exposed to the air have patches where the cells are loosely joined, and through these spaces exchange of gases takes place. Breathing or respiratory roots are only occasionally adventitious.

ROSES. Some of the loveliest of our country-side flowers belong to the very large rose family. Of the roses themselves there are the pink Dog-roses, the white Burnet-roses, the hairy Sweet Briar or Eglantine, and the white, scentless flowers of the Trailing or Field Rose. Among the wild relatives of the roses are the shrubby Blackberry, Raspberry, and Dewberry, the tree-like Blackthorn, Wild Cherries, Hawthorn, Crab-apples, and Rowan or Mountain Ash, as well as herbaceous wild plants like the Silver-weed, Wild Strawberry, Cinquefoil, Tormentil, Meadow-sweet, and Herb Bennet. Besides these British species, members of the rose family are to be found in all parts of the world, although they occur most abundantly in northern temperate regions. In warm climates, the leaves of roses are often tough, leathery, and evergreen—very different from the fine, delicate rose-leaves of Great Britain.

The flowers of roses and related plants are made up on the same general pattern (*see* INDEX, p. 65). Each flower has five green sepals, five large free petals of varying colours, and many stamens. Some flowers have only one carpel, while in others the number may be indefinite. Sometimes the carpels are free, and sometimes joined (*see* FLOWERS).

The most common British wild rose is the popular Dog-rose, so called because, since the days of the Ancient Greeks and Romans, it was believed to cure the bite of a mad dog. Its leaves are compound, being divided into seven serrated leaflets, and having two pronounced leaf-structures or 'stipules' at the base of the leaf-stalk. The stems and leaf-stalks are covered with prickles, which curve backwards. The delicate perfume of the flowers attracts bees and other insects, which collect the pollen and, incidentally, help to cross-pollinate the flowers. After fertilization, the fruits develop into scarlet 'hips', so attractive to birds, which unwittingly help to distribute the seeds.

The Burnet, or Scots Rose, is a much smaller shrub than the Dog-rose, and is fairly common near the coast. During the summer, it develops handsome, white flowers, with stamens which form a well-marked golden boss in the centre of the flower. The hips are large and globe-shaped, sometimes dull red, but more usually a rich black. Easily recognized by the fragrant smell of its rubbed leaves, the Sweet Briar or Eglantine has sticky, fragrant, reddish glands on the lower sides of the leaves. It is a more slender plant than the Dog-rose, and its pink flowers are seen in hedgerows in early summer, very often singly.

John Markham

Crab-apple flowers

John Markham

Wild Dog-rose

John Markham

Mountain Ash

John Markham

Meadow-sweet

FLOWERS OF THE ROSE FAMILY

The Field Rose has slender, trailing branches, which often extend for several metres. Its shiny leaflets are common in hedgerows and thickets, and the white flowers, in bunches of three or four at the ends of the branches, appear in the summer. They last much longer than those of the Dog-rose.

See also HEDGEROWS.
See also Vol. VI: ROSES.

RUFF, *see* WADING-BIRDS (picture, p. 15).

RUMINANTS. These are animals which 'chew the cud', a process most highly developed in CATTLE, SHEEP, and DEER (qq.v.). The stomach of a ruminant is divided into four parts as shown in the diagram. The food is cropped, and then swallowed, unchewed and in bulk, into the paunch or rumen, where it is stored until the whole paunch is filled. The beast then begins to ruminate. During this process, the food passes from the paunch into the honeycomb bag, where it is squeezed into round 'boluses' or balls of 'cud'. The balls are regurgitated, one by one, up the gullet into the mouth, and there they are mixed with saliva and chewed until they become soft and liquid. Each ball is now swallowed

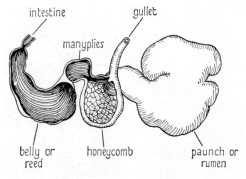

STOMACH OF A RUMINANT

again, and goes direct to the manyplies. The form of the gullet is such that dry bulky food closes the entrance to the manyplies and opens that to the paunch, whereas liquid and pulpy chewed food follows the other passage and closes the entrance to the paunch. The manyplies allows only well-chewed material to slip between its filter-like leaves into the belly, and the residue alone passes on to the gut. The process of chewing the cud allows a shy animal to swallow a large amount of food in a very short time, and to digest it at leisure.

See also MAMMALS; NUTRITION OF ANIMALS.

RUSHES, REEDS, AND SEDGES. These plants resemble grasses in usually having long, narrow leaves and inconspicuous flowers. Many of them grow in wet places, such as damp woods, beside streams, or in marshes.

The Common Rush has cylindrical leaves and clusters of flowers on one side of the stem. The stem contains a white pith which, in old days, was dipped in grease to make a rush-light. Woodrushes have flat, often hairy leaves in loose clusters at the base of the stem. The flowers have five or six green, reddish, or brown sepal-like segments and six stamens. The Flowering Rush and Bulrush are not rushes at all.

The Common Reed belongs to the GRASSES family (q.v.). It has tall, stout stems up to 3 metres high; large, flat leaves; and purplish-brown flowers with silky hairs at the base of the spikelets. It grows in marshy places and by rivers, and is used for THATCHING (q.v. Vol. IV), especially in Norfolk.

The sedges belong to a large world-wide family, including the Cotton-grass (see p. 201) and the Bulrush (not the Reed-mace, often wrongly called a Bulrush). PAPYRUS (q.v. Vol. IV), used by the ancient Egyptians for making writing material and also boats, is a sedge. Papyrus boats are still used in parts of Africa. Most sedges have solid, triangular stems; the leaves have sheaths which clasp the stem at the base and, unlike those of grasses, are not split on one side. The green, brown, or blackish flowers are in small spikes, and the male flowers usually have two or three stamens.

See also WATER PLANTS.

See also INDEX, pp. 69, 71.

S

SABLE, *see* WEASEL, Section 4.

SALAMANDER. The term 'salamander' has been applied to many creatures, all belonging to the Caudata or tailed AMPHIBIA (q.v.), but scientifically not closely related to one another. It includes the true Salamanders, represented by the Spotted Salamanders of Europe and the Newts in England; the Mexican Axolotl and the Marbled and Tiger Salamanders of North America; the Red, the Dwarf, and the Slimy Salamanders of the U.S.A.; and the Giant Salamander of Japan. Any of the Amphibia, provided it has legs and a tail, might be termed a Salamander, if we use the word in a popular sense. All Salamanders pass through a larval stage; but their tadpoles throughout their lives are much more like their parents than are those of TOADS and FROGS (qq.v.)—tailless Amphibia. Some species never lose their gills, and spend their whole lives in the water.

Salamanders are found mainly in northern countries, except for a few species which inhabit the mountainous regions of Central America. North America has many more species than Europe, Asia, and Africa. Europe has some twenty species, and there are fifteen or more in eastern Asia; but the dry regions of south-western Asia are without them. The NEWTS (q.v.) are the only members of the Salamander family which are found in Britain. The belief that the Salamander can stand fire is, of course, a legend (*see* FABULOUS CREATURES, Vol. I).

The Spotted Salamander, the common Salamander of central Europe, lives in hilly districts, and hides by day under stones or fallen timber or among decaying leaves. It is black, with large, irregular spots and patches of bright yellow on the back and limbs. The secretion

from its skin is poisonous to small animals, and for this reason it has few enemies in nature. The female carries the spawn inside her body, and the young tadpoles are born alive. It is frequently kept as a pet in England, and will live for years, feeding on worms or pieces of raw meat.

The Axolotl, a Salamander of Mexican origin, is greyish or whitish, sometimes pure white, with small yellow spots, and grows to a length of about 17 cm. In the Mexican lakes, it permanently retains its larval form, with branching external gills and crested tail, and breeds as if it were fully developed. There is another type of Axolotl found in other parts of North America that undergoes a normal METAMORPHOSIS (q.v.). In a few North American lakes this second type of Axolotl also breeds as a larval form, but this is because the water of the lakes lack iodine

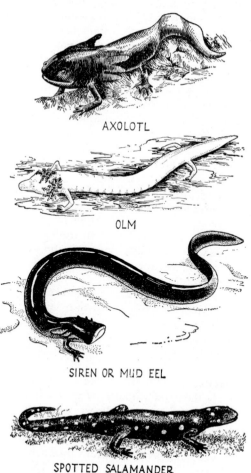

AXOLOTL

OLM

SIREN OR MUD EEL

SPOTTED SALAMANDER

TYPES OF SALAMANDER

which is needed for a gland that controls development. If they are given iodine these Axolotls develop normally. Axolotls make good pets.

The Giant Salamander of Japan is the largest Salamander known, growing to a length of about 1·5 metres. It has a heavy body, with a large head and bluntly rounded muzzle, and a dark-brown or black, thick, warty skin. It lives in mountain streams, usually fairly high up, and although found originally in both China and Japan, is now probably extinct in China. Its flesh is eaten by the country people. The Hell-bender, sometimes called the Mississippi Salamander, is of the same family as the Giant Salamander, differing mainly from the true Salamander in that it has no eyelids. The Hell-bender inhabits the rivers of the mountainous districts of the eastern States of North America, and lives entirely in the water. It has a stout body, short limbs, and a short and crested tail. Its skin is glandular and slimy to touch, and forms a thick fold along the side of the body. It is a voracious creature, being much disliked by fishermen, whose bait it often steals.

Another interesting Salamander is the Olm, a primitive, blind creature, living in the subterranean waters of the mountainous districts of south-eastern Europe. It is 25 cm long, and has a smooth, eel-like body ending in a crested tail. It is greyish in colour, except for the gills, which are coral-red. The limbs are small and feeble, with three toes on the fore-feet and two on the hind-feet. Another species belonging to the same family is the Mud Puppy or Furrowed Salamander, which is found in fresh water in the U.S.A. and Canada, living in the mud at the bottom of streams. It has eyes, and is extremely resistant to cold.

The Siren or Mud Eel, an eel-like creature with external gills, belongs to the class of two-legged Salamanders, for it has two small fore-limbs, but no hind limbs. It lives in the swamps of southern U.S.A.

SALMON. 1. This fish, often called 'king of fishes', is the most valuable of food-fishes, and supports an important industry wherever it is found (see SALMON FISHING, Vol. VI). Anglers have always counted it as their richest prize, and have developed its capture into a fine art (see ANGLING, FRESHWATER, Vol. IX). In strength and beauty it has few superiors. The average adult Salmon weighs about 10 kilograms, but very large specimens can be 35 kg and up to 1·5 metres long; Pacific King Salmon have been known to reach 45 kg. There are two main groups of Salmon, an Atlantic species and a group of Pacific species.

The Atlantic Salmon is found on the western coasts of Europe, but not in the Mediterranean, and on the eastern coasts of North America. So far as we know, there is only the one species, which, however, varies in appearance in different places or because of different habits. There is some difference of opinion as to whether Salmon are sea-fishes that breed in fresh water, or freshwater fishes that go down to the sea to feed. However, this is an unimportant matter compared to an understanding of the life history of these fine creatures.

The eggs of Salmon are large (about the size of peas) and are laid on the gravelly beds of rapid streams, where the female hollows out a shallow trough, or 'redd', and then covers the eggs with fine gravel. They take a long time to hatch—anything from 5 weeks to 5 months, according to conditions. When they hatch the baby fish, or 'fry', are small and transparent. They carry part of the yolk of the egg beneath the body, and this is gradually absorbed during the first few days, after which time the fish are able to feed by mouth. They grow rapidly, and are soon recognizable as small Salmon, called 'parr'—though at this stage they have dark bands across the body. They remain in fresh water for about 2 years, feeding on insects, crustaceans, and so on. Then a change occurs in their make-up, and a beautiful silver sheen develops on the body, covering up the parr-marks. The 'parr' have now become 'smolt', and they move down the river to the sea.

Here they remain, feeding in the rich storehouse of the ocean, and growing large and beautiful, for a varying period of time, until they are ready to return to the river in order to breed. This happens usually during the autumn, when the fish are about 3½ years old. The Salmon entering the rivers are known as 'grilse'. After spawning, they return to the sea the following spring, when they are called 'grilse-kelts'. Some, however, do not move up the rivers until the spring, when they are about 4 years old: these are known as 'small spring salmon'. Others may not leave the sea until they are 5 or 6 years old, when they are called 'maiden' fish.

Fresh from the rich feeding in the sea, the Salmon is plump and active, its flesh firm and red, and it is at this period that the fishermen set their nets or cast their lines to catch it. With the approach of spawning time, however, the female turns to dull brown, spotted with orange and red and with white-edged black spots, while the skin of the male becomes thick and spongy, and the jaws grow longer, especially the lower jaw, which becomes hooked at the end. It may be that these curious changes in structure are due to the fact that the fishes rarely feed after leaving the sea, and thus have to develop their eggs and make their journey at the expense of other tissues. After spawning, the Salmon are exhausted, and many of them are unable to reach the sea alive. Those that do, however, soon recover, and regain their bright silver coats. Some Salmon pass up the rivers to breed every year.

A SALMON LEAPING

Ronald Thompson

The life history of a particular fish can usually be found out by 'scale-reading'—that is, by examining one or more scales from the side of the body. Only the edges of the scales grow, rings being added at fairly regular intervals by growth outwards. Since the fish grows more rapidly in the sea, the rings are spaced farther apart during this period, whereas in freshwater periods they are very close together. So we find alternate 'zones' which, when added up, tell us how old the fish is, how many times it has been to the sea, and roughly for how long. Moreover, the changes that take place in the body at spawning-time leave a scar on the scale, so by these 'spawning-marks' we know how many times the fish has bred. This scale-reading is useful for many kinds of fish, but is particularly valuable when studying Salmon and Trout.

The rapid rivers up which the Salmon moves to spawn often have waterfalls or weirs; and to get over these into the peaceful waters above, the fish often make enormous leaps—in fact, the name Salmon comes from a Latin word meaning 'to leap'. To encourage the valuable Salmon up difficult rivers, 'salmon-ladders' are often built, or by-passes cut, to enable them to get past waterfalls that would otherwise be impassable. Not all Salmon go to the sea, however: some kinds, particularly in North America, are 'land-locked'—that is, confined to lakes that have no outlet to the sea.

Of the Pacific Salmon, there are several species. The King Salmon, or Quinnot, of the north, runs up rivers in enormous numbers in the spring, at the age of about 4 years, and may travel more than 3,000 km to reach its spawning-ground. The Blue-back has similar habits. The Silver-dog, and Humpback Salmon, on the other hand, run in the autumn. Once having spawned, the Pacific Salmon never reach the sea again: they are so feeble that they fall a prey to parasites and disease, and the banks of the streams are littered with their bodies.

2. TROUT. Closely related to the Salmon is

the Trout, which alters so much in different circumstances that its study has proved very difficult: indeed, for a long time it was thought that there were many different species. Almost every stream or lake has its own variety of Trout, some of them being very beautifully coloured. Those of mountain streams are generally only a few centimetres long; those of great lakes reach a large size. In addition, some of them, called Sea-trout, have a silver livery like the Salmon, and feed in the sea in much the same way. Nevertheless, they are probably all the same species, their differences being the result of the different conditions of life.

To distinguish a Trout from a Salmon it is necessary to examine the little fleshy fin, or 'adipose fin', above the tail, behind the true dorsal fin. In a Salmon, the scales, counted downwards from the hind edge of this fin to the lateral line, number ten to thirteen; while in a Trout, the number is thirteen to sixteen. The number thirteen, which might be either Salmon or Trout, is fortunately not common.

The Trout is not so important a food-fish as the Salmon; but it is a highly prized sporting fish, and has been introduced into other countries for the benefit of the angler, notably to New Zealand, where it is now more common than many of the native fishes.

The Rainbow Trout of America is very similar, but can be recognized at once because it has many black spots on its tail. Finally, mention should be made of the exquisitely coloured Char, of which there are many kinds in America and Europe. Many lakes in Britain have their own distinct varieties.

See also Vol. VI: SALMON FISHING.
See also Vol. IX: FISHING.

SALT-MARSH PLANTS, *see* SEASHORE PLANTS, Section 3.

SAND-DUNE PLANTS, *see* SEASHORE PLANTS, Section 4.

SAND-GROUSE. These birds are not GROUSE (q.v.), but belong to a separate order of their own, showing some relation to Pigeons on the one hand and Game Birds on the other; their strong flight is rather like that of the Plover. They inhabit the desert regions of Africa and western and central Asia, one species belonging to Madagascar, and another spreading to southern Europe. The colour and pattern of their plumage make the birds very difficult to see in their sandy surroundings. They have plump, compact bodies, long, pointed wings and tails, and feathered legs which are so short and have such short toes that the birds cannot perch. They associate in flocks, often going long distances across the desert to their drinking pools. They will scratch themselves comfortable hollows in the sand, and there bask in the hot midday sun; but they also can stand severe cold. They nest in slight hollows in the ground, the hen always incubating the eggs by day and the cock by night.

One species, the Pallas's Sand-grouse, occasionally makes freak migrations from its natural home in central Asia to Europe. These migrations, from which there is normally no return, are, strictly speaking, irruptions (*see* MIGRATION). On certain years, the last occasion being in 1888, enormous flocks of Sand-grouse have arrived in the spring on the east coast of Britain, and have spread over the whole country, even as far as the Western Isles. They have attempted to breed, but sooner or later the damp cold of the north-western European climate has proved too much for them. Small invasions have been recorded in other years.

SANDPIPER, *see* WADING BIRDS, Section 3.

SANDWASP, *see* WASPS, Section 2.

SAPROPHYTES. Green plants obtain food by PHOTOSYNTHESIS (q.v.)—that is, by building up sugars and starch from raw materials acted upon by their green colouring matter, or chlorophyll, in the presence of sunlight. Some plants, however, contain no chlorophyll, and so cannot feed in this way. They obtain their food either directly from the living body of another plant or animal, when they are described as PARASITES (q.v.), or from dead organic matter, when they are called saprophytes.

Saprophytes are of great importance to the farmer and gardener, because of the part they play in promoting decay. Many types of saprophytic bacteria live on dead plant and animal matter, causing it to decay, until it is reconverted into the original chemical elements from which it was formed (*see* NITROGEN SUPPLY IN PLANTS; CARBON IN LIVING THINGS). Another big group of saprophytes are the FUNGI, of which the

Harold Bastin
STUMP FLAP (*Polystictus versicolor*)
A saprophytic fungus growing on a dead stump of wood

MOULDS and YEASTS (qq.v.) are well-known examples.

A few flowering plants also live as Saprophytes, examples in Britain being *Monotropa*, the Yellow Bird's Nest, which belongs to the heather family, and *Neottia*, the Bird's Nest Orchid. Both have at the base of the stem a mass of short, thick roots (tangled like a bird's nest), and the fleshy upper part of the stem bears small, yellowish-brown scales, instead of green leaves. The Yellow Bird's Nest grows in beech-woods, and probably obtains its food-supply from the decaying beech leaves. The exact way in which these plants feed is not known, but an excess of organic matter is necessary to them.

See also BACTERIA.

SARDINE, *see* HERRING.

SAWFISH, *see* SHARKS AND RAYS.

SAWFLY. This insect is so called because its ovipositor, or egg-laying tube, is toothed like the edge of a saw, for cutting into the plant tissues where it lays its eggs. It has a large, square head, broad, ample wings, and a stoutly built abdomen. The absence of a narrow 'waist' just below the thorax will distinguish a Sawfly from its relative, the ICHNEUMON FLY (q.v.).

The larvae or CATERPILLARS (q.v.) are vegetarian, feeding mostly on trees and shrubs. They differ, as a rule, from the caterpillars of butterflies and moths in having more pairs of claspers behind the three pairs of jointed legs. In some species there is a pair on each segment of the abdomen. Caterpillars of Stem Sawflies, which bore up the stems of plants, have only

vestiges of legs. Of these, the Wheat Stem-borer is destructive to wheat, though much less so in Britain than in some other countries. Some Sawfly caterpillars are covered with a white or bluish bloom, which gives them a very mealy appearance. Others have a slimy, brownish or greyish covering that makes them look like slugs, but they shed this before they pupate. Many others are quite clean on the surface: the caterpillar of the Currant Sawfly, for instance, is pale green dotted with tiny black spots.

Most Sawfly caterpillars feed openly by daytime, but some feed only at night; others, such as the Apple Sawfly, hide in fruit, and there are some which hide in plant-stems or in GALLS (growths of plant tissues) (q.v.), which they have caused to grow round them. A few are leaf-miners, boring galleries between the upper and lower surfaces of leaves. The pupae are usually enclosed in tough silken cocoons, and often buried below ground. Some adults are short-lived, the males dying within a few hours of mating, and the females after laying their eggs, a process which takes only a few days. They are sluggish fliers, not usually flying more than a few yards. On hot summer days they may be seen resting on flowers.

See also Vol. VI: INSECT PESTS.

SCALE INSECT. These bugs, which are closely related to the APHIDES (q.v.), are recognizable by their legs, which have only a single claw and a one-jointed tarsus. The two sexes are usually very different. The females exude a powdery wax or long wax thread with which they cover themselves, forming a 'scale', and to which the skins from earlier moults are often attached. Hence the name 'scale insects' or 'mealy bugs'. The females are always wingless. Some retain their legs and are active throughout life, but others show almost every stage of degeneration; some are even found without antennae or legs, firmly attached to their food-plant by means of their mouths. In most species the males have wings; but only the first pair is fully developed, the hind-wings being very small. During their change from larvae to adults their mouth parts disappear, for when adult the males take no food.

Most Scale Insects cover their eggs with the 'scale', but in some species the eggs are protected by the dead body of the female parent. The larvae (or nymphs) emerge from the eggs as active crawlers and soon disperse themselves. Towards the end of the larval period the nymphs attach themselves to their food-plants by their mouth-parts, and the females, who remain stationary, push their mouth-parts farther and farther into the plant. At this stage the females are fertilized by the males, which move about. Scale insects secrete honeydew, as do many Aphides, and are thus often attended by ants.

Many Scale Insects are serious agricultural pests (*see* APHID PESTS, Vol. VI). For instance, the Scale Insect pest of the Citrus trees in California caused so much damage that LADYBIRDS (q.v.) had to be introduced to combat it. A few Scale Insects are of some use to man. For instance, the Cochineal Insect, which lives on species of cactus and prickly pear, provides a red dye, used among other things for soldiers' tunics. Dyes and artists' pigments, as well as a resinous varnish called shellac, are obtained from the Lac Insects of India; and the Chinese at one time used to get much of their wax for candles from another Scale Insect, the Chinese Wax Insect, that feeds on the ash tree.

There are some 150 kinds of Scale Insects in the British Isles. Because of their habit of clinging to their food-plants, many Scale Insects have been transported all over the world, especially in the export of nursery plants.

See also BUGS.

SCALES. These vary in type, shape, and function. Fish scales, for example, differ widely from the scales of a butterfly wing. Most fossil fish had bony scales, and these are still found in fish such as SHARKS (q.v.), skate, and dog-fish, whose bony scales have enamel tips that come through the surface like tiny teeth. The scales of fish such as COD, HERRING, and SALMON (qq.v.) are called 'soft' because they are completely covered with a thin, slimy epidermis or outer skin. They develop from small, nipple-like protuberances, called 'papillae', in the skin. The scales of reptiles are horny, and are securely fixed in the skin and covered over with a hard layer. The 'slough' of a SNAKE (q.v.) is not a shed skin, but is this outer covering, which bears the imprints of the scales. The scales on the wings of insects such as butterflies and moths fit together so closely that they look like one complete surface. These scales are responsible for the patterns and colours on the wings (*see* BUTTERFLIES).

SCALLOP. These molluscs are of interest on account of their habits, their food value, and the beauty of their shells. Perhaps the most familiar species is the Great Scallop, so often seen upon the fishmonger's slab. It is the largest British species, average specimens measuring about 15 centimetres in length by 13 wide. There is a striking inequality between the two valves of the shell, the lower being more deeply convex than the upper, which is almost flat. The rather thick shell is further strengthened outside by regularly spaced broad ribs, which in turn have a corrugated surface. While the lower valve generally has a whitish ground, showing delicate tints of pink and creamy yellow, the flat upper valve is more brightly coloured, the ribs often showing a rich dark-red ground with the finer corrugations brown, both colours grading to a lighter hue towards the apex. But quite the most remarkable feature in the Scallop is the row of iridescent, greenish-blue eyes, which shine like precious stones. These are placed along the two edges of the mantle, so as to receive the light when the shell is open, and they are almost as complex in structure as the eyes of the higher vertebrate animals. How much or what exactly the Scallop sees it is difficult to estimate; but undoubtedly these remarkable eyes are capable of warning their owner of approaching danger, so giving the Scallop time to retreat, and to close the valves of its shell tightly. Normally, Scallops rest on the floor of the sea, with their shells slightly gaping; but when alarmed, or if they

M. Burton

SCALLOP (PECTEN) SHOWING ROW OF GREENISH-BLUE EYES ROUND THE EDGES OF THE MANTLE

wish to seek another resting-place, they shoot through the water in a curious zigzag manner achieved by the rapid alternate opening and closing of their shells.

The Quin, or Queen Scallop, is a much smaller mollusc than the Great Scallop. The shell averages about 5 cm in breadth, both valves being slightly convex, and it is not so thick as that of the Great Scallop. Different specimens vary considerably in colour, from pure white to pale pink, yellow, red, brown, or purple. The Quin is found round the coasts of England on sandy bottoms offshore, sometimes in large numbers. The shells of many smaller species, some measuring hardly a centimetre in width, but beautifully coloured, may be found stranded on sandy shores as the tide goes out.

See also Molluscs.
See also Vol. VI: Shell-fish Gathering.

SCARAB. The celebrated beetle, to which the great naturalist Linnaeus gave the name *Scarabaeus sacer*, and others of the same kind, are called Scarabs. These insects were held sacred by the ancient Egyptians on account of their strange habit of fashioning perfectly round balls from the animal-droppings upon which they feed. These they roll about, pushing them backwards by using their legs and thrusting their heads against the ground. This curious habit has aroused attention and wonder for many centuries. It was supposed that the ball contained the insect's egg, which could be hatched only in this way; but we now know that most are used for food, generally to be eaten in the end by the insect itself. The female beetle, however, digs a hole in which she places a ball, and then, opening it, deposits an egg inside, and carefully closes it again. The soft-bodied grub which emerges from the egg eats the interior, while the outer crust becomes the cell in which it undergoes its Metamorphosis (q.v.) into a winged beetle. Egyptian sculptures and paintings are full of representations of these beetles in all sorts of curious forms, sometimes holding a ball and sometimes with their wings spread in flight. Models of them, usually of baked clay, were also made in immense numbers—probably because healing virtues were attributed to them. These, also called scarabs, are still manufactured and sold today, and a few superstitious people still credit them with mysterious properties.

See also Beetles.

British Museum (Nat. Hist.)
SACRED EGYPTIAN SCARAB PUSHING ITS FOOD-BALL

SCIENTIFIC NAMES. The biological sciences are unique in having an international language, so that any living creature, whether plant or animal, has a scientific name by which it is known throughout the world. The criticism is often made that the use of 'difficult' names is unnecessary, the common names being quite sufficient. A single example will meet this criticism. We are familiar in this country with the robin, a small bird with a red breast; but there are many other birds in different parts of the world, each having a red breast, each known by the common name of 'robin', and yet none related to the other. The only way any of these 'robins' can be accurately described is by its scientific name, which shows its true relationship. Thus, the British robin is *Erithacus rubecula*, the robin of North America is *Planesticus migratorius*, of South Africa *Caffrornis caffra*, of India *Saxicoloides fulicata*, of Australia *Petroica phoenicea*, and of New Zealand *Miro longipes*. If these universal names were not used, then the word 'robin' would become entirely meaningless, except in local use. And there are many other similar cases.

Scientific names consist of two, or three, parts. The scientific name of the common English House Sparrow, written in full, is *Passer domesticus domesticus* (L.). The first name (*Passer*) is the generic name, and shows the genus to which this and other sparrows belong. The second name (*domesticus*) is the specific name, and shows the species of Sparrow (i.e. House Sparrow, not Tree Sparrow). The third name is the subspecific name, and shows the sub-species or geographical race—that is, the European race (not the Syrian or Algerian). The letter (L.) shows that LINNAEUS (q.v. Vol. V) first gave one of these names to this bird. But Linnaeus considered the sparrow to be related closely to the Finches, and called it *Fringilla domestica*. Had he called it *Passer domesticus* as we do now, the letter L. standing for his name would not have been enclosed in brackets. Thus the scientific name for the Skylark remains the same as Linnaeus gave it—*Alauda arvensis*, and is written in full *Alauda arvensis arvensis* L. (In Linnaeus's day the three-name system, with a third name to indicate sub-species, was not used.) These names are normally written *Passer d. domesticus* (L.) or *Alauda a. arvensis* L., where the specific and the sub-specific names are the same. (Such races are known as the 'typical' race.) Where the names of the species and sub-species differ, they must both be written in full. So the Eastern Skylark (from Asia) is *Alauda arvensis intermedia* Swinhoe. (This was first named in 1863 by an ornithologist, Swinhoe). The scientific name for an animal or plant usually describes some characteristic feature of the organism. Plants with creeping runners, for example, often have the specific name *repens*, which is the Latin for 'creeping' (*Ranunculus repens*, the Creeping Buttercup). Sometimes the name may refer to the kind of place where the plant grows. *Palustris*, for example, means 'growing in a marsh' (*Caltha palustris*, the Marsh Marigold).

See also CLASSIFICATION OF ANIMALS AND PLANTS.
See also Vol. VI: BOTANICAL NAMES.

SCORPION. This animal belongs to an order of the class known as Arachnida, to which belong also SPIDERS, MITES, and TICKS (qq.v.). There are about 600 known species, found in most warm parts of the world, but not in New Zealand, Patagonia, and the oceanic islands. They are generally about 5 to 10 centimetres long.

In ancient times they enjoyed a reputation, not wholly deserved, for ferocity and venom, owing to the facts that they can run at a great speed, that they possess large, powerful pincers called 'pedipalpi', and that they carry, and freely use, a poison-bearing sting at the end of the tail. When a scorpion strikes, it arches its tail over its back and then thrusts it forward; at the same time, muscles squeeze the poison-gland, and force the poison into the wound made by the tail. The sting of a scorpion is much more

Edmund A. Robins

A FEMALE SCORPION CARRYING HER NEWLY BORN YOUNG ON HER BACK

virulent than the bite of a spider, and is instantaneously fatal to insects, spiders, and centipedes. Some scorpions are more dangerous than others: many are quite harmless to man; others may produce pain and swelling, more or less serious, and very occasionally death follows. A scorpion, however, cannot poison itself—a fact which contradicts the popular fable that a scorpion, surrounded by fire, will commit suicide.

Most scorpions are more active at night than by day. They never attack unprovoked, and, when disturbed, they generally much prefer to escape unnoticed. They lead solitary lives, and are said to be found together only when mating or when one is eating another. They seem never to drink: evidently their food provides them with all the moisture they require—so that they are well adapted to the hot sandy places in which they are usually found. Like spiders, they can survive prolonged fasts. Like spiders, too, they are slow eaters, and will spend more than an hour consuming one cockroach.

All scorpions are born alive, not in eggs, and the newly born young, like young Wolf Spiders, are carried on their mother's back until their first moult, after which they can feed themselves.

See also SPIDERS; FALSE SCORPIONS.

SCORPION-FISH. This name is given to a family of thick-set fishes, which have the sharp spines of the first dorsal fin on the back provided with a poison that can cause very painful wounds. Needless to say, they are much dreaded by fishermen. Many of them are quite fantastic in appearance, and are often beautifully coloured, generally closely resembling their surroundings. One kind, found in the South Seas, is black when living among dark volcanic rocks, mottled with deep red when found among red sea-weed, and bright yellow when caught in deep water—yellow because concealment is not necessary in the dark of the deep ocean, and because yellow colouring matter will develop in the dark better than black or red. Another kind of Scorpion-fish, found in Indian waters, is always covered with colonies of small polyps (relatives of the Sea-anemones), which grow only on this fish. The polyp helps to conceal the fish from its enemies, and itself gets transport from place to place. Such association between different animals for their mutual benefit is called symbiosis.

A species of Scorpion-fish, bright red in colour, is sometimes seen in American and British fish-shops, where it is called Norway Haddock, or the more fitting name Rose-fish. One species is often called the Lion-fish, and is found in reefs of the Indian and Pacific Oceans.

Related to these are the Bullheads, a large family of small fishes mostly inhabiting seas north of the Equator. Most live near coasts, but a few species are found in deep water. They have two dorsal fins, the first with spiny rays, and a large bony head, usually provided with sharp spines above the eyes, on the nose, and on the gill-covers. Some of them are able to make a loud noise by moving one bone of the gill-cover against another. There are several freshwater species, the Miller's Thumb of Europe, a small fish about 7·5 cm long, being common in England and Wales. Its head is broad and flattened, the same shape as the thumb of a miller, which is flat from continually testing the texture of his flour.

Bullheads, in common with certain other fishes, are capable of sudden changes in colour, generally turning pale when disturbed. Most of them have a pattern consisting of irregular blotches that help to conceal them among the weeds and corals where they live. Many of them take good care of their eggs, placing them under stones, inside broken bulbs of the bladder-wrack, inside empty mollusc shells, in crevices of rock or coral, or even making a crude sort of nest among seaweed. Sometimes the male will take the whole egg-cluster under him, embracing it with his pectoral and pelvic fins, which are prickly underneath, enabling him to get a firmer grip; and there he rests, aerating the eggs by fanning them every now and then with his large pectoral fins, until they hatch.

Gurnards, similarly, have large, bony heads, often armed with ridges and spines. The pectoral fins are long, the lowermost rays being separate, strong, jointed, and movable like fingers. By their aid, the Gurnards are able to walk about on the bed of the sea, and to feel about in the

A. Fraser-Brunner

RED GURNARD

A. Fraser-Brunner

A SEA BULLHEAD

sand or explore inside shells for food. Many Gurnards have strong, thorny plates of bone along the side, and sometimes a pair of long, bony, sword-like growths, pointing forwards above the mouth, which they may use for digging out worms and other creatures for food. These fishes are well known among fishermen for the loud grunting noises they make when caught. The larger kinds are useful as food.

SEA-ANEMONE. These gaily tinted, almost flower-like, animals are abundant in the deep rock-pools exposed at low tide all round our coasts; but they may very easily escape the un-trained eye of the casual visitor, for, when alarmed or left exposed by the receding tide, they contract their graceful tentacles and bodies until they look rather like uninviting blobs of jelly. They are found in all climates, from the cold seas of the Arctic and Antarctic to tropical regions, where they attain their greatest size and magnificence.

Anemones vary greatly in colour, shape, and size. The soft body is called the 'column'; it may be long and slender, or short and fat, and it is capable of changing considerably in a single individual—for the Anemone can expand, contract, and alter the shape of its body at will. At the top of the body-column is the 'disk', with the slit-like mouth at the centre, encircled by one or several rows of tentacles. The tentacles vary considerably in size, shape, and number in the different species. They are hollow, extremely sensitive, constantly on the move, expanding and contracting, and are armed externally with many minute, complex, stinging-thread cells used for defence and for the capture of prey. The Anemone attaches itself to the rocks by its base or foot, and normally remains in one spot, though it sometimes glides slowly over the surface or, relinquishing its hold upon the rock, relies on the flow of the tide and the waving of its tentacles to carry it to a more congenial spot. The sperms are released by the male Sea-anemone into the water; they swim into the female animal through the mouth and fertilize the egg whilst still in the ovary. The fertilized eggs hatch and partly develop inside the parent. The minute oval larvae emerge from the mouth of their parent, and by the rhythmic lashing of their hair-like cilia, swim freely through the water. They soon settle down on the floor of the sea, undergoing a METAMORPHOSIS (q.v.) into very small Anemones. The mouth of an Anemone is very elastic, and comparatively large animals are sometimes swallowed, so that the body becomes very much distended. How long they live under natural conditions is difficult to estimate, but one particular specimen is known to have lived more than 100 years.

While some species live attached to the rocks in the tidal pools and at greater depths, others live half-buried in the sand, and others are almost invariably found attached to a whelk-shell inhabited by a hermit-crab (*see* CRAB). One group of Anemones, known as *Edwardsia*, is of special interest, because in their structure they appear to make a connecting link between the Anemones and the true CORALS (q.v.). There are six British species of *Edwardsia*, all small in size and with long, slender bodies, which do not end in a flat disk, but are rounded. They live with their bodies entirely buried in the sand, only their tentacles being expanded at the surface. When the tide is out, they disappear from view, the only guide to their presence being a small roundish hole in the sand.

The largest and handsomest of our British Sea-anemones is the Dahlia Anemone, which measures sometimes as much as 20 cm across its expanded disk. It has a stout body-column, and its tentacles, though short, taper gracefully to a point, and are arranged in five rows round the mouth-disk. The Dahlia Anemone varies much in colour—pinkish-red, crimson, purple, or deep orange, while the tentacles may be snow-white or banded with delicate shades of red, white, and orange. Those that live low down on the shore among the rocks often hide themselves under a covering of fine shingle and fragments of shell; but those living in the deep rock-pools do not trouble to camouflage themselves in this way, and remain fully expanded. The Beadlet Anemone may often be found in the rock-pools between mid-tide and low-tide levels. Crimson and green are its commonest colours, but there are many intermediate tints. Generally, the base is edged by a narrow blue line, and the short, stout column is purplish-brown, with a band of brilliant azure-blue spots round its upper margin, which give it the appearance of a bead necklace—hence its popular name. It was one of these Beadlet Anemones that was taken from the Firth of Forth by the famous Scottish naturalist, Sir John Dalyell, in 1828, when it was judged to be not less than 7 years old: it not only survived its captor, but continued to flourish in captivity until 4 August 1887, when it died. The Plumose Anemone is one of the most grace-

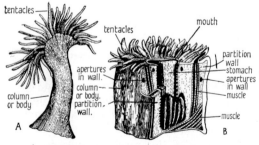

A. SEA-ANEMONE WITH EXPANDED TENTACLES.
B. CROSS-SECTION OF SEA-ANEMONE

ful and exquisitely tinted inhabitants of the deep rock-pools. It has a tall, moderately slender column, crowned with innumerable tentacles, and it varies considerably in colour. The Snakelock has long slender tentacles, and looks rather like a shaggy chrysanthemum.

SEA-BREAM, *see* SEA-PERCH.

SEA-COW. The Dugong and the Manatee are the two members of the Sea-cow family. They are MAMMALS (q.v.), but are not related to whales, although they have horizontal tail-fins, no hind legs, and flipper-like fore-legs. They live in shallow waters, never venturing out into the open sea. The Dugong is found along the coasts of the Indian Ocean and Australian Seas, and the Manatee in tropical rivers on both sides of the Atlantic. Sea-cows have small eyes and mouths, and tiny ear-holes; their thick skin is either finely wrinkled or rugged like bark, and is sometimes sparsely covered with fine hairs. They are sluggish, harmless, and not very intelligent creatures, living on seaweed and other water plants. The female produces one baby at a time, which she looks after with great care. The old belief that she nurses her young one, supported by her flippers, with her head above the water, is not true; the legend may have given rise to some of the stories of the MERMAID (q.v. Vol. I.)

Manatees (except for one species) have three rudimentary nails on their flippers: this pecularity, and the way they use their flipper-like hands when nursing their young, account for their name (derived from the Latin *manus*, a hand). They grow up to 2·5 metres long. Their remarkable mouths have prehensile upper lips, with which they can grasp and eat food without any help from their lower lips. They are now rather scarce, as they have been much hunted for their oil and hides.

The Dugong is generally smaller than the Manatee, its average length being from 1·5 to 2 metres. It has a crescent-shaped tail, and is without the nails on its flippers. Formerly Dugongs used to be seen in large herds of several hundreds, and they were so fearless of man that they would allow themselves to be touched. Now they are found in small parties only, and have become much more wary.

SEA-CUCUMBER (Holothurian). Although totally different in shape and appearance, the Sea-cucumbers are really close relatives of the STARFISH and SEA-URCHIN (qq.v.), and have derived their popular name from the tough, warty skin covering their somewhat sausageshaped bodies. Like the starfishes, Sea-cucumbers possess tube-feet; but the number and position of these vary considerably in the different species: they may be present as five regular zones, running down the entire length of the animal, or scattered over the surface of the body, or again reduced, as in the slender worm-like *Synapta*, to a circle of oral tentacles.

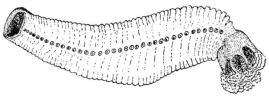

A SEA-CUCUMBER

The Sea-cucumbers are without arms and have no continuous limy skeleton, like that of the Sea-urchins; but instead they have innumerable microscopic spicules or rods and plates embedded in the tough skin, which are either perforated ovals or resemble miniature anchors. Some species are found round the coasts of Britain, among the seaweeds, or with their bodies partly buried in the sand and mud. One of the commonest is the Cotton Spinner, which may measure nearly 30 centimetres long when fully expanded. It is so called because of the mass of long whitish threads, composed of mucus combined with parts of its inner organs, which the animal spouts into the surrounding water when alarmed or injured. In tropical seas, the Sea-cucumbers grow to a large size, and, under the name of Trepang or *Bêche-de-mer*, are sold as food in the markets of the Far East. The giant of the tribe is the tropical Bessel's Seacucumber, which grows to nearly 2 metres long.

SEA-HORSE. Sea-horses are the only fishes that can use their tails for holding on to objects.

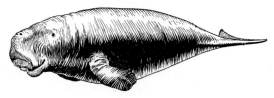

A DUGONG

They belong to a group known as the Tube-fishes, all of which have long tube-like snouts with small mouths at the end. Many different species, varying from 5 to 30 centimetres long, and found in all warm seas, all look very much alike, except for certain Australian kinds. These latter are among the most fantastic of all fishes, for they are provided with long bony outgrowths from the body, upon which are flaps of skin; so that the creatures look exceedingly like bunches of seaweed, being similarly coloured. They are often called Leafy Sea Dragons.

Sea-horses are close relatives of the Pipe-fishes, which do not have the head bent at an angle to the body, and do not use the tail in the same way. They are mostly small, worm-like creatures, having their bodies encased in rings of bone, somewhat after the fashion of flexible gas-piping.

Sea-horses and Pipe-fishes are feeble swimmers, moving about by a waving motion of the small fin on the back, and being carried from place to place by currents. The male has a

SEA-HORSE AND PIPE-FISH

A. Fraser-Brunner

pouch or fold of skin on the belly, into which the female injects the eggs. When the eggs hatch, it looks as though the male is giving birth to the young, who then remain near the father. But the report that they dart back into his pouch if danger threatens is probably not true.

SEAL. There are three separate families of seals: the Sea-lions and Sea-bears (or Eared Seals); the Walruses; and the True or Earless Seals. The Walruses live entirely in northern waters; but the other two families live on both sides of the Equator, though they are found in the greatest numbers on northern coasts. Some of these large water mammals are quite active on land on their flippers, but others have greater difficulty once they are out of the water.

The Sea-lions and Sea-bears are the most active, and spend a good deal of time on land. By turning their hind flippers forward they can walk and even run and climb rocks almost as easily as land animals. The Sea-lions are the largest—a big one being nearly 4 metres long. These seals, however, do not have the soft, woolly underfur which makes the skins of the smaller Sea-bears or Fur Seals so much sought after by the fur-hunter.

Sea-lions and Sea-bears go to their breeding places in the spring. The first to arrive are the males, who at once select stations for themselves. They fight fiercely amongst themselves for the best positions; and some of the early arrivals, which took up stations near the shore, become so exhausted that they have to yield and move farther inland. When the females arrive, each male tries to capture as many as possible for himself. In order to guard their harems, often of from ten to fifteen females, the bull seals have to be continually on the watch. Throughout the breeding season, therefore, which lasts for several weeks, they neither eat nor drink, with the result that, though at the beginning of the season they are fat and in good condition, by the end they become thin and weak. The cubs are born on land, generally one only at a birth, weighing about 5 kilograms.

Walruses, which live in the Arctic Ocean, are bulkier and less active than the Sea-lions and Sea-bears. Both male and female grow powerful tusks 50 centimetres or more long. As a rule, Walruses collect in herds; and when they are on shore or on an ice-floe they huddle together like pigs. They feed mostly on shell-fish prised off

E. O. Hoppé

COLONY OF ALASKAN FUR SEALS ON THE COAST OF ST. PAUL ISLAND, BERING SEA

the rocks with their tusks. They are very devoted to their young, and also show great sympathy with each other: the whole herd, for instance, will unite in an intelligent defence of a wounded companion. Although not at all aggressive, they will fight fiercely if attacked, and use their great tusks with considerable effect. They have a deep, full roar, and a bark which they repeat several times in succession.

The True Seals are not very active on land. They have thick, close fur, and a large reserve of fat (blubber) under the skin. The largest species is the Elephant Seal, which is also the largest of all the seals, growing to 6 metres or more long, with a girth of about 4·5 metres. It gets its name from the male's short, movable trunk. The Grey Seal lives in the north Atlantic, and is fairly common off the shores of northern Europe. It breeds on the Scilly Isles and several of the Scottish Isles, and is very common off south and west Ireland. Its voice is a gloomy

'hoo', often accompanied by angry, bear-like growls. During the breeding season the males fight fiercely amongst themselves for the females, often severely wounding each other with their teeth. One, or sometimes two, young are born after about $11\frac{1}{2}$ months. The baby has a white, woolly coat, which is shed at the end of 3 weeks and is replaced by a slaty-blue coat. At 4 weeks old, the cubs are weaned, and the mothers go off to sea leaving the young to find their way to the water unaided and unattended. The slaty-blue coat is gradually replaced by the adult coat, which varies a great deal from brown to grey.

The smaller Common Seals are found also off the coasts of the British Isles, especially on the smaller Scottish isles. They spend much of their life ashore, coming to rocks or sand-banks, usually at half-ebb, to bask in the sun and sleep. Apparently they post a sentinel, and then all lie, head to sea, ready to dive on any alarm. The young take to the water as soon as they are born,

John Markham

SEA-LIONS

and swim with ease. Common Seals are very easily tamed, and will often follow their owners about like dogs.

SEA-LILY, *see* STARFISH.

SEA-LION, *see* SEAL.

SEA-PERCH. This name is generally applied to a large number of different fishes, known collectively as the Percomorphi, a group to which the freshwater PERCHES (q.v.) also belong. All have the front portion of the dorsal or back fin supported by sharp spines; and all have one spine and five soft, branched rays on the pelvic fins. Many of them are very valuable as food. Only a few of the most important can be described here.

On the Atlantic coasts of America and southern Europe are found the Sea-bass, which often enter the mouths of rivers. They are good food, and also very good sporting fish, being much prized by anglers, particularly in Britain. They are caught with fine tackle, somewhat after the fashion of salmon. Very much larger are the so-called Groupers, of tropical seas, which are often brightly coloured. One Indian species, for instance, is vivid red with many blue spots. Some of them, usually called Jewfish, grow to nearly 2 metres or more, and weigh 250 kg, while the biggest, found in the South Pacific, is said to grow to over 3 metres long. Various other handsome kinds, such as those known as Snappers,

and a multitude of small, brilliant species, are found throughout the warmer seas of the world.

A small, brightly coloured species of Sea-perch, called the Comber, lives in the Mediterranean, and sometimes strays to the coast of Britain. The remarkable thing about this fish is that it is hermaphrodite—having both male and female organs in the same fish.

The Cardinal-fishes are related, but differ in having two separate dorsal fins. Most of them are small and handsomely marked, and live among rocks and corals. They have the habit of taking their eggs into their mouths to protect them until they hatch. One species, found recently on the coast of Florida, lives inside the mouth cavity of a large sea-snail, popping out every now and then in search of food. Strongly marked and often brilliantly coloured species belonging to the family Pomacentridae are found in coral-reefs. The most famous is a small fish with a bright orange body crossed by pearl-blue stripes and edged with velvety black. It lives inside the body-cavity of a giant sea-anemone, darting out for food—quite unharmed by the anemone's stinging-cells or digestive juices. It is sometimes called the Clown-fish, or Anemone-fish.

The Horse-mackerels, so called because many of them resemble Mackerel, although there is no relationship, are particularly common in tropical seas. Some of them, the Cavallas or Pampanos, grow very large. Most are silvery in colour, and have two small separate spines in front of the anal fin. They change very much with age, the fully grown fish being very different from the young (which have, in most cases, thread-like filaments on the fins). Some of the larger kinds, notably the Yellow-tail of America, are well-known sporting fishes; while others are of value as food.

The young of many kinds of Horse-mackerel live in the open sea, where they seek refuge from their enemies beneath the 'umbrellas' of the larger kinds of medusae, or jelly-fish, protected by the deadly stinging-cells. One species of Horse-mackerel, often called the Scad, is found in British seas, sometimes in great abundance, but is of no use as food, for it is lean and bony, with a row of strong armour-plates along the side.

The famous Pilot-fishes belong to the Perch family. They are found nearly always in the company of Sharks, and were once believed to lead them to their food—hence their name. They will often travel alongside ships, from which arose the idea that they could pilot vessels safely into harbour. In fact, they follow Sharks simply in order to pick up the scraps left over from the Sharks' meal, trusting only in their swift movements to escape being eaten themselves. They probably accompany ships to feed on the 'leavings' thrown overboard, but they may perhaps mistake ships for large sharks. They are bluish fishes with dark cross-bands, and have a keel on each side of their tails.

The Sea-breams are a family of perch-like fishes, not at all like the freshwater Bream, which belongs to the Carp family (q.v.). There are many kinds of Sea-bream, some of them, such as the Porgies of America and the Schnappers of South Africa and Australia, being valued foodfish. One species, the Red Bream, is often sold in London markets. These fishes have very strong teeth, the front ones being pointed for grasping, the back ones blunt and smooth for grinding, admirably suited for crushing the

shells of molluscs and crabs on which they feed. Perhaps the most famous species is the Red Tai, of Japan, which is as much a national emblem as the rising sun. Ebisu, the fish-god, is always shown in pictures and sculptures with a Red Tai under his arm.

Another group of Perch-like fishes is the tropical Butterfly-fishes—short and deep fishes, flattened from side to side, and with fins covered with scales. Their bright markings serve as camouflage, so that they are not easily seen in a coral-reef, with its strong light and shade. All these fishes have many close-set, bristle-like teeth in their jaws, with which they browse among the coral. Some of them, Angel-fishes, have a strong spine on the gill-cover. The bestknown is the Emperor Fish of Indian seas, a very gaudy fish, with its yellow stripes crossing a blue or brown body, and blue and white markings on head and fins. These fishes change a great deal during their life history. When very small they have tough bony shields on the head, often with big spikes jutting out over the eyes; these they lose as they grow up. Some of the Angel-fishes, when young, have a black-and-white pattern, quite different from the gaudy adult.

SEA SERPENT. As with the Loch Ness Monster, there is no scientific evidence that the Great Sea Serpent exists. Many people claim to have seen it, but most probably what they saw was one of the larger Ribbon-fishes (q.v.). It is possible that the sea contains many large creatures that we know nothing about, but the larger they are, the less likely are they to have escaped capture—particularly if they are airbreathers, and must therefore come to the surface at frequent intervals. From time to time large sea creatures have been cast ashore, and have been claimed by the less reputable newspapers to be the Sea Serpent. But expert examination has shown that they are either wellknown mammals or fish, generally in varying stages of decay. That some Plesiosaur-like creature still survives in the ocean is perhaps within the bounds of possibility, and were it to be seen swimming with its head and neck showing above water, it would be not unlike some pictures drawn of the Great Sea Serpent. But until a specimen or some part of this unknown monster is available for examination, the scientific world cannot accept it and give it a name.

See also Vol. I: Fabulous Creatures.

A. Fraser-Brunner

SOUTH SEA BUTTERFLY-FISHES

SEASHORE PLANTS. 1. Although the sea-shore constitutes one large association of animals and plants, there are many separate communities, the rocky shores, the salt-marshes, and the sand-dunes each having a characteristic vegetation. The seaweeds, which must be included, can best be seen during the period of low-water on the three days before and after new moons. At these times the tides flow to a much higher, and ebb to a much lower level than at other times (*see* TIDES, Vol. III).

2. SEAWEEDS, or ALGAE (q.v.), are plentiful where the rocks run out to sea, and also on scattered rocks on the beach, and at the foot of cliffs washed by the sea. Seaweeds grow in three levels on the shore. Green seaweeds are found highest up the beach, and are exposed to the atmosphere at all low tides, brown seaweeds are found between high and low water-level; while red seaweeds are found growing in deeper water, and are usually never exposed. Among the greens are the Sea-lettuces, with their flat, wide 'fronds'; and where fresh water runs over rocks or over the beach, grows the green, streaky *Enteromorpha intestinalis*, consisting, as its name suggests, of tubes varying in length from 2 to 30 centimetres, the ends of which are inflated into bags.

Of the brown seaweeds, the leathery Channelled-wrack, or *Pelvetia*, grows the highest on the shore, and is usually only reached at high-water spring tides. When dry, it is tough and brittle, but becomes soft and supple when moistened. The most common of the brown seaweeds, the Bladderwrack, grows lower on the shore. It consists of flat, forked branches, each with a definite vein, and with round air-bladders on either side, which buoy up the plant when it is floating in water. Still lower grow the long, strap-like fronds of the Knotted Wrack, with forked branches swollen in places to form large oval air-spaces; the flat, forked branches of the Serrated Wrack, which have toothed edges, can be recognized because they bear no air-bladders and retain their glossy olive colour when dry. Farther seawards are the large, light yellow-brown straps of the Oarweeds or Tangle-weeds. These are uncovered at the lowest spring tides only; at other times their leathery fronds may be seen at low water, rising and falling with the waves, the stems remaining attached to the rocks. They can be picked up on the beach after a gale.

Beyond the brown seaweeds, below the limit of the lowest spring tides, the red seaweeds are found. Their colour is due to a red pigment, which increases in intensity on exposure to light. Most of them have a light, airy appearance, and usually consist either of delicate plumes or of flat, fan-like membranes. The Coral Seaweed, one of the most common, owes its coral-like appearance to a coating of lime. It is purple, but fades to white when dry. Red seaweeds may be found in rock-pools or thrown up on the shore.

3. SALT-MARSH PLANTS. A salt-marsh is

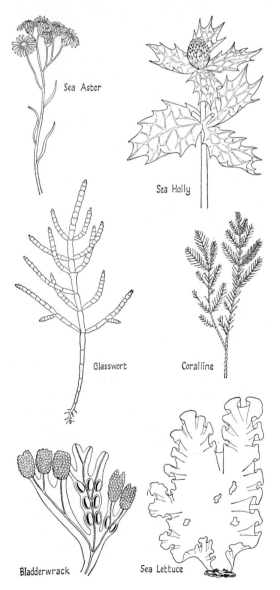

Sea Aster

Sea Holly

Glasswort

Coralline

Bladderwrack

Sea Lettuce

John Markham

THRIFT, OR SEA-PINKS (*Armeria maritima*) GROWING ON THE NORTH CORNISH COAST

Harry Meyer

SAND DUNES WITH MARRAM GRASS—STUDLAND HEATH, DORSET

gathers around the hummocks so formed, which then become colonized with other halophytes such as the Sea Aster, Sea Lavender, Seablite, Sea Plantain, and Seaside Arrowhead. As the mud becomes built up, it becomes further invaded by plants such as the Sea Thrift, Sea Purslane, Scurvy Grass, Sea Beet, and Sea Milkwort. A grass which plays an important part in the stabilization of moving mud is a species of *Spartina*, a cross between the American and European species, first known in this country about 1870, since when it has spread rapidly round the south and west coasts of Britain.

4. SAND-DUNE PLANTS. Sand-dunes are found above the high-water mark on sea-shores. They are built up by accumulations of blown sand, and are as constantly being blown away by the wind, so that they are always shifting. If there is nothing to stop their progress, sand-dunes may be blown far inland—indeed they have been known to overlie whole districts. One of the most powerful checks to the movement of sand-dunes is the growth of Marram Grass, a plant with upright shoots and sharp narrow leaves. Marram Grass has long, perennial 'rhizomes', or underground stems, as well as deep-growing, fibrous roots, which help to bind the sand together. Although the shoots are constantly being buried by the sand, they have the power of being able to force their way again to the surface. The roots are renewed at higher levels, too, the old ones remaining in the sand and helping to bind it below. In this way the level of the dune is built up—in some cases as high as 24 metres—humus being added to the soil by the decay of the roots and shoots of the grass itself. In south Lancashire, the Sea Couch Grass acts as a dune-former. It grows nearer the sea than Marram Grass, and has the advantage of being able to endure immersion in sea water. It has, however, only a limited power of upward growth through sand, and the dunes formed from Sea Couch Grass are usually smaller than those formed from Marram Grass. As the dunes are built up, the sheltered landward slopes become invaded by such plants as are able to face a deficiency of humus. At the higher levels of the dunes there is little moisture, although the sand may be quite wet at the bottom. The dunes become very hot, also, during the day, and cold at night. Among the plants which have become adapted to these conditions are the Stork's Bill, Ragwort, Cat's Ear, Sea Purslane, Sea Holly, Sea Bind-

formed where a river meets the sea, its rate of flow being slowed down so that the silt is deposited as mud. Along these estuaries, as well as in sheltered bays, the mixture of mud and sand supports a special type of vegetation. These salt-marsh plants or 'halophytes' are occasionally immersed entirely in salt water, and at all times there is a high percentage of salt in the soil. Consequently, they have to adapt themselves not only to the movement of the mud, which makes rooting difficult, but to the lack of oxygen in the waterlogged soil.

The roots of halophytes are able to absorb water from a strong salt solution; and the presence of many water-storage cells in their fleshy leaves enables them to conserve this water. The lack of oxygen is overcome by the development of large air-spaces; and to meet the shifting state of the mud the plants have long roots, or underground stems, which act as anchors. A characteristic halophyte is the Glasswort, which has a branched, rounded, fleshy stem, and resembles a CACTUS (q.v.). It is one of the first to colonize the open beach. Masses of dead seaweeds accumulate around the Glasswort plants and help to manure the mud. The mud

weed, Sea Spurge, Sea Buckthorn, the Red Fruited Dandelion, and the Sand Sedge. When the dunes have become fixed, they are invaded by other plants, such as Dutch Clover, Bird's-foot Trefoil, and Rest Harrow.

See also ECOLOGY OF PLANTS.

SEA-SLUG, *see* SLUG.

SEA SNAKE. Except for one species which inhabits a freshwater lake in the Philippines, Sea Snakes live entirely in salt water. They can be distinguished at once from all other snakes by their paddle-shaped tails. There are two sub-families: the one with ventral shields—that is, enlarged scales which enable them to move on the ground, and the other without proper ventral shields. They range from the Persian Gulf to the shores of Japan, and south through Malayan waters to the north coast of Australia and western Polynesia. One species has extended its range to the east coast of Africa, and has crossed the Pacific to the Gulf of Panama.

The first sub-family spend a good deal of their time among rocks on the sea-shore. They lay eggs—whereas the second sub-family bring forth their young alive. These latter live entirely in the water, and are active and graceful swimmers; on land, owing to the absence of proper ventral shields, they are almost helpless. They prefer sheltered waters, and are seldom found far out from the coast. On days when the sea is quite calm, they may be seen in hundreds basking on the surface of the water. They feed upon fish, some species living mainly upon eels.

All Sea Snakes are poisonous, the venom of some being very deadly. There are no records of bathers ever having been attacked by them; but the native fishermen, when hauling in their catches, often come into contact with them and get bitten. Some fifty species are known, and it is unlikely that many more will be discovered. The majority do not exceed a metre in length, but two species reach 2 metres or more; the

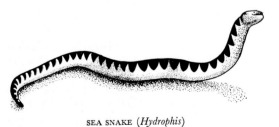

SEA SNAKE (*Hydrophis*)

most massive of these is Stoke's Sea Snake from Australian waters, which has a girth of 25 centimetres. Sea Snakes have nothing to do with the great SEA SERPENT (q.v.), which has not yet been proved to exist.

See also SNAKES.

SEA SQUIRT. On the rocks and on pier piles at low tide may be found tough, jelly-like bags, from 1 to 7 or more centimetres long, which, when touched, squirt out a fine jet of water. These are the tunicates or Sea Squirts, animals closely related to the vertebrates. There are two holes in each bag, one at the top and one at the side. The water, bringing food and oxygen to the animal, is drawn in at the top by minute hairs and ejected at the side. Although the adults are usually fixed and unable to move about, the larvae are free-swimming. They resemble the tadpoles of frogs, with round bodies and long tails, and undergo a METAMORPHOSIS (q.v.) before reaching the adult stage. Some Sea Squirts, such as the Golden-star Sea Squirt, live in colonies, the jelly-like covering containing many small animals arranged in rosettes. One tropical form, the beautiful *Pyrosoma*, is long, tubular, and phosphorescent, and floats in large numbers near the surface of the sea, lighting it up at night.

SEA-URCHIN. These belong to the same division of the animal kingdom—the Echinodermata or prickly-skinned animals—as the STARFISH and SEA-CUCUMBER (qq.v.). With the exception of the so-called Leather-urchins, Sea-urchins possess a skeleton consisting of a complete armour of plates of hard carbonate of lime, and an outer covering of skin. They are more or less globular, heart-shaped, or disk-shaped animals, and most pass through free-swimming larval stages before becoming adult. All live in the sea. Their bodies are thickly clad with spines, varying considerably in length, thickness, and number in the different species. There are five broad bands of large spines, and five narrow bands on which the spines are fewer and where the plates of the skeleton are pierced by small holes, through which the long and slender tube-feet are extended. The spines are attached by muscular fibres to round knobs or bosses on the close-fitting plates of the skeleton, and so can be moved in all directions; it is by the combined movement of the spines, together

D. P. Wilson

COMMON SEA-URCHIN MOVING ACROSS A ROCK

larly called Cake-urchins are flattened in form and more or less oval in outline, resembling, as their name suggests, little flat cakes. They frequent shallow inshore waters, where they live half-buried in the sand, their flat shape and multiplicity of tube-feet preventing them from sinking too deeply in the sand or being turned over by the waves. A very flattened form, almost circular in shape, is the Sand-dollar urchin, common on the east coasts of North America. The curious Leather-urchins of the deep sea are generally large and brightly coloured, and have thin strips of soft flesh between the hard skeletal plates. They are also rather flat and cake-like in shape. They are capable of inflicting very painful wounds with their poison spines.

See also EVOLUTION.

SEAWEED, *see* ALGAE; SEASHORE PLANTS, Section 2.

SECRETARY BIRD. Although this large, pearl-grey and black African bird belongs to the Birds of Prey, it differs from the others in appearance and behaviour. It stands over a metre high on long grey legs, and has two long tail-feathers, barred at the ends with black and white. It has an eagle-like, hooked beak, and ten long feathers projecting from the back of its head, like quill pens behind the ears of a clerk.

Secretary Birds are fairly frequently seen, generally in pairs, on the plains of South Africa, and are found as far north as Ethiopia in the east and Ghana on the west coast. They spend most of their time on the ground, and can walk faster than a man can run. But they can also fly strongly, and will soar high in the air, with head stretched forwards and legs backwards. They attack their prey—lizards, snakes, small mammals, and birds—with their strong feet, striking them so quickly that they have no time to retaliate. Although their propensity to attack large snakes is probably exaggerated, they are considered sufficiently valuable as destroyers of poisonous snakes to be protected by law.

SEEDS. 1. STRUCTURE. Inside the protective coat, or 'testa', of a seed there is a complete plant in miniature, called an 'embryo'. This can grow only if it has enough food to give it a start in life; therefore the seed contains a reserve of food, stored either within the embryo itself or outside it. The Broad Bean is a good example

with the dragging or hauling action of the tube-feet, that the Sea-urchin is able to move about on the floor of the sea. Scattered over the body are large numbers of specially modified spines, some of which have glands secreting a poisonous fluid, and are used as weapons of defence. In most species, though not in all, the mouth is provided with a complicated arrangement of teeth, called the 'lantern of Aristotle', after the famous philosopher, who was the first to give an accurate description of the Sea-urchin.

The different species vary greatly in size, form, and colour. Some have bodies reaching fully 20 centimetres in diameter. The Common or Edible Sea-urchin, which may grow to the size of a big Jaffa orange, is usually pale ruddy-brown or purple, covered with pink or purplish spines, sometimes with white tips, of moderate length and thickness. Another fairly common species, the Purple Egg-urchin, lives in holes among rocky ledges, exposed, or only partially submerged, at extreme low-tide. This has much longer spines, of a fine purple colour, though its body is smaller than that of the Common Sea-urchin. On wide sandy shores near extreme low-tide mark, the brown, heart-shaped Heart-urchin forms burrows in the sand to a depth of 20 to 25 cm, connecting with the surface by a narrow, somewhat cylindrical shaft. Occasionally, as if impatient for the return of the tide, the urchin emerges from its burrow and slowly makes its way towards the incoming waves. The popu-

of a seed with a large store of food. On the flattened edge is a long black band, a scar showing where the seed was joined to the fruit. Near this is a triangular bump, and between the two is a tiny pore or 'micropyle', through which water can pass. Most of the space in the seed is taken up by two large seed-leaves, called 'cotyledons', which contain the food reserves in the form of starch and a little protein. Where these join, there is a tiny root (the 'radicle'), and a tiny shoot (the 'plumule'), destined to bear the leaves, flowers, and fruit.

Protected by its hard coat, the dry bean-seed passes the winter in a resting condition. With the coming of the warmth and moisture of spring, the embryo gives off enzymes, which so act on the starch and protein that they become suitable for nourishing the growing seedling. The plumule and radicle, therefore, begin to grow. The radicle passes through the tiny pore or micropyle, splits the coat or testa at its point of weakness, penetrates into the soil, and begins to form branch roots. At the same time the plumule grows up. Until it has passed through the soil its tip remains bent like a crochet-hook, so that the delicate growing-point is not harmed. When it reaches the surface of the soil, the stem straightens out and continues growing into a shoot, bearing foliage leaves. Until the young seedling is established, and has developed green leaves to take over the duties of food manufacture, food is supplied from the reserves in the cotyledons. These remain below ground, gradually shrivelling up as the starch and protein are used, and finally disappearing.

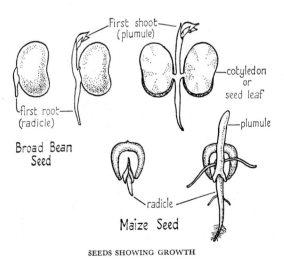

First shoot (plumule)

cotyledon or seed leaf

first root (radicle)

plumule

Broad Bean Seed

radicle

Maize Seed

SEEDS SHOWING GROWTH

Seeds such as the Broad Bean, the Scarlet Runner, and Pea remain below ground to nourish the young seedling. When the French Bean germinates, however, the cotyledons are carried above ground, and after their contained food has been used to nourish the young seedlings, they remain as two shrivelled organs at the bottom of the stem. The seeds of the Mustard and Cress differ from the French Bean in that the cotyledons, once they reach the air, soon open out and turn green, to begin the work of Photosynthesis (q.v.) or food manufacture. In the Castor Oil seeds, the cotyledons are thin and tissue-like, and do not store food; but instead an oily type of food is stored inside the seed, not directly connected to the young plant. When the seed germinates, the cotyledons remain inside the seed for some time, absorbing the food material over their whole surfaces. Then, as the shoot grows, the cotyledons are carried above ground, become green, and begin to manufacture food.

All the seeds so far described have two cotyledons, and are typical of one of the two big groups of Flowering Plants (q.v.), the 'dicotyledons'; but in the other group, the 'monocotyledons', there is only one cotyledon. To this group belong the Lilies, Daffodils, Crocuses, Tulips, and Grasses, including all the cereals. The grain of Maize or Indian Corn is a good example of the second group. This is not a true seed, but a fruit in which the fruit-wall and seed-coat are fused. On one side of the flattened grain there is an oblong area of pale colour, which indicates the position of the embryo. The rest of the grain is filled with reserve food material—chiefly starch, but a little protein. One part of the embryo is somewhat shield-shaped, and is pressed against the reserve food: this is the cotyledon. The remaining part consists of the plumule and the radicle. On germination the cotyledon gives off enzymes, which act on the starch and protein to convert them into food suitable for the growing seedling. The leaves of the plumule are enclosed in a sheath, which splits as it appears above ground. The radicle has only a short life, and before it dies off adventitious roots spring from the base of the stem, and grow into an extensive fibrous root system (see Roots, Section 5).

Seeds, therefore, possess either one or two cotyledons. In some seeds the cotyledons remain below ground, in others they appear above ground. There are many other variations, however. In the Sycamore, for example, the cotyledons are long, tightly coiled, and green—which, as they have been enclosed in a dark seed, is rather surprising. The Date-stone is a seed in which the reserve food material is cellulose—the material characteristic of the cell-walls of plants.

2. SEED DISPERSAL. It is clearly of advantage to plants that the seeds should be carried some distance from the parent and be widely dispersed, so that overcrowding is avoided; and various special devices help to achieve this end. The four chief methods are dispersal by wind, animals, or water, and by explosive or ejecting mechanisms in the fruit itself.

(*a*) *Wind Dispersal.* The seeds of some plants, such as the Orchids, are so small and light that when they are set free, they are freely blown by the wind. Others have hairs or wings which enable them to float on the wind. The winged fruits of the Sycamore, Elm, and Ash are good examples, and also those of the Hornbeam and Lime, where the 'wings' are formed from bracts. In Traveller's-Joy or Old Man's Beard (Clematis), the fruit consists of a collection of seeds (achenes) on each of which, as it ripens, the style remains as a long white plume which helps the

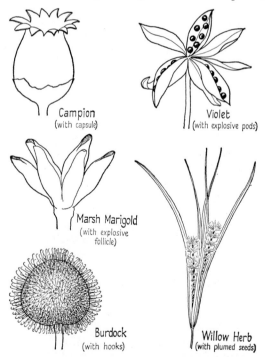

Campion
(with capsule)

Violet
(with explosive pods)

Marsh Marigold
(with explosive
follicle)

Burdock
(with hooks)

Willow Herb
(with plumed seeds)

TYPES OF FRUIT SHOWING DIFFERENT FORMS OF SEED
DISPERSAL

fruit to float in the air. The Willow, Poplar, and Willow-herb have plumed seeds. Other plumed seeds develop a ring of hairs, or a feathery appendage called a 'pappus', as in the Dandelions, Hawkweeds, Thistles, Groundsel, and other members of this family of flowers. In the Dandelion, the pappus acts as a parachute, and often travels long distances through the air. In Thistles, the pappus with its branched hairs is attached so delicately to the fruit that a light breeze is enough to separate them; the fruit falls to the ground, and the pappus, as thistledown, floats away.

Plants in which the seeds are borne in capsules bearing teeth or pores are also distributed by wind. The capsule of the Poppy, for example, is borne at the end of a long stalk which is easily shaken about in the wind, and the seeds are shaken out through the pores. Wind dispersal is probably the best method of distributing seeds over large areas; but it is probably also the most wasteful.

(*b*) *Animal Dispersal.* Seeds and fruits may be distributed by animals, either by sticking to their coats or by being eaten and then excreted by them. Some seeds have hooks which catch in the fur or wool of browsing animals, or to the clothing of human beings; so that they are carried and dropped elsewhere. The Goose-grass, Burdock, Teasel, Wood Avens, and Enchanter's Nightshade all have such hooks, and are sometimes carried great distances from the parent plant. Birds, in particular, carry seeds over wide areas —web-footed water-birds, for instance, carry seeds in the mud that clings to their feet. Charles DARWIN (q.v. Vol. V) once took 190 grammes of mud from water-fowls, and mixed it with sterilized soil—from this mud no less than 537 plants germinated. Animals sometimes distribute fruits and seeds by dropping them accidentally. Squirrels, for example, when carrying nuts for their winter hoards, often drop some on the way; rooks and jays distribute acorns in much the same manner. Even the ant is responsible for seed dispersal: it carries off oily seeds such as the Violet, Periwinkle, and Greater Celandine, not all of which reach their destination.

When fleshy fruits, such as drupes, berries, and pomes, are eaten by animals, the seeds either pass out in the droppings or are rejected by the animal after the juicy part has been eaten. In the Blackberry, for instance, the seeds pass through the animal unharmed; but in the

John Markham

TRAVELLER'S-JOY (Clematis)

Eric Hosking

DANDELION

PLUMED SEEDS DEPENDENT ON WIND DISPERSAL

Cherry, the hard stone is rejected by the bird and dropped.

(c) *Water Dispersal.* This is the least common method, and is confined to a few plants growing in or near water. The seeds of the riverside Alder, for example, have spongy coverings filled with air, and these drop into the water and float away. When the spongy covering becomes saturated with water the seed loses its buoyancy and sinks—to germinate in the bed of the stream or river. The Coconut has a fibrous mesocarp enclosing a large number of air spaces, which make it buoyant. The coconut palm grows chiefly along the sea-shore or along the banks of rivers; and the fruit, when ripe, usually falls into the water. There it floats until it is washed up on dry land or is caught in the mud, where it develops into a new plant. The Water-lily, also, is dispersed by means of a floating seed.

(d) *Ejecting and 'Explosive' Fruits.* Some fruits catapult their seeds away. When the pods of Gorse and related plants ripen, they dry and shrivel. The shrivelling takes place unequally, with the result that the two halves of the pod separate, and then twist. All this takes place so rapidly that the seeds are shot out to a consider-able distance. On a hot still day, the gentle 'pop, pop' from a group of Gorse or Broom bushes can easily be heard. The Geranium is another example of an ejecting fruit: so sudden is the splitting of the fruit that the five portions into which it divides are flung to some distance.

Probably the best example of an explosive fruit is the Squirting Cucumber. When ripe, the rough, hairy, almost prickly berries become detached from the stalk, leaving only a delicate skin at the base. The pressure of the juice inside the skin causes the berry to burst at this weak spot, and the juice containing the seeds is shot out of the hole to some considerable distance.

See also FRUITS; REPRODUCTION IN PLANTS.

SENSES. 1. Our contact with the world around us is entirely through our senses, a fact which is too often overlooked. The same is, of course, true of every animal. The five senses are those of sight, hearing, touch, taste, and smell. In addition, it is usual to speak of a sixth sense whenever we find ourselves doing something that is not obviously dependent upon one of those five. This fact alone is sufficient to warn us that we have not explored completely the field of sensory experience, even so far as human beings are concerned. Much less fully do we understand the senses of animals—indeed, so long as we are unable to get inside the mind of an animal, so long shall we be unable to understand fully its sensory experiences in relation to our own.

Let us see how little we know of an animal's sensory experiences by comparing the behaviour of a man and a dog. A man is more aware of the world from what he sees than from what he feels, hears, tastes, or smells. Next in order of importance comes touch, with hearing following third: smell and taste have but a limited importance to him. To a dog, however, smell appears to be far and away the most important sense, with hearing second, sight a poor third, and touch of little importance. Taste is so closely linked with smell that it is often difficult to tell where one begins and the other ends. If, then, we had the sensory experiences of a dog, the world would probably appear as a place in which every object had its characteristic scent or perfume. We should recognize each other by smell. We should find our way home by smell. We should not eat without first smelling our food. We should know if our companions were pleased or angry, sad or happy, tired and energetic, by the scent they gave off. Again, we should be much more aware of sound: we should be aware of noises now too highly pitched for us to hear, just as we should recognize smells which, as human beings, we are not aware of. Our sight, on the other hand, would be defective compared with what we have now. Our appreciation of colours would be limited; the outlines of common objects would be blurred: only things close at hand would be at all clearly seen. Touch would be limited to a gross appreciation of solid objects, although the lips would probably be more sensitive as tactile organs. Therefore, though a dog has a brain, eyes, nose, tongue, and so on, very like those of human beings, the world must appear to him very different. We can be reasonably sure that even greater differences must exist between our own experiences and those of other vertebrates, such as birds, reptiles, and fishes, even though their brains, nervous systems, and sense organs are built on essentially the same pattern as our own. It is of supreme importance to recognize this great difference between the sensory experiences of man and animals, and also between one animal and another; otherwise our interpretation of behaviour will be seriously at fault. Nevertheless, it must be recognized that all behaviour and all sensory experiences have a common origin and fit neatly into an evolutionary sequence.

The senses, and as a consequence the sensory experiences, of the invertebrates depart even more widely from those of human beings. While it is true that the higher invertebrates, such as insects, crustaceans, and molluscs, have eyes comparable with those of vertebrates, though of different structure, the other senses are very different. Most invertebrates have no ears, but some, such as crickets, which produce sound, have auditory pits. For the most part, however, the antennae are the main sensory organs, and probably in them are lodged organs of smell, taste, and touch, and even, it may be, senses which have no parallel in the vertebrates. In the lower invertebrates—sponges, sea-anemones, worms, and starfish—sensory appreciation is limited to an ill-defined touch, taste, and light-perception. In the lowest animals of all, the protozoa, although the protoplasm appears to possess the dawning senses of taste (ability to select food-particles from among indigestible matter), sight (reaction to light stimuli), hearing (sensitivity to vibrations), and touch (reaction to changing temperatures, chemicals, or electric currents), all responses are on the part of the protoplasm as a whole. With the evolution of the multicellular animal, certain cells began to take on separate functions, and the senses tended more and more to be localized in special organs; and the more highly the animals evolved, the more localized and specialized the organs became.

2. SIGHT. The eye in its most highly developed form may be compared with a camera. Both possess a LENS (q.v. Vol. VIII) through which rays of light are allowed to pass and strike upon a sensitized film. In both there is a shutter for controlling the passage of light, and also a diaphragm for cutting down the amount of light when it is too intense. In dealing with the eye, we use the term retina for the sensitized film, eyelid for the shutter, and iris for the diaphragm. There is, however, one important difference between the eye and a camera: whereas the sensitized plate or film of a camera can produce a negative image only after further treatment by chemicals, and can be used only once, the eye is able to produce a never-ending series of positive images which, in the higher animals, are stored up in the brain as memories.

The eye and its function of sight in the highest

animals can be best understood by seeing how the eye is evolved from the lowest animals to the highest. In the most primitive animals, the protozoa, there is an obvious response to light, some moving away from light and some towards it. In some protozoa, however, there is somewhere in the body a pigment spot, usually black, brown, or red, the possessors of which always react more strongly and rapidly to the stimulus of light. This same tendency is seen more and more marked as we pass from the unicellular protozoa to the multicellular metazoa, and upwards through the metazoa from the less highly organized to the more highly organized animals. Thus, in the jellyfishes and the worms, the pigment spots are already becoming larger; and in the mollusca, crustacea, and insects, a definite eye has been formed.

There is a considerable variety of eye-pattern in the animal kingdom, the eye becoming more complex the more highly organized the animal. From the simple pigment spot of the protozoa, a retina slowly evolves by the laying down of more and more pigment granules. At a later stage, a lens is added; and this has the effect of concentrating the light rays on small areas of the retina, thus producing on it an image of the object from which the rays have been reflected. In general terms, sight in the lowest animals is no more than a vague reaction to the stimulus of light; but in the higher animals there is also the formation of an image. The degree to which this image is formed varies from one type of animal to another: fishes and reptiles, for instance, can

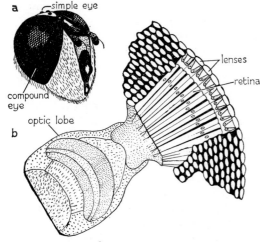

a. HEAD OF INSECT; *b.* SECTION OF COMPOUND EYE AND OPTIC LOBE

probably appreciate only vague shapes and, more particularly, movement in objects around them.

The best-developed sight is 'stereoscopic sight' —that is, sight capable of seeing things in the solid. This is possessed by man (*see* EYE STRUCTURE, Vol. XI) and certain birds and mammals with eyes close together instead of one on each side of the head. An elephant, with an eye on each side of the head and directed away, can almost certainly see only a flat picture of the world around; whereas a cat, with the eyes close together and pointing in the same direction, as are human eyes, must be able to appreciate solid forms as we do, and therefore has stereoscopic vision. A bird, to whom sight is perhaps the most important of the senses, has very highly developed and efficient eyes.

3. HEARING. The ear, the organ by which we hear, is not the fleshy flap on the side of the head, although in everyday speech we are accustomed to speak of it as such. This is merely the instrument for catching the sound waves and directing them towards the *tympanum*, or ear-drum. The middle and inner ear, the mechanism by which the more highly developed animals hear, consist of a complicated apparatus of small bones and cartilages, lodged in a cavity in the skull, from which a nerve, the auditory nerve, runs to the brain, enabling us to translate vibrations of air into what we call SOUND (q.v. Vol. III). Similar sound vibrations will travel through air, water, and earth; and almost all animals respond to one or other of these vibrations, according to whether they live on land, in the water, or under the earth.

In the animal kingdom, hearing has a different meaning according to the group of animals with which we are dealing. As the protozoa are sensitive to light even though they have no eye, so some animals—for example, earthworms—are sensitive to vibrations, whether of air, water, or land, without showing any sign of a structure which could be called an ear. The sensitivity of earthworms, for instance, to vibrations in the ground makes them withdraw into their burrows when a thrush runs across the lawn. The simplest form of ear known, in some of the lowest animals, is a minute pit in the skin, known as an auditory pit, lined with sensitive protoplasmic hairs, and containing a tiny pellet of lime. This is connected to the nervous system by one or more nerve-fibres. The ears of the higher animals are similar in form to 'those of human beings (*see* Ear Structure, Vol. XI). The bigger outer ears of many animals make effective instruments for catching the sound waves.

Closely related to hearing, whether through the highly organized ear of a higher animal or through an auditory pit, is the sense of balance, both hearing and balance being perceived through the ear.

4. Feeling (Touch). The 'tactile' or touch sense was the first sense to appear in the course of Evolution (q.v.). It is located throughout the skin, although it is more highly developed in some parts than in others. The human finger-tips, for example, have a more highly developed tactile appreciation than, say, the back of the neck; and the palms of the hands are more

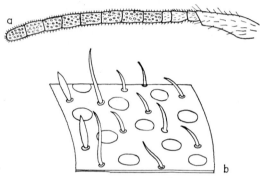

a. ANTENNA OF HONEY-BEE WORKER; *b.* PORTION OF A SEGMENT SHOWING THREE TYPES OF SENSE ORGANS SENSITIVE TO TASTE AND SMELL

sensitive still. The sense is conveyed by means of fine nerve-fiberes nding just under the skin; and in the higher animals, especially in those parts more highly sensitized, such as the finger-tips, their minute touch-corpuscles are made up of highly branching nerve-fibres encased in cushions of tissues. In such animals as insects, where the body is covered with a horny layer, the sense of touch works through sensory hairs projecting from the surface—in particular, through the antennae; and in mammals where the body is covered with fur there are long, very sensitive hairs, such as those on a cat's face, which perform the same function.

5. Taste. The taste-buds, the special organs of taste, consist of groups of narrow, rod-shaped cells in the skin of the mouth and, more particularly, of the tongue and soft palate. In fishes, they are found on the outer surface of the gills also. They are comparable with the touch-

corpuscles, and like them are connected by nerve-fibres to the central nervous system.

6. Smell. The sense which enables us to perceive a scent or perfume is spoken of as the 'olfactory' sense. In the vertebrates this is lodged in the nose, and is dependent upon a mucous lining richly supplied with nerve endings derived from the olfactory nerves in the brain. In only a few vertebrates, notably the whales, is there no sense of smell; in fact, in many animals it is the most developed of the senses. In invertebrates there is no organ which may be called a nose, although it is clear that some, such as insects, have a sense corresponding to the sense of smell, which is probably located in the antennae. The mechanism of smell is very imperfectly understood, but probably scent or perfume is the result of stimulation by minute particles which bombard the mucous membrane.

See also Nervous System; Brain.

SHARKS, RAYS, AND CHIMAERA (Rattails).

1. These fishes are quite distinct from the true bony Fishes (q.v.), and from a study of Fossils (q.v. Vol. III) it is thought that they developed separately from a group of very early bony fishes which invaded the sea far earlier than the true fishes. In the sea they lost their bony skeleton and, as in the modern species, developed a cartilaginous (gristly) skeleton.

There are two rather distinct groups, which have probably been separate for many millions of years—the Sharks and Rays (Elasmobranchii) and the Chimaeras (Holocephali).

The skeleton, though formed only of cartilage, is fairly complete, and the gills are supported on jointed rods of cartilage, called gill-arches. Except in the Chimaeras, each gill has a separate opening at the side of the head. In most cases there are five openings on each side (though occasionally there are six or seven); and just behind the eye there is a valved hole, called a 'spiracle'. This in Skates is sometimes enlarged, allowing water to pass over the gills.

Most Elasmobranchs are covered with bony scales or denticles, being all that remains of the bone of their distant ancestors. The teeth are simply enlarged and specialized denticles. There are usually several rows one behind the other, the new ones being formed at the back. The front teeth, which are the largest, are used for biting; as these are worn out or lost, those behind move up to replace them.

The fins of Sharks and Rays are supported by numerous horny rays upon a complicated skeleton of gristly rods; but these are not visible from outside, as they are completely covered by skin and muscle. Most members of the family can be recognized by the shape of the tail, the end of the body being turned upwards so that most of the tail fin lies beneath it. It is easy to distinguish the male from the female, also, since the former has a pair of stiff finger-like 'claspers' attached to the pelvic fins.

Some Sharks and Rays bear their young alive, somewhat after the fashion of mammals; but others, such as the Port Jackson Shark and some of the Rays, lay a sort of egg, encased in a strong horny capsule, sometimes called the Mermaid's Purse.

2. SHARKS. Most sharks are rather long-bodied, fish-shaped animals, with the eyes and gill-openings on the side of the head. They have two pairs of fins, the pectoral fins behind the head corresponding to our arms, the pelvic fins, farther back on the belly, corresponding to legs. They have one or two dorsal fins on the back, an anal fin below the tail, and the typically shaped caudal fin at the end of the tail. The body is covered with denticles pointing backwards, so that the skin feels fairly smooth if rubbed towards the tail, but very rough when rubbed in the opposite direction. This skin, when dried, is call 'shagreen'. Sharks usually swim with a side to side bending of the body. They feed for the most part on smaller, bony fishes.

Many different kinds of shark are known in the various seas of the world, a few entering fresh water. The most primitive kinds are the rare Frilled Shark of the North Atlantic and Japanese waters, and the more common Cow-sharks. Among the more specialized sharks are the fierce mackerel-sharks, including the well-known Porbeagle, sometimes caught off the coast of Britain during the summer months, when it may damage the nets of fishermen. This shark, which grows to about 3·5 metres long, has a large mouth full of frightful teeth, and a keel on each side of the tail, to help its swift surface-swimming. The famous Man-eating Shark of tropical seas, a relative of the Porbeagle, grows much larger, often as long as 9 metres. It is by far the most voracious of all, and there are many stories of its attacks on bathers and pearl-divers. The great naturalist Linnaeus considered it to be the animal, wrongly called a

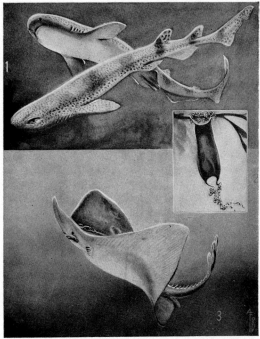

A. Fraser-Brunner

TYPICAL SHARKS AND RAYS

1. Spotted Dogfish—a small species of shark; 2. A 'Mermaid's Purse'—the horny egg-case of the Dogfish; 3. A Skate swimming with its broad 'wings'.

whale, that swallowed the prophet Jonah. Other large sharks have also been responsible for the death or injury of men, particularly some of the Cub-sharks of the West Indies. Related to them is the Blue Shark, a handsome species that follows the mackerel to the British coast during the summer.

The Hammerhead is a strange creature, much like a Cub-shark, but with the sides of the skull so drawn out that the eyes, fixed on broad stalks, are wide apart. The Thresher, another curious species, has a tail-fin as long as the rest of the fish. It is said to beat the water vigorously with this long tail to round up schools of fishes so that it can charge into the terrified mass and eat its fill. Quite different are the Carpet-sharks, harmless creatures, broad-bodied, with large heads provided with fleshy fringes. They live at the bottom of the sea, having a complicated pattern for concealment, the best-known species being the Wobbigong, of Australia.

The various Dogfish, also known as Cat-sharks or Roussettes, found throughout the temperate seas, are quite small and harmless—some being useful as food (*see* ROCK SALMON). They lay eggs which are protected by horny oblong capsules attached to weeds by means of tendrils at the corners. These are occasionally found washed up on the shore after a storm.

Some sharks have a strong spine in front of each dorsal fin. One of these, the strange Port Jackson Shark of the Pacific, has a big, clumsy head, and heavy, scroll-like teeth for crushing molluscs and crustaceans. It lays its eggs in spiral cases that spin round and round in strong currents instead of being washed away. The common Spur-dog, or Picked Dogfish, is another of these spiny sharks. This and its relatives usually have no anal fin, and do not grow very large; some of them are jet-black, with luminous areas on the body, and inhabit very deep water. Their young are born alive (*see* DEEP-SEA FISHES).

The largest of all sharks, and the largest living fish, is the great Whale-shark, which may be as much as 12 metres long. This rather rare monster is quite harmless, however, having very feeble teeth. Several have been caught off Florida during recent years. Almost as large and equally harmless is the Basking Shark, which is remarkable for its very long gill-openings. Both these large sharks feed on PLANKTON (q.v.), which they draw into their mouths with large quantities of water, and filter off, much as the whalebone WHALES (q.v.) do by means of the large sieve-like gill rakers. The Basking Shark is so called because, when not feeding, it spends much time merely floating, or basking, on the surface of the ocean. Occasionally, when a Basking Shark dies or is killed, its decomposed remains are washed up on shore, the jaws and gills having nearly always fallen away, leaving the small skull on the end of what looks like a long neck. When this happens, it is almost

A. Fraser-Brunner

CHIMAERA OR RABBIT FISH (MALE ABOVE, FEMALE BELOW)

certain that a newspaperman will photograph it, and it will be described in the papers as a SEA SERPENT (q.v.). It is an event such as this that keeps the old legend of the Sea Serpent alive.

Among the curios often brought home by travellers are the 'saws' of the Sawfish. This is a rather wide, flattened shark of the tropics, which may grow to a large size. The snout is lengthened into a long flat blade, on each side of which is a row of teeth (really modified denticles) set in sockets. With this weapon the Sawfish drives into shoals of fishes, making great havoc, after which it feeds at leisure on the bodies. Another flattened shark is the Monk-fish, or Angel-shark (often marketed as 'Rock Salmon'), which has only one gill-opening on each side, and rather broad pectoral fins, very like those of a Ray.

The flesh of many kinds of Shark is eaten in different parts of the world, and the Chinese value the dried fins of some species very highly, making them into soup.

3. RAYS AND SKATES. These are closely allied to the Sharks, but are very much flattened, the pectoral fins being joined on each side to the head, so that the fins and head together form a disk. The eyes and spiracles are on top of the head, the nostrils, mouth, and gills underneath. The tail is usually slender, and there is no anal fin. The most shark-like kinds are the curious Guitar-fish, with a narrow disk and pointed snout, and the Torpedoes, or Electric Rays (*see* ELECTRIC FISHES), which have a rounded disk. Both these have rather thick tails, and bear their young alive.

The Skates have bigger pectoral fins, and a slender tail, bearing the little dorsal fin near its end. They lay eggs in horny cases, called 'skate-barrows', which are oblong in shape, with a stiff tube at each of the four angles. Some of the Skates grow very large, and are valuable as food.

Sting-rays have tails drawn out into long whip-lashes. Instead of a fin at the end, there is a strong spine, with a groove that contains poison, and this can inflict a very painful wound. Sting-rays are found in warm seas, and can often be dangerous to fishermen.

Largest of all is the great Devil-fish or Manta of tropical waters, which has the pectoral fins drawn out to points, like great wings, and may be as much as 6 metres from tip to tip. On each side of the very big mouth is a sort of tentacle, which is used like a hand to push food into the mouth. Devil-fishes seem to be fairly harmless creatures, unless attacked.

Most Skates and Rays live on the bed of the sea, feeding mainly on molluscs, crustaceans, or carrion, which they crush with their flat teeth, the most notable exceptions being the surface-loving Mantas. They all swim by wave-like movements of the edges of their great pectoral fins.

4. CHIMAERAS. These silvery-coloured creatures, often called Rat-tails or Rabbit-fishes, are extraordinary fishes in appearance. A few species are all that remains of a one-time widespread group. They are found mostly in deep water. They have long tails, drawn out to a fine point, and teeth quite unlike those of Sharks, consisting of flat, bony plates called 'tritors', which form a sort of beak. In addition to the usual claspers, the males have small extra ones on the front of the pelvic fins and above the eyes. The dorsal fin extends along the back, and has a strong spine, which is said to be poisonous, at its front end. Chimaeras feed on a great variety of worms, molluscs, and crustaceans, and are themselves eaten by many larger fishes. They lay eggs in horny capsules, one end being drawn out into a long point, which sticks in the mud, serving as an anchor.

See also Vol. VI: SHARK FISHING.
See also Vol. IX: BIG-GAME FISHING.

SHEARWATER, *see* PETREL, Section 5.

SHEEP. These belong to the order Artiodactyla (even-toed hoofed animals. They are hollow-horned RUMINANTS (q.v.), as are also ANTELOPES, CATTLE, and GOATS (qq.v.). They eat mostly grass, which they digest at leisure by 'chewing the cud'. Both sexes of wild sheep usually have horns, those of the males being much larger than those of the females, and, as a rule, curved outwards from the side of the head in more or less of a circle. Their outer hair is short and stiff and not woolly, as is that of the domestic breeds; but they have an undercoat of wool.

There are nearly a dozen wild species, all essentially mountain animals, mostly living in Europe and Asia. There is one species in the Rocky Mountains of North America, and one, unlike all the others, in North Africa. Among the best known of these wild species are the fine American Bighorns, which stand about a metre

Paul Popper

MOUFFLONS OF CORSICA

high, and have massive horns. Some of these sheep are remarkably agile, making tremendous leaps from rock to rock. The lambs, when only a few days old, can follow their mothers up the steepest cliffs. In the great heights of the Altai and Pamir mountains of central Asia live the Argalis, great wild sheep as large as donkeys, with massive horns sometimes up to 1·5 metres long, measured along the curve. The Pamir Argalis are also known as Marco Polo's Sheep, for he first wrote about them in the 13th century. In the mountains of Corsica and Sardinia live the Moufflon, which are about 68 centimetres high, and have dark reddish-brown coats with a white saddle-patch. The Barbary Sheep, or Udad, of Africa are up to a metre high, and have a great mass of long hair on their throats, chests, and fore-limbs, and thick, hairy tails. They live in the Atlas mountains, and are said to be able to go for several days without water. The rams of these wild sheep, with their massive horns, are magnificent animals, very different from the domestic sheep.

It is difficult to trace the origin of the domestic sheep, as they do not appear to be directly descended from any of the wild species existing today. But as they were domesticated so very long ago, they may well be descended from species that no longer survive. Domestic sheep differ from wild sheep, not only in having wool instead of hair coats, but also in having naturally long tails—though these are usually docked. The only wild sheep to have long tails are the African Barbary Sheep.

See also Vol. VI: SHEEP.

SHEEP MAGGOT-FLY, *see* BLOWFLY.

SHELDRAKE, *see* Ducks, Sections 1 and 2.

SHIELD BUG. These rather robust, flat, broad insects are amongst the largest of British Bugs (q.v.). Thirty-eight species, many of which are brightly coloured, are found in Great Britain. A triangular horny plate, which is the dorsal part of the thorax, extends backwards over the abdomen, reaching at least to the base of the membraneous part of the wing, and often reaching to the end of the body. The eggs are laid, usually in batches, on leaves and stones, and the growing Shield Bugs moult five times before they assume their adult, fully-winged, condition. The young, or nymphs, are often brightly, and quite differently, coloured from the adults.

Shield Bugs are not molested very much by other animals, probably on account of an unpleasant odour they give off; but toads, which so often attack insects that other animals reject, seem to like them quite well. Shield Bugs generally feed on plant juices, but some attack animals, especially other insects. Some are found on trees, and others on low-growing, herbaceous plants; but none of those in Britain seems to do any serious damage. One British species, a deep metallic blue insect, the nymphs of which are scarlet, is found at the base of sedges and heather; it is said to feed on other insects, especially on Flea-beetles, and their larvae. Two very beautiful species, one shining black with white mottlings, the other purple-bronze, are often found on white and dead-nettle. The common bright green species, found on Birch trees, has a strong smell. Others, of various shades of brown, may often be seen on tree-trunks, especially those of Oak.

SHIELD BUG

SHIPWORM. This mollusc lives in the timbers of ships and the wood of breakwaters and harbour works. At first sight it is hardly recognizable as a mollusc, for it has a long, slender, worm-like body, from 15 to 30 centimetres long. At one end of the body are the pair of small, globular-shaped valves of the shell, while the other end carries a curious pair of small, racket-shaped plates, which are chiefly used to close the entrance to the burrow in which the Ship-

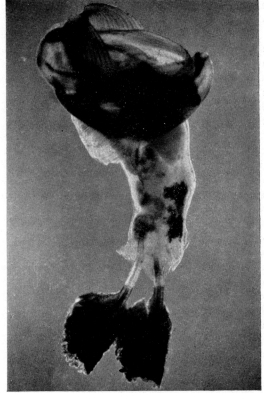

Robert Clarke

ADULT SHIPWORM

The shell is in front, and at the hind end of its long, wormlike body are its two breathing siphons

worm lives. The outer surfaces of the valves of the shell have a file-like texture, and as the animal can rock them from side to side, giving a grinding action to the series of toothed ridges, they form a very effective tool for boring. As it bores, the Shipworm lays down a shelly lining to its tunnel. The female Shipworm sheds her eggs into the sea, and the larvae, hatching from them, can swim freely to fresh timbers, where they start boring operations on their own account.

All kinds of timber seem to be attacked by Shipworm: pine and other relatively soft woods are rapidly destroyed, while even teak and oak do not escape. The tunnel is usually bored in the direction of the grain of the wood, only swerving to one side when an extra hard knot or an iron nail is encountered. In the days of wooden sailing-ships, the depredations of the Shipworm were an ever-present danger; but the practice of sheathing a ship's timbers with metal below the water-line gave safety from this menace. In the 18th century, the havoc wreaked by Shipworms on the piles and timber-work of the sea-dikes often caused serious damage and inundations along the coast of Holland. As an example of the speed at which Shipworms work, a piece of pinewood pile measuring 23 cm in diameter, after being in use for 5 years, had become so bored away as to contain scarcely any solid timber. Indeed, 4 to 5 years' submergence in the sea is generally enough to destroy any wooden piles, unless they have been well studded with broad-headed iron nails. But no matter how tortuous or crowded together the tunnels of the Shipworm may become, they rarely, if ever, encroach upon each other. There are only two species of Shipworm in Britain.

Another, closely related, mollusc, which causes extensive damage to marine timbers, is a species of Piddock (q.v.), the Wood Piddock. It shows a marked preference for birch, pine, and oak. Unlike the Shipworms, it generally bores against the grain, in a slightly diagonal direction, going only deep enough to bury itself in the timber; and it does not secrete a shelly lining to its burrow. It has a small, rather globular-shaped shell, composed of two glossy, semi-transparent valves. It is always to be found at work on the timbers of old groins and breakwaters.

See also Mollusc.

SHREW. Although they are often called Shrew-mice, shrews are not mice, but belong to the Insectivora (q.v.,) or insect-eating order of mammals, as do Moles and Hedgehogs (qq.v.). They eat a variety of food, such as worms and slugs, as well as insects. Shrews can be recognized by their long, sensitive snouts, small eyes, and soft, silky fur. They live in Europe and the temperate and semi-tropical parts of Africa, Asia and America. The four species found in Great Britain are the Common Shrew, Pigmy Shrew, Water Shrew, and Scilly Shrew.

Common Shrews are about 8 centimetres long, with tails nearly 4 cm long. They have thick, velvety coats, brown on top and whitish below. They are extremely active, foraging for food unceasingly by day and night, and eating an amazing amount—about their own weight every 24 hours. They die if they are without food for more than a few hours. The foul, musky smell which they give out from glands on each flank protects them from certain of their enemies; but, nevertheless, they are killed and eaten by moles, stoats, weasels, owls, and kestrels. Dogs and cats also kill, but do not eat them. Shrews can run at a speed of about 4 km/h, and they can also leap a distance of some 60 cm. They climb up trees in search of insects, and also swim.

Shrews are always very quarrelsome among themselves, but particularly so in March, when they often kill and eat each other. They build their breeding-nests under logs, in tree-holes, and in banks. These are woven of dry grass, shaped like a cup, and have a loose lid. Litters of from five to seven young are born in the spring and summer. They stay in the nest, and are fed by their parents until they are almost fully grown. In summer, shrews live in grass or thick cover, either making nests of their own or using those of mice and voles. In the autumn they migrate to other ground, and in winter retreat to hedge-rows, gorse, and piles of leaves and sticks. In the autumn, very large numbers are found dead. This abnormal mortality at only one season may be on account of a shortage of food; but it is now thought that it is due merely to their normal span of life being only 18 months. They are said to die also in thundery weather.

Pigmy or Lesser Shrews are smaller than Common Shrews, being only 5 cm long. There

COMMON SHREW   *A. R. Thompson*
This is one of the smallest British mammals

are not so many of them in Great Britain, although they are by no means rare, and they are the only shrews found in Ireland. Scilly Shrews or Blair's Shrews are the same size as Pigmy Shrews and, as their name denotes, are found in the Scilly Isles.

Water Shrews are a little larger than Common Shrews, and have shiny, velvety fur which throws off water without becoming wet. Their colour varies from blue-black to dark brown. On the underside of their tails they have a 'keel' of stiff hairs which helps them in swimming, and they have a fringe on the side of the hind feet for the same purpose. They are about day and night, winter and summer, spending most of the time in the water, and preferring clear, slow streams and backwaters to muddy and swift waters. They come up every half-minute to breathe, and rarely venture far from the bank. Instead of using all four legs when swimming, like most mammals, they wriggle their bodies like fish and use their forelegs only to steer. On rising to the surface, they often leap clear of the water. Like all shrews, they have large appetites. In the water they turn over the stones in search of fish-spawn, small fry, caddis-flies, and other insects and larvae. As this food does not always satisfy them, they search for food on land, even killing and eating each other. They make their nests of grass, moss, roots, or oak-leaves, deep down in small, mole-like galleries in the banks of streams, with entrances above and below water. A litter of from five to eight young is born in May, and probably a second litter later on in the year. In autumn Water Shrews travel away from their usual homes, and sometimes live away from water. Like the Common Shrews, large numbers die each autumn.

SHRIKE (Butcher Bird). This large and varied family includes the scarlet Minivets of India and east Asia, the black and white Magpie Larks and Piping Crows of Australia, as well as the typical Shrikes, among which are the Red-backed Shrike, the British species, and the European Great Grey Shrike, a winter visitor to Britain. Of the 200 or more species, however, the majority are found in Africa, where they are, perhaps, the most characteristic bird of the open thorn-scrub country. There are only two species in North America, and none in South America.

The Red-backed Shrike is not uncommon in

Eric Hosking

COCK RED-BACKED SHRIKE FEEDING HIS FAMILY

localities in the southern half of England. It winters in Africa, and is one of the latest birds to arrive in Britain, and one of the earliest to depart. The cock bird has a blue-grey head, reddish-brown back, white throat, and pinkish underparts. It and other members of the family earn their name of Butcher Birds because of their habit of neatly impaling their victims on thorns or spikes in a sort of larder near their nests. They have powerful bills, the upper part being hooked and toothed, and with this strong weapon they attack not only insects, but small birds, field-mice, frogs, and lizards. They are very agile and quick in their movements, shooting out like an arrow on their prey, and very seldom missing their mark. They build a largish nest in a hedge or low bush—not in a tree, as do most members of the family.

The Great Grey Shrike, a rather larger bird, some 25 centimetres long, breeds in central and northern Europe. It builds in forest trees, often in an oak-tree on the outskirts of a wood. It lines its large nest with a great deal of soft material—feathers, fur, wool, and hair. It visits the east coast of Britain fairly regularly in the winter. The Woodchat Shrikes of central and southern Europe also occasionally visit Britain.

SHRIMP, *see* Prawns and Shrimps.

SHRUBS, *see* Flowering Plants.

SIGHT, *see* SENSES, Section 2.

SILK MOTHS. The common Silkworm (belonging to the family Bombycidae) is the only insect that has been entirely domesticated by man, and it is doubtful whether it exists anywhere in the wild state now. For thousands of years it has been bred in captivity for the silk the caterpillars produce when they spin their golden cocoons. The moths have lost their power of flight, although they still retain their wings, and the caterpillars have no inclination to wander, relying upon man to feed them daily with mulberry leaves. The story of how two Persians, nearly 1,500 years ago, stole some of the precious eggs from a 'silk farm' in China, and smuggled them into Europe hidden in hollow staffs, is too well known to be told in detail here. But from this small stock it is said that the great silk industries of France and Italy have sprung into being (*see* SILKWORMS, Vol. VI).

Each female silk moth lays 200 to 400 eggs, which lie dormant all the winter, and hatch in the spring, when the mulberry leaves burst from their buds. Sometimes in late springs it is necessary to keep the eggs in a cold place to prevent their hatching before the leaves are ready; and at other times they can be forced in special incubators. The caterpillars, or silkworms, which are smooth and putty coloured, crawl about from leaf to leaf on the tray where they are fed, moving only a few centimetres in search of food. If mulberry leaves are scarce, they can be fed on lettuce, though lettuce is not suitable for commercial purposes. They change their skins several times, until they reach a length of 6 or 7 cm. When they are ready to spin their cocoons, the yellow silk begins to show through their skins. The worms attach their cocoons to bunches of straw, twigs, or spirals of paper. When finished, the cocoons are about 4 cm long, and golden-yellow or sometimes pale green, light apricot, or white. Each cocoon consists of an outer case of coarse silk (called floss silk in commerce), and inside this is a closely woven sheet made from a continuous double thread of silk. The brown chrysalis lies inside the cocoon. Except for a few that are kept for breeding purposes, the pupae are killed inside the cocoon before the silk is wound off. Cocoons vary in their yield of silk from 450 metres of thread to nearly 2,000 metres.

Many moths belonging to the family Saturni-idae are also silk producers. The EMPEROR MOTH (q.v.) is the only British representative of this group, which includes such giants as the Atlas Moth (*see* Colour Plate opp. p. 64), the Tussore Silk Moth, the Indian Moon Moth with long sweeping tails to its wings, and the lovely North American Robin Moth. In contrast to the common silk moth, which is insignificant and of a plain creamy colour, the other large silk moths are strikingly beautiful, most of them having characteristic large eye-spots on their wings. Their caterpillars, too, are marked in brilliant colours and decorated in surprising profusion with bright tubercles, warts, and hairs. Although some of them are bred in captivity, notably the Tussore Silk Moth and the Chinese Oak Silkworm (which produces light buff shantung), none has ever reached anything like the commercial importance of the Chinese Mulberry Silkworm.

The silkworm of Greek and Roman times is a relative of the LACKEY MOTH (q.v.). It was cultivated in Persia for over 2,000 years before the introduction of these Chinese species.

See also Vol. VII: SILK INDUSTRY.

SILVERFISH. This insect is about 8 millimetres long, wingless, and covered with silvery-white scales. At the end of its body are three slender tails, from which the common name 'Bristle-tail' has arisen. The newly hatched insects look like their parents, except in size, and so are said to be without a METAMORPHOSIS (q.v.). They usually moult six times while they are growing up. Silverfish move with great speed, and are often seen skimming quickly over the floor as they make for cover. They are commonly found in old houses, especially in kitchens near bread-bins. A liking for starchy food may make them a nuisance in libraries, as they will attack the bindings of books for the sake of the paste.

SILVERFISH

The Firebrat is another species, often larger and with dark markings on top. It has similar habits, and is usually found in the warmth of fireplaces and ovens.

See also Vol. XI: HOUSEHOLD PESTS.

SILVER-Y MOTH, *see* NIGHT-FLYING MOTHS.

SISKIN, *see* FINCHES, Section 3.

SKATE, *see* SHARKS AND RAYS, Section 3.

SKELETON, *see* ANATOMY.

SKIN. This is the flexible covering of the body of the higher animals, from which may grow HAIR, FEATHERS, SCALES, HOOFS, NAILS AND CLAWS, and HORNS (qq.v.). (The hard external

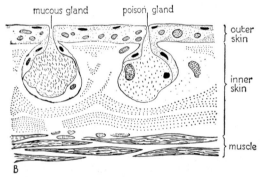

A. SECTION OF BODY WALL OF AN EARTHWORM
B. SECTION OF SKIN OF AN AMPHIBIAN (SALAMANDER)

skeleton of crustaceans, and the chitinous covering of insects are not, strictly speaking, skin.) In the lower invertebrate animals the skin is often only one cell thick and may have small movable projections or 'cilia' which help the animal to move and feed. In the higher animals the skin is not a single, simple covering, but consists of a number of layers, the outer of which is periodically renewed.

In some animals, notably the amphibia, RESPIRATION (q.v.) may take place through the skin. In mammals, the skin possesses sweat glands which help to keep the body at a constant temperature.

In some animals, the outer covering (fur, feathers) is moulted annually, or even more often, but in others the process is much more gradual, and less obvious.

See also Vol. XI: SKIN (Human).

SKIPPERS (BUTTERFLIES). These small insects, so called because of their habit of skipping swiftly from flower to flower, are traditionally regarded as butterflies, though they differ from true BUTTERFLIES (q.v.) in many respects, and are probably best classified by themselves. They have large heads, prominent eyes, and thick, often very hairy bodies. Their antennae are clubbed like those of butterflies, and sometimes hooked. Their rather small wings are usually brown, orange, black, or grey, with lighter or darker patterns. Some, e.g. the Dingy Skipper, rest with their wings sloping downwards, like moths; but most hold their hind-wings horizontally and tilt their fore-wings upwards. The Regent Skipper of Australia, more primitive than any other butterfly, has the front and hind-wings in the male coupled together by means of bristles, as have most moths. The simply-formed caterpillars of Skippers often feed on grasses, but also on some other plants such as irises, lilies, and palms. They shelter beneath silken webs or spun leaves, as do those of many moths, a few being stem-borers. The smooth, long-shaped pupa lies in a loosely spun cocoon—another difference from true butterflies which do not spin cocoons.

About 3,000 species are known, many of which are South American. Of the eight species breeding in Britain, four, the Dingy, Grizzled, Large, and Small Skippers, are quite common and fairly generally distributed. It has been recently discovered that the Chequered Skipper, long thought to be confined to a few Midland woods, has a darker and more greenish variety on the west coast of Scotland. The Lulworth Skipper is confined to parts of the Dorset and Devon coasts, and the Silver Spotted Skipper to

S. Beaufoy
SMALL SKIPPER ($\times 2$)

chalk or limestone country. The Essex Skipper occurs on both sides of the Thames and in the Fen district and Wiltshire.

SKUA, *see* GULLS, Section 5.

SKUNK, *see* WEASEL, Section 5.

SLATER, *see* WOODLOUSE.

SLAVE-MAKER ANT, *see* ANTS, HABITS OF.

SLOTH. This is a South American mammal, about the size of a fox-terrier, belonging to the same order as the ANT-EATERS (q.v.)—the Edentata—the members of which have no front teeth. Its name 'sloth' arose because its ungainly, slow, cautious movements give an impression of indolence. In fact, it is not particularly more slothful than any animal living in rather prescribed surroundings. It is found only in the tropical forests, where it lives high up in the trees, hanging upside-down from the branches, and never coming down to the ground except to pass from one tree to another. Its body is adapted for this kind of life: it has very long front legs, and its feet end in long, hook-like claws, by means of which it hangs from the branches.

Sloths have very thick coats of long, coarse, brownish-grey hair, which grows in the reverse direction from that of other animals, corresponding to their normal upside-down position. Their fine under-fur is striped brown and orange. The most extraordinary thing about their coats is that a microscopic plant grows in grooves on the longer hairs, giving the coat a greenish tinge. In consequence, the animals look very like the lichens which grow on the boughs of their native tropical forests; and when they go to sleep rolled up in a ball, their heads tucked between their arms, they look amazingly like the lichen-covered knots. This camouflage is, in fact, their only defence, for they are harmless, unaggressive animals.

Sloths live in pairs or in small families. They move and eat at night, living on leaves and fruit, which provide them with so much moisture that they do not need to seek water. The young are born singly, and the baby sloth clings to its mother's hair with its claws, its arms round her neck. There are two main types of sloth—those with three toes on the fore-feet, and those with

Zoological Society of London

THREE-TOED SLOTH OF SOUTH AMERICA

only two. Some prefer dry districts, and others those which are permanently flooded; but otherwise their habits are much the same.

SLOW-WORM. This legless lizard of England and Europe belongs to the family Anguidae. Because it has no limbs, it looks like a snake; but it is a true LIZARD (q.v.) with eye-lids, a fleshy tongue, ear-openings, and vertebrae of the lizard type. It has the vestiges of a pelvis, but no shoulder girdle. As in many other lizards, the tail is fragile; and if the creature is carelessly handled, it will be cast off—hence its scientific name *Anguis fragilis* (fragile snake). The tail can be regrown, but it has never the same length or appearance as before.

The Slow-worm is common in many parts of England and Scotland, being found on heaths, in open woods, and in gardens. On fine days it may be seen basking in the sun; but those looking for it will more often find it hiding under stones or fallen timber. It is easily caught, and has never been known to bite. It feeds mainly on worms and slugs, particularly the small white kind. The young are born alive in September, and are beautiful little creatures, striped lengthwise with gold or yellow on a black background. The adult is brown, with or without darker stripes, and sometimes with blue spots. When fully grown, it reaches a length of 36 cm, of which the tail forms about one-half.

The so-called Glass Snakes are members of

A. R. Thompson

FAMILY OF SLOW-WORMS
The young Slow-worm is about 6 weeks old

nary garden slugs, whose bodies always taper away to end in a slender tail. The Carnivorous Slug spends most of its time beneath the surface of the soil, where it hunts for worms, being able to elongate its body so as to enter their burrows. It also preys upon some of the caterpillars and beetle larvae which feed upon plant roots.

The Great Grey Slug, measuring about 15 cm in length, has a small oval shell, hidden beneath the mantle and covering the breathing apparatus. It usually keeps its spotted and yellowish-grey body fully stretched out when at rest, with the tail-end slightly curved towards the mantle. It often haunts larders and dairies, as it likes cream, milk, butter, and other animal food, while fresh green plants are distasteful to it. On the other hand, the Tree Slug, which to look at might easily be mistaken for a half-grown Great Grey, is totally different in habit, living chiefly among the branches of trees, particularly beech and walnut, and also frequenting lichen-covered rocks. It descends from one branch to another by means of a thread of slime secreted from its slime-glands.

In the slugs belonging to the genus *Arion*, which includes many garden and field pests, the shell is represented by a few disconnected granules of limy substance. Of these, a familiar example is the large Black Slug, which is by no means always black—brown, red, and yellow specimens being not at all uncommon, while even white ones are sometimes found. This slug grows to fully 13 cm in length, the red and dark-brown ones being really handsome creatures. They devour ripening fruit and tender vegetables, and, when green-food is scarce, eat almost anything they can find, from smaller slugs to dead birds and mice, and even stray pieces of damp paper. The smaller Garden Slug is all too common and familiar a native of our gardens, hiding away during the day-time under damp

the same family, being lizards, not snakes, in spite of their legless, snake-like form. They differ from snakes in having a deep fold of skin along the side of the body. Four species are known: one inhabits south-east Europe, two the Indo-Chinese region, and one North America. They live on small rodents, other lizards, and sometimes snakes.

See also LIZARDS.

SLUG. The land slugs are very similar in structure and habit to the land SNAILS (q.v.), and they are, in fact, probably descended from shell-bearing ancestors, although only a few species now develop a small single shell. While many species seriously damage crops and garden plants, others are harmless or even mildly beneficial, as they feed on their own vegetarian relatives, on worms, and insects. Some 600 species are known, of which nineteen are British.

One of the most interesting of the British species is the Carnivorous Slug, which is about 8 centimetres long, and has a small oval shell at the hind end of the body. It is yellowish-brown, and at once attracts attention by the shape of its body, slender in the fore-part and increasing in girth behind—exactly the reverse shape of ordi-

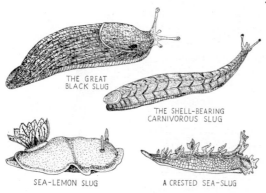

THE GREAT BLACK SLUG

THE SHELL-BEARING CARNIVOROUS SLUG

SEA-LEMON SLUG

A CRESTED SEA-SLUG

stones or boards and garden rubbish, and coming forth as night descends to start upon its nocturnal raids among the garden crops and flowers (*see* Pests and Diseases, Vol. VI).

The Sea slugs are very different in appearance and resemble the Sea snails in structure (*see* Snail, section 4). Some Sea slugs have rows of plume-like papillae arranged along their backs, and the majority are truly elegant creatures, their varied shapes and soft lovely colours in some cases being protective, and in others conspicuous and warning (*see* Protective Coloration). Some feed entirely upon seaweeds; while others are more or less flesh-eating, browsing upon living sponges, hydroids, sea-anemones, and corals. Some frequent the deep rock-pools exposed at low tide, and shallow waters offshore; while some, such as the Gulfweed Sea-slug, are found only in the open sea, where they live on floating seaweeds. A familiar British Sea slug is the Sea-lemon Slug, which both in colour and shape is rather like a lemon that has been cut in half lengthways. At one end of its body it has a pair of ear-like tentacles, and at the opposite end a circlet of plume-like gills, which can be withdrawn into a special body-chamber. It is found near low-tide mark, feeding upon living sponges.

See also Molluscs.

SMELL, *see* Senses, Section 6.

SMOOTH SNAKE. This is the rarest of the three British snakes—indeed not many people in England have ever seen it. It is restricted to the heather country of the south, particularly that of Hampshire and Dorset. It can be distinguished from the Adder (q.v.), which in general appearance it resembles most, by its more slender body,

and the absence of a defined neck. Its colour is different, also, being grey or reddish above, with dark-brown or black transverse bars or paired spots, and no zigzag marks. The belly is brown, grey, or reddish, either uniform, or speckled with black. The pupil of the eye is round, instead of slit-like as in the Adder. It grows to a length of 60 cm. The Smooth Snake feeds mainly upon lizards and slow-worms, but will also eat small mammals, which it kills by constriction—for it is not poisonous. It will bite when first caught, but is easily tamed and can be trained to feed from the hand, and, for a snake, shows much intelligence. It is widely distributed over Europe, but was not recorded in England until 1859.

Related to the Smooth Snake is the beautiful Leopard Snake of southern Europe. The particular colour-variety from which it derives its name is greyish or pale brown above, with a series of large, dark brown or bright red spots with black edges, arranged transversely with the smaller ones on the sides of the body. Underneath it is white chequered with black, or nearly all black. This snake, which is nearly a metre long, feeds on small creatures, which it kills by crushing them in its coils.

SNAIL. **1.** There are hundreds of different kinds of snails to be found on land, in fresh water, and in the sea. All possess a well-developed head, which usually bears a pair of small eyes, and one or two pairs of horns, or tentacles, which can be pushed out or withdrawn. Inside the mouth, there is a rasping tongue-ribbon, or 'radula', for breaking down the plant or animal matter upon which these molluscs feed. The spiral shell is secreted by glands on a part of the body called the 'mantle', the fleshy folds of which are also arranged to form a chamber containing the breathing organs. In many of the marine species the hind end of the foot carries a structure called the 'operculum', which forms a perfectly fitting lid when the animal retires within its shell. It is a permanent structure, and increases in size as the snail grows. Most land snails have no operculum; but in late autumn, when about to retire for their winter sleep, they secrete from their foot-glands a temporary lid, composed of a mixture of hardened slime and lime, which closes the mouth of the shell and shuts out the winter cold. When they awaken in early spring, this temporary door is moistened from within and dissolves away. The land snails generally lay eggs. In some species these are enclosed in hard shells, and the young, on hatching out, are already completely formed, only differing from their parents in size. The majority of marine snails, however, pass through a larval stage, and at first are totally unlike their parents in appearance, being minute oval creatures, with a girdle of fine hair-like cilia which, by rhythmical lashing movements, enable them to swim about.

2. LAND SNAILS. The different species of land snails have become accustomed to live under the most varied conditions, so that there are few places, from the ice-bound lands of the Arctic and Antarctic to the humid swamps and sun-scorched deserts of the tropics, where some kind of snail is not found. Because of their nocturnal habits, however, they are apt to escape notice, for most of them have their regular hiding-places, to which they return after their nightly foray, and there, safely hidden from view, they sleep away the hours of daylight. They vary greatly in size, and many possess beautifully coloured shells. Our two largest British species are the common Garden Snail and the Edible or so-called Roman Snail, which was cultured by the Romans for their kitchens in special 'nurseries'. It can be found in the chalk and limestone hills of southern England. It has a large handsome shell, usually creamy-white, marked with three to five spiral bands of a pale-brownish tint.

In South America, the West Indies, and Tropical Africa, there are giant land snails with shells measuring over 15 centimetres long. Many of these giant snails live in the forest trees, and some lay hard-shelled eggs nearly as large as those of a pigeon.

3. FRESHWATER SNAILS. These abound in rivers, ponds, and lakes all over the world. Two of the British species must be familiar to anyone who has gone pond-hunting or kept an aquarium—the Great Pond Snail, which has a large greyish or yellow-brown spiral shell, and the Ramshorn Snail, which has the whorls of its reddish-brown shell coiled in the same

GREAT POND SNAIL

plane, and measures about 2·5 centimetres in diameter. Several species serve as the intermediate hosts for parasitic worms which cause various diseases in cattle, sheep, horses, and man.

4. SEA SNAILS. Strictly speaking, the term 'Snail' should not be applied indiscriminately to the hosts of marine molluscs possessing spiral-shaped shells, for many of them are quite unlike the land snails both in structure and appearance, while all are 'water-breathers', obtaining their supplies of oxygen from the water bathing their gills. The round-mouthed sea snails most nearly approach the true land snails. They are nearly all vegetarians, and are therefore found only between tide-marks on shore, and in the shallow waters off-shore where seaweeds abound. Familiar examples are the Periwinkles, which in many ways resemble their cousins, the true, air-breathing land snails. Indeed, one species, the Rough Periwinkle, prefers to be out of the water for long periods at a time, and lives so far up the shore that even at the highest tides it is not completely immersed in water. In contrast to the dull-coloured common Periwinkle, there are some members of the family with yellow, red, white, orange, or pale-green shells of smaller size and smoother surface. Another familiar family of sea snails is the Top-shells, to be found feeding on the seaweeds in the rock-pools. Their shells are cone-shaped, something like a peg-top, and, in the British Painted Top-shell, are creamy flesh-coloured, with deeper pink or red wavy markings, the animal itself being bright ruddy-brown, with long and slender pinkish horns.

See also MOLLUSCS.

T. Huxley

GARDEN SNAILS

SNAKES. These are reptiles of the order Squamata, which includes also the LIZARDS (q.v.). Many lizards with elongated bodies and no limbs, such as the SLOW-WORM (q.v.), look like snakes; but snakes have certain characteristics which, when taken together, will always distinguish them. The eyes of snakes are without lids, the eyeball being covered with a transparent skin shaped like a watch-glass; there is no ear opening; the body is greatly elongated and is without limbs, except in some of the BOAS (q.v.) and other primitive snakes, in which there are tiny vestiges of a hind pair protruding from the body on each side of the vent; the tongue is long, deeply forked, and can be drawn back into a sheath.

Altogether, some 2,500 species of snake are known. They are found all over the world except in Polar regions. Some, for example the English snakes, live in fields, woods, and on heaths; some live in the desert, others in the thickest jungle; some pass their lives in fresh water; while the SEA SNAKES (q.v.), with one exception, live in the sea. Some live on the ground; others, such as the Cat Snakes of south-west Asia and north Africa, live in trees; others again, such as the Blind Snakes, spend their lives underground, and have bodies adapted for this life. Snakes are most numerous in tropical countries, and those that live in temperate climates spend the cold months in a state of torpor. They have been found in the Himalayas and in the Andes at heights of 3,000 metres.

Scientifically, the snakes are divided into eleven families, three of which are poisonous and eight non-poisonous. The non-poisonous can be divided again into the Solid-toothed Snakes, which are harmless, and the Back-fanged Snakes, whose bite is poisonous to the creatures they feed on, but hardly ever to man. The division between these two groups is, however, not clearly defined. The Back-fanged Snakes are so called

Zoological Society of London

KING COBRA

because the back teeth of the upper jaw are enlarged and grooved to carry the venom, which comes from a special gland, originally part of the upper labial gland. The majority of non-poisonous snakes belong to the family Colubridae. It is by far the largest of the families, including some two-thirds of all the snakes known. The three families of poisonous snakes are as follows: the Elapidae, which include the COBRAS and KRAITS; the SEA SNAKES (Hydrophiidae); and the VIPERS (Viperidae) (qq.v.).

The ability of snakes to swallow food much exceeding their own girth is well known. This is possible because the bones of the jaws are only loosely attached to the skull and to one another, and are freely movable. The size of some of the objects devoured by snakes is almost incredible. The Egg-eating Snake of Africa, with a neck no thicker than the little finger, can swallow a fowl's egg. It has a mouth and gullet specially modified, so that when the snake's mouth closes over the egg, the muscles of the gullet contract, and small teeth in the neck break the shell. The snake then swallows the contents and ejects the fragments of shell. A python in Australia has been known to devour a kangaroo, and an Indian python, a leopard. Some snakes kill their prey by constriction—that is, by squeezing them in their coils so that they suffocate, no bones being broken in the process. To help them in swallowing their enormous meals, most snakes are well provided with salivary glands, from which the saliva is poured out during the process of swallowing—they do not lick their food all over before starting a meal, as is often stated.

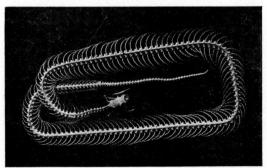

By permission of the Trustees of the British Museum (Nat. Hist.)

SKELETON OF A SNAKE

YOUNG PYTHON SWALLOWING A MOUSE

Douglas Fisher

All snakes are flesh-eaters. The Milk Snake of eastern North America, and some other snakes, are accused by farmers of sucking the milk from cows; but it is doubtful if any snake could do this, even if it wanted to.

The tongue of a snake is an organ of touch and smell, and when it is seen flickering, in the way we know so well, it is collecting scent particles which are then passed on to the organ of scent, a structure lying above the palate, close to the nostril. From there the sensation passes by means of a thick bundle of nerve fibres to that part of the brain concerned with the sense of smell.

All snakes are covered with SCALES (q.v.), which on the head are large and usually regular in shape and position, but on the body are smaller, and vary in shape, numbers, and arrangement. The number of scale-rows on the body is a valuable means of identification. The scales on the belly, known as 'ventral shields', are broad—in most species nearly as broad as the body. Only in the Sea Snakes and some burrowing snakes—Blind Snakes, for example—are they absent or very small. The Wart Snake, which lives in brackish waters in Malaya, has small, hard, rough scales and no proper ventral shields, so that it is almost helpless on land. There are two kinds of viper—the Rattlesnake of North America, and the Viper of south-western Asia—both known as Side-winders, for they are able to travel in a sideways as well as in a forward direction. They do this particularly when trying to escape. Some snakes are known as Flying Snakes—and the term is not entirely incorrect. No snake can fly in the real sense of the word; but some can plane through the air from a higher to a lower altitude, in the same way as the Flying Frog, the Flying Lizard, and the Flying Squirrel (*see* FLIGHT). The snakes known to be able to do this are the Golden Tree

Snake and the Painted Bronze-back, two well-known snakes of the East. In 'flight', the scales of the belly are contracted to produce a concave surface, the body is straightened and made rigid, and the creature planes through the air at a steep angle.

The largest snakes in the world are the Pythons and the Boas, both of which are known to reach 9 metres in length; the smallest, the burrowing snakes *Typhlops* and *Leptotyphlops*, are only a few centimetres. Most snakes lay eggs; but a few produce their young alive. All embryo (unhatched) snakes are provided with an egg-tooth to enable them to break the 'shell', which is of whitish, parchment-like skin, containing only a small amount of lime.

There are some 600 species of poisonous snakes, of which about 150 carry a poison strong enough to kill a man. The poison of snakes is injected into their victims through specialized teeth, known as fangs. These convey the venom from the poison gland (a modification of the salivary gland) either through a tube or along a groove in the fang. To provide an antidote to snake-bite, snakes are kept in captivity, and the venom is periodically extracted, to be used in the making of anti-venine. The first 'snake park' was opened at São Paulo, Brazil; and there are now others at Johannesburg and Port Elizabeth in South Africa, at Kasauli in India, at Nha-Trong in Indo-China, and at Bangkok in Thailand. The snakes are kept in open-air enclosures, provided with shelters or retreats, into which they can retire during the day-time. Periodically they are 'milked' by pressing on the venom gland so that the venom is discharged into a small dish. When dried, it becomes crystalline, and in that state will remain unchanged for years. Venom kept for 40 years has been shown experimentally to be just as active as when fresh.

The distribution of snakes is interesting. There are no snakes in Ireland (from where, according to the legend, they were cast out by St. Patrick), or in New Zealand. There are no poisonous snakes in Madagascar. The majority of the snakes in Australia are poisonous, the most deadly being the Elapid known as the 'death adder'; but there are no Cobras, Kraits, or Vipers there. There are no Elapid snakes in Europe, where the only poisonous snakes are the Vipers. In Britain there are only three Snakes: the GRASS SNAKE, the SMOOTH SNAKE, and the poisonous ADDER (qq.v.).

SNIPE, *see* WADING BIRDS, Section 4.

SOLAN GOOSE, *see* GANNET.

SOLE, *see* FLATFISHES.

SONG, *see* ANIMAL LANGUAGE.

SPARROW. This name has been given to many small brown birds, including the Hedge Sparrow, which is not a sparrow at all (*see* THRUSH). It belongs properly to a group of thick-billed, finch-like birds, of which the House Sparrow is a typical example. Sparrows are natives of almost every part of the Old World, but not Australasia. They were, unfortunately, introduced into America, because it was hoped that they would keep down noxious insects—but they are so much more seed-eaters than insect-eaters that any good they may do is far outweighed by their depredations on seeds and grain-crops. They increase in numbers very fast, for they generally produce three broods in a season. They build rather untidy nests, generally placed in some part of a building. Occasionally they build in a hedge or tree, and then they construct a dome to protect the nest from the weather. Sparrows are very particular to keep their plumage in good order, not only taking frequent water-baths, but also, in summer, enjoying dust-baths.

Another species, the Tree Sparrow, found locally in Britain, is much less inclined to frequent human habitations. It is rather differently marked, having a chestnut crown and black patches on the cheek. In the Mediterranean countries the Spanish Sparrows are serious pests. They nest in very closely packed and noisy colonies. In South Africa the Black-breasted Sparrow, in West Africa the Grey-headed Sparrow, and in Arabia the Golden Sparrow are the common species.

See also FINCHES.

SPIDERS. These are not insects: they form the largest and most widely distributed order of the class of animals called Arachnida, which also includes the SCORPIONS, HARVESTMEN, FALSE SCORPIONS, MITES AND TICKS (qq.v.), as well as the marine King-crabs and several less important creatures only to be found in the tropics. The bodies of all these animals are in two parts: in front, the head and chest closely joined, forming the cephalothorax, and behind, the abdomen. They have a pair of jaws, a pair of 'pedipalps', or pincer claws, and four pairs of legs, all of which are attached to the cephalothorax. These features, and their lack of antennae, distinguish the Arachnida from INSECTS (q.v.). Spiders secrete silk through tubular spinnerets, usually six in number, placed at the tip of the abdomen. They use the silk for a variety of purposes, the most characteristic being the spinning of a web to ensnare their prey.

DIAGRAM OF A SPIDER

Not all spiders spin webs: many hunt for their food in quite an ordinary way, usually at night. Others have developed particular habits, usually shared by all members of a family, which help them in hunting. For example, the Wolf Spiders—the small brown spiders so common in woods and pastures from spring to autumn—run fast enough to pursue their quarry and overtake it. Crab-spiders lurk among fallen leaves and pounce unexpectedly upon their victims. Their popular name is descriptive, for they are flattened in form, with crab-like legs, and a habit of darting sideways. A few of them lie hidden in flowers, and seize the butterflies and other insects which alight on the petals. Jumping-spiders have better eyesight than other spiders; they stalk their quarry, approach-

WOLF SPIDER

ZEBRA SPIDER

ing it stealthily until near enough to leap upon it. The little Zebra Spider, common all over Britain, is often to be seen hunting on walls and fences in bright sunshine. It has a habit, common to all spiders, of trailing behind it a drag-line of silk, fastened at intervals. If the spider misses its footing, the drag-line, like a mountaineer's rope, saves it from falling to the ground.

The drag-line habit is important, because it suggests a possible explanation of how spiders first started to make webs; and the web is interesting because it is almost the only trap constructed by any animal. If a spider continued to use the same hiding-place, the approaches to it must soon have become coated with threads of silk—and as soon as the spider had learnt that the trembling of these threads gave notice of the passing of an insect, the 'web-idea' had come into being (see INTELLIGENCE). The webs of the most primitive spiders do, in fact, consist of a roughly circular mat surrounding a hole, in which the spider waits: the rough, bluish-looking webs, to be seen, for instance, in the corners of windows, are familiar examples of this primitive type of web. The spider will obviously catch more if he extends the area of the 'mat'; and the house-spiders, which spin 'cobwebs' in the corners of our rooms, illustrate this development. The spider lives in a silk tube, the trap part of the web being a hammock-like sheet, sometimes—as in the space between two rafters of a shed roof—of a great size. The web-forms which evolved from this are often seen in hedges and on bushes.

Most of the small spiders of Europe belong to the family Linyphiidae, which includes the 'Money-spiders'. These do not use the tubular shelter, but hang themselves upside-down under a sheet or hammock—a characteristic which makes the family easily recognizable. Above the sheet is a supporting maze of threads, which checks the flight of insects and throws them down on to the sheet beneath. The spider seizes them from below and drags them through it. A family of small, brightly coloured spiders, known as Theridiidae, use the superstructure without the sheet for their irregularly tangled webs. Lastly, the perfection of web-spinning is found in the cart-wheel, or orb-web, spun by the Garden Spider, and other members of its family, Argyopidae. This has been so successful that it is found all over the world, sometimes reaching a large size.

In addition to all these there are spiders, not

THREATENING DISPLAY IN REPTILES

Above: Frilled Lizard of Northern Australia erecting its frill in defiance
Below: The Red-tailed Pipe Snake of S.E. Asia rearing its tail and showing red in warning

to be found in Britain, which dig a hole in the ground, line it with silk, and close it with a silk trap-door, covered with earth and other materials so that it exactly resembles its surroundings. These Trap-door Spiders include the largest species known, and are sometimes misnamed Tarantulas. Some are also called Bird-eating Spiders, for they are able to attack and consume small humming-birds. Ordinarily, however, spiders eat insects; and the stories told of their killing mice, snakes, and fish are either chance occurrences, or are records of the special habits of peculiar species.

It is clear that, to be able to detect their prey by the vibrations of the threads of their silk webs, spiders must have an extremely delicate sense of touch—as indeed they have. Their bodies and legs are covered with hair-like 'setae', many of which are perhaps merely protective, but some of which are certainly sensitive organs of touch. The finest of them are believed to respond to the air-waves which convey sound, and to provide the spider with its only means of 'hearing'. There are organs on the legs which appear to detect scents; but, on the whole, a spider leads a life in which almost every sensation is of touch, every event a vibration.

Among the most remarkable of spiders' habits are their peculiar methods of courtship, different in different families. The male Jumping-spider performs a kind of dance in front of the watching female; the Wolf Spider waves his decorated forelegs in front of her; the male Grab-spider climbs upon the female and tickles her; and the Web-spider drums on the sheet of the web or tweaks its threads. The result of these peculiar actions of the male spider is to suppress the female's usual inclination to leap upon, kill, and eat any moving creature that approaches her. Hence a male, as soon as he begins his courtship, is comparatively safe, and often he lulls the female into a passive trance. After mating, he usually escapes at his best speed. The popular belief that female spiders always eat their mates is an exaggeration; but it sometimes happens towards the end of autumn, when the females are likely to be hungry and the males less active.

All spiders start life as eggs, usually laid in masses in a silk cocoon. Generally, the female pays little attention to her cocoon after it is completed; but the female Wolf Spider fastens her cocoon to her spinneret and drags it about

Mustograph

TRAP-DOOR SPIDER

with her. Newly hatched Wolf Spiders ride for a time on their mother's abdomen. Spiders do not go through a larval stage, as do most insects, but resemble their parents when they hatch. They grow by periodic castings of their skins, and the sex of a spider is usually impossible to tell until it is mature.

When spiders bite they paralyse their victims with poison secreted from glands in their jaws. The venom has an effect on such small animals as mice, moles, or sparrows; but only a few spiders, and no British spiders, are dangerous to man. The largest spiders are not the most dangerous: the most poisonous spiders are the American 'Black Widow' and its relatives in other countries (*see also* TARANTULA).

The well-known phenomenon 'gossamer' is produced by young spiders of many species, and adults of a few, in their peculiar method of MIGRATION (q.v.). When the weather is suitable, they climb up fences and railings, turn their heads towards the wind, raise their abdomens, and exude silk. The drop of silk is drawn out by the breeze into a long thread, and when sufficient buoyancy is

BLACK WIDOW

T. Huxley

CRAB SPIDER ATTACKING A BEETLE

attained, the spider lets go and drifts away. These aerial journeys may reach heights of a thousand metres or more, and cover distances of hundreds of kilometres. Similar to this, but nothing to do with migration, is the rarer 'rain of wool'. Sometimes a sudden rise of temperature stimulates the many thousands of spiders on the ground to secrete silk, and the earth becomes carpeted with a sheet of silk. Rising currents tear this, and pieces are borne into the air—but not carrying spiders.

There are about 22,000 different species of spiders, of which about 500 are British. The largest are found in central America, and have a body-length of about 9 centimetres: the smallest species are less than a millimetre long.

SPIROGYRA, *see* ALGAE.

SPONGE. This animal holds a peculiarly isolated position in the animal kingdom; for its exact relationship to other forms of animal life is very obscure, and there are many problems concerning its daily life and reactions that remain to be solved. Indeed, although a few species grow to a great size—for example, the Neptune's Cup Sponges which reach nearly a metre high—they appear in many respects to be most nearly allied to those microscopic single-celled animals known as collared-monads, which belong to the simplest forms of animal life, the PROTOZOA (q.v.).

Some sponges, such as the common Bath Sponge, build a skeleton of horny fibres, others a more elaborate skeleton of silica or of calcium carbonate. Scattered over the entire surface of a sponge, in addition to the easily recognized large holes or oscules, are thousands of tiny pores, opening into equally minute canals, which branch and pierce the tissues of the sponge in all directions. Each fine division of the branching canals ends in a spherical chamber, the walls of which are lined with special collared cells. These cells carry a protoplasmic collar or funnel, with a whip-like 'flagellum' or slender outgrowth, springing from the base inside the collar. By the lashing of the flagella of hundreds of thousands of collared cells, a continuous flow of water is drawn through the body of the sponge, entering at the pores and leaving by the oscule, bringing food and oxygen, and carrying away waste matter. The collared cells engulf tiny food particles brought in with the current. At intervals groups of cells form buds, with the flagella on the outside. The buds swim to a new place, settle, and grow into another sponge.

It is possible, by squeezing a living sponge enclosed in a piece of very fine silk, to separate the tissues into their component cells, and to observe under the microscope their movements in a small glass dish filled with sea-water. The separate living cells are seen for a time to move about freely, but gradually to draw together until they form a little mass, which is the beginning of a new sponge. Because of the behaviour of its cells, a living sponge must be regarded, not so much as a single individual, but rather as a colony of cells, in which each cell is more or less

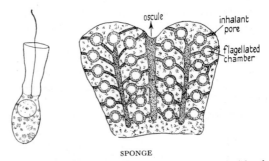

SPONGE

Left, Collared cell (each flagellated chamber is lined with collared cells). *Right*, Section of a sponge showing canal system

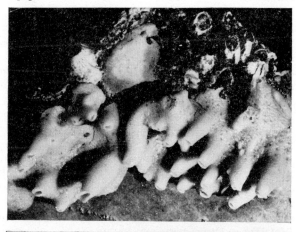

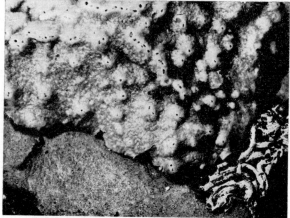

M. Burton

THE THREE COMMON BRITISH SPONGES

Left, The Purse Sponge growing on seaweed; *Top right*, The Crumb-of-bread Sponge growing on rock; *Bottom right*, *Hymeniacidon sanguinea*—a brick-red or tan sponge, growing on rocks

independent of the rest, and is capable of changing its form and function as occasion may demand—and yet as one in which a bond of union exists, so that all work together to make one harmonious whole. No less wonderful are the skeletons built up by certain of the sponge cells. The spicules from which they are formed are composed of silica, or of calcium carbonate, extracted from the water which passes through the canals. These take on the most beautiful and varied shapes, such as slender needles, stars, forks, or anchors, mostly microscopic in size, though in some species they are several centimetres, and in one species nearly a metre long.

Sponges are divided into the following four orders: (1) the Calcarea, which have spicules of calcium carbonate, and are found mostly in shallow seas; (2) the Hexactinellida, which have skeletons composed of six-rayed spicules of silica, and are mostly deep-sea forms. They include the beautiful Venus's Flower-basket, the Glass-rope Sponge, and the curious Single-stem Sponge, which has one great spicule, about a metre in length, standing erect with its base buried in the mud, and the sponge itself embracing it at the middle; (3) the Tetraxonida, which have four-rayed spicules of silica. They include the common Crumb-of-bread Sponge, which grows in green or yellowish-white masses on rocks, seaweeds, and shells, between mid and low-water mark all round our coasts; the large goblet-shaped Neptune's Cup Sponges from the warm sea around the coasts of the Indonesian islands; and also the Freshwater Sponges, which form greenish, slimy masses on lock-gates; and the burrowing Cliona Sponge, which is a shell-boring pest of the Oyster; (4) the Keratosa or Horny-skeletoned Sponges, which include the Bath Sponge and other commercial sponges, all possessing skeletons composed of a network of spongin-fibres, and chiefly obtained from the eastern Mediterranean and the West Indies.

SPOON-BILL, *see* STORK.

SPORES, *see* REPRODUCTION IN PLANTS, Section 3.

SPRAT, *see* HERRING.

SPRINGBOK, *see* ANTELOPE.

SQUID, *see* CUTTLEFISH AND SQUIDS.

SQUIRREL. This RODENT (q.v.) belongs to a sub-family of the large family Sciuridae, the other sub-family of which includes the MARMOTS (q.v.). Squirrels are found in wooded districts of most parts of the world, except Madagascar and Australia. They range in size from as small as a mouse (Borneo and West Africa) to as large as a cat (Malaya), and in colour from bright

RED SQUIRREL

Mansell Coll.

chestnut-red to deep, blackish-grey or clear, pale grey. There are some very beautiful striped species in tropical countries, among the commonest of which are the little Indian Palm Squirrels, to be seen in large numbers running about most Indian villages. In general, they have slender, agile bodies, long, bushy tails, well-developed, pointed ears, and feet adapted for climbing. They mostly live in trees, leaping from branch to branch and running down the trunks head-first; the heavier-built tropical squirrels are less arboreal. Squirrels are among the most thrifty of animals, and are for ever storing food away for future consumption. They make holes in the ground to hold hundreds of nuts—though they often forget where their stores are. They sleep with their heads covered by their tails. Although they can swim well, they do not much care for water.

In the British Isles, there are both red and grey squirrels. The native Red Squirrel used to be much more numerous than it is now; but its numbers have been reduced by epidemic diseases, and it is being replaced in many districts, particularly in southern England, by the more robust American Grey Squirrel, which was introduced into England at the end of the last century. The Red Squirrel changes colour a good deal during the year, owing to two moults, one in October and another in May. Its tail starts dark, but gradually bleaches and thins through the year. Squirrels are very active during the day; but, being timid, they usually dart behind a trunk and climb up the far side of a tree at the sight of a human being. When they are scared, they scold and chatter. They eat acorns, beech-mast, haws, bark, fungi, fruit, seeds, and, very rarely, eggs and young birds. They sit up to eat, holding their food in their hands, and wasting a good deal of it. In autumn they spend a lot of time on the ground, picking up food to be stored for the winter. In very cold climates Red Squirrels hibernate for some of the winter; but in England they take only a few long sleeps. At the mating season in early spring, the males fight amongst themselves; but by February or March both sexes are busy building nests, called 'dreys', of sticks, bark, and moss. They usually make these in conifers or in hollows in other trees, sometimes using as a foundation an old crow's, sparrow-hawk's, or wood-pigeon's nest. The nests, unlike most birds'-nests, have roofs and side entrances, like those of magpies.

John Markham
GREY SQUIRREL

tree to another. As they always lose height when they glide, they have to climb to a considerable height before attempting to fly to the lower branches of the next tree. They are very playful creatures, delighting in racing up and down the trees and chasing each other about.

STABLE-FLY. This bloodsucking insect, sometimes called the Biting House-fly, is common in most country places throughout the summer. It frequents outbuildings on farms, and also comes into houses. Both male and female Stable-flies suck blood from horses, cattle, dogs, and occasionally human beings. The Stable-fly can easily be distinguished from the HOUSE-FLY (q.v.) by its proboscis, which is elongate, rigid, and cannot be drawn back. It breeds chiefly in horse manure, and completes its development from egg to adult in from 3 to 4 weeks.

STAG BEETLE. About the largest beetle found in the British Isles, and the most remarkable in its appearance, is the common Stag Beetle, *Lucanus cervus*. It is not known in the north, but is quite common round London. Its larvae, which take 3 years to reach maturity, feed upon old decaying tree-stumps or at the base of rotting posts. The beetles emerge to fly about in early summer; but their adult life lasts only for

Additional nests are built close by, so that the young can be transferred to them in case of danger. As a rule two or three young are born, naked and blind, in March or April, with often a second litter in August.

Grey Squirrels (sometimes called tree-rats) are larger than Red Squirrels. They cause a great deal of destruction by eating buds and young shoots, and by stripping the bark off deciduous trees. They tear off ripe and unripe fruit in gardens, and also eat grain, nuts, seeds, young birds or rabbits, and carrion. In consequence, farmers kill them whenever they can. Unlike Red Squirrels, Grey Squirrels usually live in deciduous woodland, and in the autumn often leave the woods for hedgerows and fields. Their nests, which are domed, with hidden entrances at the side, are usually built in deciduous trees. The first litter of young is born between March and May, and a second litter appears in June or July, with possibly a third in August or September. The parents turn their young out of their nest before the coming of the winter.

Flying Squirrels, most of which belong to south-east Asia, have flaps of skin joining their limbs so as to form a parachute, by means of which they can glide up to 60 metres from one

British Museum (Nat. Hist.)
THE COMMON STAG BEETLE, MALE AND FEMALE

a few weeks. The enormous, antler-like horns, peculiar to the male, are really its jaws. The females are so unlike the males that they were once thought to be quite different insects. Their small jaws are really more useful instruments than the formidable-looking horns of the male. Four different kinds of Stag Beetle occur in Britain, all of them passing their early stages in rotting wood. In the whole world nearly 1,000 kinds are known.

See also BEETLES.

STARFISH. The common Five-armed Starfish may be found in the rock pools or stranded on the sands near low-tide mark on most shores round British coasts, and must be one of the most familiar members of that great and remarkable division of the animal kingdom, the Echinodermata, or spiny-skinned animals, which also includes the SEA-CUCUMBERS and SEA-URCHINS (qq.v.). The body is disk-shaped, and from it grow out five symmetrically arranged arms, which gradually taper to their blunt-pointed ends. The upper surfaces of both the body and arms are pink, red, or purple. If the starfish is turned over on to its back, it is possible to see the mouth, from which radiate five narrow grooves, one along each arm. These grooves are crowded throughout their length with tubular bodies with sucker-like ends—the tube-feet, by means of which the starfish creeps about and also grasps its prey. The tenacity with which these tube-feet can adhere to any object is remarkable. The whole of the Starfish's body wall is supported by a network of somewhat rod-like plates embedded in the tough skin, forming a partial skeleton; while scattered over both the upper and under surfaces are numerous very minute, pincer-like organs, which keep the surface of the body clean by grasping any minute organisms or floating particles that otherwise would settle on the skin. The mouth is very elastic: the degree to which it can be stretched to take in some extra large object is quite remarkable.

The sex of the starfish is difficult to discern without dissecting the animal. At the spawning period, the female liberates a great mass of minute eggs into the sea, where they are fertilized by the sperm of the male. From the egg develops a larva, quite unlike the parent. After some weeks of free swimming, the larva fixes itself to a rock or seaweed by little sucker-like disks at its front end, and then undergoes a METAMORPHOSIS (q.v.), transforming its body into that of a baby starfish, with the five-ray shape.

Of the many other species of true starfishes to be found in British waters, it is possible here to mention only one or two of the more interesting. The Lingthorn, a large and handsome starfish with five to seven long, flat, and rather slender arms, is fairly abundant in shallow waters offshore. It has a habit of parting rather readily with one or more of its arms when in danger, or if roughly handled during capture. This violent dismemberment is common among starfishes, though it happens to some more easily than to others. The loss of one or two arms causes only temporary inconvenience, as new limbs are gradually grown. The Rosy Cribrella is a fine rosy-red, and has five rounded, tapering arms with narrow grooves on their under-surface, the tube-feet being arranged in two rows. Very handsome and striking in appearance is the common Sun-starfish, so named because of its resemblance to the conventional drawings of the sun seen on such places as the sign-boards of ancient country inns. It varies a good deal in colour from the typical fine orange-red to a somewhat purplish-red tint. The arms are quite short and stout, and number from eight to sixteen. The common Cushion-starfish, found on the south, west, and northern coasts of England, has such short arms that the starfish really looks like a small five-cornered cushion, bright red, yellowish-white, or mottled. The Bird's-foot Starfish, another of our British Cushion-starfishes, is thin and flat, and the narrow deeply set grooves spreading across the under-surface help to intensify its resemblance to the webbed foot of a wading bird.

The beautiful Brittle Stars all have small, disk-like bodies and long slender arms composed of a number of joints. The common Brittle Star is one of the handsomest of our British species. The upper surface of the body-disk is covered with short spines, except for five pairs of bare, almost wedge-shaped plates, standing out in marked contrast to the darker portions of the body, which may be rose-red with grey scales, white spotted with red, or brown with ruddy markings. The long arms are covered with stout, short spines growing out at right angles, and the animals move about by snake-like movements of these arms. The Sand Stars have very short

M. Burton

THE SUN-STARFISH

M. Burton

A BRITTLE STAR

spines, lying close to the sides of the slender arms and making each look like the tapering end of a lizard's tail. The remarkable Gorgon-head Brittle Stars are the largest of Brittle Stars, and their long, slender arms repeatedly fork so as to form a regular crown of interlacing branches. The giant Arctic species measures more than 30 cm from tip to tip of its many-branched, out-stretched arms.

The Feather Stars and the Stalked Crinoids or Sea-lilies are so distinctive in character as to be placed in a separate division, called the Crinozoa—literally, lily-like animals. Instead of crawling about mouth downwards by the aid of their tube-feet, like all the starfishes, they remain more or less permanently fixed in one spot, mouth upwards, the Sea-lilies growing on long, slender stalks, and the graceful Feather Stars being anchored by little clawed hooks to seaweeds and stones. They are the only living representatives of a great group which swarmed in the seas of past geological ages. The Rosy Feather Star is not uncommon in shallow water off British coasts. It has a small disk-shaped body, from which arise five arms, each divided almost at its base into two—giving the little starfish the appearance of possessing ten slender rays. From the middle of the back of the body-disk arise the

M. Burton

COMMON STARFISH (*Asterias rubens*) SHOWING STAGES IN
THE REGENERATION OF THE ARMS

clawed hooks, by means of which the creature anchors itself to the weed or stone upon which it rests.

The stalked Crinoids or Sea-lilies are all cup-shaped animals with slender branching arms; they grow on long jointed stems, permanently attached to some suitable base on the floor of the sea. They are found in most parts of the world, but mostly live at considerable depths.

STARLING. Until the second part of last century, the Starling was not a common British bird; but it has increased enormously of late, and is now found in large numbers in all parts of the country, even more migrating from northern and central Europe to winter in Britain. Although flocks of Starlings do great damage to fruit-orchards, as a whole the Starling is a useful bird, for it destroys the larvae of harmful insects. It not only searches assiduously for grubs in the grass and earth, but it also picks parasites off the backs of sheep. One species of African Starling, the Oxpeckers, feed mainly on the ticks which they peck from the backs of animals—cattle, elephants, rhinoceroses, and antelopes; and they have feet provided with sharp, curved claws which enable them to keep their hold on the animals' backs.

From a distance the common Starling appears to be a dull, black bird; but observed closely, in the sunlight, its dark plumage is seen to be shot with brilliant greens and purples, and spotted with buff. It has a song of its own, heard all the year round; but it is a very good mimic, also, imitating not only the songs of other birds, but any other sound which has caught its attention. It builds a large, untidy nest in any suitable sheltered situation, a crevice in a cliff, wall, or building, a hole in a tree (hollowed out, perhaps, by a Woodpecker for its own use), a Sand-martin's burrow enlarged, or even the entrance to a rabbit-hole. After the nesting season is over, Starlings band together in flocks, sometimes of many thousands. A huge cloud of birds can often be observed in the evening, circling and wheeling in the air about their chosen roosting place, and then suddenly dropping down to their perches.

Among the other species of Starlings is the Rosy Starling, or Rose-coloured Pastor, a lovely bird, with a black crest, head, wings, and tail, and a rose-coloured back and breast. This bird sometimes visits Britain from southern Europe.

STARLINGS ROOSTING

Eric Hosking

The Indian Mynas are the common Starlings of southern Asia. The Glossy Starlings of Africa and the Grackles of Asia are near relatives of the true Starlings. They are mainly forest birds, feeding on fruits among the highest branches of trees, and rarely coming to the ground. Several species have been kept in zoos, where they have learnt to repeat words and tunes perfectly.

The Crested Cassiques of tropical America are sometimes called the Starlings of the New World, though perhaps they are more closely related to the ORIOLES (q.v.). They are small, black and citron-yellow birds, which live in colonies, hanging their long, bag-shaped nests in groups from the twigs of tall forest trees, or even sometimes from telegraph wires. These nests are made of closely woven grass, and have long narrow necks, on the side of which is the entrance.

STAR SLIME. This whitish, jelly-like substance is sometimes found lying on the ground in open places in the country, particularly in late summer and autumn. Popular legend has for years associated it with 'shooting stars'—Pembrokeshire shepherds being said to have called it 'pwdre sêr', the 'rot of the stars'. Actually, the jelly is formed from the gelatinous lining of the oviducts (egg-passages) of frogs or toads which may have been devoured by birds, possibly crows, the internal organs having been left untouched. When exposed to moisture, the jelly swells to such an extent that the oviducts are split open. With advancing decomposition, the jelly sometimes persists for some time after the tissue from which it originated has become unrecognizable.

STEMS. 1. (*a*). The main work of stems is to support the leaves and to display them so that they gain the maximum benefit from the light of the sun. Roots have a fairly constant environment; but the shoot is exposed to wind and rain, to the heat of day or the chills of night, and must adapt itself to meet these different conditions. Whereas most kinds of roots look much alike, the shoots—stem and leaves—differ so greatly that plants can generally be identified from them.

A second function of the stem is to display the flowers and, later, to suspend the fruits and seeds. The stem also acts as a connecting-link between root and leaves, all the water and dissolved salts absorbed by the root from the soil passing up through a passage in the stem, called the 'xylem' or wood, into the leaves. If a green stem is placed in red ink for a few hours, and then cut across, this passage will be seen to be stained red. Some of the foodstuffs manufactured in the leaves, too, pass down the stem to the roots through a separate series of vessels called the 'phloem' or 'bast'. So the stem is like a seaport where raw materials and manufactured products are constantly crossing each other.

Besides the ordinary aerial stems which grow erect, some stems, such as those of the Moneywort, Creeping Jenny, and Ground Ivy, grow along the surface of the ground; and some grow underground. In addition, some act as storage organs for food: some, such as those of the CACTUS and other succulent plants which live in dry regions, store water. In some plants, such as many ALPINE PLANTS, the stems are so short as to be almost non-existent, and the leaves are arranged in a tight rosette. CLIMBING PLANTS (qq.v.), on the other hand, have long, weak stems which are able to grow upwards only by using supports.

(*b*) BUDS. The stem bears buds, which grow into flowers and leaves. As buds are delicate, there are often elaborate devices to protect them from the weather, from insects, or from fungal diseases. The arrangement of the growing leaves inside a bud shows it to be no more than a condensed shoot—as can be seen if a big leaf-bud, such as a Brussels Sprout, is carefully unravelled, or if small buds are uncoiled with needles and tweezers. Leaf-buds appear at the growing-tip of the stem, which is concealed and protected by the young leaves, and also in the angle (the 'axil')

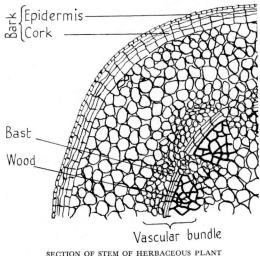

SECTION OF STEM OF HERBACEOUS PLANT

made by last year's leaves with the stem. These side buds often do not develop unless something happens to injure or check the growth of the bud at the tip. The 'dormant' buds, for example, on a hedge or fruit-tree are stimulated to growth when the tip-buds are trimmed or cut off by PRUNING (q.v. Vol. VI).

(c) AGE OF A STEM. This, and the amount of growth a stem has made in a season, can be told in the following manner. Young buds are covered with tiny scale-leaves, which drop off as the bud unfolds and the shoot begins to grow. When they drop, they leave scars, called 'girdle scars' because they run around the stem. As each girdle scar shows the beginning of a new year's growth, the length of the stem between two adjacent sets of scars shows the amount of growth in any one year. In the branches of trees (for these, also, are stems) the scars are, of course,

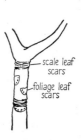

scale leaf scars

foliage leaf scars

shed with the bark; but as long as they persist on a branch, the age can be calculated. These girdle scars are very plainly seen on the Beech and Horse-chestnut twigs. In one British tree, the Wayfaring Tree, there are no scales to the buds, for these are well protected by hairs; and so the age of the twigs cannot be calculated in this way. Naked buds occur also in tropical lands, where there is no unfavourable season from which the buds must be protected.

(d) CORK. Stems are liable to become infected by myriads of moulds, mildews, and other fungal diseases, either from the air, or indirectly through attacks by insects. Just as animals are covered with a SKIN (q.v.), one of the functions of which is to keep out diseases, so young plants are covered by a compact layer of cells which forms a skin, or 'epidermis'. As the plant gets older and its girth increases, this epidermis is often replaced by a layer of cork, formed from a row of cells situated below the epidermis. The walls of the cork cells become impregnated with a material through which water or water vapour cannot pass—a fact made use of in ordinary bottle-corks, which are made from the corky tissue of a Mediterranean tree called the Cork-oak.

(e) BARK. Since water cannot pass through the corky layer, all the cells outside it die off. In places, however, small gaps called 'lenticels',

consisting of loosely packed collections of cells, occur in the cork, and allow air to pass in for the respiration of the tissues beneath. Lenticels can be seen clearly as pale spots on the shoots of the Elder, and the dark streaks on bottle-corks mark the lenticels in the bark from which they were made. Each year, a new cork layer is formed just below the old, and the layer of tissue outside the cork, already dead because it is cut off from the plant's food and water supply, becomes a little thicker. This dead layer is the bark of a tree. When a tree is wounded, as, for instance, by the breaking of branches or the cutting of initials, a special process of cork-formation takes place to heal the wound. Owing to the formation of successive layers of cork round the wound, the initials (often cut on the smooth surface of a beech trunk, for instance) become more and more indented as the years go by.

2. UNDERGROUND STEMS. (a) Tubers. The colourless appearance of the tubers of potatoes, and the branches which bear them, suggest that they are typical underground roots. But those who have stored potatoes know that the potato produces shoots—a function performed only by stems. The potato tuber, then, although it develops underground, is a stem, not a root. Its shoots develop from the 'eyes', which are young buds arranged in the axils of very much reduced scale leaves, and which, when the potato is planted, grow upwards and become leafy stems. The potato tuber is a stem which has become greatly swollen to act as a storage organ, storing chiefly starch, with a little protein. This nourishes the plant until the leaves are sufficiently

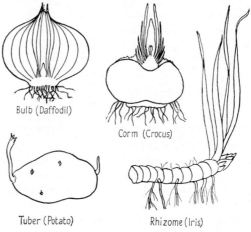

Bulb (Daffodil)

Corm (Crocus)

Tuber (Potato)

Rhizome (Iris)

TYPES OF UNDERGROUND STEMS

formed to manufacture food for themselves (*see* PHOTOSYNTHESIS). Other examples of stem tubers are the Chinese and Jerusalem Artichokes, though they differ slightly in structure, and contain different food materials.

(*b*) The RHIZOME (as seen on the Iris, for example) is another type of underground stem. Superficially, rhizomes appear to be roots; but examination shows that they bear leaves and buds. They grow almost horizontally, just below the surface of the ground; but during the spring and summer, the tip turns upwards, carrying the leaves and flowers above the soil, where they continue at first to be nourished by food stored in the thick, fleshy rhizome. So the direct onward growth of one year's length of rhizome comes abruptly to an end; and, next year, the rhizome grows in a slightly different direction. Since they are stems and cannot absorb solutions from the soil, rhizomes produce adventitious roots underneath, which serve both for absorption and for anchorage. Solomon's Seal has a fleshy, food-storing rhizome in which the round scar or 'seal' is left by the decay of a whole shoot, lately the bearer of foliage leaves and flowers. Slender rhizomes are found in Wood Anemone, Reeds, Sedges, and Grasses—those of Couchgrass (Twitch) being only too well known because of the difficulty of getting rid of it from the garden.

Some plants with sturdy tap-roots, such as Carrots, Primroses, and Radishes, appear to have their leaves growing from the top of the root. This topmost part, however, is not a root, but a short, thick, vertical stem or rhizome, known as the root-stock.

(*c*) CORMS. Crocuses, Gladioli, and Montbretia supply another example of an underground stem modified for food storage—the corm. Here, the main stem is round and globular, and is surrounded by a number of loose, scaly leaves, which, when removed, reveal small buds in their axils. In early spring, one of the uppermost buds bursts forth and produces a flower and green foliage leaves, while the base of one of the other buds begins to swell, eventually forming the corm for the following year. During the spring, food manufactured by the foliage leaves is stored in this young, developing corm, the old corm shrivelling up. In late spring, when growth has ceased, the new corm remains in the soil in a resting condition until the following spring. The roots of some corms have a special structure

which enables them to contract and pull the corm into the soil to the most suitable depth.

(*d*) BULBS. In the corm, the stem portion is by far the most prominent and important part, the leaves being merely protective scales. In bulbs, however, the swollen, fleshy, pale-coloured leaves which act as storehouses of food form the bulk, the stem being a relatively insignificant, small, bun-like structure, which gives off adventitious roots round its edges. The bud grows from the centre of the upper surface, and finally produces the foliage leaves and flowers, nourishment for the growing shoot being supplied from the fleshy leaves. In Tulip bulbs, the stored food is starch; in Onions, sugar. In Lily bulbs, the fleshy leaves overlap at their margins and are called scaly bulbs. Like corms, bulbs have contractile roots, able to pull the bulb down to the required depth in the soil. These can be seen very clearly if a hyacinth bulb is grown in a glass.

See also PLANTS; ROOTS; LEAVES; FLOWERS.

STICK CATERPILLAR, *see* PROTECTIVE COLORATION, Section 3; LOOPERS.

STICK INSECT AND LEAF INSECT. These are remarkable creatures, nearly related to our COCKROACHES (q.v.). They closely resemble either the twigs of their food-plant or its leaves, and are therefore good examples of animal CAMOUFLAGE (q.v.). Stick insects are green, brown, or grey-brown, with cylindrical, stick-like bodies, often they have projections, like thorns, and a few species even have grey-green lumps giving the effect of moss-grown twigs. They are natives of tropical and semi-tropical countries, but they can be reared easily enough at home on privet and ivy. They are not very entertaining pets, however, for during the day-time they cling quite motionless to their food-plant with two or three of their legs, the rest being either pressed close to the body, or stuck out in an angular manner. It is, of course, important for an insect relying on concealment to escape its enemies that it should act its part well—and a stick that started to walk about would very soon attract attention. Stick Insects, therefore, move and feed only at

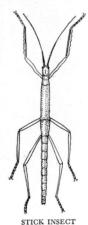

STICK INSECT

night. In many species, including one found in Britain, males are very rare indeed, and many generations can be raised in succession without producing even one (*see* REPRODUC-TION IN ANIMALS). The eggs are dropped to the ground, each enclosed in a hard capsule with a lid, through which the newly-hatched insect escapes some months later.

Leaf Insects are flat and broad. The females have shorter wings but broader bodies than the males. Their wings are bright green, and ribbed so as to resemble very exactly the veins of leaves. There are growths on the sides of their legs, also, which are flat, green, and leaf-like (*see* Colour Plate opp. p. 336). They, too, remain still during the day. Leaf Insects inhabit the Far East, especially the islands of the Indian Ocean.

See also PROTECTIVE COLORATION (Insects).

STICKLEBACK. The Three-spined Stickle-back, known to most people as the 'Tiddler' (or perhaps by some other name, such as Sharpling

A. Fraser-Brunner

THREE-SPINED STICKLEBACK

The male is swimming round to keep intruders away from his nest

or Bandie), is a very common freshwater fish in Britain and Europe, and is found across Siberia, in Japan, and in northern America. It is equally at home in brackish water and sometimes lives in the sea. Sticklebacks are small fishes, with the first dorsal fin composed of separate, stout spines, and the pelvic fins on the abdomen com-posed of one strong, sharp spine each, and one small soft ray. The tail is very slender, and along the side there is a series of large plates of bone, which vary in number, fish from inland waters having as few as three near the shoulder, those near the sea having a complete set.

At mating time, the male Three-spined Stickleback develops a brilliant dress of shining green, with a bright red chest. He builds a nest in the water plants and fights off other males who come near. He courts one or more females and persuades them to lay their eggs in his nest. He then guards the eggs and protects the young ones when they hatch.

A less common kind, found in more southern localities, is the Ten-spined Stickleback, a fresh-water fish which has similar habits, but which, as its name indicates, has ten spines on the back instead of three. Another and larger kind, the Fifteen-spined Stickleback, which sometimes reaches nearly 18 cm long, lives only in the sea or in brackish water at the mouths of rivers.

STINGING NETTLE, *see* PLANT DEFENCES.

STOAT, *see* WEASEL, Section 2. See also VOL. VI, WILD ANIMALS ON THE FARM.

STORK. This very long-legged, long-beaked bird is a relative of the HERON (q.v.), and also of the Ibis, the sacred bird of ancient Egypt, and of the strange-looking Spoonbill. There are about 20 species, spread over most of the world, other than very cold regions, and generally living and breed-ing in communities. They have plump bodies, with large wings and short, rounded tails; long strong, naked legs; long beaks with sharp points; and a plumage which is predominantly white and black. They have no song, their only noise, often surprisingly loud, being made by the snap-ping of their beaks. They are strong fliers, and frequently soar to great heights. In many places they are looked upon with great favour, almost reverence, not only because they are useful scavengers, but because they are proverbial for the care of their young—from which reputation,

Eric Hosking

EUROPEAN WHITE STORKS AT THEIR NEST

Eric Hosking

WHITE STORK IN FLIGHT

perhaps, has grown the nursery legend that the stork brings the baby.

The common European White Stork, a typical stork, is a handsome bird standing over a metre high, with pure white plumage, long black wing-feathers, and a red beak and legs. It is particularly common in Holland, Germany, and Poland, and spreads also over western and central Asia and parts of India. It is an occasional visitor to Britain. It migrates in vast flocks to Africa for the winter. The White Stork frequents human habitations, standing on roof-tops and building its flat nest of sticks on chimney-tops and roofs. The birds, which mate for life, return to the same nest year after year, adding to it until it becomes a bulky structure. Three to five pure white eggs are laid. The Black Stork is a smaller, much less common, and much shyer species, which frequents secluded swamps, and nests in tall trees. Another species closely related to the White Stork is the African White-bellied Stork, a still smaller bird, found very commonly in the Sudan and farther south, and much venerated by the natives of the Sudan.

The largest of all the Storks are the huge, ugly Adjutant Storks, or Marabou, of Africa and southern Asia. They are over 1·5 metres long, with enormous, thick, wedge-shaped beaks, bare heads and necks, and long pouches hanging from the throat. The Indian Adjutants are common in some parts, especially in Calcutta, where they used to perch in numbers on the

parapets of Government House during the rains. In many places, they are protected because of their good work as scavengers. The tropical regions of America, Africa, and Australia have other very large Storks, about 1·5 metres long, with very long beaks.

The Ibis, which belongs to a different family related to the Storks, is a smaller bird, with much shorter legs, and a long, slender, slightly curved beak. The Sacred Ibis is now no longer found in Egypt, but belongs to the swampy regions of the Sudan near the Upper Nile, where it nests in colonies. It is white, with a black head, neck, and tail-feathers. Other species are found in Madagascar, Australia, New Guinea, and

Booth Steamship Co.

A SPOONBILL STANDING ON A TURTLE

eastern Asia. The Glossy Ibis is a species belonging to Europe and western Asia, occasionally visiting Britain, and found also in North America. The Scarlet Ibis is a brilliant bird, with scarlet plumage and black tips to the wings, found in tropical America and the West Indies.

The Spoonbill is a white bird, rather over 75 cm long, with a long, drooping crest, black legs, and an enormous, wide, black beak. It used to breed in Suffolk and Sussex some 300 years ago, and is still a fairly frequent visitor to the east coast in the summer. It lives near marshy lakes or sandbanks on rivers over most of the world, using its great, broad, spoon-shaped bill for fishing up small aquatic animals in the shallow water.

Harold Bastin

THE HUGE ADJUTANT STORK

STURGEON. These fishes, which are mostly large, resemble SHARKS (q.v.) in the shape of their tails, in having their mouth underneath, and in the fact that their skeletons are almost entirely cartilaginous. But features of the gills and the presence of an air bladder show that they are more closely allied to the bony FISHES (q.v.). Together with the Paddle-fish, Sturgeons are the survivors of a group which were once much more widespread. They are clumsy, sluggish creatures, with a long, bony snout, below which are barbels or 'whiskers' for feeling in the mud. The mouth, which has no teeth, can be stretched out like a telescope to suck up the small creatures on which they feed. The skin is rough, and along the back is a row of very large bony plates, or 'bucklers', while on each side are two rows of smaller ones.

There are many kinds of Sturgeon found in Europe, northern and central Asia, and North America. Many of the larger ones are marine, moving only a short distance up rivers to spawn; but some of the smaller kinds spend their lives in fresh water. The common Sturgeon of the Atlantic sometimes visits Britain. In this country it is called a royal fish, since, according to an old law, any Sturgeon caught belongs in theory to the Sovereign. The flesh is good to eat, though coarse and beefy, and in places where Sturgeon abound they provide a very important fishery. Their eggs are prepared as the highly prized delicacy called caviare.

In the Mississippi Valley of America is found a very curious Sturgeon, called the Paddle-fish, Spoonbill, or Shovel-fish, because of the shape of its snout. This is expanded to form a large, paddle-shaped blade, nearly as big as the body. Another, with a somewhat similar snout, is found in the great rivers of China.

SUNDEW, *see* INSECTIVOROUS PLANTS, Section 3.

SURINAM TOAD. This primitive AMPHIBIAN (q.v.), not really a TOAD (q.v.), inhabits central America and the Guianas. It lives entirely in the water, and is tongueless and toothless. Its fingers end in star-shaped tips, and its toes are broadly webbed. It is remarkable for the way in which its young are produced—the eggs, when laid, being placed on the back of the female by the male, where they sink into wrinkles of the skin and develop in the pouches thus formed. The tadpoles do not leave their cells until they have completed their METAMORPHOSIS (q.v.) into the adult, after 80 days. The Surinam Toad stands captivity well.

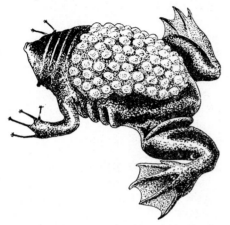

FEMALE SURINAM TOAD CARRYING HER EGGS ON HER BACK

SWALLOW. The Swallow tribe includes not only the Swallow, but also the House Martin and Sand Martin. They are all birds with stream-lined bodies, long wings, and long, generally forked tails; and all feed on insects, which they catch on the wing. They are found in most parts of the world, those species that breed in the cooler regions of both hemispheres migrating to warmer climates for the winter.

The Swallow is the largest of the group, being about 20 cm long. It is distinguished from the House Martin by its more deeply forked tail and its chestnut-red forehead and throat. It winters in South Africa, and the earliest birds reach the south of England towards the end of March. During April they come in great numbers, returning usually to the same district in which they spent the previous summer. As soon as they are mated the pair begin to build their nest of mud and straw, a task which sometimes takes several weeks. The nest is a saucer-shaped struc-ture, made by the plastering on of tiny beakfuls of mud with water and saliva. The inside is shaped and polished with the beak, and lined with wool and feathers. Swallows prefer to build under cover and in the dark, the rafters of farm buildings or the wide chimneys of old-fashioned houses being favourite sites. Four or five white eggs with reddish spots are laid, and sometimes as many as three broods are produced. The fledglings of the latest brood sometimes fare badly, as their parents' migratory instinct proves stronger than their parental instinct, and they

desert the nest to join the noisy gatherings collecting on telegraph wires, trees, and fences, ready for the autumn flight. Strangely enough, the young swallows of the earliest broods are the first to migrate, setting off some two or three weeks before their parents, and finding their way by some uncanny instinct to the winter quarters, to which the older birds soon follow.

The House Martins usually arrive in their breeding quarters a little later than Swallows. They are rather smaller birds, with more white in their plumage, and a rather heavier flight. They build cup-shaped nests of mud, which they fasten on the wall of a building under the shelter of the eaves, or in the angle of a beam. The entrance is by a small hole near the top. In coastal districts colonies of Martins often build against the cliff face under the shelter of an over-hanging rock. Their nests are sometimes attacked and taken over by Sparrows, against whom the Martins can put up no fight. The Martins gather for flight in the autumn, often making the migratory journey in company with Swallows.

Sand Martins, the smallest, least conspicuous, and least noisy of the group, do not frequent human dwellings, as do their relatives, but seek nesting sites in sand-pits or quarries, railway cuttings, or steep, sandy river-banks. They prefer to live near water where flies breed freely. They dig a nesting tunnel in the sand, generally nearly a metre long—though much longer tun-nels have been found. The tunnel usually slopes

Eric Hosking

PAIR OF SWALLOWS AT THEIR NEST

HOUSE MARTIN

Eric Hosking

SAND MARTIN

Eric Hosking

slightly upwards towards the nest for the sake of drainage. It is said that, after two or three years' tenancy, the nest becomes so foul and flea-infested that a new tunnel has to be dug. The Sand Martin is more vigorously attacked by these parasites than the Swallow, partly because it takes neither dust baths nor the frequent plunges into water that the Swallows enjoy so much.

The Crag Martin of the Alps and southern Europe resembles the Sand Martin. In America the Purple Martin is a well-known bird, which generally nests in hollows in trees.

SWALLOWTAIL BUTTERFLIES. This family is characteristic of tropical forests, the Birdwings of the East Indies, for instance, being some of the largest and finest butterflies known (*see* BUTTERFLIES AND MOTHS, TROPICAL). Of the 850 known species, however, 27 occur in North America and one in the British Isles. Male and female Swallowtails often differ considerably in form and colour, the females being without the tails, and often achieving safety by mimicking several different species (see picture, p. 333). The wide-ranging African *Papilio dardanus*, for instance, has so many different guises that it has been aptly described as the most surprising butterfly in the world.

The English Swallowtail, which has a wingspan of 7·5 cm, is pale yellow, with black bands and blotches on the fore-wings, and a broad band of dark blue and two red eye-spots on the hindwings near the two 'tails', which occur in both sexes. The butterflies fly during May and June, and often again in August, at Wicken Fen and along the Norfolk Broads. The females lay their spherical eggs singly on milk parsley, a plant almost restricted to the marshes of eastern England. There is also a Continental race of this Swallowtail, which occasionally migrates to the southern counties of England, particularly Kent, and in favourable seasons has been known to breed, though it never establishes itself. It lays its eggs on wild or cultivated carrot. These two races of the same species, therefore, not only differ in appearance, but also in locality, habitat, and habits: it is from such differences that new species of butterflies evolve. This insect ranges through Europe as far as India and China, and shows many slight variations in pattern, different from the heavily marked British race.

The young black and white caterpillars re-

S. Beaufoy

SWALLOWTAIL WITH WINGS CLOSED

S. Beaufoy

SWALLOWTAIL WITH WINGS OPEN

semble bird-droppings so closely that they are likely to be passed over by insect-eating enemies as objects unsuitable for food. Later, they assume strong warning colours, vivid green with black bands and orange spots. These, together with the unpleasant smell coming from a fleshy, forked organ extended repeatedly from behind the head, serve to remind would-be enemies that the caterpillar's body is unpleasant to taste and is best left alone (*see* Protective Coloration, Section 2). The chrysalis is found on the stem of a reed, attached by the tail to a silken pad and supported round the middle by a silken girdle. This silk represents the remains of a cocoon similar to that made by the caterpillars of many moths.

See also Butterflies.

SWAN. This close relative of the Geese and Ducks (qq.v.) is found in the wild state in many parts of the world, and in all types of climate. Excepting the Black Swan of Australia, swans all have white or mainly white plumage. In summer they live near inland waters, but in the winter they frequently seek the sea. Swans feed chiefly on water-plants, insects, and small molluscs. They feed by dipping their long necks under the water, sometimes standing straight on end, as ducks do, to reach down far enough.

Swans mate for life, and return yearly to the same nesting site. Their nests are untidy erections of sticks and vegetation, more than a metre across and about a metre high. They are placed near the water, sometimes on an islet. Generally about eight large, greenish-white eggs are laid, which the 'pen' (female) incubates for 5 weeks, while the 'cob' (male) guards the nest with great ferocity. While he is 'busking'—that is, swimming with wings raised and head thrown back in an aggressive attitude, it is unwise to go near him, for a swan can kill a dog or seriously cripple a man with blows from its open wing or elbow-joint. The 'cygnets', or young swans, are covered with dark greyish down, which lightens as the birds grow older. They soon take to water, following their mother in search of food; but if danger threatens, the mother takes them on her back, holding up a foot for them to scramble up by. She cleans and dries them very thoroughly when they return to the nest. When autumn comes the swans migrate southwards, flying in large groups, generally in a deep **V**-formation, very high and very fast.

Eric Hosking

MUTE SWAN

John Warham

AUSTRALIAN BLACK SWAN

The European wild swans are called the Mute Swan, the Whooper, and Bewick's Swan. The Mute Swans are supposed to have been brought to England by Richard I when returning from a crusade. They live here now in a partly domesticated state, though they breed in a wild state over much of the Continent. For many hundreds of years in England swans were called 'birds royal', because only the King or those with a licence from the Royal Swineherd might keep them. An individual or a city company with a licence to keep swans received a special 'upping mark', which had to be cut on the bill of every swan once a year. The ceremony of 'swan upping' is still held on the Thames every year, for the swans on the Thames are still regarded as the property of the Sovereign and of the Dyers' and Vintners' companies.

The Whooper Swan nests in Iceland, Scandinavia, and within the Arctic Circle, and visits the coasts of Britain in the winter. It is often called the Whistling Swan from the curious noise its wings make as it flies. Bewick's Swans, rather smaller birds, are rarer winter visitors. All three species are rather alike; but the Mute Swan has

an orange beak with black at the base, and carries its neck in a graceful curve, and its secondary wing feathers raised over its back; while the other birds have yellowish beaks with black tips, hold their necks more stiffly, and carry their wings flat on their backs.

There are two species of swans in North America, the Trumpeter Swan, the largest of all, and the Whistling Swan. In South America, especially in Chile, is the Black-necked Swan; and in Australia lives the Black Swan, first discovered in 1697 by a Dutch explorer. This bird is completely black, except for its white flight-feathers and its coral-red bill.

SWIFT. It is common to associate this bird with the SWALLOW (q.v.), which it superficially resembles. Like the Swallow, it has a streamlined body, long wings, and a forked tail. It is almost always seen on the wing, using its short beak and wide gape to catch its insect food. It is, however, no relation to the Swallow, being actually more closely related to Humming-birds and Nightjars. As well as the typical Swifts which visit Europe, there are several other species widely distributed in America and Asia.

The Swifts are among the latest of the migrant birds to arrive in Britain and the earliest to depart, spending less than 4 months here. They winter in South Africa, and arrive in Britain about the beginning of May, announcing their arrival with their loud, harsh, screaming cry.

Harold Bastin

NEST OF THE EDIBLE SEA SWIFT

saliva, and fasten them on to the walls of caverns. The nests of the Borneo Edible Swifts are highly prized by the Chinese, who use them for soup. The Asiatic Tree Swifts make tiny nests of bark and saliva, large enough to hold one egg, and fasten them on to the side of a thin bough.

SWIFT AND GHOST MOTHS. These are the most primitive of all moths except the GOLD AND PURPLE MOTHS (q.v.), although they are highly specialized in some ways. Their long, narrow fore-wings have a small flap, which projects beneath the smaller hind-wings to couple the two together, and this takes the place of the bristles by which the fore and hind-wings of most moths are linked. The larvae bore in roots, stems, and trunks, attacking a wide range of plants, and often taking 2 years to complete development. The pupae have flexible abdominal segments bearing spines, which enable them to push their way out of the soil when the moths are ready to emerge.

Of some 250 known species the majority are in Australia and New Zealand, and include some of the largest and finest moths—the Bent-wing of New South Wales, for example, having a wing-spread of 23 centimetres. The Bent-wing is orange-brown, patterned with silver, and has a raised eye-spot on each fore-wing, so that, when at rest, it closely resembles a lizard's head. Its giant caterpillar bores in the trunks of eucalyptus trees, causing much damage.

The largest of the five British species is the Ghost Moth, the silvery-white males measuring about 5 cm across, and the pale yellowish-brown females about 1 cm larger. In June the males perform a 'ghostly' dance at dusk, swaying to and fro about a metre above the ground in rough meadows. Here they are sought by unpaired females, who thus reverse the usual role of the sexes. After mating the female scatters her eggs while hovering. The whitish larvae feed on the roots of grasses, dead nettle, dock, or dandelion.

The Gold Swift, common in woody districts in June, is not quite so large. Both sexes are yellowish-brown, the male being distinguished by silver spots. Although less conspicuous than the Ghost Moth, it hovers in the same way, and emits a pineapple scent attractive to females. The females of the Common Swift sit on grass stems in rough meadows on fine summer evenings, vibrating their wings as they await the yellowish-brown males. Their whitish cater-

Eric Hosking

SWIFT

They build their nests in crevices in walls or holes under the eaves, constructing them of straw, dead leaves, or any other material which they can pick up in the air, bound together with their own saliva. Swifts, as their name suggests, are perhaps the fastest fliers of all British birds. The Alpine Swift is even more rapid than the British variety. They twist and turn in the air like bats, and soar very high up into the sky. In summer, non-breeding birds may spend the night high in the air, and on some evenings, just as it is getting dark, flocks may be seen ascending into the sky. Though so agile in the air, their long wings and very short legs make them extremely awkward on the ground. They never come to the ground if they can help it, but if brought down, they have great difficulty in rising again. Neither can they perch, for all their four toes are directed forwards—an arrangement which, however, makes them well able to cling on to vertical surfaces. When ready to migrate in the autumn, they do not gather in swarms on telegraph wires, as swallows do.

The most interesting of the Asiatic Swifts are the Edible Swifts, which build nests composed mainly (with one species, entirely) of their own

pillars have shining brown heads, and brownish raised dots with a few hairs on the body. They may feed for 2 years, either on the roots of weeds, or sometimes on lettuce and root crops.

The name Swift refers to the rapid flight of the moths. The most active British species is the Map-winged, which flies in June and July on heaths and in wooded districts, particularly in northern Britain, north Devon, and Somerset. The Orange Swift, a late-summer species, flies in early evening among bracken, or among the higher branches of trees. Though widely distributed in Britain, it is more common in the south and east.

SWINE. These animals belong to the order Artiodactyla (even-toed hoofed mammals). There are two main branches of the Swine family—the true pigs of the Old World, and the Peccaries of America. The HIPPOPOTAMUSES (q.v.) are fairly closely related, but are not included in the family. Many species of swine have become extinct, and in many places where they used to be common they have been exterminated by man.

The best known of the true pigs is the wild boar, which is still common in the larger forests of Europe and in parts of North Africa and Asia.

There used also to be many in the British Isles, but the last was killed before 1600. The European wild boar is a powerfully built, blackish-grey animal, about 1·5 metres long, and nearly a metre high. The male has formidable tusks, growing from the lower jaw and projecting beyond the upper lips, the edges of which are sharpened against the upper tusks. They are powerful weapons, capable of ripping open a horse at a single stroke. Like all wild pigs, the wild boars like to wallow in mud, turning up the ground with their snouts in search of food. The female has one or two litters a year, of from six to ten. The young of all wild swine are lightly striped.

The Indian wild boar is one of the fiercest animals in the world. It will charge men, horses, even elephants, without a moment's hesitation, however badly wounded it may be. It can run very fast, but cannot keep up its high speed for very long. These wild boars make their lairs in any convenient covert, in tall grass, reeds, sugarcane, in bushes, or in the forest. In the mornings and evenings they go out to look for food, devastating the crops in cultivated districts, but elsewhere eating roots and the carcasses of dead animals. The old boars lead a lone life, while the females and young collect in droves of

Paul Popper

A FAMILY OF WART HOGS IN THE KRUGER NATIONAL PARK, TRANSVAAL

Paul Popper

EUROPEAN WILD SOW AND FAMILY

usually from ten to twelve head. PIG-STICKING (q.v. Vol. IX) is still a favourite and often dangerous sport in India.

In the damp forests of Celebes and Borneo in the East Indies live the Babirusas or Pig Deer, so called because of their long, curving tusks and long, slender legs. The male has four curved tusks, one pair growing from the lower and the other from the upper jaw, projecting through the skin. They are excellent swimmers, not only entering lakes to feed on water-plants, but also crossing the small channels of the sea which separate one island from another.

In Africa, south of the Sahara, live the Bush Pigs (or Bosch-varks). These have rather long, greyish-brown hair—the Red Bush Pig or River Hog of West Africa being certainly the most handsome member of the swine family.

The most hideous wild pig is the African Wart Hog. It has an enormous head, with a huge warty protuberance below each eye, huge tusks growing from the upper jaw, a massive, almost cylindrical body, and a long tail. Very often a

Wart Hog will occupy the deserted burrow of an AARD-VARK (q.v.), and before going down it he always turns round and goes in backwards so as to be ready with his tusks to gore any pursuing enemy. As recently as 1904 another large black wild pig, named the Forest Hog, was found in the forests of Equatorial Africa.

The wild pigs of America are called Peccaries. There are two kinds: the Collared Peccary and the larger White-lipped Peccary, both of which eat mostly fruit and roots, and live in the hollows of trees or in burrows dug by other animals. The White-lipped Peccaries are beasts of uncertain temper, and have been known to rush at human beings, squealing with fury and gnashing their sharp, razor-edged tusks. Their tusks are capable of inflicting terrible wounds, and dogs used in hunting them are frequently cut to ribbons by the vicious creatures. When food is scarce, large herds of the Peccaries make long migrations.

See also Vol. VI: PIGS (Domestic).

SWORDFISH, *see* MACKEREL.

T

TADPOLES, *see* FROGS.

TAPEWORM, *see* WORMS, Section 6.

TAPIR. This animal, which belongs to the order Perissodactyla (odd-toed hoofed mammals), as do the RHINOCEROS and the HORSE (qq.v.), has kept much of the original characteristics of the primitive ancestors of the hooved mammals, having changed hardly at all in the course of thousands of years. Though it must once have had a much wider distribution, it now lives in the jungles of the Malay Peninsula and Borneo, and in Central and South America. It is a very strange-looking, ungainly beast, with an elongated snout, with which it hooks foliage into its mouth. Its legs are short and stout, and its tail short and thin. It has a thick, smooth skin, scantily covered with very short hairs.

The single species living in the Malay region is coloured black and white. The newly born young are brown or velvety black, with very vivid, yellow, longitudinal stripes on their sides, and white stripes beneath their bodies. This striking colouring makes an effective camouflage on the occasions when they are left alone by

Zoological Society of London
MALAY TAPIRS

their mother in the thick vegetation. They take on the colour of the adults when they are from 4 to 6 months old. Malayan Tapirs are very seldom seen, and little is known of their habits, because they remain hidden in the interior of the country, avoiding inhabited parts.

There are four species of Tapir in Central and South America, the best known being the Brazilian Tapir. The adults are blue-black or brown all over; but the young have the same conspicuous striping as those of the Asiatic species. They live in the thickest parts of the forests, avoiding all open spaces, and journeying in search of food and water along regular pathways made by themselves. They eat palm-leaves and young plants, fallen fruits or swamp grasses, beginning their feed in the early evening and probably continuing throughout the greater part of the night. In the early morning they go to the banks of the river to drink. They are fond of gambolling in the water and rolling in the soft mud, until their hides become thickly plastered —which probably protects them against insect bites. Except in the mating season they are nearly always about alone, walking slowly, deliberately, and quite silently, with their snouts close to the ground. If frightened, however, they will rush blindly forward, crashing through the bushes, or splashing through water. They swim and dive, and have no difficulty in crossing the largest rivers. As a rule they are perfectly harmless animals; but when they do attack—for instance, in protection of their young—they do so fiercely. The only sounds they make are a shrill whistle, of little volume in comparison with their size, and a loud snort when disturbed.

TARANTULA. This name (from the town Taranto in south Italy) was given in the 16th century to a spider, common in Europe, and now known as *Lycosa tarantula*. The bite of this spider was traditionally believed to be peculiarly dangerous: it was supposed to induce a general melancholy which would prove fatal, unless a cure could be achieved in time—the only cure being said to be music. The victims, known as *tarantati*, used to summon a musician, who would play a selection of tunes, or *tarantellas*, until he found one which inspired them to dance. They went on dancing for a long time with increasing speed and vigour, until at last they were exhausted—when the poison was supposed to have been sweated out of their bodies. During the

Mustograph

TARANTULA SPIDER AT THE MOUTH OF ITS BURROW

TEETH AND TUSKS. Teeth are used to tear off and break up food in the first process of digestion; tusks are greatly enlarged teeth which, in such animals as wild boar, are used for defence and for digging, and no longer serve to break up food.

As animals feed on a great variety of foods, from grass and flesh to seeds and nuts, it is to be expected that their teeth will be of many different kinds. In RODENTS (q.v.) or gnawing animals, such as rats, squirrels, or beavers, the teeth are slender and sharp, growing continuously from the base as they are worn away at the top. So if a rodent loses a tooth, the one opposite the gap, having nothing to grind against, will grow abnormally long, and in the course of time will prevent the animal from feeding, and so cause it to starve. Horses and other grass- and grain-eating animals have broad and flat back teeth, which act as millstones (as the name molars indicates), and sharp front teeth for biting off the grass. CARNIVORA (q.v.), or flesh-eating animals, such as dogs and cats, have sharp front teeth for killing, and knife-edged molars for tearing the flesh, which is very little chewed. In animals using a mixed diet, such as man, the teeth are adapted for tearing, biting, and grinding.

Teeth are modified in various ways to meet the special needs of particular animals. The hollow poison fangs of poisonous snakes are modified teeth; and the teeth of snakes in general point backwards, so as to prevent their victims from escaping while being swallowed. Some reptiles and fishes have several rows of teeth in either jaw; and the frog has teeth in the upper jaw and on the palate, but none on the lower jaw.

Most mammals are born without teeth, so that the mother can suckle the young without injury; but in some young seals the canine teeth are already developed and extremely sharp, so that they would hurt the mother were they not very much to the side. Mammals normally have two sets of teeth: the small 'milk-teeth', which are soon lost, and the permanent teeth which last throughout life. In other animals, such as fish and reptiles, there are no milk-teeth, the

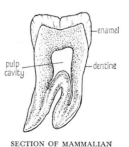

SECTION OF MAMMALIAN
MOLAR TOOTH

Middle Ages, when whole communities were at times affected by what is now known as mass-hysteria, their peculiar behaviour would usually be ascribed to the local spider.

There is, in fact, no support for the belief that *Lycosa tarantula* is more venomous than any other small European spider. In America, the name is commonly applied to all the larger 'trap-door spiders'—those which live in silk-lined burrows, closed by a trap-door. These, again, are not necessarily more venomous than the rest. Dangerous spiders do exist—the best known being undoubtedly the Black Widow, a spider more conspicuous for its red and black colouring than for its size. Its bite can have painful and even fatal effects, but it certainly does not induce any desire to dance.

See also SPIDERS.

TARSIER, *see* LEMUR.

TASMANIAN DEVIL, *see* MARSUPIAL.

TASTE, *see* SENSES, Section 5.

TEAL, *see* DUCK, Section 2.

young animal being born with a permanent set. Many animals, including some of the Edentata (*see* ANT-EATER) and all birds except fossils, are without teeth—the serrations on the edges of some birds' beaks being merely horny projections.

Teeth are made of a hard white 'dentine', a substance much like bone, and, like bone, composed largely of calcium. The outer covering, known as enamel, is derived from the epidermis, or outer layer of skin. The teeth of mammals have a fleshy central pulp containing the nerve.

See also Vol. XI: TEETH (Human).

TERMITES. These insects are often called 'White Ants'; but this is a most misleading name, as ANTS (q.v.) and Termites have little in common, excepting that both are 'social insects'.

There are many species of termites in the tropics and in warm temperate countries, but none in the British Isles. They make nests of various types, the simplest being galleries in decaying tree-trunks. The species tunnelling these often attack also the dry timber of buildings and furniture: thus a table, apparently perfectly sound, may be so riddled inside that it is a mere shell, ready to collapse almost at a touch. Other species throw up 'termitaria', large structures of earth, excavated below ground and cemented together by saliva. These buildings are usually about 2 to 4 metres high (though they may reach even 6 metres), and are so hard that they are difficult to break open, even with a pickaxe. Other termites have their nests below ground— all that can be seen from above being a number of small mounds.

Termite communities, often composed of thousands of individuals, are divided into four groups or 'castes'. Only two of these are able to breed, but all four include both males and females. The first of the two reproductive castes is believed to be the original stock from which the other castes have sprung. Its members have two pairs of large, elaborately veined wings. At certain times, when the weather suits them (as, for example, during a rainy season), they leave the nest in very great numbers, to form new colonies. They are not good fliers, and it is unusual for a swarm to travel any great distance. As several colonies generally swarm at the same time, this allows interbreeding to take place. Of these large swarms very few individuals survive, most being destroyed by birds, lizards, and mammals; but of the few who remain alive, each pair tries to form a new colony. The first action of the 'royal pair', as they are called, is to break off their wings along a line near the base. Both take part in building, as the beginning of the future nest, a small underground cavity called the nuptial chamber; and here they remain for the rest of their long lives. A queen of this caste may live in the chamber till she is about 10 years old. She devotes herself entirely to laying eggs, the enlargement of the nest being carried out by certain of her offspring. She increases enormously in size, being said to grow to about 20,000 times the bulk of one of her worker offspring. This enormous increase in bulk is made possible by the stretching of the softer cuticle between the hard plates, which, fitting close together, formed her protective covering when she was her original size. These plates now appear as small, widely separated, dark brown rectangles upon her pale-coloured, swollen body. The head and thorax keep their original size and appearance; the increase is in the abdomen. At the height of her activity she may be producing a million or more eggs a year.

The second reproductive caste is made up of individuals whose wings never develop beyond the rudimentary stage. The members of this second, small-winged caste do not mate for life, as do the royal pair. Their use in the community may be to assist in maintaining it at full strength, to increase its numbers, or to continue the colony if the royal queen dies, either of old age or by accident. It is certain that the colony can outlast the life of its foundress, and can be maintained solely by the small-winged caste. In a

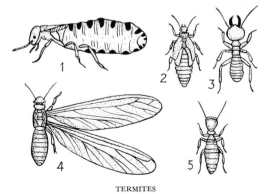

TERMITES

1. Queen; 2. Nymph; 3. Soldier; 4. Winged Male; 5. Worker

very few species there is a third reproductive caste, a completely wingless one. Though the females of these two castes may increase in size, they never grow so enormous as the original queen. It seems that she, only, is able to produce new members of her own caste; and, so far as we know, it is members of her caste only which leave the habitation to start new colonies.

The other two castes, both wingless, consist of 'workers' and 'soldiers'. Though these, too, include both males and females, the development of their reproductive organs is arrested at an early stage, so that they are sterile. The workers are the most numerous. They are the first to be produced by the royal queen, and are fed to begin with on her saliva. They become adult after about 7 months, and do not partake of their normal food until well developed. As the queen increases in size, and in consequence becomes more and more helpless, she is tended by workers. Her diet is changed to soft food, which the workers specially prepare. They enlarge the habitation, building it up to its great size, and also look after the eggs and young nymphs.

The soldiers have very large heads and strong horny armament. They are of two types: one with very robust jaws, and the other with small jaws and a long horny projection. The soldiers are regarded as the defenders of the colony. The worst enemies of termites are ants, and the soldiers attack these and prevent them from entering the colony. (Some writers, however, say they are the first to run away when the habitation is broken open, though others maintain that they act with courage, adopt threatening attitudes, and attack intruders.) Apart from their stout armour and strong jaws, certain types of soldier are provided with poison glands, the contents of which can be discharged through a 'frontal pore' at approaching enemies. Ants are said to be put completely out of action by this means.

When the large-winged offspring of the royal pair are ready to make their flight, the workers bore holes in the wall of the habitation to let them out, and many workers and soldiers assemble as if to bid them a ceremonious farewell. It is not yet clearly known what determines which of the offspring of the royal pair shall become members of their own caste and which will belong to the other castes, though it is possible to tell, when they leave the eggs, what they are going to be when they grow up. Occasionally, members of the sterile castes are known to have partly recovered the lost characters of the reproductive castes. Thus, egg-laying female soldiers have occurred, and their offspring have become workers; and soldiers have sometimes been found with small, undeveloped wings.

Adult termites live on wood and other vegetable matter, as well as upon refuse; but the young nymphs are fed on saliva. Many species have special flagellates (see PROTOZOA) in their gut which digest wood particles. Termites cannot do this by themselves and starve if their flagellate are killed, even though they continue to eat wood as usual.

Certain species of termites have taken to what might be called horticulture. In their nests are special chambers, called 'fungus gardens'. The floor of these consists of decaying wood, well manured by the termites themselves. This manure apparently contains the spores of timber-attacking fungi, which pass unharmed through the bodies of the termites and then germinate in the decayed wood on the floor. The gardens, which are usually near the chamber where the royal pair remain imprisoned, form nurseries for the young nymphs, which graze upon them almost like sheep. Some of this fungus material is used also by the workers to make up the food upon which the old queen is fed.

TERN, see GULLS, Section 2.

TERRAPIN, see TURTLES AND TORTOISES, Section 3.

THRUSH. 1. This very large family, closely related to the WARBLERS (q.v.), is distributed all over the world, and contains many of our best-known British birds. The ROBIN, REDSTART, NIGHTINGALE, and BLUE BIRD (qq.v.), all members of the thrush family, are described in separate articles. The family also includes the Blackbirds, Fieldfares, Chats, and Wheatears, as well as the Redwings of northern Europe, the Dhyal Birds of south-east Asia and Madagascar, and the Shamas of southern Asia.

The thrush family as a whole have rather delicate, slender bills, suitable for collecting their food of insects, grubs, and berries. The nestlings always have a speckled plumage, and this speckled pattern sometimes remains in the adult stage—as, for instance, in the Thrushes

Eric Hosking

MISSEL-THRUSHES AND FLEDGLINGS

themselves. Many members of the family are migratory, though some make only short journeys. Great numbers of Thrushes and Blackbirds come to Britain every autumn from northern Europe to winter in the milder climate, and the Fieldfares and Redwings are winter visitors only. Practically all the family are fine songsters, their song being their means of declaring to other members of their species their claim over the territory in which they breed and find their food (*see* ANIMAL TERRITORY). The family may be divided into several groups: the Thrushes themselves; the Blackbirds, which are very closely related; the Chats and Wheatears; the Robins, Redstarts, and Nightingales; and the Hedge Sparrow, which is often classified as a Warbler.

2. THRUSHES. The Song-thrush (or Mavis) has a song as rich and varied as the Nightingale's, though in the opinion of many people hardly as finished and perfect as that of some Warblers. It feeds mainly on the ground on slugs and worms—its method of cracking the shells of snails against a stone being well known. Near the sea, thrushes often eat sea-molluscs, such as whelks. The Song-thrush builds a characteristic cup-shaped nest, made chiefly of grass, and lined with mud and decayed wood. It is one of the earliest British birds to start breeding, and rears several broods in a season. The Missel-thrush, a larger bird, its breast spotted rather than speckled, is so named because it eats mistletoe berries, which other birds reject. It is also often called the Stormcock, because its loud song is heard on stormy days in winter. It builds its nest in a fork of a tree, the nest being, as are most nests of this family, a cup-shaped structure of materials such as grass on a mud foundation, but without the mud lining of the Song-thrush. When the young are fledged, they gather in family parties to hunt for feeding grounds, until the autumn, when many fly farther south.

Fieldfares are common in northern Europe, where they breed in colonies, nesting frequently in birches and fir-trees. Redwings, also northern birds, make migratory flights in large flocks, flying chiefly by night, across the North Sea to Britain or central Europe. They feed very much more on worms and insects than on berries, and therefore are apt to suffer badly during a protracted period of hard weather. It is, in fact, their flanks, not their wings, which are red. In southern Europe, southern Asia, and Africa are the Rock Thrushes, among them the Blue

Thrush, shy birds which nest in remote places in holes in rocks or walls.

3. BLACKBIRD AND RING OUZEL. The Blackbird, Shakespeare's Ouzel Cock 'with orange-tawny bill', does not breed as far north as many of the thrushes, and often migrates to a milder climate for the winter. The cock is a fine songster and a good mimic. The Blackbird's loud, cackling alarm-note is frequently to be heard, especially during that anxious period when the fledglings are making their first flights. The Ring Ouzel, in appearance like a Blackbird with a white patch on the chest, is a mountain-loving bird, much more shy and wary than its relation, and breeding in solitary places among rocks and heather. In Switzerland it nests in fir-trees, feeding on the berries of the mountain ash, and making raids on cherry orchards and vineyards.

4. WHEATEAR AND CHATS. This group contains the smallest members of the family, the little Whinchat and Stonechat, each about half the size of a Blackbird. They inhabit open country, especially that covered with gorse or broom. The Wheatear and Whinchat migrate for the winter; but the Stonechat is a resident. These birds are not shy; but they are restless and very careful not to reveal the whereabouts of their nests. The Wheatears build in suitable crevices in banks or walls or among rocks; the Chats generally build under a whin or gorse bush a most skilfully concealed nest, which the female bird approaches through the grass from some little way off. The cock of the Stonechat is a brightly coloured little bird, with a shiny black head and a bright red-brown breast. The name Chat has come from the sound, like the clash of two pebbles, which the bird makes; it has also a sweet but short song. The Chats are typical birds of Africa, where there are several species. There are other species in western Asia and Europe; and the Black Chat is a common bird in India and Burma. North America also has a species. (*See also* pictures on pp. 154-5.)

5. The HEDGE SPARROW (Dunnock) belongs to the Accentors, which are closely related to the thrushes and also to the warblers: it is no relation to the House Sparrow, which is a finch. Its shallow nest of roots and moss is usually placed low in a hedge or bush—so poorly concealed that it often falls victim to the birds'-nester. Cuckoos also frequently make use of it, though the Cuckoo's egg rarely matches the light-blue eggs of the Hedge Sparrow. The Alpine

Eric Hosking
WHEATEAR COCK BIRD

Accentor, which resembles the Hedge Sparrow, is found in the high mountains of Europe, such as the Alps.

6. DHYAL BIRD AND SHAMA. These graceful little birds, to be found especially in India, are closely related to the Robin, which they resemble in much of their behaviour and in their charming song. Their plumage is mainly black and white, the Shamas having chestnut under-parts and long tails.

TICKS, *see* MITES AND TICKS.

TIGER. The Tiger and the LION are the two largest members of the CAT (qq.v.) tribe. Most tigers are smaller than lions, but some—for instance, a full-sized Bengal Tiger—are actually larger. Tigers range over a vast area in Asia: from Mongolia, south-west to the Caucasus, and southwards to Java and southern India, but not Ceylon. The Mongolian Tigers, some of the largest, grow thick, rather pale, woolly coats; while those of Sumatra and Java are very much smaller, and have deep, rich-coloured coats. The big cats of Africa, the LEOPARDS, and those of South America, the JAGUARS (qq.v.), must not be confused with tigers.

The tiger's yellow coat striped with black, although so vivid when seen in the zoo, is a wonderful camouflage in the animal's native surroundings. Tigers generally lie concealed in long grass or in the forests until evening, when they start out on their nightly prowl. The Indian

Ewing Galloway, N.Y.

A TIGER COMING OUT OF THE JUNGLE TO A WATER-HOLE

Tiger generally hunts alone. During the very hot season he takes up one definite 'beat', haunting river banks and patches of fresh, long grass close to swamps. He shelters from the burning rays of the sun in caves, or among the grass-grown ruins of deserted cities. Sometimes he takes a mud-bath in the shallow waters at the river's edge, and afterwards rolls in the dry sand. Very often he swims a river in search of prey. Tigers are very poor tree-climbers; but when attacking hunters they will spring as much as 5 metres from the ground into the fork of a tree.

The tigress is a devoted mother, and will protect her young with great ferocity. The number of cubs in a litter varies from two to six. As soon as they are old enough, she trains them thoroughly in the technique of hunting, and they generally stay with her until they are nearly 2 years old. Young tigers are more wanton in their killing than old ones, often destroying much more than they need to eat. Very young cubs are easily tamed; but tigers do not breed as freely as lions in captivity, and the cubs are more difficult to rear.

A typical jungle tiger lives chiefly on deer, wild pigs, and antelopes; but he sometimes eats cattle, and small animals such as porcupines, monkeys, and peafowl. He kills large prey by dislocating their necks. A wild bull buffalo is about a match for him; but he occasionally kills a young elephant or an adult bull gaur. He will eat his kill even when it has become putrid. In captivity, if not properly fed, he has been known to eat his own offspring. Tigers living near a village feed almost entirely on the small native cattle—unless, of course, they are man-eaters. Between meals they are sluggish and stupid and rarely show fight.

A regular man-eater is usually an old tiger which has grown too feeble to hunt other game; if there is a scarcity of food for her cubs, a female will attack human beings. Cattle-stealers sometimes become man-eaters after they have got used to the sight of man and have lost their fear of him. A man-eater will seize an unsuspecting native by the neck, and drag the body to a quiet spot where it can eat it at leisure, without fear of interruption. It eats only the fleshy parts, and then goes out to get a fresh victim for its next meal. Man-eaters are very wary, and big-game hunters find them the most difficult of all tigers to kill (*see* BIG-GAME HUNTING, Vol. IX).

In many parts of India and in Burma, tigers are regarded with superstition, and the natives will not kill them.

TIGER MOTHS AND FOOTMEN. The

family Arctiidae contains some 3,500 species, of which 29 occur in Britain. The Tigers, with which are grouped the Ermines, Clouded Buff, Muslin, and Flunkeys, are usually larger and more robust, have wider wings, and are more brightly coloured than the Footmen. Their caterpillars are 'woolly bears', most of which hibernate and complete their development in the spring. Most insect-eating animals quickly learn to associate the conspicuous colours of these moths and their larvae with distasteful qualities, and consequently leave them alone (*see* PROTECTIVE COLORATION). Cuckoos, however, eat hairy caterpillars freely.

The largest British species is the common Garden Tiger, the female sometimes measuring nearly 8 cm across the wings. The fore-wings are cream with large, dark-brown markings, and the hind-wings are deep reddish-orange with blue-black spots. These spots are sometimes so large that they are almost blotches, or sometimes so small that most of the wings are clear red. All-black specimens occur, and also others with the red colour of the hind-wings replaced by yellow, or with almost pure white, or with sooty-brown hind-wings—but they are very rare. The caterpillars, most easily seen on sunny days in April and May, when they are nearly full-grown, occur in most country lanes along the foot of hedgerows, round haystacks, or in farm-yards where nettle patches grow. They are jet-black, with numerous white spots or tubercles, each bearing tufts of long, black, silky hair tipped with white, while along the sides and by the head the hairs are reddish-brown. They feed on low-growing weeds such as stinging-nettle, dead-nettle, dandelion, plantain, and dock, and spin a loose cocoon of silk before turning into the chrysalis. The moths emerge in July or August, about 3 weeks after pupating; but as they fly only at night they are not so well known as the caterpillars.

The Cream-spot Tiger has velvety-black upper-wings with about eight cream-coloured spots, butter-yellow hind-wings with five or six black spots, and a patch of red on the body near the tail end. The caterpillar, a less striking 'woolly bear' than the Garden Tiger, feeds in much the same sort of places and on the same kind of weeds. It is most frequent in the southern and south-western counties of Britain. The much smaller Wood Tiger has yellow and black patterns on all four wings, the under-wings of the female being sometimes flushed orange or red. The moths are usually found in late May to early July in clearings in woods or on mossy moorland banks, and the caterpillars, rather gay-looking with their russet hairs, hibernate in thick, soft tussocks. The Ruby Tiger of southern England is crimson-rose, with black dots and a black border on its hind-wings. In the north, darker and duller varieties with little or no ruby colouring are found on moorlands where, in spring, their light brown, silken cocoons can be picked off heather stems. The quite common brownish caterpillars are thickly tufted with dark hair. They feed on a variety of weeds, and hibernate when fully fed.

The White, Water, and Buff Ermines, and the Muslin Moth are all nearly 4 cm across, and white or buff with black spots. The Water Ermine is restricted to fens and marshes; but the others are common garden species, the hairy caterpillars feeding on mint, lily of the valley, and many other low-growing plants. The male and female of the Clouded Buff differ in appearance and habits: the yellowish-white males have dark central spots and pink edges to both fore- and hind-wings; the females are orange with a central spot on the fore-wings and heavy black markings on the hind-wings. Though the males fly by day when disturbed, the females are rarely seen until the evening.

The black and yellow banded caterpillar of the Cinnabar Moth feeds on ragwort in waste lands and fields, the caterpillars being sometimes so abundant that they completely strip the rag-wort. An unsuccessful attempt was made about 1930 to introduce the Cinnabar to New Zealand, so that it might control the weed. The Cinnabar Moth has sooty fore-wings with a vermilion stripe and two vermilion spots, and vermilion hind-wings (*see* Colour Plate, p. 336).

The Feathered, Speckled, and Crimson Speckled Footmen, better known as Flunkeys, are nearer to the Tigers than to the true Foot-men. The Speckled Flunkey is restricted to parts

S. C. Bisserôt

GARDEN TIGER MOTH

of Dorset and Hampshire; the other two are rare immigrants, though the Crimson Speckled has a wide range, extending into Africa, India, Australia, and New Zealand.

The Footmen, of which there are 16 British species, are mostly yellowish or greyish in colour.

Derek Whiteley

CINNABAR MOTH AND LARVA

They have long, narrow fore-wings, which they fold along the body when resting—so presenting the stiff appearance which has suggested their common name. They mostly have a wing-expanse of about 2·5 cm, though the largest British species, the Four-spotted, measures over 4 cm. Their hairy caterpillars feed on lichens. There are many of them in Australia, where they largely replace the Tiger Moths.

The Scarlet and Jersey Tigers are the only British representatives of another family with warning colours, the Hypsidae. The Scarlet Tiger has blue-black fore-wings with nine or ten creamy spots, and rich scarlet hind-wings dotted and banded with black. Though very local, it has occurred in many counties as far north as Staffordshire, most frequently on river banks on the chalk, but also on sandstone, on sand-dune marshes, and in clearings in woods. The yellow-spotted, black caterpillars feed on comfrey, nettle, and other plants, and hibernate when quite small in curled leaves on the ground. They feed up rapidly in the spring, and pupate low down amongst withered grass or dead leaves, emerging during June. A Berkshire colony of Scarlet Tigers, which was under observation for a period of years, was estimated to vary from 1,000 to 10,000 individuals. The Scarlet Tiger is exceptionally suitable for such population studies because of its restricted habitat and conspicuous coloration. The Jersey Tiger, common in the Channel Islands, but in Britain restricted to south Devon, is a gaudy moth, the fore-wings being metallic blue-green with 'tiger' stripes of pale cream, while the under-wings vary from scarlet to orange or yellow, with three or four dark blotches. The caterpillars, also, are brighter than other Tigers, being greyish-brown, striped with orange and yellow, and covered with short, bristly, brownish hairs.

TITS (Titmice). These small birds, with short, strong bills, are to be found in most parts of the world. The family includes many species, several of which are common British birds. They feed principally on insects, which they hunt for in places such as the bark of trees and fruit buds, often perching with great agility upside down or in other odd positions.

Tits build lovely cup-shaped nests of moss and other soft materials, lined with feathers and wool —that of the Azure Tit of Siberia is chiefly of fur. The nests are generally placed in well-covered

Eric Hosking

LONG-TAILED TIT AT ITS NEST

holes in trees or walls; but the Great Tits and Blue Tits specialize in finding odd places, such as upturned flower-pots, letter-boxes, or the base of a discarded Crow's nest. Some tits, such as the Long-tailed Tit of Britain, the Penduline Tit of South Europe, and the New Zealand Creeper, build much more elaborate nests. The Long-tailed Tit builds, in a tree or bush, a deep, domed, bottle-shaped nest, woven of materials such as moss, lichen, wool, and spider's webs, and lined with a great number of feathers. The entrance is by a small hole high up on one side. When incubating, the bird sits with her long tail bent backwards over her head, sometimes even sticking out through the entrance-hole. The Penduline Tit hangs her woven nest like a deep hammock from a branch (*see* picture, p. 45). The New Zealand Creeper's nest is rather like that of the Long-tailed Tit—wool, moss, and vegetable fibre felted together into a pear-shaped bag, with a small entrance on one side. Many of the tits lay large clutches of up to twelve or fourteen white eggs, speckled with red. They generally rear two broods in a season.

The Great Tit, Coal Tit, and Blue Tit are all common residents in Britain, generally spending the winter in parties. These three species, although very closely related, have sufficiently different feeding habits to enable them to inhabit the same territory without interfering with each other. The Great Tit can eat larger insects than the other two, and occasionally even kills small or weak birds. The Coal Tit eats seeds as well as insects, and hunts its food on the ground as well as among the trees. The Blue Tit uses its delicate little bill to extract minute insects and grubs from the bark of trees or from fruit-tree buds. The Marsh Tit frequents woods near marshy country or along river banks; while the Crested Tit lives farther north and feeds partly on pine-seeds.

The Bearded Tit (Reedling or Reed-pheasant) is not very much like a typical tit—indeed it has more the build of a finch, and is classified separately. Its name comes from the long, beard-like feathers on the sides of the throat. Its blue-grey, chestnut, and buff colouring makes it blend well with its surroundings in the reed-beds and marshes of Norfolk. A few breed in Norfolk, where they build nests of reeds and flat grasses

CRESTED TIT

Eric Hosking

lined with reed-flowers, and placed in the reeds near the water.

TOAD. The name, if strictly used, applies only to members of the family Bufonidae (Latin, *bufo*, a toad); but it is used for many different kinds of tailless AMPHIBIA (q.v.). The general opinion that toads have thick-set, rather clumsy bodies, and a dry, warty skin is not true of all members of the family. The majority of the *Bufo* genus live on the ground; some (*Nectophryne*) live in trees, and have adhesive pads on their fingers and toes, like the Tree Frogs; while the Malayan *Pseudobufo* spends most of its life in water.

The genus *Bufo*, with more than 100 species, is found all over the world, except in Australia and Madagascar. Identification of many of the species is often difficult, for the differences between them are slight. England has two species, the Common Toad and the Natterjack. Other well-known species are the Green Toad of Europe and North Africa (closely related to the Natterjack), the common Asiatic Toad, the Malayan Giant Toad, which reaches a length of 20 centimetres and is the largest of all the toads, the Common American Toad, and the Giant Toad of tropical America. The latter, up to 15 centimetres long, has now been introduced into sugar plantations to destroy insect pests.

Toads lay their eggs in strings—as opposed to frogs, which lay them in clusters. The tadpoles of the Common Toad can be easily distinguished from those of the FROG (q.v.) by their smaller size and blacker colour. Toads seem to like to breed in certain ponds. The larval stage lasts about 2 months. When first the baby toads leave the water, they measure little over 1 cm in length, and for some time they live near the pond, hiding under leaves or stones by day. A sudden shower of rain will bring them out of their hiding-places—and this occurrence has given rise to the stories of 'showers of toads'.

The Natterjack is distinguished from the larger Common Toad by its smoother skin, which is greenish in colour and has a yellow stripe down the back. Also, having shorter hind legs, it usually runs rather than hops. It is much the rarer of the two species, being found only in certain localities—particularly sandy places, where it is often found in numbers. In the breeding season, male Natterjacks are very noisy, and on still evenings their loud calls can be heard a long way off.

The tadpole of the Natterjack is very small, about 2·5 cm in length, and it remains a tadpole for only about 6 weeks. When they leave the water, the young toads measure nearly 1 cm in length; by the end of the second summer they are still less than 2·5 cm long, and they do not reach maturity until the fourth or fifth year.

S. C. Bisserôt

COMMON TOAD

The average length of the fully grown toad is about 6 cm.

The Midwife Toad, a native of central and western Europe, is so named because of the way in which the male carries and cares for the eggs during the early stages of their development. After the eggs are laid, the male pushes his legs through the mass so that they become wound round him in a sort of figure-of-eight. Then, leaving the female, he carries the eggs about with him for the next 3 weeks or so, moistening them regularly with dew or even immersing them in water. At the end of that time he takes them to the nearest water, and the young, already partly developed, escape from their covering membrane and continue their lives as tadpoles in the ordinary way.

Spadefoot is a name applied to the toads of two genera inhabiting Europe and North America. The foot is provided with a strong, shovel-shaped tubercle, by which the creature can dig itself into the soil, where it remains concealed during the day. The skin exudes a secretion which smells like garlic—and in Germany they are sometimes called Garlic Toads.

Toads can become very tame in captivity and may live for 40 years.

TOADSTOOL, *see* Fungi.

TORTOISE, *see* Turtles and Tortoises.

TORTOISESHELL BUTTERFLIES, *see* Vanessinae.

TOUCAN. This fantastic-looking, brilliantly coloured bird is an inhabitant of the tropical forests of South and Central America, spreading as far north as Mexico. It is a relative of the Woodpecker. Toucans have beaks out of all proportion in size to the rest of their bodies. The Toco Toucan of South America, for instance, a bird of about 60 cm long, has a beak which extends a quarter of its total length. This beak, which makes the bird look top-heavy, is actually very light, being made of a fine network of bony fibres which give strength without weight. It is generally highly coloured, as are the naked parts of the bird's head. The plumage in most species is predominantly black and green. Toucans are mainly fruit-eaters, living in large or small flocks in the high forest trees, and flying with ease and grace over the tops of the forests. During

Booth Steamship Co.

TOUCAN OF TROPICAL AMERICA

the heat of the day they rest motionless in the branches, but otherwise are constantly on the move. They nest in hollow branches of fruit-trees.

TRANSPIRATION OF PLANTS. During cold weather the insides of greenhouses are often covered with water; and if a potted plant with a leafy shoot is put under a glass jar for a few hours, water will appear on the glass. This condensed water may have come either from direct evaporation from the soil, or else from the plants themselves. All land plants give off water-vapour which in certain circumstances, such as in the greenhouse, may condense as liquid drops. A fair-sized oak-tree may give off as much as 680 litres of water a day, while a plant of Indian Corn, during its life of 26 weeks, may give off 9 litres of water. The process of giving off water is known as transpiration.

That green plants should transpire is natural, since the cells of their leaves are saturated with water, which, with its dissolved mineral salts, is constantly being supplied by the roots for the process of food manufacture or Photosynthesis (q.v.). The air surrounding these leaves is more or less dry. The thousands of tiny pores or 'stomata' on the leaves take in from the atmosphere the carbon dioxide necessary for photosynthesis, and at the same time let out water-vapour.

The leaves are almost entirely responsible for the loss of water-vapour from green plants. If, for instance, the leaves are greased on both sides, so that water cannot escape through them, transpiration will practically stop. In normal leaves, which lie horizontally to the ground, most transpiration takes place from the lower surfaces, where the majority of the stomata are found. The Lilac leaf, for example, has 24,800 stomata per sq cm on the under and only one on the upper surface; whereas the Holly leaf has 9,700 stomata per sq cm on the under surface and none on the upper. As might be expected, leaves such as Grasses and Irises, which grow upright, have an equal number of stomata on each surface. Some WATER PLANTS (q.v.), however, the leaves of which lie out on the surface of the water, have all their stomata on the upper surface.

The passage of water-vapour through each of the stomata is controlled by two guard cells. As these swell or shrink, the pores automatically open and close. As a rule the stomata are open in the light and closed in darkness, and so transpiration takes place mostly during the day and practically ceases at night. In time of drought, when the soil is dry, the guard cells shrink, closing the stomata, and transpiration is reduced. When there is plenty of water in the soil, however, transpiration occurs freely.

The intake of water through the roots is not the only factor which affects transpiration. The humidity or amount of water-vapour in the atmosphere, for instance, is a consideration. Water evaporates much faster in a dry atmosphere than in a damp one, and at first transpiration continues rapidly in a dry atmosphere, until the air becomes so dry that the guard cells shrink and close the stomata. Wind, also, by drying the atmosphere increases transpiration, so that plants in exposed places often suffer from excess of transpiration, and need shelter. The intensity of light, by affecting the rate of photosynthesis, also affects the rate of transpiration.

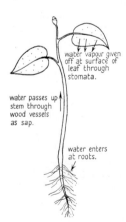

water vapour given off at surface of leaf through stomata.

water passes up stem through wood vessels as sap.

water enters at roots.

PLANT TRANSPIRATION

It is probable that humidity, temperature, light-intensity, wind, and the amount of water available in the soil, all interact together to control the rate of transpiration—although it has recently been shown that slight changes in the degree of opening of the stomata affect the rate of transpiration much less than was formerly supposed.

Transpiration is not, however, a purely wasteful process. The reason for the flow of water from deep roots to the top of a tall tree has never been satisfactorily explained; but transpiration probably plays a most important part in bringing this about. As water is lost by the cells bordering a stoma, so it is absorbed by these cells from the surrounding ones. This loss and absorption proceeds as a chain process in the leaf-cells until the veins are reached. These veins contain the wood vessels, which stretch in long tubes down to the roots, and make what amounts to a closed system of pipes. As water is sucked out of these vessels at the top, it is probable that a state of tension is set up, which causes water to be sucked in by the root-cells from the soil. Thus, by continual loss of water, transpiration is probably the means of starting a flow of water containing mineral salts from the roots to the leaves, where it is indispensable for photosynthesis. But the flow of water through a plant is also thought to be helped by a force exerted from below, a force the existence of which is known, and which is called ROOT PRESSURE (q.v.).

The upward transpiration stream in plants is closely associated with the transport of water containing the food substances made by photosynthesis. This 'translocation stream', as it is called, goes out to all parts of the plant, taking with it food for immediate use or for storage, as well as water and dissolved gases for respiration and other purposes. Together, the transpiration and translocation streams correspond to the BLOOD SYSTEM (q.v.) of animals.

See also RESPIRATION IN PLANTS.

TREE-CREEPER. This inconspicuous little brown and greyish-white bird has a long, curved bill, strong, curved claws, and a long, stiff tail. It spends much of its life running up the trunks of trees with quick, jerky movements, probing the crevices of the bark for insects. As soon as it has crept up one tree, it flies down to the base of the next tree and starts again. Insects form the bulk of its food, though it also eats some seeds and grain. This bird is to be seen fairly commonly in all wooded districts of Britain, and during the winter it often joins bands of Tits and Goldcrests in search of food. It nests in a crevice of a tree, often between the trunk and a piece of loose bark, or a thick ivy stem. There is a closely related species in North America.

The Wall-creeper is a larger relative, to be found in the mountains of central and south Europe. It has a grey head and back, and large, rounded, blackish wings, marked with a crimson band and white spots. It spends its time hunting for insects over the faces of rocks or among boulders, climbing about with jerky hops, and helping itself by opening and closing its wings.

TREES. Though so different in height and shape, a broad-leaved tree is as much a FLOWERING PLANT (q.v.) as a tulip. Its trunk is its STEM (q.v.). Its FLOWERS, FRUITS, LEAVES, and ROOTS (qq.v.) are similar to those of other plants, and its reproduction is carried out by the same methods. The ECOLOGY (q.v.) and distribution of trees are determined, as in plants, by soil, temperature, and rainfall (*see* WOODLANDS; TROPICAL JUNGLES).

There are two main kinds of trees: (*a*) broad-leaved trees, many of which shed all their leaves in the autumn (*see* TREES, BROADLEAVED, Vol. VI); (*b*) those which bear their seeds exposed in cones and always have narrow or needle-shaped leaves, and which are not true flowering plants (*see* CONIFERS). Most conifers shed their old leaves and grow new ones to take their place all the year round.

See also Vol. VI: PALM TREES; TIMBER; FORESTRY; ARBORICULTURE.

TREE SHREW (TUPAI). This insect-eating mammal of Asia, though it looks very like a Squirrel, is not related to it. It is usually placed among the INSECTIVORA (q.v.); but in the opinion of some scientists is related more closely to the LEMURS (q.v.) and Primates (*see* MONKEYS). Tree Shrews have the long, sensitive snouts peculiar to the Insectivora; but, like Squirrels, they have bushy tails as long as their bodies, and live in trees. They show the same movements as Squirrels, too, often sitting up to eat and holding their food between their forepaws. They usually find enough insect food in the trees; but sometimes they hunt for it on the ground—in Malaya often entering houses for the purpose. Their rat-like heads and thievish expressions make them not very attractive. Among themselves they are quarrelsome—though, in fact, they are quite easily tamed. Their usual call is a short, peculiar, whistling sound which, when they are angry, changes to a loud, shrill cry.

TROGON. These tropical forest-birds carry, perhaps, more brilliant plumage than any other birds. The skins of the American Trogons, in particular, have been sought after so keenly that some species have been almost exterminated. The majority of Trogons belong to South and Central America, one species reaching as far north as Texas and Arizona. Another species belongs only to San Domingo, and one only to Cuba. There are four species in tropical Africa, and others in south-east Asia.

One of the most spectacular of the Trogons is the Quetzal of Guatemala. The male bird has a brilliant metallic green head, chest, back, and wings, deep blood-red underparts, and some white and black on the outer tail-feathers. It carries a large, rounded crest, long, drooping wing-plumes, and a very long tail, with the two middle plumes extended about four times as long as the rest—nearly 2 metres altogether. The female is much less adorned. The characteristic colouring of the typical Trogons, birds which range from southern Brazil to Mexico, is metallic blue and green above, and yellow, scarlet, and crimson beneath. They live, generally in pairs, in the forest, feeding on fruit and berries, and uttering at intervals their curious cries.

The African Trogons are shy birds, and not a great deal is known of their behaviour. One species belongs to East Africa, another to Central Africa, a third to West Africa, and a fourth to Zanzibar. They are said to lay four white eggs in a hole in a tree. One of the Asiatic species, the Red-headed Trogon, eats insects rather than fruit, catching its prey on the wing, as a Fly-catcher does.

RESPLENDENT QUETZAL

The Colies or Mouse-birds, exclusively African birds, and closely related to the Trogons, live generally in small flocks, and creep about fruit-trees with the help of their claws and beaks, hanging head downwards to reach the fruit. They are said even to sleep in that inverted position.

TROPICAL JUNGLES. The vast forests of the tropics form a girdle round the globe, and, whether in Africa, America, or the East, are in many ways alike. In some regions, where there is a definite dry season, the trees shed their leaves and have a resting-time (like our own trees in winter) till the rains return and the new leaves appear. But in hilly areas near the equator, where there is almost daily rain, there are great stretches of evergreen forest. Here the climate is one long moist summer, always hot and always damp, providing ideal conditions for the exuberant growth of plants. The trees grow to immense heights, often to 90 metres, forming a dense canopy, under which the air is always heavy with moisture. The light is dim, and there is a weird stillness below the canopy. The forest seems to be built on different levels. On the ground are the shade-loving shrubs; and above them woody climbers (*see* CLIMBING PLANTS) struggle ever higher towards the hidden sun—many of them beginning their race for light and air, not from the ground, but from nooks and crannies in the trees. Among the rope-like stems of the climbers are layers of filmy FERNS (q.v.), and perched plants or 'epiphytes', or even parasites, fastened on the branches of the trees (*see* PARASITIC PLANTS). MOSSES (q.v.) and lichens shroud the stems and branches; and even the leaves are veiled with minute ALGAE (q.v.). Seen from below the canopy looks green and brown; but in reality it is the home of many vivid and striking ORCHIDS (q.v.) which, hoisted on the shoulders of the giant trees, flaunt their glowing blossoms.

Sometimes the plants which grow on other plants and live at their expense become so strong that the overburdened tree beneath gives up the struggle and dies. The parasitic fig-tree, for example, sprouts from a seed lying in the fork of another tree, and begins to send long roots to the ground. These long suckers form a network round the trunk of the supporting tree, and after they have reached the ground, they become strong and woody. The smothered supporting tree dies at last, leaving a trellis-work fig-tree in its place. The strands of the trellis fuse together gradually, till the fig-tree has developed a huge trunk, and becomes one of the forest giants.

A particularly interesting example of a tropical parasitic plant is Rafflesia, a native of the Malayan forests, which grows on the roots of vines. The roots, stems, and leaves of the plant become reduced until they are little more than colourless threads growing through the soil and piercing the roots of their vine host to extract food. The flower, on the other hand, is far from reduced—one species, in fact, has the largest-known flower in the world. This is usually red, and can measure up to a metre across. It has a repulsive smell, rather like that of decaying fish.

In those jungles where the sky cannot be seen at all because of the dense canopy, the undergrowth is usually scanty, the forest floor being covered merely with a carpet of pale FUNGI (q.v.) and with a scattering of dead leaves from the giants overhead. But where the sunlight can penetrate, the undergrowth becomes so thick that one can scarcely see a metre ahead. There is no grass in the true tropical forest, owing to the lack of sunshine; but where a stream flows or there is a clearing from a fallen tree, there is a rich plant life, with coarse grasses, like those of the bushlands, at the fringes of the forest.

The inexhaustible variety of plants found in the hot, damp climates of these forests grows with such incredible rapidity that areas which have been cleared and then neglected become completely grown over and unrecognizable within a few years. Although evergreens predominate, there is also a considerable proportion of deciduous trees, many of which burst into flower twice, and several even as much as four times, in a year. The mighty Teak of the Indian and Burman jungles sheds its leaves in the dry season. With the evergreen trees, leaf-shedding occurs in a sporadic fashion; and also—which is more remarkable—flowering takes place sporadically throughout the year, instead of at any fixed season. In consequence, fruits also, including pulpy fruits, are available for animal food at all seasons. The flowers are often borne directly on the older stems or trunks of the trees and occasionally even on the roots. The flowers of the COCOA tree (q.v. Vol. VI) of West Africa, for example, are borne on the trunks.

The number of different trees to be found in these forests is immense: there may be as many

TYPICAL TROPICAL JUNGLE IN EQUATORIAL AMERICA

as 200 different kinds to the square kilometre. They include a large number of such important trees as the Camwood, Ebony, Rubbers, and Mahoganies of enormous size, scented and otherwise, which are distributed in tropical forests throughout the world. Banana Palms are typical of the tropical forests of the Old World; the Ginger plant occurs in the Indo-Malayan forests; while the American forests contain Arrowroots. Coniferous trees occur only on the higher lands, because they cannot survive where the temperatures are too high.

See also ECOLOGY OF PLANTS.
See also Vol. III: FORESTS, Section 2 and 3 (a).
See also Vol. VI: FORESTRY; RUBBER; BANANAS.

C. A. Gibson-Hill

RED-TAILED TROPIC-BIRD OF THE INDIAN OCEAN

TROPIC-BIRD. Called by sailors the 'Boatswain', this ocean bird, rather smaller than a common gull, frequents the tropical regions of the Atlantic, Pacific, and Indian Oceans. It belongs to the same group of birds as the CORMORANT, GANNET, PELICAN, and FRIGATE BIRD (qq.v.). It has predominantly white plumage, some species having red bills and black on the wing-feathers, and others yellow bills and a little red on the tail-feathers. All have webbed feet and two very greatly elongated tail-feathers. Tropic-birds often follow in the wake of ships for long periods, showing boldness in pursuing food. They breed in large companies on the Bermudas and Pacific Islands, nesting in holes in the rocks or in trees, and laying one dark-brown, mottled egg.

TROUT, *see* SALMON, Section 2.

TRUFFLES, *see* FUNGI.

TSETSE FLY. This blackish, dark-brown, or yellowish-brown insect is found only in tropical Africa. It is about the size of one of its near relatives, the HOUSE-FLY (q.v.); but it can easily be distinguished by the way it shuts its wings—folding them flat, one exactly over the other, upon the abdomen, beyond which they project considerably. Its skin-piercing and blood-sucking proboscis projects a short distance in front of its head. The female produces one larva at a time, which drops, fully grown, on to the ground and burrows at once into the ground to pupate. The pupa is enclosed in a puparium, the last larval skin.

Tsetse Flies occur in Africa from the Congo on the west to Uganda and the Great Lakes in the east; but they are confined to patches of forest, where they have moisture, warmth, and shade. The tracts they inhabit are called 'fly-belts'. They carry and transmit PROTOZOA (q.v.) which cause deadly tropical diseases, the most serious to mankind being 'sleeping-sickness'. 'Nagana' is a devastating cattle disease also transmitted by Tsetse Flies.

TSETSE FLY

See also FLY.

TUATARA. This solidly built reptile, somewhat lethargic in its movements, grows to a length of 60 cm. Although externally shaped like a LIZARD (q.v.), it differs in so many structural characters that it cannot be placed even in the same order. It digs a burrow in the ground, with a spacious chamber at the end, and this it shares with a bird, usually a species of PETREL (q.v.). The birds are allowed to breed there; but no other Tuatara is allowed to enter the burrow. It remains at home through the day, coming out after dark to hunt for its food, of small vertebrates, insects, and whatever it can pick up on the sea-shore.

It is of particular interest to scientists as being the most primitive of all living reptiles: it is the sole survivor today of an order—the Rhynchocephalia—that was once spread widely over Europe. At the beginning of the last century, the Tuatara was common on the main islands of

Zoological Society of London

TUATARA

New Zealand; but with the advance of the white man it has vanished, and is now found only in some of the islets in the Bay of Plenty, where it is preserved by Government order.

TUNNY, *see* MACKEREL.

TURBOT, *see* FLAT-FISHES.

TURKEYS. These birds, originally natives of North and Central America, form a small group of birds hunted for food. The Aztecs of Mexico had domesticated Turkeys long before the arrival of the Europeans, who introduced them into Europe after the Spanish conquest of Mexico, about 1500, and into England at least as early as 1541. The Turkey soon became a favourite table-bird, quite displacing the PEACOCK (q.v.). Mexican and North American species are still to be found wild in the eastern states of North America, from Mexico to Canada. It was found there by the 17th-century pioneers to North America, and has since then been the traditional dish for the American feast of Thanksgiving Day. How the name 'Turkey' originated is uncertain: perhaps the bird, being introduced to Britain from southern Europe, was thought to have come from Turkey. Turkeys of Central America are resplendent birds, with plumage of green, bronze, blue, and gold, and 'eyes' on the tail-feathers like those of peacocks; but are too delicate to be domesticated. Cock Turkeys perform elaborate dances, with spreading of the tail and fluffing of the plumage, as part of their courtship display in the spring (*see* ANIMAL LANGUAGE). The Mexican Indians, thinking that the Turkeys danced to bring rain to the dried-up country, invented a 'turkey dance' themselves, which they performed as part of the magic to bring rain.

See also Vol. VI: TURKEYS.

TURTLES AND TORTOISES.   1. These creatures belong to the Order Chelonia or Testudines (Latin, *testudo*, a tortoise), which includes all the shelled reptiles, such as the Marine Turtles, the Mud or Soft-shelled Turtles, the Land Tortoises, the Freshwater Tortoises, the Terrapins, and the Side-neck Tortoises. The Chelonians differ from all other reptiles in having a more or less developed bony shell enclosing all the organs of the body, and into which the head and limbs can be withdrawn. Classification is based partly on the method of withdrawing the head, which can be done either by bending the neck vertically in an S-shaped curve, or by bending it sideways.

The shell can be divided into two parts, the upper being called the 'carapace', and the lower the 'plastron'. The two meet along the side of the body (the junction being called the 'bridge'), leaving a large aperture in front and behind for the passage of the head and limbs. The ribs and vertebrae of the back are solidly joined to the carapace, with the result that the upper bones of the limbs lie inside the ribs, instead of outside them, as in all other animals. In most species the bony shell is covered with horny plates. None of the Chelonians has teeth, the jaws being furnished with horny cutting margins. They lay rounded or oval white eggs: in the Marine Turtles these have a parchment-like covering; in all the others, there is a hard, chalky shell.

2. TURTLE. The name covers two very distinct groups—the Marine Turtles, which inhabit the oceans, and the Mud or Soft-shelled Turtles, which live entirely in fresh water.

The Marine Turtles can be recognized by their broad, paddle-shaped limbs, often furnished with claws, but without distinct digits, the fore-limb always being longer than the hind. They live entirely in the sea. There are five species, four belonging to one family, the Cheloniidae, while the fifth, the Leathery Turtle, which differs widely in structure from the others, forms a separate family by itself.

The members of the Cheloniidae are the Green Turtle, the Hawksbill Turtle, the Loggerhead, and Kemp's Turtle, the latter a rare creature found only off the east coast of North America.

The Green or Edible Turtle gets its name from the green colour of its fat. Turtle soup is made from the flesh. The natives of many tropical islands enjoy eating the meat and fat. From the horny shell of the carapace of the Hawksbill is obtained commercial tortoise-shell. The flesh is not usually eaten; but the eggs of both species, and also those of the Loggerhead, are eagerly sought after as food, and the collecting of them is a regular industry, often under Government control. The eggs, as big as golf-balls, are laid on sandy beaches in holes dug by the female. Usually several batches are laid, the Green Turtle and the Loggerhead laying between 300 and 500 each season, the Hawksbill not so many. They are sold in the native markets, but to European taste are flavourless and rather gritty in texture. The Green Turtle is a vegetarian, living largely on sea-grasses; the Hawksbill and the Loggerhead are mainly flesh-eating. The shell of the Hawksbill seldom exceeds 85 cm in length; that of the other two reaches 100 cm. The home of all three is in tropical waters; but they occasionally find their way to the coasts of England.

The Leathery Turtle (or Luth) is the largest of all the living Chelonians, reaching a length of about 2 metres and an estimated weight of 450 kilograms. It is inedible. It differs from all other Chelonians in the construction of its bony shell, this being composed of small, interlocking plates, not connected with the backbone or ribs. It is generally found in tropical waters, but appears to be scarce everywhere, except on the coasts of Ceylon and southern India. It is an occasional visitor to English shores. It feeds mainly on shell-fish and marine plants; but, as it spends most of its life in the deep sea, very little is known of its habits. Like the other marine species it comes ashore to breed; but the young, once they are hatched and have escaped to the sea, are not seen again until they are ready to breed.

The Mud or Soft-shelled Turtles are so called because their bony shell is covered with skin instead of with horny plates. They live in slow-flowing rivers with muddy bottoms, and may be found also in lakes. The limbs are not flipper-shaped; but the toes are broadly webbed and are provided with sharp claws. The bones of the carapace and plastron are smaller than in other Chelonians, and there is no bridge holding them together. The snout is long and tubular in shape,

with nostrils at the end which enable them to breathe in the water without exposing any other part of the body. The neck is long, and the head can be shot out and withdrawn with lightning-like rapidity. Most of the species are fierce in disposition and, when fully grown, are dangerous to handle.

Mud Turtles are found in many parts of Asia, Africa, and North America. They feed on fish, frogs, and molluscs, and are not particular whether their food is alive or dead. In captivity they will eat rice, bread, and other vegetable food. In many of the Indian and Indo-Chinese temples, they are kept in a semi-domesticated state, soon learning to come for food when called.

3. TORTOISE. The term tortoise is a useful name for all those Chelonians which cannot be included under the word turtle. It covers the Freshwater Tortoises, the Terrapins, the true Land Tortoises, the Side-neck Tortoises, and many others with more specific names, such as the Snappers, the Box Tortoises, the Painted, and the Musk Tortoises.

The name Terrapin covers all edible species (eight or ten) of Freshwater Tortoises inhabiting the U.S.A., the best known being the Snappers and the Diamond-back Terrapin. The Snappers, including two species, the Alligator Terrapin and the Common Snapper, have large heads, long tails, rugged shells, and fierce dispositions. When interfered with, they stand on the defensive with open mouths, looking as fierce as they can, and ready to bite anyone who tries to handle them. The Alligator Terrapin grows to 38 centimetres long, the Common Snapper not quite so long. They live in fresh water, and eat both animal and vegetable food. Another species of Terrapin common in the U.S.A is the Painted Turtle, which has an almost black carapace, handsomely margined with yellow; the plastron is entirely yellow or marked with black or dark brown. The name Musk Tortoise is given to three species of Terrapin on account of the unpleasant odour which, on the slightest provocation, they give out from glands by the thighs. They are known also as Stinkpots.

Land Tortoises, as their name implies, live entirely on land—some in desert regions far from water. They are all vegetarians. The limbs are club-shaped, the digits compactly joined to one another and provided with sharp claws. The carapace in most species is deeply convex, so that legs and head can be completely with-

Mansell Coll.

TURTLES HATCHING OUT
The eggs have been laid in a sandy hollow, and incubated by the heat of the sun

drawn. The family, the Testudinidae, includes the Greek Tortoise from the Mediterranean, often seen in captivity in England, the Giant Tortoises of the Galapagos and Mascarene Islands, the Hinged Tortoises of South Africa, and the Gopher Tortoises of North America.

The long life of the Giant Tortoises is proverbial: it is beyond doubt that one of them has lived for at least 150 years; and it is said, though there is no authentic record, that they have reached 200 or 300 years of age. The Hinged Tortoises are so called because the hinder part of the carapace is joined to the front part by a hinge of gristle, enabling the creature, when the legs are withdrawn, to close that end of its house. A similar but much more perfect modification can be seen in the Box Tortoises.

Side-neck Tortoises are freshwater tortoises scientifically known as the Pleurodira. They are found only in the southern hemisphere, in Australia, South Africa, and South America; and, except for the marine turtles, they are the only turtles or tortoises in Australia and New Guinea.

The name Side-neck has been given to them because, when attempting to conceal the head under the shell, the neck is bent horizontally sideways, instead of in the more usual S-shaped curve. As most of the species have very long necks, the attempt is not very effective. There are also other characteristics in the skull, vertebrae, and shell by which they differ from other Chelonians. Not many of the species have popular names. Some of those in Australia are called Snake-necked Tortoises, and perhaps the best known of all is the Mata-mata of South America. The largest member of the group is the Giant Amazon Tortoise, with a shell measuring 76 centimetres in length.

Box Tortoise is a general term given to certain species of tortoise which can close their shells both in front and behind, so that the head and limbs are completely hidden—a very effective method of defence against their enemies. So perfect is the closure in some species, that the blade of a knife cannot be passed between the two portions of the shell. None of the Box

Tortoises grow to more than 20 centimetres in length. Some are found in open woodland country; others spend most of their lives in rivers, lakes, and ponds. They are natives of the East and of North America.

See also REPTILES.
See also Vol. VI: TURTLE FISHING.

TUSSOCK MOTHS. Under this heading are grouped the members of the family Lymantriidae, which include the Tussocks themselves, the Vapourers, the Gypsy Moth, the Gold-tail, and the Black Arches. They are medium-sized brown, grey, or white moths with strongly combed antennae—especially in the males. Their mouth-parts are degenerate and they do not feed. The females of some species are quite unable to fly, having only tiny undeveloped wings. Some have tufts of hair at the end of their bodies, which they utilize to cover their eggs. The caterpillars are always hairy, and some bear conspicuous tufts or brushes. They feed mainly on broad-leaved trees, some species being serious pests in Europe and America. Eleven species have been recorded in Britain; but the Reed Tussock and Gypsy Moths are now extinct, and the Black V-Moth a very scarce immigrant.

The common Pale Tussock is a drab, greyish moth, with darker cross-bands on the fore-wings; its caterpillar is an exquisite shade of primrose-yellow, with whitish or greenish hairs, four thick brushes of yellow hairs on its back, and a larger thin, reddish tuft at its tail. Between the brushes are velvety-black areas clearly displayed when the caterpillar, on being disturbed, curls up. This caterpillar is common in hop-fields, though it attacks the hops too late in the season to do much harm. The moths fly in May and June. The Dark Tussock is chiefly a northern and Scottish species, but also occurs in Dorset and Kent.

The male Vapourer, a small, foxy-brown moth, with a white spot on each fore-wing, is frequently seen in towns, flying in the sunshine during July and August. When the grey, almost wingless female emerges, she lays her batch of eggs on her empty cocoon, which is attached to a twig, or some such support. The caterpillars, which hatch in the spring, are brightly coloured smoky-blue, dotted with red, and have four thick brushes of yellow hair on the back, a pair of fine pencils of black feather-like hairs in front, and a dark-grey or brownish tuft behind. They feed upon a variety of trees and bushes, and some-

times swarm in London parks. The Scarce Vapourer, which is very local, has more white on the wings of the male, but is otherwise like the Vapourer in appearance and habits.

The pure-white Brown-tail is a coastal species occurring in Kent and Sussex. The female lays her eggs on various trees in clusters of 200–400, and covers them with hairs from her tail. The young larvae make a tent by drawing together several leaves with silk, and there they hibernate. In the spring they quit the old shelters, constructing new ones, and feeding on buds and young leaves, sometimes completely stripping the trees. The full-grown caterpillar is blackish-brown, with an interrupted white line on each side, and two vermilion spots near the hind end. Its hairs are barbed and hollow, and contain a poisonous substance which causes an irritating rash on the human skin. In badly infested areas the poisoned hairs are sometimes carried by the wind and may lodge in clothing. Brown-tails are spread over most of Europe. Early in the century they were introduced into the eastern United States, where they caused much damage to fruit- and oak-trees. They became such a menace that action had to be taken to reduce their numbers—the most successful method being the destruction of the winter webs in which the larvae hibernate.

The female Gypsy Moth, about 6 centimetres across, has creamy wings marked with black. Her body is so large that she cannot fly, and she usually lays her eggs in July in a cluster near the cocoon from which she has emerged, covering them with brownish down from her tail. The smaller, brown male is a strong flier. The Gypsy Moth is common on the Continent, even in Paris, where its hairy caterpillars, which are brown, with blue and red warts arranged in two rows down the back, feed from May to July on the plane trees of the boulevards. They were introduced into Massachusetts, U.S.A., in the 19th century in an attempt to cross them with the Silkworm Moth; but some escaped and spread so fast that in 20 years they were a serious nuisance over 900 square kilometres. Steps taken to exterminate them were not persistent enough, and by 1905 they were defoliating trees over six times that area. It has cost millions of dollars to get the pest under control, and constant vigilance is still necessary, as the young larvae are very buoyant and easily carried by the wind, as well as being transported by man.

Both sexes of the common Gold-tail are silky-white. The female measures over 4 centimetres across, the male slightly less, but has one or two black spots near the hind margins of the fore-wings. The Gold-tail caterpillar is black, with a red stripe down the back and white tufts at the side. It hatches in August, hibernates, and in the spring is a familiar sight on hawthorn, fruit-trees, and roses. It pupates in a cocoon made of silk and barbed hairs from the caterpillar's body. When the female emerges in June or July she sweeps up many of these hairs with her golden tail, and then, when she lays her eggs, the hairs, as well as part of her own tail-tuft, stick to the eggs and serve to protect them. Both male and female Gold-tail raise their golden tails when disturbed.

The black and white caterpillars of the White Satin Moth hibernate, and in the spring feed on poplar, sallow, and willows, becoming full grown in June or July. The moth, which measures about 5 cm across, has also been introduced into the United States, where it is now a pest.

The Black Arches or Nun Moth, ranging from about 4 cm across in the male to 5 cm in the female, has white fore-wings with zigzag black markings, greyish hind wings, and an abdomen tinged with pink. The eggs are laid on the bark of trees such as spruce, pine, oak, and apple, and the vari-coloured caterpillars hatch in the spring. Though widely distributed in Britain it has never become a serious pest; but the spruce plantations of central Europe are periodically defoliated.

The caterpillars of another member of the family, the Mexican Silk Moth, construct nests of silk which the natives spin into cloth (*see* SILK MOTHS).

S. Beaufoy

CATERPILLAR OF PALE TUSSOCK MOTH

S. Beaufoy

PALE TUSSOCK MOTH

U V

UMBRELLA BIRD, *see* CHATTERER.

UNDERGROUND STEMS, *see* STEMS, Section 2.

UNDERWING MOTH, *see* NIGHT-FLYING MOTH.

VANESSINAE (Butterflies). These form a subfamily of the Nymphalidae, to which family also belong the FRITILLARIES, PURPLE EMPEROR, and WHITE ADMIRAL (qq.v.). The Vanessinae include some of the most gaily coloured butterflies seen in the British Isles, the Peacock, Comma, and Tortoiseshells being permanent residents, while the Camberwell Beauty, Painted Lady, and Red Admiral are immigrants. The caterpillars are shiny, and often live in colonies until nearly full grown. The pupae, which hang by their tails, usually bear gold or silver spots—because of which the name 'chrysalis', meaning 'golden', came to be used for the pupae of all butterflies.

The Red Admiral is a gay, black and red immigrant from North Africa and the Mediterranean coasts. The female lays only a few eggs, one at a time on each patch of nettles visited. The caterpillar folds the nettle leaves over in a flap and secures them with fine threads of silk. When ready to pupate, it fastens itself by a silk pad to the top of a little 'tent' of folded leaves, within which it turns into a chrysalis. The butterflies emerge in late July, and compete with other Vanessinae for the best positions on the buddleia bushes and, a little later, on Michaelmas daisies. In autumn they are often seen feeding from rotting fruit in orchards, or from sap exuding from trees. Recent evidence suggests that many more Red Admirals hibernate in Britain than hitherto believed, though most still come as migrants.

The strongly flying, pink and brown Painted Lady is the most cosmopolitan of all butterflies, and has been seen in most parts of the world where butterflies can live. It breeds continuously along the Mediterranean coast, and periodically migrates—though what causes these large-scale movements is unknown. Most years a few are seen in southern England, two or three influxes occurring during the summer; though sometimes they appear in large numbers. On arrival, the females lay their eggs on thistles, nettles, or burdock leaves. The caterpillars are spiny, with streaks of lemon-yellow on their greyish skins. They feed singly, and are often found on thistles, each one lying along the mid-rib of the leaf, covered by a few threads of silk hooked on to the prickles. They crawl away from the plant to pupate, and hang up amongst thick undergrowth. The pupa is ash-grey and studded with golden dots, which sparkle in the sunshine. The butterflies fly in the evening long after most butterflies have settled down. They do not survive the winter.

The rich reddish-brown Small Tortoiseshell is one of the commonest hibernating butterflies in the British Isles, its dark underside being well adapted for concealment. It often spends the winter in houses, sleeping in a corner, behind a picture, or in the fold of a curtain; but on sunny winter days it may become active, and is sometimes found fluttering in a window. If the butterfly is allowed to fly out into the cold it will almost certainly die, for it does not normally leave its winter quarters until March. The females lay their eggs in large batches on the undersides of stinging-nettle leaves, several generations appearing throughout the summer. On hatching, the tiny black caterpillars spin a web between the stems, and live together until they reach the last skin—when they are about 2 cm long, and have changed to greenish-grey with yellowish stripes along their back and sides. They then wander away and bask in the sunshine in groups of two or three. They wander still farther to pupate, the chrysalis being dirty brown, ornamented with gilt points (*see* pictures, p. 63).

The Large Tortoiseshell is more nearly related to the Peacock and Camberwell Beauty than to the Small Tortoiseshell. Once common in most southern counties of Britain, it became increasingly scarce in the early part of this century. Recently, however, it has been seen in some numbers in the eastern counties and Kent. The females lay their eggs in batches round the twigs of elm trees or the stems of sallow bushes, and the caterpillars usually feed in large colonies on the upper branches. They frequently drop to the ground when ready to pupate, and then wander in search of a suitable site. Large numbers of pupae have been found hanging in rows under the eaves of sheds or woodland cottages.

The Peacock is easily recognized by the four large 'peacock eyes' on its brilliant plum-red wings, and by its black undersides. The caterpillars, which have inky black, spiny bodies, feed only on stinging-nettles, and live in large colonies in a common web. In the autumn the butterflies haunt buddleia bushes, feasting on the rich nectar before retiring into hibernation in late September. Although sometimes found indoors, Peacocks usually spend the winter in old barns, outhouses, hollow trees, or rabbit burrows, where they remain until the first warm days of spring. Peacocks have recently been found in many parts of Scotland, where they have long been absent.

The Camberwell Beauty is most often seen along the east coast of England, to which it occasionally migrates in the autumn from Scandinavia. It has never been known to breed here, for only a scattered few succeed in surviving the winter. The butterfly, which is dark purple with a yellow edge to its wings, is called in Scandinavia the Mourning Cloak butterfly. The females lay their eggs on sallow bushes. The spiny black caterpillars are curiously marked with eight large, round red patches on the back. In Scandinavia the butterflies hibernate among stacked pine-logs.

The Comma is so called because of the little white marks, like commas, on the underside of each orange-brown hind-wing. No other British butterfly has such ragged wings, which make Commas resemble the dead leaves, among which they usually hibernate. In the spring they may be seen feeding from sallow catkins. The females lay eggs on a variety of plants, including elm, red currant, hops, and stinging-nettles. The caterpillars are the brightest of British Vanessine larvae, being patterned in reddish-brown on the back for the first five segments, then in white to the tail. The butterflies mate after hibernation, some of the first brood of cater-

S. Beaufoy

PEACOCK BUTTERFLY

S. Beaufoy

PAINTED LADY BUTTERFLY

S. Beaufoy

CAMBERWELL BEAUTY BUTTERFLY

pillars producing butterflies in early summer. These early summer offspring are more tawny and less ragged than the late summer ones. They pair immediately and produce a second brood in September. During the 19th century the Comma declined, and became extinct in most districts, though it still survived in Herefordshire and neighbouring counties. Since 1920, however, it has increased again, and now even reaches into Scotland.

See also BUTTERFLIES; HIBERNATION.

VAPOURER MOTH, *see* TUSSOCK MOTHS.

VENUS'S FLY-TRAP, *see* INSECTIVOROUS PLANTS, Section 5.

VIPERS. 1. These poisonous snakes of the family Viperidae are distinguished from other poisonous snakes by having the poison-fangs attached to a movable bone, the 'maxillary'. When not in use, the fang lies backwards in the mouth in a horizontal position. The vipers are divided into two sub-families: the true Vipers and the Pit Vipers—so called because they have a pit in the side of the face between the eye and the nostril. To the Pit Vipers belong the Rattlesnake of America and a large genus inhabiting south-west Asia and South America.

The typical viperine head, bluntly triangular and mounted upon a narrow neck, is fairly distinctive of the whole group; but it is found on many other snakes besides vipers, some quite harmless. Snakes of the Viper family are mostly thick-bodied, with shortish tails, slow in their movements, and when molested they will often stand their ground rather than retreat. The bite of many of them, particularly the larger species, is often fatal to man; the bite of others results in pain and swelling round the bitten place, but will not cause death.

2. TRUE VIPERS. The only British Viper is the ADDER (q.v.); but there are other kinds in southern Europe. Most vipers are to be found in the warmer parts of the world. Among these are many so-called Horned Vipers, which have extensions of the scales projecting from the head or snout. The Egyptian Horned Viper, like the African Egg-eater and the Saw-scaled Viper of India, has the scales on the side of the body placed obliquely and roughened like the teeth of a saw. By throwing the body into folds and rubbing these scales against one another, the snake

can produce a hissing sound. The Saw-scaled Viper is very common in some of the dry areas of north-west India, and causes many deaths each year by its bite. In an attempt by the authorities at the end of the last century to reduce the numbers of this deadly snake, nearly a quarter of a million were killed annually for several years, but without any apparent effect upon their numbers. On one occasion, when the reward was raised from 6 pies to 2 annas a head, 116,000 specimens were brought into Government offices in 8 days.

Largest of all the African Vipers is the gorgeously marked Gaboon Viper, which grows to a

GABOON VIPER

length of 1·5 metres, and bears the longest fangs—3 or 4 centimetres—of any snake known. In spite of these, it is said to be quiet, and will even allow itself to be picked up without attempting to bite. The Night Adder of South Africa is remarkable in that the poison gland, instead of being at the back of the head as in most snakes, is in the forepart of the body. A long duct connects it with the fang. The Puff-adder of Africa has a thick body, and may reach 1·5 metres in length.

3. THE PIT VIPERS include a number of well-known species. One of the largest of these is the Fer-de-Lance of Central America, which has a body as thick as a man's arm and is up to 2 metres long. It is sluggish, and will strike rather than try to escape, its bite being said to be very deadly. Another species, much feared by the natives of the Amazon forests, is the red, brown, and black Jaracara. The Bush-master, which may reach 4 metres long, lives in thick forest in tropical South America, and is reddish-yellow above, with a longitudinal series of large brown spots,

Rattle enlarged

DIAMOND RATTLESNAKE

each of which contains two light spots. The Water Moccasin of North America has the unusual habit among vipers of spending much of its time in the water. The Bamboo Snake of India, another Pit Viper, often seen in bamboo clumps in gardens, is green with a yellowish tinge; but, though its bite may be painful, it is not dangerous to man. Among the best known of the Pit Vipers is the Rattlesnake, some twenty-five species of which are known, inhabiting Central and North America, especially the U.S.A. Rattlesnakes are so called because their tails end in a series of horny, interlocking segments—the rattle—which, when vibrated rapidly, produces a dull, hissing sound. The number of segments varies greatly, because the end ones are continually getting damaged and dropping off. Six to ten is a common number; more than fifteen is rare. A new segment is added every time the skin is cast—or, more precisely, a new one is revealed—for fresh segments are being continually formed at the base of the rattle, but are not exposed until the skin is cast. As a group, Rattlesnakes are heavy-bodied reptiles, slow in their movements, and, when menaced, often prepared to stand their ground rather than retreat. Their fangs are very large, and the larger species can inject a powerful dose of venom. In the northern part of the U.S.A., where the weather is cold enough for them to hibernate, they often congregate in hundreds, and, coiled together in masses, spend the winter in sleep. They often return to the same place year after year, and have been known to travel many kilometres to reach it.

Many theories have been put forward to explain the function of the rattle; but the answer really is that we do not know. That it acts as a warning to creatures near is generally recognized; that it was originally designed for that purpose is not so easy to believe. The habit of vibrating the tip of the tail when alarmed is common to many other snakes, both poisonous and non-poisonous; but having no rattle, they do not make a noise. Moreover, if, as we now believe, snakes have little power of hearing, the Rattlesnake cannot even be aware of the sound it is making.

See also SNAKE.

VIRUSES. Although the existence of viruses has been known since the end of the 19th century, their scientific study is one of the newest branches of biology. Viruses are too small to be seen with an ordinary microscope, and before the invention of the ELECTRON MICROSCOPE (q.v. Vol. VIII) we knew of their presence only by the symptoms they produce in human beings and animals when they cause diseases such as measles, mumps, yellow fever, small-pox, foot-and-mouth disease, influenza, and the common cold. Although many viruses can exist outside other living things, they can only multiply inside living CELLS (q.v.), and it is not certain whether they should be regarded as living or non-living. In many cases they are passed from one animal or plant to another by blood-sucking or sap-sucking insects, so that it is possible to prevent the spread of illnesses such as yellow fever by attacking the mosquitoes which carry them. Similarly many serious plant diseases can be controlled if the greenflies which spread them are eliminated. The best seed potatoes come from Scotland because it is too cold there for the greenflies to survive, and the potatoes, therefore, are free from disease. Though many viruses which infect plants have been isolated and examined under the electron microscope, very little is known even now about their structure and life-history. Many of them have been found to be identical with chemical substances called nucleoproteins, and there is little doubt that these substances are in fact viruses, since they produce typical disease symptoms when injected into a healthy plant. Much research work is in progress concerning viruses, and some of the mysteries of their structure and life-history should soon be solved.

See also Vol. VI: ANIMAL DISEASES; PLANT DISEASES.

VOLE. This rodent is related to the MOUSE (q.v.); but it has a short tail, small eyes and ears, and a blunter head. Its teeth are also different, being typically herbivorous—that is, adapted to bite the toughest fibres and grasses on which voles feed, rather than the seeds and softer vegetable foods eaten by mice. The word 'vole', a Norse word meaning 'field', was first used for all field mice; but it is now strictly used for mice with herbivorous teeth. There are many different species of voles, including the Musk Rat and Lemming, in Europe, North America, and northern Asia, three, the Bank Vole, the Field Vole, and the Water Vole, being common in Britain.

Bank Voles are most like mice. They are very

John Markham

A FIELD VOLE

active, and can climb nimbly, swim, and jump out of a box over 20 centimetres deep. Though they are mainly nocturnal, they come out into the sunlight, especially in spring; and though they spend most of the winter in their burrows, they do not hibernate. They particularly like to live in ivy-clad banks, where they dig shallow burrows under the ivy or exposed roots of bushes. They often use mole-runs, sharing them with mice, shrews, and even rats. The Bank Voles drill smaller burrows leading from the mole-runs into sleeping-rooms and stores, which they line with chewed grass. They are quarrelsome animals, and will kill and eat the less bold Field Vole; but they do not defend their young. The female has from two to four litters of from four to eight young a year.

Field Voles or Short-tailed Voles live in rough grassland and moorland. They are much less active than the other voles, neither jumping nor climbing. They make a burrow in the ground, at the bottom of which they construct the nest, and store tight balls of grass for winter food. Normally, they have about the same number of litters and young as the Bank Vole; but in certain years, generally following mild winters, they reproduce at an abnormal rate. In these years

the 'vole plagues', as they are called, are responsible for the devastation of large areas, especially on the Continent. In one district in Germany, for instance, two million Field Voles were destroyed during one of these plagues.

Water Voles (often mistakenly called Water Rats) are not unlike Brown Rats, but their muzzles are blunter. They live by sluggish rivers and dikes, and make long, rambling burrows in the banks. They are almost entirely vegetarian, feeding on water-plants. They usually dive with a loud plop to avoid the pursuit of some of their enemies, and rise to the surface of the water under cover of leaves brought from the bottom.

Musk Rats or Musquashes of North America are as much as 28 cm long, with long, scaly tails, which they use as rudders when swimming. They dig their burrows in banks, hiding the entrance beneath the surface of the water. The tunnel turns upwards until it reaches above high-water level, where a large chamber is hollowed out. Here the Musk Rat lives and rears his family during the summer. With the approach of cold weather, he begins to build a winter home. This is a large, dome-shaped structure of mud, sticks, and reeds, resting on the bottom of a shallow pond or swamp, and rising over a metre above the surface. In some winters dozens of these houses are to be seen; but in others there are few or none—for the Musk Rats seem to know if there is going to be a severe or mild winter, and make their plans accordingly. Some years ago Musk Rats were imported to a fur farm in Britain. A certain number escaped and became wild, causing considerable destruction to river embankments. A law now orders their destruction wherever they are found, and none is thought to have survived.

The Lemmings of the mountains of Scandinavia are also voles. They are nearly 13 cm long, with soft, yellow-brown coats marked with dark-brown spots. They select dry places for their burrows, and during the day sit quietly in or near the entrance. If a human being appears, they become very excited, sitting up on their hindquarters and making ready to attack—and, indeed, they have been known to bite the legs of intruders coming too close to their holes. They eat grass, reindeer moss, birch catkins, and roots, and build nests of dry grass lined with hair, in which litters of five or six young are born. Lemmings are best known for their remarkable 'migrations'. Periodically they, like Field Voles, increase enormously in numbers; and, following such a period, they set off in huge numbers across the country, finally reaching the sea and drowning (see MIGRATION). Why they do this no one knows—but presumably scarcity of food is the basic reason.

VULTURE. This large Bird of Prey is closely related to the EAGLE and HAWK (qq.v.), but differs from them in having a more or less bare head and neck, blunter claws, and the habit of feeding upon the carcasses of dead animals. True Vultures are restricted to the warmer regions of the Old World. American Vultures, the largest of which is the enormous CONDOR (q.v.), belong to a different family, although their habits are much alike.

The best-known Vulture is the Griffon Vulture, which is found in the greater part of Africa and Asia, as well as in eastern and southern Europe. This large, brown bird, with a ruff of white feathers round the lower part of the neck, is a metre or more in length, with enormous, powerful wings. The Griffon Vulture finds its food by the aid of its keen sight. It circles high up in the air, scanning the ground below over a wide area. When it sees a carcass, it begins a

rapid, plunging descent, which is observed by other vultures at a distance. Soon a number of these great birds are gathered round the carcass, gorging their fill. They can go for long periods without food, but on making a good find they will stuff themselves until they cannot fly—and, indeed, can hardly stand. Griffon Vultures build very large nests of sticks and grass on an overhanging ledge of a cliff, several nests often being placed close together. They lay one greyish-white egg. The young bird often stays in the nest until it is 3 or 4 months old, growing extremely fat on the food brought by its parents.

Among other true Vultures is the Black Vulture, to be found in Mediterranean countries and eastwards to India and China. Unlike the Griffon, the Black Vulture prefers wooded country, and usually nests in trees. This repulsive and ungraceful-looking bird serves a very useful purpose as a scavenger in hot countries where, without its services, disease might arise from putrefying carcasses. The white Egyptian Vulture, a smaller bird, little more than 60 cm long, inhabits the Mediterranean countries and western Asia, and has occasionally wandered as far north as the British Isles.

The huge Lammergeyer or Bearded Vulture,

Zoological Society of London

LAMMERGEYER VULTURE

Paul Popper

VULTURES ASSEMBLING TO GORGE ON A CARCASS ON THE PLAINS OF INDIA

found from southern Spain to China, seems to form a link between the true Vultures and the Eagles. Its habits are those of Vultures, but it is more eagle-like in appearance. It dwells in mountainous regions, building its huge nest of sticks on a rock ledge. It appears to be very fond of bones, which it cracks by dropping them on rocks from great heights. It also eats tortoises, breaking their shells in the same way. It is now becoming very scarce.

W

WADING BIRDS. 1. Plovers and plover-like birds form a group of Wading Birds, almost all of which belong to one family and have many characteristics in common. They include the Plovers; the long-legged Stilts and Avocets; the Curlews; the Sandpipers, Redshanks, Greenshanks, Dunlins, Godwits, and Phalaropes; the Snipe and Woodcocks; and the Oyster-catchers. Some waders belong almost entirely to warmer countries—the Pratincole, for instance, inhabits the Mediterranean countries and parts of Asia, and the beautiful Sun Bittern inhabits tropical America.

All these birds are migratory to a greater or lesser extent. Some only migrate from their inland breeding-quarters to spend the winter on the coasts; others migrate from their summer quarters in the tundra lands of arctic Europe and Asia to winter in tropical Africa. Many species which breed in Britain have their numbers greatly increased in the winter by flocks migrating from farther north (*see* MIGRATION). During the winter, therefore, members of this family are to be found in almost all parts of the world. Long legs, suitable for wading in the watery land where they generally live, and long, thin bills, suitable for probing in the sand or mud for food, are their characteristics. Most species prefer open marshy or boggy moorland, some live on the banks of rivers or lakes, and others on river estuaries or low sandy coasts. Almost all nest on the ground, generally making very little in the way of a nest, and laying four eggs, pear-shaped and with reddish-brown markings on an olive-greenish or buff background—an excellent protective coloration for moorland country. Most wading birds also are themselves equipped with a speckled plumage of reds, greys, and whites, which makes them able to depend on CAMOUFLAGE (q.v.) as their principal protection

from enemies. All waders can walk and run with great ease, the chicks being able to run from the time they are hatched. The chicks are hatched with a good covering of down, and also with very effective protective coloration.

Most wading birds have a characteristic cry, generally a clear, wild, often melancholy note. The Curlew's plaintive 'Cur-lew' reaches far over the moors. The Redshank, a noisy bird, keeps up a continuous 'Too-oo-ee'. The Common Sandpiper calls 'Wheet, wheet, wheet'. The Golden Plover makes a clear 'Tlu-ee', and the 'Pee-wit' of the Lapwing is well known. The Oyster-catcher makes a shrill 'Kleep-kleep', which changes to 'Pic-pic' when the bird is alarmed. Most waders are noisy in their courtship, the male having a piping, trilling nuptial song. During the courtship season the males have a variety of display habits. The Lapwing makes a series of bowings and short erratic flights, and also fight each other. The Redshank and the Curlew raise their wings before the female, and then, half lowering them, beat time with rapid quivers. Then they hover in the air, uttering a bubbling song. The Woodcock makes a slow flight with plumage fluffed out, uttering at the same time a deep, repeated croak, varied by a shrill screech. In the spring the Ruff grows ear-tufts and a remarkable ruff of feathers around the neck, the colour of this courtship adornment varying considerably from bird to bird. The Ruff spreads out his gay plumage before the female, the Reeve, and runs round with quick steps, or spars with a rival. In contrast to other members of the family, the Ruff is often polygamous, there being generally more Reeves than Ruffs. The female of the little Red-necked Phalarope is larger and more brightly coloured than the male, and it is noteworthy that the roles of the sexes are partly reversed, the female taking the more active part in the courting, even fighting other females, and keeping guard over the nest while the male does the incubating.

2. The CURLEWS, the largest of the family, vary from 53 to 66 centimetres long. They are marsh and moorland birds, keeping away from cultivation. In winter, they can be seen flying in a V-formation from the moors to sandy coasts. Great numbers of them migrate from arctic Europe to winter in northern Britain. They are graceful birds with very long, slender, turned-down bills, which they use to probe for insects

The late Arthur Brook

THE CURLEW OF MARSH AND MOORLAND

and worms in the sand or soft soil. The Whimbrel is a smaller Curlew, which breeds to some extent in the Outer Hebrides, Orkneys, and Shetland Isles.

3. The SANDPIPERS, smaller, gracefully built birds with long, slender bills, form a very large group of the waders. The Common Sandpiper is a lively, restless little bird, which lives on banks of rivers or lakes, or on river estuaries. It continually bobs its head and jerks its tail, and makes frequent flights across the river. It is a very common bird in Scotland. The Redshanks and Greenshanks, found on coastal marshes and

The late Arthur Brook

THE GREENSHANK WITH ITS NEST IN THE HEATHER

lakes, are larger relatives, distinguished by their long red or green legs. The little Dunlins are among the commonest of all birds of the seashore, where they probe for worms in the wet sand or mud. They breed on high moors farther north. Like many members of this group, such as the Sanderling, Knot, and Godwit, the Dunlin has a marked change of plumage between summer and winter, being much paler in the winter (*see* pictures, pp. 266 and 267).

4. SNIPE and WOODCOCK are both valued as table birds. Snipe are difficult to hit, for when 'flushed' (roused to flight) they make a very swift, corkscrew zigzag for some 50 metres before flying straight. In the nesting season, cock snipe sometimes make wide, circular flights ending in a sudden descent, with wings half-closed and tail spread out. During the descent, the vibration of the stiff outer tail-feathers makes a curious noise known as 'drumming', somewhat like the bleating of a goat. Snipe are common on boggy moors in Scotland and north Britain, but less often seen in the south. Woodcock are heavier, larger birds, with shorter legs. They live in open woodlands, where some are resident, and to which others migrate in large flights for the winter. They are nocturnal birds, feeding in marshes and ditches at night, and sleeping among low trees by day. A Woodcock is known to be able to carry a chick, held between its thigh and body, when it is flying (*see* picture, p. 72).

5. PLOVERS have shorter, stouter bills than other members of the family. Golden Plovers mostly spend the summer in the tundra lands of northern Europe and Asia, often wintering in Britain or passing on their way farther south; but one species is a resident of Britain, chiefly in the north. Like other waders, they are quick runners, and can be seen running sideways or backwards on the look-out for enemies. The little Ringed Plover is a very common shorebird, and associates with the Dunlin and other waders. The Lapwing, Peewit, or Green Plover is common throughout Great Britain. It is a handsome bird, carrying a long, turned-up crest on the back of its head. The female uses many tricks, as do other waders, to distract enemies from her nest. She runs some distance before rising, and then sometimes feigns an injured leg or wing.

6. The OYSTER-CATCHER, a rather stouter, shorter-legged bird with a long, thickish bill, is black and white, with dull red legs. It inhabits

John Warham

RED-NECKED AVOCET NESTING

shingly river-banks or sea-shores, feeding on shell-fish, sea-worms, and shrimps—but not, as one might expect, on oysters. Its main food is mussels, the shells of which it prises open with its beak. Oyster-catchers are very noisy birds, and in winter form small flocks, gathering on reefs and islets. The little red-legged Turnstone is an exclusively sea-shore bird, spending most of its time on the very edge of the waves, turning over stones in search of food.

7. The STILTS and AVOCETS are distinguished from other members of the family by their very long legs. Neither is resident in Britain, though one species of Stilt is a rare visitor, which has bred once, and one species of Avocet has nested in recent years in fairly large numbers on Haver-gate Island off the Suffolk coast. Both birds are essentially marsh-birds, often standing in water up to their knees on the look-out for food. When they fly, they stretch their necks out in front and trail their long thin legs behind.

WAGTAILS AND PIPITS. These birds have slender bodies, slender, insect-eating bills, and longish tails. Wagtails generally have longer legs and tails and brighter plumage than Pipits. They are distributed over most of the world, the majority belonging to Europe and Asia. Several species are resident in the British Isles, though most make at least short southward journeys in the autumn: the Grey Wagtail, for instance, rarely nests in the eastern or southern districts of England, though it may often be seen there in the winter. Some migrate long distances in flocks.

Wagtails are conspicuous for their charac-teristic run and flight. They walk or run, instead of hopping as do most birds, making a quick,

sudden dash to catch an insect, and, when they stop, wagging their long tails up and down many times. Their flight is quick and erratic, with graceful dippings and risings in quick suc-cession. They feed on insects and small aquatic animals—for most Wagtails like to live near water. They generally nest on or near the ground, in a hole in a bank or wall, among rocks, or in a hollow tree. Pied Wagtails sometimes nest in a thatched roof. The nest is made of grass and moss, lined with hair and feathers. Four to six eggs are laid, and two broods are often reared in a season.

The best-known Wagtails are the Pied or Water Wagtail, the Grey, and the Yellow Wag-tail. The Pied Wagtail is the most common, frequenting not only rivers and pools, but gar-dens and farms. Its near relative, the White Wagtail, is well known on the Continent. The Grey Wagtail, with its blue-grey back, black throat, and yellow underparts, is essentially a water bird, frequenting rocky mountain streams, and uttering its short, pretty song from the tops of willow trees. In the summer, the cocks will attack fiercely any intruder on their territory. The Yellow Wagtail is a smaller, very graceful little bird, with brown-grey back and bright yellow throat and underparts. It is somewhat local in distribution, frequenting damp meadows rather than streams. Its close relation, the Blue-headed Wagtail, rarely visits Britain, but is found commonly in meadows and cornfields in most parts of Europe. Both these species nest in tus-socks of dry grass. Another relative, the Yellow-headed Wagtail, belongs to Siberia and east Russia, and winters in India.

Pipits have predominantly brown and buffish-white plumage. They are not unlike LARKS (q.v.) in appearance and way of life. The Tree Pipits are not arboreal birds in spite of their name; but they often perch on high trees to sing. They also have the habit of rising from a tree into the sky about 12 metres, and then sailing down in spirals with tail spread and wings partly extended, singing as they come. In the late summer, they gather in flocks to feed in stubble-fields, and then migrate in flocks.

The Meadow Pipit, or Titlark, prefers moor-land country, peat bogs, and rough, undrained meadows, and nests in holes in the grass or heather. Meadow Pipits have the same habit of singing on the wing as have Tree Pipits. The female, if disturbed when brooding, never rises

Eric Hosking

THE PIED OR WATER WAGTAIL

straight from the nest, but runs some little distance through the grass first. Cuckoos very often lay their eggs in Pipits' nests (*see* pictures, p. 111). The Rock Pipit lives near rocky sea coasts, and nests among the rocks.

WAINSCOT MOTH, *see* NIGHT-FLYING MOTHS.

WALLABY, *see* KANGAROO.

WALRUS, *see* SEALS.

WAPITI, *see* DEER, Section 5.

WARBLERS. As their name indicates, these birds are noted for their fine song: in particular the Garden Warbler and the Blackcap have lovely, ringing, lively songs, thought by many people to be as fine as that of the THRUSH or NIGHTINGALE (qq.v.) to which they are closely related. Warblers are little birds with, for the most part, a sober brown or greenish plumage. The rare Dartford Warbler is exceptional in having a tawny breast. They are of slender build, with slender, insect-eating bills. They feed mainly on insects, which many of them catch on the wing, rather in the manner of Flycatchers. Since an insect diet is not available in northern countries, such as Britain, in the winter almost all Warblers migrate southwards. Species of Warblers are to be found over most of the world, though there are very few in the Americas. The family includes the Whitethroats, Chiffchaffs, Blackcaps, and Wood Wrens. Some of them, especially the White-

throat and Willow Warbler, are among the commonest of British birds.

The Whitethroat, rather larger than many of the family, can be heard from mid or late April till early September singing its hurried, lively song, and can be seen making its quick, jerky movements and short flights in gardens, orchards, and any rough ground covered with rank vegetation. It nests for preference in a bank of thick nettles, but low bushes or brambles will serve instead. It shares a habit with other members of the family of feigning lameness to distract attention from its nest or fledgelings. The Lesser Whitethroat, a rather smaller bird, is much less common.

The Blackcap and Garden Warbler are much alike in habits, though the Blackcap is the earlier to arrive in the spring. They frequent woods, orchards, and rough common land—being no commoner in gardens than any other Warbler. The male Blackcap, in particular, is a pugnacious bird, and protects his own territory fiercely, especially against the intrusions of the Garden Warbler. Both are shy birds, and will stop singing if disturbed.

The very common, yellowish-green Willow Warbler is to be found in most localities in Britain—even in London parks—and has no particular connexion with willows. The Chiffchaff is common also, and is to be heard singing its little song, 'chiff-chaff', all day long from the tree-tops. Another lover of trees is the Wood Warbler or Wood Wren, which delivers its song of a few clear notes with a hurried end from high up in tall oak or beech trees. It nests on the ground, often among dead bracken.

The Sedge and the Reed Warblers are quite common near slow-flowing, reed-grown streams. The Sedge Warbler, as well as singing its own charming song, mimics the songs of other birds. It nests in dense, tangled vegetation. The Reed Warbler builds a deep cup of grass and moss, which it suspends between four reeds, where it sways with the wind. The Grass-

John Warham

SPLENDID BLUE WREN

An Australian Warbler

Eric Hosking

CHIFFCHAFF AT ITS NEST

hopper Warbler has a curious 'reeling' cry, except for which it would be little noticed, because it takes cover quickly, hiding in the undergrowth.

WART HOG, *see* SWINE

WASPS. 1. All Hymenoptera with stings, except BEES and ANTS (qq.v.), are included among the Wasps. An important thing to remember is that only the females sting.

Like bees, wasps may conveniently be divided into two groups, those which are social in habit and those which are solitary. The social wasps are those which live in an organized community, consisting of a queen and a large number of daughters, the workers, who are usually smaller than their mother. These tend the offspring of the queen, but produce none of their own. The solitary species, on the other hand, do not live in communities: a single female wasp builds a protected cell, places food in it, lays an egg on or near the food, and then takes no further interest in it. Most species of wasps are solitary in habit.

Adult wasps are very fond of sweet things, and visit certain flowers in search of nectar. The spring-flowering Cotoneasters attract large numbers of queen wasps, and later in the season the flowers of Figwort and Snowberry attract their workers. But wasps, unlike bees, usually have short tongues, and can get nectar only from flowers with shallow corollas. In late summer, ripe fruit will attract large numbers of the social wasps. The larvae, however, must have animal food, and to get it the female wasps prey mostly upon other insects—though some hunt only spiders.

Social wasps use their sting only for defence, and rely on their powerful mandibles and strong legs for killing and overpowering their prey. The Common and German Wasps of this country may often be seen hawking amongst low vegetation in search of flies and caterpillars. They are clumsy hunters, striking at far more flies than they are ever able to seize and destroy. Once she has caught a fly, the wasp bites off its head, legs, and wings, and chews the body up into a pulpy mass, which she carries to her nest to divide among the hungry grubs. She swallows the more liquid part of the prey, and later regurgitates it from her stomach to feed the grubs. The solitary wasp, however, although she stings in defence, uses her sting chiefly for injecting into her prey a minute quantity of poison, which paralyses but does not kill her victim. She then carries or drags the helpless victim to her burrow, where it remains alive until the tiny wasp-grub hatches and begins to devour it.

2. SOLITARY WASPS: Solitary wasps are found all over the world, especially in the tropics, and there are many British kinds. Of these, one of the so-called Potter Wasps, *Eumenes coarctata*, is a small, black and yellow insect, with a long, slender waist. The female builds (usually on a twig of heather) a little hollow round cell, about the size of a pea, with a small hole in the side. Then she catches and paralyses some small caterpillars, which she stuffs into the cell. Finally, she lays an egg among them, and closes up the hole with mud. As soon as the tiny grub hatches, it begins to eat the caterpillars. When it is full grown, it turns into a pupa (chrysalis). The following summer, as an adult wasp, it gnaws its way through the hard wall of the cell, and flies away.

A very common British wasp, of which there are several kinds, is *Odynerus*. Most of them nest in holes in walls or in the deserted burrows of other insects, especially in wooden posts. They all collect caterpillars as food for their young.

The name 'Sand Wasp' is used rather loosely for a vast number of wasp-like insects which move extremely rapidly, enjoy very hot sunshine, and nest in sand or dry soil. Among the best-known Sand Wasps are the Spider-hunting Wasps, Pompilidae. They move in a quick and jerky manner, darting swiftly over the ground in short spurts, and will not fly unless hard pressed. The females store their burrows with spiders. On a hot day, one of these little wasps may often be seen dragging along a big spider to her burrow. In some tropical countries, especially South America, these wasps are often very large, with a wing-expanse of up to 10 centimetres. These amazons of the insect world are able to attack some of the largest-known spiders and, because of their agility, are almost always victorious. The Sphecidae, another large group of Sand Wasps, select their prey from a great variety of insects, including flies, beetles, grasshoppers, caterpillars, and cockroaches, though any one species of wasp confines itself to one kind of prey. Whatever insect happens to be used, the wasp paralyses it with her sting before carrying it off to her burrow.

Some of the best-known Sand Wasps belong to the genus *Cerceris*, mostly black and yellow insects with a preference for dry, sandy regions. So far as we know, nearly all the species attack weevil beetles, stinging them and carrying them off to their burrows. *Cerceris arenaria*, a British species, is found in July and August on the sandy commons of southern England. It makes vertical burrows, often in very hard ground, and stores its cells with weevils. Another British species, *Cerceris rybyensis*, uses the small bees known as *Halictus*—a good example of how the habits of closely related species of Sphegid wasps can differ.

One of the most interesting Sand Wasps is *Ammophila*. This is a large, black, slender-bodied insect, with a partly red abdomen separated from the rest of the body by a long, thin stalk or waist. These wasps build their cells in burrows in dry, sandy places, and stock them with caterpillars. Where a species uses only one caterpillar for each cell, its victim is so large that the wasp cannot fly with it, but must drag it over the ground, often as far as 75 metres, to her burrow. On her way home, she often leaves her prey for a moment to take a short flight to survey the ground, so that she may be able to continue her journey on foot in the right direction. When she reaches her burrow, she leaves her prey at the entrance, disappears into the burrow for a final inspection, and then, reappearing, seizes the caterpillar in her long, sickle-shaped jaws, and slips backwards into the hole, dragging her victim after her. Having laid an egg on the caterpillar, she reappears, and with rapid move-

SOLITARY WASP, *Cerceris*

ments of her front legs scrapes the surrounding sand to fill the mouth of the burrow. And now a remarkable performance takes place: the *Ammophila* finishes her job with a tool! She selects a small pebble or stone and uses it as a mallet to ram down the sand at the mouth of the burrow, until all trace of its exact position has been smoothed out.

Under this general term 'Sand Wasp' are included the elegant little insects known as Mutillidae. The females are, without exception, wingless; the males are fully winged, much larger, and unlike the females in shape and colour. The females are brightly coloured, their abdomen being sharply marked with spots and bands of dense white hair. They are said to sting fiercely. They usually lay their eggs in the cells of other solitary wasps or of solitary bees; but one African species lays its eggs in the pupae of the harmful TSETSE FLY (q.v.), which the grubs destroy. Only two species of Mutillidae occur in the British Isles, one of which, *Mutilla europaea*, lays its eggs in the nests of certain species of Bumble-bees.

Female *Ammophila* carrying paralysed caterpillar to her burrow

The Methocidae, a small family of blackish wasps with wingless females, related to the Mutillidae, has particularly interesting habits. The single British species attacks the fearsome larva of the common Tiger-beetle in order to lay her eggs on the grub's body. This grub lives in a burrow in the ground, the mouth of which it blocks with its flattened head and thorax. Any passing insect which crawls over the flattened head is immediately seized by the larva in its sickle-like jaws and dragged down into the burrow to be eaten. How then can the little wasp lay her egg on the body of this ferocious larva? She allows

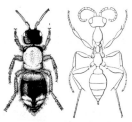

Left, Sand Wasp, *Mutilla europaea*, or velvet-ant. *Right*, The ant-like Wasp, *Methoca ichneumonides*

herself to be caught in the grip of the beetle grub's jaws, and then, at the moment when she is being held aloft, before being dragged down into the burrow, she drives her sting home between the legs of the larva, so that it sinks back paralysed into its burrow. After laying an egg on her victim, the wasp fills up the burrow with sand, and goes forth in search of another beetle larva. But things do not always turn out according to plan, and occasionally a wasp has been seriously mutilated by a Tiger-beetle larva.

3. SOCIAL WASPS (VESPIDAE): these include the common wasps of the British Isles. There are seven species in Great Britain, the largest, but by no means the most vicious, being the Hornet. Their life history is very like that of the BUMBLE-BEES (q.v.), the main difference being that wasps need animal food, such as flies and caterpillars, and build a nest of wood-pulp or papier-mâché. After sleeping through the winter, hidden away among dry leaves or beneath loose bark, or even among the folds of a window curtain, in late spring the queens seek out places in which to build their nests. Some British wasps, such as the Tree Wasp, *Vespula sylvestris*, and the Hornet, *Vespa crabro*, nest in hollow trees; others build their nests in the open, on the branch of a tree, or in a bush. But the wasps which are such a nuisance in late summer, such as the Common Wasp, *Vespula vulgaris*, are nearly always underground builders.

The wasps' building material consists of wood fibres scraped by their powerful mandibles from wooden objects, such as posts. The fibres are mixed with saliva and worked to a pulp, which is then applied by a worker to the rim of a cell, and drawn out between the two edges of the wasp's mandibles to form a thin strip of paper, like a ribbon. The queen wasp builds a tiny nest in a suitable hollow under the ground—a beautifully made and fragile piece of work, about the size of a golf-ball. The Common Wasp uses soft decayed wood for her nest. This has two or three outer covers, which give it its familiar spherical shape, and a tiny comb, securely fastened by a short central stalk of hardened wood-pulp to a rootlet, or some other object, sticking out from the roof of the chosen cavity.

The comb consists of a single layer of cells, with their mouths opening downwards. At any one time it contains eggs, larvae, or grubs at different ages, and pupae hidden beneath white

QUEEN HORNET

S. C. Bisserôt

silken cappings. The queen toils from dawn until dusk to provide food for her large family. If there is a long spell of very cold or wet weather, she and her brood may die of starvation; but if all goes well, the first workers appear some time in June, about 4 weeks after the eggs are laid. They soon take over the tasks of fetching wood-pulp for nest-building and food for the larvae; while the queen, her wings frayed from long use and her bright colours faded, devotes herself to laying eggs. The little colony grows rapidly, reaching perhaps 2,000 workers towards the end of the summer. In late August and early September the workers begin to build combs composed of larger cells, in which the queen lays eggs. From these the workers rear perfect females or queens, perhaps several hundred, though only a few of them will survive to found nests the following summer. The workers also rear a great number of males, who leave the nest with the young queens on fine days in autumn for mating. The males can often be seen flying around the tops of trees or up and down hedgerows, looking for the females. After pairing has taken place, the queens at once search for a sheltered spot in which to hibernate; but the males continue to fly about in large numbers on sunny days, jostling

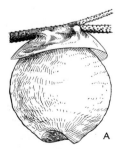
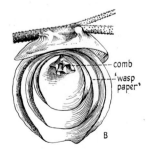

A. NEST OF TREE WASP. B. CROSS-SECTION OF TREE WASP
NEST

each other for a place at the ivy blossom. When hard weather comes, they soon die of cold and starvation. The old queen mother, exhausted from her labours of egg-laying, drags herself about feebly among the empty, mouldering combs until she, too, with her few remaining workers, falls a victim to the cold and damp of the last autumn days.

The Hornet, the largest British wasp, has a similar life history to that of the common social wasps. It usually nests in hollow trees; but often it will hang its nest from the rafters of an out-house or shed. Besides those described here, there are other sorts of social wasp, especially in South America, many having interesting habits which are not yet fully understood. But the social wasps, taken all together, form only a small part of the total wasp fauna of the world.

WATER-BEETLE, *see* BEETLES.

WATER-BOATMAN. Two different families of bugs are known as Water-boatmen. One, the Notonectidae, are robust insects about a centi-metre long, often seen resting with the head downwards, the tip of the abdomen at the sur-face of the water, the rest of the body submerged, and the two long hind-legs stretched out straight like a pair of oars. Their leg strokes appear very deliberate, and with a few rapid movements they are well below the surface of the water. In America they are known as Back-swimmers, because of their habit of swimming upside down.

The Notonectidae should be handled with care, because they can stab the skin with their beaks, and the wound may be very painful. They often attack tadpoles and small fish; and they can make a shambles of an aquarium in a very short space of time. The Notonectids have an interesting way of holding a store of air for breathing under water. A keel runs along the middle of the under-surface of the body, from each side of which rises a row of stiff hairs; these hairs, together with others rising from the sides of the body, imprison the air that is used by the Boatman when sub-merged. The bugs lay their eggs in the stems of water-plants, and the nymphs, when they hatch, look very like their parents, except that they

WATER-BOATMAN

are whitish in colour, much smaller in size, and lack wings.

In America, and sometimes also in Great Britain, the name Water-boatman is reserved for another family, the Corixidae, which are also called Lesser Water-boatman. These are much less formidable than the Notonectids, have much flatter bodies, and do not swim on their backs. They can be seen when the water is clear, paddling about near the bottom of the pond with a gentle movement of the hind legs, very different from the vigorous, purposeful strokes of the Notonectids. A few British species are about a centimetre long, but most are much smaller. Their reserve air-supply is held be-tween the wings and the abdomen. So far as we know, they are largely vegetarian, scraping up organic matter with their spade-like fore-legs.

See also BUGS.

WATER-PLANTS. The majority of these, such as the Bladderwort and Water-milfoil, have greatly reduced roots, and can absorb water all over the surface of the plant. Roots, when present, serve mainly for anchorage. Water-plants have no need of woody tissue for support or for conducting water from the roots; but many of them, especially in their under-water parts, possess large air-spaces in the tissues, so that a supply of oxygen for breathing is assured, even to the submerged organs. Many water-plants, such as Water-lilies and some Pondweeds, have leaves which float on the surface of the water, and differ from those of most other plants in having pores (or stomata) on the upper surfaces only (*see* TRANSPIRATION). Thus they can take in carbon dioxide needed for building up food-stuffs. To prevent the stomata from being flooded, these floating leaves have long stems, which allow for changes in the water-level. Some tropical water-plants have leaf-stalks shaped like corkscrews, which stretch or twist to keep the leaves floating at the right level. The Giant Water-lily of the Amazon has leaves large enough to support the weight of a baby, with the edges upturned all round to prevent flooding.

Shallow water-plants often have two kinds of leaves: normal leaves growing above the surface of the water, and others growing below the water, with no stomata, which absorb gases from solution in the water. Many plants living sub-merged in flowing water have finely divided

Marsh Marigolds

Eric Hosking

Water Crowfoot

Eric Hosking

John Markham

Yellow Water-lilies (*Nuphar lutea*)

Lotus Lilies

Paul Popper

WATER PLANTS

Harold Bastin

Victoria regia, THE GIANT WATER-LILY OF THE AMAZON

leaves which expose a far greater surface for the absorption of gases. Some Water-crowfoots, for instance, have both lobed floating leaves and thread-like submerged leaves. The Arrowhead of the ponds has arrow-shaped leaves growing above the surface, and ribbon-shaped leaves below, which spread freely in the water.

Some water-plants live in marshes, and some in ponds and streams. The soil in marshes, though waterlogged, is not peaty and sour as in bogs; but it is deficient in oxygen, and so marsh plants usually have large leaves with big air-spaces for the passage and storage of oxygen. In some marshes the dominant plant is the Osier Willow, while in others it is the Rush. Other marsh-plants are the Meadow-sweet, Ragged Robin, Wild Iris, Marsh Mallow, Water Mint, Water Forget-Me-Not, and the Marsh Marigold. The latter, with its sturdy rootstock holding the plant firmly in the soil, is a typical marsh-plant. Because of its large air-spaces, the whole shoot is spongy, while the yellow flowers are large, and readily attract insects.

The nature of the soil, the depth of water, and the position with regard to trees, affect the supply of mineral salts to pond-plants, as well as affecting the temperature and the amount of light which they get. Some plants live in shallow water with their roots in mud and their leaves above or floating on the water; others live in deep water, are not rooted at all, and float freely on or just below the surface of the water. There are also plants which are rooted in the mud, but whose leaves are entirely submerged. Shallow water-plants are much like those in marshes, but may include others—Reeds, Sedges, and Bulrushes, Arrowheads, Water Plantains, and Horsetails, for example. Freely floating plants include the insectivorous plant, the Bladderwort (*see* INSECTIVOROUS PLANTS, Section 4), the Frogbit, with its rosette of leaves, few hanging roots, and starry white flowers, and the Duckweeds, with their small leaves and long white roots hanging freely in the water. Examples of plants rooted in the mud but with submerged leaves are the Water-violet, the Water-milfoil, the Water-starwort, and the Canadian Pondweed. The latter is well known as a nuisance in reservoirs: it reproduces itself simply and very freely, since any detached piece becomes a new plant. It was introduced to Britain over 100 years ago, and now inhabits practically every expanse of water in the country.

The plants of streams and rivers differ with the strength of the current, though some, like the Floating Meadow-grass and Water-crowfoot, occur both in swiftly running water or almost dry mud, their leaves being long and narrow when in swiftly flowing water, and short when in mud. All marsh and pond-plants may also occur in sluggish streams and rivers, the banks of which are often lined with alders and willows.

See also ECOLOGY OF PLANTS.
See also Vol. VI: WATER GARDENS.

WATER SCORPION. In Britain there are two species of aquatic bugs known as Water Scorpions. In one, called *Nepa*, the body is broad and extremely flat; in the other, called *Ranatra*, it is a long and very narrow cylinder. Both types are found all over the world, although they are rare in Australia. The name of Water Scorpion is given more particularly to the *Nepa*. The *Ranatra* is often called the Water Stick-insect.

Though these bugs spend their time in the water, their second and third pairs of legs are better fitted for walking than for swimming. The front pair of legs is used neither for walking nor swimming, but for catching prey. They are distinctly 'elbowed', and the part farthest from the body can close down at the 'elbow' to fit into a groove in the nearer part, in exactly the same way as the blade of a penknife fits into the haft, so that any victim captured between the two is helpless.

At the other end of the body is a breathing-tube composed of two slender pieces, each of which is grooved on its inner side, the tube being formed when they come together. The mouth of the tube can be pushed to the surface when the insect is resting in shallow water, so that it can obtain air. At the base of the tube are two 'spiracles' or breathing-pores, by which the air is passed into the body.

These insects are carnivorous, feeding upon other small insects and animals. They often stalk their prey, relying greatly on concealment. The broad, flat, brown *Nepa* lies well hidden in the mud at the bottom of the pond. The olive-brown *Ranatra* may be found in similar places, its long legs and cylindrical body looking like the

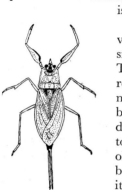

WATER SCORPION

stalks of decaying vegetable matter. It often clings to aquatic plants and submerged grass, where it is equally well protected. If Water Scorpions were unable to harmonize completely with their surroundings, and so conceal themselves, they would be helpless. They can swim when necessary, but only slowly, and chiefly by means of the hind legs, which act together like the legs of a frog. On land, they crawl awkwardly by means of the second and third pairs of legs, which move alternately, as is usual in walking animals; and they wave the first pair in front as they do so. Most have undeveloped wing muscles and can very rarely fly. Beneath the drab wing-cases lie a pair of purplish-red hind-wings and a bright red upper abdomen, banded with black—the one patch of colour on an otherwise uniformly brown body.

See also BUGS.

WAXWING. This small bird, of which there are about ten species, is to be found in the northern regions of Europe, Asia, and America. The Japanese Waxwing breeds in parts of Siberia, and winters in China and Japan. The Bohemian Waxwing breeds in Scandinavia and other northern countries, and comes south for the winter, in some seasons crossing the North Sea in large flocks to winter in the eastern counties

Paul Popper

WAXWING

of Britain. The Cedar Bird belongs to North America.

Waxwings are small birds with long wings, short legs, short, slightly hooked beaks, and silky plumage. The inner quills of the wings are tipped with red, horny appendages, almost like sealing-wax. The Bohemian Waxwing is a colourful bird, the male having a reddish-chestnut head and crest, grey-brown back, blackish wings tipped with white and yellow, a blackish tail ending in a broad band of yellow, and purplish-red underparts. Waxwings perch in an erect position, and if startled, raise and spread out their crests. These gay little birds, feeding in flocks on the red berries of the mountain ash above a snowy ground, are a most attractive sight. The Cedar Birds of America, smaller and less colourful, come down to the lower lands in the winter to feed on the berries of the red cedar, on which they become very fat. Waxwings make nests of coarse, dry grass in the fork of a tree, the eggs being pale blue, marked with purple-black spots.

WEASEL. The Weasel family belongs to the Carnivora (q.v.) or flesh-eating order of mammals, and is distributed widely over the northern hemisphere. The most important members are the Weasel itself and its close relatives, the Stoat, Polecat, Marten, Skunk, and Mink, as well as the Wolverine, Otter, and Badger, which are described in separate articles. Most of the family are greedy, bloodthirsty animals, and several of them have a vile smell, which they use as an excellent weapon of defence, giving it out whenever they are attacked or annoyed. Weasels and their near relatives all have long, slender bodies and short legs. The family includes some of the most valuable fur-bearing animals in the world.

1. Weasels are the smallest of the British carnivora, but are most savage hunters, probably even more courageous than Stoats. The males are 15 to 20 cm long, with short tails, and the females are somewhat smaller. Their coat is chestnut with white underparts, sometimes becoming entirely white in the winter in very cold climates. Weasels and Stoats look very much alike; but the Weasel is the smaller and has a less bushy tail, while the Stoat is the browner and has a black tip to its tail. They both give out a repulsive smell.

Weasels are widespread in country districts, living in hedgerows, woods, and among stones.

Eric Hosking

WEASEL

Mice, voles, and rats form their main food; but although so small, they sometimes kill game, hares, and rabbits. They will continue to hunt and kill their prey long after they have satisfied their hunger. When out hunting, they advance by small leaps, stopping at intervals to sit up on their haunches and have a good look round. With their snake-like bodies, they can follow most of their smaller prey into their holes and hiding-places. They usually make their nests in holes in banks, dry ditches, or in hollow trees. The female has a litter of four or five young, which, if necessary, she will defend with fury and desperation, risking her own life rather than leaving them. The young family is taken out regularly on hunting excursions, after having first been taught to use their teeth on half-dead mice and other small creatures.

2. Stoats normally have a brown coat tinged with yellow; but in Scotland and all very cold regions it becomes white in the winter, whereupon the Stoats are known as Ermines. The white winter coat not only makes the Stoat inconspicuous in the snow, but also helps to conserve the heat generated by its body—for white fur is a bad conductor of heat. The winter coat of Scottish Stoats is too coarse to be of any commercial value; but Ermine from the very cold, northerly regions is highly prized.

Stoats will go almost anywhere after their prey—they will enter rats' and moles' burrows, climb trees, and even cross very wide rivers. In order to attract birds within their range, they tumble and writhe like snakes on the ground. When moving in packs, they have sometimes attacked dogs and even human beings. They overcome their prey by a final rush, seizing the

Harold Bastin

STOAT

Harold Bastin

POLECAT

victim by its throat or on the artery behind the ear. They then drag it back to their nests to be eaten, often pulling and pushing beasts as much as four times their own weight. They carry back stolen eggs by holding them under their chins, and rolling them on the ground. In Britain, a litter of from five to eight young is born in April or May.

3. POLECATS are also savage, evil-smelling creatures, the males being about 56 cm long, with longish tails, and the females always a few centimetres smaller. The Polecat's fur is almost black with a purple sheen, and through it shows a buff undercoat. They live in woods and hilly thickets, sleeping by day in their nests, and hunting by night. Small prey, such as rats and mice, rabbits, lizards, and snakes are their main victims,

though sometimes they will attack geese, turkeys, and hares, biting them on the throat or at the back of the neck. Very occasionally they have been known to attack human beings. The sexes live together for most of the year, and during the mating season (February to April) they make long night journeys. Their nests have two chambers, one lined with leaves for the young, and the other used as a larder for storing food. A litter of four or five young is born in April or May, and there is often another litter later in the year. The young are very pale when born, and do not become the colour of the adults until about 8 months old, though they are fully grown at 3 months. In winter, Polecats sometimes nest in deserted buildings.

Polecats live in Europe, Asia, and America.

Eric Hosking

PINE MARTEN

Paul Popper

LITTLE SKUNK

They used to be quite common in certain parts of the British Isles, but are now almost extinct, except in the remoter parts, especially of Wales. The domesticated ferret (*see* FERRETING, Vol. IX) is believed to be descended from the Asiatic Polecat, and although its domestication took place a very long time ago, the dark-coloured Ferret still looks much like a Polecat.

4. MARTENS do not have the unpleasant smell of the first three animals. They are found in many parts of Europe, Asia, and America, the different species varying very little. The only one now to be found in the British Isles, and that only rarely, is the Pine Marten. It is about 45 centimetres long, with a bushy tail, and fur which is rich brown, except on the chest, where the colour varies from yellowish-white to bright orange. Pine Martens are wild and shy, and, as they mostly live in trees, are rarely seen. They creep swiftly from branch to branch in pursuit of birds and squirrels, but also come down to the ground to kill small prey and to raid the farm-yard. When they are being chased they travel by long leaps, spitting and hissing like cats or uttering shrill, loud cries. Four or five cubs, with fine, white hair, are born once a year. They remain blind for about 3 weeks.

The Beech or Stone Marten and the Sable are found on the Continent and in Asia. The largest species is the fine, black-grey Fisher Marten of North America. All Martens are trapped for their fur, that of the Sable being so much sought after by fur-trappers that the animal has now become very rare.

5. SKUNKS, which live only in America, have by far the most nauseous smell of all the weasel family. Whenever they are provoked or irritated, they discharge an amber-coloured liquid with a vile odour from a pair of glands under the tail. The Canadian Skunk, the best-known species, is about the size of a small cat. It has jet-black fur, with broad bands of white from head to tail, a white line down the face, and a black, bushy tail. The Skunk is not afraid to walk abroad, because this conspicuous colouring warns other animals off, reminding them of the Skunk's smell. The Skunk walks very slowly and deliberately, and, because of its fearlessness, is very easily trapped.

6. MINKS are small amphibious animals about 40 cm long, with thick, bushy tails, and a smell almost as bad as that of the Skunk. Their thick, glossy fur varies in colour from dull yellowish-brown to rich chocolate-brown. There are three species found in North America, eastern Europe, and Siberia. Minks never live far away from water, making their nests either in a hole in the bank of a river or lake or in a hollow log. They eat frogs, crayfish, mussels, water-birds, and various small water mammals, following their prey almost entirely by scent, and hunting them both by day and by night. Although Minks frequently make attacks on poultry, they are not nearly as destructive as some of the other members of this family. For many years now, Mink fur has been very highly valued, the best skins being obtained from the American species. When caught alive in a trap, the Mink's face, never very prepossessing, is said to take on an almost diabolical expression.

See also Vol. VI: FUR FARMING.

WEAVER BIRD. Weavers form a large group of small, finch-like birds, found principally in Africa, but also in parts of Asia and Australasia. They are so named because of their elaborate and beautifully made nests, which they generally place close together in large communities. The majority build nests of grass and twigs suspended from trees or between the stalks of two or three reeds. The exclusively African Sociable Weaver Birds carry community building much farther. A flock of birds builds one enormous, umbrella-shaped erection of grass, difficult to distinguish at a distance from the thatched roof of a native hut, and fixed among the branches of a large tree. Under its shelter are constructed numerous little tunnels, leading to individual nesting chambers lined with feathers. The birds use these chambers not only for nesting, but also during other seasons as shelter against the violent tropical rains. The structure lasts from year to year, being repaired by the community as need arises.

The African Whydah Bird is included among the Weavers. There are several species, the Paradise Whydahs, in particular, being remarkable for the extremely long tails and brilliant plumage of glossy black and scarlet or crimson which the cocks carry in the mating season. During the rest of the year the cocks carry a much less conspicuous yellowish-brown plumage, like that of the hens.

Not very distantly related are the Tanagers of tropical America. There are altogether some 400 species of these finch-like birds, most of which are very brilliantly coloured, the typical

MEXICAN DESERT

The thick leaves of the Cactus plants store moisture and resist heat. The colouring of the Horned Toads makes them difficult to see against their background

Zoological Society of London

LONG-TAILED WEAVER-BIRD

colouring being blue and yellow. The splendid Scarlet Tanager, the 'Red-bird' of America, has a scarlet body and black wings. This bird winters in tropical America, but goes northwards in the summer, and is to be seen occasionally even as far north as Canada. Tanagers are very shy, and it is generally easier to hear their pleasant song than to see the birds themselves.

WEEVER-FISH. These small fishes of European and African coasts belong to the SEA-PERCH group (q.v.). They have two dorsal fins, the first with five grooved spines, and also a large grooved spine on the gill-cover, all provided with poison-glands. The sting of these spines is much dreaded, especially by shrimpers—for, as the Weevers feed principally on shrimps, they are often found in their company. Since the Weever has the habit of burying itself in the sand, with just the tips of the dorsal spines above the surface, it is liable to be trodden on, with painful results to a bare foot. There are two British species.

WEEVIL. Beetles known as weevils have the head drawn out to form a snout, at the end of which is the mouth with its tiny jaws. The snout may be of various lengths, sometimes very short. It often serves as a kind of gimlet to bore a hole in which the female places an egg. For instance, the Nut-weevil bores into the growing nut, and inserts an egg, from which hatches the familiar fleshy white grub.

There are over 35,000 known species of weevil, all feeding upon vegetable food of some kind, and many being extremely destructive. The tiny Rice weevils destroy great quantities of stored rice and grain, and the big Palm-weevils kill the trees which produce coconuts. Very common in Britain are the Leaf-rolling Weevils, brightly coloured beetles which cut and roll the leaves of birches and other trees to form the funnel-shaped or barrel-shaped objects so often found hanging from them. The mother-beetle cuts with her jaws from the edge of the leaf to the midrib, and then rolls up the partly separated half, laying an egg inside the roll. The grub is protected by the roll, and feeds upon the interior of it until it drops to the ground ready to pupate. The little barrel-like cases, skilfully shaped from oak-leaves, are the work of a bright red weevil.

Some kinds of weevil have lost the wings which they formerly carried beneath their wing-covers. The wing-covers in these have become firmly joined together, forming a solid armour. Such weevils are very lucky, because most birds find them too indigestible to eat. Many weevils have their bodies covered with extremely minute stalked scales, rather like the feathers of birds. These are often a brilliant green; but sometimes they are golden-green, blue, or red, mixed together or combined to form attractive patterns. The scales, like those of butterflies' wings, are very easily rubbed off.

Bark-beetles, which are related to the weevils, burrow between a tree and its bark, causing the latter to fall off and reveal, at times, curious patterns traced in the wood. The female penetrates the bark and then gnaws a tunnel beneath it, laying eggs at regular distances along each side. Each little grub eats its way straight into the soft layer beneath; so that many side-galleries are gnawed steadily outwards from the original tunnel. These increase in size as the grubs grow larger, and are made to diverge more and more in order to keep separate. The result is a very complicated and attractive pattern. Each grub, when it reaches full size, undergoes at the end of its gallery a METAMORPHOSIS (q.v.) to the beetle-form; then, biting a round hole through the bark, it escapes.

See also BEETLES.
See also Vol. VI: INSECT PESTS.

A. Fraser-Brunner

A BLUE WHALE STRANDED

WHALES. The whales are mammals—warm-blooded animals that suckle their young—and they belong to the order Cetacea, which includes Porpoises and Dolphins. Many of the young ones still have a few bristles round their mouths; but, otherwise, whales have lost the thick fur coat that most mammals wear in order to keep in the body heat. Instead, they have under the skin a thick layer of a very oily substance called blubber. They have become fish-shaped because this is the best shape for an animal that spends its life in the water. As whales never leave the water, they are more perfectly streamlined than the SEALS (q.v.), which spend part of their time on land. Their front legs have become 'flippers', somewhat resembling in shape the breast fins of fishes, and to all outward appearance their hind legs have been completely lost.

The most noticeable feature distinguishing whales from fishes is that the great tail-flukes are placed horizontally, whereas the tail-fin of the fish is upright, its movement being from side to side. Although some fishes bear living young, none suckles them, as do the whales. The whale has a double heart with four chambers, just like the human heart. It breathes, not by gills, but by lungs; and its skeleton is very much like that of other mammals, and quite unlike that of a fish. Because whales breathe by lungs, they have to come to the surface of the water every so often

to get a supply of fresh air, and to rid themselves of the old used air. This is called spouting. The breath is puffed out from the nostril as a warm vapour—but it immediately condenses in the cold air into a sort of mist, and looks like a fountain of water.

All whales eat living animal food: some feed on small creatures such as prawns; many on fish; some on cuttlefish; but only one, the Killer Whale, attacks other warm-blooded animals. Most whales are harmless, timid creatures, showing great affection for one another, as well as for their young, which are both born and nursed in the water. Most pairs have one baby about once a year. Whales are found in all the oceans. They generally swim together in herds known as 'schools', often numbering several hundreds. The two main groups into which they can be divided are, firstly the Toothed Whales, which include the Sperm Whale, Narwhal, the Killer Whale, and the Dolphins and Porpoises; and, secondly, the Whalebone Whales, one of which is the giant Blue Whale, the largest animal alive today.

The Toothed Whales, as their name suggests, all have teeth in their jaws. The largest is the Sperm Whale, the males of which are sometimes 18 metres long. When attacked, the Sperm Whale is a very dangerous creature, and in the old days, when harpoons were thrown by hand from small craft, it used to upset the boat by its furious charge. Melville's Moby Dick, which bit off a man's leg, was a Sperm Whale. These whales are so valuable that they have been killed in large numbers, and are now less common. The head has a huge hump, consisting mainly of a reservoir for spermaceti. In the living animal this is a liquid oil; but it turns solid on being cooled, and is used for making ointments and candles. An even more valuable occasional product is ambergris, which is used for making perfumes. It appears to be formed in the intestines of the whale, and is sometimes found floating on the sea, looking rather like a dirty grey sponge, but a real treasure for the lucky finder. The ferocious Killer Whale feeds on seals, porpoises, and sea-birds, as well as on large quantities of fish. Occasionally Killers are seen off the coast of Britain. They hunt in packs, swimming at great speed. On more than one occasion they have been known to leap half out of the water on to ice-floes in an attempt to seize the sledge dogs of polar explorers.

The Narwhal, only about 5 metres long, lives in the Arctic Seas. In the male, one of the two teeth develops into a slender tusk, twisted in a left-handed spiral, up to 3 metres long. This great spear may possibly be used in fights with other whales. A number of the small Toothed Whales, especially those with beak-like jaws, are called Dolphins. They are found in nearly all the seas of the world, and occasionally off the coasts of Britain. They accompany ships for miles, playing gracefully round the bows. A few swim also in tropical rivers—one in India is blind, and finds its food by poking about in the mud with its beak. Porpoises, about 1·5 metres long, are the best known of all the whales that come near the British coast. They swim in large schools, tumbling and rolling in play, keeping close to the shore, and sometimes ascending the larger rivers.

The Whalebone Whales have, instead of teeth, a row of long, horny plates, called the 'baleen' or whalebone, hanging down from the roof of the mouth on each side of the huge tongue. These whales feed by taking in a huge mouthful of water—together with any small animals that may be in it—and forcing it out again through the baleen, which acts as a sieve, holding back the small animals to be swallowed. Whalers in the old days found that some of the Whalebone Whales were slower and easier to catch than others; and as they were also the most profitable,

A. *Fraser-Brunner*

KILLER WHALES ATTACKING A RIGHT WHALE

SPERM WHALE CATCHING A GIANT SQUID
The used air is coming out of the animal's nostril

A. Fraser-Brunner

having a good deal of oil of good quality, they were called Right Whales, a name still used today. Right Whales are clumsy creatures, not more than 15 metres long. The Greenland Right Whale was hunted so successfully for its oil and whalebone during the last three centuries, that it is now very rare, and is found only in Arctic seas.

The whaling industry has now centred on the Rorquals or Fin Whales. They are much faster than Right Whales, and their blubber is not so rich in oil. The largest is Sibbald's Rorqual or the Blue Whale, which is 30 metres long—the largest living animal known today. In recent years, Rorquals have been killed in enormous numbers for their oil, which is mainly used for the manufacture of soap and margarine. To protect them, an international agreement now prohibits more than a certain number being killed each year.

See also Vol. VI: WHALING.

WHEATEAR, *see* THRUSH, Section 4.

WHELK. The various species of Whelks are all active, carnivorous molluscs, which prey upon their sedentary bi-valved relatives by first boring a neat round hole through one of the valves of their victim's shell, and then literally eating the unfortunate owner 'out of house and home'. In this way they may cause considerable damage

on the oyster-beds by attacking the young oysters. They also do valuable service, however, as natural scavengers, by seeking and devouring the bodies of dead fish and other marine animals.

Large numbers of the Common Whelk are collected and used by fishermen in line-fishing. The shell of the large Red Whelk measures 10 to 20 cm in length. This is also known as the 'Roaring Buckie', because if you hold the mouth of a large shell against your ear, you seem to hear the sound of the waves roaring. The Netted Dog-whelk is very common on sandy shores, where large numbers may be found half-buried in the sand near low-tide mark. It has a stout, conical-shaped shell, strongly ribbed in two directions, so forming a network pattern. The shell is a dull buff colour, tinged with bands of blue and brown, a full-sized specimen measuring more or less 3 cm in length. The Thick-lipped Dog-whelk, also found near low-tide mark, has

S. C. Bisserôt

THICK-LIPPED DOG-WHELKS
Acorn barnacles are also clinging to the rocks

a smaller shell, and looks quite different from its Netted relative, the ridges across the whorls of its shell being stronger, and the white outer lip of the shell much thicker. The colour varies from white or pale flesh-colour to a pale brown. The smallest of our British species is the little Dwarf Dog-whelk, less than a centimetre in length, and found on the coasts of Dorset, Devon, and Cornwall. It has a few spiral ridges on its shell, and its general colour is yellowish-white with tawny tints, with the white lip of the shell shading to brown on its inner surface. Although the home of this dainty little Whelk is off-shore in deeper water, empty shells are often left stranded by the tide, and are frequently appropriated, also, as temporary homes by young Hermit-crabs (*see* CRAB).

See also MOLLUSCS.

WHITE ADMIRAL BUTTERFLY. This velvety-black butterfly, with a white bar across each of its wings, is the only British representative of the Limenitinae, a sub-family of the Nymphalidae, to which belong the FRITILLARIES, VANESSINAE, and PURPLE EMPEROR (qq.v.). The name 'Admiral' is a corruption of 'Admirable'. This graceful and powerful butterfly used to be mainly confined to the New Forest, but can now be seen on the wing in July and August in most wooded districts in southern England. The females spend most of the day fluttering amongst the undergrowth, searching for sprays of honeysuckle on which to lay their eggs. The males haunt the tangled masses of blackberry blossom for nectar, and are often seen in company with Silver-washed Fritillaries. On hatching, the caterpillar makes its way to the tip of a honeysuckle leaf, and eats part of the leaf away from each side of the midrib. When it is not feeding, it lies along the midrib, where it can easily be found before it retires into hibernation in the autumn. Its winter shelter, a folded honeysuckle leaf, is prevented from falling by being attached to the stem with silk. In the spring the caterpillars cast off their dark olive-green winter coat, and appear in a brilliant light-green coat, matching the young growth of the honeysuckle. On their backs they have long, reddish spines. They pupate on the food-plant, hanging head downwards suspended from a silk pad. The chrysalis is green with beautiful shining silver markings, and is unique in shape, being grotesquely swollen in places and having two sharp projections on its head.

S. Beaufoy

WHITE ADMIRAL BUTTERFLY ON BRAMBLE FLOWER

WHITE ANT, *see* TERMITE.

WHITE-FLY, *see* Vol. VI: INSECT PESTS.

WHITES (Butterflies). These largish butterflies, together with the YELLOWS and WOOD WHITE (qq.v.), belong to the very large family Pieridae. Two, the Large and Small Cabbage Whites, are among the most common butterflies in the British Isles. All Whites and Yellows have six fully-developed legs, all of which they use for walking. The Marbled White, in spite of its name, is a member of the BROWN family (q.v.).

The male Large Cabbage White has no markings on the upper side of his wings, except for a black tip. The female, however, has two large, black spots on each fore-wing, and a streak running towards her body. The British-bred Whites, which have two broods a year, are often reinforced by enormous migrations from the Continent. The female lays her eggs in batches of a dozen to a hundred on the underside of a cabbage leaf, and also on nasturtium, rape, jack-by-the-hedge, and mignonette. The caterpillars, which are greyish-yellow speckled with black, and have an unpleasant smell, live in communities. When they are in their last skin, however, and fully fed, they leave the food-plant and crawl away to a wall or nearby fence. There, they pupate, attached by the tail to a silken pad and supported by a girdle.

S. Beaufoy

LARGE CABBAGE WHITE BUTTERFLY WALKING ON ITS SIX
LEGS

S. Beaufoy

GREEN-VEINED WHITE BUTTERFLY SHOWING UNDERSIDES OF
WINGS

This butterfly is a great pest in the vegetable garden—indeed, were it not that only a small proportion survive to reach maturity, the cultivation of cabbages would be impossible. In some years, as it is, they do cause serious devastation (*see* BUTTERFLY AND MOTH PESTS, Vol. VI). Many larvae die from bacterial diseases, and others are infested by Braconid Wasps, which pierce the newly hatched caterpillar and lay 20–100 eggs within its body (*see* ICHNEUMON FLY). The pupae, also, are freely eaten by birds.

The Small Cabbage White is almost an exact miniature of its large relative, except that the male usually has two spots, one on each forewing. (In the spring brood the spots are often missing.) The caterpillars, however, are quite different. The Small Cabbage White caterpillar is green with a fine yellow line along its back and sides, and it feeds alone, not in exposed colonies like the Large Cabbage Whites. There are three distinct broods, in spring, summer, and autumn; but they usually overlap, and are frequently reinforced by immigrants from the Continent— so that the butterfly appears to be breeding continuously from March to early October. It was introduced into America about 1860, and within 30 years had spread all over the United States. In 1930 it was accidentally imported into New Zealand, where it rapidly increased. In both countries the Braconid parasites have been deliberately introduced in order to control the spread of the Whites.

The Green-veined White, although often confused with the Small Cabbage White, is not a garden butterfly, but frequents damp places, country lanes, open glades, and ridings in woods, where the markings on its underside harmonize well with the grasses among which it rests. The green colour is due to the intermixing of black and yellow scales. The males produce a scent, like lemon verbena, which appears to attract the females. The caterpillars, much like those of the Small Cabbage White, feed mostly upon jack-by-the-hedge and horse-radish. A brilliant lemon-yellow Irish form has been bred in captivity for many years.

The Orange Tip has blotched green and white undersides, which harmonize well with green and white flower heads. The male alone has the brilliant orange tips to the wings. A yellow form occurs in the Isle of Man. The female lays her eggs in May amongst the flower-clusters of jack-by-the hedge, charlock, or cuckoo flowers. These are at first cream-coloured, change within a few hours to bright orange, and then fade until, as the tiny caterpillar begins to show through the semi-transparent shell, they appear almost black. The caterpillars may often be found during the day resting lengthways upon the long pods of jack-by-the-hedge. They are bluish-green, finely dotted with black, with a white stripe along the sides. Young larvae are often carnivorous, attacking others of the same kind. They also, like the BLUES (q.v.), secrete a sweet fluid attractive to ants, whose attendance gives them considerable protection. The extremely angular

S. Beaufoy

ORANGE TIP BUTTERFLY SHOWING UNDERSIDES OF WINGS

chrysalides may also be found attached to the stems of jack-by-the-hedge.

The Bath White derives its name from a piece of needlework executed at Bath in the 18th century, which portrayed a specimen said to have been found near that place. This species is a rare migrant, and has only appeared in 27 years from 1824 to 1944, not more than 370 individuals altogether being recorded. In 1945, however, it reached the British Isles in unprecedented numbers, along an 800-km front from Kent to Co. Kerry. At a distance the Bath White can easily be mistaken for the Green-veined White. Both sexes, however, have a large square black spot on each upper wing, and the female has a band of black markings on the outer margin of the lower wings. It may be distinguished from the female Orange Tip by the less complete black tips to the fore-wings and the more compact green marbling on the underside. The orange eggs closely resemble the pollen-bearing anthers of the mignonette, the most usual food-plant. The lilac and yellow caterpillar has been known, especially in 1945, to feed also on mustard and sea-radish.

The Black-veined Whites became extinct in the British Isles about 1922. They were last seen in any numbers in the Canterbury district of Kent about 1914. Before that, they used to breed in the New Forest and several other parts of southern England and Wales. The butterfly is quite unmistakable, being larger than the Large Cabbage White, and its wing-veins are heavily etched in black—as its name

suggests. The wings are semi-transparent, especially in the female, and, unlike most butterflies, they have no fringes round the edges. The caterpillars live in colonies in a slight web, and on the Continent feed on plum, blackthorn, and others of the prunus family.

WHITETHROAT, *see* WARBLERS.

WHITING, *see* COD.

WIDGEON, *see* DUCK.

WINKLE, *see* SNAIL, Section 4.

WIRE-WORM. This is the grub of certain of the Click-beetles or Skipjacks (so called from their habit of jumping into the air by striking the surface on which they lie). Click-beetles are narrow-bodied insects, generally found amongst herbage. When they are alarmed, they draw their legs close to their bodies and slip to the ground. If they happen to land on their backs they cannot easily get on their feet again as their legs are so short. They get out of this difficulty, however, by bending the body until it rests upon the head and the tip of the tail, and then straighten out so suddenly that they strike the ground and spring upwards, turning over at the same time—and so regaining their feet.

The grubs of the Click-beetles are slender, whitish or brownish creatures; some kinds feed upon rotting wood, and some devour other insects, while some are the hated wire-worms— amongst the worst enemies of our crops. These abound in cultivated soil, where, unseen, they can feed upon the roots of corn, potatoes, vegetables, strawberries, and almost any cultivated crop. Fortunately, we are befriended by many kinds of birds which prey upon the wire-worms, and search the fields for them or follow behind the plough, devouring those which are brought to the surface.

See also BEETLES.
See also Vol. VI: BEETLE PESTS.

CLICK-BEETLE
(ADULT OF WIRE-WORM)

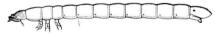

WIRE-WORM

Ewing Galloway, N.Y.

GREY TIMBER WOLF OF AMERICA

WOLF. Wolves belong to the same group as the DOG, and are therefore close relatives of the Fox and JACKAL (qq.v.). They are widely distributed over Asia and North America; and though they have now disappeared from Britain and most of Europe some still live in the wilder and more mountainous districts, especially of eastern Europe. They are very numerous in many parts of Russia, but are not to be found in Africa or Australia. Wolves live both in forests and in open country. They hunt by day and by night, generally alone or in pairs, but sometimes, especially in winter, in family parties. Normally they are shy, suspicious, and cowardly animals; but when they are hungry, or when hunting together in parties, they grow fierce and aggressive. Wolves have on frequent occasions attacked and killed human beings, and in America they will attack animals as large as the bison or moose. They do not stalk their prey and then spring on it, as do the cat family, but run it down in the open. Their long, elastic gallop is deceptive—indeed few people would think that a wolf could out-distance a very fast horse. They have, too, a wonderful power of endurance, running for long distances without slackening pace. Their cry is a loud prolonged howl. A single wolf can make so much noise that many a traveller has thought himself surrounded by a pack of wolves, when there was but one a few kilometres away.

A wolf's lair is usually either in a rocky cavern, in a hole in the ground, or in the hollow of a fallen trunk. The she-wolf generally produces from three to four cubs in the spring, and while they are young she feeds them with the flesh of animals which she herself has swallowed and then regurgitated, partially digested.

In North America live the Grey Timber Wolves, the White Arctic Wolves, and a small wolf called the Prairie Wolf or Coyote. The Coyote is a crafty and cunning, but very cowardly, animal, which lives in burrows and feeds on various small mammals and birds. Cubs, captured young, become very tame, but never lose their shy, skulking habits. In the open bush country of Brazil and the Argentine lives the Maned or Red Wolf, which is rather like a large fox on stilt-like legs. It towers above the tufted grass, and so is able to follow the movements of its small prey.

Wolves can rarely be tamed so as to eradicate their wild instinct—sooner or later they nearly always attack their owner. Domestic dogs and wolves are very closely related; but it is not at all certain that the wolf is the only ancestor of the domestic dog: it may well be a product of several wild species (*see* DOG BREEDS, Vol. IX).

WOLF SPIDER, *see* SPIDERS.

WOLVERINE. This mammal, also known as the Glutton, is a very strong and fiendishly savage, bear-like relation of the Martens, Stoats, and WEASELS (q.v.). It is powerfully built, under a metre long, with a short, bushy tail, and it has a smell almost as bad as that of the Skunk. Its dark-brown fur is rather coarse, long, and thick. Wolverines live in the forests of northern Europe, Asia, and America, rarely stirring abroad before nightfall. On the very few occasions when they have been seen about during the day, they were reported as sitting up and shading their eyes with their paws, as if suffering from the unaccustomed light. In spite of their clumsy-looking appearance, they run fast, climb trees with ease, and swim rivers in chase of prey. Generally they live alone in underground holes —frequently the deserted lairs of bears. The four to five young, which are born in June or

The Times

OAK-TREE ON ASHTEAD COMMON, SURREY

July, remain with their mother until the following winter, after which they have to shift for themselves.

Wolverines are extremely greedy, and will devour any animal they can kill. Their sharp teeth and claws enable them to bring down a deer or caribou, although they prefer smaller game, and would far rather steal from others than hunt for themselves. They rob traps set for other animals, pulling the trap to pieces and removing the bait or the captured animal. After they have satisfied their hunger, they bury the rest of the booty, defiling it with their nauseating scent so that no other animal will touch it. They have also a curious habit of stealing and hiding things for which they could have no possible use—they have, for instance, been known to remove and hide the entire contents of an uninhabited hunting-lodge, including such articles as guns, axes, knives, cooking utensils, and blankets.

WOMBAT, *see* MARSUPIAL.

WOODCOCK, *see* WADING BIRDS, Section 4.

WOODLANDS. 1. Two thousand years ago most of Britain was covered by vast forests of different types. Today, most of the land has been cleared for agriculture or for towns; but all the main types of woodland are still represented, some being dominated by a certain type of tree, such as the Oak, Beech, or Pine. The woodlands of Britain are made up either of deciduous trees, the most common being Oak-woods, Beech-woods, Ash-woods, and Birch-woods, or of coniferous trees, which are generally found at high altitudes and with pines as their dominant trees.

2. OAK-WOODS. There are two types of oak-wood in Britain, damp oak-woods, generally found in the south of England on clay or loam soils, and dry oak-woods, which are usually on the drier, shallower, and more sandy soil of the Pennines and other places. The typical damp oak-wood tree is the Pedunculate Oak, which can be recognized by its stalked acorns and by its shining, peculiar-shaped leaves. The typical tree of dry oak-woods is the Durmast or Sessile Oak, in which the flowers, and consequently the acorns, have no stalks, and the leaf-blades taper to the stalk and have star-like hairs on their under-surfaces. There are many crosses between the two kinds of oak, however, and the two sometimes live in such close association that it is difficult to distinguish a true damp oak-wood from a dry oak-wood. Durmast oak-woods are found extending up hill-sides to altitudes of between 350 and 450 metres. Up to a height of 240 metres the trees grow to a moderate size; but above this they are stunted by the wind, and increasingly sparse.

Whether the Pedunculate or Durmast Oak is dominant in a wood, the plants found with them are much the same—although in the damp woods there is usually a greater profusion of undergrowth and of shrubs. Among the oaks are often found the Ash, Field Maple, Birch, Wild Cherry, Alder, Wych Elm, Rowan or Mountain Ash, and, sometimes, Hornbeam; but these usually grow on the edges of the wood and in the more open glades, as they are not able to compete with the oaks when these grow closely together. The rich shrub population of the damp oak-wood is made up of Hazel, Hawthorn, Blackthorn, Dogwood, Privet, Guelder Rose, and Willows. Most of these also occur in dry oak-woods, but not so profusely. The carpet plants in oak-woods vary according to the type of soil. In woods of Pedunculate Oaks, where the soil is light and dry, large areas may be covered with Bracken, Bluebells, Wood Sanicle, Dog's Mercury, Anemones, Primroses, and Meadow-sweet; in open places Foxgloves often flourish. In the south of England, these plants occur also in the Durmast woods; but in the more hilly regions of the north the ground flora is of a healthy type, and includes Bilberry, Ling, Heath Bedstraw, Wild Sage, and Tormentil.

3. BEECH-WOODS occur mainly in the south of England, their chief need being a warm, dry, well-aerated soil, preferably chalk or limestone: they never flourish on waterlogged ground. The finest beech-woods in Britain occur on the southern slopes and escarpments of the chalk hills of the North and South Downs, and of the Chilterns, as well as on the limestone ridges of the Cotswolds. The most striking feature of a beech-wood is the dense shade made by the leafy canopy, and consequently the scarcity of ground vegetation—unlike the abundant carpet vegetation found in oak-woods. Beech-woods are the home of the characteristic SAPROPHYTES (q.v.), such as Bird's Nest Orchid and the Yellow Bird's Nest, which get their nourishment from the decaying beech leaves. On the outskirts of beech woods and in glades where light penetrates, considerable sheets of Dog's Mercury, Wood Sanicle, and Bluebells may occur, the first being better able than most plants to flourish in shade. The three common kinds of Violet—Hairy, Wood, and Dog—Wild Strawberry, Arum Lily, Herb Bennet, and Enchanter's Nightshade may also be found. Very few trees can compete with the Beech; but Ash, White Beam, Yew, and Wayfaring Tree sometimes occur in clearings.

4. ASH-WOODS are found on chalky soils, particularly those which are poor in humus. They occur on the limestone hills of the north and west of England, and grow particularly well in the Peak District of Derbyshire. Where the chalk soil is damp, as in the Isle of Wight, they may replace beech-woods. Ash-woods extend well up hill-sides to a height of 350 metres, above which they merge into a zone of hawthorn scrub. Ash trees cast less shade than either oaks or beeches, and so their ground vegetation is often extensive. With the Ash grows a great variety of lime-loving, woody plants, including Wych-elm, Hawthorn, Yew, Juniper, Aspen, Hazel, Bramble, Ivy, and, in the south of England, Traveller's Joy. Where Hazel occurs, it often forms dense thickets, the shade of which hinders the growth of floor plants. Ash-woods in well-drained soils have carpets of Dog's Mercury and Moschatel, Ground Ivy, and Hairy St. John's Wort. Those soils which are wet in the spring but drier later, have Garlic, Wild Strawberry, Globe Flower, and Red Campion; while in marshy places ash-woods have a ground vegetation of Meadow-sweet, Kingcup, Great Butterburr, and Valerian. The floor carpet of ash-woods, especially in summer, often consists of one dominant herb—there may be nothing but patches of Dog's Mercury or Ground Ivy.

5. BIRCH-WOODS occur in both chalky and non-chalky soils above the limit of oak-woods on hill-sides—and Birches will grow farther north than most trees. In the moorland peat of the Pennines, and in Scotland, the remains of birch trees show how widely they once spread. The Rowan or Mountain Ash is frequently present in birch-woods. Quite often, especially on sandy soils, the Birch accompanies the Oak, and the abundant supply of light seeds also enables it to invade heaths. The Birch does not produce dense shade: and the well-developed ground vegetation is heathy in nature, including Bracken,

BEECH WOOD ON THE COTSWOLDS

PINE-WOOD (ROTHSEN FOREST, INVERNESS)

BIRCH-WOOD (FRILSHAM COMMON, BUCKS.)

Ling, and Bilberry, as well as MOSSES (q.v.), which tend to accumulate moisture.

6. PINE-WOODS. Most of the pine-woods of Britain are the descendants of trees originally imported from abroad, the original primitive pine forests being restricted to a few areas in the central part of Scotland. The dominant pine of these original Scottish pine-woods is a variety of the imported pine, and both have come to be called the Scots Pine or Scotch Fir. Provided the roots of the Pines can get a hold, pine-woods are found on all dry soils, on ground that is deep and sandy as well as on partially drained bogs.

When pine-woods are thick, the shade is so dense that all the lower branches, except at the edges of the wood, die off. There is little ground vegetation, the only plants to be found being a few Mosses, Fungi, and the Yellow Bird's Nest. In such woods there is a natural scarcity of nitrates, which are usually formed from decaying humus—and the Pine gets its necessary nitrogen with the help of FUNGI (q.v.) which invade its roots, forming mycorrhiza, and pass on to the tree the organic matter they use as food. At the edges of these dense pine-woods, Bracken, Bilberry, Ling, Bell-heather, Bramble, and herbs such as Tormentil, Heath Bedstraw, and Wood Sorrel may occur, and these are also found in pine-woods where the trees are more widely spaced (*see also* ECOLOGY OF PLANTS).

See also CONIFERS.
See also Vol. III: FORESTS.
See also Vol. VI: TREES, BROADLEAVED; TREES, CONIFEROUS.

WOODLOUSE (Slater). Woodlice are common in every garden, where they hide during the hours of daylight under flat stones and rotten wood. They are the only members of the Crustacea completely adapted for spending the whole of their lives on land, and they possess the beginning of a tracheal system for breathing air, as is found in insects. They are active creatures when disturbed, crawling rapidly away in search of a fresh hiding-place—though some species, the Pill or Armadillo Woodlice, have the habit of curling up into a ball when alarmed. The two other species common in our gardens are the Brown Woodlouse, which has a brownish body with two rows of yellowish spots on the back; and the Grey Woodlouse, which is greyish-blue. The largest British species, about 2 centimetres long, is the Sea Slater, commonly found on the sea-shore in rocky places well above high-water mark, where only the salt spray will reach it.

T. Huxley
WOODLOUSE (× 2)

See also CRUSTACEA.

WOODPECKER. There are many species of Woodpeckers distributed over most of the world, but not in Australasia and the Pacific Islands. Woodpeckers vary in size from the Great Grey Woodpecker of Malay, 46 centimetres long, to the tiny Piculets of tropical America, some of which are only 8 centimetres. Most of them spend their lives in trees, hunting for insects and grubs; but some, such as the Ground Woodpeckers of Africa, the Golden-winged Woodpeckers (or Flickers) of the U.S.A., and the Pampas Woodpeckers of Argentina, find most of their food on the ground—in river banks, hill-sides, or the mud walls of buildings.

The typical Woodpeckers have short legs and strong claws adapted for climbing; stiff, pointed tail-feathers on which the birds support themselves when climbing; strong chisel-shaped beaks for digging into the wood and ripping off bark; and long tongues which the birds can shoot out to catch an insect. Woodpeckers have sticky tongues, like those of ANT-EATERS and CHAMELEONS (qq.v.), very convenient for licking up insects. Although they eat a certain amount of other food, such as fruit, berries, and nuts, their main food is insects and grubs—and they are particularly fond of ants. They breed in nesting holes in trees, laying pure white eggs, generally four or five in number, on nothing more of a nest than the wood-chippings left over from the excavation. The entrance hole is only just large enough for the bird to enter, and is marvellously symmetrical. The fledglings stay in the nest a long time, and are conspicuously noisy. Woodpeckers are shy birds, more often heard than seen. They quickly put the trunk of the tree between them and any intruder. Their general practice when hunting food is to start at the bottom of a tree and work upwards. They tap the trunk to see whether the wood is sound or not, and then rip off the bark from any likely sounding spot, to excavate for grubs and insects beneath. One group of Woodpeckers, the Sapsuckers of America, tap trees such as birches and maples, and feed on the sap which they draw. In the course of 2 or 3 years of such tapping, a family of Sapsuckers will kill a full-grown tree.

In Great Britain there are three species—the Green Woodpecker and the Greater and Lesser Spotted Woodpeckers. The quite common Green Woodpecker is conspicuous with its parrot-like colour of green, with crimson head, and yellow rump. It is often called the Yaffle, because of its cry like a harsh laugh, which it utters continuously as it makes its rather heavy, dipping flight from tree to tree. The Greater Spotted Woodpecker, a smaller bird with bright pied plumage and crimson crest, is less rare than is usually thought, but it is so shy that it is not easy to see. The Lesser Spotted Woodpecker is still smaller, about as large as a Chaffinch. Both birds in the spring make a curious jarring noise, almost like a rattle, by tapping their beaks very rapidly against a bough. This is quite unlike the normal tapping in search of food.

The Wrynecks, grey-brown birds about as big as Larks, are close relatives of the Wood-

G. K. Yeates

GREEN WOODPECKER OR YAFFLE

peckers, with the same long, sticky tongues, but with less strong beaks. Their plumage is mottled, their backs marked with little wavy black lines. They winter in tropical Africa and India, but breed in Europe, visiting many parts of Britain. They are often called Snake Birds, for they twist their long necks in a snake-like fashion and hiss like snakes when disturbed. Their cry is a monotonous, piercing 'guee-guee-guee'.

WOOD WASP (Horntail). People who live near places where timber is stored are often surprised by the entry into their houses of a large, black and yellow insect. It looks like a huge wasp, and, being thought to possess an extremely powerful sting, it causes considerable alarm. It is, however, quite harmless, and is one of the common species of British Wood Wasp. These insects are closely allied to SAWFLIES (q.v.). There are eleven British species, another common one being steely-blue in colour. They are over 2·5 cm long, with a horn at the end of the abdomen. The Wood Wasp's ovipositor or egg-laying organ, the so-called tail, which gives the appearance of a sting, extends below and beyond the 'horn', and is continuous with the lower surface of the abdomen for about half its length. It is used to drill through the bark of a suitable tree and deep into the wood beneath, an egg being inserted each time this is done. The larvae burrow into the heart-wood, and live there for about 2 years, after which they pupate in the galleries they have formed, each in a silken cocoon in which are entangled particles of chewed up wood.

At the base of its ovipositor the Wood Wasp has a pair of cavities containing a fungus that attacks decaying, but not sound, timber. When the insect lays its eggs deep in the timber, it also leaves there some of this fungus, which eats its way through the timber. The larva, when hatched, travels in its wake, probably feeding upon partially digested material prepared, as it were, in advance, but apparently not feeding on the wood. We have here an interesting example of what is called 'symbiosis', in which two living things are acting together for the benefit of both. In this instance the fungus gains entry by the drilling operations of the Wood Wasp, and the larva of the Wood Wasp finds its route and its food prepared for it by the fungus.

The eleven species of British Wood Wasps are

Eric Hosking

GREAT SPOTTED WOODPECKER AT NESTING HOLE

YELLOW-TAILED GIANT
WOOD WASP

divided into two groups, one attacking coniferous trees, the other deciduous. In the latter group there are two species, both largish, mostly black insects; one of these attacks willows and the other alders. Both groups only bore into trees which are unhealthy or diseased, particularly those suffering from over-crowding or from fungal diseases.

See also Vol. VI: TREES, PESTS OF.

WOOD WHITE BUTTERFLY. This small, delicate butterfly has dead-white, black-tipped wings, and a long, thin, pointed body. It is the only British representative of the sub-family Dismorphinae, belonging to the WHITE family (q.v.), of which 98 out of the 101 species live in Central and South America. It is extremely local, but, although it disappeared from many of its haunts at the beginning of this century, there are numerous signs of its revival. The male butterflies appear in sunny woodland glades in May, and a few form a second brood again in July. The females usually remain in the shade of the undergrowth, only coming out to lay their eggs on clumps of bird's-foot trefoil or tufted vetch. The caterpillar is vivid green with a yellow stripe above the legs. The narrow, angular chrysalis is yellowish-green with a pinkish stripe along the sides.

WOOLLY BEAR CATERPILLAR, *see* TIGER MOTH.

WORM. 1. The word 'worm' is really only a convenient descriptive term for a large assortment of animals possessing more or less elongated bodies. In the higher forms they are composed of a series of rings or segments, as in the common Earthworm; many of the lower forms, however, are unsegmented, in some cases leaf-like, and often have complex life-histories. These include Flatworms, Ribbon-worms, and Roundworms, parasites in the bodies of other animals. The higher forms, the ringed worms or Annelids, include the familiar Earthworms, the Freshwater Worms, and the very numerous and beautiful marine Bristle Worms. These latter rank among the highest forms of worm-life, possessing paired appendages called false-feet, and a more or less highly developed head, often bearing 'jaws', tentacles, and feelers.

2. EARTHWORMS. These are of considerable importance to agriculture, for by their constant burrowing and their habit of breaking and carrying down fallen leaves in autumn, they help both to turn the soil and to keep it fertile (*see* EARTHWORMS, Vol. VI). At the same time, earthworms can become a nuisance to those who like a tidy lawn—although their casts make an admirable top-dressing. The body of the Earthworm is covered from end to end by a smooth cuticle, which helps it to glide between the particles of soil. On each segment of its body are tiny bristles, called 'chaetae', normally eight to each segment. These enable the worm to fix one part of its body securely to the ground while another part is being moved. The Earthworm also helps itself through the soil by the sucking act of its pharynx. This draws some of the earth into its body, the digestible parts being absorbed as food, and the rest being passed through the body and ejected, forming little heaps called worm-casts.

There are many different species of Earthworms, varying considerably in size, colour, and choice of dwelling-place. The Brandling, which every angler values for use as bait, lives in manure heaps; the less familiar Tree-worm climbs trees; while other species frequent the roots of certain plants growing in swamps or on the banks of streams. Java is the home of a very large Earthworm said to grow to a metre or more long; it is called *Perichaeta musica* from the fact that, as it creeps about on the surface of the earth at night, it produces a sharp clinking sound, probably caused by the bristles of its body striking against stones lying in its path. Tasmania possesses a giant Earthworm which sometimes reaches nearly 2 metres in length; it is said to make a gurgling noise as it slithers back into its burrow in the ground.

3. FRESHWATER WORMS. The common little pond Blood-worm, measuring from 1 to nearly 5 centimetres long, is one of the most familiar of the freshwater worms. It often occurs in such numbers as to give a red tinge to the mud. About half the body is hidden in the little mud tube which the worm has formed as its home, the remainder protruding into the water and constantly waving backwards and forwards.

D. P. Wilson

FRILLED TOPPED SANDY TUBES OF THE SAND-MASON

4. MARINE WORMS. The marine Bristle Worms (*Polychaeta*) form a large and very important group, the members of which are characterized by possessing bodies externally divided into a series of rings or segments, bearing numerous bristles. These may grow out on projections, called false-feet, on each side of each body-ring, or from depressions in the tissues of the skin. Bristle Worms also possess tentacles and external breathing organs, called 'branchiae'. There are two main groups, the wandering worms, with well-developed false-feet, and the tube-forming worms, which lead a more or less sedentary life in tubes constructed from various materials. All have a METAMORPHOSIS

(q.v.) before reaching the adult stage, the larva being quite unlike its parents, and possessing one or more girdles of hair-like structures, called 'cilia', by which it swims through the water. At certain seasons of the year these larvae swarm in immense numbers in the surface waters of the seas, providing some of the food of various larger sea animals. One of the most familiar of the burrowing sea-worms is the common Lug-worm, which throws out from its burrows the little mounds composed of ropes of sand and mud so often seen on flat, sandy shores when the tide is out. It has a long, cylindrical, blackish or bronzy-green body, measuring up to 25 or 30 centimetres long, the first thirteen segments bearing bright-red, branching gill-filaments. The so-called Red Cat-worm, used by sea-anglers for baiting their lines, is a typical example of the wandering worms, and is characterized by its long, slender, segmented body, flat head, and large, horizontally moving jaws. It varies a good deal in colour, from a fleshy-red to a yellowish-brown or greenish hue, and burrows in the sand and mud on shore between tide-marks. Among the giants of the family is the Creeper, which grows to 46 centimetres long, and lines the walls of its burrow in the sand or mud with mucus secreted by the large, leaf-like lobes of its false-feet. One of the most unwormlike of the wandering worms is the Sea-mouse, often found on wide, sandy shores at low tide. Its body, which may be 25 or 30 cm long, is oval in outline, the whole of the back being covered by a soft, dense, mouse-grey felting; while down each side of the body runs a prickly armature of bristles and compound hairs, displaying the most beautiful iridescent hues; in addition, its numerous false-feet bear long, stout, sharp-pointed bristles, which may be of service as weapons of defence.

The tubes formed by the sedentary marine worms are very varied, both in structure and composition. In some species they may consist merely of hardened

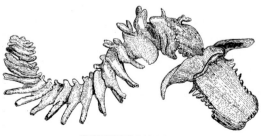

VARIFOOTED SEA-WORM

FAN SABELLA

PEACOCK WORMS—TUBE-DWELLING BRISTLE WORMS

mucus secreted by the worm; while in others the mucus forms a lining, as well as a natural cement by which particles of mud, sand, minute fragments of shell or small pebbles are held together so as to form an elaborate tube; in a few species, a single coiled or slightly curved tube of carbonate of lime is secreted. On shores where there is a mixture of sand and mud the Fan Sabella builds a tube which looks like a piece of narrow-bored rubber tubing sticking out of the sand. Sometimes the Fan Sabella may be seen at work in a pool, lengthening its tube; and then the worm, with its red or brown, feathery gill-tufts fully expanded and banded with bright colours looks like some delicate flower on a slender stalk. Sometimes, near low-tide mark on a clean sandy shore where there is an admixture of sand and fragments of shells, one may see what look like miniature trees, their trunks and branches coated with glistening sand-grains, fragments of shell, and pebbles: these are the work of another tube-building worm, the Shell-binder, which selects and collects the materials for its elegant tube with its long, slender tentacles. In a similar place the Sand-mason worm

uses nothing but carefully selected sand-grains of a certain size for its tiny tube. This is slightly conical in shape, and only one sand-grain in thickness, the grains being embedded in a liberal cementing of mucus, which makes both the inner and outer surfaces quite smooth.

Sometimes at the bottom of rock pools, on stones or on old scallop or oyster shells, one may see pinkish or greyish tapering tubes composed of carbonate of lime, about 8 cm long, marked at irregular intervals with encircling ridges, and slightly coiled at the narrow end. These have been formed by a Serpulid worm, which possesses special lime-secreting glands for the purpose. It is a small but very handsome worm, with magnificent plume-like gills which spread out like broad fans on the head, and are composed of bright red, slender filaments. One of its horns, or antennae, is transformed into a brightly tinted conical-shaped plug for closing the entrance of its tube.

5. LEECHES, animals used in the old days by surgeons for 'bleeding' (see Vol. XI, MEDICINE, HISTORY OF), also form a group of the Annelids. Leeches live on the blood or juices of other animals. They have suckers at either end, by which they attach themselves to their hosts, the mouth being in the front sucker. They pierce the skin of their victims with saw-edged jaws, and inject into the wound a fluid which stops the blood from coagulating. They store the blood they suck in a large pouched crop to await digestion. Some, such as the Medicinal Leech, live in fresh water; some, such as the Horse-leech, live also in damp places on land, and prey on earthworms and other invertebrates; others, such as the Warty Rock-leeches which infest sharks and rays, live in the sea.

6. Parasitic Worms. These are small, usually slender animals, such as Ribbon-worms, Flat-worms, and Roundworms, which dwell as parasites in or on the bodies of other animals or plants.

The Ribbon-worms are mostly marine, ranging from a millimetre or so to several metres long, living in the mud, and feeding on Bristle Worms. The Flatworms include the Planarians, Flukes, and Tapeworms. The Planarians are small, flat and unobtrusive animals, living among decaying vegetation and feeding on small

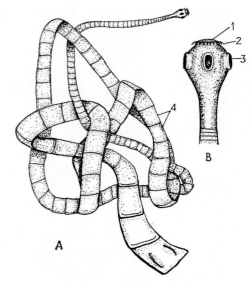

A. tapeworm; B. 'head'
1. Rostellum; 2. Hooks; 3. Sucker; 4. Segments

molluscs and insects. The Flukes are small, leaf-like Flatworms, which cling by suckers to the bodies of larger animals, and may be found, in some cases, on the outside of the body, in other cases, in the internal organs where their presence is the cause of a variety of diseases. The Tapeworms are usually parasitic in the stomach or intestines, and are of particular interest since, while all parasitic worms become modified to a greater or lesser extent, the Tapeworms represent the most extreme case. A typical Tapeworm consists of a cylindrical head, armed with a crown, or rostellum, of hooks and several suckers. Although this part is spoken of as the head, it is no more than an organ for clinging to its host and budding off at the free end a never-ending series of segments which in time become filled with eggs. There are no sense-organs in the head, and no mouth, nor does the animal possess limbs. In fact, it possesses very few organs other than those devoted to reproduction. The mouth, stomach, and intestines are unnecessary, for the parasite feeds on the fluids of its host, which it absorbs over its whole surface.

The Roundworms are mainly free-living, but some are partially or wholly parasitic. They are found in almost all situations on land, in fresh water, or in the sea. Some attack animals, some cause disease in plants, whereas others merely feed on decaying matter.

See also Vol. VI: Parasitic Worms.

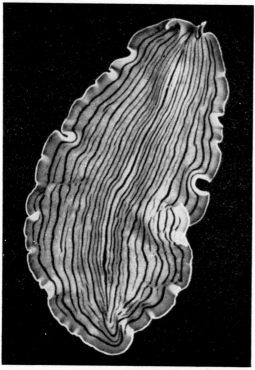

D. P. Wilson

A FLATWORM

WREN. About 100 species of Wrens are known, a great many in South America, and others in North America and the Old World, principally in the cooler regions.

The common European Wren, to be found in nearly every hedge and garden in Britain, is a tiny, russet-brown bird, with a pointed, slightly curved bill, a compact little body, and short, rounded wings and tail, the latter carried tilted up over its back. For its size it has a powerful and sweet song, which can be heard at all seasons and in all weathers. It is an insect-feeder. Wrens nest in thick bushes or hedges, in sheltered banks or ivy-clad walls, or in the thatch of cottage roofs. The nest is a domed construction, rather large for the size of the bird, with a neat hole on one side. The outside is made of dry leaves felted together with moss and lichen, and the inside is lined with finer moss and feathers. Six or eight eggs are generally laid—though much larger clutches, up to 16, have been known. The pair bring up several broods in a season, and care for them assiduously. The cock has a curious habit of building the framework of several nests—these unfinished nests, called 'cocks' nests', being probably used for shelter in cold weather, when the birds will creep into any convenient hole and huddle together for warmth.

There are different races of the common Wren in the Scottish Isles and on St. Kilda's Isle, these being larger and of varying shades of plumage. The St. Kilda Wren has a very loud, penetrating song.

The Warbling Wren or Organ Bird of the Amazon forests has a lovely and peculiar song. Sometimes the notes sound unmistakably like those of a boy's voice, at other times like the notes of a flageolet. The Cactus Wrens are a

G. K. Yeates

WREN AT ITS NEST IN THE IVY

larger group, species of which are to be found from California and Texas to South America. They build large, pouch-shaped nests in cactus plants. These nests are made of twigs and dry grass, lined with feathers, and measure as much as 30 centimetres from the narrow entrance-passage to the end. The Willow Wrens, Wood Wrens, and Golden-crested Wrens are not true Wrens, but belong to the WARBLER group (q.v.).

Y Z

YAFFLE, *see* WOODPECKER.

YAK. The Yak is a very strong, hardy, and sure-footed member of the Ox Tribe, which lives in the high regions of Tibet and central Asia. It has been domesticated, and plays much the same part in the lives of the people of these regions as the camel does for the Bedouin Arabs: they drink its milk, eat its flesh, use its hide and hair for tent covers and clothing; and employ it as their main means of transport. Indians use its tail as a fly-whisk. It has such powers of endurance that it has been of great value on exploits such as the EVEREST Expeditions (q.v. Vol. III); but it cannot stand heat.

The wild Yak, which is larger than the domesticated kind, stands not quite a metre in height and has long horns. It has a blackish-brown coat, with a long mane of hair on its throat and all along the underside of its body, reaching nearly to the ground. The herds often number hundreds or even thousands. Yaks are shy and wary animals, but can be very fierce in defence. When alarmed, the older bulls and cows place themselves in the centre, and, on the approach of the hunter, the whole herd takes flight, galloping away with heads down and tails in the air.

See also CATTLE, WILD.

YEAST. If some baker's or brewer's yeast is examined under the microscope, it will be seen to consist of oval cells, separate or loosely joined in long chains. Each cell is composed of a mass of protoplasm containing a small central body or nucleus, and is surrounded by a thin cell-wall. Yeast is a fungus, and, like all FUNGI (q.v.), it contains no green colouring matter, or chlorophyll, and so cannot build up its own food from raw materials by PHOTOSYNTHESIS (q.v.). Since yeasts obtain their food by absorbing dead organic matter, they are called SAPROPHYTES (q.v.).

The common method of reproduction in yeasts is by budding. When the cell has reached a certain size, a small outgrowth appears, gradually swells, and finally separates off as another yeast cell. At maturity each bud has the same structure as the parent cell, and repeats the process of budding. In this way colonies of yeast cells, looking like bunches of grapes, may be built up. When conditions are unfavourable to this method, another process of reproduction begins. The cell contents divide into four portions. Each portion, or spore, as it is called, surrounds itself with a thick wall, and later, when the wall of the original cell breaks down, it escapes to form a new yeast plant. With this thick wall, spores can withstand frost, drought, or other adverse conditions, and, being small and light, they are easily blown about in the atmosphere, which contains many millions of them. In the brewing industry, where specially cultivated yeasts are used, great care is taken to see that spores from other yeast strains do not fall into the fermenting material from the atmosphere, and so spoil the flavour of the beer.

Yeast is of enormous use to man, for every year tonnes of yeast cells are used to promote fermentation necessary for the making of bread, beer, wine, and other things. Its value lies in

TIBETAN YAKS

YEAST CELLS

its peculiar method of anaerobic respiration (*see* RESPIRATION IN PLANTS), by means of which it is able to oxidize sugars into alcohol and carbon dioxide. It is this carbon dioxide, given off in great quantities, which causes bread to rise.

There are several kinds of yeasts. That used in beer-making is known only under cultivation, but wine yeast is found in the soil in vineyards. Most fruits have wild yeasts growing on them and feeding on their sugar. Wild yeasts are used in making cider. Yeast also contains relatively large quantities of Vitamin B2, and is often used as a tonic. It also produces valuable plant proteins; and factories have been set up in the West Indies especially to manufacture these yeast proteins on a big scale.

See also FERMENTATION.

YELLOW-HAMMERS, *see* FINCHES, Section 7.

YELLOWS (Butterflies). These largish butterflies belong to the same family as the WHITES (q.v.), and have many of the same distinguishing characteristics, including six fully developed legs. The Brimstone is a common British resident, but the Clouded Yellows are migrants.

The Brimstone is one of the first hibernating butterflies to awaken in the spring. It has often been suggested that the word 'Butterfly' takes its origin from this 'Butter-coloured fly', so conspicuous because of its early appearance. The male is brilliant yellow, and the female the lightest shade of pale greenish-yellow, the most conspicuous marking being an orange spot near the centre of each wing. Both sexes have hooked tips to the fore-wings and points on the hind-wings, making them quite distinct from other British butterflies. The undersides resemble the yellowing ivy leaves among which they winter. In spring the females fly a long way looking for buckthorn bushes, the only food the caterpillars will eat. The caterpillar lies along the upper surface of the leaf's midrib, and is exceptionally difficult to see, as it is the same colour as the buckthorn. It has a white line running the

length of the body just above the legs, which decreases the intensity of shadow. It pupates underneath a leaf or on a twig, attached by a silken girdle. The butterfly emerges in July. Hibernated individuals are sometimes still on the wing in July, making a span of life of about a year—the longest of all British butterflies. Before going into hibernation the Brimstone haunts fields of clover and lucerne, or flower gardens, apparently without the urge to wander.

Clouded Yellows are rich orange-yellow butterflies, with deep black-bordered wings. They migrate to the British Isles from the Mediterranean region, usually arriving in late May and early June, and in some years spreading over southern England in vast numbers. The females immediately disperse in search of clover or lucerne fields on which to lay their eggs, while the males chase over hills and downs, soon wearing themselves out and dying. In warm weather the dark-green caterpillars, which have conspicuous side stripes of alternating yellow and orange, are fully grown within six weeks. In another fortnight the butterflies emerge, beautifully fresh-looking as compared with their parents. Sometimes the Clouded Yellows do not reach England until the end of August or September, in which case the young caterpillars have no time to feed up before being nipped by early frosts. A variety of the female Clouded Yellow, called *helice*, has white or cream wings, instead of orange-yellow.

The Pale Clouded Yellow is primrose-yellow, the paler female bearing a strong resemblance to the *helice* just described, but being less heavily marked with black. Its caterpillar resembles that of the Clouded Yellow and feeds on the

S. Beaufoy

CLOUDED YELLOW BUTTERFLY

same plants. A much rarer species, the Berger's Clouded Yellow, which is easily confused with the true Pale Clouded Yellow, has the tip and front edge of the fore-wings rounded and the black markings of both wings less extensive. It is said to be faster and wilder on the wing, and to be attached to chalky or limestone areas where the Horseshoe Vetch, its only food-plant, grows. The caterpillars are green, streaked with yellow, and spotted with prominent black dots—very different from those of the Pale Clouded Yellow. These species visit Britain less frequently than the Clouded Yellow and penetrate less far north.

YELLOW UNDERWING MOTH, *see* NIGHT-FLYING MOTHS.

YEW, *see* CONIFERS.

YUCCA MOTH. The Yucca Lily plant of Mexico and the southern United States produces seeds only after pollination by the small white Tineid moth; and this moth depends on the seeds of the Yucca plant as food for its larvae.

The female moth flies by night from flower to flower. When she has collected the sticky pollen from the stamens by means of a pair of peculiar scrapers in her mouth-parts, she visits yet another flower to lay her eggs. She inserts her long flexible ovipositor into the ovary, and there she lays one or more eggs. She then climbs up the style of the flower to the funnel-shaped opening of the stigma, which she fills with pollen from the compact mass carried under her head, pressing it down firmly. As a result the ovules are fertilized and develop into seeds—enough both to feed the Yucca moth caterpillars and to propagate the plant. The special adaptations of the Yucca moth in structure and behaviour, so that it is able to serve the Yucca plant and, incidentally, provide for its own sustenance, are unparalleled in insects, except among BEES (q.v.). Usually the association of insects and flowers leads to much greater modification of the flower than of the insect.

ZEBRA. These animals are closely related to the HORSE (q.v.) and the Ass, the main differ-

Mansell Coll.

SOUTH AFRICAN ZEBRA AT WATER-HOLE

ence being their striped coats. They once lived in Asia, Europe, and North America, but are now found only in Africa, where they are declining in numbers, two species being already extinct.

The largest species is Grévy's Zebra, which lives in droves in the open plains of Abyssinia, Somaliland, and northern Kenya. It stands about 13 hands, and has wide ears and rather narrow stripes down to its feet. The mare carries her young for about 12 months. When the foal is born, its mane extends from its shoulder to the tuft of its tail. The Mountain Zebra, once common in the mountainous districts of Cape Colony, but now almost extinct, is a small, sturdily-built animal, standing about 11½ hands. It is striped all over, the stripes on its hindquarters being broad, and the horizontal ones meeting the transverse ones to form a distinct pattern known as the 'gridiron'. A fold of loose skin at its throat forms a dewlap. A slightly different type of this Zebra is found in South-West Africa.

A long time ago in Cape Colony there were vast herds of reddish-brown Zebras with very few stripes and rather upstanding manes. They were called Quaggas, in imitation of their cry. So ruthlessly were they hunted for their flesh and hide, however, that they became extinct in the wild state about 1870. They had several near-relatives, among them being Burchell's, Chapman's, and Grant's Zebras. Burchell's Zebra, an animal with a striped body but white legs, used to be common north of the district occupied by the Quagga; but it, too, has now been exterminated. Chapman's Zebra of Bechuanaland is a similar type, but is striped all over; while Grant's Zebra, still quite common in East Africa, has very distinct black and white stripes. Many efforts have been made to break in and train Zebras, but in general these have not been successful. One pair of Zebras, however, were trained and driven in Hyde Park in the early years of this century.

ZOOLOGICAL GARDENS, *see* ZOOLOGICAL GARDENS, Vol. IX.